American Archival Studies:

READINGS IN THEORY AND PRACTICE

EDITED BY

Randall C. Jimerson

THE SOCIETY OF AMERICAN ARCHIVISTS • CHICAGO

THE SOCIETY OF AMERICAN ARCHIVISTS
527 S. Wells Street, 5th Floor
Chicago, IL 60607 USA
312/922-0140 • fax 312/347-1452
info@archivists.org • www.archivists.org

First printed in 2000
Printed in the United States of America

ISBN 0-931828-41-4

"'Mind and Sight': Visual Literacy and the Archivist" and "Digital Communications: Documentary Opportunities not to be Missed" appear courtesy of *Archival Issues*, the journal of Midwest Archives Conference (MAC).

"At the 'rim of creative dissatisfaction': Archivists and Acquisition Development," "The Documentation Strategy and Archival Appraisal Principles: A Different Perspective," "'The Surest Proof': A Utilitarian Approach to Appraisal," "The Power of the Principle of Provenance," and "Descriptive Practices for Electronic Records" appear courtesy of *Archivaria*, the journal of the Association of Canadian Archivists.

"Reinventing Archives for Electronic Records: Alternative Service Delivery Options" appears courtesy of *Archives and Museum Informatics Technical Report* No. 18.

Library of Congress Cataloging-in-Publication Data

American archival studies: readings in theory and practice/edited by Randall C. Jimerson.
   p. cm.
Includes bibliographical references and index.
ISBN 0-931828-41-4 (alk. paper)
   1. Archives–United States–Administration–Study and teaching. 2. Archives–United States–Administration–Philosophy. 3. Archives–United States–Administration. 4. Archivists–United States. I. Jimerson, Randall C. II. Society of American Archivists.

CD3021. A75 2000
025–dc21

00–044537

Table of Contents

Preface

The essays reprinted in this volume represent important recent American writings on archives and the role of archivists in modern society. They are collected here in order to make them more easily accessible to archival students and practicing archivists, indeed to anyone who wants to explore archival issues in greater detail than can be found in introductory texts. This volume supplements, but does not replace, two previous compilations of articles by North American archivists. *A Modern Archives Reader*, edited by Maygene Daniels and Timothy Walch, remains an important collection of classic essays and basic writings on archival functions. But after 15 years, it needs to be supplemented with more recent scholarship that reflects new developments in the field. The second model for the current volume is *Canadian Archival Studies and the Rediscovery of Provenance*, edited by Tom Nesmith, which presents a selection of some of the best writings by Canadian archivists.

Seeking to combine the best features of these two earlier collections, I have selected some of the most important recent writings by American archivists. These articles provide important perspectives both on basic elements of archival practice and on fundamental principles in archival theory and methodology. Since this volume is intended to supplement the publications in the Society of American Archivists' (SAA) Archival Fundamentals Series, it takes its basic structure from the topics covered by these manuals, with the addition of separate sections for archival history and electronic records. However, these essays are not intended to provide a basic introduction to these topics, but rather to articulate specifically American perspectives, issues, and concerns. Although I have written an interpretive introduction examining the American search for archival identity, this volume is not organized or selected to represent this theme.

This is not an "official" compilation, nor is it a comprehensive or fully balanced presentation. Although I have consulted widely with fellow archivists in selecting articles for inclusion, this is not a volume produced by committee. In the end the responsibility for selection has been mine alone. This has required many hard choices, since a single volume cannot include all deserving articles. In making these selections, I am fully aware that many archivists familiar with the professional literature in the past 15 years will find something missing, or will question inclusion of some of the articles, or will find unbalanced coverage of some topic of interest or concern to them. When the SAA Publications Board discussed my preliminary list of articles in 1998, its members could not find common agreement and referred the selection back to me. In a very real sense, then, this is my own personal selection of the "greatest hits of the 80s and 90s," as one colleague called it.

I hope that this volume will stand on its own as a reflection of the best of archival writings in the United States during recent years. Stay tuned. There is more coming, as archivists broaden their research and scholarship to meet the demands of an increasingly complex and challenging world of modern records.

* * *

In compiling this volume, I have received valuable assistance from many people. Above all, I have benefited from the comments and suggestions of my current and former graduate students at Western Washington University and the University of Connecticut. In their frank assessments of a wide variety of archival literature, they have not been influenced by personal and professional friendships with the authors, and they have generously shared their assessments of numerous articles and books.

David Haury, SAA publications editor, has contributed valuable suggestions during a long editorial process. Members of the SAA Publications Board have been very supportive and have given me wide latitude in selecting articles. In making these difficult choices I have received advice and recommendations from Richard Cox, Phil Eppard, Tim Ericson, Mark Greene, Linda Henry, Bill Maher, Jim O'Toole, Helen Tibbo, and some anonymous sources who returned questionnaires without giving their names. Tom Nesmith, Mark Greene, and Jim O'Toole offered thoughtful and often convincing critiques of early drafts of my introduction. Special thanks go to Teresa Brinati, managing editor of SAA, for her patient guidance and support through the entire process. The results are, of course, my own responsibility, and none of these friends and colleagues should be blamed for my errors of omission and commission. Many excellent articles could not be included due to space limitations, and the final choices were mine alone.

This volume could not have been completed without the support of my colleagues at Western Washington University, particularly George Mariz, chair of the Department of History. Geri Walker, of the Bureau for Faculty Research, approved funding to convert previously published articles into electronic format. Laurie Rossman cheerfully completed the time-consuming process of scanning these articles, so that I only had to complete copyediting and formatting for each article.

I also want to acknowledge my own archival teachers and mentors. When I first entered the archival profession in 1975, Fran Blouin, Bob Warner, Tom Powers, and Mary Jo Pugh of the Bentley Historical Library, University of Michigan, offered me the benefit of their own professional expertise and guidance. At Yale University Larry Dowler gave me opportunities and encouragement to grow as a professional archivist, and at the University of Connecticut Norman Stevens allowed me to continue my professional development. None of this would have been possible — or worthwhile — without the love and companionship of my wife, Joyce, and our daughters, Laura and Beth.

RANDALL C. JIMERSON
Bellingham, Washington

Introduction:
American Archivists and the Search for Professional Identity

by **RANDALL C. JIMERSON**

The most striking feature of the American archival profession in recent years is its ongoing search for identity and for public acceptance as a socially significant profession. Many of the important developments in the field since the early 1980s have either derived from or eventually contributed to this quest for professional identity and recognition. At times this has stirred passionate debates over the nature of American archives, the role of archivists in society, the relationship between archives and other professions, and the education necessary for archivists, among other topics. These issues provide the historical context for examining the recent archival literature represented in this volume.

The search for professional identity has led American archivists to develop external initiatives to increase public awareness of archival resources and services, partly in order to obtain increased funding and higher salaries. Within the profession there have been initiatives to improve standards of archival practice. Whether explicitly or implicitly, these efforts have often been closely related to underlying goals of increasing professionalism and gaining public recognition. This process of professionalization can be understood by examining its three broad manifestations: developing internal standards for professional recognition; enhancing the public image of archives and archivists; and strengthening the research and theoretical foundations of the profession.

By the late 1970s American archivists had identified three potential internal standards by which archivists and their institutions could be judged worthy of professional status. These standards could measure the professionalism of archival education programs (guidelines for graduate education), of individual archivists (certification), and of archival repositories (institutional evaluation). Although some archivists supported only one or two of these methods, those who advocated all three believed that in combination they would provide a strong basis for defining minimum standards for professionalization of archivists and archival institutions. However, there was no common agreement on these proposed methods for setting professional standards, not even universal acceptance that any such efforts were needed or practicable. Such disagreements led to heated discussions that still continue within the American archival profession, even though two of the three internal standards have been adopted.

The debate over professional education of archivists goes back to the early twentieth century. In 1909 Waldo Gifford Leland stated, "Of special knowledge, aside from technical matters, the archivist should have a training both historical and legal." Samuel Flagg Bemis reiterated this emphasis on historical preparation in a major 1938 report. "It is the historical scholar who dominates the staffs of the best European archives. We think it should be so here, with the emphasis on American history and political science."[1] By the 1970s the debate over the preferred method of education centered around two disciplines: history and library science. Those who advocated history as the proper background for educating archivists espoused the traditional view that archives was a historical discipline, requiring knowledge of historical methodology, historiography, and the origins and development of institutions.[2] Advocates of library science stressed the methodologies of cataloging, reference service, and providing access as common elements that archivists could learn from the increasingly sophisticated field of library science.[3] This debate was so divisive that when the Society of American Archivists (SAA) issued its first guidelines for graduate archival education in 1977, it deliberately sidestepped the question of whether such programs should be based in a particular discipline.

The Society of American Archivists' tentative and gradual steps toward professional standards can be seen clearly in the successive efforts to define guidelines for archival education, from 1977 to 1994. The 1977 "Guidelines for a Graduate Minor or Concentration in Archival Education"[4] outlined basic components of a one-semester course on archival theory and methods, to be followed by a practicum and an optional independent study. This very modest educational program envisioned grafting archival education onto existing programs in either history or library science, but not a full curriculum in archives administration. Ten years

---

1   Leland and Bemis quoted in F. Gerald Ham, Frank Boles, Gregory S. Hunter, and James M. O'Toole, "Is the Past Still Prologue? History and Archival Education," *American Archivist* 56 (Fall 1993): 718.

2   For one example of this perspective, see Ibid., 718-29.

3   For one example of this perspective, see Nancy E. Peace and Nancy Fisher Chudacoff, "Archivists and Librarians: A Common Mission, a Common Education," *American Archivist* 42 (October 1979): 456-62.

4   Guidelines published in *American Archivist* 41 (January 1978): 105-6.

later SAA revised its education guidelines in response to "the profession's continuing growth, the increasing complexity of its mission in the information age, and a recognition of the challenges faced in gaining adequate resources and developing a stronger theoretical basis for professional work." The 1988 guidelines were designed for multicourse programs "in related fields or fully independent graduate programs in archival administration." SAA now called for archival education programs to be administered by a full-time faculty member, who would teach core courses. Adjunct instructors could be hired to supplement such course offerings, but they should not constitute the entire faculty.[5]

Meanwhile, Canadian archivists had established a small number of graduate education programs, which provided an alternative model. The Canadian education programs, most notably at the University of British Columbia, offered a wide array of courses specifically designed for archives students and leading to a separate degree of Master of Archival Studies (MAS). According to Terry Eastwood, director of the MAS program at UBC, "The knowledge which archivists need to do their job and on which their techniques are based must be distinctive because the nature of archives — a centuries-old form of documentation — is distinctive, and therefore archival education must be distinctive."[6] Thus, graduate archival education in Canada gained recognition as a separate discipline.

By the early 1990s American archivists began planning a significant revamping of the graduate education guidelines, using the Canadian MAS programs as a model. The 1988 guidelines seemed increasingly inadequate to provide archivists with sufficient preparation to manage the complexities of modern records, including electronic records. Sensing competition with librarians and computer/information scientists, archivists also recognized the need to enhance the education requirements and professional status of their discipline. In 1993 SAA circulated for comment draft guidelines for an American MAS degree. After review by the Standards Board, the SAA Council in June 1994 approved the "Guidelines for the Development of a Curriculum for a Master of Archival Studies Degree." These new guidelines pointed in the direction of a more formal educational program, which could exist independently of either library science or history. The MAS guidelines outlined the basic elements of an archival studies program, including contextual knowledge (e.g., organizational history, legal and financial systems), archival knowledge (including both records management and "archival science"), and

---

5   "SAA Guidelines for Graduate Archival Education Programs," in *Directory of Archival Education, 1993-1994* (Chicago: Society of American Archivists, 1992), 10-14.

6   Terry Eastwood, "Nurturing Archival Education in the University," *American Archivist* 51 (Summer 1988): 228-53; see also Luciana Duranti, "The Archival Body of Knowledge: Archival Theory, Method, and Practice, and Graduate and Continuing Education," *Journal of Education for Library and Information Science* 34 (Winter 1993): 8-24.

complementary knowledge (e.g., conservation, library and information science, history, etc.). Additional components would include a practicum and scholarly research.[7] Although no full MAS program had been established in the United States as of January 2000 the MAS guidelines have influenced several graduate studies programs to modify their curricula in response to the MAS model.

The second effort to establish minimum qualifications for professional archivists involved creating a certification process by which individuals could gain recognition for their professional experience and knowledge. Initiated as an alternative to creating an accreditation process for educational programs, certification provided a relatively simple process by which archivists could establish their credentials as members of a profession. Much of the impetus for certification came from a belief that archivists should identify standards for professional qualifications rather than allow employers to set their own criteria for what constituted a professional archivist. From the start, the proposal for certification stirred deep controversies, with some archivists seeing it as an essential step toward professional recognition and others denouncing it, on one hand, as elitist and divisive and, on the other hand, as insufficient.[8] Although discussions of certification at both national and regional professional meetings indicated significant divisions within the profession, SAA Council approved the process for certification of individual archivists in February 1987.

The first archivists to be certified did so by submitting detailed applications outlining their archival experience, educational background, and professional service. This "grandparenting" process enabled experienced archivists to be certified by petition. Following a brief period for grandparenting, all future applicants would have to gain certification by passing an examination. SAA quickly established the independent Academy of Certified Archivists, which continues to establish criteria for membership, administer the examination, and monitor a process of recertification. Although certification still occasionally stirs passionate debates, it is well established as a means for archivists to demonstrate at least some minimal competency and knowledge of professional principles.

The third effort to establish professional standards within the discipline of archives did not fare as well. Proposals made in the 1980s to create a process for institutional evaluation of archival repositories arose from the same impulse as identifying professionally accepted methods of

---

7   "Guidelines for the Development of a Curriculum for a Master of Archival Studies Degree" *Archival Outlook* (September 1994): insert.

8   "The Certification of Archivists: An Early Opinion Survey," *SAA Newsletter* (November/ December 1985): 4; "Archival Certification Plan," *SAA Newsletter* (August 1986): 6-9; William J. Maher, "Contexts for Understanding Professional Certification: Opening Pandora's Box?" *American Archivist* 51 (Fall 1988): 408-27; Rand Jimerson, "Forum on Certification," *New England Archivists Newsletter* 13, no. 3 (July 1986): 14.

managing archives and caring for records. In 1982 SAA developed a draft process for institutional evaluation and compiled a handbook outlining "the essential elements and characteristics of a sound historical records repository." Basic principles for assessment and evaluation of archival institutions covered the areas of legal and governing authority, financial resources, staff, physical facilities, building archival and manuscript holdings, preservation, arrangement and description, access and reference, and outreach. These criteria would be the basis for a self-study process or a peer review site visit.[9] SAA hoped that institutional evaluation would improve the professionalism of archival institutions and create a process for measuring professional practices. By establishing guidelines and standards for archival institutions, these evaluation reports could be cited to justify increased support from parent institutions. Despite optimistic goals, the difficulties of administering such a program and the potential liability to legal action eventually led SAA to abandon the initiative.

While these efforts to establish internal professional standards for archivists were under way, American archivists had also begun a more systematic approach to planning for the profession. In 1982 SAA established a Task Force on Goals and Priorities, which published its recommendations under the title *Planning for the Archival Profession*, in 1986. Seeking to promote consensus on archival goals and objectives, the Task Force sought to clarify the professional identity of American archivists. The first step was to define a mission for the entire profession: "To ensure the identification, preservation, and use of records of enduring value."[10] The Task Force's report identified broad goal statements for this threefold mission, with 15 objectives and dozens of activities needed to achieve these goals and objectives. The report also listed priorities for action.

One of the basic assumptions outlined in *Planning for the Archival Profession* was that archives needed greater public support. "Present conditions, which are inadequate to ensure the identification and preservation of archival records, will not improve unless there is greater support for archival activity from outside the archival community," the report stated.[11] Concerned with their professional identity, archivists had begun efforts to enhance their public image and recognition as members of a profession that provides significant benefits to society. The problems seemed daunting. Frustrated by years of neglect, by inadequate funding and institutional support, and by popular stereotypes of archivists as

---

9 SAA Task Force on Institutional Evaluation, *Evaluation of Archival Institutions: Services, Principles, and Guide to Self-Study* ([Chicago]: Society of American Archivists, [1982]); "Principles of Institutional Evaluation," *SAA Newsletter* (July 1986).

10 Society of American Archivists Task Force on Goals and Priorities, *Planning for the Archival Profession: A Report of the SAA Task Force on Goals and Priorities* (Chicago: Society of American Archivists, 1986).

11 Ibid., 4.

dusty inhabitants of underground warrens, archivists asked how these
images could be changed. The result of this neglect, revealed in a series of
statewide historical records assessment studies, was a "cycle of poverty"
from which archives seemingly could not escape.[12] Changing the stereotypes seemed essential to gain greater visibility and support for their
important work. In 1984 SAA President David Gracy announced formation of a Task Force on Archives and Society, which would examine these
concerns and suggest remedies. As Gracy declared, "The archival service
to society — the obtaining, preserving, and making available of the permanently valuable records and papers of our institutions and our people
— has fallen to its saddest condition since modern archival institutions
took root in this country fifty years ago with the founding of our
National Archives."[13]

   One of the major initiatives of the Task Force on Archives and
Society was to commission a survey of resource allocators, those administrators who controlled the budgets of archival repositories, to determine their attitudes toward archives and archivists. This study, conducted by Sidney J. Levy and Albert G. Robles, concluded that resource allocators viewed archives as useful and important, but also saw archivists as
quiet, benign, and powerless: "Archivists are perceived as quiet [and]
profes-sional, carrying out an admired but comparatively subterranean
activity." Archivists would not be likely to demand additional resources
and support, and thus would not compete successfully with those programs that seemed essential to the institution's existence and success.
The Levy-Robles report thus indicated that archivists faced significant
obstacles both in securing the necessary funding to maintain and
expand their programs and in gaining public recognition as a dynamic
and significant profession. Part of the problem was that, "Archivists'
professional identity is unclear." To overcome this, Levy and Robles recommended, "archivists need to define more coherent identity objectives,
and communicate greater freshness and distinctiveness in imagery by
their training, programs, self-assertion, publicity, advertising, and relevance to modern life."[14] A recent study of popular literature confirmed
that these stereotypes and images of archivists persist in the public
imagination.[15] The public image of archives and archivists thus suggests
stagnation and irrelevance.

---

12 Lisa B. Weber, ed., *Documenting America: Assessing the Condition of Historical Records in the United States* (Atlanta: National Association of State Archives and Records Administrators, 1984).

13 David B. Gracy, "Our Future is Now," *American Archivist* 48 (Winter 1985): 13.

14 Sidney J. Levy and Albert G. Robles, *The Image of Archivists: Resource Allocators' Perceptions* (Chicago: Society of American Archivists, 1984), iv-v.

15 Arlene B. Schmuland, *The Image of Archives and Archivists: Fictional Perspectives* (M.A. thesis, Western Washington University, 1997), and "The Archival Image in Fiction: An Analysis and Annotated Bibliography," *American Archivist* 62 (Spring 1999): 24-73.

The Task Force on Archives and Society suggested steps to overcome these unflattering stereotypes. The starting point would be self-assessment, as archivists reevaluated how they looked at themselves as professionals. Archivists could enhance their prestige by building on the profession's perceived virtues and by using archival knowledge and skills to gain a competitive edge. Archivists would need to communicate their needs more effectively to resource allocators. In addition, archival outreach suggested opportunities to present a more positive image of the profession both to researchers and to other constituencies.[16] By presenting archives as important repositories of essential evidence for institutions and of research materials for a wide range of potential users, archivists sought to overcome the negative images. Outreach would be essential for public visibility.

To take advantage of outreach opportunities to assist researchers, archivists recognized that they needed to investigate their research constituencies, rather than operate under possibly false assumptions about who did or could make use of archival sources. Lawrence Dowler outlined a research agenda related to the availability and use of records, suggesting that archivists need to answer such questions as: "What do users use, how do they use it, what do they do with what they use, and how do they find their way to the archives in the first place? Who, in fact, are archival users?"[17] Conducting user studies of the type suggested would require systematic research rather than relying on impressionistic or anecdotal evidence. This type of formal research was exactly what some American archivists had recently begun to advocate as a means of enhancing archival practice and strengthening its basis in archival theory.

In separate articles published in 1981, Gerald Ham and Frank Burke each called for greater emphasis on research into archival issues. Ham proposed a series of archival strategies for survival in an age he described as "the post-custodial era." These strategies included inter-institutional cooperation, outreach, planning, and research and development. The neglect of research into archival matters had become a serious impediment for the profession. "We need new tools, new methodologies and theories, if we are to make operational the programs on our agenda for the 1980s," Ham declared. Archival research was hampered by a lack of infrastructure and resources to support research, by a dearth of "teacher-researchers," and by a preoccupation with daily practice and the "craft aspects of our work." Research and development were needed in all aspects of archival work. This could only occur if archivists could focus their attention on research.

---

16   "Archivists' Resource Allocators: The Next Step," *SAA Newsletter* (January 1987): 8-9.

17   Lawrence Dowler, "The Role of Use in Defining Archival Practice and Principles: A Research Agenda for the Availability and Use of Records," *American Archivist* 51 (Winter/Spring 1988): 74-86.

Ham thus concluded that there was a great need for "an institute for archival research," which could both assist archivists in improving their practice and also enable them to conduct theoretical studies.[18]

In "The Future Course of Archival Theory in the United States," Frank G. Burke started a debate over archival theory that threatened to divide the profession between those who advocated development of theoretical principles as the basis for professionalization and practitioners who denied there was any archival theory to examine. Burke challenged American archivists to consider the "universal laws" of archives and to examine the fundamental questions concerning the nature of records, the reasons that records are created, why human organizations function as they do, the nature of decision-making processes, the role of archives in society, and other essential issues. In searching for pure theory and "immutable laws" of archives, Burke concluded that, "there has been no elucidation of archival theory in the United States and little, if any, in the rest of the world."[19] Such theory could not develop "in the hot, agitated atmosphere of the workplace, under the glare of the imperative for pragmatic solutions," but would have to grow in the academic "cloister" as certain archivists moved from the workplace to classroom settings in which they could commune with other academic colleagues. Burke outlined several broad areas for investigation, calling for archivists to develop a "new philosophy of archives as records of human experience."[20]

Burke's call for increased emphasis on archival theory immediately created controversy. The first formal rejoinder came from Lester J. Cappon, who reviewed "the pragmatic course of practice and theory" as a basis for evaluating Burke's arguments. Cappon stated that the essence of archival theory lies in confirming the truth of the records; for the archivist, "the concern is with not the substance of the texts, but, rather, the genuine origin and continuous preservation of the records." This is the central archival principle of provenance, which developed, according to Cappon, from "common-sense practice," not from abstract theory or universal laws of archives. "Overarching archival principles emerged empirically," and this is the proper basis of archival theory.[21] Cappon argued that Burke's concern for finding truth in the records had "lured the author into theory of history, beyond the archivist's domain." Burke's list of questions for investigation "pertain not to archival theory but to cultural issues derived from evaluation of the records," and thus "blur the

18 F. Gerald Ham, "Archival Strategies for the Post-Custodial Era," *American Archivist* 44 (Summer 1981): 207-16.

19 Frank G. Burke, "The Future Course of Archival Theory in the United States," *American Archivist* 44 (Winter 1981): 42.

20 Ibid., 42, 45.

21 Lester J. Cappon, "What, Then, Is There to Theorize About?," *American Archivist* 45 (Winter 1982): 19-21.

distinction between historical and archival theory."[22] Although agreeing with Burke that the kinship of the archivist and the historian should be strengthened through "an alliance of archives with history," Cappon concluded his essay with the plea, "let us not compromise the status of archives as a separate discipline, maintaining the *integrity* of the records as its first principle."[23] Even in their disagreement over what constitutes archival theory, both Burke and Cappon thus sought to strengthen the professional identity of archivists and to define the intellectual contributions of the discipline.

A more direct challenge to the existence of archival theory came from John W. Roberts, who argued that "what passes as archival theory" consists of two strains. One strain "is archival but not theoretical, and deals with the practical, how-to, nitty-gritty of archival work. . . . The other is theoretical but not archival, and is concerned with historiography."[24] Roberts contended that the "thinking work of archives" is rooted in subject knowledge, and that, "It is subject specialization that makes an archivist competent, not functional expertise."[25] This disdain for archival methodology and practice mirrored his dismissal of archival theory, which Roberts argued, "is largely irrelevant to archival work, promotes an undesirable stratification within the profession, and is intellectually frivolous."[26] Calls for developing archival theory, he charged, "may derive less from an objective need for more archival theory than from an emotional need on the part of an archival community seeking greater professional acceptance."[27] Roberts deliberately took an iconoclastic position, which he reiterated in two subsequent conference papers. His dismissal of the theoretical basis of archives reflected an expression of the underlying pragmatism that characterizes the American archival profession. As the profession moved to embrace theory, Roberts fought a rearguard protest. Yet he clearly recognized that one of the motivating factors for emphasizing archival theory was the desire for professional recognition. This was part of a broader effort to redefine the profession.

While Roberts complained that American archivists were becoming preoccupied with theory, other critics charged just the opposite. European and Canadian archivists, in particular, have criticized Americans for ignoring or violating archival theory developed over centuries of study concerning the nature of records. According to Jean-Pierre Wallot, then

---

22 Ibid., 23-24.

23 Ibid., 24-25 (emphasis in original).

24 John W. Roberts, "Archival Theory: Much Ado About Shelving," *American Archivist* 50 (Winter 1987): 67.

25 Roberts, "Archival Theory: Myth or Banality?" *American Archivist* 53 (Winter 1990): 115, 118.

26 Ibid., 111.

27 Roberts, "Much Ado About Shelving," 66.

National Archivist of Canada, "It is Canadians' perception that, despite the evident European influences decades ago on the work of Theodore Schellenberg and Ernst Posner in the United States, American archival practice is still largely based on serving the needs of researchers, particularly historians." Wallot contrasted this to Canadian archival practice, which "is now more rooted in European archival theory and indigenous explorations into the 'contextual history' or provenance of the record in a wide sense."[28] The problem with American archivists was not that they were becoming too enamored of archival theory, as John Roberts had charged, but that they had abandoned theoretical concepts in favor of meeting current demands for service. Wallot urged Americans to focus on the records themselves, not on their subject matter.

A further critique came from Dutch municipal archivist Joan Van Albada. After attending the SAA annual meeting in 1990, Albada complained that, "The majority of the sessions were not archivist-oriented but collector-oriented, whether the collectors were librarians, manuscript curators, or documentalists." He denigrated the MARC-AMC format for cataloging archives as "the American disease," because of the fact that "in the U.S. more and more often archives are arranged and described out of context, in conformity with a praxis more useful to librarians."[29] Thus did he dismiss the entire historical manuscripts tradition in the United States, insisting that the only valid archival techniques were those based on public archives principles.[30]

Similarly, in a lengthy review of the SAA Archival Fundamentals series, Terry Eastwood of the University of British Columbia complained that American archivists "work from practice to theory," and charged that "the homegrown and pragmatic *modus operandi* . . . remains deeply engrained in the profession in the United States." After criticizing most of the publications in this SAA series for not providing "a comprehensive statement of fundamental theoretical concepts and the methods and practices flowing from them," Eastwood concluded that "to do that would still seem to run against the grain of the pragmatic and under-developed state of archival science in the United States."[31] Rather than developing a coherent body of theory about the nature of records, on which methodology and practice could be based, Americans had derived theory inductively from archival practice.

---

28 Jean-Pierre Wallot, "Free Trade in Archival Ideas: The Canadian Perspective on North American Archival Development," *American Archivist* 59 (Spring 1994): 386-87.

29 Joan Van Albada, "On the Identity of the American Archival Profession: A European Perspective," *American Archivist* 54 (Summer 1991): 398-402.

30 For a discussion of these two archival traditions, see Richard C. Berner, *Archival Theory and Practice in the United States: A Historical Analysis* (Seattle: University of Washington Press, 1983).

31 Terry Eastwood, "From Practice to Theory: Fundamentals U.S. Style," *Archivaria* 39 (Spring 1995): 138, 149.

This is precisely the approach that Harold Pinkett had applauded in a 1981 article. Pinkett began by quoting Max Lerner: "In the European sense Americans have had little 'grand theory,' whether of the state, the economy, the society, the culture, Nature, or God." Likewise, historian Henry Steele Commager had found "an intense practicality" in American thought, and believed that pragmatism could almost be called the "official philosophy of America." Without apologizing for this pragmatic approach to problem solving, Pinkett observed that, "American theory has evolved essentially from European archival principles adapted to deal with unique characteristics of American record-making and record-keeping practices, from concepts of the democratization of the use of archival materials, and from innovative thinking about archival interest in the management of current and semi-current records." Although recognizing that "American archival theory does not exist as a systematically formulated body of ideas," Pinkett concluded that it does "represent a group of principles that provide a firm foundation for current archival practice."[32] Thus, Pinkett accepted the pragmatic nature of American archival practice as a culturally influenced phenomenon. To be American is to be practical, not theoretical. It also means seeking individualistic solutions rather than accepting collectivistic standards.

Since the founding of the colonies, many Americans have believed in their own exceptionalism and the irrelevance of European approaches to solving American problems. The Revolution severed ties with a monarchical and hierarchical Europe, where rulers and nobility enjoyed rights and privileges that offended the American quest for democracy and egalitarianism. The distrust of external authority heightened the individualism that has largely defined the American character. Americans think of themselves as practical, innovative, and resourceful people who can solve their own problems. This American pragmatism, which sometimes appears as a strain of anti-intellectualism, has strengthened the egalitarian disdain for overarching theory. According to J. Rogers Hollingsworth, "most Americans of the eighteenth and nineteenth centuries placed a premium on such non-intellectual tendencies as rough and ready habits, rapid decisions, and quick seizure of opportunities. Experience was preferred to speculation, pragmatism to idealism, the inventor to the pure scientist."[33] In the twentieth century these national characteristics led many American archivists to believe that they must solve problems unique to their times and their society and to adopt European practices selectively.

---

32 Harold T. Pinkett, "American Archival Theory: the State of the Art," *American Archivist* 44 (Summer 1981): 217, 222.

33 J. Rogers Hollingsworth, "American Anti-Intellectualism," *South Atlantic Quarterly* 63.3 (1964): 269. The classic analysis of American individualism was Alexis de Tocqueville, *Democracy in America*.

This apparent conflict between theory and practicality, and between individualism and collectivism, has led some American archivists to a crisis of professional identity. They see archivists in Europe and Canada enjoying a clearer sense of professional purpose, a greater unity of agreed-upon principles and methods, and a stronger recognition and respect from the public. Much of this, of course, is a matter of degree; much of it comes from a longer history as a profession. However, a major portion of this difference comes from cultural perspectives and the greater interest and higher regard for history in European countries. The United States remains a relatively young nation, and Americans continue to focus attention on the future and to regard the past with suspicion or disdain. Part of this comes from the Revolutionary War heritage, in which a new democratic nation shed its ties to a European past in order to forge a new egalitarian identity committed to a better future for mankind. This American phenomenon has not boded well for history, at least for historical objectivity. Instead Americans, when they have paid attention to their own history, have often filtered it through patriotic or nostalgic lenses or have imagined conspiracies and dark secrets. Examples of these tendencies abound, from Disneyland's Main Street USA to Oliver Stone's film, *JFK*. Such popular culture approaches to history run diametrically opposed to the realm of archives, which values evidence, authenticity, and historical objectivity.[34]

In looking to European and Canadian archivists for alternatives, some American archivists have concluded that developing a comprehensive body of theory and establishing agreed-on standards are necessary for public recognition and professional identity. Theory focuses attention on fundamental principles. Professional standards can enhance professional unity, increase opportunities for cooperation, and demonstrate a commitment to common goals. Together, theory and standards offer the promise of professionalization and higher status in the public's perception of archivists. As Richard Cox wrote in response to Frank Burke's 1981 article, "Burke is correct, however; without any commitment to the development of theory, the archival community lacks one of the essential features of a profession, and weakens its incentive for improving practice and meeting its mission to document society."[35] Frederick Stielow stated even more directly the linkage between theory and professionalization: "Theories are tools that provide a context for understanding and solving problems, tools that can become synonymous with professionalism and the building of a knowledge base."[36] Advocates of archival theory thus

---

34 William J. Maher, "Lost in a Disneyfied World: Archivists and Society in Late Twentieth-Century America," *American Archivist* 61 (Fall 1998): 259-65.

35 Richard J. Cox, "American Archival Literature: Expanding Horizons and Continuing Needs, 1901-1987," *American Archivist* 50 (Summer 1987): 314-15.

36 Frederick J. Stielow, "Archival Theory Redux and Redeemed: Definition and Context Toward a General Theory," *American Archivist* 54 (Winter 1991): 26.

presented this approach as one solution to the problems identified in the state assessment reports and the Levy-Robles report on the image of archivists. They argued that archival theory would help to improve the professional identity of American archivists and ultimately lead to increased funding and support.[37]

Essential to this proposed development of archival theory would be increased emphasis on archival research, as Ham and Burke had advocated. "The quality of archival knowledge is mainly attributable to the literature that defines, debates, and refines the profession's practices and the reasons for these practices," Richard Cox stated in 1987. "The condition of the literature indicates much about the condition of the archival profession."[38] Cox concluded that although some improvements had been made, both were in poor shape. In a 1994 article on archival research, Cox was even more pessimistic, stating that, "There is virtually no substantial research going on in archival science."[39] He blamed this on the current state of archival education, a lack of research opportunities, a lack of reward mechanisms, and prevailing attitudes toward research. In calling for a stronger research basis for the profession, Cox stated:

We as a field badly need research that
- explores all archival functions.
- is replicable.
- is well-designed from a research methodology perspective.
- builds on and refines earlier research.
- draws on relevant research in other fields.[40]

Research of this caliber would significantly improve the profession's foundations in underlying principles and theory, Cox suggested, and would enhance American archivists' identity as a profession.

As American archivists encounter increasingly complex problems of modern records in the information age, we have been forced to move beyond "how we do it good" reports on local practice and to examine the underlying assumptions, theories, and methods of the discipline. The archival literature is beginning to catch up to these needs. As James O'Toole stated in 1990, "While there will always be a need for a significant body of case studies (both positive and negative), the archival literature of the future will be healthy to the extent that it promotes

---

37 Richard J. Cox, "Professionalism and Archivists in the United States," *American Archivist* 49 (Summer 1986): 229-47.

38 Cox, "American Archival Literature," 307, 317.

39 Richard J. Cox, "An Analysis of Archival Research, 1970-92, and the Role and Function of the *American Archivist*," *American Archivist* 57 (Spring 1994): 279.

40 Ibid., 288.

research into archival theory, archival practice, and even archival history."[41] O'Toole, Cox, and others have pointed out the relatively unso-
phisticated level of much of the recent archival literature, the paucity
of strongly conceptualized research studies, and the need for a more
rigorous approach to professional writings. As Max Evans wrote in
1986, "It is ironic that although we are a profession concerned primarily
with documentation, we have not created a permanent body of documentation, or precedent, upon which we can base future decisions and
which we can use to train future generations of archivists."[42] Despite
such problems, there have been noticeable improvements in the
archival literature in the years since Frank Burke called for renewed
attention to archival research.

Two major influences that have helped to shape the recent archival
literature in the United States are an expanded publication program
undertaken by the Society of American Archivists and a major research
program sponsored by the Bentley Historical Library. SAA first began a significant expansion of its publications program, beyond the quarterly journal the *American Archivist*, with the release of the Basic Manuals Series in
1977. The series was intended to provide the "types of publications most
useful to advance the profession and to improve archival theory and practice."[43] During the 1980s, SAA also began publishing additional monographs, reports, brochures, and manuals. Its publications list began to
offer volumes from other publishers in an effort to provide convenient
access to relevant archival literature. In addition to the SAA publication
program, two regional archival associations began to publish their own
journals, providing further outlets for professional research and writing.[44]

By the early 1990s SAA recognized that more detailed publications
were needed, focusing more clearly on basic archival principles rather than
on practical how-to advice. The resulting Archival Fundamentals Series
consisted of seven volumes designed to "discuss the theoretical principles
that underlie archival practice, the functions and activities that are com-

41 James M. O'Toole, *Understanding Archives and Manuscripts* (Chicago: Society of American Archivists, 1990), 47.

42 Max J. Evans, "The Visible Hand: Creating a Practical Mechanism for Cooperative Appraisal," *Midwestern Archivist* 11, no. 1 (1986): 9.

43 C. F. W. Coker, Jan Shelton Danis, and Robert M. Warner, "Foreword," in David B. Gracy II, *Archives & Manuscripts: Arrangement & Description* (Chicago: Society of American Archivists, 1977), v. The first five manuals focused on basic archival functions: arrangement and descrip-tion, appraisal and accessioning, reference and access, security, and surveys. Later manuals in the series covered topics such as exhibits, public programs, machine-readable records, and con-servation, with specialized manuals devoted to religious archives, museum archives, and related topics.

44 In 1972 the Society of Georgia Archivists began publishing *Georgia Archive* (renamed *Provenance* in 1982). In 1976 the Midwest Archives Conference began *The Midwestern Archivist* (renamed *Archival Issues* in 1992).

mon within the archival profession, and the techniques that represent the best of current practice."[45] Separate volumes addressed understanding archives and manuscripts, selection and appraisal, arrangement and description, preservation, providing reference services, and management; a final title was a glossary. Although the Fundamentals Series still did not provide a fully articulated corpus of archival theory, it represented a significant advance from the Basic Manuals Series, as SAA moved toward a more comprehensive offering of introductory publications for the profession. During the 1990s, SAA also continued to expand its own publications list, including several joint publishing ventures with Scarecrow Press, and to offer reprints of archival classics, such as T. R. Schellenberg's *Modern Archives: Principles and Techniques*. The readily available archival literature is thus far greater than what could be found even a decade ago.

The second major initiative that has enhanced the American archival literature since the mid-1980s is the Research Fellowship Program for Study of Modern Archives, sponsored by the Bentley Historical Library of the University of Michigan from 1983 to 1997. The idea for this fellowship program emerged from a 1977 National Endowment for the Humanities conference on setting priorities for the archival profession, but the announcement of its first fellowships came shortly after calls by Gerald Ham and Frank Burke for a new commitment to archival research. The program thus met a need that was just beginning to be articulated. The goals of the fellowship program were stated thus:

> (1) to encourage advanced research on topics in archival administration of concern to the archival profession and the user community; (2) to enrich the professional literature by raising the level of discourse on archival problems through published material produced by the Research Fellows; and (3) to experiment with one vehicle promoting research, i.e., individual fellowships, and to evaluate its appropriateness for the archival profession.[46]

With funding from the Andrew W. Mellon Foundation, NEH, and the University of Michigan, the Bentley fellowship program enabled archivists and other researchers to spend a month or more at the University of Michigan conducting research away from the pressing deadlines and distractions of busy workplaces. By requiring research fellows to spend at least part of the month of July in Ann Arbor, the program also ensured lively discussions of research projects and cross-fertilization of ideas. This was the institute for archival research that Ham had advocated. The

---

45 Mary Jo Pugh, "Preface," in Fredric M. Miller, *Arranging and Describing Archives and Manuscripts* (Chicago: Society of American Archivists, 1990), 1.

46 Marjorie Rabe Barritt, *A Decade of Sponsored Research: The Bentley Historical Library's Research Fellowship Program for Study of Modern Archives* (Ann Arbor, Mich.: Bentley Historical Library, 1994), 1.

Bentley program immediately began to contribute to the professional literature, as research fellows published articles and presented papers at conferences. In its first 11 years the program supported 51 individual studies and 9 team projects, resulting in publication of 35 articles and reports and 5 books.[47] This represented a significant contribution to expanding the archival discourse and enriching the professional literature.

The American archival literature is thus finally achieving a respectable critical mass just as the national boundaries of the archival profession are beginning to blur and perhaps become irrelevant. Within the past two decades, an increasing international exchange of ideas has taken place among archivists from all continents. Joint international conferences are becoming more frequent, and national conferences in all parts of the archival world have invited speakers from abroad. Study tours of American archivists visiting China, Russia, and Australia have been complemented by delegations from many countries visiting the United States. The archival literature has been enriched not only by publishing authors from other nations but also by joint international research efforts, such as the Vatican Archives Project. More than at any time since the 1930s, American archivists have joined the international professional discourse going on in Europe, Australia, Canada, and even China, Russia, and the Third World. We are all recognizing our common goals, our common principles, and our common destinies. We may not yet be on the threshold of a single world of archives, but as we enter a new millennium we are coming closer to recognizing our global professional identity.

Given these international perspectives, how can the Society of American Archivists justify a seemingly parochial publication limited to writings by American archivists? The answer lies, I think, in the value that such perspectives have both for archivists in the United States, seeking to understand their professional identity and the issues that have emerged in recent years within the profession, and for our colleagues from other nations, seeking to understand the peculiarly American tensions between archival theory and practical solutions to daily problems. Americans on the whole will not easily accept theoretical constructs independent of practical applications.

Rather than lament Americans' seeming lack of intellectual rigor or resistance to abstract truths, I think we should celebrate a national inclination toward meeting daily problems directly with a good dose of common sense. Archival theory will guide us in our approaches to meeting the needs of preserving the essential records of society and providing access to evidence that can ensure accountability and protect rights of citizens. It will enable us to make correct choices among alter-

---

47 Ibid., 1, 7-10.

natives. But theory devoid of practical applications will stifle us and prevent us from completing our daily tasks as we fulfill our professional obligations. Theory is based on experience. Since the days of Schellenberg, this has been the distinctly American contribution to the world of archives. Theory and practice cannot be separated. They must work together to ensure the preservation of archival records and the rights and guarantees that they protect. This recognition is what defines the American archivist.

Part One:
Understanding Archives and Archivists

To understand the nature of archives and the responsibilities of archivists, one must understand the forms and purposes of human communication, the desire to preserve and use information, and the important role played by archivists in documenting organizational functions and significant aspects of modern society. The articles included in this section indicate some of the varieties of approaches to these concerns taken by archivists and others.

In his 1990 SAA presidential address, John Fleckner reflected on the motivations and rewards of an archival career. "'Dear Mary Jane': Some Reflections on Being an Archivist" is both a very personal professional memoir and a thoughtful examination of the important roles archivists play in society. For anyone considering a career in archives — or for experienced archivists seeking to recapture the enthusiasm with which many of us joined the profession — this is a good starting point.

The nature and uses of archival records are explored in the next two selections. "To Remember and Forget: Archives, Memory and Culture," written by geographer Kenneth E. Foote, examines the meaning of memory in society, and the role of archives, both in ensuring that certain events, individuals, and groups will become part of our collective memory and in expunging representations of tragic events that we want to forget. Dedicated to preserving the past and the records of individuals and organizations, archivists may react indignantly at being asked to assist this collective forgetting. But they also take part in this process by the very nature of archival selection, acquisition, and appraisal.

In "The Symbolic Significance of Archives," James M. O'Toole continues Foote's discussion with an examination of the ways that archival records are used not simply to convey information or to record transactions, but also to symbolize and perpetuate memory of events, cultural values, and important aspects of society.

Archivists have traditionally focused much of their attention on managing textual records, but they increasingly recognize the importance of visual records, sound recordings, electronic records, and other media for recording transactions, conveying information, and documenting society. Elisabeth Kaplan and Jeffrey Mifflin provide a valuable reminder of the importance of understanding these new media. "'Mind and Sight': Visual Literacy and the Archivist" examines the interrelationship of visual and textual records and the need for archivists to become familiar with visual awareness. Similar concerns also relate to archivists responsible for sound recordings and electronic records, which are examined in later selections.

1

"Dear Mary Jane":
Some Reflections on Being an Archivist

JOHN A. FLECKNER

Abstract: Written in the form of three letters to a recent college graduate and archival intern, this essay presents a personal perspective on the role of the archivist in modern society and on the personal and professional satisfactions of being an archivist. In describing his own professional experiences, the author reflects on how he became an archivist, on the pleasures of mastering archival practice, and on the common set of values and commitments shared by members of the archival profession.

This address is written in the form of three letters to a recent college graduate who spent nearly a year as a volunteer and intern in the Archives Center of the Smithsonian Institution's National Museum of American History. For Mary Jane Appel the year was an opportunity to experience archival work firsthand and to consider her future before entering graduate school. For me, our conversations were an occasion to recollect and reflect on my own career choices and on the archival mission.

Dear Mary Jane:

You asked me how I became an archivist. Really, it was elegantly uncomplicated. After too many years in graduate school, pursuing a vague notion of teaching college-level history, I recognized that university jobs weren't to be found, even if I somehow managed to complete a dissertation. I recognized too that moving office furniture — my latest in a string of minimum-wage jobs — helped to feed my small family and to nurture my identification with the proletariat, but starved my mind and spirit.

Reprinted with permission of the *American Archivist* 54 (Winter 1991): 8-13. John A. Fleckner gave this presidential address at the fifty-fourth annual meeting of the Society of American Archivists in Seattle on August 30, 1990. Abstract added for this volume by the editor.

Still, I was so naive that it took a University career counselor to recognize that my history background might be anything other than an economic liability. Leaning back in her chair, she pointed out her office window to the State Historical Society of Wisconsin just across the street, and she directed me to a recently established graduate program in archives administration. The instructor — yes, it was Gerry Ham — would make no promises about the prospects for a job, but with a sly smile he offered that all his previous students were working. I didn't need a weatherman — as they said in those days, the early 1970s — to tell me which way the wind was blowing.

So, it was an accident in good guidance that got me in the door. But it was the experience of doing archival work — beginning with simplest class exercises and then a formal internship — that sealed it for me. I loved the combination of handicraft and analytical work and I loved the intense, intimate contact with the "stuff" of history. Before I completed my internship, I knew I wanted to be an archivist. I never considered the long-term prospects, the career ladders, or the alternatives. No, I didn't visualize my future at all.

As a graduate student, of course I had done some research in archives — at the Library of Congress, the College of William and Mary, and especially the State Historical Society. But the archivists had taken all the fun out of it — the materials were antiseptically foldered, boxed, and listed. Wheeled out on carts, they were like cadavers to be dissected by first-year medical students. On occasion, perhaps, I even donned white gloves. The documents always seemed lifeless.

Now, as a would-be archivist, they thrilled me. Of course, now I was in charge of these would-be archives. I would evaluate their significance, determine their order, describe their contents, and physically prepare them for their permanent resting places. Still, it was not so much this heady feeling of control that awed me but more the mystery, the possibilities of the records themselves. Unlike the research forays of my graduate student days, I now came to the records without preconceived questions and I didn't judge them solely by their contributions to my puny research interests. Now I didn't have to ignore those portions that fell outside my research design. No, the records could speak to me in whatever voices my curious ears could hear, with whatever messages I could understand.

I recall my first collection as an intern, the first I would take charge of from beginning to end — is it possible I still remember this more than twenty years later, like a first date? It was the records of a local settlement house. The building itself had been razed, a casualty of 1960s urban renewal. I knew nothing of the settlement house, although I lived nearby and could still see remnants of the Italian-American neighborhood it once served. Of the collection I especially remember the photographs, some of them taken for a neighborhood garden contest. Old men in undershirts and women in house dresses, amidst great clusters of tomato vines, stared out at me from four decades before. And the minutes and reports, dutifully prepared by the students and imitators of Jane Addams, with their predictable WASP views, recorded a world they had come to make over and which now, only a few decades later, had vanished.

It was my job, I knew, to be imaginative in listening to these records. My judgments would be critical to building paths to them for generations of researchers, across the entire spectrum of topics, and into unknown future time. Pretty heady stuff for someone who had devoted much of his — admittedly quite brief — adult life to writing term papers for required courses. (Years later I still was crushed to learn that despite my best efforts and great enthusiasm the collection had to be entirely reprocessed — a learning experience for both intern and supervisor.)

The archival enterprise held another attractive feature for me. For all the opportunity to reconstruct the past captured in these documents and to imagine the future research they might support, I had a well-defined task to accomplish, a product to produce, techniques and methods for proceeding, and standards against which my work would be judged. There was rigor and disicipline; this was real work. And, as good fortune would have it, I soon was getting paid to do it.

Well, Mary Jane, this has gone on perhaps too long but your questions brought back a rush of recollections.

Sincerely,
John

Dear Mary Jane:

Your question about the satisfactions of being an archivist gives me some pause. Like most folks, I suppose, I go off to my job each morning with little thought to what it is that sustains my enthusiasm, in this case for some 20 years. Perhaps these reflections will convey to you, and even reveal to me, something of what being an archivist means.

Some background: My father and my grandfather were, among other things, craftsmen, skilled machinists. Whether for lack of aptitude or — I suspect — in quiet rebellion, I turned away from industry to more academic interests. But who knows better than archivists that our pasts — personal and communal — are never left entirely behind. And how fitting, then, that today my mastery of the craft of "doing archives" should be so important to my sense of personal and professional identity.

I didn't become a skilled archivist overnight, of course. After an introductory class and an internship, I served, in effect, an extended apprenticeship (although we never called it that and only now do I recogn.ze what it really was). Senior colleagues, whose critical attention to

my work was never clouded by our warm personal relationships, honed
my skills. In those ancient days, before word processing, I rewrote and
retyped finding aids, memoranda, and reports until I met their high standards. I accompanied my colleagues to courthouses, university campuses,
attics, and basements. And they stood over my shoulder as I analyzed
records, proposed processing plans, and replied to reference inquiries. In
a spirit of personal generosity and professional pride, they passed on to
me their craft and their wisdom. I wish I had been as grateful then as I
am now.

I began to understand the payoff for all this attention when I ven-
tured out on my own. The Crawford County courthouse in Prairie du
Chien, Wisconsin, stands out in memory. My task was to survey a great
jumble of nineteenth-century court records — some of them among the
oldest in the state. Stored in a damp basement, the records were adjacent
to the prison cell in which the Winnebago Indian leader Red Bird had
died in 1828. A single naked light bulb revealed the iron manacles still
hanging from the walls of the tiny rooms. It was an eerie place and a true
archival challenge. But I mustered my archival knowledge and trusted my
budding archival instincts, and I succeeded in making sense of the
records, producing an intelligible survey report, and thereby initiating a
long process that eventually saved some of these treasures.

Since then I have exercised, and expanded, my archival skills in
many locations — although very few have been as exotic and unpleasant
as the Crawford County courthouse basement. And, on many of these
occasions, I have been taken aback by the awe that the ordinary practice
of archival techniques can inspire in nonarchivists. Part science, part art,
and — when done properly — part showmanship, our ability to quickly
understand and evaluate the record — especially when it is old, large, or
complex — is a unique facet of our craft. So too is our ability to satisfy
research inquiries by applying our complex understandings of how and
why the historical record is created. Perhaps in modesty, or perhaps
because we devalue the everyday and familiar, we fail too often to appreciate our unique archival skills and capabilities.

Most often, of course, my exercise of archival mastery has no audience. I smile only to myself at how quickly I recognize a pattern of
arrangement in a complex body of papers and how I determine the correct provenance of a misplaced file. No one else will fully appreciate the
concise accuracy of my well-constructed scope note. And, like a surgeon,
I do bury my mistakes: the unidentified negatives, left behind for disposal and only later fully appreciated; the series misinterpreted and scheduled for destruction. Successful archivists relish their unseen accomplishments and learn from them; they don't brood over their mistakes, seen
or unseen.

Mary Jane, you've noticed that these days precious little of my time
is spent appraising, arranging, or describing archives. Is it nostalgia for

"real" archival work that sustains me now, you might ask (if you were less discreet)? Well, as manager and administrator, much of the satisfaction is secondhand. The funding proposal I help to write and to massage through the bureaucracy enables David — with temporary staff — to turn an embarrassing backlog problem into an important research resource. With my advice and assistance Barbara scrounges time from our in-house editor and designer, coordinates staff review of her narrative text, selects illustrations, and the Archives Center finally has a brochure announcing its program and services. Faith and I pore over a potential donation, as she reflects on its appropriateness to our collection. A consensus emerges and she carries through with the acquisition.

Often, my role in all this is only to facilitate the work of others: clearing roadblocks in "the system," recognizing and encouraging good work, coordinating efforts. At other times I represent the Archives Center and its 15 staff members in the complex and unending rituals of budget and policy planning that are the soul of the modern bureaucracy. And, at appropriate moments, I lead — most often, I hope, by example; least often by direct command. My leadership — once again, I hope — sets larger goals and standards and motivates and facilitates my colleagues' efforts.

Some days it doesn't work so well. We have our crises of confidence and our fallings out. Yet, in the long run I know it does work. We have created a viable archival program. Historical records are preserved and used. We have the support of our colleagues (and the respect of our competitors). The individual efforts of dozens of people combine to achieve our goals. It is a different satisfaction from the exercise of my individual professional skills to achieve mastery. I like them both.

Sincerely,
John

Dear Mary Jane,

As I reread my letter to you about the pleasures of mastering archival practice, I realize it neglects a critical source of the satisfactions I find in my archival career. As a professional archivist, I have joined a community of colleagues who share not just a common occupation but a common set of values and commitments. We join in this profession in mutual self-interest and in the pursuit of the larger public interests that we espouse.

This notion of "profession" is much debated these days and much abused in the public parlance. After all, what do we make of "professional" wrestling except that it is done in public for large amounts of money?

Well, we archivists rarely qualify on either score, but we do have many of the other manifestations: a journal long on footnotes and short on photographs; annual conventions where we stay up too late (or at least we did when we were younger), and an esoteric jargon requiring a regularly revised glossary. More seriously, we do share a body of common knowledge, practices, and standards for our work. Indeed, much of our expanding professional literature, our educational endeavor, our certification program, and our committee work are devoted to these matters.

But the notion of a "profession" also harkens back to a more old-fashioned idea: the idea that as "professionals" we have something to "profess," something more than devotion to the latest techniques. And further, that in this act of "professing" we tie our own self-interest to the well-being of the larger society so that our "profession" is not merely that of a self-interested clique, but, instead, a legitimate claim on behalf of the greater public interest.

Well, Mary Jane, you might ask what, then, do I profess as an archivist? Most simply put: that what we archivists do is essential to the well-being of an enlightened and democratic society. No, not every step or each day is so vital, but the sum of all our efforts makes a critical dfference. Of course, like all grand and abstract claims, this one is at once self-evident and layered with complex meanings. In my two decades in the profession, I have begun to discover something of its essential truth for me.

The archival record — and here I mean the total of what we look after as well as the underlying principles of records keeping — is a bastion of a just society. In a just society, individual rights are not time-bound and past injustices are reversible. Thus the archival record has sustained the claims of Native American peoples to lands and liberties once unjustly denied them. And the archival record will help to secure justice for the victims of government actions 40 years ago downwind from the Hanford, Washington, nuclear installation.

On a larger scale — beyond the rights of individuals — the archival record serves all citizens as a check against a tyrannical government. We need look no further than the Watergate and Iran-Contra scandals to see that without the documentary record there could have been no calling to account, no investigation, no prosecution. And that record — the tapes, the documents, and all the rest — stands as witness in the future to those who would forget or rewrite that past.

The absence of outright scandal and of irreversible injustice is no guarantee of an enlightened and democratic society. The archival record assures our rights — as individuals and collectively — to our ownership of our history. As archivists who maintain the integrity of the historical record, we guard our collective past from becoming the mere creation of "official" history. Fortunately, today there is little threat to us from a centralized Orwellian tyranny. Yet the continuing struggles of individuals and groups neglected or maligned by the dominant culture remind us that central governments are not the only oppressors. African Americans, Native Americans, and others are now recreating from the surviving historical record a sense of their historical peoplehood too frequently denied to them in the past. And they are struggling also to assure that the historical record in the future does greater justice to the richness and truths of their pasts.

The history of the United States is uniquely one in which we — as individuals, as ethnic groups, as localities, as generations — continually reinvent ourselves and then, like Huck Finn, light out for new territory. All this places a special burden on the American archivist. Our society values the present and the future above all. And yet, from time to time, we turn back, almost in panic or desperation, to rediscover and rethink where we have come from. Today, for example, we ask how the nation fared in a previous era of massive immigration and how we brought the natural environment to its current precarious state. If we are successful as archivists, the historical record will speak for this past in a full and truthful voice. And, as a society, we will be wiser for understanding who and where we have been.

As I write these words, I am struck — as always — by the magnitude of our profession's ambitions and responsibilities in contrast to our miniscule numbers. And then I recall — as I usually do — that it is precisely the breadth of our professional values that ties us to a wider community of professions, institutions, and individuals. Our allies are all those who struggle to understand and protect the past for the benefit of the future. We are, from this enlarged perspective, truly the partners of librarians, museum professionals, folklorists, archaeologists, and all the others who preserve the cultural record in its material form. We are the colleagues of political leaders and scholars, of jurists and journalists, of architects and artists who would be faithful to the integrity of the past in their interpretation of it.

Well then, this is my joy in doing archives. To be, at once, a master practitioner — with esoteric knowledge and uncommon skills — and a participant in the most profoundly and universally human of all undertakings: to understand and preserve the past on behalf of the future.

Mary Jane, I would like to tell you much more about my profession: about the sense of shared commitment to the archival mission; about the spirit of generosity and collegiality; about the lifelong friendships. I would tell you, too, about the Society of American Archivists, which embodies so much of the profession and through which we have accomplished so much on its behalf. And, lastly, I would tell you of my hopes for the profession: that we will overcome centrifugal forces and embrace all who care for the historical record in all its forms; that we will articulate the public interest in preservation of the record; and that we will increase public understanding and support for our essential mission.

I would like to tell you all this, but perhaps better, I invite you to join me in this profession, to share in our commitments, and to discover for yourself the larger (and smaller) meanings in what we do. If this is your calling, I assure you lifelong challenges, a sense of community through participation, good friends, and more than a few good times. Let me know; I expect to follow this path for a good while longer. I hope you will come and walk with us.

Sincerely,
John

2

To Remember and Forget: Archives, Memory, and Culture

KENNETH E. FOOTE

Abstract: The idea of archives as collective memory is sometimes employed as a metaphor for discussing the social and cultural role of archives. It is argued here that the idea is more than a metaphor and is supported by theories that would view collections of documents and material artifacts as means of extending the temporal and spatial range of communication. Archives, along with other communicational resources such as oral and ritual tradition, help to transfer information — and thereby sustain memory — from generation to generation. Two examples illustrate the interrelationship of archives and memory within this broadened view of communication and culture. The first arises from attempts to find ways to warn future generations of the location of radioactive waste repositories. The second revolves around pressure to efface from cultural landscapes evidence of tragic events that people wish to forget.

The Memory Metaphor

Archivists have long been interested in the theoretical dimensions of their work as well as its institutional and social goals. With a view toward improving archival documentation strategies, some writers have drawn attention to the question of why societies maintain archives.[1] In addressing this broader question, archives are sometimes said to be society's collective memory. From this perspective, archives transcend the immediate tasks of documentation, education, enrichment, and research to help sustain cultural traditions and values. Although the view of archives as

---

Reprinted with permission from the *American Archivist* 53 (Summer 1990): 378-93.

1   Frank Burke, "The Future Course of Archival Theory in the United States," *American Archivist* 44 (1981): 40-46; Lester Cappon, "What, Then, Is There to Theorize About?" *American Archivist* 45 (1982): 19-25; F. Gerald Ham, "The Archival Edge," *American Archivist* 38 (1975): 5-13; Andrea Hinding, "Toward Documentation: New Collecting Strategies in the 1980s," in *Options for the Eighties: Proceedings of the Second Annual Conference on American College and Research Libraries,* eds. V. Massman and M. Kathman (Greenwich, Conn.: JAI Press, 1982); Michael Lutzker, "Max Weber and the Analysis of Modern Bureaucratic Organization: Notes Toward a Theory of Appraisal," *American Archivist* 45 (1982): 119-30; Society of American Archivists, Task Force on Goals and Priorities, *Planning for the Archival Profession* (Chicago: Society of American Archivists, 1986).

collective memory is sometimes employed metaphorically, it is a claim that can be placed on firmer theoretical foundations. Previous writings in anthropology, sociology, linguistics, and semiotics argue that material objects, artifacts, and documents — including those contained in archival collections — play a special role in human communication.[2] Unlike verbal and nonverbal action, which is ephemeral and disappears as it occurs, the physical durability of objects, artifacts, and documents allows them to be passed from person to person and from place to place over long periods of time. Their durability defines them as communicational resources that can be used to transmit information beyond the bounds of interpersonal contact. The first of the two key points of this article is, then, that archives can be seen as a valuable means of extending the temporal and spatial range of human communication.

The coevolution of writing systems and early civilizations provides an example of the relationship between the use of documents and communicational range. Although many factors were involved in the rise of early civilizations, the beginning of complex social organization seemed to require a means of notating the spoken word.[3] Writing allowed information to be transferred from place to place and from year to year, even if the information pertained at first only to commonplace business transactions and government decrees. In this way, documents and archives facilitated transfers of information that were difficult to accomplish through means such as oral and ritual tradition.

Yet, the fact that documents and artifacts can extend the temporal and spatial range of human communication does not mean they are the only resource available for meeting this need. Oral and ritual tradition can serve a similar function and, indeed, *memory* may even be said to reside in the institutional mission of organizations such as archives, museums, universities, some government agencies, and the like. In this light, the idea of *collective memory* assumes a double meaning. First, as discussed in sociology and psychology, collective memory refers to beliefs and ideas held in common by many individuals that together produce a

---

2   Kenneth E. Foote, "Object as Memory: The Material Foundations of Human Semiosis," *Semiotica* 69 (1988): 243-68, and "Space, Territory, and Landscape: The Borderlands of Geography and Semiotics," *Recherche Semiotique/Semiotic Inquiry* 5 (1985): 158-75. The case made in those two articles is based on a number of sources: Victor Yngve, *Linguistics as a Science* (Bloomington: Indiana University Press, 1986); Ferrucio Rossi-Landi, *Linguistics and Economics* (The Hague: Mouton, 1977) and *Language as Work and Trade: A Semiotic Homology for Linguistics and Economics* (S. Hadley, Mass.: Bergin and Garvey, 1983); Mary Douglas and Baron Isherwood, *The World of Goods: Towards an Anthropology of Consumption* (New York: Norton, 1979); Jean Baudrillard, *Le système des objets* (Paris: Gallimard, 1968); and Pierre Bourdieu, "Le marche des biens symboliques," *L'Année sociologique* 22 (1973): 49-126.

3   Jack Goody, *The Interface Between the Written and the Oral* (Cambridge: Cambridge University Press, 1987), 1-56, and *The Logic of Writing and the Organization of Society* (Cambridge: Cambridge University Press, 1986); Roy Harris, *The Origin of Writing* (London: Duckworth, 1986), 76-157; Geoffrey Sampson, *Writing Systems* (London: Hutchinson, 1985), 46-61.

sense of social solidarity and community.[4] In the second sense — of interest here — the term implies that many individuals and organizations act *collectively* to maintain records of the past, even if these records are shaped by the demands of contemporary life. From this perspective, the activities of, say, archives and museums are interwoven. Each particular institution may sustain a *representation* of the past quite specific to its institutional mandate, but these representations can be interrelated.[5]

The value of this point is that it guards against assuming that collective memory is invested in any single type of human institution, such as the archives. Any view of the past conserved by the archival record can be placed, profitably, in the context of the representations maintained by other institutions. The task of assessing this archival contribution is made no easier by the variability in the way different societies come to sustain important information. In one society, oral and ritual traditions may predominate, while in another society they may be allied with archival records, written documentation, and even elements of material culture such as monuments and memorials.[6]

This second key point — about the collective, interdependent nature of institutional memory — implies that the cultural role of the archives is hard to isolate from the contributions of other institutions and traditions.

Setting archives in such a broad context, however, gives us a better understanding of how social pressures influence and shape the archival record. No matter how tempting it is to discount these forces, understanding the force of their influence is a natural outgrowth of viewing archives in relation to, rather than as set apart from, the goals of other cultural institutions.

The two key points of this discussion can be set in bolder relief with examples, the first of which arises from recent attempts to isolate high-level radioactive wastes from living ecosystems. Warning future generations about the location of waste sites is a serious public policy issue and raises the possibility of archives being used to help communicate across spans of time greater than any single civilization has ever endured. The second example emphasizes some of the forces that shape a society's view of its past. It derives from study of landscape history and the selective way in which tragedies and acts of violence have been marked with

---

4   Maurice Halbwachs, *The Collective Memory*, trans. F. J. and V. Y. Ditter (New York: Harper & Row, 1980) and Edward S. Casey, *Remembering: A Phenomenological Study* (Bloomington: Indiana University Press, 1987).

5   Mary Douglas, *How Institutions Think* (Syracuse: Syracuse University Press, 1986), 69-90.

6   Jan Vansina, *Oral Tradition as History* (Madison: University of Wisconsin Press, 1985). The literature of oral history is of interest also in this regard, including David Stricklin and Rebecca Sharpless, eds., *The Past Meets the Present: Essays on Oral History* (Lanham, Md.: University Press of America, 1988) and William W. Moss, "Oral History: An Appreciation," *American Archivist* 40 (1970): 429-39.

monuments and memorials in order to outline an almost mythological representation of the national past.

Sustaining Warnings for Ten Millennia

Since the dawn of the Atomic Age during World War II, the United States has produced large quantities of high-level nuclear waste. These radioactive by-products of weapons production and commercial power generation require up to 10,000 years to decay into less dangerous isotopes. No solution has yet been found to the problem of this material's safe disposal. Current plans call for its solidification and burial deep in stable geologic formations. However, quite apart from uncertainty about natural processes that might breach the storage chambers, human violation of the waste dumps is an important concern. No matter how securely the waste is stored, it is virtually impossible to prevent people from disturbing the waste — intentionally or unintentionally — during the next ten millennia. If some of the buried waste becomes of value to future generations, it may even be "mined."

Recognition of the dangers of possible human penetration of waste deposits led to the formation of a Human Interference Task Force by the U.S. Department of Energy in 1980.[7] The task force included specialists in semiotics and communication and was charged with proposing long-term warning systems for disposal sites.[8] It recognized from the start that disturbance of the sites by future generations could never be completely prevented. Indeed, the task force was unwilling to assume responsibility for safeguarding the waste from deliberate violation. However, it did accept the obligation to reduce the likelihood of inadvertent, ill-informed penetration of the storage areas.[9] Long-term communication regarding the location of waste deposits was seen as crucial to this goal.

The key to understanding the interplay of archives and communication in this instance lies in the task force's pursuit of long-lasting means

---

7   The following discussion summarizes an argument found in Kenneth E. Foote, "Object as Memory: The Material Foundations of Human Semiosis," *Semiotica* 69 (1988): 253-59.

8   Thomas A. Sebeok, *Communication Measures to Bridge Ten Millennia* (Columbus, Ohio: Battelle Memorial Institute, Office of Nuclear Waste Isolation, 1984) and Percy H. Tannenbaum, *Communication Across 300 Generations: Deterring Human Interference with Waste Deposit Sites* (Columbus, Ohio: Battelle Memorial Institute, Office of Nuclear Waste Isolation, 1984).

9   Battelle Memorial Institute, Office of Nuclear Waste Isolation, Human Interference Task Force, *Reducing the Likelihood of Future Human Activities That Could Affect Geologic High-Level Waste Repositories* (Columbus, Ohio: Battelle Memorial Institute, 1984); U.S. Department of Energy, *Statement of Position of the U.S. Department of Energy in the Matter of Proposed U.S. Nuclear Regulatory Commission Rulemaking on the Storage and Disposal of Nuclear Waste (Waste Confidence Rulemaking)* (Washington, D.C.: Department of Energy, 1980); U.S. Environmental Protection Agency, "Environmental Standards for the Management and Disposal of Spent Nuclear Fuel, High-Level and Transuranic Waste," *Federal Register* 47, 29 December 1982, 53196. U.S. Nuclear Regulatory Commission, "Disposal of High-Level Radioactive Wastes in Geologic Repositories, Technical Criteria," *Federal Register* 48, 21 June 1983, 28194.

of communication employing a variety of transmission techniques. Durable physical markers at the storage sites were seen as a long-lasting, but insufficient, technique (Figure 1). It would be impossible to hope that such markers could retain their meaning for 300 generations, or that they would even remain physically intact. After all, some of the most durable building materials known are, by virtue of their durability, prime quarry for scavengers. The task force therefore proposed that other techniques be employed to supplement the warning conveyed by physical markers.

Written documents maintained in on-site vaults and off-site document collections would be the most important of these supplements. At the site of the waste deposit, written warnings could be placed in an above-ground document vault to explain the nature and danger of the radioactive materials. In this way, detailed information about the design and layout of the storage area would be available for careful study. Future generations would be encouraged to periodically translate the documents from their original languages into languages that may emerge over the next 10,000 years, thereby enhancing the effectiveness of the on-site written documents. The task force saw periodic translation of the materials

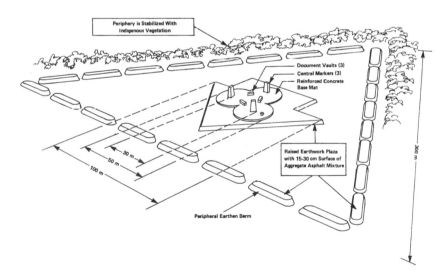

Figure 1. A schematic plan of the surface marker for a nuclear waste repository. The plan mirrors the shape of the proposed nuclear waste warning symbol. Monoliths are combined with document vaults in the plan, which includes a geodetic survey coordinate marker. (Source: Battelle Memorial Institute, Office of Nuclear Waste Isolation, Human Interference Task Force, *Reducing the Likelihood of Future Human Activities That Could Affect Geologic High-Level Waste Repositories* [Columbus, Ohio: Battelle Memorial Institute, 1984], 87, with permission.)

as a means of creating a sort of temporal "relay system" of information transmission.

In addition to this relay system of translation, the task force proposed distributing information about the disposal sites and their location to off-site library and archival collections. Printed records produced on acid-free paper were judged the most durable for distribution, but microfilm, magnetic tape, and electronic storage media were viewed as possible alternatives if periodically copied and replaced.[10] Entrusting the care and updating of these new records to established libraries and archives would serve to extend their longevity. History has shown that collections gathered by libraries and archives have been maintained with care for long periods — in some cases for many centuries — without serious disruption.[11] Worldwide distribution of warning messages in this manner would mean that the potential loss of a record from any one place would be offset by the conservation of copies in other collections.

The task force also recommended that information about nuclear waste sites be added to maps and included in the national land survey system. Maps were seen as an effective means of communicating with future generations because they are used extensively, are produced in great number, and are constantly revised under the supervision of established national, state, and local government agencies. To encourage mapping of the waste sites long into the future, each site would have established vertical and horizontal reference points within the national geodetic survey system. These reference points would provide surveyors and cartographers with the incentive to retain information about the location of the storage areas. Furthermore, it was recommended that the locations of waste storage sites be included in recently created *geographical information systems*. These are large computer databases developed by government agencies and private corporations to store plat and tax maps and plans of public utility systems. Geographical information systems are among the largest databases ever created in the world of computer technology. The high cost of their creation provides some assurance that investment in their maintenance will continue long into the future. The task force concluded that this plan of distribution would extend the longevity of warnings by again entrusting their care to a variety of established and long-lived organizations.[12]

Beyond the use of records stored in onsite vaults and off-site document collections, the task force considered the possibility of employing oral tradition to communicate with future generations.[13] Disagreement exists among historians, anthropologists, and folklorists about the

---

10 Battelle Memorial Institute, "Reducing the Likelihood," 67.

11 Ibid., 72.

12 Abraham Weitzberg, *Building on Existing Institutions to Perpetuate Knowledge of Waste Repositories* (Columbus, Ohio: Battelle Memorial Institute, Office of Nuclear Waste Isolation, 1982).

13 Sebeok, *Communication Measures.*

effectiveness of oral traditions in accurately transmitting information over long periods of time.[14] Instances can be found in which factual information has accurately been maintained orally for hundreds of years, but in many other cases oral tradition has fallen far short of sustaining factual accuracy. Of all the means of conveying information, oral tradition was judged the most difficult to assess in terms of potential long-term effectiveness. Legend-like tales and stories might well arise, or be created, to convey the dangers of the waste deposits. But the task force held little confidence that such stories would transfer enough information to guarantee safety, unless one or more of the other long-term communicational techniques succeeded, too.

Finally, as part of its recommendations, the task force suggested creation of a universal biohazard symbol as a twofold aid to communicational durability. First, the symbol would depict the deadliness of the waste in a form that could be marked on a wide variety of monuments and written documents. Second, use of a single legible symbol would permit its meaning to be assimilated more readily and accurately into oral and social traditions.

Taken together, these efforts reflect the varied resources societies have at their disposal for extending the temporal range of communication. Given the need to communicate through ten millennia, the Human Interference Task Force recommended that both durable markers and documentary records be employed as the cornerstones of long-term warning systems. The task force did, however, find value in other communicational resources, such as legend-like stories. The task force also argued that synergistic relationships can be expected to emerge from the interplay of communicational resources. For example, the longevity of markers and written records could be improved significantly if their safekeeping could be made an ongoing concern of existing human institutions, such as libraries, archives, and government mapping agencies. The conclusions imply that even though documents and markers may be the preeminent means of sustaining memory in human communication, they are not the only way, and they benefit from interaction with other communicational resources.

The Effacement of Memory

If archives can play a part in extending the range of communication, they can just as readily be implicated in any attempt to thwart communication by diminishing its temporal and spatial range.[15] In George Orwell's novel *1984*, the Ministry of Truth ("Minitrue" in the language of

---

14   Battelle Memorial Institute, "Reducing the Likelihood," 74, and W. L. Montell, *The Saga of Coe Ridge: A Study in Oral History* (Knoxville: University of Tennessee Press, 1970).

15   Further discussion of the following issues can be found in Kenneth E. Foote, "Object as Memory: The Material Foundations of Human Semiosis," *Semiotica* 69 (1988): 259–63 and in "Stigmata of National Identity: Exploring the Cosmography of America's Civil Religion" in *Person, Place, Thing: Essays in Honor of Philip Wagner*, ed. S. T. Wong and M. E. E. Hurst (in press).

Newspeak) revised records to reflect current dogma. By translating documents from Oldspeak into Newspeak, Minitrue workers could manipulate the past to support "goodthink." In real life, people do sometimes choose to keep secrets, to lie, and to distort information to control others. Bureaucracies and corporations may seek to control the flow of damaging information by destroying incriminating records and employing oaths of secrecy.[16]

Despite the prevalence these days of paper shredders in high government offices, professional archivists would not condone effacement of records in their care. Nonetheless, as was earlier made clear, archives are subject to the same social pressures that shape the collective memory of other institutions. Perhaps archivists are more successful in resisting these pressures, but effacement does sometimes occur with respect to representations of the past maintained by other institutions and by society at large. Insight into how such forces aid *forgetting* can be gained by turning to the history of places that have been stigmatized by violence and tragedy.

These are cases stemming from landscape history, an active area of research in contemporary geography. To draw a parallel with archival theory, this research has stressed, among other themes, the interrelationship between cultural landscape and collective memory. Such studies are based on observations of the close connection between the places a society values and that society's view — or "myths" — of its past.[17] Like archives, cultural landscapes can be said to maintain a representation of the past. In some early civilizations and primitive societies, this representation was legible in the layout of cities and villages that were designed according to sacred cosmological principles.[18] In modern secular societies, the organizational principles that guide the shaping of cities and landscapes are considerably more complex and elusive. Yet, as the historian Catherine Albanese has noted, Americans are not without a sort of "civil religion," despite claims to the contrary.[19] This civil religion has attained a sort of cosmographical representation in the American landscape, in the national

---

16 Sissela Bok, *Secrets: On the Ethics of Concealment and Revelation* (New York: Vintage, 1984) and *Lying: Moral Choice in Public Life* (New York: Pantheon, 1978).

17 Foremost among these works are those of David Lowenthal, including "Past Time, Present Place: Landscape and Memory," *The Geographical Review* 65 (1975): 1-36, and *The Past Is a Foreign Country* (New York: Cambridge University Press, 1985), 185-259. Other related works are: John B. Jackson, *The Necessity for Ruins* (Amherst: University of Massachusetts Press, 1980); John Gold and Jacquelin Burgess, eds., *Valued Environments* (London: George Allen & Unwin, 1982); and Yi-Fu Tuan, *Landscapes of Fear* (Minneapolis: University of Minnesota Press, 1979).

18 Paul Wheatley, *The Pivot of the Four Quarters: A Preliminary Enquiry into the Origins and Character of the Ancient Chinese City* (Chicago: Aldine Publishing, 1971), 225-476.

19 Catherine L. Albanese, *Sons of the Fathers: The Civil Religion of the American Revolution* (Philadelphia: Temple University Press, 1976).

parks, battlefields, museums, monuments, and memorials that are maintained at public expense and are the object of pilgrimage by tourists.[20]

One of the most interesting aspects of this landscape cosmography is the selectivity with which sites are commemorated to recall great victories, watershed events, historical turning points, and the women and men who made sacrifices for the cause of nationhood. Not infrequently, however, darker events — tragedies and massacres — are marked as well. The value of turning to episodes of violence and tragedy lies in the fact that the memory of such events is so prone to be held in tension. A society's need to remember is balanced against its desire to forget, to leave the memory behind and put the event out of mind. Few events produce such strong ambivalent feelings as acts of violence, and as societies grapple with these feelings in public debate, the struggle comes to imprint itself on landscape. If a tragedy seems to illustrate a lesson of human ethics or social conduct worth remembering, or if it demands that warnings be forwarded to future generations, tension may resolve in favor of a permanent monument or memorial.[21] If the violence fails to exemplify an enduring value, there is greater likelihood of the site, artifacts, and documentary record being effaced, either actively or passively. As geographer David Lowenthal has written, "Features recalled with pride are apt to be safeguarded against erosion and vandalism; those that reflect shame may be ignored or expunged from the landscape."[22]

This point about effacement can be illustrated with striking, but contrasting, examples from Salem, Massachusetts, and Berlin, Germany. Today in Salem, no one knows exactly where the town's "witches" were executed.[23] Soon after the witchcraft episode of 1692, witnesses retracted their testimony and the trials were discredited. Through the years, the exact location of the site of the executions was forgotten (Figure 2). Tourists visiting Salem today can stop at the Witch Museum (the building and site are unrelated to the events of the seventeenth century), and visit

---

20 An informal but provocative account of cosmographical representations and "pilgrimage" routes to be found in the capital cities of Europe is provided by Donald Horne, *The Great Museum: The Re-Presentation of History* (London: Pluto Press, 1984).

21 In this context it is useful to recall that the etymological root of the word *monument* is the Latin verb *monere* — "to remind, to warn." Monuments may arise from other impulses, but their power to remind and to warn often overshadows secondary considerations. Further insight into this issue is offered by Kurt Forster, "Monument/Memory and the Mortality of Architecture," *Oppositions* 25 (1982): 1-19; Alois Riegl, "Der moderne Denkmalskultus, sein Wesen und seine Entstehung," in *Gesammelte Aufsätze* (Augsburg: Dr. Benno Filser, 1929); and John Ruskin, *The Seven Lamps of Architecture* (London: J. M. Dent, 1907), 182.

22 David Lowenthal, "Past Time, Present Place: Landscape and Memory," *The Geographical Review* 65 (1975): 31.

23 Sidney Perley, *Where the Salem "Witches" Were Hanged* (Salem, Mass.: Essex Institute, 1921). For an account of the witchcraft episode, see Paul Boyer and Stephen Nissenbaum, *Salem Possessed: The Social Origins of Witchcraft* (Cambridge: Harvard University Press, 1974).

Figure 2. View from Gallows Hill toward Salem, Massachusetts. No record
was kept of the site of the executions of 1692; only the general location can
be surmised. The witchcraft trials and the reputation they lent the town
remain a divisive issue in Salem. This is particularly true now, in light of the
suggestion by some citizens to raise a memorial in 1992 during the tricenten-
nial year of the witchcraft episode. (Photograph by author.)

a house where it is believed accusations were leveled against some of the
victims. The sense of shame engendered by the trials, combined with
Salem's subsequent growth as a prosperous seaport, led to the passive
effacement of the execution site. All records of the site, both oral and
written, were lost. Still, with the tercentenary of the trials approaching in
1992, the executions remain part of Salem's public life. Proposals to raise
a memorial, and thereby publicly accept the event as a valid part of
Salem's past, are countered by the desire of many to leave the episode
unmarked and unremarked.

In Berlin, buildings closely associated with Nazi power have been
destroyed. The Berlin Wall was originally begun close to the heart of the
former Nazi government district as an intentional means of breaking
apart this stigmatized area. The site of the Gestapo headquarters remains
vacant more than 40 years after the building's destruction. In Berlin, this
conscious effacement of buildings was based on renouncement of this
vicious genocidal episode, as well as on the belief that effacement would
waylay attempts to create pro-Nazi monuments. The destruction of
Spandau Prison, following the death of Rudolph Hess, was predicated on

Figure 3. The rail siding leading to the Nazi death camp at Auschwitz. Memorials to the victims of the Holocaust are among the most compelling reminders of twentieth-century genocide. In Berlin and elsewhere, symbols of Nazi power were effaced. (Photo by Dr. Lisa Nungesser.)

the latter motive. Some Germans go so far as to call for the razing of all remaining Nazi buildings, such as the libraries and galleries that still stand in Berlin and elsewhere.[24]

In Germany, of course, this active effacement of buildings has been matched by the demand that sites of Nazi atrocities be memorialized for eternity. Without question, the Holocaust has inspired some of the most forceful memorials of modern times (Figure 3). The pressure to sustain these sacred places is growing ever stronger as members of the last generation of Holocaust survivors seek, in their remaining years, to leave enduring testimony to the evil of the Holocaust.

---

24 The fate of these sites of Nazi terror is an active topic of debate in Germany and is discussed in Reinhard Rürup, ed., *Topographie des Terrors: Gestapo, SS und Reichssicherheitshauptamt auf dem "Prinz-Albrecht-Gelände"* (Berlin: Verlag Willmuth Arenhövel, 1987); Gottfried Korff and Reinhard Rürup, eds., *Berlin, Berlin: Die Ausstellung zur Geschichte der Stadt* (Berlin: Nicolai, 1987), 543-60; and Benedikt Erenz, "Der Ort, der Stört," *Die Zeit*, 9 September 1988. Debate about the disposition of this "landscape of terror" is closely related to attempts by Germans to come to terms with the Nazi legacy, a topic discussed by Lucy S. Dawidowicz, *The Holocaust and the Historians* (Cambridge, Mass.: Harvard University Press, 1981) and Richard J. Evans, *In Hitler's Shadow: West German Historians and the Attempt to Escape from the Nazi Past* (London: I. B. Tauris and Co. Ltd., 1989). This debate is likely to increase in intensity in the wake of East and West German unification; many sites are likely to be reappraised in light of this development.

These cases bring to mind other events of violence and tragedy where calls for monuments divide opinion and provoke heated public debate. Generally, this debate is resolved in favor of one of four outcomes for landscape: sanctification, designation, rectification, or effacement. As was the case above with respect to concentration camps, sanctification entails construction of a memorial — perhaps a building, monument, or park — and ritual dedication of a site to the memory of an event, martyr, great individual, or group of victims. Designation revolves around the marking of an exceptional event without the religious overtones borne of sanctification. Rectification occurs, generally, after accidental tragedy, when a place or building is "put right" and reused. As was noted above for Salem and Berlin, effacement occurs both actively and passively after particularly shameful events and involves obliteration of the evidence of violence.

The most striking aspect of all four outcomes is the length of time required for transformation to occur. Even in cases where tragedy sites become transfigured into shrines of national, state, or civic identity, their sanctification frequently involves a lengthy struggle. In the first place, as many historians have noted, historical conceptions of a national past are almost entirely retrospective and take time to evolve.[25] The American Revolutionary and Civil Wars had to be won, for instance, before people became interested in identifying key events of the struggle. Second, as has been noted above, tragedies carry intense equivocal meaning and people may hesitate to sanctify sites of tragedy without first reinterpreting their meaning. The initial horror of a tragedy usually must pass before its significance can be assessed and its site sanctified. As a consequence, years or decades may pass before sites achieve the status of national shrines. Until then, the sites may lie abandoned and virtually ignored.

Nowadays, the Boston Massacre of 1770 is viewed as the first act of violence of the Revolutionary War era, but more than 100 years passed before it was permanently marked (Figure 4). Even after this was accomplished, people argued against the marker on the grounds that the massacre was little more than a street fight, an undignified provocation of British troops unfit for commemoration as part of America's "glorious"

---

25 Some of the most useful sources in this large literature are Eric Hobsbawm and Terence Ranger, eds., *The Invention of Tradition* (Cambridge: Cambridge University Press, 1983); George Allan, *The Importances of the Past: A Meditation on the Authority of Tradition* (Albany: State University of New York Press, 1986); Bernard Lewis, *History: Remembered, Recovered, Invented* (Princeton, N.J.: Princeton University Press, 1975); Richard Johnson, Gregor McLennan, Bill Schwarz, and David Sutton, eds., *Making Histories: Studies in History-Writing and Politics* (London: Hutchinson, 1982); Michael Kammen, *Selvages and Biases: The Fabric of History in American Culture* (Ithaca, N.Y.: Cornell University Press, 1987); John Lukacs, *Historical Consciousness, or, The Remembered Past* (New York: Harper & Row, 1968); Patricia N. Limerick, *The Legacy of Conquest: The Unbroken Past of the American West* (New York: Norton, 1987); and Paul Thompson, *The Voice of the Past: Oral History,* 2nd ed. (New York: Oxford University Press, 1988).

Figure 4. The Boston Massacre marker in Boston's State Street. The hub of the memorial is believed to lie where the first blood of the Revolutionary War was shed by Crispus Attucks on 5 March 1770. This memorial was laid in 1886. A monument commemorating the massacre was built several blocks away on the Boston Common in 1888. (This and following photos by author.)

struggle for independence.[26] Similarly, many years passed before Texans sanctified the Goliad and Alamo battlefields, both sites of needless massacres (Figure 5). In fact, the Alamo was almost lost to urban development before it was rehabilitated and enshrined to mark an almost mythical view of Texas's origin as a republic and state. The same delay occurred in the cases of Chicago's civic tragedies: the Fort Dearborn Massacre of 1812 and the Chicago Fire of 1871. Initially these were viewed as at least inauspicious, and perhaps even shameful, events. Only later did they become reinterpreted — and marked — as episodes demonstrating Chicago's civic spirit as a hardworking, enduring, and enterprising city.

In contrast to these landscape "stigmata" of national, regional, and local identity, places go unmarked and even unnoticed when defaced by other types of violence. Accidents, for example, seem to have little effect on landscape, unless they claim many victims of a single group and induce a feeling of community loss. Society seems to find little redeeming value in accidental tragedy. Once the immediate causes have been deduced and rectified, the site of an accident is usually forgotten. As a

---

26 Franklin J. Moses, "Mob or Martyrs? Crispus Attucks and the Boston Massacre," *The Bostonian* 1 (1895): 640-50.

Figure 5. A memorial raised outside Goliad, Texas, in 1936 at the gravesite of those men massacred by Mexican troops after surrendering during the Texas Revolution. The battle sites of the Texas Revolution, like those of the American Revolution, went unmarked for many years before being sanctified. It took Texans a century to mark the sites associated with origins of the republic and state. The Goliad site is perhaps less celebrated than the Alamo massacre site in San Antonio, possibly because the Alamo's defenders died fighting whereas the soldiers of Goliad surrendered before being executed.

result, the sites of many accidental tragedies have remained unmarked or have been reused. Among these are the sites of many of the worst accidental tragedies in American history, such as the Iroquois Theater fire (1903) and the Our Lady of Angels School fire (1958), both in Chicago, and the Cocoanut Grove fire (1942) in Boston. By isolating, cleansing, and returning such sites to everyday use, people absolve them of guilt in a manner common to other ritual processes.[27]

In the case of accidental tragedy, the passage of time is a useful means of absolution. But when a tragedy is not accidental, rectification resulting from the healing action of time is not always acceptable, and this is where social pressure is most outwardly evident. People may be so outraged and shamed by the appearance of violence in their community, perhaps caused by someone they knew and trusted as a neighbor, that they demand active, not passive, effacement. In the case of many mass murders, for instance,

---

27 Victor Turner, *The Ritual Process: Structure and Anti-Structure* (Chicago: Aldine, 1969) and Arnold Van Gennep, *The Rites of Passage* (Chicago: University of Chicago Press, 1960).

Figure 6. Site of the former home of serial murderer John Gacy in an unincorporated area known as Norwood Park northwest of Chicago. The house was disassembled during the police search for victims in 1978-79. The remains of the structure were bulldozed shortly after completion of the investigation. Effacement is one common response to particularly shameful acts of violence, although a sense of stigma may still remain attached to the site itself.

people have not hesitated to destroy the site of the massacre — or even the murderer's home — as soon as possible after the violence (Figure 6).[28] Apart from assassinations of prominent individuals, which tend to inspire memorials, the general trend is for murder sites to be rectified gradually, as are places of accidental tragedy.[29] But slow decay is unacceptable in instances of particularly heinous crimes. In some cases, the sense of shame and stigma is so great that a place, once effaced, will remain isolated and

---

28 Perhaps the best known of these demolitions followed the 1984 mass murder in a fast-food restaurant in San Ysidro, California. The restaurant was razed and the land donated to the City of San Diego. There are, however, many less well-known cases. During the course of the investigation of a serial murder in a suburb of Chicago in 1978-79, the killer's house and garage were leveled by public officials (Figure 6). In the case of a series of murders discovered in 1957 in Plainfield, Wisconsin, the killer's house was destroyed by arson. Many sites of mass murder are rectified, but about half are effaced.

29 For example, see the Martin Luther King, Jr., Memorial shown in the cover illustration for this issue [Editor's note: Figure 7 in this volume]. The memorial is on the balcony of the Lorraine Motel in Memphis, Tennessee, where King was assassinated; it was created by the motel's owner, Walter Bailey. It took nearly 20 years for supporters of a memorial to gain public funding that would convert the motel into a civil rights educational center. Similar tensions have been aroused by attempts to memorialize victims of American violence of the 1960s at Kent State University, Jackson State University, and the John F. Kennedy assassination site in Dallas, and with respect to the Vietnam Veterans Memorial in Washington, D.C.

unused indefinitely, never to be reincorporated into the activities of daily life.[30] Perhaps the "silence" of these sites actually does "speak" to the senselessness of the violence as eloquently as any monument would.[31] In the end, all these cases show how social pressures shape landscape into an acceptable representation of the past. The disposition of the tragedy sites comes to mirror society's view of its own motives and aspirations.

Implications for Archival Appraisal and Retention

The issue of sustaining or effacing memories of tragedy has a direct bearing on debate concerning the collection and appraisal of archival materials. In 1970 historian Howard Zinn faulted archivists for neglecting to collect records documenting significant social minorities outside the mainstream of American life.[32] In a sense, Zinn was maintaining that archives err in favor of preserving records of dominant social groups at the expense of the less powerful. As the discussion of tragedy shows, the issue of selectivity is even more involved. The American landscape, too, is notably silent in regard to these less powerful groups. Few monuments mark the course of American racial and ethnic intolerance. But even with respect to the activities of dominant groups, powerful forces may intervene to influence the record of the past, regardless of whether it is represented in the landscape or in an archival collection.

The Dallas County Historical Foundation had difficulty raising funds to open an exhibit entitled "The Sixth Floor" in the former Texas School Book Depository from where Lee Harvey Oswald is alleged to have shot President John Kennedy. The foundation's fundraising efforts were hampered by a division of public opinion concerning the exhibit. Some people felt that an exhibit was needed, whereas others believed it would only serve to glorify the assassin, since Dallas had already built a cenotaph honoring President Kennedy.[33] The Historical Museum of South Florida was severely criticized for collecting the motorcycle of a black man whose alleged murder by Miami police in 1980 sparked a major riot. Some museum sponsors withdrew their support in the wake of rumors that the motorcycle was to be put on display.

---

30 Shame and stigma may have a powerful effect on the shaping of landscape and the archival record. Future research in this area is supported by a suggestive literature on shame and stigma and their bearing on interpersonal relationships, including Erving Goffman, *Stigma: Notes on the Management of Spoiled Identity* (Englewood Cliffs, N.J.: Prentice-Hall, 1963); Agnes Heller, *The Power of Shame: A Rational Perspective* (London: Routledge & Kegan Paul, 1985); and Edward Jones et al., *Social Stigma: The Psychology of Marked Relationships* (New York: W. H. Freeman, 1984).

31 Bernard P. Dauenhauer, *Silence: The Phenomenon and Its Ontological Significance* (Bloomington: Indiana University Press, 1980) and Peter Ehrenhaus, "Silence and Symbolic Expression," *Communications Monographs* 55 (1988): 41-57.

32 Hinding, "Toward Documentation."

33 Candace Floyd, "Too Close for Comfort," *History News,* September 1985, 9-14.

Figure 7. The balcony of the Lorraine Motel in Memphis, Tennessee, where the Reverend Martin Luther King, Jr. was assassinated in 1968. Tragedies such as assassinations of public figures often carry intense equivocal meaning and efforts to sanctify the sites often meet considerable resistance. This small memorial was erected by the motel's owner soon after the assassination. Efforts to create a larger memorial took many years but culminated in the creation of the National Civil Rights Museum on the site in 1991.

Archivists have never come to terms with the concept of the cultural effacement of memory. They have long recognized the necessity of selective retention, but have done so to avoid squandering limited archival resources on redundant or relatively unimportant records. Similarly, they have accepted the necessity of restricting access to certain records, at least temporarily, in order to balance national security, personal privacy, or competitive business considerations against the value of public availability. But the possibility that a positive purpose might be served by conspiring to efface the collective memory of a particular event is alien to prevailing archival values, at least in contemporary Western civilization. The point here is not to realign those values, but to help understand the conflicts inherent in any society's attempts to remember and deal with its past. A critical role for archives may well be to serve as a countervailing force to effacement as a "source of last resort."

For archivists, the idea of archives as memory is more than a metaphor. The documents and artifacts they collect are important resources for extending the spatial and temporal range of human communication. This view implies that attitudes toward the past, as well as visions of the future, can sometimes condition collecting policies. In regard to the long-term storage of nuclear waste, it may be imperative that archives be employed to protect future generations from danger. Conversely, the history of tragedies exposes the power of social pressure to shape society's view of the past as represented in cultural landscapes and, by extension, archival collections. At the same time, the examples discussed in this article suggest how much remains to be learned about the dynamics of collective memory. Theorists must eventually come to terms with how archives, as communicational resources, are to be related to other means of memory conservation, and why some events are so well documented and stir so much interest while others leave such a small mark on the historical record, to the point where archives become a memory of last resort. Pursued in these directions, research can yield insight into the relationship of societies to their archives so that the concept of memory is not overlooked — or forgotten — in archival theory.

3

The Symbolic Significance of Archives

JAMES M. O'TOOLE

Abstract: *Although most archival records are created to accomplish a practical, utilitarian purpose, this essay explores some of the more "symbolic" aspects of recordmaking and record-keeping. It argues that archivists should understand such issues as: the mixture of practical and symbolic values in records; the effects of symbolic meaning on the forms that records take; the occasions when the act of recordmaking is more significant than the record itself; the ceremonial uses of records; and both the reverence for and the hatred of records as objects.*

More than a decade ago, Frank Burke called on archivists to ponder some of the fundamental issues of their profession. Rather than focus so exclusively on the day-to-day tasks of appraising, arranging, describing, and providing reference services for documentary collections, Burke urged his colleagues to raise their sights to consider larger questions, questions that had no simple answers. Why are there archival records in the first place? Why do humans make written records so abundantly, and why do they leave them behind for future uses? "Is the impulse a purely practical one," he wondered, "or is there something in the human psyche that dictates the keeping of a record, and what is the motivation for that act?" Why, in short, is there anything on which we may work our archival magic? [1]

Burke's challenge has gone largely unaddressed, and some have even doubted the benefit of any inquiry that reaches beyond the urgent but pedestrian demands of daily professional practice. No less a figure than Lester Cappon, a member of the founding generation of American archivists, believed that, in the end, there was very little for archivists to theorize about. Others have resorted to a grosser and more waspish anti-intellectualism. Those who waste time on larger questions, they maintain, suffer from a status anxiety so acute that they will resort to any tactic

---

Reprinted with permission from the *American Archivist* 56 (Spring 1993): 234-55.

1   Frank G. Burke, "The Future Course of Archival Theory in the United States," *American Archivist* 44 (Winter 1981): 40-46; the quotation is on page 42.

to make archival work seem more important than it really is. "Shut up," they seem to say, "and just shuffle the damn papers."[2]

This naysaying to the contrary notwithstanding, some archivists have periodically attempted to address the questions of where archives come from and why. In doing so, they have exhibited a remarkable unanimity of opinion by emphasizing, as Burke noted, the inescapably practical nature of the recordmaking and recordkeeping processes. Works of the leading archival theorists have all emphasized the utilitarian motivations for the making of written records. These records, they say, provide immediate advantages not available to purely oral cultures. Sir Hilary Jenkinson, still acknowledged as the premier writer on archives in English even though he is infrequently read in the United States today, began his classic study by defining archives as records that had been "drawn up or used in the course of an administrative or executive transaction (whether public or private)." His American disciple, T. R. Schellenberg, concurred. Records are compiled by an institution "in pursuance of its legal obligations or in connection with the transaction of its proper business." Records constitute "evidence of its functions, policies, decisions, procedures, operations, or other activities," and when they acquire additional usefulness for "reference and research purposes," Schellenberg said, they truly become archives. The recordmaking process is the result of "purposive and organized activity," usually relating to administration, business, or the demands of the legal system. Even with personal papers, "purposive" activities are responsible for creating the records that might eventually be deposited in an archives. The very words made the point: transaction, policies, evidence, administrative, proper business. Archives are straightforward and inevitably practical.[3]

Explorations of archival history seemed to confirm the belief that these motives for records creation were paramount. Surveying what was then known of archives in the ancient world, Ernst Posner concluded that the desire for "control of material, men, and manmade installations" was

---

2   Lester J. Cappon, "What, Then, Is There to Theorize About?" *American Archivist* 45 (Winter 1982): 19-25. For the hostility toward posing larger questions, see, for example, the letter to the editor by Laura K. O'Keefe, "Forum," *American Archivist* 54 (Winter 1991): 4. In just two sentences, O'Keefe (who boasts that she has never read an article in a professional archives journal) manages to call archival theory "unnecessary," "counter-productive," "foolish," and "self-deluded," and she accuses (on the basis of what evidence is not clear) those who attempt it of being motivated solely by a desire to impress nonarchivists. Another "Forum" letter writer (Richard Lytle) in the same issue celebrates the "attack" on archival theory, concluding bluntly: "there isn't any."

3   Hilary Jenkinson, *A Manual of Archive Administration* (London: Lund Humphries, 1966; reissue of revised 2nd edition, 1922), 11; T. R. Schellenberg, *Modern Archives: Principles and Techniques* (Chicago: University of Chicago Press, 1956), 16, 13, 68. These same themes of the legal and administrative purposes of archives were repeated by Schellenberg's contemporary, Margaret Norton; see *Norton on Archives: The Writings of Margaret Cross Norton on Archival and Records Management*, edited by Thornton W. Mitchell (Carbondale: Southern Illinois University Press, 1975), especially 3-31.

responsible for the production and accumulation of archives. In the process, he identified six "constants in record creation": the laws of a particular jurisdiction; records of administrative precedent; financial records of all kinds; land records; records that asserted control over individuals (tax and military service obligations, for instance); and "notarial" records through which the state certified and endorsed transactions between individuals.[4] More recently, Trudy Peterson found "counting and accounting," which she called the "most fundamental acts of an organized people," to be at the core of recordkeeping.[5] Perhaps because these and other prominent archival writers came predominantly from government records backgrounds, they tended to focus almost entirely on those practical aspects of human affairs which demanded that some record be left behind for future reference, convenience, precedent, or other pragmatic purpose.

Today, scholars in several areas of specialization have begun to address the broad subject of literacy in history, exploring the ways different societies have made the transition from a purely oral culture to one in which writing is available and even commonplace. In the process, they are expanding significantly our understanding of the role that written records and archives play in human affairs. William V. Harris, for instance, studying literacy in ancient Greece and Rome, has added considerably to Posner's six "constants." The utilitarian purposes of records are all there (in rather more detail than in Posner), Harris acknowledges: records may indeed be used to prove ownership, to maintain financial accounts, to provide receipts, and so on. Beyond these, however, other purposes are also evident: records honor distinguished persons; they commemorate brave individuals and deeds; they dedicate objects and people to the gods; they fix the religious calendar and prescribe the precise form of prayers; they even increase the potency of curses. Another classicist, Rosalind Thomas, has explored the ways in which literacy may be used primarily to supplement oral communication, and she has identified a number of "nonliterate" and even "non-documentary" uses for writing, including the ceremonial and purely decorative.[6]

Medievalists, too, have begun to examine the motivations behind recordmaking that show up in sharp relief in societies making the transition (never smooth, complete, or linear) from orality to literacy. Those human activities that formerly could be transacted only by word of

---

4   Ernst Posner, *Archives in the Ancient World* (Cambridge, Mass.: Harvard University Press, 1972), 34. For an important challenge to Posner's "rationalist" view of ancient archives, see Rosalind Thomas, *Literacy and Orality in Ancient Greece* (Cambridge: Cambridge University Press, 1992), 93-100.

5   Trudy Huskamp Peterson, "Counting and Accounting: A Speculation on Change in Recordkeeping Practices," *American Archivist* 45 (Spring 1982): 131-34.

6   William V. Harris, *Ancient Literacy* (Cambridge, Mass.: Harvard University Press, 1989), 26-28, 50-56, and 66-93. Thomas, *Literacy and Orality in Ancient Greece*, 74-88.

mouth could now be accomplished in writing as well; watching societies decide, in effect, when to speak and when to write could highlight the different roles of the two forms of communication. In the process, a good many nonpractical aspects of recordmaking began to emerge. M. T. Clanchy, whose work has enjoyed something of a vogue among archivists, has discussed these dynamics in Norman England. Monastic chronicles were seen by their authors as demonstrations of divine providence, for example, while, in a merging of mundane and higher concerns, practical documents like deeds and charters were often kept in shrines, chapels, and reliquaries. Not only were such places relatively secure in a generally uncertain world, but the physical proximity of the documents to the relics of the saint under whose patronage they had been assembled also symbolized their importance. The quintessential written record, the Domesday Book, had a meaning far beyond its inventories of property and feudal obligation, and it was, in its first few centuries, used only infrequently in practical administration. For the Normans, it was important principally as a "majestic and unchangeable memorial" of their triumph. For the Saxons, it was a pointed and humiliating reminder of their defeat: even their domestic animals were now subject to William the Conqueror and his successors.[7] Rosamund McKitterick and Brian Stock have extended this study to continental Europe. McKitterick has shown that the mere possession of books and manuscripts was a sign of status in Carolingian France and that, in times of war, they were protected physically with as much care as art work and church plate. Stock maintains that, by the twelfth century, even saints' relics generally needed some kind of accompanying documentation if they were to be considered valid and thus efficacious.[8]

Archivists can profit from this recent scholarship by thinking again about the human needs and activities that call records into being. Jenkinson, Schellenberg, Posner, and the rest are right in identifying the utilitarian and functional nature of some (perhaps even most) archival records, but we are beginning to appreciate that that is only part of the story. Hugh Taylor, for instance, has argued that many human "acts and deeds" were first memorialized in ceremonies involving highly symbolic documents, which took on practical import and usefulness only later.[9]

---

7   M. T. Clanchy, *From Memory to Written Record: England, 1066-1307* (Cambridge, Mass.: Harvard University Press, 1979), 7, 18, 125-27.

8   Rosamund McKitterick, *The Carolingians and the Written Word* (Cambridge: Cambridge University Press, 1989), 155-57; Brian Stock, *The Implications of Literacy: Written Language and Models of Interpretation in the Eleventh and Twelfth Centuries* (Princeton: Princeton University Press, 1983), 244-46.

9   Hugh Taylor, "'My Very Act and Deed': Some Reflections on the Role of Textual Records in the Conduct of Human Affairs," *American Archivist* 51 (Fall 1988): 456-69. I have explored some of the motivations for recordmaking very briefly in *Understanding Archives and Manuscripts* (Chicago: Society of American Archivists, 1990), 10-13.

Archivists should now focus attention on those aspects of the records-creation process which are not practical, if only because such an expanded view will be valuable to them in their daily work. Appraisal decisions, for example, must be founded on a reasonably complete understanding of the nature of records and the roles they have played; if some of those roles are ignored, the appraisal will necessarily be flawed. Similarly, archival description that slights the significance and possible uses of records will remain imperfect. In preservation planning, the archivist must always balance the survival of the information and the survival of the record conveying it. Sometimes (with most newspaper clippings, for instance) one cares only about the former, but sometimes (with an organization's "founding documents," perhaps) one will care about both. Outreach and exhibit programs that feature only the records of "counting and accounting" will be pretty dull stuff. Without denying the importance of immediate and enduring utility in the making of records, archivists should think about the polar opposite of that motivation: not the practical, but the *im*practical reasons for the creation of records.

What follows is a preliminary exploration of this nonpractical side of the equation — what I am calling, for lack of a better term, the "symbolic" nature of archival records. When does the true significance and meaning of a record derive less from what appears in its surface text and more from its symbolic standing-in for something else?[10] Are there cases in which records contain practical information, but in which the real significance is larger and more symbolic? When are records made in such a way that their symbolic nature is emphasized over their practical character? When is the act of recordmaking more important than the record that is made? When and how are records put to ceremonial and even religious purposes? When are records revered primarily as objects, with their content and meaning de-emphasized, and, conversely, when are records despised? Examining these questions can offer archivists a fuller sense of the context, and ultimately the meaning, of the materials in their care.

---

10 By phrasing the question in this way, I mean deliberately to separate this inquiry from one founded more explicitly in diplomatics, the "old science" for which Luciana Duranti has been teaching us to find "new uses." See her multipart work, "Diplomatics: New Uses for an Old Science," in *Archivaria* 28 (Summer 1989): 7-27; 29 (Winter 1989-1990): 417; 30 (Summer 1990): 4-20; 31 (Winter 1990–1991): 10-25; 32 (Summer 1991): 6-24; 33 (Winter 1991-1992): 6-24. Duranti herself limits the strict applicability of diplomatics (the internal analysis and criticism of documents) to those records "which result from a practical administrative activity," though she seems open to the possibility that the diplomatic outlook may also be applied, *mutatis mutandis*, to some private documents as well; see 28 (Summer 1989): 15-16. In any event, the symbolism I mean to explore here relates more to records as records than to their internal, textual, and narrative structures.

Practical Values and Symbolic Values

Any archivist who has supervised a collection knows that an ingenious researcher can find uses for records that no creator, collector, or curator ever imagined. Thus, virtually any archival record, no matter how esoteric or bizarre, might be put to a use that could be fairly characterized as practical. Even so, there are certain kinds of records in which the symbolic values outweigh the practical values. These are records that may indeed contain practical information, information that may be used to answer direct questions, but their symbolic character is nonetheless predominant.

Most obvious of these are common family Bible records. Someone — usually successive generations of someones — records the names and dates of births, marriages, and deaths, often together with other information, in the family Bible. Some of these Bibles (or just the pages containing the family data) eventually show up in archival collections. The personal information recorded in the family Bible may indeed be put to a practical purpose — When was Uncle Louis born? When did he marry Aunt Louise? — even though that same information is usually recorded elsewhere, often more reliably and certainly more officially, by public authorities. Still, the family Bible may be put to a practical use. We can check the records whenever we want, without having to travel to the county record office or the state vital statistics bureau, waiting for them to open, and perhaps having to pay a fee to learn what we want to know.

The real significance of the family Bible record, however, is larger than that. Like family quilts or other keepsakes, the Bible is part record, part artifact. We make and value these records because of the way they reconstruct the family across time and space. There they all are, relatives we ourselves may never have known, assembled together by name with their biographical details duly noted. What is more, by making such records, we make the family ours. "There's my grandmother," we say, feeling the personal link and wanting often to touch the name written on the page. The responsibility for entering new information (at the time of major passages in our families' lives) is usually taken seriously, with completeness and accuracy highly prized. The people whose names are thus recorded are different from the mass of humanity because they are our people. The power of that symbolic reconstruction of the family is substantial and, often, emotional.[11]

---

11   On the nature and use of family Bible records, see Gilbert H. Doane, *Searching for Your Ancestors: The How and Why of Genealogy*, 5th ed. (Minneapolis: University of Minnesota Press, 1980), and Ralph J. Crandall, *Shaking Your Family Tree: A Basic Guide to Tracing Your Family's Genealogy* (Camden, Maine: Yankee Books, 1986). An even more graphic reconstruction of the family can be seen in the multigenerational forms, often called "fan charts," in which family members are represented as spreading out from a single individual (often the compiler). For examples of "family group forms" and "pedigree forms," see the appendixes to Crandall's manual and Val D. Greenwood, *The Researcher's Guide to American Genealogy*, 2nd ed. (Baltimore: Genealogical Publishing Co., 1990), 47-48.

School diplomas are another example of records that, though they contain some practical information, are usually put to a symbolic rather than practical purpose. The diploma does indeed convey some specific facts about its subject: that an academic program at a specified school has been completed and a particular degree or rank has been received at a given date. The text of the diploma often contains some language about the bearer being entitled to all the "rights and privileges" that come with the degree, though most recipients would be hard pressed to identify what those are. Because of their formulaic nature, diplomas may also contain some information that is either untrue or questionable: references to the graduate as a "youth," for example, are increasingly inaccurate in the age of the "nontraditional" student. Despite this apparently high level of information content, however, diplomas have a very limited practical usefulness. Potential employers might possibly ask to see a copy of an applicant's grade transcript, but seldom do they want to see a copy of the diploma.[12] Even if they were to do so, using the diploma would be problematic, since often these documents are written in a language (Latin) that most people cannot read. And yet which of these two records do we prize? Do we frame our transcript and hang it on the wall? No, it is the diploma that we value, the framed diploma that we want the reassurance of seeing in our lawyer's or dentist's office. The diploma is symbolic of achievement. It represents the years of hard work, the long nights of study. It conveys the prestige of the institution granting it. What is more, we demand a certain "look" from diplomas: even when printed and mass-produced, they must appear to be original, hand-lettered manuscripts. The diploma is important for these symbolic reasons, not for the particular information it contains.

Wills and epitaphs may be highly symbolic records. Wills, which became common in Western culture in the twelfth century, surely have a direct and practical purpose: that of ensuring that the deceased's wishes on the distribution of property are carried out. For most of its history, however, the will had a larger purpose. It was a religious as well as legal document. A will not only provided for one's heirs; it also offered the occasion to confess one's faith, to acknowledge one's sins, and to support various pious causes. Making out a will was, therefore, "a religious, almost sacramental act."[13] Epitaphs, too, may convey useful information. Westerners of all ranks of society revived the classical aristocratic practice of writing epitaphs in the twelfth century and, over time, these

---

12 The only instance I am aware of in which persons had to produce photocopies of their diplomas was in the process of certification of archivists by petition, apparently to forestall the possibility that petitioners would lie about their credentials; see "Certified Archivist Petition," *SAA Newsletter*, July 1989. This practical usefulness of diplomas is too silly to warrant further comment.

13 Philippe Ariès, *The Hour of Our Death*, translated by Helen Weaver (New York: Oxford University Press, 1981), 196; see his entire discussion of wills, 188-201.

inscriptions became increasingly informative. They presented the basic data of the subject's life and death, but they also often invited "a dialogue between the dead writer and the living reader." One could put them to a practical purpose — Who is buried here? What were the facts of their lives (birth, death, family relationship)? — but their symbolic evocation of the deceased was at least as important. They were, says the leading historian of Western attitudes toward death, "an invitation not only to prayer but to literal memory, to the recollection of a life with its peculiar characteristics and actions, a biography."[14] Useful information was surely present in these records, but their real meaning was more symbolic than practical.

Record Form and Symbolic Meaning

Some records are created to perform useful purposes, but their physical form and the way they are made invest them with an equally important symbolic meaning. Religious archivists of many denominations, for example, collect the membership and sacramental records from local parish churches or congregations. In some religious traditions, these records have a direct and practical usefulness. In order to be married in the church, for instance, one may be required to produce a copy of one's baptismal record. With the passage of time, these records take on a secondary practical use, that of supporting genealogical research. Quite often, however, these practical records are made in a very impractical way. The record books are often huge and heavy: an archives where the author once worked held a volume of parish baptismal records that measured 11 by 17.5 inches and weighed 16 pounds. Such a book is difficult to use because of its heft, and it presents a number of preservation challenges to the archives. It is so ungainly that its covers give out, its spine cracks, and pages tear loose from the binding.[15] Most county courthouses could provide similar examples of the registration of land titles, deeds, or probated wills kept in such outsized volumes.

Is it purely accidental that the late-nineteenth-century priests keeping those baptismal records had chosen to do so in such a big book? To be sure, they may well have had some practical considerations in mind, buying a big book so they would not have to buy a succession of small ones; nor should we minimize the effect of inertia, in which recordkeepers continue to rely on certain forms simply because "we've always done it this

---

14 Ariès, *Hour of Our Death,* 230; see his full discussion of epitaphs, 216-33. I am told that the latest innovation in this regard is a videotaped message from the deceased, recorded prior to death.

15 This was a volume of baptismal records, 1871-1887, for Saint Mary's parish, Lawrence, Massachusetts, now held by the Archives of the Archdiocese of Boston. The archives holds a number of such books, some with larger physical dimensions than this one, weighing between 10 and 20 pounds.

way."[16] Might there not also have been, however, an unspoken connection between the record being made and the way it was made? Might there not have been an intention to underline the authority of the record by giving it a physically impressive appearance?[17] Surely a baptismal record in such a volume was official, and lasting, and *true* — perhaps even "more true" than if it had a different, less imposing form. Making records that were thought to have an enduring effect and applicability in such a solid, apparently (though seldom really) permanent form was not coincidental.

Furthermore, is it not possible or even probable that the image of the biblical Book of Life provided an unconscious model for these kinds of records? The notion of a "master record" in which each person's actions are set down is an ancient one, deriving from both the Hebrew (Daniel 12:1ff., for example) and Christian (Revelation 5:1ff., for example) Scriptures. By the thirteenth century, popular belief, supported by ritual and iconography, held that every individual had a metaphysical book in which the good and evil deeds of life were itemized. The traditional funeral hymn, *Dies Irae*, painted the role of such records in the Last Judgment vividly: *"Liber scriptus proferetur, / In quo totum continetur, / Unde mundus judicetur"* ("Lo! the book exactly worded, / Wherein all hath been recorded, / Whence shall judgment be awarded"). A more modern hymn, popular in several Protestant denominations, asks, "In the book of Thy kingdom / With its pages so fair, / Tell me, Jesus, my Saviour, / Is my name written there?" A sixteenth-century fresco depicted the judgment of the dead, each with a small book worn around the neck like an identification badge.[18] Such images have lodged in the popular mind: think of *New Yorker* cartoons in which the deceased faces Saint Peter at the pearly gates, with the gatekeeper sitting at a tall scribe's desk, consulting the contents of a large volume and rendering his decision on admission to heaven. With sacramental records, the manner of recording was obviously intended to send a message that was as important as content. The medium was not the only message, but it was a message of at least equal importance.

Seals and other aspects of the appearance of documents also affect the symbolic significance of the records. Diplomas are prepared with elaborate calligraphy or are at least printed with an unusual typeface; somehow, a

---

16 On inertia and resistance to change in recordkeeping, see JoAnne Yates, *Control Through Communication: The Rise of System in American Management* (Baltimore: Johns Hopkins University Press, 1989), 21-22, 271-74.

17 For an interesting parallel, see the discussion in Rhys Isaac, "Books and the Social Authority of Learning: The Case of Mid-Eighteenth-Century Virginia," *Printing and Society in Early America,* edited by William L. Joyce, et al. (Worcester, Mass.: American Antiquarian Society, 1983), 228-49.

18 Most of these examples are from Ariès, *Hour of Our Death,* 104–5. Ariès also cites a pious manual from the eighteenth century in which each person is described as possessing two t ooks, one for good deeds and the other for bad. I am grateful to Timothy Ericson for providing m? with a copy of the words and music to "Is My Name Written There?"

common typewriter or computer printer just will not do for such occasions. They frequently include two-dimensional representations of seals. Clanchy has argued that the expanding use of seals in Norman England helped make charters of all kinds more acceptable in a culture just emerging into literacy. Seals did have a practical aspect, helping to prevent forgery and ensure legitimacy. Beyond that, though, impressed wax looked more majestic than simple written letters and, since seals had originally been the exclusive prerogative of kings and nobles, they added the weight of traditional authority. A seal looked (usually wrongly, as things turned out) as though it would last longer than the parchment to which it was affixed, thereby preserving more successfully the intentions of those who drew up and received the document. The seal was, in short, "a relic, which could be seen and touched in order to obtain from it that authentic view and feel of a donor's wishes which no writing could adequately convey."[19]

The demand for seals became and has remained a cultural commonplace. Even in our own literate age, when written documents are so numerous and so readily acceptable, we still seem to feel that certain documents require them or other symbolic trappings. A colleague at the Vermont State Archives has called an example of this perception to my attention. Notaries public in Vermont are not required by statute to own and use a seal; in fact, some of them do, but many do not, and this can create problems. How, without this expected symbol of office, is one who encounters a notarized document to know that the notarization is valid? Other records must be used to fill the "symbolism gap." The state archives does so and is called upon regularly — about a thousand times each year — to verify that such and such a person was indeed a notary at the time indicated. What is more, in the process of making these certifications, the archives often receives complaints that the notarized documents just do not "look right." One foreign consul in particular complained that the document should have been sealed with wax and festooned with colorful ribbons.[20]

The general appearance of records has been important to their meaning from the beginning of their widespread use and acceptability, and this remains true today. In the Middle Ages, scribes devoted themselves not merely to the transmission of information in documents, but also to more aesthetic concerns. Works such as the Book of Kells and the Lindisfarne Gospels were prepared not so much for their usable information (the even-then readily available Gospels) as for the devotional nature of preparing them. Making such objects was, Clanchy concludes,

---

19 Clanchy, *From Memory to Written Record*, 229, 245.

20 D. Gregory Sanford to author, 18 December 1989, in author's possession. Notaries in Vermont had formerly been required to use seals, but this provision was repealed in 1983; see *Vermont Statutes Annotated* (Cumulative Pocket Supplement, 1991), Title 24, chapter 5, section 444. The movement for change came from police officers, who were *ex officio* notaries but who found it cumbersome to affix a seal to every statement they took from a victim, witness, or suspec

Records and the Last Judgment. Written records figure prominently in William Blake's painting *The Day of Judgment* (1808), depicted in this contemporary engraving. God holds an open book on his lap, while angel scribes record the judgment scene. Other figures display record books specifying the fate of the saved (*left*) and of the damned (*right*). (Source: Colleen McDannell and Bernard Lang, *Heaven: A History* [Yale University Press, 1995])

"an act of worship in itself," and the writing was "aimed at God's eye more often than at communicating information to fellow human beings." Elsewhere, the use of various kinds of color — royal manuscripts written in gold letters on parchment sheets dyed purple, for example — underlined the authority of documents and enhanced their force.[21] Even today, citations of various kinds are prepared with a similar concern for visual appearance: award certificates; commendations to retiring employees; collective expressions of gratitude; documents on paper manufactured to look something like parchment and contained in leather folders. The significance of the appearance of such physical objects as seals is implicit in the twofold meaning of the word *impress:* to stamp with a seal in wax, and to have a noticeable and lasting impact on the mind.

Recordmaking and the Record Made

In many instances, the symbolic significance of records derives from the act of recordmaking rather than from the record that results. Writing one's congressional representative is the most obvious example. Only the naive assume that the legislator actually opens the mail, reads and ponders individual constituent opinion, and decides how to vote on that basis. Simply writing the letter is what is important here. Once received, the incoming mail is typically collected, tabulated, and summarized by the staff: so many constituents urge a "yes" vote, so many want a "no." There is even, as Hugh Taylor has pointed out, a kind of implicit hierarchy of value: handwritten, "personalized" letters carry more weight, telegrams and telephone calls somewhat less, and preprinted postcards count practically not at all.[22] Letters of recommendation may sometimes operate under the same dynamic. Do we really read them line for line and consider their contents? Are we not more inclined to note simply that they do or do not exist? Are we not often impressed merely by who has (or has not) written them? In all such cases, the act of writing is as important as the message or information conveyed.[23]

Signing one's name may sometimes be a largely symbolic act. To be sure, signatures most often have a practical importance. The autograph at the bottom of a check is what the bank uses to determine whether to honor it — though as for that, the bank will accept the obviously printed, nonoriginal signature on your payroll check, even as it hands over to you

---

21 Clanchy, *From Memory to Written Record*, 226; McKitterick, *Carolingians and the Written Word*, 143-44.

22 Taylor, "'My Very Act and Deed,'" 468. The groups (unions, political lobbying organizations, etc.) to which the author belongs generally urge him to "personalize" letters when writing a public official in the hope that this will win a better hearing.

23 Keeping a diary may be another expression of this impulse; see Thomas Mallon, *A Book of One's Own: People and Their Diaries* (New York: Ticknor and Fields, 1984).

in return paper currency that bears something made to look like an auto-graph signature, even though it plainly is not. Signing guest books of various kinds (at funerals, for example) is a way of expressing presence, solidarity, and sympathy, but the subsequent use of such books to determine who attended, while certainly possible, is probably rare. The archivist of a small women's college has told me that at her institution's recent sesqui-centennial celebration, attendees at each of the various events were asked to sign a scroll, headed by the date and a description of the event. At the end of the anniversary year, all the separate scrolls were pasted together, one after another, to form one single scroll that is 169 feet long![24] No one could argue that this is primarily a practical record. What mattered here was the act of making the record, all those alumnae signifying their participation, principally to one another, while they were still there. The impact of signing was emotional.

Social historians who study the level of literacy in a given society have long understood the difficulties of using signatures alone as a measure. Some people may be able to sign their name without being able to read or write anything else. Some may be able to sign their names but, for a variety of reasons, do not do so. A modern business executive's correspondence may be signed (with or without identifying initials) by a secretary, for example, or even signed with a signature stamp or by a machine. Similarly, the absence of an autograph on a medieval or early modern document may tell us nothing about the literacy of its originator.[25] In other instances, the use of a signature may be what one historian has called "a socially significant sign." Consider, for example, the case of an early eighteenth-century New England farmer who had achieved enough success to need at last to keep an account book. This was an important achievement, and he demonstrated its intensely personal meaning by writing inside the cover of the book the following inscription: "John Gould his Book of accounts I say my Book my owne book and I gave one shillin and four pence for it so much and no more."[26] A farmer who was barely getting by had no need to keep a written record of his financial condition; he knew it all too well. This more successful farmer had practical reasons for keeping accounts, but these did not exclude or overwhelm the larger significance entailed in his

---

24 Zephorene L. Stickney to author, 11 December 1989, in author's possession. The final scroll was, Stickney points out with undeniable understatement, "a nightmare to assemble."

25 The literature on this subject is enormous. For some interesting discussions of the problem, see P. Collinson, "The Significance of Signatures," *Times Literary Supplement*, 8 January 1981, 31; David Cressy, *Literacy and the Social Order* (New York: Cambridge University Press, 1980); and Kenneth A. Lockridge, *Literacy in New England: An Enquiry into the Social Context of Literacy in the Early Modern West* (New York: Norton, 1974).

26 Quoted in Laurel Thatcher Ulrich, *Good Wives: Image and Reality in the Lives of Women in Northern New England, 1650-1750* (New York: Vintage, 1982), 44; original in Essex Institute, Salem, Massachusetts. On this topic, see also Franz Mural, "Varieties and Consequences of Medieval Literacy and Illiteracy," *Speculum* 55 (April 1980): 237-65.

Symbolic Recordmaking. Zephorene L. Stickney (left), archivist of Wheaton College (Massachusetts), displays the scroll compiled during the college's anniversary celebration. The scroll, 169 feet long, is draped down a three-story stairwell. (Toby Pearce Photo, Gebbie Archives and Special Collections, Wheaton College, Norton, Mass.)

having to make records. The fact of making the entries in the account book represented social and economic success.

Even records that might have a use in upholding tradition or establishing precedent could be valuable primarily for the act of making them. The classicist Mary Beard has described one such example from ancient Rome. The Arval Brotherhood, a priestly cult devoted to prayer and sacrifice on behalf of abundant crops and the health of the emperor and his family, kept a regular chronicle of its rituals. These annual inscriptions, dating from about 40 B.C.E. to 300 C.E., became increasingly detailed and "informative" over time, but there is no evidence that they were ever actually read or used in any way once they had been made. In 14 C.E., for example, a tree collapsed in the brotherhood's sacred grove, a serious ritual defilement of the space. To cleanse the sanctuary, the tree was burned where it fell and none of its wood carried off; the procedure describing this purification was dutifully recorded in that year's chronicle. When other trees fell in the same spot, however, first 25 and again 70 years later, they were simply chopped up and the wood put to another use.

The record of the first procedure provided no precedent or necessary prescription for the future and was apparently never even referred to after the fact. "The activity of the writing was part of the activity of the ritual," Beard concludes, "and not an external, utilitarian record of it."[27]

Ceremonial and Religious Uses of Records

If the making of records can be an action full of symbolic significance, so can their use. Records are often put to a number of broadly ceremonial and even expressly religious purposes. Just as the alumnae signified their presence at the college anniversary events by ceremonially signing the long scroll, so other records may be created or used in various sorts of ritual procedure. In such cases, the record is valued not principally for the information it contains but rather for its symbolic or liturgical character.

From the first, writing has often been associated with religious and even magical powers. Saints Cyril and Methodius, the "apostles to the Slavs," whose bags were packed with both a written alphabet (Cyrillic) and the Christian religion, understood this connection. In practice, the teaching and use of writing was often reserved to the priestly classes, but beyond that, those religions which made use of writing usually proved to be successful and enduring. The great "Religions of the Book" — Judaism, Christianity, and Islam, certainly; but even Buddhism and Hinduism — were easier to spread because their basic texts and tenets could be written down preserved intact and distributed geographically. What is more, since religious texts were believed to capture and fix God's own words and intentions, they possessed an authority that was harder to challenge than purely oral traditions. Interpretations of particular passages might vary, but the text itself remained firm. Indeed, no small amount of effort went into its preservation, word for word, in "authorized" versions. Praying became a matter of repeating certain phrases precisely, as in the case of the Lord's Prayer, even if its language ("hallowed be Thy name," for instance) became increasingly distinct from everyday speech. Writing had the pragmatic value of helping to spread particular religious beliefs, but it also promoted their authority and acceptability.[28]

---

27 Mary Beard, "Writing and Ritual: A Study of Diversity and Expansion in the Arval Acta," *Papers of the British School at Rome* 53 (1985): 114-62. The story of the trees is on pages 138-39. Beard suggests that there may have been a connection between recordmaking and social status, that more detailed records were made as the social and economic position of the Arval priests declined, with recordmaking becoming a form of validation; see 147-49.

28 For a good overview of the connections between writing and religion, see Jack Goody, *The Logic of Writing and the Organization of Society* (Cambridge: Cambridge University Press, 1986), especially Chapter 1. See also Goody's discussion of the spread of Islam in Africa around the year 1000 C.E. in his *The Interface Between the Written and the Oral* (Cambridge: Cambridge University Press, 1987), 125-38. For introductory discussions of the liturgical significance of the written word in early Christianity, see George Galavaris, "Manuscripts and the Liturgy," *Illuminated Greek Manuscripts from American Collections*, edited by Gary Vikan (Princeton: Princeton University Press, 1973), 20-25, and Otto Pacht, *Book Illumination in the Middle Ages: An Introduction* (New York: Oxford University Press, 1986), 10-12.

Given such a close association between religion and writing, one should expect to find written records and books put to use in religious ceremonies of all kinds. In Greece and Rome, written prophecies, complex spells, and instructions on what to do and not do at particular shrines were common. Jewish Torah and law scrolls were treated as cultic objects, handled with great care when in use, and buried in cemeteries when damaged or replaced. Early Christian writings, which were probably responsible for the ultimate triumph of the codex over the scroll, were invested from the first with religious significance. Processions led by someone carrying aloft a book or scroll (often elaborately decorated), the ceremonial kissing of written holy words, the distribution of texts to scattered sectarian communities (as in the Epistles of Saint Paul), all offer evidence of the connection between records and ritual.[29]

These connections were not confined to ancient times but may still be seen in religious practices today, especially in denominations that retain a high degree of ritual. Weekly Jewish sabbath services, for example, have a ceremonial display of and reading from the Torah at their core. Accompanied by the chanting of the congregation, the scroll of the Torah is taken from the Holy Ark and leads a procession to the reader's desk; members of the congregation come forward and reverence it by kissing it with their fingers, prayer shawls, or (in some instances) their own prayer books. After the reading, the scroll is lifted up, some of its text exposed to view, then rerolled and returned to its place of honor. Some yearly Jewish festivals (Simhat Torah, for example, celebrated every autumn) are devoted not only to the reading of the content of the revelation but also to acts of ceremony honoring the object itself. In another example of the ceremonial use of documents, Jewish marriage ceremonies include the ritual signing of a document called a *ketubah* by the bride and groom in front of the witnesses. This document is the lineal descendant of the civil marriage "contract," but its practical uses today are limited. The parties still need a marriage license from the state, and the *ketubah* is written in Aramaic, a language few can read.[30]

Records also play an important role in Roman Catholic and Episcopal ceremonies, especially during the ordination of priests and bishops. At the ordination of a Catholic bishop, the presiding celebrant asks the officers attending the bishop-elect whether he has a mandate of

---

29 Harris, *Ancient Literacy*, 154, 218-21; Colin H. Roberts, *Manuscript, Society and Belief in Early Christian Egypt* (London: Oxford University Press, 1979), 15-20; Colin H. Roberts and T. C. Skeat, *The Birth of the Codex* (London: Oxford University Press, 1983), especially chapters 8 to 11. For a discussion of the darker side of the connections between writing, religion, and magic, see the examples offered in John G. Gager, ed., *Curse Tablets and Binding Spells from the Ancient World* (New York: Oxford University Press, 1992).

30 For a discussion of all these ceremonies, see Abraham E. Millgram, *Jewish Worship* (Philadelphia: Jewish Publication Society of America, 1971), 179-81, and 327-28.

appointment from the pope. The document, usually a hand-lettered and sealed parchment, is then produced. It is first ceremonially shown to those participating on the altar and then held up before the entire congregation, ostensibly for them to satisfy themselves that the document, and therefore the appointment, is valid, before its contents are read aloud. Later, the presiding officer places an open book of the Gospels on the head of the bishop-elect while the prayer of consecration is said. Immediately thereafter, the head is anointed while two other priests hold the book over it. In Episcopal ceremonies, the procedure is similar. Documents attesting to the valid election of the new bishop are read, a declaration of loyalty is signed by him ("in the sight of all present," the prayer book prescribes), and a copy of the Bible is presented.[31]

Colleges and universities are equally good places to observe the ceremonial use of records, frequently focused on the diploma. At some institutions the text of the degree is read during the commencement ceremony, often in the original Latin and without translation. For most participants, the high point of any graduation exercise comes as their names are called and diplomas are received. Parents and friends crowd around, eager to record on film the precise moment at which the diploma is handed over. So central is this symbolic act involving the document that the ceremony may even be arranged to create a deliberately false impression. At the author's own university, students march across the stage as their names are called and receive from the dean the large, flat leather folders containing their diplomas — except that the diplomas are not actually in them! The folders are empty. Only after all grades have been recorded and averages computed (and library fines paid, of course), usually weeks after the graduation ceremony itself, does the diploma arrive at each student's house by mail. In some cases, students will have failed classes, and their degrees will remain to be completed, even though they have already participated in the ceremony and thereby appeared to have graduated. There are other document-based university rituals. At the Massachusetts Institute of Technology, for example, new presidents are installed in a ceremony that includes the handing over of a copy of the school's charter as a symbol of their taking office. This copy has no practical or legal significance; the president probably does not read it, then or ever, and the original alone (a legislative document kept in the state archives)

---

31 For a description of the Catholic ceremony, see *The Rites of the Catholic Church* (New York: Pueblo Publishing, 1980), 87-100. There is a similar procedure in consecrating the leaders of religious and monastic communities of both men and women, in which those being installed receive a copy of the rule of the order; *Rites*, 122, 130-31. For the Episcopal ceremony, see *The Book of Common Prayer* (Kingsport, Tenn.: Kingsport Press, 1977), 513-21. Earlier practice in the Church of England called for a Bible to be placed on the neck of the bishop-elect as he knelt in prayer, symbolizing the burden of responsibility that came with the office; see Marion J. Hatchett, *Commentary on the American Prayer Book* (New York: Seabury Press, 1980), 529.

Ritual Uses of Records. An open book of the Gospels is placed like a yoke on the shoulders of Jeremiah J. Minihan during his consecration as an auxiliary bishop of the Roman Catholic Archdiocese of Boston in 1954. (Courtesy of Archives, Archdiocese of Boston [Murray Papers])

constitutes "the record." The only certain result is to multiply the number of copies of the charter, all of them useless, in the presidents' papers in the institute's archives. Still, the installation ceremony is deemed to be incomplete without this ritual use of the document.[32]

Records Revered as Objects

Where documents are put to religious and ceremonial uses, the records are revered as objects in themselves more than they are valued for their contents. Such reverence is not attached to all records, to be sure, but with those special enough to warrant it, the sentiment is genuine and lasting. The aura surrounding the Domesday Book offers a good example.

The Domesday survey was compiled by agents of William the Norman just 20 years after his conquest of England, and the resulting record became important in royal administration. Its precise practical uses changed with time, however. The particulars of feudal obligation went out of date quickly, but the completeness of the survey meant that its record of lands and rights had an enduring utility. In 1256, for example, almost 200 years after its compilation, it was used in a legal case to force the inhabitants of Chester to pay for the repair of a bridge, since the Domesday Book indicated that maintaining the bridge had always been their obligation. Well into the nineteenth and even twentieth centuries, the book was still being cited in court proceedings. By that time, its pages had pretty much ceased to yield any relevant evidence, but litigants and lawyers continued to search it in the increasingly vain hope of supporting their cases. The universal and almost mythic respect which had, by that time, grown up around it made it seem the logical starting point for all inquiries.[33]

The more purely historical meaning of the Domesday Book emerged gradually, and in that it achieved an unrivaled symbolic value. Not just any primary source, it was so comprehensive and so ancient that it came to occupy a central psychological position, even when it was cited in support of patently ridiculous assertions. In 1919 an editorial writer called for efforts to preserve an oak tree in Essex on the grounds that the tree had been specifically mentioned in Domesday. The document's name said it all. A twelfth-century administrator, writing when the book was only 90 years old, recognized this. "The book is metaphorically called by the native English, Domesday, i.e., the Day of Judgment," said Richard Fitz Neal, Henry II's treasurer. "For as the sentence of that strict and terrible last account cannot be evaded by any subterfuge, so when this book is

---

32 Helen W. Samuels to author, 1 November 1989, in author's possession.

33 The best history of Domesday and its meaning is Elizabeth M. Hallam, *Domesday Book Through Nine Centuries* (London: Thames and Hudson, 1986). For the changing uses of the book, see 32-73.

appealed to on those matters which it contains, its sentence cannot be quashed or set aside. . . . Its decisions, like those of the Last Judgment, are unalterable."[34] Even the procedure for making copies of information from the Domesday Book was designed to reinforce its symbolic centrality. Well into the seventeenth century, clerks making copies or extracts from it were required to do so in a script that mimicked that of the original, a style of handwriting that had long since gone out of common use.[35]

By the nineteenth century, Domesday had emerged as a largely symbolic museum piece with tremendous sentimental value attached to it. It was rebound several times between increasingly elaborate covers, and the first photographs of some of its pages were produced and sold in the 1860s. An "octocentennial" was held for it in 1886, inaugurating an ongoing pattern of exhibits, lectures, and even spoofs in *Punch*. During the First World War and again in the Second World War, it was stored in a prison in the countryside, far out of harm's way in London, and in 1952 it was the center of a minor controversy when the deputy keeper of public records — it was Hilary Jenkinson! — closed the museum where it was on display, claiming the impact of budget cutbacks.[36] The stature of the Domesday Book may be the exception rather than the rule, of course, but it still demonstrates the power of the impulse to revere some documents as objects.

In the American context, the symbolic analogs to Domesday are the Declaration of Independence and the Constitution. In their early history, both documents moved around with the Continental Congress or the seat of government. In the nineteenth century, the Constitution's travels were particularly wide-ranging and not necessarily happy. During the evacuation of Washington in 1814, for instance, it was thrown into a linen sack with some other loose papers and stored in a vacant grist mill a few miles up the Potomac River. Later on, it continued to move from here to there, and at midcentury it was kept (probably without intentional irony) at the Washington Orphan Asylum. Only gradually, as interest in "tradition" increased, did concern for the document itself grow. By the 1920s, both the Constitution and the Declaration were on display at the Library of Congress, but the dedication of the National Archives building in 1933 touched off a 20-year tug of war between the two federal agencies for the rights to possess and exhibit them. When the library finally gave

---

34 Quoted in Hallam, *Domesday Book*, 32. The use of the Judgment Day metaphor indicates that the image of the all-inclusive Book of Life (above, n. 18) was common even then.

35 Hallam, *Domesday Book*, 60. The preservation and use of an ancient script would also be evident later, even after the perfection of movable type printing. Many early type fonts were designed to look like particular styles of handwriting; see Lucien Febvre and Henri-Jean Martin, *The Coming of the Book: The Impact of Printing, 1450–1800*, translated by David Gerard (London: NLB, 1976), 78-83.

36 On the physical care of Domesday and its modem adventures, see Hallam, *Domesday Book*, 153-72.

Shrines for Records. The "high altar" in the main hall of the National Archives, Washington, D.C. This reliquary displays the Declaration of Independence and the Constitution of the United States. (Courtesy of Earl MacDonald, National Archives and Records Administration)

them up to the National Archives in 1952, the transfer was accomplished with all the pomp and solemnity of a medieval procession of saintly relics. The boxed pages were brought down the library steps through an honor guard of 88 servicewomen, loaded into an armored personnel carrier, and escorted down Pennsylvania Avenue by the Army and Air Force bands. Once at the archives, they were greeted by the president and chief justice and installed in exhibit cases, appropriately called the "Shrine of Freedom," specially built to hold them. "We are engaged here today in a symbolic act," President Harry S Truman said. "We are enshrining these documents for future ages."[37]

---

37 On the early travels of the Constitution and Declaration, see Michael Kammen, *A Machine That Would Go of Itself: The Constitution in American Culture* (New York: Vintage, 1986), 72-75. For the slowly emerging interest in them as objects, compare Kammen's accounts of the 1887 centennial and the 1937 sesquicentennial of the Constitution in his *Mystic Chords of Memory: The Transformation of Tradition in American Culture* (New York: Knopf, 1991), 445, 457. On the twentieth-century bureaucratic struggle for the two documents, see Milton O. Gustafson, "The Empty Shrine: The Transfer of the Declaration of Independence and the Constitution to the National Archives," *American Archivist* 39 (July 1976): 271–85; the same story is told, in not quite so lively a way, in Donald R. McCoy, *The National Archives: America's Ministry of Documents, 1934–1968* (Chapel Hill, N.C.: University of North Carolina Press, 1978), 254-56.

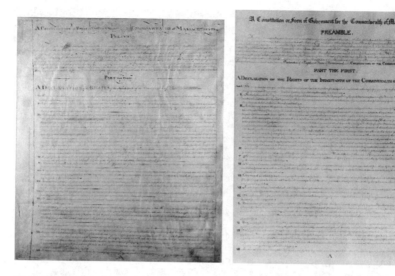

Two Constitutions. The deteriorated 1780 Constitution of Massachusetts (left) and its 1894 "perfect" copy. (Courtesy of Massachusetts Archives)

Truman said more than he knew, and there is much work still to be done in understanding the easy equation, explicit in his remark and implicit in much architectural practice, of archives and shrines. Why are so many archives buildings massive and fortresslike? Why is such solidity (stolidity?) the not-so-subtle message of their designers and occupants? Why do we feel that the importance of the documents that archives hold is best served by imposing physical surroundings? What messages do these structures send about the accessibility and "user-friendliness" of archives?

As with the empty diploma folders, constitutions are important enough as revered objects that we may even be willing to deceive the public at large in order to preserve the aura that surrounds them. The story of the Massachusetts Constitution of 1780 offers a good example. Massachusetts boasts the oldest written constitution in the world that is still in effect; it is largely the work of John Adams. The original was written on nine sheets of parchment, each more than two feet square, shortly after its adoption, and it was stored and occasionally displayed throughout the nineteenth century by the secretary of the commonwealth. In 1893 the secretary reported to the legislature that the original manuscript of the Constitution was "in such a condition that, in my judgment, it should be copied without delay. In several places the ink has faded so as to be hardly visible." The legislature authorized the making of a copy and specifically invested that copy with "the same force and effect as the original." Within a year, a "perfect" copy had been made. "Parchment of the same size as the original was procured," the secretary reported after the work had been completed, "on which the copy was written line for line, with interlineations and marginal notes wherever such appeared in the original, and with special care to reproduce punctuation and capitalization."[38] The copy was exact, literally "line for line": Even when a word was divided over two lines in the original, it was rendered that way in the copy. Though they did not attempt to replicate eighteenth-century orthography, the craftsmen who copied the Massachusetts Constitution more than a century after it was written were scrupulous in making their work look as much like the original as they could. A mere transcription or printed version of the text for legal or informational purposes was not sufficient; the document was important enough as a document that the copy had to be as nearly "perfect," visually and physically, as possible.

The remarkable features of this case do not end there. As noted, the copy was declared to be the legal equivalent of the original, which now became, in effect, irrelevant or unnecessary. The significance of that designation went beyond questions of constitutional law. Perhaps typically for anything involving Massachusetts government, an elaborate and apparently intentional deception then began. The original document was retired to a specially built walnut case — one is tempted to say "reliquary" — stored first in the secretary's own office and eventually in the state archives. The copy was then put on exhibit (where it remained until 1984) but without any indication that it was not the original. Thousands of tourists and schoolchildren were invited to look on their constitution without any knowledge that they were seeing an 1894 copy rather than the 1780 original. Few suspected, since it looked "old enough." The symbolic meaning of the document was so important that lying — or at least failing to tell the whole truth — was permissible to preserve its mystique.

Not every archival record is the Domesday Book or the Declaration of Independence, but these extreme examples highlight nonetheless the ways in which other, "lesser" records may be revered as objects. In virtually any institutional context, some documents may take on the character of a relic more for what they are than for the information they contain. The charter of a business organization, the original deed to the property of a hospital or social welfare institution, the handwritten diary of a founding religious missionary — all may be symbolic documents that are carefully preserved, pointed to and handled with awe, and taken out

---

38 *Second Report of the Secretary of the Commonwealth of Massachusetts for the Year Ending December 31, 1893* (Boston, 1894): 13; Chapter 58 of the Resolves of 1894, original papers, Archives, Commonwealth of Massachusetts, Boston; *Third Annual Report of the Secretary of the Commonwealth of Massachusetts for the Year Ending December 31, 1894* (Boston, 1895): 15. I am grateful to Albert H. Whitaker, archivist of the commonwealth, for permitting me to examine both the original constitution and the copy.

periodically to be shown to distinguished visitors. Virtually every archives has such documents, to which it accords a certain pride of place.

Hostility Toward Records

If records can be revered as talismanic objects, they may also be despised. Records may evoke as much hostility as reverence. A democratic revolution in first-century Greece led to the burning by a mob of the city archives, for instance, an action one historian has described as "certainly . . . not a unique event" in classical times. Opposition to central authority in the Roman Empire could likewise spawn local hostility toward the records of administration, perhaps taxation records in particular. During the French Revolution, any document written in fancy script and adorned with seals or other trappings was deemed to be ipso facto a legacy of feudal oppression and was therefore marked for destruction.[39]

Destroying records may be an important instrument of war, politics, or religion. The victorious frequently symbolize and even celebrate their victory by gathering up and destroying the books and records of the vanquished. An estimated 120,000 Christian manuscript books were thrown into the sea by the Islamic captors of Constantinople in 1453. During the Peasants' Revolt in Germany almost a century later, the destruction took a more deliberate and targeted form: Lutheran peasants attacked Catholic monasteries and religious houses, intent not only on the pious work of burning "idolatrous" books of the old faith but also, in the same stroke, eliminating evidence of debt and work obligations. During the wars of religion in sixteenth-century France, book burning seemed to become a favorite type of "street theater," competing with rival processions for the most common form of party identification. In one instance, a Catholic mob hanged a Protestant printer and burned his "seditious" volumes as part of the same public ceremony.[40] Few actions are more symbolically straightforward than consigning the written words of an opponent to the flames. Is there a more graphically direct symbol for the destruction of ideas thought to be dangerous?

As Orwell knew, control of the past was critical to control of both the present and the future. The constant rewriting of the historical record,

---

39 Harris, *Ancient Literacy,* 128, 211; Ernst Posner, "Some Aspects of Archival Development Since the French Revolution," *American Archivist* 3 (July 1940): 161-62.

40 Marc Drogin, *Biblioclasm: The Mythical Origins, Magic Powers, and Perishability of the Written Word* (Savage, Md.: Rowman and Littlefield, 1989), 74, 84; Barbara S. Diefendorf, *Beneath the Cross: Catholics and Huguenots in Sixteenth-Century Paris* (New York: Oxford University Press, 1991), 56, 65. See also the revisionist argument that it was the enduring religious hostility among pagans, Christians, and Moslems (rather than the cataclysm of warfare) that led to the destruction of the great ancient library, in Diana Delia's "From Romance to Rhetoric: The Alexandrian Library in Classical and Islamic Traditions," *American Historical Review* 97 (December 1992): 1449-67.

the annihilation of old, outdated "facts," and their replacement by the new ones of changing orthodoxies were all essential government monopolies in the negative utopia of *1984*. Such absolute controls, however, are by no means confined to fiction. The first Qin emperor of China, who unified the country and began construction of the Great Wall, reinforced his position at the head of a "new world order" by destroying all previous historical writings in 213 B.C.E. History would literally begin with him. When his successors sought to reconstruct the past around this deliberately created gap, they did so by carving classic Confucian texts in stone and placing them strategically around the empire, a practice that continued until the end of the eighteenth century. Even at that, the inscriptions remained controversial, and these tablets were periodically smashed during local uprisings.[41]

More recently, the political upheavals in Eastern Europe have offered examples of hatred toward written records. In January 1990, for instance, a mob stormed the headquarters of Stasi, the East German secret police. The protestors broke up the furniture, scattered the agency's surveillance files on the floor, and proceeded to stomp on them in what one newspaper temperately called "a show of popular frustration." Significantly, the mob did not destroy the files — indeed, just one month before, leaders of the democratic movement in East Germany had acted to prevent the destruction of secret police files in the interests of preserving evidence of government abuse and of identifying informers — but simply vented their wrath on them by physically abusing them.[42]

In this and in similar cases elsewhere in East Germany and in other collapsing Communist bloc countries, the records had great symbolic significance. They certainly had been created to accomplish a practical purpose — in this instance, the systematic violation of human rights by the government. To the democratic movements, however, the records had been transformed, at least temporarily, into something else: symbols of all that was wrong with the regimes they were now overthrowing. To destroy the records, or at least to scatter them around on the floor and to feel the satisfaction of grinding them underfoot, had more to do with symbolism and psychology than with the utilitarian aspects of record-making and recordkeeping.

---

41 Drogin, *Biblioclasm*, 82-83; see also John King Fairbank, *China: A New History* (Cambridge, Mass.: Belknap Press, 1992), 54-57. Orwell's famous dictum — "Who controls the past controls the future; who controls the present controls the past" — is in *1984* (New York: Signet, 1982), 32. There is a need for more study of hostility toward books and records, a study that might start with the treatment of the subject in works of fiction such as *1984* and Ray Bradbury's science fiction classic, *Fahrenheit 451*.

42 *New York Times*, 16 January 1990. For examples of the mob moving to protect the files from destruction (often by their fleeing Communist masters), see the *New York Times*, 6 and 8 December 1989.

Conclusion

The argument throughout this exploration is not that archival records have symbolic meaning to the exclusion of practical meaning or use. Probably most of the records archivists encounter, especially those functional and instrumental records of modern bureaucratic organizations, will exhibit far more practical than symbolic characteristics. Those archival theorists and writers who concentrated on the records produced by "purposive" activities were not mistaken; they simply did not see the entire picture. As a corrective, we should begin to explore in further detail — in part, simply by multiplying the number and kind of examples considered here — the symbolic aspects of archival culture. One view is not "right" and the other "wrong"; what we need is a more balanced vision.

Such an exercise in balancing may have a usefulness to archivists even in their everyday practice. As noted at the outset, appraisal, arrangement, description, reference, and outreach programs may all be enhanced by a fuller understanding of the roles, both practical and symbolic, that records have played. More fundamentally, archivists have always maintained that they are interested first and foremost in the context of their records. They have taken the principles of provenance and original order, both of which require an understanding of the contexts in which records were originally created and used, as their central professional guides. To understand records, archivists say, one must understand as much as possible about the circumstances that produced them. Achieving that understanding demands that we look not only at the practical, utilitarian context of records but at the symbolic context and meaning as well. If we continue to overlook that aspect of our work, our task as archivists remains only half done.

4

"Mind and Sight": Visual Literacy and the Archivist

ELISABETH KAPLAN AND JEFFREY MIFFLIN

Abstract: Contemporary culture is increasingly captured by and reflected in visual materials. Preserving and providing intellectual access to visual records will become an increasingly important aspect of archival work as such materials proliferate and are widely available in electronic form. Visual literacy, an evolving concept best defined as the ability to understand and use images and to think and learn in terms of images, is an essential skill for archivists and researchers using visual materials. Archivists of all media should strive to increase their visual literacy because of the complex ways in which visual and "traditional" textual documents interrelate. Archivists can approach visual literacy by becoming familiar with levels of visual awareness; participating in the ongoing discourse about the nature of literacy, including the relationships between visual and textual literacy; and increasing understanding of the special characteristics of image-creating technologies as well as the conventions and modes of expression associated with particular media. Expanded visual literacy will help archivists to understand and better describe visual resources as well as traditional documents and other materials of record. The results, improved finding aids and catalog records, will keep pace with anticipated expanding requirements of the research community.

Most archivists recognize that contemporary culture is increasingly captured by and reflected in visual and audiovisual documents and that the proliferation of such materials presents new challenges to the archival profession. Archivists have demonstrated their appreciation of these challenges by organizing conference panels, workshops, committees, professional associations, and Internet discussion groups dedicated to exploring archival issues related to visual media. The concerns voiced in these forums have, with few exceptions, focused on understanding the physical aspects of the media for practical ends. Preservation techniques, scanning equipment and methods, and the technological manipulations needed for multimedia applications are among the most frequently discussed topics.

Reprinted with permission from *Archival Issues* 21, no. 2 (1996): 107-27. This article grew out of graduate papers prepared at the University of Massachusetts, Boston, and Simmons Graduate School of Library and Information Science. The authors would like to thank James M. O'Toole, Allan B. Goodrich, and James B. Hill.

These efforts to deal with physical and practical aspects of visual materials are essential, but archivists should also devote corresponding attention to underlying intellectual issues. Case studies on use and interpretation of visual materials in specific historical and cultural contexts, examinations of the complex and shifting relationships between print media and audiovisual media, and focused explorations of the technology and material characteristics of visual media in relation to their intellectual contents will become increasingly necessary as these materials come to constitute more of, and interrelate more closely with, the contemporary archival record.

An adequate knowledge base supports any practice, and understanding the characteristics of visual materials is crucial to archival practices such as appraisal, arrangement, and description. Furthermore, a level of competence and sophistication with the intellectual issues presented by a record's visual content is increasingly important for archivists of *any* medium. Contemporary, overlapping, and obsolete document forms are peculiarly interrelated. New materials of record require archivists to rethink their perceptions about concurrent or previously used document forms, and therefore to rethink their conceptions of archival theory and practice. "A new medium," as Walter Ong has observed, "transforms not only the one which immediately precedes it but often all of those which preceded it all the way back to the beginning."[1]

Explorations of the present dimensions of literacy and its future are of increasing philosophical and practical importance. "What will be the intellectual character of the new society, [and what will constitute the] 'literacy' of its people?" asked the editor of a 1982 issue of *Daedalus* entitled "Print Culture and Video Culture." How should those who engage intensively with documents — archivists and historians, for instance — conceive of, cope with, respond to, and prepare for these changes?[2]

More specifically, how should archivists approach visual materials in an informed manner, or approach "traditional" materials with a knowledge of their relationship to visual materials? The declaration that this is a culture reliant on visual communication, and that all members of such a culture require a particular set of abilities for interpreting images, is by now familiar.[3] How can archivists achieve a professional consciousness of these

---

1 Walter Ong, *Interfaces of the Word: Studies in the Evolution of Consciousness and Culture* (Ithaca: Cornell University Press, 1977), 90.

2 Stephen S. Graubard, "Preface," *Daedalus* 111 (1982): vii.

3 Consider, for example, Stephen S. Graubard's observation that "we live in the century of the 'moving image,' but have only barely begun to consider the cultural and social implications of that fact" (*Daedalus* 114 [1985]: v). This issue of *Daedalus* was titled "The Moving Image." More recently, see "Visual Images Replace Text as Focal Point for Many Scholars," *Chronicle of Higher Education*, 19 (July 1996): A8-A15.

skills? Understanding the visual content of documents entails facility with a complex and little understood set of skills, described in this paper as "visual literacy." Visual literacy is essential for people bombarded by television, news photos, advertisements, digital images on the World Wide Web, and other aspects of our contemporary super abundance of visual stimulation. Yet how is visual literacy practiced? What individual skills does it require? Does it involve a solely interpretive set of skills, or has it an expressive component as well? How does it relate to other communications processes? Is visual literacy merely a component of human cognitive development, or is it learned, and thus tied to culture-specific conventions for communication? If the latter, then by what methods can it be taught? If visual communication is a form of "literacy," then to what extent can the dimensions of visual information be understood by analogy to language? By extension, to what extent can visual materials be understood by analogy to traditional textual materials? Whether archivists consciously consider these questions or not, they affect daily archival work. Whether they realize it or not, archivists who work with visual materials, even on an occasional basis, grapple with visual awareness on several levels.

Archivists, like others, will have to wait for a full understanding of the implications of visual materials. Additional research and additional hindsight are required. In the meantime, there are ways in which archivists can begin to gain an interesting and useful understanding of visual literacy issues. This paper serves as a preliminary articulation of questions about the nature of visual expression and interpretation and a preliminary application of those questions to the archival profession. It suggests that archivists will benefit from an increased facility with levels of visual awareness, and that such facility can result from investigation on at least four frontiers:

- an increased attention to the scholarship on history of literacy generally, as well as to the discourse on visual literacy
- an increased awareness of the conventions or modes of expression employed by visual materials such as film, photography, and video, and the levels of analysis at which such materials can be understood
- an awareness of how historians and others in related disciplines are facing visual awareness issues, and an exploration of the possibilities of collaboration
- a review of the efforts of archivists over the years in relation to these issues

The Evolution of a Concept

In a written text, perception, understanding, and expression of the building blocks and the ways of putting those blocks together are referred to as *literacy*, a set of skills traditionally associated with reading and writing. What, then, is literacy's equivalent when it comes to visual materials?

Scholarship on visual literacy is best viewed within the framework of the larger literature on the history of literacy in general, which has enjoyed renewed attention since the early 1980s. At the risk of oversimplification, it might be stated that this literature redefines the concept of literacy from its traditional definition, the ability to read and write, to a complex set of shifting, evolving, overlapping communications processes; processes driven by changing technology, occurring in overlapping stages, and more complex than has been allowed in the past.[4]

An immediately striking feature revealed by a survey of literature on the concept of visual literacy is the variety of terms applied by scholars to the concept. The interpretive aspect of the process of "doing" visual literacy, by which visual information is mentally registered and processed, is described variously in the literature as *reading, listening, hearing*, and *decoding*. The expressive component, by which information is communicated through visual means, is described as *writing, speaking, composing, encoding*, and *uttering*. These terms imply a variety of approaches to the concept, including explicit analogies to traditional literacy, and careful attempts to sidestep that analogy.[5]

The term *visual literacy* was first developed and popularized in the late 1960s by John L. Debes, coordinator of education projects at the Eastman Kodak Company. Debes described his idea tentatively at first: "When I say visual literacy what I have in mind is a great dim shape, the outlines and importance of which are not yet clear."[6] What was clear, according to Debes, was that some sort of confluence of "knowledge, theory, and technology" was underway, embodied in a concept whose time had come. "I think of visual literacy," he wrote, "as a great amoeba-like entity with pseudopods reaching out in many directions. I see those pseudopods labeled with the names of sources such as semantics, linguistics, philosophy, psychology, the industrial, vocational, and graphic arts, psycholinguistics, art, and screen education."[7]

---

4 A typical traditional definition of literacy is found in *The American Heritage Dictionary*, 2nd college edition (Boston: Houghton Mifflin, 1985). The recent works relating to the history of literacy are numerous and include the works of M. T. Clanchy, Richard D. Brown, Walter Ong, Eric Havelock, Rosalind Thomas, Jack Goody, and Harvey J. Graaf.

5 In addition, the word *text* is applied in its traditional sense by some scholars to mean written or printed works, and in its deconstructionist sense by others to describe images, sounds, and virtually any other form of communication. Many scholars neglect to define their terms, with confusing results.

6 John L. Debes, "The Loom of Visual Literacy," *Audiovisual Instruction* 14 (1969): 25.

7 Ibid.

Debes convened the First Annual National Conference on Visual Literacy, held in Rochester, New York, on March 23, 1969, attended and sponsored by diverse groups, including university and high school educators, English teachers, audiovisual instructors, art teachers, and representatives from Eastman Kodak, the University of Rochester, and Syracuse University.[8] At the conference, Debes attempted a fuller formulation of the concept:

> Visual literacy refers to a group of vision-competencies a human being can develop by seeing and at the same time having and integrating other sensory experiences. The development of these competencies is fundamental to normal human learning. When developed, they enable a visually literate person to discriminate and interpret the visible actions, objects, and symbols, natural or man-made, that he encounters in his environment. Through the creative use of these competencies, he is able to communicate with others. Through the appreciative use of these competencies, he is able to comprehend and enjoy the masterworks of visual communication.[9]

By the mid-1970s, visual literacy ceased to be solely a concept and became a self-described movement. Perhaps because it coincided with widespread concerns in the early 1970s about the impact of television on young children, and perhaps because experts in a variety of disciplines began simultaneously to recognize that contemporary culture is increasingly likely to be reflected in, captured by, or represented by visual media, the idea of visual literacy caught on immediately. In addition to the disciplines Debes foresaw as contributing to the discussion on visual literacy, scholars in education, art theory, film theory, history, film history, media and communications studies, sociology, and semiotics all began to address the topic. Some embraced the phrase and used it explicitly, while others grappled with the same issues, but for the most part rejected the term itself. By the mid-1980s, the volume of literature on visual literacy was enormous, and a number of newly established journals devoted considerable attention to the concept. Still, visual literacy continued to be plagued by foggy definition and inconsistent application.[10]

---

8 Laverne W. Miller, "Some Thoughts on Visual Literacy," *Choice* 22 (March 1985): 937. From this conference sprang the International Visual Literacy Association (IVLA), an eclectic interdisciplinary group that has met and published its proceedings annually since then. In 1970 Debes and Clarence Williams founded the Center for Visual Literacy at the University of Rochester.

9 Debes, "The Loom of Visual Literacy," 27.

10 Journals include *The Journal of Communication, Visible Language, Media and Methods, The Journal of Visual and Verbal Languaging,* and *Visual Resources.*

A few voices noted that the lack of a consistent theory and definition of visual literacy was problematic, both for the entire discussion, and for its practical application. In an important essay summarizing the literature to 1982, instructional technologist John A. Hortin stated the problem in this way:

> Many authors have mentioned sources for a theoretical foundation of visual literacy but failed to give a thorough analysis or satisfactory explanation of the theory and its link to practice. For instance, no one has satisfactorily explained the analogy between visual language and verbal language. We need an historical, analytical study of the philosophical origins of visual literacy.[11]

Hortin continued, "it is necessary to know the meaning and theoretical foundations of visual literacy before one can use visual literacy effectively."[12] In 1986 educator Richard Sinatra noted that:

> The meaning of visual literacy has not been clearly defined in functional, realistic terms. This is undoubtedly due to the expansiveness of the concept, the meaning of visual itself, the academic leanings of [those] applying the terms, and preoccupation with the forms and techniques of media communication. . . . A major problem for visual literacy enthusiasts is that they have been using a catch-all term to mean anything that is delivered through visual sensory output.[13]

The most recent attempt to formulate a theory of visual literacy is found in Paul Messaris's 1994 *Visual 'Literacy': Image, Mind, Reality*, which draws from a range of disciplines to deconstruct assumptions that have accompanied the concept from the start. Messaris attacks the premises that visual images are arbitrary and culture-bound; that visual literacy (defined as familiarity with a visual language or grammar) is necessary for visual comprehension; and that visual literacy and verbal language are analogous. As he writes, "strictly speaking, of course, the term 'literacy' should be applied only to reading and writing. But it would probably be too pedantic and, in any case, it would surely be

---

11   John Hortin, "A Need for a Theory of Visual Literacy," *Reading Improvement* 19 (1982): 260.

12   Ibid., 261.

13   To illustrate this point, Sinatra cites a 1976 conference at which delegates were asked for definitions of visual literacy. "Analysis of the 62 definitions indicated that 52 different phrases were used to define the adjective 'visual,' and that 3 major meanings evolved for the word 'literacy'. . . ." Richard Sinatra, *Visual Literacy Connections to Thinking, Reading, and Writing* (Springfield, Ill.: Charles C. Thomas, 1986), 45-46.

futile to resist the increasingly common tendency to apply this term to other kinds of communication skills (mathematical 'literacy,' computer 'literacy') as well as the substantive knowledge that communication rests on (historical, geographic, cultural 'literacy')."[14]

Hortin's 1982 proposal that "visual literacy is the ability to understand and use images and to think and learn in terms of images, i.e., to think visually"[15] is probably the most useful definition to date, because of its simplicity, inclusiveness, and refusal to rely on the conventions of language for its definition.

In sum, the volume of recent literature devoted to visual literacy demonstrates that it is an idea whose time has come, while its meaning and application continue to evolve.

The Need for Increased Awareness

Those who appraise, arrange, describe, and provide access to visual materials must be able to understand and express by means of the written word the contents of the collections. These processes of perception and translation occur on several levels, and it may be useful to consider three such levels, with accompanying examples.

A first level of visual awareness might be described as an immediate or *superficial* one. On this level, the viewer determines what a photograph, piece of film or video, or other material, is "of." For example, when viewed cursorily, a sample of unedited campaign footage from the Robert F. Kennedy Film Collection at the John F. Kennedy Library depicts the 1964 New York Senate campaign and is immediately identifiable as images "of" Robert Kennedy, in various settings: greeting crowds in Harlem; speaking at a press conference at a midtown hotel; or riding in a convertible with Ethel Kennedy. A superficial look at Robert Capa's famous still photograph of the D-Day invasion shows an allied soldier with rifle and equipment, hunkered down in the surf, drifting or crawling in shallow water. His face bears an expression of fear counterbalanced by determination.

On a second level, the Kennedy footage is "about" much more. "Aboutness" refers to *concrete* subject content and includes, for example, various aspects of politics and culture in the mid-1960s: standard protocol for political campaigns; minority and women's participation in the political process; dynamics between ethnic neighborhoods in American cities; New York City life, commerce, and architecture; and much more. The process by which the viewer perceives these subjects differs from that which occurs on the superficial level. The concrete level demands more

---

14 Paul Messaris, *Visual 'Literacy': Image, Mind, Reality* (Boulder, Colo.: Westview Press, 1994), 2.

15 Hortin, "A Need for a Theory of Visual Literacy," 261-62. This article includes a succinct summary of successive definitions of visual literacy and a useful bibliography from 1969 to 1982.

complex ways of thinking about the images and requires specific historical knowledge of circumstances or events, participants, techniques, and
more. The second level of visual awareness can also disclose more
"about" Capa's 1944 invasion photo. Omaha Beach, on June 6, 1944, was
raked continuously by machine gun fire from German pillboxes. The soldier was about to stumble into a dangerous melee, visible just ahead, lit-
tered with the bodies of maimed and dying comrades. The crossing had
been rough. Fear is daunting. Courage is sustaining. And so forth.

Most archivists accept that an adequate level of specialized historical
background knowledge is vital to the ability to process a collection. An
archivist with appropriate background knowledge can recognize elements
from the superficial and the concrete levels of visual perception and find
ways to express them. Between general historical knowledge and research
into the specific historical background of the materials, such information
can be adequately perceived, translated, and conveyed in a finding aid or
catalog record.

The third level of visual awareness is considerably more elusive. It
has little to do with the superficial contents or the concrete subject matter of the document, but involves instead the perception of the document's purely visual, or *abstract* elements. These elements cannot be as
easily expressed with words, and the perception of them entails an
understanding of the realm of conventions associated with the visual.
While the second level requires a sharp eye coupled with a measure of
basic historical knowledge, the third level is distinctly more subtle,
requiring the same sharp eye as well as a particular set of sensibilities and
skills, and a knowledge base that, like facility with history and historiography, must be learned. This form of expertise requires sophistication
with conventions and technology for both visual perception and visual
expression; an understanding of the conventions of particular media in
their particular context (e.g., television in the 1960s, political advertisements relating to a particular campaign, filmmaking techniques at the
turn of the century, the evolution of nineteenth-century still photography, etc.); an ability to critically dissect a document composed of elements such as time, light, sound, and motion; and an ability to translate
these elements into a verbal description. Of additional importance is a
level of awareness of other components of visual materials, which can
include symbol, organization, ambiguity, space, sequence, rhythm,
moment, and point of view, as well as historical contextual matters such
as what the film's creators intended to express visually, possible expectations of original viewers, and possible perceptions of subsequent viewers.

Footage from the Robert Kennedy Collection can serve as one example. Archivists who experience (view, listen to) a document must understand the building blocks from which the document is constructed and
ask questions about the way the document uses these building blocks to
communicate information. The building blocks begin with a vocabulary

that includes such elements as camera angle, perspective, and editing techniques. Questions arise from an analysis of the vocabulary as applied to the particular document. Why, for instance, did the director choose to film Kennedy from certain angles? Why is the camera handheld at certain times and on a dolly at others? Is it significant that the image is jerky at times, smooth at others? What is the effect of the swift panning of the vast crowd, and the effect of lengthy close-ups of individual faces in the crowd? What do those faces tell us, and how does the way in which they are filmed convey director Charles Guggenheim's intention or vision? Guggenheim adapted to television *cinema verité* techniques borrowed from directors associated with the French New Wave. How were these techniques used to evoke emotion in the viewer? How do these techniques stand up over time? Are they ambiguous, even disturbing, or trite or formulaic ways of sending messages to viewers? To what extent is the viewer required to think actively about, and engage with, the images to understand them, and what will viewers, familiar with the conventions for contemporary visual communication, absorb passively?

Level three of visual awareness can also guide interpretation of Capa's D-Day photo, raising questions as well as answering them, but in all cases leading closer to a fully informed perspective. Capa, for example, was a photographer who sold images to the press, whose reputation and career had been built upon action photos taken in dangerous situations. His invasion photos were intended for the broadest possible publication (newspaper readers in America, in unoccupied Europe, and perhaps elsewhere). His point of view as a socialist was one of sympathy with the common man. He took no interest in darkroom techniques, and generally considered his work done once he had frozen a newsworthy moment on his negative strip.[16] Did Capa intend to emphasize the indomitability of the common man by pointing the lens down and showing the soldier crawling or drifting, instead of charging, as heroes stereotypically do? Is the image blurred to suggest violent motion, or commotion, confusion, or fear, or because the photographer himself was partially submerged behind a steel fortification and may have been trembling from cold or fear? Were the negatives improperly dried and therefore blurry? Did Capa specially choose this man to represent so many others, or was his first choice lost when all but eight of his 106 Omaha Beach negatives were accidentally destroyed by a careless darkroom technician?[17] What is the significance of his choice of camera, lens, focus, exposure, moment? What was he intending to express, and how were viewers likely to receive his photograph in 1944, and how today?

---

16 Richard Whelan, *Robert Capa* (New York: Knopf, 1985), 15.

17 Ibid., 210-215. Some extensive quotes from Capa's own account of his D-Day assignment and its aftermath are found in Cornell Capa, ed., *Robert Capa* (New York: Grossman, 1974), 68-71.

Possibilities for a visually literate interpretation of an image, whether moving or still, are enhanced when the image is maintained by an archives in context with related materials. Images created by the same photographer help explain one another, as do related collections. The tremendous importance of photographer's notes, for example, is illustrated by the practices of Dorothea Lange, whose habit was to summarize each day's picture-taking in notes setting the context and recording short biographies of people depicted. Lange felt that half the value of her work was lost if pictures were not adequately documented by notes. "I don't like the kind of written material that tells a person what to look for or that explains the photograph," she told an interviewer. "I like the kind . . . that gives background . . . without directing the person's mind. It just gives him more with which to look at the picture."[18] These vitally important written materials are what film historian Thomas Cripps has called the "paper trail."

"Seizing the Light: the Appraisal of Photographs" by Ballard and Teakle attempts to outline some criteria for assessing the research value of photographs:

> The aim is to recognize the original intention of the photograph — its particular cultural use by particular people. This is rarely given within the picture, but is developed in its function or context. . . . What was the purpose for the record being created, when, by whom, in what context? Photographs cannot be meaningfully employed unless . . . creator and context are understood. Visual literacy requires the same critical analysis as verbal literacy. Familiarity with the changing conventions of photography is essential to reveal the full meaning of historical images. Every photograph is altered in some way by the bias of the creator (intentionally or unintentionally), the nature of the apparatus, the film processing and printing and the unique interpretation . . . by each viewer. Photographic evidence of a particular event or location is often inaccurate or misleading because it is incomplete.[19]

Historians and Visual Awareness

Some of the best insight into the nature of visual literacy comes from the field of history. Increasingly, historians have expended a great deal of effort exploring the possibilities of "reading" and "writing" with visual

---

18 Beaumont Newhall, *Dorothea Lange Looks at the American Country Woman* (Fort Worth, Tex.: Amon Carter Museum, 1967), 71.

19 Cilla Ballard and Rodney Teakle, "Seizing the Light: The Appraisal of Photographs," *Archives and Manuscripts* 19 (May 1991): 44-46.

materials and of teaching those skills to students. Their recognition of the importance to their discipline of visual materials has led to a substantial body of literature.[20]

As early as 1924 Johan Huizinga's magisterial *The Waning of the Middle Ages* called attention to the value of visual evidence in garnering historical insight. Huizinga saw nothing in "traditional" documents that illustrated the range of emotional experience that he knew (from art) existed in the late medieval period. He turned to different sources as a way of eliminating this blind spot, and in particular proceeded to analyze the paintings of the Van Eyck brothers and their successors. Van Eyck portraits, for example, often included a meticulous visual inventory of the sitter's possessions and clues to the sitter's emotional state. Depiction of private space as a key to the state of mind of those who fill it became common in painting of subsequent centuries.[21] Such portraits/interiors have, of course, more obvious and accessible uses for historians interested in objects used or displayed, and their relationship to space, and to people in the space. Photographs, being less subjective, and including a greater wealth of detail, are even more useful for purposes of historical understanding than paintings. As with other media, there are pitfalls in the interpretation of photography, which can be overcome to some extent by visually literate scrutiny and insight.

Until recently most historians have neglected non-traditional sources in constructing their theses. The pattern of research codified by Leopold von Ranke in the nineteenth century (historians should rely on original written records methodically analyzed and interpreted) still prevails,[22] but many historians now want, in addition, oral histories, visual evidence, and other sources of information.[23] The mid-to-late-twentieth-century discovery of the photograph as a legitimate source may be related to an awakening interest in women's history, minorities, the poor, and other topics less well documented by written records than the topics

---

20 Investigations in archives-related disciplines in addition to history will enhance archival understandings of visual literacy. Valuable insights can be drawn from work already done in such fields as art and film theory, art history, museology, and philosophy of art, all of which customarily discuss visual information in terms of interpretation, expression and analysis. In addition, the writings of artists themselves can be quite enlightening. This approach would of course entail the momentary setting aside of divisions between art and "non-art" materials, an act that could be instructive. As Hugh Taylor has written, "The line [between archival records and art] is by no means clear-cut and points up the dilemma of a culture that distinguishes art from record in an uneasy dichotomy." Hugh Taylor, "Documentary Art and the Role of the Archivist," *American Archivist* 42 (October 1979): 425.

21 Johan Huizinga, *The Waning of the Middle Ages* (London: Edward Arnold & Company, 1952), 222-96.

22 Michael Thomason, "The Magic Lantern Revisited: The Photograph as a Historical Source," *Alabama Review* 31 (April 1978): 83.

23 Hugh A. Taylor, "Documentary Art and the Role of the Archivist," *American Archivist* 42 (October 1979): 417-19.

favored by previous generations of historians.[24] (Still photographs
have often been included in histories or biographies as illustrations in
the form of 8- or 16-page inserts of plates, but such inclusion has
almost always been an afterthought, a visual bonus to attract readers
and book buyers. Such images were supported by, not used as support
for, the historical text, ordinarily based on traditional written documents.)[25]

Artifacts and the American Past by Thomas Schlereth analyzes reasons
why historians have so often distrusted or disregarded visual evidence
and why many have yielded to a begrudging acceptance. The American
Historical Association Conference in 1939 featured as a principal speaker
Roy Stryker, who had engineered the Farm Security Agency's concerted
drive to document, with the camera, depression-era conditions and the
effects of the government's effort to alleviate them. Schlereth believes
that Stryker's session, "Sources and Materials for the Study of Cultural
History: Documentary Photographs," was a catalyst in the promotion of
visual literacy for historians. He adds that the kinds of questions historians have traditionally asked

> have not been phrased in ways that photographic data can answer
> directly . . . as students of the word, with a large investment in
> careful verbal analysis, many historians . . . have tended to deprecate
> new types of visual evidence that threaten primacy of verbal commu-
> nication. . . . To be sure, historical photography has significant
> limitations as historical evidence. Yet, after all the methodological
> rejoinders have been issued, all questions of veracity and representa-
> tiveness raised, and all the problems of adequate citation and verifi-
> cation noted, historical photography still survives as an important
> evidential node enormously valuable to the historian . . . The his-
> torian must judge.[26]

In short, the level of visual literacy of the researcher is an aid to
interpretation and a possible safeguard against being misled.

Schlereth alerts researchers to a number of common pitfalls. "The
camera," he warns, "can lie, as often and as clearly as any other tool
wielded by people intent on telling lies. And even . . . where the photographer is . . . honest . . . his picture will show only what the particular
lens on the camera is capable of showing in the way of depth, clarity, and

---

24 Marsha Peters and Bernard Mergen, "'Doing the Rest': The Uses of Photographs in American
    Studies," *American Quarterly* 29 (Bibliography Issue 1977): 280-82.

25 Walter Rundell, Jr., "Photographs as Historical Evidence: Early Texas Oil," *American Archivist* 41
    (October 1978): 373.

26 Thomas J. Schlereth, *Artifacts and the American Past* (Nashville, Tenn.: American Association of
    State and Local History, 1980), 14-15.

spatial relations . . . We would have seen more than what the frame or the exposure allows us to see. Cropping of a scene cuts off the viewer from other details that may well be relevant to an understanding of the picture." The book discusses problems related to long exposures and historical photographic processes and warns that manipulation can occur at every stage, regardless of era. Historians using photographic evidence must remember that photos are not a facsimile of total past scenes and events, but only a partial reflection of past reality. "Moreover, the photographer exerts enormous control over that reflection and the information and insight it conveys."[27] Of special significance is Schlereth's advice that the negative, the primary source of photographic evidence, can seldom be altered without showing signs. The historian, therefore, should examine negatives whenever they are available for inspection.[28]

Historians began to demonstrate an interest in the relationships between moving image materials and the historical tradition around 1949. This interest was first a German, then a British, and by the mid-1960s, an international phenomenon. One scholar has compiled a list of nine academic conferences devoted to history and film between 1968 and 1975, most of which took place in Europe.[29]

Only gradually did historians in the United States begin to address the topic. Articles on issues relating to moving image materials began to appear in the 1970s in *Radical History Review,* the *Journal of Contemporary History, Oral History Review,* and in the American Studies literature. A 1982 article in the British *Historical Journal of Film, Radio and Television* proclaimed that "research and writing in . . . the field of documenting historical research through reference to films [is] growing. In the United States we are now coming into what might be called the 'second generation' of . . . historians with a bent for using films as documentation." The author also observed, however, that this field was still far from the mainstream of historical research, noting that "the documenting of history through films [has] developed as [a] comparatively idiosyncratic" pursuit, and describing the individuals attracted to this form of research as "mavericks."[30]

But by the early 1980s, historical film reviews appeared regularly in the major historical organs in the United States, such as the *Journal of American History* and *American Historical Review,* and the mainstream professional organizations had begun to sponsor conferences on film and

---

27 Ibid., 43-47.

28 Ibid., 45.

29 Nicholas Pronay, "The 'Moving Picture' and Historical Research," *Journal of Contemporary History* 18 (1983): 366.

30 Paul Monaco, "Research-In-Progress: A Sampling from the U.S.A.," *Historical Journal of Film, Radio and Television* 2 (1982): 180.

history, to organize committees on the subject, and to give annual awards to innovative historical work with film and video.[31]

Previous generations of historians had treated moving image materials with reactions ranging from "bemused indifference to outright hostility," as one observer has suggested.[32]

By the time the *Journal of Contemporary History* devoted its entire July 1981 issue to "Historians and the Movies: the State of the Art," the relationship of visual materials to history had become a topic of legitimate, if not widespread, interest among historians. As historian-filmmaker Nicholas Pronay observed,

> There . . . has been a noticeable change of attitude concerning the difficulties which this non-written record material presents for the historian, or indeed about the desirability of using it at all. [A] growing proportion of our profession came to consist of those who were already brought up in a society in which the moving picture, televised or projected, provided the primary form of communication. . . .[33]

Debates about history and moving image materials have centered around a set of issues that are never more than temporarily resolved. These issues include the legitimacy of moving image documents as historical evidence;[34] the potential of moving image documents for

---

31 The Committee on Radio, Television, and Film Media of the Organization of American Historians was established in the late 1970s. In 1994 the American Historical Association expanded the award categories in its teaching prize to include innovations with moving image media. The American Studies Association has made film criticism a regular topic of discussion in its meetings since the late 1970s.

32 Daniel J. Walkowitz, "Visual History: The Craft of the Historian-Filmmaker," *Public Historian* 7 (1985): 53. In addition, Paul Smith has pointed out that "the criticisms . . . of film regarded as record can be levelled at other forms of source material: written and printed documents, for instance, may equally be partial, subjective, tendentious, emotive, and even forged. Nothing has been more curious in discussions of film's role in historical studies than the degree of suspicion directed against it by historians who are prepared to accept verbal material with far less critical apprehension. . . . It is largely the comparative unfamiliarity of film, decreasing with each new generation of historian, which has earned it such suspicion. . . . " Paul Smith, *The Historian and Film* (New York: Oxford University Press, 1976), 6.

33 Pronay, "The 'Moving Picture' and Historical Research," 366.

34 With continued attention at professional conferences, and with the publication of such landmark works as historian John E. O'Connor's *American History/American Film: Interpreting the Hollywood Image* (New York: Ungar, 1979) and *American History/American Television: Interpreting the Video Past* (New York: Ungar, 1983), skeptics could no longer deny the validity of the research value of moving image documents with their previous self-assurance. As O'Connor wrote in 1990, "In their various publications the contributors to this volume have been arguing for nearly two decades that historians should expand their horizons and begin to do justice to the study of moving images. Now it is time to press that issue further. There are important areas of historical scholarship where the researcher who ignores the close study of moving image evidence has failed to cover the subject; and the number of these areas is sure to increase in the future." John E. O'Connor, *Image as Artifact: the Historical Analysis of Film and Television* (Melbourne, Fla.: Krieger, 1990), 1ff.

portraying history;[35] the necessity of visual literacy skills for historians and students;[36] and fundamental concerns about the nature of images versus the nature of language.[37]

Visual Literacy and the Archivist

Archivists, as well as historians, should explore the ideas behind visual literacy, and define visual literacy in practical terms applicable to archival

---

35 Historian Arthur Marwick was convinced that moving images could not represent history, though they could help to enhance students' interest. "Film," he wrote, ". . . is not suited to the presentation of a complex historical narrative, and is most certainly unsuited to complex historical analysis" (Smith 1976, 153). In contrast, most contributors to the special 1983 issue of the *Journal of Contemporary History* agreed that no fundamental barrier exists between images and print for the presentation of history. When the December 1988 issue of *American Historical Review* devoted its "Forum" to the topic, four of the five contributors agreed that it is indeed possible to present legitimate history on film, and these four expressed a readiness to move on to a deeper analysis of the problem. As Robert Rosenstone, a pioneer advocate of the potential of history on film, wrote, "I no longer find it possible to blame the shortcomings of historical films either on the evils of Hollywood or the woeful effects of low budgets, on the limits of the dramatic genre or those of the documentary format." At stake, as Rosenstone suggested, was a fundamental dilemma of historical definition, with vast implications for the discipline. Perhaps it was not the limitations of film that caused problems, but the limitation of traditional conceptions of history. "Can one really put history onto film," he asked, ". . . or does the use of film necessitate a change in what we mean by history, and would we be willing to make such a change?" His challenge is profound. Do the conventions of textual historiography (traditional conceptions of primary and secondary sources, stylistic customs, citations, bibliographies, statistics, etc.) enable historians to present history in its most objective and authentic form? Is it only through the use of such conventions that historians can present rich, complex, and subtle analyses of historical events or issues? Might images permit complex analyses as well, using the conventions of visual, not textual, communication? Hayden White suggests that visual history (history presented by means of moving image media) represents a challenge to traditional history and historiography not unlike the challenge presented by feminist historiography: not only new answers, but new kinds of questions must be formulated, questions that ultimately require reevaluation of the entire framework of the discipline. Hayden White, "Historiography and Historiophoty," *American Historical Review* 93 (1988): 1199.

36 "Visual literacy is an essential tool for citizenship in contemporary America," wrote O'Connor in 1990. "It would be easy to teach students to be cynics (or to reinforce them in their cynicism), but this would be neither productive nor educational. Not long ago, the naive presumption was common that whatever people saw on the news they accepted as fact. Today, people are so ready to disbelieve news reports, and especially news analysis, that 'media bashing' has become an effective political tool." John E. O'Connor, "History in Images/Images in History: Reflections on the Importance of Film and Television Study for an Understanding of the Past," *American Historical Review* 93 (1988): 1208. Training in visual literacy skills is essential for historians. Historian Daniel Walkowitz has argued that despite historians' increased recognition of visual media as legitimate tools for writing and teaching history, the point of these efforts is lost if "neither historians nor their students have learned to 'read' images." Daniel Walkowitz, "Visual History: The Craft of the Historian-Filmmaker," *Public Historian* 7 (1985): 54.

37 When these issues are confronted, they are generally discussed in terms of a debate over the validity of the analogy between images and language. To what extent can images be compared to language, and can methodological approaches to textual documents be applied to visual materials? See especially Smith, 1976; Robert Rosenstone, "History in Images/History in Words," *American Historical Review* 93 (1988): 1173-85; John Schott in Barbara Abrash and Janet Sternburg, eds., *Historians and Filmmakers: Toward Collaboration* (New York: The Institute for Research in History, 1983); Pronay, "The Moving Picture"; Joshua Brown, "Visualizing the 19th Century," *Radical History Review* 38 (1987): 114-25; and O'Connor, *Image as Artifact*.

methods and archival records. Though all participants in contemporary culture regularly interact with visual materials, the interactions of historians and archivists with these document forms are particularly ripe for examination because both groups engage intensively with documents on a professional basis and in a variety of complex ways. Furthermore, as has been recently observed, the "perception of information [is] affected by its manner of transmission," and this is a "critical issue for archivists."[38]

Surprisingly, neither library schools nor archival degree programs offer a special track for training visual resources specialists, and very little attention is devoted to visual materials in the general curriculum.[39] "Guidelines for the Development of a Curriculum for a Master of Archival Studies Degree," approved by the Council of the Society of American Archivists on June 5, 1994, do not mention a need for archival trainees to become oriented in the administration of visual resources.[40] Nor did the Association of Canadian Archivists Education Committee make any specific recommendations about visual materials in its 1988 report, "Guidelines for the Development of a Two-Year Curriculum for a Master of Archival Studies Programme."[41] A 1993 report published in the *American Archivist* delineating important areas for education of future archivists and historians fails to mention visual literacy skills, though it does refer to "the inclusion of many new types of sources in archival repositories."[42] A 1994 issue of the *American Archivist* was devoted to a discussion of pressing current archival issues, upcoming concerns, and priorities for future research, yet visual materials were mentioned only in passing, indicating that these issues have lost, or perhaps not yet been accorded, the urgency they deserve.[43] Nevertheless, the archival literature has for many years included references to the importance of the intellectual issues presented by abstract visual awareness.

In 1968 John B. Kuiper, as head of the Motion Picture Section of the Library of Congress, wrote in reference to moving image materials that archivists must first reevaluate their traditional methods and, second, rethink their intellectual approaches in the wake of the proliferation of moving image documents. "Inevitably," he wrote, ". . . as archivists . . .

---

38 James K. Burrows and Mary Ann Pylypchuk in Barbara Craig, *The Archival Imagination: Essays in Honor of Hugh Taylor* (Ottawa: Association of Canadian Archivists, 1992), 250.

39 This absence is demonstrated by an examination of the Society of American Archivists' *Directory of Archival Education, 1995-1996.*

40 Society of American Archivists, "Guidelines for the Development of a Curriculum for a Master of Archival Studies Degree," *Archival Outlook* (September 1994): eight-page insert.

41 Association of Canadian Archivists, "Guidelines for the Development of a Two-Year Curriculum for a Master of Archival Studies Programme," *Archivaria* 29 (Winter 1989-90): 128-41.

42 "Special Report: Historians and Archivists: Educating the Next Generation," *American Archivist* 56 (Fall 1993): 732.

43 Margaret Hedstrom, issue ed., "Special Issue: 2020 Vision," *American Archivist* 57 (Winter 1994).

we must be concerned with . . . education . . . as well as with the problems of availability, cataloging, selection, and acquisition, although there is no doubt that these problems must also be given fresh treatment." "We serve," he wrote, "as the bridge between our collections and the clearer understanding of the century that our collections undoubtedly provide."[44]

Ten years later, archivist Walter Rundell's groundbreaking article on still photography addressed the expressive uses of visual materials. Still photographs, first viewed as "adjuncts to literary sources and for display," gradually came to be viewed by other scholars as "original sources themselves," with expressive potential in their own right.[45] Rundell's article was important, in part, because it alluded to the uniqueness of the image as a mode of communication and implied that new ways of understanding images, not bound by textual conventions, were in order. In addition, it demonstrated the ways in which modes of literacy overlap and in which new modes are made to bear the conventions of older ones.[46]

Several broad-based analyses of groups of photographs on related historical themes have been completed with satisfying results. Joan Schwartz, for example, examined the extant photographic record of British Columbia prior to its incorporation into the Canadian Federation, looking at many intersecting factors, including boosterism, attitudes toward the wilderness, the necessity for professional photographers to produce images they could sell, the difficulty of reaching remote locations with heavy equipment and chemicals, and the problems of depictions associated with limitation of the medium during the period under study. She reminds historians using photographs as source material to always ask: who made it, who was expected to receive its message, and what was it meant to convey? She concluded, in part, that pre-confederation British Colombian photography focused on the alteration of the wilderness by humans rather than on the beauties of nature, due to both the emotional need of settlers to feel that they had re-created a home environment similar to that which they had left and the desire to attract additional settlement. While the image itself can be analyzed for certain types of information, its use by a buyer can tell something else; for example, a mass-produced photograph of a famous sternwheeler or Indian village may be found in a photo album of the type commonly kept in a Victorian parlor.[47]

In 1979 Hugh Taylor reiterated Kuiper's suggestion that traditional archival methods be reevaluated in the context of new forms of record

---

44 "The Historical Value of Motion Pictures," *American Archivist* 31 (October 1968): 390.

45 Walter Rundell, "Photographs as Historical Evidence," *American Archivist* 41 (October 1978): 373.

46 On the latter point, see also Rosalind Thomas, *Literacy and Orality in Ancient Greece* (New York: Cambridge University Press, 1992).

47 Joan M. Schwartz, "The Photographic Record of Pre-Confederation British Columbia," *Archivaria* 5 (Winter 1977-1978): 17-44.

and recognized that visual materials have their own special qualities and requirements quite separate from those of written documents. In "Documentary Art and the Role of the Archivist," an article on art objects (Canadian landscape paintings) as archival record, Taylor made several important observations that apply to the present discussion. He warned that "to those of us brought up on history written entirely from textual records, the written word has a certain respectability, a deceptive precision, a convincing plausibility that masks its limitations," and that "our literary training has often caused us to 'read' pictures 'literally' without being aware of certain rules and conventions that are in sharp contrast to the rules of alphabet, grammar, and syntax." In spite of this, he advised, "we must all learn to describe pictorial content in words if we are to retrieve it."[48]

The most recent and most ambitious attempt to address the intellectual issues attending moving image materials was the organization of a conference by the International Council of Archives, held in Ottawa in 1990, and titled "Documents that Move and Speak." Conference participants consisted of an impressive international array of archivists, librarians, and media specialists, and discussions embraced a broad spectrum of issues. Many participants advocated the need for archivists to expand their conceptual horizons in regard to the significance of audiovisual media. Jean-Pierre Wallot, National Archivist of Canada, noted that "the challenge confronting archivists is not just the physical aspects of moving image and sound documents, but also the intellectual aspects." He continued that "we should not conclude that the key questions confronting archivists in this area are simply questions of technology."[49] Participants also noted the importance of studying new and changing media of record both on their own terms and within the context of older document forms and literacy patterns. "Moving image and sound documents should not be studied in isolation. They form part of the new information record of the twentieth century which will have an impact on all aspects of the archival profession. Thus, they must become part of a plan to assess the role of the archivist in this new age."[50] Hugh Taylor continued in the same vein in his presentation at the conference, chiding archivists for not pursuing these issues further.

> Archives are a subset of the whole communication process, and the media we use affect our individual perceptions and impact on society as a whole. As archivists we could have become aware of this since

48 Hugh Taylor, "Documentary Art and the Role of the Archivist," *American Archivist* 42 (October 1979): 427.

49 Jean-Pierre Wallot, in his welcoming speech. National Archives of Canada, *Documents That Move and Speak: Audiovisual Archives in the Information Age*, (New York: K. G. Saur, 1992), 12.

50 Ibid.

the 1960s through the works of Marshall McLuhan, Harold Innis, Walter Ong, and many others, but we have been slow to recognize this aspect in our search for meaning and value. We were all reared for the most part on the heavy gruel of text.[51]

These calls to action have resulted in relatively little output in terms of archival research and publications, yet the problems persist. For a variety of reasons, attention to visual literacy issues will be a priority for archivists as the century draws to a close. Descriptive access, for example, may be the most important, most problematic, and least explored aspect of audiovisual archives administration. It is the point at which visual literacy skills become crucial. The translation process, entailed by providing descriptive access, confounds even seasoned audiovisual archivists.

Extensive description of visual materials is vital for preservation of documents and for ease of reference for researchers. Because of the physical difficulties presented by moving image collections in particular, researchers are extremely dependent upon access to preliminary descriptions of the materials, rather than to the materials themselves. As one film archivist observed in 1983, "Film cataloging is the least visible activity of a film archive. Yet, an accurate, professional description of both filmographic and technical information about the collections is the pivot upon which the other activities depend."[52] The substance of Clive Coultass's 1976 diatribe on the importance of descriptive tools for moving image materials holds true today, though the practices he mentions are now dated.

It is impossible for any one person to view all of the [archives'] footage, and detailed information necessarily has to be provided by the subject index cards, shot sheets or other documentation, which can only go so far and might not adequately give an impression of the visual composition of a shot, or it can be obtained from one or

---

51 Taylor, in "Documents that Move and Speak," 19.

52 Early archival writings on moving image materials acknowledge this fact. See, for example, the 1956 statement that "the more informative the descriptions are, the less the need to consult the film itself in searching. Frequent screenings of films for reference purposes is expensive, both in time and damage to films. Since archival holdings often include unedited films lacking narration or other documentation, the records description task of the archivist is a major responsibility. It is of the greatest importance that his descriptions be accurate, for finding aids not founded on careful research can bring discredit on him and his agency." Hermione Baumhofer, "Film Records Management," *American Archivist* 19 (July 1956): 242. For a more recent statement, see Sheila Intner's comment that "new nonbook media materials . . . and increasing popularity of older media forms seems to indicate a need for more and better summary notes. Catalogers, who write them, need to accept responsibility for doing the job and getting the help they need to do it well." Sheila Intner, "Writing Summary Notes for Films and Videos," *Cataloging and Classification Quarterly* 9 (1988): 72.

other individual who has personally seen different parts of the collection. The danger . . . is that one senior film librarian may accumulate a great deal of knowledge himself and, even though he may transfer the basic details to the cards, he can be so harassed by pressure of demand and shortage of staff that his own intimate acquaintance with the collection is only sporadically passed on to his subordinates, themselves busy with day-to-day administration and with scarcely any time to look at film.[53]

Archivists need to be able to describe visual materials in terms meaningful to researchers with various levels of sophistication. Even an understanding by the archivist that there are several levels of visual awareness can provide for better description. Certainly, a description that goes beyond the first level of visual awareness, as discussed earlier, can be a great help to a researcher. If the finding aid can use the vocabulary of visual communication by briefly noting such aspects as camera angle, distance, and shot composition, so much the better. Though these terms may mean nothing to some researchers, they function as codes to others, who understand that such specifics are part of the "language" of visual communication and can interpret them as such. "Medium-shot low angle pan of crowd faces with occasional close-ups interspliced" means a great deal more to a visually sophisticated researcher than does "crowd scenes." Without editorializing or imposing inappropriate interpretation, the former connotes an entire style of visual expression; places the document within a historical context of the genre; and gives clues as to the intentions of the director, the deliberate and the unplanned elements of the footage, possibilities for interpretation, and other considerations, while the latter reveals none of this content.

Heightened access to visual materials through multimedia databases will solve neither the visual literacy problem nor ameliorate the challenges of visual description. It may, instead, accelerate the urgency of the problems facing archivists. Such collections cannot benefit researchers if archivists do not possess the knowledge and skills necessary to provide adequate verbal descriptions of the visual contents of digitized images. Descriptive tools, such as catalog records and finding aids, will become increasingly important as visual documents continue to proliferate and as access to the images, or digitized representations of them, increases. As Alfred Willis wrote in the "Visual Resources" chapter of the *Guide to Indexing with the Art and Architecture Thesaurus*, "Computer technology has made possible the digitization of images, but attacking the problems of managing disembodied visual images in

---

53 Coultass, in Smith, *The Historian and Film*, 44.

computerized image banks is a matter of urgent concern for visual resources specialists."[54] And, one might add, for all archivists.

Spurred on by the advent of image digitization, and by the general increase in volume of visual materials, efforts to improve techniques for providing descriptive access to moving image collections in particular have increased in recent years. These efforts have proceeded on three fronts: attempting to provide archivists with standardized vocabulary for describing the form and content of moving image materials; reaching consensus on the kinds of data to be included in descriptions; and providing means of sharing descriptive information from repository to repository. These three tasks are linked and interrelated: as the trend toward emphasis on data sharing increases, and as researchers' expectations rise, standardization becomes imperative. Archivist Clive Cochrane summarized the problem, describing the current state of film archives in the U.K.: "Because of the different practices employed by archives and libraries, those working with moving image materials possess a variety of skills, knowledge and attitudes and no professional body plays a dominant role."[55] Nevertheless, impressive efforts have been made in these three directions by dedicated archivists and librarians in recent years.[56]

The "Visual Resources" chapter of the *Guide to Indexing with the Art and Architecture Thesaurus* lays out the theoretical issues underlying these practical problems eloquently, but offers no facile solutions:

---

54 Alfred Willis, "Visual Resources," in Toni Petersen and Patricia Barnett eds., *Guide to Indexing with the Art and Architecture Thesaurus*, 2nd ed. (New York: Oxford University Press, 1994), 165.

55 Clive Cochrane, "An Overview of the Trends in the Collection and Use of Moving Images in the U.K.," *Journal of Documentation* 49 (1993): 289-90.

56 Eileen Bowser's 1991 comment that "At present there is no universal standard for genre and subject terminology" for moving image materials remains true in 1996. Eileen Bowser and John Kuiper eds., *A Handbook for Film Archives* (New York: Garland, 1991), 103. The major efforts to provide controlled vocabulary specifically for audiovisual materials include the *Art and Architecture Thesaurus* and Martha Yee's *Moving Image Materials: Genre Terms* (Washington D.C.: Library of Congress, 1988). There are no universally or even nationally accepted standards for cataloging methods and no agreement on data elements for catalog records. See National Archives of Canada, *Documents That Move and Speak* (New York: K. G. Saur, 1992), 156. The now-obsolete MARC VM format and Wendy White-Hensen's *Archival Moving Image Materials: A Cataloging Manual* (Washington, D.C.: Library of Congress, 1984) provide the basic tools for film cataloging, but neither has been satisfactory for cataloging unedited footage. Both are at present undergoing major revisions. See Martha Yee and Linda Tadic, "Report of the AMIA Cataloging and Documentation Committee," *Views: The Newsletter of the Visual Materials Section, Society of American Archivists* (9 April 1995): 4. Agreement on data element definitions and cataloging standards becomes increasingly important as multi-repository databases of descriptive information on audiovisual collections are expanded. At this writing, data sharing utilities for moving image materials include: local online film archives catalogs, which are accessible via the Internet; the national bibliographic utilities (RLIN, OCLC), which accept MARC VM records; and the National Moving Image Database (NAMID), conducted under the auspices of the National Center for Film and Video Preservation at the American Film Institute. NAMID's goal is to serve as a comprehensive database of descriptive information about film and video holdings in the United States. These massive databases have a great potential, but as Roger Smither cautioned in an important article in 1987, "The cause for concern in the film archival world is precisely the fact that common

Managing intellectual access to visual resource collections involves the coding or translating of the information inherent in those items, primarily information about the cognitive and/or aesthetic content of the subject depicted. The complex task of translating the information contained in images into words and other codes . . . is complicated by uncertainty about how human beings derive information from pictures and the differing intellectual and disciplinary perspectives of users. The difficulty of expressing certain qualities of pictures in verbal language is not necessarily due only to an imperfect command of the language, or to some kind of imperfect "visual literacy," but rather to the real limits of verbal and visual communication themselves. It would appear that some qualities of the [image] are simply indescribable in words. . . . These problems are not ones of theory only. . . . The problems associated with the disparate nature of what one can "see" in a visual resource are mirrored by those associated with what one can say or ask about it as well. Researchers' disparate questions about the images in visual resources collections drive the information retrieval function. In handling them, catalogers are reminded again and again just how difficult it is to specify in words what information is conveyed by a particular image.[57]

Archivists who do not possess a basic understanding of the history of the media of record, its technology, the conventions of visual communication, and the history of shifts in modes of literacy will experience additional (and unnecessary) difficulties in creating the tools needed to meet such challenges.

A Call to Expand Our Role

Archives and archivists are well positioned in the 1990s to provide some much-needed grounding for the use and interpretation of visual materials: by playing an important role in promoting visual literacy; alerting researchers to possible problems in interpretation; and managing collections of visual materials more effectively.

Archivists should make a special effort to keep related materials together. On the most basic level, this means keeping together images that were created together. Subject access and cross-referencing can always be provided, but loss of context results in loss of information.

---

standards for data exchange are being developed not only well after the perception of the usefulness of shared data, but also after the development of the first potential contributions to a global database." He continues, "The viability of data exchange depends on the consistency of the data shared." He cites in addition "a tendency to assume that the introduction of new technology in some way automatically results in an improvement in services and circumstances. This is simply not confirmed by experience." Roger Smither, "Formats and Standards: A Film Archive Perspective on Exchanging Computerized Data," *American Archivist* 50 (1987): 329, 332, 333.

57   Willis, "Visual Resources."

Photographers' notes and other complementary sources should be sought out, preserved, and made available. If donors of collections are asked a few extra questions, they may well remember having seen notebooks or scribbled-upon negative sleeves or film cans somehow misplaced or otherwise separated from the images they describe.

Transferring an image to another repository is appropriate if doing so reunites a broken collection or enhances the usefulness of resources. Users should always be informed about the existence of other repositories with images relevant to their research, and this means that archivists must communicate among themselves.

Users of visual resource documents may benefit from the examination of accompanying archival materials, such as written notes, negatives, outtakes, unedited camera originals, and still photos, which permit them to see the *processes* by which choices are made, allowing far richer and more complete understanding of the documents than would be afforded by viewing the final product in isolation. Negatives, for example, are the part of a photographic record closest to what the lens actually saw and are difficult to alter without a trace. They should be available for inspection by users of a collection and can often be viewed sufficiently without being removed from protective enclosures. Archives should keep a light box in the reading room next to the always available supply of white cotton gloves. Many researchers who use collections containing visual materials are familiar with such procedures and possibilities. Most archivists, however, are not prepared by education or training to recognize, understand, and convey information about visual communication on this third level and should take steps to upgrade their skills. Archives should maintain a shelf or two of reference books about the history of visual media, including details about technological change and analysis of the social contexts of, for example, film or photography in various periods. Patrons should be made aware of these reference works and staff members should be given the time and encouragement to peruse them. (Of course, a thoughtful rejection of published conclusions is always a possibility.)

Archivists should learn what they can about the authenticity of images they accession through examining provenance and otherwise tracing the history of a collection. Ask donors, or creators, if possible: "How was it made, and when? Was it, or a related image, ever exhibited or published? Where was it kept? How did it come to you?" Increasing potential for high-tech image alteration will make such considerations especially important in the future.

Visual media are a stimulus to the memory and can be shown to knowledgeable informants as a way of opening them up in oral history interviews or when compiling notes on the history of a family, a town, a religious institution, a college, or business. The circumstances under which such recollections were preserved should always be noted as part of the record, including the catalog number or other identifying label of each *aide-memoire.*

Archivists should promote a symbiotic relationship with researchers, who, after all, have more time to focus undivided attention on details and who often come to a project with some degree of subject expertise. Archivists can bring to this exchange of information their own special insights.

Above all, archivists should ask the right questions about visual collections and encourage patrons to do the same. Archivists need to be able to help researchers understand aspects of the collections that may not be obvious or may be masked by misconceptions about the medium. We cannot afford to consider such skills the exclusive domain of film or photograph specialists any longer. All media, even traditional textual ones, can benefit from visually literate interpretation, and background on the conventions associated with communications media and document forms enhances archival work tremendously. With regard to visual materials, this understanding of the history of the media and their unique conventions is at the heart of the concept of visual literacy. Automation will eventually integrate the retrieval of all media, and the entire media spectrum may be retrieved in a complex search. Archivists should be prepared to guide researchers through at least some of the pitfalls and sources of confusion, providing information needed for balanced interpretation, explaining why images may not be what they seem.[58]

Archivists do not have to become experts in visual literacy, just they do not have to become systems analysts or computer programmers to appreciate the archival issues and challenges posed by textual electronic records. But archivists, as much as historians, do have a responsibility to become familiar with such challenges and issues in the documentary landscape. There are a number of ways in which we can enhance understanding of our collections and improve our practices. We can begin by attempting to understand levels of visual literacy and upgrade our descriptions accordingly. We can peruse available sources on the technology and history of visual communication and on the aesthetics of photography, film, and video. We can and should engage in the already active discourse on visual literacy, on shifting modes of literacy, and on the impact on our society of new document forms. Attention to these issues should be a required component of any archival education program.

Preservation policies presume that information contained in the documents is worth preserving. Making the informational content of archival documents, including visual materials, accessible requires the creation of adequate descriptive tools, in the form of finding aids, catalog

---

58 See Hugh Taylor, "2020 Vision," *American Archivist* 57 (Winter 1994): 140.

records, and guides. The creation of such tools requires skills and a knowledge base that hinge upon thoughtful consideration of changing definitions of literacy, the possibilities and limits of translation, and the nature of communication through language and image. What is the worth of carefully preserved or digitally scanned materials if their informational content is not accessible to researchers?

Improvements in Dutch lens grinding in the late sixteenth century made available several innovations in visual aids, including improved spectacles and primitive microscopes, which attracted much attention as novelties.[59] A northern European coin of the period circulated the following wisdom in the form of a Latin motto, worth considering today:

> Of what use are lens and light
> To those who lack in mind and sight?[60]

As archivists, we shape the record of the past because, in part, we do serve as the bridges between collections and users. We are, as such, in a unique position to respond to the challenges posed by changing media, by the evolving nature of the documentary record. We can build better bridges. It is a big responsibility, but a fertile and promising endeavor.

---

59 Derek Birdsall and Carlo Cipolla, *The Technology of Man: A Visual History* (London: Penshurst Press, 1979), 146.

60 Helmut Gernsheim and Alison Gernsheim, *A Concise History of Photography* (London: Thames and Hudson, 1971), 7.

Part Two:
Archival History

Faced with daily demands on their time, archivists often focus on the methods and techniques of their professional responsibilities. It is important from time to time to step back and examine the theory behind professional methodology and the historical development of archival principles. This historical perspective reveals both the professional connections between modern archivists and their predecessors and the ways archivists have responded to challenges in the past.

The first two articles in this section were both written as graduate student papers, and each received the SAA's Theodore Calvin Pease Award for the best student paper of the year. In "Liberty, Equality, Posterity?: Some Archival Lessons from the Case of the French Revolution," Judith Panitch examines this critical period in the development of archival concepts and the role of archives as "sites of memory." She demonstrates the importance of archives both in political contests over remembering and forgetting the past and in reflecting the cultural norms and values of society. Luke Gilliland-Swetland looks at the development of the American archival profession from two different strands of thinking about and caring for archival records. "The Provenance of a Profession: The Permanence of the Public Archives and Historical Manuscripts Traditions in American Archival History" outlines the early debates over American archival identity by analyzing the two traditions identified by Richard Berner.

The Society of American Archivists has played an important role in uniting the members of the profession, in fostering communication and debate on archival issues, and in providing opportunities for professional development and education. SAA was joined in these goals by regional, state, and local professional associations, beginning in the early 1970s. In "The Blessings of Providence on an Association of Archivists," J. Frank Cook delineates some of the growing pains of the SAA. As archivist of SAA, Cook uses these archival sources to trace important developments and debates over the nature of the profession and the role of the Society.

5

Liberty, Equality, Posterity?: Some Archival Lessons from the Case of the French Revolution

JUDITH M. PANITCH

Abstract: The French Revolution has been widely regarded as a turning point in archival history, yet few have probed the complexity and numerous contradictions of this transitional period. Rather than smoothly ushering in a new concept of archives or archival practice, the Revolution fostered two divergent tendencies. Records and documents from the Old Régime were reviled and frequently destroyed, even as archival structures were developed to care for new records of the Republic and for selected records from the past. This article explores both of these tendencies in order to provide a fuller picture of archival development during the Revolutionary period. Yet the very fervor surrounding archives during that time also provides the basis for more universal reflection. The battle over the appropriate formation and content of archives demonstrates the extent to which they are, above all, cultural institutions and the ways in which archival documents are frequently of importance as much for their symbolism as for their content. This article concludes by examining the ways in which archives, as "sites of memory," are very much products of their time, invested with a meaning that may be changed — as during the French Revolution — by changing beliefs and values.

The title of Ernst Posner's well-known article "Some Aspects of Archival Development Since the French Revolution" makes manifest what has since become an archival commonplace: that the French Revolution represents a landmark event in the evolving conception and administration of archival institutions. The advances of that era, writes Posner, were threefold.[1] First, "the framework of a nationwide public archives administration was established," encompassing existing but defunct depositories, as well as active record-producing public entities. Second, "the state acknowledged its responsibility respecting the care of the documentary heritage of the past." And finally, the Revolution

---

Reprinted with permission from the *American Archivist* 59 (Winter 1996), 30-47. This article received the Society of American Archivists' Theodore Calvin Pease Award in 1995 for the best research paper written by a student in an archival education program.

1 Ernst Posner, "Some Aspects of Archival Development Since the French Revolution," *American Archivist* 3 (July 1940): 161-62.

definitively established the principle that archival records should be accessible to the public.

So familiar are these assertions that they resurface regularly and without elaboration throughout the literature. Robert Bahmer's article entitled "Archives" in the *Encyclopedia of Library and Information Science,* for example, draws liberally upon Posner to reaffirm that the "concept of an archives as a public service agency . . . did not reach its full development until the French Revolution." James O'Toole also recapitulates Posner, observing that, "as in so many other things the French Revolution proved a watershed event" in archival history, while Charles Kecskeméti pronounces in passing that the "history of modern archives starts with the French Revolution."[2] Indeed, the more this dictum is repeated, the more skeletal and axiomatic it becomes, until the Revolutionary era appears, above all, as a moment of rapid but essentially unproblematic transition. Such a perspective appears itself to have originated with Posner's article, in which his own necessarily selective discussion conveys an impression of continuous progress, as though a short-lived period of destructive furor rapidly gave way to more enlightened concepts consolidated in a few key laws.

Not surprisingly, however, this development hardly proceeded so tidily. If the Revolution was, in the words of one twentieth-century scholar, "perhaps the most complex phenomenon which it has ever been given to historians to study,"[3] then its relationship to and treatment of archives prove no exceptions. Rather than exhibiting a direct and discernable evolutionary path, archives more properly reflect the influence of two opposing tendencies that had consequences for all cultural and historical institutions and artifacts of the day. On the one hand, they suffered in the by-now infamous campaign to eradicate all traces of the defeated monarchy. Statues were torn from their pedestals, books burned, and church façades defaced in a frenzy of Revolutionary vandalism that sought to eliminate any sign of a hated and shameful past. At the same time, a mood of conservation had taken hold, resulting in the establishment of museums, libraries, and archival repositories. Some felt that remnants of the past ought to be retained for pedagogical purposes; others wished to immortalize the founding of the new egalitarian Republic. In either case, these warring propensities toward preservation and destruction defined an era. "The Revolution," writes historian Michel Delon, "is contained

---

2 Robert Bahmer, "Archives," in *Encyclopedia of Library and Information Science,* vol. 1 (New York: Marcel Dekker, 1968), 516; James M. O'Toole, *Understanding Archives and Manuscripts* (Chicago: Society of American Archivists, 1990), 29; Charles Kecskeméti, "The Professional Culture of the Archivist," *American Archivist* 50 (Summer 1987): 412.

3 Léon Delessard, "La Révolution Française et les Archives Départementales," *Mémoires de l' Académie des sciences, arts et belles lettres de Dijon* (1944), 167. This and all other unascribed translations in the text are the author's original versions, prepared for this paper.

entirely in this alternation between brutal elimination of the past and its sublimation as testament, between amnesia and memory, between vilification and historic neutralization."[4]

By their very nature, archives proved a privileged and fertile field upon which this battle played out, both in popular attitudes and, more significantly, through the numerous legislative mandates to which Posner alludes. Their turbulent history bears recounting all the more because so few scholars of this century have comprehensively addressed the issue. Posner's essay remains focused principally on developments subsequent to the Revolution, while Robert-Henri Bautier's much-cited address, "La phase cruciale de l'histoire des archives," concentrates upon preceding centuries. Amédée Outrey and Vida Azimi have both written rather theoretical articles probing specific attitudes and events of the period, while Carl Lokke provides a helpful but ultimately non-interpretative chronology. Brenneke's classic *Archivkunde* has yet to be translated from the German.[5] Most existing studies, in fact, belong to the highly charged and partisan historiography of the nineteenth century and must be treated with some caution, if no less interest.

In the first place, then, the fate of archives during the Revolutionary period casts light upon a lively chapter of French cultural history, illuminating values and mentalities of a remote and unsettled era. More immediately, a careful reading of Revolutionary discourse and actions, both detrimental and favorable toward archives and documents, promotes a more thorough understanding of archival development during that defining period. The origins of Posner's assertions become apparent and, so fleshed out, his conclusions reclaim their deserved complexity and nuance. Finally, and more universally, I believe that this chaotic episode of archival history reveals much about archives themselves, suggesting specifically their fundamental fragility and malleability. The Revolution's raging debates and contradictory impulses thus prove intrinsically interesting, even as they provide eventual material for more abstract theorizing about the nature of archives and about our ongoing relationship as human beings to our own documentary heritage. It is, in many ways, the

---

4 Michel Delon, "La bibliothèque est en feu: Rêveries autour du livre," *Bulletin des Bibliothèques de France* 34, no. 2-3 (1989): 120.

5 Robert-Henri Bautier, "La phase cruciale de l'histoire des archives: la constitution des dépôts d'archives et la naissance de l'archivistique, XVIe-début du XIXe siècle," *Archivum* 18 (1968): 139-49. Amédée Outrey has written several legally and historically oriented articles, including: "La notion traditionnelle des titres et les origines de la législation révolutionnaire sur les archives: La loi du 7 september 1790," *Revue historique de droit français et étranger* (1955): 438-63; and "Sur la notion d'archives en France, à la fin du XVIIIe siècle," *Revue historique de droit français et étranger* (1953): 277-86; Vida Azimi, "La Révolution française: déni de mémoire ou déni de droit?" *Revue historique de droit français et étranger* 68, no. 2 (1990): 157-78; Carl Lokke, "Archives and the French Revolution," *American Archivist* 31 (March 1968): 23-31; Adolf Brenneke, *Archivkunde* (Leipzig: Koehler & Amelang, 1953).

very extremity of the Revolution, itself demanding closer scrutiny, which
also permits transcendence of its own particularity, and, as in so many
matters, demonstrates the era's worth as the touchstone it has become.

Before examining the changes that archives underwent, it is helpful
to recall how they were viewed at the start of the Revolution. The
eighteenth-century concept of archives was far more restricted than
our current definition of the term allows, referring at that time exclusively to documents conferring legal or economic advantage upon the owner
or named party. Diderot and d'Alembert's *Encyclopédie,* an authoritative
source for contemporary thought on most any topic, makes this understanding explicit: "Archives se dit d'anciens titres ou chartres qui contien-
nent les droits, prétensions, priviléges & prérogatives d'une maison,
d'une ville, d'un royaume" ("Archives is the term used for those old titles
or charters which contain the rights, pretensions, privileges, and prerogatives of a house, a town, or a kingdom"). The *Encyclopédie* further
defines *titre* as "any act which establishes some right," and *chartres* as
"very old titles, as from the 10th, 11th, 12th and 13th century, or at least
anterior to the 15th century."[6] This legalistic definition prevailed through
the last days of the monarchy, and was so well ingrained in political and
scholarly consciousness that it was repeated virtually unaltered in leading
legal texts of the day.[7]

The power of archival records, then, could be vast, for upon them
rested the entire legal, political, and economic legitimacy of the monarchy and nobility. Robert-Henri Bautier compares them to an "instrument
placed at the disposition of those in power" and to "an arsenal of judicial
and political arms."[8] So crucial were archival records that sovereigns
maintained them in secrecy. Furthermore, in an administration not so far
removed from Louis XIV's declaration that "l'état c'est moi," even official
State archives were understood to "constitute the personal documentation of the sovereign and to remain at his personal disposition."[9] The
same prerogative applied to any holder of *titres* or *chartres.*

Given their importance, it is understandable that, early in the
Revolution especially, archives were a hated and frequently attacked symbol of feudal oppression. Seen as preserving "documents written in [legal-
istic] 'code' to serve the rights of some and subjugate the rest,"[10] they
provided a natural lightning rod for revolutionary outrage. This sort of

---

6 *Encyclopédie ou Dictionnaire raisonné des sciences, des arts et des métiers* (Paris: Briasson, 1751-1765):
   vol. 1, 619; vol. 16, 359; vol. 3, 220.

7 For a detailed study of contemporary use and understanding of the term *archives,* see Outrey,
   "Sur la notion d'archives."

8 Bautier "La phase cruciale," 141.

9 Ibid., 144.

10 Azimi, "La Révolution française," 164.

spontaneous, visceral hostility manifested itself especially during the period of the *Gran' Peur,* the rural insurrections that gripped the country-side during the summer of 1789, following the fall of the Bastille. The peasant, writes Philippe Sagnac, "took his own Bastille, invaded the châteaux, ran straight to the seigneurial archives, held at last in his hands the charters, monuments of his own servitude, and delivered them to the fire."[11] Much like attacks on other symbols of oppression — defacement of churches, coats of arms, statues, and carriages, for example, and even the strangling of game birds on seigneurial manors — this mutilation and destruction of records can best be construed as a metonymic assault against the nobility and the seigneurial system, an act of displaced retri-bution that might in some cases have even had practical consequences for the peasants whose debts and obligations had just gone up in flames.

In many ways, this image of the patriotic peasant and avenging sans-culotte plays to some of the most enduring myths of the Revolution. In the end, however, the effects upon archival records were isolated, modest, and little-documented. Of far greater magnitude are those instances in which the government actively initiated the wholesale destruction of records. In what reads now as a series of harrowing directives purporting the purification of France and the obliteration of dangerous or painful reminders of the past, the state itself became the author and authorizer of a more systematic revolutionary vandalism.

A series of laws promulgated between 1789 and 1793 abolished most titles and privileges and appropriated to the government the properties of nobles, the clergy, emigrés, the condemned, and, of course, the monar-chy, along with the written records belonging to and granting land and benefits to these classes. While some of the confiscated documents did in fact wind up in the archives of the new regime, and others were trans-ferred in sales to profit the state, those remaining were put to more dra-matic patriotic use. On May 12, 1792, for example, the Legislative Assembly decreed that papers of the nobility and the orders of knight-hood, which were then being housed in the Augustine Convent in Paris, should be burned in the Place Vendôme (although titles to nationalized properties and items of particular historical interest were spared).[12] A sim-ilar bonfire on June 19 of that year was praised on the floor of the Assembly by no less than Condorcet, rationalist mathematician and one of the last remaining *philosophes* in these early days of the Terror:

---

11 Philippe Sagnac, *La Législation civile de la Révolution française (1789-1804)* (1898; reprint, New York: AMS Press, 1973), 85.

12 Armand Gaston Camus, "Mémoire sur les dépôts de chartes, titres, registres, documents et autres papiers qui existaient dans le département de la Seine, et sur leur état à l'époque du 1er janvier 1789, sur les révolutions qu'ils ont éprouvées et sur leur état au 1er nivôse de l'an VI," in Félix Ravaisson, *Rapport adressé à S. Exc. le ministre d'Etat au nom de la commission instituée le 22 avril 1861* (Paris: Panckoucke, 1862), 322.

It is today that, in the capital, Reason burns, at the foot of the statue of Louis XIV, 600 folio volumes attesting to the vanity of this class whose titles will at last disappear in smoke. . . . [W]e must enfold all depositories [of titles] in a common destruction. You must not retain at the nation's expense these ridiculous hopes which seem to threaten our equality. Do not believe this goal unworthy of you, for it is a question of combating the most idiotic, but most incurable of passions, namely vanity. [13]

He then introduced, and there was passed, a resolution requiring "all titles and genealogies found in public repositories [to be] burned," pending extraction of any having potential financial value for the state.

It was measures such as this, coupled with a new law of July 17, 1793,[14] that authorized the destruction *en masse* of archival records in the provinces, where, it is generally acknowledged, the most extensive and spectacular campaigns took place. Frequently incorporated into patriotic festivals or instructive exercises, the disposal of these records inspired unfettered flights of the patriotic imagination. Papers, writes Serge Bianchi, "were baptized with derogatory names: rags, ecclesiastic cartridges, cannon fodder, playthings, magic papers, certificates of deception, childishness, lying titles . . .,"[15] and the circumstances of their destruction were no less spectacular. An official from the city of Mantes, for example, reported that "[b]eneath the tree of liberty was lit a fire into which were thrown all *orders of priesthood*, feudal titles, and tapestries bearing the fleur de lys. . . . Around the fire, the citizens and our priests danced a carmagnole to the sound of music composed by citizens of our community."[16]

Numerous variants of this scenario are recounted in fairly lurid detail by the archival histories of the nineteenth century,[17] but of greater interest than any specific degradations is the force motivating this destructive agenda. Unlike the spontaneous insurrections of the *Gran' Peur*, the state now actively sponsored and encouraged manifestations of violence in the furtherance of its own ideological and political agenda. Destroying the

---

13 *Archives Parlementaires de 1787 à 1860: recueil complet des debats legislatifs et politiques des chambres françcaises,* First series (Paris: Paul Dupont, 1879-1913): vol. 45, 378. Hereafter refered to as *AP.*

14 Article 6 of the law proclaims that any holders of feudal titles are "required to deposit them within three months at the local clerk's office. Those deposited before August 10 will be burned that very day in the presence of the general Communal Council and citizens; the rest will be burned three months later." Cited in Henri Bordier, *Les Archives de la France* (1855; reprint Geneva: Mégoriotis, 1978), 327.

15 Serge Bianchi, *La révolution culturelle de l'an II: Elites et peuple, 1789-1799* (Paris: Aubier, 1982), 166.

16 Bordier, *Les Archives,* 336. Emphasis in original.

17 See especially Bordier, *Les Archives,* 333-40 and Le Marquis Léon de Laborde, *Les Archives de la France: Leurs vicissitudes pendant la Révolution, leur régénération sous l'Empire* (Paris: Renouard, 1867), 233-44.

symbols of the old regime demonstrated the extent of one's hatred of that government and, conversely, one's devotion to the Republic. At the same time, large-scale, irreversible obliteration of the monarchy and nobility's legitimizing and functional operating documents would seem to prevent any reversion to that system in both symbolic and practical terms. The new administration skillfully channeled popular passions so that, observes Philippe Sagnac, "What had been insurrectional in 1789 became legal in 1793."[18] Moreover, it became, from the State's point of view, both useful and desirable.

Despite the high-sounding Revolutionary rhetoric that accompanied the disposal of monarchic, feudal, and religious documents, a good number fell victim to more prosaic, primarily economic, concerns. We have already mentioned the government's policy of auctioning for profit seized and nationalized properties, with the dispersion of titles this procedure entailed. In other cases, the financially foundering Republic took a more high-volume approach, remanding papers of the appropriate size and composition to the nearest arsenals for use in manufacturing munitions. A law of January 15, 1793, instructed that local directorates that "possess depositories of paper and parchment in their various quarters will allow the representatives of the Minister of the Navy to proceed freely and without delay in the sorting [of these papers] and the removal of those which they judge suitable for artillery use."[19] Other documents were claimed for paper making, in order to economize on the use of linen.[20]

The extent of cultural losses resulting from this state-sanctioned vandalism are to this day unknown and unknowable. As a recent paper by Annie Regond prudently cautions:

> We too often forget that the exact state of our cultural heritage
> . . . that is, books, archives, art works and buildings, was not
> known with any precision at the beginning of the Revolution. In
> the same way, we know even less about the exact extent of
> destructive acts, their dates, the perpetrators, or their motiva-
> tions. . . . In fact, we completely lack any systematically derived
> data which might allow the broad synthesis that could constitute
> a sound basis for reflection.[21]

---

18 Sagnac, *La Législation civile de la Révolution française,* 149.

19 Cited in Edgard Boutaric, "Le vandalisme révolutionnaire: les archives pendant la Révolution française," *Revue des questions historiques* 12 (October 1872): 350.

20 De Laborde, *Les Archives de la France,* 241.

21 Annie Regond, "'Vandalisme révolutionnaire' et protection du patrimoine pendant la Révolution française: pour une enquête nationale," in *Révolution française et "vandalisme révolutionnaire,"* ed. Simone Bernard-Griffiths, Marie-Claude Chemin, and Jean Ehrard (Paris: Universitas, 1992), 131.

Authors since the Revolution, however, have not been deterred from proffering their best estimates, extrapolations, and flights of fancy, especially during the nineteenth century, when interest in archival history, and in the Revolution more generally, intensified markedly. Between 1870 and 1914 "several thousand studies on the Revolution filled journals and periodicals,"[22] and the most comprehensive studies we now have to work with date from this period. In many cases these accounts — considering the lack of hard data that Regond so regrets — provide the best overall portrait readily available. At the same time, their authors make no pretense of hiding or disguising their own opinions, which must be accounted for in the attempt to derive a more objective appreciation of the Revolution's archival advances and errors.

On the one hand, Henri Bordier, writing in 1855 as former Archivist of the Empire, is the principal exponent of the view that Revolutionary vandalism, while regrettable, was not on the whole as extensive or as deleterious to archives as might be supposed. "It is incontestable," he writes, "that an enormous number of papers and parchments were sold or burned in that terrible year of 1793," but these were, he claims, documents "almost entirely lacking historic or literary value."[23] More specifically, in a study of some 15,000 addresses to the Convention, a forum in which, he avers, speakers never hesitated to "proclaim their patriotism and give all possible proofs of it," Bordier found only 64 that discussed the burning of records in the provinces. Of these, a mere 16 identified the records with any degree of specificity.[24] His scientific method may be questionable, but Bordier expresses confidence that very few truly significant records were eliminated and even that, on occasion, "entire archives, said to have been destroyed by revolutionary vandalism . . . were later found lying about ignored in some corner of the prefecture or town hall."[25] For the most part, modern historians adhere to this general view. "A little skepticism regarding destruction statistics . . . is in order," cautions Carl Lokke, while Paul Gerbod concurs that archival repositories in France's municipalities certainly "suffered the consequences of abandonment or of the bonfires celebrated in popular jubilation[, but] the majority survived."[26]

Bordier's contemporaries, on the other hand, were far less sanguine, chief among them the Marquis Léon de Laborde, who penned a still-cited

---

22 Marc Bouloiseau, *The Jacobin Republic*, trans. Jonathan Mandelbaum (Cambridge: Cambridge University Press, 1983), 153.

23 Bordier, *Les Archives*, 329.

24 Ibid., 332.

25 Ibid., 326-27.

26 Lokke, "Archives and the French Revolution," 31; Paul Gerbod, "Vandalisme et anti-vandalisme du pouvoir politique de 1789 à 1795," in Bernard, et al., *Révolution française et "vandalisme révolutionnaire,"* 295.

inquiry, notable both for its comprehensive scope and for the florid vehemence of the author's prose. De Laborde, a politician and art scholar, was named Director of the Imperial Archives in 1856. A titled noble who prospered during the regime of the Emperor Louis-Philippe, he has been termed "one of the most violent adversaries of the Revolution."[27] His revealingly titled treatise, *Les Archives de la France, Leurs vicissitudes pendant la Révolution, leur régénération sous l'Empire*, represents a frontal attack on the Republic, focusing upon, but hardly limited to, its handling of the nation's archives. Even such a proponent of de Laborde's conclusions as Edgard Boutaric, writing in the *Revue des questions historiques* in 1872, terms the work "a passionate plea against the Revolution . . . essentially true, but with a partisan aspect: which has damaged his credibility."[28] In assessing the consequences of Revolutionary policies, de Laborde calculates that "more than 10,000 archives were affected and more or less devastated, that they contained a billion documents, that more than two thirds were destroyed, and that the order of the remaining third was thrown into upheaval."[29]

Hostile as de Laborde's account may be, even he makes clear that willful revolutionary ravages reflect only part of the story. As Serge Bianchi reminds us, "The idea of Jacobin vandalism gives a false sense of

---

27 A. Giry, "Archives," in *La Grande Encyclopédie: Inventaire raisonné des sciences, des lettres et des arts* (Paris: H. Lamirault, 1886), 749. We might additionally note that the Marquis's family history certainly must have contributed to his hostility regarding the Revolution: His father, Alexandre-Louis-Joseph, had been forced to flee to England during this period and eventually served in the Austrian Army, while his grandfather, Jean-Joseph, was arrested and guillotined during the Terror. (See *La Grande Encyclopédie* at "Laborde," vol. 21, 688.)

28 Boutaric, "Le vandalisme révolutionnaire," 334. The extent of de Laborde's partisanship may be clearly seen in passages such as the following:
> All were swept up in the spirit of the rights of man and the conquests of civil liberty; the old regime was shouted down, all our history vilified; France, throwing off her garment which she deemed too worn, claimed to be starting a new sort of humanity, superior to the preceding sort, and which had need of neither experience nor tradition. Archives suffered in this explosion of spirits; they had no importance and offered no interest simply because they conserved the laws and traditions of another time. So the old regime was abhorred, none wished to learn from it; and, the better to destroy it, it was resolved to destroy anything which might call it to mind." (de Laborde, *Les Archives de la France*, 18-19)

That Boutaric himself was no friend of the revolution is made clear by his proposal to study chronologically, "the general measures which were taken during the Revolutionary period to confiscate, transport, move, pile up, make scrap of, dismember, divide into small piles, obliterate [and] scribble upon these secular archives which go from Dagobert to Louis XVI, and which make of us, I would say the first, the most ancient of modern peoples" (Boutaric, "Le vandalisme révolutionnairre," 340).

29 De Laborde, *Les Archives de la France*, 125. We might note, without much surprise, that de Laborde was violently critical of Bordier. In an interesting footnote to the history of archival history, the latter riposted with his own publication, in which he chides that "we have rarely seen such bitterness spill from the pen of a functionary, whose duties would instead seem more conducive to a calm and discreet seriousness" (Bordier, *Les inventaires des Archives de l'Empire: Réponse à M. le Marquis de Laborde, Directeur Général contenant un Errata pour ses préfaces et ses inventaires* (Paris: Librarie Bachelin-Deflorenne, 1867), 2.

history. The archives and museums of the Year II are its antithesis. It is
just as true to affirm that the defense of our history was born in the Year
II, as to prove that the Jacobins and sans-culottes destroyed the symbols
of the Ancien Regime's 'governing elite.'"[30] That Bianchi should single
out archives as an example of Revolutionary conservation is not inciden-
tal, for their consolidation and organization represent a massive feat of
planning and dedication; one which has, moreover, been far more
meticulously documented than the corresponding destruction of
archives and can thus be studied a bit more dispassionately. This is not
to say that this aspect of the archival past is any less convoluted. Indeed,
rather than standing in unequivocal opposition, the impulses toward
destruction and conservation are frequently intertwined, with the latter
containing disturbing elements of the former. A brief chronology will
highlight some of the more significant developments and contradictions
in this history.

The gains made in archival theory and management can again best
be appreciated through comparison with the state of archives under the
Ancien Régime. We have seen that archival documents, as judicial and
economic instruments, were primarily of interest to their owners, who
understandably preferred to keep close watch over them. The result was
an unregulated multiplicity of archival repositories. As Bordier writes:
"The King of France had his 'trésor des chartes,' the parliament its registers; the Church, monasteries and communes all had their charter rooms;
each body jealously guarded its own archives; no depository was connected
with any other, and it was impossible to imagine ever uniting them
all."[31] An account conducted in 1770 identified 405 archival repositories
in Paris and 5700 outside the capital, including 1700 monasteries and
1780 seigneurial seats.[32] Through the series of confiscations and aban-
donments mentioned earlier, many of these documents rapidly fell under
control of the Republic, which additionally was generating records of its
own conduct and decisions.

It was in fact these latter legislative records that inspired the
Assembly's concern for archival preservation. In one of its earliest acts,
dated July 29, 1789 — a mere two weeks after the fall of the Bastille —
the members approved their own rules of procedure, including provision
for establishment of a legislative repository:

---

30 Bianchi, *La révolution culturelle de l'an II*, 172-73.

31 Bordier, *Les Archives*, 1.

32 Ibid., 326; Giry, "Archives," 740. Giry objects that many private and religious archives had been
    overlooked in this census and that we can, "without exaggeration, place at over 10,000 the
    number of archives in France at the end of the Ancien Régime." This is a figure repeated by
    Langlois (Charles Langlois and H. Stein, *Les Archives de l'histoire de France* [1891; reprint,
    Nendeln, Lichtenstein: Kraus Reprint, 1966], p. iv.)

> Choice will be made . . . of a safe place for the deposit of all
> original documents relating to the operation of the Assembly, and
> there will be constructed cabinets having three keys, of which
> one will be given to the president, the second to one of his secre-
> taries, and the third to the archivist, who will be elected from
> among the members of the Assembly by a majority vote.

The act additionally instructs the Archives to house original copies of
all laws, as well as one of the two official copies of the minutes for each
session, and to communicate these items only to the President or
Secretaries of the Assembly, or upon their written orders.[33] On August 4,
the Assembly elected as archivist Armand-Gaston Camus, a well-known
lawyer and scholar, admired, according to Lokke, for his "unquestioned
probity" and "exemplary private life,"[34] but just as likely chosen in tribute to his impeccable Republican credentials.[35] Camus immediately proposed reclassifying the documents under his control and renaming the
"Parliamentary Archives" as the "National Archives." Except for a two-
and-one-half year imprisonment by the Austrians from 1793 to 1795, he
served at its head until his death in 1804.

The organization and operation of the new National Archives were
finally consolidated under the Law of September 12, 1790,[36] which proclaimed it "the repository of all the acts which establish the Constitution
of the Kingdom, its laws, and its division into departments." The
archivist was to be elected for a term of six years, over the objections of
Camus, who wished the appointment to be permanent.[37] Two commis-
sioners were also elected from among the members of the Assembly. The
law established the specific duties of the archivist, including the requirement that he "live in the place where the archives will be established; he
may only leave for important reasons, after notifying the commission-
ers," and that he furnish to the Assembly an annual report on his work
and the Archives' holdings. The Archives was to be open to the public
three days a week, from 9 A.M. to 2 P.M., and from 5 P.M. to 9 P.M. Thus
was established a single, unified institution with responsibility for all

---

33 *AP,* vol. 8, 302-3.

34 Lokke, "Archives and the French Revolution," 25.

35 Outrey, "La notion traditionnelle," 444. De Laborde takes a characteristically less charitable view
of the new archivist: "The functions [of the office] were few, and well within his abilities" (*Les
Archives de la France,* 5-6); "his exile [in an Austrian prison] had suggested to him no new or reasonable ideas regarding the organization of archives, he understood them no better than before
his departure" (*Les Archives de la France,* 99).

36 *AP,* vol. 18, 572-74 and 646-49. (The law was actually debated over the course of two sessions,
on the fourth and ninth of September.)

37 See Outrey, "La notion traditionnelle," for details of this heated debate. Under the Ancien
Régime, most archival officials did in fact hold life-long appointments, but the Assembly found
such an arrangement at odds with its democratic spirit.

documents relating to the new administration, and open for the first time to the general public.

The legislation examined up to this point would seem to cleave neatly in two: Elaborate measures were devised to safeguard the records of the Republic, while, conversely, documents relating to the Old Regime were ordered burned, sold, or recycled. Yet such a characterization, however convenient, unjustly oversimplifies legislative and archival history and minimizes the vision of those who established the heart of the modern French archival system. From the outset of the Revolution, numerous voices were raised in defense of the nation's cultural heritage, newly wrested from the privileged and religious classes. The Decree of June 19, 1790, abolishing hereditary nobility and titles, for example, explicitly forbid citizens under "pretext of the present decree, to attack the monuments placed in churches, the charters, titles and other documents concerning families or properties, or the decorations in any public or private place."[38] Concern for the monuments of the past continued to grow, long before the Abbé Grégoire, in his 1794 reports to the Convention, actually coined the term *vandalism* and decried its excesses as "counter-revolutionary."[39] If nothing else, as Bordier points out, it was still necessary to "see and sort [old titles] before pronouncing their condemnation."[40] From these considerations, both elevated and venal, was born a series of measures designed to bring some order to the masses of old records suddenly in the possession of the new republic.

The first such measure, the law of August 7, 1790, mandated the consolidation "in a same and single location" of several Ancien Régime repositories in Paris.[41] Apparently, this reorganization presented logistical difficulties — most notably a lack of space — and it was only undertaken in response to the new Law of 12 brumaire Year II (November 2, 1793).[42]

---

38 Cited in John Hall Stewart, *A Documentary Summary of the French Revolution* (New York: MacMillan, 1951), 143.

39 Grégoire, "Rapport sur les destructions opérés par le Vandalisme, et sur les moyens de le réprimer;" "Second Rapport sur le Vandalisme;" and "Troisième Rapport sur le Vandalisme" (Paris: Imprimerie Nationale, 1794). In fact, Grégoire makes few specific references to archives at all. Boutaric suggests that he ignored them because he simply did not care about their fate: "[T]he conservation of documents had no interest at all to Grégoire or his colleagues: they concerned a past whose memory it was necessary to erase. At the most, it was thought that a few items should be saved to attest to the history of progress and the human spirit, by pointing out [earlier] errors and showing just how wretched men had become under the fatal influence of the monarchy" (Boutaric, "Le vandalisme révolutionnaire," 327). Grégoire's lack of attention, however, seems equally likely to stem from the fact, as we have seen, that archives were conceived as legal, and not cultural, institutions, and thus fell outside his scope. Still, the growing concern for France's heritage is unmistakable.

40 Bordier, *Les Archives*, 329.

41 *AP*, vol. 18, 652.

42 *AP*, vol. 78, 1270-77.

Under this law, records were assigned to either of two repositories, an "administrative and land section" ("partie domaniale et administrative") or a "judicial and historical section," both under control of the Archivist of the Republic. The law further directed the city of Paris to "remit to the two sections of the National Archives the titles, minutes, and registers which it had removed from other repositories."

Even at this preliminary stage, three features characteristic of the Revolution's subsequent archival legislation begin to emerge. The first is a tendency toward both physical and administrative centralization, "the desire," as Camus himself later characterized it, "to make all revolve around a center, and bring everything toward unity."[43] At the same time, as *fonds* were combined, the archivists sorted individual records according primarily to document type and content. Although certainly foreign to modern principles of arrangement in their obliteration of any previous, naturally occurring order, these schema did reflect contemporary French archival practices, drawing heavily upon the passion for encyclopedic classification that so characterized the Enlightenment.[44] Finally, the entire operation was marked by an ideological component no less pronounced — indeed allied with — the very spirit that promoted the burning of records beneath the Tree of Liberty. In proceeding with sorting operations under the law of 12 brumaire, wrote Camus, "we adopted the principle of letting nothing remain which bore the stamp of servitude, but to conserve [only] that which could provide evidence of public or private ownership, or which could be used for instruction."[45] Most frequently, the documents "bearing the stamp of servitude" were those consigned to the bonfire or the arsenal. Thus conservation proceeded hand-in-hand with destruction.

These tendencies were amplified by the Law of 7 messidor Year II (June 25, 1794), "the veritable code of the National Archives and for all the repositories . . . in the Republic."[46] Between the titles and documents amassed under the Law of 12 brumaire, and those confiscated from nobles, emigrés, the clergy, and others, the Convention's Committee on Archives rapidly felt itself deluged, as well as pressured to turn these papers to best fiscal advantage. Their response was this law, proposed in an impassioned endorsement by Julien Dubois:

---

43 Camus, "Mémoire sur les dépôts de chartes," 336.

44 Bautier, "La phase cruciale," 147. According to Nancy Bartlett, "the tradition of the Enlightenment's Encyclopedists still inspired efforts at universal codification systems among leading French curators" as late as the middle of the nineteenth century. (Nancy Bartlett, "*Respect des Fonds*: The Origins of the Modern Archival Principle of Provenance," in *Bibliographical Foundations of French Historical Studies* [Binghamton, N. Y.: Haworth Press, 1992], 108.)

45 Camus, "Mémoire sur les dépôts de chartes," 335.

46 Ibid., 336.

When statues of tyrants have been toppled, when file and chisel spare no emblems of feudalism or monarchy, republicans can only view with indignation the traces left in manuscript collections of so many offenses made to human dignity. The first impulse which moves us is to deliver all these titles to the fire and make vanish the slightest vestiges of so hated a regime. Only the public interest can and should limit this laudable zeal. . . . Far from wishing to cool [this passion], it is precisely to proscribe what is rightly reprehensible that we urge a severe examination, and are wary only of an ill-considered haste which could offend justice, harm the public fortune, and cause us later regret.[47]

The innovations of the law were twofold. First, the National Archives was confirmed as "a central repository for the entire Republic." It was to have jurisdiction over all other repositories, monitoring their operations, and in many cases appropriating documents from them. At the same time, the law detailed a more elaborate sorting system than that previously employed. Valid titles documenting state ownership of property would continue to be sent to the "section domaniale" and legal documents to the "section juridique." Furthermore, "charters and manuscripts proper to history, the sciences, and the arts, or which are useful for instructive purposes" would be sent to the Bibliothèque Nationale or to local libraries. Finally, the Committee earmarked for automatic destruction "purely feudal titles," as well as land titles "without any utility" because they referred to property already disposed of. To this end, the law authorized formation of a "Temporary Title Agency" ("Agence Temporaire des Titres") and the appointment in each department of local officers (*préposés au triage*). These committees were allotted six months to complete their task. In all other respects, previous laws on archives still remained valid, including the right of "any citizen . . . to request in any repository . . . consultation of the records contained therein."

The effects of the law were far-reaching and ultimately controversial. It is undeniable that the Agence Temporaire des Titres was forced to make rapid, summary judgements regarding an enormous quantity of documents and that its members had moreover to carry out their work at the ideological height of the Terror. Lokke repeats an earlier determination that "upwards of 500,000 kilograms (550 tons) of records" were marked for destruction in Paris alone. Frequently records awaiting triage were transferred to poorly equipped holding areas, where they were subject to harmful conditions and neglect. Not unexpectedly, the Marquis de Laborde criticizes the work of the Agency as even more reprehensible than the wholesale vandalism committed by those who did not know better:

---

47 *AP*, vol. 92, 177-82.

The Commission of 1794 . . . shared all the prejudices of the moment, presumed to date everything, even history itself, from the establishment of the Republic, saw in the old archives merely a fiscal resource to appropriate the property of churches, convents, corporations, princes, emigrés, and the condemned, and, if it set aside several charters, treatises, and diplomas in a very small number for the sake of curiosity, it was only for the purpose of sending them off most illogically to the public libraries.[48]

Bordier, on the other hand, asserts that "[e]ven while making certain concessions to the Revolution's destructive tendencies, concessions which were indispensible at the time, [the Law] nevertheless firmly reasserts the ascendancy of science and enumerates most clearly those practical measures to which we owe the salvage of so many precious items which remain to us today."[49]

Interestingly, at least part of the disagreement between de Laborde and Bordier would seem to stem not from political differences, but from their assessments of Revolutionary archival theory. De Laborde particularly laments what we might today call the Commission's disregard for principles of provenance and original order:

To introduce into the unity [of an archives], in which all parts hold together, the dissolving force of a triage which arbitrarily reassigned items to land, judicial, and historical sections, was to alter completely the archives and diminish the significance of the items so isolated. . . . The triage ordered by the Convention disturbed, by its arbitrary and absurd divisions, all archives which, as I said, had been arranged over the centuries in an intelligent and continuous order. This triage . . . ruined archives by separating them.[50]

A more tolerant Bordier, continuing his dialogue with the Marquis, argues that:

The great crime of Camus and [his successor] Danou, according to M. de Laborde, is to have accepted the ideas of the Convention regarding archives, and to have persevered . . .: 1) in the Revolutionary plan to classify all documents in land, judicial, and historic sections, without thought to their provenance; 2) in the pretension to centralize in the general Archives all items of historic interest which could be found in the departments and in

---

48 De Laborde, *Les Archives de la France*, 72.

49 Bordier, *Les Archives*, 8.

50 De Laborde, *Les Archives de la France*, 85-87.

conquered nations. These two charges are equally unacceptable, because the men who lived during the Revolution and at the beginning of this century considered archives from a perspective other than our own; they were dealing with a question of militancy, where we have a question of art; they argued amidst the difficulties of a new situation, while we talk about facts with the wisdom of long experience.[51]

Whatever their operating methods, archival commissions certainly required more than six months to realize the Convention's vision. Members were appointed to the Agence des Titres on November 8, 1794; in 1796, the decree of 5 floréal Year IV (April 24) authorized the reorganization of the agency, which functioned for another five years under various names. Work in the provinces ended earlier, when the Law of 5 brumaire Year V (October 26, 1796) closed local agencies. The next significant reorganization of the nation's archives did not occur until 1800, when the pressures and constraints of Revolutionary politics, economics, and ideology had eased considerably, and once the framework of France's archives had been firmly established. As Boutaric observes, "From here on, we enter a period of conservation of documents."[52]

This tour through archival history began by accepting the thesis of Ernst Posner: that the French Revolution altered fundamental conceptions about the nature, mission, and administration of archival repositories. In examining the content and implementation of certain defining laws of that era, culminating in the Law of 7 messidor, we have observed the ways in which the Revolutionary government appointed itself curator of all records from both the Old and New Regimes; undertook their management through a centralized nationwide system; and confirmed every French citizen's right of access to these documents. This approach has worked backward toward the origin of Posner's conclusions, filling in their outlines and reaffirming that very image of innovation that the Revolution itself worked so hard to perpetuate.

At the same time, however, it is useful to retain some distance from the sweeping and infectious spirit of novelty inherent in Revolutionary rhetoric. Tocqueville's classic study, *L'ancien régime et la Révolution*, demonstrated the similarity between many administrative institutions of the Old and New Regimes; much the same claim can be made for their cultural institutions. In its "concern for the preservation of its cultural heritage," writes Jacques Solé, "the revolutionary era . . . appears to be

---

51 Bordier, *Les Inventoires des Archives de l'Empire*, 4. Nancy Bartlett's article on the origins of "Respect des Fonds" again provides a more thorough discussion of the history of the principle of provenance and of de Laborde's and Bordier's roles in its development.

52 Boutaric, "Le vandalisme révolutionnaire," 357.

guided as much by continuity as by rupture."[53] In the case of archives, this continuity manifests itself in several ways. First, as Bautier has pointed out, "the archival guardians of the Ancien Régime were members of the Revolution's triage agencies and provided the National Archives with their first 'clerks': they are really the ones who founded the French Archives, and they did so according to traditional concepts, as expressed in theoretical treatises and the work of practitioners."[54] In other words, arrangement proceeded along the principles of encyclopedic classification outlined earlier. Moreover, while politics and ideology unquestionably colored the massive triage projects imposed by the Legislature, it is remarkable just how frequently the Republic's archivists managed to introduce their own more professional interpretations of the law. Even de Laborde acknowledges, with tremendous relief, the numerous occasions upon which individual archivists, under their own initiative, chose to retain documents that should ordinarily have been marked for destruction.[55]

More frequently overlooked amid examinations of upheaval and evolution is the continuity that prevailed regarding the fundamental conception of archives. They were considered legal instruments on the eve of the Revolution, and so they remained at its end. It was never, after all, the intention of the French Revolution to do away with or to limit property. Records of legal ownership — both old and new — therefore merited continued careful attention. Similarly, the Declaration of the Rights of Man, with its subsequent elaboration in the laws of the Republic, was considered the ultimate "title" granting rights to all citizens. Its security required special vigilance. To be sure, political realities had their effect on the particular documents or types of documents that archival repositories henceforth contained. Outrey points out, for example, that the actual debates of the Assembly "were envisioned as a sort of title," which that body ordered transcribed, published, and housed with its archival materials, in contrast to the earlier practices of the monarchy and parliament.[56] More conspicuously, those documents suddenly deprived of their legal authority — such as feudal titles, genealogies, and adjudicated land titles — were swept out of archives and consigned as "historic monuments" to libraries, or were destroyed entirely. The measures taken to reorganize and reorder archival establishments were "above all intended to facilitate the administration of the nation and its departments, and to better document its services."[57] The

---

53 Jacques Solé, *La Révolution en questions* (Paris: Seuil, 1988), 308.

54 Bautier, "La phase cruciale," 148.

55 De Laborde, *Les Archives de la France*, 139-42.

56 Outrey, "La notion traditionnelle," 443.

57 Robert-Henri Bautier, "Les Archives," in *L'Histoire et ses méthodes*, ed. Charles Samaroun (Paris: Pléiade, 1961), 1133.

notion of archives as a site of historical or cultural scholarship had yet to take hold; their purpose at the close of the Revolution remained unaltered.

Whatever their novelty, or lack thereof, it is clear that archives were very much shaped by the Revolution's ongoing vacillation between preservation and obliteration. The paradox, like so many puzzles resulting from the interplay of human beliefs and passions at a time of turmoil, may defy satisfactory resolution. Yet these two impulses need not be seen as divorced entirely one from the other. This final discussion will seek to situate the Revolution's simultaneous destruction and salvation of archives into a broader context, giving it a sense in terms of both the very particular circumstances of the era, and, more generally, of society's relation to the records it creates.

On the one hand, the desire to destroy the records of the Ancien Régime appears to be, first and foremost, an intuitive, cathartic, and eminently understandable expression of rage, directed at one of the most prominent symbols of a hated and vilified class. Viewed with a bit more distance and dispassion, however, the impulse for destruction appears not merely as an act of negation and denial, but also the necessary prelude and counterpart to more constructive institutions, as though the past had to be put definitively to rest if it were not to endanger the emergent Republican future. This thesis of the tabula rasa has been developed at some length by Serge Bianchi in his influential book *La révolution culturelle de l'an II*. In order to regenerate society, he proposes:

> It was necessary to extirpate the roots of the irrational and corrupt Ancien Régime . . . to destroy the signs, symbols, beliefs and values of 'the age of shadows and fanaticism.' It was necessary to eliminate the 'gothic,' 'barbarous' vestiges of the monarchy, of feudalism, of traditional religion. . . . As long as the seeds of the old social system and of superstition persisted, the Revolution would have no firm foundation.
>
> The tabula rasa was inseparable from the new system of values . . . [although] the project aroused some reserves [because it was] assimilated to a simple campaign of 'revolutionary vandalism.'[58]

Bianchi's particular interest is in the many idiosyncratic customs that characterized the revolutionary landscape: the imposition of a new calendar, for example; the secular festivals that replaced religious celebrations; the rechristening of towns (by which St. Denis became Franciade and countless villages were suddenly known as "Montagne"); or the penchant for "revolutionary names" (Brutus, Marat). All demanded the abolition of tradition, the effacement of the past, in order to take root and acquire

---

58 Bianchi, *La révolution culturelle de l'an II*, 157.

their own authority. Such a concept takes on uncanny descriptive relevance in the case of archives, which, we have seen, formed the conceptual and practical basis for the hated institutions of the Old Regime. Their destruction struck symbolically at the heart of the old order, obliterating the very vision of history inscribed in feudal deeds, titles, and other documents, clearing the stage for the constitution of a new history. "Never," writes Vida Azimi, "has there been such a will to escape from history," as during this period. For the sanctioned "vision of time, the Revolution substituted the vision of emptiness, absolute nothingness from which could emerge a universe without precedent."[59] The destruction of historical records — that is, of the historical record — permitted the construction of a new civilization from the foundation up.

At the same time, the Revolution was just as concerned with establishing archives as with eliminating them, and this concern extended — albeit belatedly and rather brutally — to the records of the old regime as well as the new. True, these records were preserved neither intact nor in context. They were sorted and reordered, frequently abandoned and misused. Those that survived were promptly reclassified and relocated. But the Revolution undeniably "saw itself as a child of the Enlightenment and as having a cultural and more specifically educational vocation . . . reflected in the determination to destroy and to preserve at the same time. In effect, the revolutionary government assigned itself the role of managing nationalized cultural properties."[60] The new nation, in other words, saw fit to retain selected monuments of the past, but only on condition of redefining them for posterity. The brave new Republic could indeed accommodate documentary reminders of its predecessor regimes, but only by wholly appropriating these vestiges, placing them in newly conceived institutions dedicated above all to the glorification of the Republic.

Such interpretations depend upon the specific confluence of circumstances that determined the Revolution's conduct in archival matters, the specific awareness that certain records embodied the prerogatives and privileges of the past while others symbolized the promise of a new society. Framed in these terms, the frequently confusing, contradictory mass of Revolutionary actions and attitudes indeed appears more coherent. At the same time, we may also wonder whether any intrinsic properties of archives might additionally have contributed to their fate. Does the French Revolution, in other words, hold any more universal lessons for archives, or can it provide at least a starting point for more theoretical reflection?

---

59 Azimi, "La Révolution française," 159.

60 Bronislaw Baczko, "Vandalism," in *A Critical Dictionary of the French Revolution*, ed. François Furet and Mona Ozouf, trans. Arthur Goldhammer (Cambridge, Mass.: Belknap Press, 1989), 866.

It is not my intention to elaborate a semiotics of archives based on a single case, but the symbolic allure of records has already been suggested and this line of thought bears development. The issue has been touched upon in recent archival literature, most notably by James O'Toole, who asserts that "there are certain kinds of records in which the symbolic values outweigh the practical values."[61] Particularly striking about the Revolutionary era is the way in which some records (principally the founding documents of the new order) appear invested of equal parts practicality and symbolism, while the significance of others (remnants of the Ancien Régime) shifted abruptly and entirely from the realm of practicality to that of pure symbolism.

To consider how this can be, it is fruitful to step beyond the scope of purely archival thought into that of psychology and sociology, through the concept of collective memory. Pierre Nora's introduction to the essays he assembles in *Les Lieux de Mémoire* proves particularly evocative in this regard and relevant to our own train of thought.[62] In his essay, Nora defines memory, specifically collective memory, as a sort of living heritage, the "unself-conscious, commanding, all powerful" repetition of tradition that links a society to its past. Opposed to memory is history, "which is how our hopelessly forgetful modern societies, propelled by change, organize the past. . . . [H]istory is a representation of the past," which attempts to analyze, totalize, and make sense of it.[63] It is the fate of memory in a historically oriented age to be distilled into *"lieux de mémoire"* (sites of memory); the places, objects, and rituals that a society designates as links to the past and as emblematic of its current identity.

Without quibbling over Nora's terminology or his very obvious agenda of identifying the components of a French national identity, I believe two of his premises, one explicitly stated, the other less so, to be particularly relevant. First is the tendency of modern societies to set aside and privilege certain places, institutions, or other *"lieux"* as important links to the past, valuable precisely because of these associations. It is hardly accidental that Nora epitomizes archives as a *"lieu de mémoire"*: "Modern memory is, above all, archival. It relies on the materiality of the trace, the immediacy of the recording, the visibility of the image"; an "obsession with the archive . . . marks our age"; and "no society has

---

61 James M. O'Toole, "The Symbolic Significance of Archives," *American Archivist* 56 (Spring 1993): 238.

62 Pierre Nora, "Between Memory and History: *Les Lieux de Mémoire*," trans. Marc Roudebush, *Representations* 26 (Spring 1989): 7-25. Aspects of this issue have also been explored by Kenneth Foote (see, for example, "To Remember and Forget: Archives, Memory, and Culture," *American Archivist* 53 (Summer 1990): 378-92), but Nora's discussion remains more general and, I believe, provides a broader basis for reflection.

63 Nora, "Between Memory and History," 8. I shall leave aside, as does Nora, the question of when, exactly, the "modern" era can be said to have started.

ever produced archives as deliberately as our own."[64] Even more important is the suggestion that the true significance of any *"lieu de mémoire,"*
archives included, is societally determined. They are above all "spectacular symbols,"[65] and so must possess all the malleability of any sign. Their
significance may consequently alter, increase, or vanish altogether, as the
society that invests them with meaning itself evolves.

Both of these declarations seem, to me, profoundly descriptive of the
archival case of Revolutionary France. As the new Republic repudiated its
monarchic past, old records were vacated of their meaning and import.
Functionally useless, because they were irrelevant in practical terms,
uninteresting because they reflected values deemed archaic, they could
instead be made to stand for the myriad sins of the Ancien Régime and
were treated — or mistreated — accordingly. Their significance lay no
longer in their specific content, but in their association with the past. For
the Minister of the Interior to consider "[a]ll old papers with gothic writing . . . [to be] nothing more than feudal titles, reflecting the subjuga-
tion of the weak by the strong"[66] merely epitomizes this change in perception. To honor or treasure such papers would be suspect, but sacrificing them to the "patriotic holocaust" or treating them as just so much
scrap paper was proof of Republican virtue.

At the same time, the Republic's concern for protecting its own
records, and eventually select records of its predecessor regimes, demonstrates an increasing appreciation for the defining power of archives and
for their potential authority as a *"lieu de mémoire."* The creation of new
repositories helped the Revolution to affirm its own identity, while the
triage and reclassification of old records guaranteed that a particular
interpretation of the past would be imposed upon succeeding generations. The Revolution, writes Bautier, "was the first time that such a considerable plan encompassed the archives of an entire regime — political,
administrative, feudal, religious — exceeding even the notion of State
Archives and instead forming the Archives of the 'Nation.'"[67] But it was
also around these very archives that the notion of "the nation" could in
part crystallize and take hold in the collective consciousness.

Constitution of the new National Archives, which glorified the
achievements of the Revolution and marginalized or minimized all that
went before, appears in this light as essential to the political and psychological legitimacy of the New Regime.

To suggest that such considerations actively or explicitly shaped the
archival policies of the French Revolution would, of course, be excessive.

---

64 Ibid., 13.

65 Ibid., 12.

66 Cited in de Laborde, *Les Archives de la France,* 23-24.

67 Bautier, "Les Archives," 1133.

Indeed, much of the history we have examined reflects above all the very pragmatic concerns born of unique historic and cultural circumstances. If archives and records attracted such vehement reactions or elaborate legislation, it is in part because they mattered in quite practical terms to the functioning of the Republic and in the lives of its citizens. In this sense, study of the Revolution and its treatment of archives is of interest as it illuminates the passions of the past and the origins of certain modern concepts and assumptions.

Yet it is difficult, given the era's intense preoccupation with archives, to escape the impression that some more fundamental impulse is also at work. The significance of archival records clearly extends beyond the information they contain, for only this broader symbolism would seem capable of incorporating such enduring extremes of both revulsion and reverence. It is in characterizing these properties that the utility of Nora's *"lieu de mémoire"* notation becomes apparent. Archives in this schema appear nothing less than a sacred space in modern society, specifically designated to convey a vision of the nation's past, its origins, and its identity. National archives are respected, at least in part, because they give meaning to the nation, confirming its legitimacy, and — perhaps nowhere more clearly than in the case of Revolutionary France — its vital mythologies. Creating new archives and reinventing the old thus constituted a founding act of the new Republic.

But if archives bring meaning to the nation, it is ultimately national consensus that in turn confers upon archives their meaning and mystique. Should consensus change, should the nation advance or evolve or disappear altogether, then archival records may be reconsidered and redefined, perhaps even rejected. Modern archival theory and practice, of course, would likely preclude the wholesale destruction and reorganizations that marked the Revolution, yet this period makes clear a relationship that has not changed. Far from standing as enduring monuments to the past, archives instead appear somewhat fragile, eternally subject to the judgement of the society in which they exist. Neither atemporal nor absolute, the meaning they convey may be manipulated, misinterpreted, or suppressed. That the archives of the past are also the mutable creations of the present is perhaps one of the most enduring and vivid lessons of the French Revolution.

6

The Provenance of a Profession: The Permanence of the Public Archives and Historical Manuscripts Traditions in American Archival History

LUKE J. GILLILAND–SWETLAND

Abstract: *This article broadens the definitions used in Richard Berner's* Archival Theory and Practice in the United States: A Historical Analysis *to distinguish between two competing perspectives within the archival professional community: one that views archivists as members of a larger community of historian-scholars with a responsibility to interpret the documents in their care, and one that defines archivists as information-management professionals with a responsibility to act as "gatekeepers" for the materials under their control. These differing views influenced the establishment and development of archival institutions early in the twentieth century and continue to shape more recent debates concerning the status of archivists as professionals.*

In 1983 Richard C. Berner looked back at the development of almost two centuries of American archival theory and practice. His monograph, *Archival Theory and Practice in the United States: A Historical Analysis,* identified two traditions that had informed archival administration in this country.[1] The first, an indigenous historical manuscripts tradition dating back almost to the birth of the country, had been shaped by private antiquarian-collectors, such as Peter Force and Jared Sparks, and was institutionalized in places such as the Massachusetts Historical Society, the Library of Congress, and the American Antiquarian Society. By the early twentieth century, these institutions and their successors had come to draw upon the theory and practice of librarianship for the

Reprinted with permission from the *American Archivist* 54 (Spring 1991): 160-75. This article received the Society of American Archivists' Theodore Calvin Pease Award in 1990 for the best research paper by a student in an archival education program. The author gratefully acknowledges William K. Wallach and Frank Boles of the Bentley Historical Library, University of Michigan; Maynard J. Brichford, University of Illinois Archives; and Anne J. Gilliland-Swetland, for their support and helpful comments.

1 Richard C. Berner, *Archival Theory and Practice in the United States: A Historical Analysis* (Seattle: University of Washington Press, 1983).

subjective —management of their holdings. Practices such as item-level descriptive control, the imposition of predetermined classification schemes for cataloging purposes, and the reliance on several types of nonintegrated access tools served these institutions well, Berner argues, because the materials collected were suited to such management and because librarianship provided the only paradigm of intellectual control then available in America (although other options were already emerging in European archival literature by the 1880s).

objective ✓   An alternative paradigm for the administration of historical records, drawn from the public archives tradition of France and Prussia, was subsequently imported to America. Championed by an emerging group of state archivists, such as Waldo G. Leland, Victor H. Paltsits, Dunbar Rowland, Thomas McAdory Owen, and Margaret Cross Norton, the public archives paradigm advocated use of the concept of provenance, that is, keeping records "as nearly as possible in the same order or classification as obtained in the offices of origin," for the management of the official records of state governments.[2]

For its advocates, the concept of provenance provided a strikingly "objective" alternative method of description, based upon arrangement, in contrast to the "subjective" classification schemes, based upon subject content and borrowed from librarianship for use in manuscripts repositories. Indeed, so strong was their faith in the power of provenance that in 1912 Victor H. Paltsits, chairman of the Public Archives Commission, suggested that provenance provided the only basis for the "scientific" management of records.[3] The historical manuscripts repositories, however, sure of the uniqueness of their nonrecord materials and secure in their status as the keepers of America's past, ignored the concept of provenance.

Despite its advocates' enthusiasm, the continental public archives tradition clearly underwent a kind of intellectual "indentured servitude" in America. Berner describes in detail the slow and sometimes faltering steps by which American archival theory and practice was erected upon the bedrock of European provenance in the twentieth century. The practice of describing records at the series level, a direct application of the principle of provenance, provided an alternative to item-level manuscript cataloging. Progress toward replacing numerous disconnected access tools with an interconnected hierarchy of finding aids constituted another extension of the principle of provenance.

As both historical manuscripts repositories and official archives contended with the increasing volume of contemporary materials created in the post–World War II era, the provenance-based paradigm provided a

---

2 Ibid., 13.

3 Ibid.

compelling solution to the increasing physical backlogs and confusion of intellectual access points to materials. By the late 1950s, a "consensus seemed to be jelling" among the spokesmen for the historical manuscripts repositories that this developing archival paradigm could more effectively answer their institutions' needs than could their continuing use of techniques borrowed from librarianship.[4] It was "fated," Berner argues, that the historical manuscripts repositories would steep in the traditions of librarianship until the "drift of history" nurtured the archival paradigm and saved America's documentary past from a tradition brewed by provincial amateur historian-librarians and preserved in glorified gentlemen's clubs.[5]

Berner's use of the concept of consensus regarding the utility of provenance leads him, however, to erroneous conclusions. His narrow definition of tradition renders his insights irrelevant in understanding the larger development of American archival theory and practice beyond the topic of arrangement and description, to which his analysis is largely confined.

Berner uses the concept of "consensus" repeatedly to describe a state of affairs within the archives and manuscripts community rather than to analyze the process by which that state of affairs was achieved. He fails to acknowledge the dynamic, often conflicting process by which consensus is achieved. The archival paradigm came to be widely accepted in the 1950s because it provided solutions to the problems faced by archivists. In Berner's analysis there appears to have been no viable alternative to it. His concept of consensus may be illusory because it does not recognize that individuals shape agreed-upon principles in different, often contradictory ways, in response to diverse sets of experiences, needs, and goals. In other words, did broad acceptance of a key principle such as provenance necessarily mean that individuals and institutions interpreted and used that principle in the same way?

Finally, consensus, like coalition governments, must be continually reconstructed. According to Berner, the ascendancy of the archival paradigm in the 1950s is the denouement of American archival practice. In the last three decades, therefore, archival principles and practices have built upon, but never challenged, the state of affairs reached in the 1950s. Berner's definition of consensus, however, fails to capture the complexity of the profession's widespread acceptance of the concept of provenance in the 1950s, allowing him to posit a consensus where none existed.

The second limitation of Berner's analysis appears when one attempts to fit his conclusions into an understanding of the overall development of the archival profession in the twentieth century. The

---

4 Ibid., 48.

5 Ibid., 111, 36–37. For other statements representative of this perspective see 7, 16, 20, and 23.

large body of literature on American archival history chronicles a profession that has continually and strenuously debated any number of issues, including the desirability of professionalization, standards of education and training, the role and implications of automation, the importance of the historical perspective and training to the vocation of archivists, and most recently, certification. It is difficult to square Berner's concept of a consensus regarding provenance in the 1950s with the three ensuing decades of such professional debates unless one accepts that developments in the realm of principles and practices bear little or no relationship to developments in the rest of the profession's life.

Berner's model can be modified, however, in a way that provides a framework within which many of these diverse aspects of the profession's development can be better understood. This article employs Berner's distinction between the historical manuscripts and public archives traditions, but uses the concept of tradition in a much broader sense. Berner has used the term *tradition* exclusively in reference to observable actions, objective practices, and public statements of intellectual rationale; in this article the definition will be expanded to include the subjective values and the less tangible professional awareness of identity and mission that animate and give meaning to those public actions. Rather than simply describe behavior, such an approach offers a contextual framework within which the reasons for these behaviors may be better understood.

This broader definition demonstrates that American archival history can be characterized by two traditions whose advocates have perceived themselves to be at odds with one another. Defenders of the historical manuscripts tradition perceived themselves as members of a community of humanities scholars and, by extension, as historian-interpreters of the documents they preserved. Advocates of the public archives tradition perceived themselves to be professionals with mastery over a body of specialized theory and practice; consequently they viewed their role as administrator-custodian of the documents they preserved.

These traditions represent two fundamentally different perspectives. In reality they are, of course, not mutually exclusive, but may be seen as competing "ideal types." This approach offers an alternative to the consensus archival historians whose determination to find and preserve the unity of our diverse professional community has minimized the very real historical differences of opinion between various groups of archivists and manuscripts curators.[6]

---

6 It is disturbing that in recent debates over the importance of the historical perspective to the archival enterprise and in the literature on certification there has been an attempt to preempt difference of opinions by branding these differences of opinion as unimportant, subjective, and divisive. It may indeed be true, as Richard Cox suggests, that the positions advanced by each side in the historian/archivist debate need not be seen as mutually exclusive (Richard J. Cox, 50

During the early part of the century, differences between the public archives and historical manuscripts traditions were most evident in debates about the nature, role, and social value of archival repositories. More recently the focus has shifted to consider the nature and role of the archivist as professional. Thus, while the questions have changed, the underlying concerns and competing ideals have remained the same. The purpose of this article is to explore the nature of each tradition's continuing ideals and to examine the changing contexts in which those ideals have been applied.

Institution Building: Public Archives or Historical Manuscripts?

Numerous historians, attempting to understand the development of the increasingly complex bureaucratic organization and nature of American government and society in the twentieth century, have identified turn-of-the-century Progressive thought as one of the primary catalysts for, and manifestations of, these social and political developments. While arguments over Progressivism have provided a rich ground for scholarly dispute, historians have agreed that new and powerful ideas about society and government informed public discourse in the first decades of the twentieth century.[7]

Central to Progressive thought was a belief that scientific principles and techniques could, and must, be applied to the management of every aspect of an increasingly complex world. In the first years of the new century, commitments to scientific principles, specialization, and professionalization were a sign that one stood upon the cutting edge of modernity. It is hardly surprising that a new generation of academic historians committed to scientific research in primary sources began to examine the historical recordkeeping practices of their country. As a result, the historical profession followed through on the reports of the American Historical Association's newly created Public Archives

---

"Archivists and Historians: A View From the United States," *Archivaria* 19 [Winter 1984-85]: 185-90). People, however, act in accordance with their understanding of reality and the meanings they give to it, not in accordance with reality itself. For other examples of how this charge of divisiveness is frequently leveled, see Donald N. Yates, "To the Editor," *American Archivist* 50 (Summer 1987): 303; John W. Roberts, "Author's Response," *American Archivist* 50 (Summer 1987): 304; and Christopher L. Hives, "Bolotenko, the Debate, and the Future," *Archivaria* 19 (Winter 198-5): 7.

Also disturbing is the fact that this same homogenization is apparent in the writing of American archival history itself. Three of the leading archival historians writing today, Richard Berner, J. Frank Cook, and Richard J. Cox, as represented in works cited in these notes, all exhibit a tendency to view the history of the profession in descriptive, almost self-congratulatory terms, instead of in analytical, self-critical terms.

7 One of the classics on Progressivism is Robert H. Wiebe, *The Search for Order, 1877-1920* (New York: Hill and Wang, 1967); for an overview of the more recent literature see Daniel T. Rodgers, "In Search of Progressivism," *Reviews in American History* 10 (1982): 113-32.

Commission and played an active role in lobbying both state and national government for the creation of repositories dedicated to the preservation of historically important materials.[8]

Within this broad movement by academic historians to establish repositories and to influence the mission of those repositories in the first three decades of the twentieth century, a small number of individuals were beginning to envision the mission and nature of these institutions differently. By 1935, this group, which constituted the Committee of Ten on the Organization of Archivists and was led by Solon Buck, Waldo G. Leland, and Curtis W. Garrison, was laying the groundwork for the emergence of a professional organization independent of both the American Historical Association and the American Library Association. The initiative of the Committee of Ten led to the establishment in 1936 of the Society of American Archivists (SAA).[9]

SAA
1936

Archival historians have argued that the establishment of the SAA was a clear indication that a new profession was emerging as a force to be reckoned with — that of archivists who saw themselves and their work as fundamentally different from historians and librarians, or at least with different ideas of how and why materials should be preserved and managed.[10] There appears, however, to have been little substantive difference between the members of the AHA's Public Archives Commission and the Committee of Ten, which shaped the early mission of the SAA, as to the perception of who would use archival repositories and why. Both groups agreed that archival repositories, and especially the newly created National Archives, should serve the ends of scholarly historical research.[11] Indeed, archivists and historians even agreed with their antiquarian-collector predecessors about why historical materials should be preserved to a greater extent than their newfound commitment to the new scientism allowed them to admit.

---

8 A full analysis of the emergence of scientific history is provided in John Higham, *History: Professional Scholarship in America* (Baltimore: The Johns Hopkins Press, 1965). Berner discusses the role of the historical profession in the early archival movement. See also Mattie U. Russell, "The Influence of Historians on the Archival Profession in the United States," *American Archivist* 46 (Summer 1983): 277-85; Victor Gondos, Jr., *J. Franklin Jameson and the Birth of the National Archives, 1906-1926* (Philadelphia: University of Pennsylvania Press, 1981); and John David Smith, "The Historian as Archival Advocate: Ulrich Bonnell Phillips and the Records of Georgia and the South," *American Archivist* 52 (Summer 1989): 320-31.

9 A more complete consideration of the organization of the Society of American Archivists can be found in J. Frank Cook, "The Blessings of Providence on an Association of Archivists," *American Archivist* 46 (Fall 1983): 374-99.

10 Consistently, the secondary literature suggests that the SAA's outlook was different from that of the AHA's. See, for example, ibid., 376-77. The author has not found any evidence offered in support of this distinction.

11 This perception, that academic historians were to be the primary users of repositories, is well documented in the already cited works of Berner and Russell. See also George Bolotenko, "Archivists and Historians: Keepers of the Well," *Archivaria* 16 (Summer 1983): 5-25; and Wilcomb Washburn, "The Archivist's Two-Way Stretch," *Archivaria* 7 (1978): 137-43.

It was only with the emergence of a small group of state archivists, with Margaret Cross Norton as their most articulate spokesperson, that a substantive challenge was advanced to the historical profession's conceptualization of the role of archival repositories in society. Norton, the state archivist of Illinois, truly brought the new scientism of Progressive reform, in the form of European archival principles, to the American archival scene. Like all importers, she was selective, ignoring the fact that, unlike American public archives, the European public archives tradition embraced both official records and nonofficial or private papers, and that the European tradition itself had been developed in part as a way to facilitate historical research.[12] Norton adopted those European principles and practices that provided solutions to the problems she perceived to be confronting American archivists. The problems she perceived and the solutions she offered all conformed to the Progressive scientific reform outlook.

Like her Progressive contemporaries, Norton targeted state government as the critical arena in need of bureaucratic efficiency to better serve the needs of the public. Archivists, Norton wrote, should be intent upon building archives as an "efficiency proposition," dedicated to the "scientific handling" of official records.[13] Historical libraries managed by historians were not archives, she argued. The confusion to the contrary was not merely unfortunate, for it threatened the very preservation of the nation's legally important documents.[14] Historians had a research agenda that was fundamentally at odds with the mission of an archives. The latter, as Norton saw it, was primarily to serve the administrative needs and public accountability demands of its institution and the needs of scholars only secondarily.

In one way, however, Norton shared common ground with the historical camp. Like the historians and the historian-archivists, Norton saw the fundamental goal of anyone interested in the preservation of America's documentary heritage to be the establishment of institutions for that purpose. However, she clearly believed public archivists to be in competition with the historian-archivists in the fight for scarce resources.[15] She used a proto-records-management argument to sell public archives to state legislators. Although some archival historians have suggested that Norton was

---

12 The limitations of Norton's understanding of the continental tradition is discussed at some length in Bolotenko, "Archivists and Historians."

13 Margaret Cross Norton, *Norton on Archives: The Writings of Margaret Cross Norton on Archival Records and Records Management*, ed. Thornton W. Mitchell (Carbondale: University of Illinois Press, 1975), 7-8.

14 The need to distinguish between administrative archives and the research repository informs much of Norton's argument in Chapters 1 and 2 of *Norton on Archives*. For specific statements see 4-7 and 14.

15 For example, Norton states: "If the archivist can convince his fellow officials that he can render them a service which will in turn add to their own efficiency, he will tap a source of support infinitely greater and more potent than that of historians," Norton, *Norton on Archives*, 15.

really attempting to preserve history in the form of archives, the entire
tenor of Norton's writings and activities demonstrates her commitment to
a view of records administration in support of institutional functions that
is fundamentally at odds with the views of her contemporaries in the historical camp.[16] By advocating the administrative, rather than the research,
role of archives, Norton emphasized the European custodial role for
archives and archivists, rather than the American manuscripts interpretive
role. These two competing roles, rather than the narrower development of
descriptive practices based upon arrangement according to provenance,
dramatically shaped all subsequent American archival theory and practice.

To explore more clearly the challenge of the public archives tradition
in an American setting dominated by the techniques and mission of the
historical manuscripts tradition, it is analytically useful to distinguish
between developments within the archivists' professional association and
the diverse ways in which the provenance-based archival paradigm was
interpreted and utilized within archival repositories. To understand these
two divergent strains of development between 1936 and the mid-1960s is
to appreciate more clearly just how illusory the consensus, which Berner
suggests the profession achieved in the 1950s, really was.

Public Places: Professional Associational Politics. After its
establishment in 1936, the Society of American Archivists quickly became
the arena in which the public archives tradition (represented by Norton,
her colleagues, and increasingly by the National Archives) came into conflict with the historical manuscripts tradition. The history of the society's
first 20 years is marked by an ongoing debate between the Norton-National
Archives bloc, which advocated the administrative use of archival materials
and the implementation of records management principles for administrative records, and a bloc of members representing manuscripts repositories
and state archives operating within the historical manuscripts tradition,
which advocated the historical research use of archival materials.[17] The
debate between the two interests manifested itself in numerous ways: in the
first contested elections for SAA president in 1949 and 1953; in the early
1950s movement to change the site of the national meetings so as not to
favor the Washington-based National Archives staff members who comprised the majority of the SAA membership; and over the editorial policy of

---

16 Maynard Brichford, for example, has taken the position of apologist in suggesting that Norton's
   emphasis on the administrative rather than scholarly function of archives was meant "to restore
   a balance that is lost when only scholarly research needs are considered." See Maynard
   Brichford, "Academic Archives: Überlieferungsbildung," *American Archivist* 43 (Fall 1980): 457.
   On the other hand, Wilcomb Washburn and George Bolotenko (see note 11) are resoundingly
   critical of Norton's position and its influence on the profession.

17 The fullest history of the Society of American Archivists is found in J. Frank Cook, "The
   Blessings of Providence." Cook describes the power struggle between the contending traditions
   in these and other conflicts, but he does not analyze the effects of that power struggle on the
   development of the profession.

the society's primary publication, the *American Archivist*.[18] This last manifestation of the debate between the two interests was especially critical in that control of the official organ of the profession provided a means to shape the profession's discourse to the benefit of either the public archives or the historical manuscripts interests. Needless to say, when Norton assumed the editorship in 1945, the *American Archivist* was devoted to articles on the technical aspects of archival administration. Under her direction, the journal was purged of the influence of historical scholarship, no longer publishing articles that detailed the scholarly use of archival materials. Norton's reshaping of the editorial policy of the *American Archivist* was emblematic of the attempt by advocates of the public archives tradition to redirect the outlook of the archival community's professional association in the years from its founding until the mid-1960s. When the National Archives lost its independent agency status and became part of the General Services Administration in 1956 it also relinquished much of its leadership role in SAA. Even this realignment within SAA, however, did not arrest the growing strength of the public archivists within the society.[19]

Private Places: Internal Repository Practices. If the challenge offered by public archivists to the defenders of the historical manuscripts tradition was highly visible in the first decades of the SAA's history, the impact of the public archives paradigm on the administration of records in numerous repositories during this period, though widespread, was less dramatic. Most private or nongovernmental repositories operating in America during the first half of the twentieth century were rooted in the historical manuscripts tradition, utilizing principles and practices borrowed from librarianship to advance the enterprise of historical scholarship. The quest for the scientific management of records as a function of government had little real impact on these repositories. Few of the newly established repositories abandoned the sense that the keeping and the using of records were activities appropriate to historians.[20] Aware, moreover, that public archivists

---

18 Ibid., 384-87. On the importance of the *American Archivist* to the profession, see Richard J. Cox, "American Archival Literature: Expanding Horizons and Continuing Needs, 1901-1987," *American Archivist* 50 (1987): 309-12.

19 Cook, "Blessings of Providence," 93.

20 Recently, several pieces have appeared in the archival literature that argue that the high number of trained historians working as archivists manifests the continuing importance of the historical perspective to the profession. The strongest case is made by Russell, "Influence of Historians," 281; but see also Bolotenko, "Archivists and Historians," 15; and Leslie J. Workman, "To The Editor," *American Archivist* 46 (Summer 1983): 261-62. Russell's article, by equating type of degree with outlook, is potentially misleading. An excerpt from Herman Kahn's 1970 presidential address, which Russell cites to demonstrate the profession's recognition of the primacy of historical training, in fact contradicts her interpretation (Russell, "Influence of Historians," 282). Kahn saw that, as the Society of American Archivists is increasingly suggesting, post-employment on-the-job training is what really makes an archivist. Within diverse institutions, that on-the-job training can engender dramatic changes in how individuals perceive their mission as archivists. In short, in a world as diverse and as hands-on as current American archival practice, educational training is not synonymous with professional outlook.

eschewed collecting nonofficial or private papers, the historian-minded administrators in historical manuscripts repositories did not think archival practices germane to their institutions or to their professional and social responsibilities as partners in the scholarly interpretation of private historical materials.[21]

After 1945, this situation changed. The same glut of paper that overcame the historical manuscripts outlook at the National Archives precipitated the adoption of archival principles by some traditional manuscripts repositories. Just as the National Archives developed a records management program as an administrative response to the flood of paper, so too, manuscripts repositories that had begun to collect records characterized by volume and an integral structure searched for better ways to administer those records. Following the lead of the Library of Congress, major historical manuscripts repositories began incorporating the central practices of the public archives tradition, using arrangement according to provenance as the basis for intellectual and physical control over holdings. Soon they implemented series- rather than item-level description and cataloging and developed an integrated hierarchical system of finding aids.[22] It would be erroneous, however, to suggest that in adopting the practices of the archival paradigm, these manuscripts repositories also adopted the outlook of the public archives tradition, that is, preserving records for administrative and public needs. Historical manuscripts repositories accepted, rather, what appeared to be better methods for achieving "traditional" goals, that is, preserving records of enduring value for use in historical scholarship by historians.

The widespread acceptance of the basic concept of provenance, therefore, demonstrates not the dominance of the public archives tradition, as Berner suggests, but rather the multiplicity of ways in which principles and practices could be adopted, interpreted, and pressed into the service of diverse institutional needs. Believing that the primary function of an official archives was its legal function, Margaret Cross Norton had developed an extensive argument regarding the role of the principle of provenance in establishing the *archival,* by which she meant *legal,* quality of a record. "The necessity for acceptable certification [legal authenticity]," Norton wrote, "is the basis for the adoption of provenance as the basis for the classification of archives."[23] Historical manuscripts repositories, however, adopted the principle of provenance because it provided a powerful tool for understanding the historical context

---

21 This is the basic tenet of Berner's analysis as laid out in the first three chapters of *Archival Theory and Practice.*

22 For a detailed treatment of changing practices at the Library of Congress and several other large manuscripts repositories during this period see ibid., Chapter 3.

23 Norton, *Norton on Archives,* 28.

(rather than the administrative or legal context) in which the materials were created since contextualization is the *sine qua non* of all sound historical scholarship.[24] It was this understanding and use of the principle of provenance that accounts for its widespread adoption by historical manuscripts repositories in the middle decades of the twentieth century.

The Rise of Academic Archives and the Transition from Institutions to Practitioners

Although joined by a common commitment to see archival repositories established, the advocates of the two traditions that came into conflict in the first decades of the century offered radically different ideas about the nature and role of these institutions. The rapid establishment of numerous nongovernmental institutional archives, especially in academic institutions, in the late 1960s and 1970s dramatically refocused archivists' attention on the nature and role of the archivist as a professional. This altered vision occurred for two reasons.

The establishment of numerous archives within stable institutions such as colleges and universities answered what had been a basic concern of the profession: the quest for institutional security. The widespread establishment of such archives also brought a new generation of young and energetic archivists into the ranks of the profession. Eager to enhance the professional status of archivists, this large and active group refocused the attention of the profession upon itself rather than its institutions. The key debates that have filled the pages of archival journals in the last three decades have all addressed a basic question of self-identity: what is the nature and role in society of the archivist as professional? The opposing positions that have been advanced in these debates, however, are yet again products of the two competing archival and manuscripts traditions.[25] To understand both the continuity and the reconfiguration of these two traditions in the 1960s and 1970s, it is necessary first to understand the nature of academically based archives that were established during this period and then to assess the impact of academic archivists on the profession.

archivist as professional

In the 1960s and 1970s, American institutions of post-secondary education experienced tremendous growth. Self-conscious about their importance and influence, many colleges and universities accepted the responsibility for what Maynard Brichford has called *überlieferungsbildung*, the handing down of culture or civilization.[26] This sense of self

---

24 Bolotenko, "Archivists and Historians," 10-11.

25 For two different positions in this debate, see Cox, "American Archival Literature," 309-12; and Maynard J. Brichford, "Who Are the Archivists and What Do They Do?" *American Archivist* 51 (Winter/Spring 1988): 106-10.

26 Brichford, "Academic Archives: Überlieferungsbildung," 449-60.

and purpose prompted institutions to establish archives to document their own history and role in American society. The prestige associated with establishing an archives was also linked to a more basic need: that of managing the flood of paper that accompanied rapidly increasing enrollment, curricular expansion, and bureaucratic complexity. Even when answering these pragmatic concerns, however, the university was also accepting and demonstrating its ability to handle the cultural responsibilities that had always been, and that were now even more demonstrably part of its cultural mission.[27]

The rapid expansion of post-secondary educational institution dramatically altered the American archival landscape. What had brought together the two differing traditions of public archivists and historian-archivists in the first decades of the twentieth century was a shared desire to establish archival repositories. By 1979, however, an SAA survey identified 900 academic archives in the United States, half of which had been established within the last decade.[28] Clearly the SAA founding generation's goal of seeing the establishment of more institutional archives had been realized. Despite the ever-present shortages of financial and physical resources, an institutional infrastructure was acknowledged and relatively secure. The time seemed right to turn to other priorities, such as enhancing the professional status and public image of archivists, an agenda that would serve in part to perpetuate society's commitment to its archival caretakers.

The combination of principles and practices adopted by these newly established academic archives for the management of their holdings also helped to shift the attention of archivists away from solely institutional concerns. As discussed above, earlier institutional practices had demonstrated a clear commitment either to the archival mission (archives as a response to administrative needs) or to the historical mission (archives as a response to the needs of historians). This trend continued in the 1950s when provenance-based practices were adopted, but used differently, by institutions operating in both the public archives and historical manuscripts traditions. The academic archives of the 1960s and later, however, appear to have been equally committed to both missions,

---

27 While most archival historians agree that one of the major catalysts for the establishment of college and university archives stemmed from a traditional commitment to scholarly research, several writers on this topic have suggested that the prestige value associated with archives and their records management capabilities account for their establishment on college and university campuses during these decades. Arguably, these two reasons are related. See Brichford, "Academic Archives," 455; Annabel Strauss, "College and University Archives: Three Decades of Development," *College and Research Libraries* (September 1979): 435-37; and Patrick M. Quinn, "Archivists and Historians: The Times They Are A-Changin'," *Midwestern Archivist* 2, no. 2 (1977): 7.

28 A more complete analysis of the results of this survey is provided in Nicholas C. Burckel and J. Frank Cook, "A Profile of College and University Archives in the United States," *American Archivist* 45 (1982): 410-28.

often functioning as both the official archives for their institutions and as a repository for nonofficial but historically and culturally significant documents. This reality of academic archives functioning with a dual mission was decidedly different from the traditional expectations of either public archivists or manuscript curators.

[margin annotation: academic archives]

As early as the 1940s, when only a handful of academic archives existed, the Society of American Archivists' Committee on College and University Archives was debating the appropriate function of academic archives. Should they be committed to preserving only the official administrative records or should they also be committed to preserving the nonofficial papers that document student and campus life, and the work of their scholarly communities? Put another way, should academic archives primarily serve the administrative, or the scholarly research needs of their parent institutions?[29] By the 1970s it became clear that the holdings of the majority of academic archives included official, nonofficial, and personal materials, and that academic archives were usually serving both the needs of administration and of scholarly researchers, not to mention members of the public, genealogists in particular.[30] This did not mean, however, that the longstanding debate over the appropriate role of the academic archivist was resolved. Rather, the growing number and influence of academic archivists participating actively in the profession placed this debate in the center of the profession's public discourse.

The most obvious result of the emergence of large numbers of academic archives in the 1960s and 1970s was that academic archivists became the numerically superior group within the Society of American Archivists; by 1970 one-third of the SAA's membership comprised individuals working in academic settings, a percentage that has continued to grow in the last two decades.[31] Many archival historians agree that this active group of archivists reshaped the SAA in the late 1960s and 1970s, turning it into a truly professional association.[32] Through the energy of these archivists, the governance of the SAA was democratized, its committee structure was reorganized, and a paid executive director was hired.

---

29 These debates are chronicled in more detail in J. Frank Cook, "Academic Archivists and the SAA, 1938-1979: From Arcana Siwash to the C & U PAG," *American Archivist* 51 (1988): 437; and Strauss, "College and University Archives."

30 For a fuller discussion see Cook, "Academic Archivists," 440-41; Strauss, "College and University Archives"; and Nicholas C. Burckel, "The Expanding Role of a College or University Archives," *Midwestern Archivist* 1, no. 1 (1976): 3-15.

31 Cook, "Academic Archivists," 434-39; and Cook, "Blessings of Providence," 89-95.

32 A thorough discussion of the importance of academic archivists in the SAA is provided in Cook, "Academic Archivists"; Cook, "The Blessings of Providence"; and Cox, "American Archival Literature," 309-14. On the general changes in the SAA during the 1970s, see Philip P. Mason, "Archives in the Seventies: Promises and Fulfillment," *American Archivist* 44 (Summer 1981): 199-206.

In the last two decades, the most active committees in the SAA have been dominated by academic archivists. In addition to establishing a core of professional literature and encouraging research and writing on archival topics, the SAA's College and University Archives Section has provided standards for institutional evaluation and professional education that have come to be accepted as standards not only for college and university archives and archivists, but for the profession in general.[33]

Along with their numerical superiority and energy, these academic archivists brought an increased self-consciousness of archival work as a career.[34] Defining the nature of that career has been the central concern of the profession in the late 1970s and 1980s.[35] Professional discourse has increasingly turned to considerations of professional issues, such as image, certification, and building public awareness of, and confidence in, the archivist as a competent manager of the nation's documentary past.[36] What animates these various discussions of professional image, however, are still the two traditionally competing ideals of the archivist as professional: humanist historian-scholar or expert documentary manager. The two competing ideals of the 1930s have emerged again, facing off upon a stage called professionalization.

In the most dramatic manifestation of this conflict, a literary firestorm in the Canadian archival journal, *Archivaria,* engendered by George Bolotenko's 1983 article "Archivists and Historians: Keepers of the Well," it is not hard to discern these competing understandings of the archival mission.[37] For Bolotenko, the movement to redefine the archival profession in

---

33 A "Core Mission and Minimum Standards for University Archives" was first developed by the University of Wisconsin System Archives Council in 1977. See *College and University Archives: Selected Readings* (Chicago: Society of American Archivists, 1979), 215-27. That document provided the basis for the SAA's Guidelines for College and University Archives (published in the *SAA Newsletter,* January 1979, 11-20), which in turn influenced the assessment checklist in the *Archives Assessment and Planning Workbook* edited by Paul McCarthy (Chicago: Society of American Archivists, 1989).

34 This view shows up frequently in the literature. See, for example, Terry Cook, "Clio: The Archivist's Muse," *Archivaria* 5 (1977-78): 198; and J. Frank Cook, "The Blessings of Providence," 95.

35 Richard J. Cox, "Professionalism and Archivists in the United States," *American Archivist* 49 (1986): 241-42. In this piece, Cox provides a sociological analysis of the development of the profession, concluding that archivists "should not limit their quest for increased professionalism by dwelling on their small numbers, but should concentrate instead on their potential for employment. They should realize that their efforts to improve professional standards can open up additional avenues for societal influences" (p. 245). Cox can only take this particular position, or indeed write a piece advocating professionalization, in large part because an institutional infrastructure exists that already provides employment opportunities for a substantial number of archivists.

36 Cox, "American Archival Literature," 312-14.

37 Bolotenko's "Historians and Archivists: Keepers of the Well" (*Archivaria* 16 [Summer 1983]: 5-25) elicited numerous responses, both pro and con, in 17 (Winter 1983-84): 286-308; 18 (Summer 1984): 241-47; and 19 (Winter 1984-85): 4-7, 28-49, 185-95. They concluded with Bolotenko's final piece on the subject, "Instant Professionalism: To the Shiny New Men of the Future," 20 (Summer 1985): 149-57.

a way that does not privilege the mission to preserve history and serve historians is a manifestation of a much broader cultural assault on the humanistic tradition. "The archivist," Bolotenko asserted in a follow-up article, "is perceived as an anachronism ill-reconciled to the modernist forces of today which, to the exclusion of broad cultural content, stand largely on the twin foundations of utility and technique."[38] Bolotenko, standing firmly in the historical manuscripts tradition, perceives the proper role of archival repositories and archivists to be that of a partnership with academic historians committed to the broad interpretive role in our society.

Like his forebears in the historical manuscripts tradition, Bolotenko, convinced that archival materials are inherently unique and require special handling, endorses the concept of provenance because it provides historians with a way to preserve the unique organic relationship between the historical activity and the records that document that activity. It is the culmination of the historical manuscripts tradition's cooptation of provenance as a historical technique that allows Bolotenko to turn the table of provenance on Norton by arguing that it is historians, not public archivists, who truly respect provenance. Bolotenko's view of those whom he characterizes as the new Nortonians is that of a group concerned with ends over means. He feels that the new Nortonians advocate information management and technique, undermining the archivist's mission to preserve the humanistic tradition in a world whose *geist* is rationalization, bureaucracy, administration, and efficiency.

If Bolotenko's perceptions replicate the outlook of the historical manuscripts tradition, the rebuttals to Bolotenko manifest the permanence of the competing public archives tradition. Richard Cox and other critics of Bolotenko see the mission and responsibilities of archivists as fundamentally different.[39] If Bolotenko can be criticized for exhibiting a siege mentality when he stridently avers that the humanistic tradition is under attack by technocrats from within the profession, Cox and others exhibit the same mentality when they argue that the enterprise of preserving records is threatened by external forces.[40]

Like the Progressive scientific reformers so well represented by Norton in the first half of the twentieth century, Cox sees the political

---

38 George Bolotenko, "Of Ends and Means: In Defence of the Archival Ideal," *Archivaria* 18 (Summer 1984): 245.

39 Richard J. Cox, "Archivists and Historians: A View From the United States," *Archivaria* 19 (Winter 1984-5): 185–90, Carl Spadoni, "In Defence of the New Professionalism: A Rejoinder to George Bolotenko, "*Archivaria* 19 (Winter 1984-5): 191-95; Carl Spadoni, "No Monopoly for 'Archivist-Historians': Bolotenko Assailed," *Archivaria* 17 (Winter 1983-4); 291-95; Anthony L. Rees, "Bolotenko's Siege Mentality," *Archivaria* 17 (Winter 1983-4): 301-02; and Bob Taylor-Vaisey, "Archivist-Historians Ignore Information Revolution," *Archivaria* 17 (Winter 1983-84): 305-07.

40 This is the basic premise of Cox's argument in "Archivists and Historians"; see also Richard J. Cox, "Archivists and Public Historians in the United States," *Public Historian* 8 (Summer 1986): 29-45.

and social institutions of modern society arriving at a new plateau of complexity and interdependence.[41] He argues that society can only be saved from itself and from the products of the "information age" if new information management skills, wielded by experts, can be contrived to master the complexity of increasingly voluminous textual and nontextual records. Also, like the Progressive reformers, Cox views the profession's lingering commitment to the ideal of the archivist as interpreter-scholar as a self-indulgent and dangerous luxury. Maintaining this fiction, Cox warns, is to "accept perpetuation of the most serious of our problems and doom our profession to stagnation and even obsolescence."[42]

If the *Archivaria* exchange over professional identity exposes the fault line in the profession, that line is also evident in several other of the professional debates that have captured the attention of the profession in recent years. The arguments raised in the debate over the certification of archivists, for example, provide striking examples of the permanence of the public archives and historical manuscripts outlooks. George Bolotenko would agree in spirit with William W. Moss of the Smithsonian Institution, who argues that "certification brings with it an unfortunate tendency to substitute vocational education for liberal education as the foundation of the profession."[43] To accept certification, Moss warns, is to surrender our "pursuit of a vision that integrates our thesis with that of other great intellectual disciplines" and to accept a "future of technocratic functionalism."[44] Conversely, supporters of certification, eager to further the professionalization of archivists, offer a set of rationales with which early Progressive reformers would have been very familiar.[45]

Conclusion

The development of the American archival profession can best be understood as the continuing interaction of two broadly conceived outlooks, those of the public archives and historical manuscripts traditions. Each of these traditions has developed and offered its own ideals, originally for archives as institutions, and more recently, for archivists as professionals. These two traditions continue to shape professional discourse, as evidenced

---

41 Cox, "Archivists and Public Historians," 38-41.

42 Cox, "Archivists and Historians," 185.

43 William W. Moss, "Commentary: To the Editor," *SAA Newsletter* (September 1986): 9.

44 Ibid.

45 The certification debate has generated a large body of argument on both sides, which appeared in the *SAA Newsletter* between July 1985 and July 1989, and the *American Archivist* (see, for example, "The Forum," *American Archivist* 52 [Spring 1989]: 140-42). For an analysis of the debate, see William J. Maher, "Contexts for Understanding Professional Certification: Opening Pandora's Box?," *American Archivist* 51 (Fall 1988): 426-27. A more recent statement of the humanist position on the certification issue is provided in Clark A. Elliott, "Comment on the Archival Profession," *American Archivist* 53 (Summer 1990): 376-77.

by the similarities between the Progressive scientific reformers/historian-archivists debate of the 1930s and 1940s and the more recent historians/information managers debate of the 1980s and 1990s.

The outcome of this continued interaction is, unfortunately, less obvious. Clearly, we live in a different age than Margaret Cross Norton and her contemporaries. Broad cultural trends have provided the profession with a new range of options for action. Both Richard Cox and George Bolotenko would agree that the archival profession has been confronted with a profound challenge in the last decades of the twentieth century. For Bolotenko, the challenge is the anti-humanistic undercurrents of modern life that require archivists to strengthen their ability to interpret and provide contexts of meaning for modern records. For Cox, the challenge is the "information age," which is requiring archivists to fundamentally reconceptualize the ways in which they think about and manage modern records.[46]

Archivists who advocate the reestablishment of closer ties with historians should recognize that they are proposing to identify with a profession that has found itself increasingly marginalized as society looks to the sciences, both hard and soft, for leadership.[47] The decision to forge stronger links with librarians and information managers, however, will lead to identification with another profession that has little professional status or social power.[48] Increasingly, archivists seem to be choosing this latter path: accepting that we are responsible to our records first and to our records' users second, and that our mission is not to aid in the interpretation of the records under our care but only to manage those records in a way that enables diverse user communities to do the job of interpretation.[49] Although the recent interest in user studies would suggest that many archivists are resisting this tendency to subordinate users to records, a close inspection of the user-study literature reveals that the goal of these studies

---

46 For example, Cox writes: "The spectre of archivists being absorbed into another profession or severely weakened in the competition for resources is a very real possibility," Cox, "Professionalism and Archivists," 245; see also p. 241. For Cox's recommendations that archivists become proactively involved with records administration through the development of documentation strategies, see Cox, "Archivists and Public Historians," 38-41.

47 For a representative consideration of this problem, see Terry Cook, "Clio: The Archivist's Muse." It has been suggested that the emergence of the new social history and of public history as a subdiscipline are responses to this very problem of marginalization. See, for example, Cox, "Professionalism and Archivists," 242; Cox, "Archivists and Public Historians"; and Berner, *Archival Theory and Practice,* 109–10. Interestingly, Cox observes that archival literature, like many brands of academic literature, has little appeal to a wider audience. See Cox, "American Archival Literature," 317.

48 For a more complete consideration of this topic see Cox, "Archivists and Historians"; Cox, "Professionalism and Archivists," 239-41; Bolotenko, "Archivists and Historians," 17; and Bolotenko, "Instant Professionalism."

49 There are numerous examples of this outlook in the literature. Particularly striking examples can be found in Berner, *Archival Theory and Practice,* 76; Spadoni, "No Monopoly for 'Archivist-Historians'" 295; and Spadoni, "In Defence of the New Professionalism," 194-95.

is not unequivocally user-centered.[50] Ironically, in backing away from the interpretive role (and in focusing on the management role) as a way to enhance our claims to being disinterested and expert professionals, we are surrendering one of the characteristics of a profession, that is, the privilege of providing cultural leadership based upon the ability to interpret a specialized body of material.[51]

As this article has suggested, however, this professional self-reorientation is not complete, nor is it occurring without debate. Developments within the profession during the last three decades have strengthened the profession and expanded the range of options available to respond to the challenges ahead. The profession, through SAA and regional archival associations, has begun to take a more active role in shaping how American society thinks about its documents — both past and present — and its archivists. As early as 1965, SAA president W. Kaye Lamb observed in his presidential address that the "archivist has ceased to be primarily a custodian — a caretaker — and has become a gatherer of records and manuscripts" and that the archivist has assumed a "dynamic" and "active" role to supplant his formerly "largely passive" role.[52] Several of the significant professional initiatives of the ensuing two decades — the publication of the SAA Task Force on Goals and Priorities' *Planning for the Profession,* and the development of documentation strategies, standards for archival description, and the AMC format for use in national databases — would seem to have substantiated Lamb's vision of a transformed profession flexing its newfound muscle in the emergent information age.[53]

---

50 The original challenge to the archival profession to examine its institutions' users and their needs was provided by Elsie Freeman in "In the Eyes of the Beholder: Archives Administration From the User's Point of View," *American Archivist* 47 (Spring 1984): 111-23. A number of pieces responded to that call. See, for example, Paul Conway, "Research in Presidential Libraries: A User Survey," *Midwestern Archivist* 11, no. 1 (1986): 35-56; William J. Maher, "The Use of User Studies," *Midwestern Archivist* 11, no. 1 (1986): 15-26; and Lawrence Dowler, "The Role of Use in Defining Archival Practice and Principles: A Research Agenda for the Availability and Use of Records," *American Archivist* 51 (Winter/Spring 1988): 74-95.

Roy C. Turnbaugh has argued, however, that too often user studies erroneously privilege reference services over the appraisal, preservation, and disposition of records of enduring value. An accurate definition of use, Turnbaugh contends, should reflect these key archival activities (Turnbaugh, "Archival Mission and User Studies," *Midwestern Archivist* 11, no. 1 [1986]: 27-33).

51 See Cox, "Professionalism and Archivists," for a more complete discussion of this point.

52 W. Kaye Lamb, "The Changing Role of the Archivist," *American Archivist* 29 (January 1966): 4.

53 *Planning for the Profession: A Report of the Society of American Archivists' Task Force on Goals and Priorities* (Chicago: SAA, 1986). Lamb was not alone in seeing the profession in these terms. See, for example, F. Gerald Ham, "The Archival Edge," *American Archivist* 38 (1975): 5-13; and F. Gerald Ham, "Archival Strategies for the Post-Custodial Era," *American Archivist* 44 (Summer 1984): 207-16.

The classic conservative response to this perspective on the profession was offered by Gregory Stiverson, "The Activist Archivist: A Conservative View," *Georgia Archive* 5, no. 1 (1977): 4-14.

If, however, the profession is to remain vital, if it is to retain the support of its constituents and realize its mission to preserve and transmit our cultural legacy, it must finally reconcile the competing traditions that have divided it since its birth. However archivists effect that resolution, the choice will have far-reaching consequences that cannot be fully envisioned or controlled and for this reason alone, archivists would do well to reflect upon the past it continues to confront.

The apparent impasse suggested by the recent debate between Bolotenko and Cox should not be insurmountable, although a fundamental reorientation is required. Clearly, both Bolotenko and Cox are sincerely committed to the same goal, that of preserving documents for posterity. Each believes that his understanding of the role of archives and of archivists provides the best path to follow in order to realize that goal. How then is one to judge objectively which is the better path? In many ways, the discourse as currently constructed does not enable members of the profession to make an informed choice. In his analysis of the debate over certification, William J. Maher observed that "both the cause and a consequence of the thinness of arguments on both sides is that the debate has become quite emotional."[54] Much of Maher's reflection on the certification question is applicable to many of the other debates that have captured the attention of the profession in recent years. Discussions of issues have degenerated into polemical diatribes and apocalyptic visions. The emotional passion that animates these debates keeps the participants from addressing the very real concerns of those on the opposite side of the fence.

To find a way through the impasse, archival historians and the rest of the profession must lay aside their advocacy long enough to understand why they have taken the stance they have. A few years ago, Cox offered a challenge to the profession. "It is vital," he suggested, "that we know as much as possible about the development of the profession to aid our continued self-study, reevaluation, and progress, especially in time of unusual stress and change. We need to direct the historian's perspective not only to the records under our care but to our profession as well."[55] Archivists have been exposed to much description and little analysis, much thinking and writing that reinforce our *a priori* assumptions and little critical self-analysis about the costs and implications of social and professional change. Believing that archivists' shared hopes for the future as a profession can only be realized if they understand their past, the author repeats Cox's challenge.

---

54 Maher, "Contexts for Understanding Professional Certification," 426-27.

55 Richard J. Cox, "American Archival History: Its Development, Needs, and Opportunities," *American Archivist* 46 (Winter 1983): 31.

7

The Blessings of Providence on an Association of Archivists

J. FRANK COOK

Abstract: *This history of the Society of American Archivists from its founding (1935-37) to the appointment of a paid executive director (1974) is organized into three periods: "I. Growing Up in Depression and War, 1935-45," in which are outlined the founding of the society and its relationships with other organizations, especially the American Historical Association; the role of the National Archives in the affairs of the society; the development of the* American Archivist; *and the impact of hard economic times and war. "II. Coming of Age, 1946-57," in which are discussed the society through its twenty-first year; international archival relations; the committee structure; SAA as a national voice for the profession; the tensions between state archivists and the National Archives; the establishment of Fellows; and the growing complexity, and resulting problems, of the maturing association. "III. The Professionalization of the Association, 1958-74," in which is reviewed the development of the society into a truly professional association designed to meet the many and conflicting demands of a varied membership. The issues examined include the threat of fragmentation and the rise of regional archival groups; the decline in interest in international archival matters; independence for the National Archives and Records Service; the Loewenheim case at the Franklin D. Roosevelt Presidential Library; tensions within the SAA leadership; internal operations and problems with committees; growth patterns of membership and budget within SAA; the increasing role of state archivists in the affairs of the society; attitudes of state archivists toward NARS; the rise of the institutional archivists; education and training programs; and the search for funding for the executive director position as the culmination of the work of the Committee of the 1970s to democratize SAA and make it more responsive to the needs of the membership.*

Growing Up in Depression and War, 1935-45

Three events in the mid-1930s gave birth to the archival profession in the United States: the establishment of the National Archives in 1934; the funding of surveys by the Works Progress Administration of federal,

Reprinted with permission from the *American Archivist* 46 (Fall 1983), 374-99. This article is an expanded version of the presidential address delivered at the 47th annual meeting of the Society of American Archivists on October 5, 1983, in Minneapolis, Minnesota. The author is grateful for the cheerful and competent manner in which his colleagues on the staff at the archives at the University of Wisconsin-Madison, especially Nancy Kunde, Steve Masar, and Bernie Schermetzler, not only carried out their duties, but also aided him as he tried to serve the society.

state, and local records in 1935-37; and the organization of the Society of
American Archivists in 1935-37. With the National Archives finally a
reality, the Public Archives Commission of the American Historical
Association (AHA) came to an end. A number of archivists saw that
another type of organization was needed to further the interests of the
profession and to cope with both the mass of historical records located
by the surveys and the flood of current records being generated by
governments expanded to ease the economic crisis of the era.

The chair of the 1935 AHA conference of archivists, A. R. Newsome,
secretary of the North Carolina Historical Commission, and Solon J. Buck,
director of publications for the National Archives, worked together to have
the conference consider the establishment of a national professional organization for archivists. Although they originally contemplated an institute
for the leading practitioners of archival administration, the founders soon
realized that such a limited membership would be too narrow to meet the
needs of archivists around the country. Theodore C. Blegen, superintend-
ent of the Minnesota Historical Society, addressed the conference on the
"Problems of American Archivists." After describing the period as one of
fruition for the "archival movement," he called for the creation of an
"Institute of American Archivists" as a clearinghouse and center for discussion of problems and experiences of archivists at the federal, state, and
local levels. Blegen called for this institute to prepare scholarly and bibliographic publications; conduct experiments and investigations; provide
education and training; develop the theory and practice of archival administration, especially in regard to uniform standards and rules; and foster
cooperation among archivists and repositories.[1]

Following his address, which could still serve as a charter for the
society, the 51 conferees at the AHA luncheon agreed unanimously to
establish an association at the next AHA meeting. A steering committee,
called the "Committee of Ten on the Organization of Archivists," was
charged with drafting a constitution. Three members of that committee —
Buck, Waldo G. Leland of the American Council of Learned Societies and
one of the real "fathers" of the profession, and Curtis W. Garrison,
archivist of Pennsylvania — served as an executive committee. During
discussion on the motion to consider forming the new association, a
desire for a broadly based national, and even international, group of
archivists, historians, librarians, and others involved in the administration of archives became evident. In the constitution adopted in 1936, it
was declared that: "The objects of The Society of American Archivists

1 Waldo Gifford Leland, "American Archival Problems," *AHA Annual Report* (1909): 342-48;
   Proceedings of SAA annual meetings, 1936 and 1937, 41-46, SAA Archives, Series 200/3/1, box 2,
   folder 11. (Hereafter, citations to the SAA Archives will be as follows, using the above citation as
   an example: 200/3/1, 2/11); P. C. Brooks to G. H. Scholefield, August 1940, 200/3/1, 2/20;
   Bulletins of the National Archives 2 (November 1936).

shall be to promote sound principles of archival economy and to facilitate cooperation among archivists and archival agencies."[2]

In the months following the 1935 meeting, the Committee of Ten
planned for the 1936 meeting to be held in conjunction with the dedication of the National Archives building, originally planned for the spring.
President Franklin D. Roosevelt's campaign schedule forced delay after
delay until the dedication scheme was abandoned in favor of meeting
again during the AHA convention in Providence, R. I. Julian P. Boyd of
the Historical Society of Pennsylvania addressed the group on the impact
the Historical Records and Federal Records surveys had on the increasing
interest in preserving historical documentation. Given this new interest,
Boyd declared that the proposed association of archivists could build on
the achievements of these surveys and that "probably no new profession
ever found itself brought into existence under more favorable auspices."[3]

The 1936 meeting is known to archival historians as the organizing
meeting, and not as the first annual meeting. The 96 men and 29 women
who voted to form the society in 1936 came from 23 states, Canada, and
Cuba. The District of Columbia alone had 61 in attendance, all but 5 from
the National Archives. New York was the only state represented by more
than 5 members. Twenty of the members were employed in state archives;
the remainder came from a wide variety of institutional repositories. The
attendees approved the draft constitution and elected a president, vice president, secretary, and treasurer to one-year terms and a 5-member council to
staggered terms of up to five years. The eager and overambitious members
adopted a constitution that provided for 12 committees, spreading the
active membership too thinly; many of these committees were all but inactive for a number of years.[4]

The question of who should be eligible for membership in the society
arose at the very beginning. Individual membership was restricted "to
those who are or have been engaged in the custody or administration of
archives or historical manuscripts or who, because of special experience or
other qualifications, are recognized as competent in archival economy."
After developing professionally for many years as a suborganization of the
AHA whose members were more interested in accessibility and use of manuscripts and archives than in preservation, arrangement, or description,
archivists had to find their own identity apart from historians. Librarians
also had an interest in the archival field; and the American Library
Association formed a committee on archives in 1936. SAA president

---

2 A. R. Newsome to S. Buck, 14 March 1936, 220/1/2, 1/4; 200/5/1, 1/17; "Report on a Luncheon
   Conference of Archivists," 200/5/1, 1/18; 200/3/1, 2/7.

3 R. D. W. Connor to Newsome, 13 May 1936, 200/3/1, 2/7; *Washington Post,* 30 December 1936,
   p. 7; *Proceedings,* p. 20.

4 200/5/1, 1/17; 200/3/1, 2/7.

Newsome expressed irritation with "library imperialism" when it appeared in 1937 that a proposed joint program sponsored by SAA and ALA would be dominated by librarians who did not understand the implications of archival administration.[5] SAA faced a dilemma. Many of its members and much of its potential support inevitably came from historians and librarians, but the archivists feared domination by the older associations. Without the dues of historians and librarians, however, the financial health of the infant society would have been poor indeed. In an effort to ensure professional purity, the council insisted on a pro forma election of every applicant for membership. There is no evidence of anyone ever having been rejected, and certainly not on the grounds of being an historian or a librarian rather than an archivist. Though its formal policy may have discouraged some would-be applicants, the society generally resisted efforts to restrict membership. Lester J. Cappon expressed the society's view when he wrote that "the broad basis of membership has been one of the strongest features of the Society in giving it flexibility to extend its influence, and nurture its growth." In an effort to extend its influence, the society also met on occasion with allied professional groups, most notably the American Association for State and Local History.[6]

While searching for its identity among the historians and librarians, the SAA also had to cope with its own peculiar institutional and geographical conformation. With more than 40 percent of those at the Providence meeting employed by the National Archives, the involvement of this agency was essential to the early success of the society; but charges of domination by the National Archives are not justified. Solon Buck devoted much time and energy to the SAA, as did other National Archives officials, such as Philip C. Brooks, the first SAA secretary. Brooks reported that the Archivist of the United States, R. D. W. Connor, was "anxious to cooperate in every way" with the society; but "he is also anxious, I feel, not to have too much of the control of the Society concentrated in The National Archives." The National Archives, for example, did not want the editor of the proposed journal to be its employee, a policy that remained in effect until the late 1940s.[7]

---

5 SAA Constitution, Section 3, "Membership"; P. C. Brooks to A. F. Kuhlman, 8 April 1938, 200/3/1, 2/17; Brooks to Newsome, 24 June 1937, 200/3/1, 2/10; Brooks to H. L. White, 1 July 1939, 200/3/1, 2/14.

6 Newsome to Brooks, 13 July 1937, 200/1/2, 1/2; *American Archivist* 5 (January 1942): 53-54; Lester J. Cappon, "The Archival Profession and the Society of American Archivists," *American Archivist* 15 (July 1952): 197.

7 Brooks to Boyd, 16 January 1937, 200/4/1, 1/1; Brooks to Newsome, 15 January 1937, 200/1/2, 1/2; Donald R. McCoy, *The National Archives: America's Ministry of Documents, 1934-1968* (Chapel Hill: University of North Carolina Press, 1978), pp. 93-97; *Annual Report of the Archivist of the United States: Second Report, 1936*, p. 33; *Third Report, 1937*, pp. 69-70 *Fourth Report, 1938*, pp. 5-6; William F. Birdsall, "The American Archivists' Search for Professional Identity, 1909–1936; Ph.D. dissertation, University of Wisconsin-Madison, 1973); and Birdsall's oral history interview with Brooks, 24 April 1973, in the SAA Archives.

SAA President Newsome recognized that "the [National] Archives certainly will be of the greatest value to the Society, and the Society should not expect to be a burden to the Archives. There is a division line which could not be crossed with propriety and wisdom." The concentration of a large number of skilled archivists in one city able and willing to offer their services to their professional association gave the National Archives a major voice in the SAA. For a number of years, the society was affected by what Newsome once referred to as "the peculiar density of membership in Washington." Given the economic conditions of the late 1930s and the travel restrictions imposed by the federal government during World War II, it is hard to imagine how the society could have avoided being a largely East Coast organization. The National Archives has provided the society with a great number of its leaders, but it is also evident that all sections of the country and all branches of the profession have been represented among the officers and council. For example, of the first 27 presidents, only 9 came from the National Archives. Given the number of members from that institution and its leadership position in the profession, especially in the early years, one-third of the presidents should have come from it. The success the SAA enjoyed in this period is due to two groups: those at the National Archives and a vigorous body of state archivists who cooperated to build both a profession and a professional association.[8]

In 1937 SAA members traveled to Washington, not to dedicate the National Archives building (a ceremony that apparently never took place but which would be a fitting part of the fiftieth anniversary in 1984) but to hold the first annual meeting. Though in formal existence for only six months, the society already had plans to publish both proceedings of the 1936 and 1937 meetings and a quarterly journal to be known as the *American Archivist.* After paying a registration fee of 50 cents and enjoying a good meal for barely twice that amount, the registrants settled back to hear Newsome deliver the first of his three successive presidential addresses.

Newsome began with an analysis of the society's horoscope. The society "was born under the influence of Capricorn, the goat, and will be ruled by Saturn. These astral influences predestine that its nature will be prudent, ambitious, persevering, melancholy, cold, dry, and perhaps archival." Acknowledging that "archivists no longer recognize astrology as an exact science" but were nevertheless interested in the future of their society, he announced his topic: "The Objectives of the Society of American Archivists." Newsome saw the first third of the twentieth century as an "era of archival pioneering in the United States" and predicted

---

8 Newsome to Brooks, 12 February 1937, 200/3/1, 2/10; Newsome to Brooks, 20 May 1939, 200/1/2, 1/16; Morris L. Radoff to Brooks, 1 September 1945, 200/9/1, 1/27.

that the second third would be "a new era of remarkable archival fruition" in which the society would seek three major objectives: (1) "to become the practical, self-help agency of archivists for the solution of their complex problems" and "strive to nationalize archival information and technique"; (2) to seek "the solution of archival problems involving external relations with all archival agencies, with learned societies, and with the public"; and (3) "to encourage the development of a genuine archival profession in the United States" in which the society would "set training standards and advance archival administration through its meetings and publications." One need not examine a horoscope to know that these are still the objectives of the society after 46 years.[9]

Publishing the *American Archivist* quickly became the primary means of fulfilling these three objectives. The first issue appeared in January 1938, after a long search for an editor that delayed not only the journal but also the publication of the proceedings of the 1936 and 1937 meetings. The *American Archivist* appeared in the standard format of a history journal, reflecting the preference of editor Theodore C. Pease, professor of history at the University of Illinois. Though some members asserted that "the quarterly should be more of a trade journal than exclusively a magazine of scholarly articles," Pease devoted his editorial work largely to publishing the scholarly uses of historical manuscripts and an analysis of the European archival tradition. The first major article, for example, was devoted to a study of manuscript repair in archives in Great Britain and Europe and required most of the space in the first two issues. More space was given to the use of archival materials in the writing of history than to articles on technical aspects of archival administration, in spite of the announcement in the first issue that "The *American Archivist* will in its contents emphasize the concrete and practical over the general."[10]

Tensions developed between the editor and Council during the war years over both editorial policy and the inability of the editor to attend most annual meetings. In 1945 Pease resigned and was replaced by Margaret Cross Norton following her term as president. In spite of heavy duties as the archivist of Illinois, she immediately gave the journal a vigorous, practical format more in keeping with her view that the journal "should be a trade publication." Articles on practical methodology, as well as features on the technical aspects of the craft, and photographs began to appear. The professional archivist found Norton's approach of more value than the ponderously learned style of Pease; but the society owes the first editor and his institution a great debt. Pease struggled for

9 *American Historical Review* 43 (October 1937): 232, and (April 1937): 625; Newsome to Brooks, 17 May 1939, 200/1 /2, 1/16; 200/9/1, 1/1; *Proceedings*, pp. 61-64.

10 Brooks to M. C. Norton, 15 January 1937, 200/1/2, 1/2; *American Archivist* 1 (January 1938): v-vi.

years to coax articles out of members not accustomed to writing papers and labored to turn talks delivered at annual meetings into pieces worthy of a scholarly journal. Likewise, the University of Illinois served the society with an annual contribution of $500 (equal to one-fourth of the society's budget) to support editorial work, leaving the meager financial resources of the SAA responsible only for printing and mailing. Most older members of the society remember the generous contributions of the National Archives to the editorial work of the *American Archivist* for some 25 years; but it is important to note that in the first, crucial years the primary support came from personnel and institutions in the Midwest. It is true that many articles in the journal were written by National Archives employees, but only because Washington attracted many bright, articulate archivists interested in writing, not because the journal was a house organ of the National Archives.[11]

The early years of the society were, of course, devoted to establishing the society and developing the journal into the respected voice of the profession; but the leadership wanted also to make significant contributions to the profession at large and not have the SAA become just a social club. The society prepared model, uniform archival legislation to be used by the various states in drafting records laws. The secretary sent copies of these models to many public officials and noted in his 1940 report that 11 states had made use of them.[12]

At the 1938 meeting the members "unanimously voted that the president appoint a committee to recommend to the society the proper pronunciation" of *archives, archivist,* and *archival.* The committee dutifully reported back a year later with the correct pronunciations. Having spent years explaining to taxi drivers what an archivist is and attempting to cope with complaints of why the word *archivist* is not pronounced like *archives,* I wish that the special committee had not been so speedily discharged.[13]

The coming of the war forced the young society to mature rapidly. Archivists had to think about the preservation of current records for both historians and the war effort itself. Waldo Gifford Leland, in his 1940 presidential address, spoke of "The Archivist in Times of Emergency." Seeing the impact of the war on European archives, he urged American

---

11 "Criticism of Editorial Policy, 1943-45," 200/3/1, 3/26; Norton to Cappon, 15 January 1944, 200/3/1, 3/9. Brooks to Pease, 12 January 1944; Norton to Karl L. Trever, 14 January 1944; L. J. Cappon, "Comments on Editorial Policy and Procedure," 24 February 1944; Buck to Norton, 21 March 1945; and Brooks to Cappon, 4 April 1945, all in 200/3/1, 3/26; "The Change in Editorship of the *American Archivist*," *American Archivist* 9 (July 1946): 233-35.

12 A. R. Newsome, "Uniform State Archival Legislation," *American Archivist* 2 (January 1939): 1-16; "The Proposed Uniform State Public Records Act," *American Archivist* 3 (April 1940): 107-15, 4 (January 1941): 53-54; 5 (July 1942): 194.

13 *American Archivist* 2 (April 1939): 125; *American Archivist* 3 (January 1940): 56.

archivists to prepare for the national emergency, not only in their repositories but also by offering their assistance in the preservation of current vital government records. The Committee on the Protection of Archives Against the Hazards of War and the Committee on the Emergency Transfer and Storage of Archives were established and began cooperating with the appropriate government agencies. Few SAA members saw combat, but many played vital roles in securing and improving the recordkeeping procedures of the federal government. Two committees on writing the history of the war were formed, and the membership passed a resolution at the 1944 business meeting urging support of the waste paper salvage program, provided citizens first consulted an archivist regarding "segregating valuable papers from the useless ones."[14]

Born in the economic hardships of the Great Depression and buffeted in its youth by war, the small (fewer than 300 members in 1945) and poor (an annual budget of around $3,000 with a $1,000 war bond as a reserve fund) society enjoyed a glorious moment. President Franklin D. Roosevelt liked archivists, and in 1942, amidst a war going badly, he took the time to tell the society so! At its 1941 annual meeting, the society named him its first honorary member; and SAA president R. D. W. Connor sent the membership certificate to Roosevelt on his sixtieth birthday. Roosevelt thanked Connor for the honor and expressed his "lifetime interest in the building up of archives throughout the nation — especially because of my personal interest in the naval history phase and the local Dutchess County material." Roosevelt went on to urge the society to work hard in building up public support for "the duplication of records by modern processes like the microfilm so that if in any part of the country original archives are destroyed, a record of them will exist in some other place."[15]

The fury of war impressed archivists, not only with the fragility of records, but also with the tenuousness of the society's relations with archivists in other nations ravaged by battle. The SAA had always been open to foreign members, but the coming of war made it impossible for many of them to attend meetings or even pay their dues. In 1944 the dues of $5 a year were reduced to $1.50 for foreign members, and those unable to communicate with the society because of the war were still carried on the rolls. At the conclusion of the war, the SAA gave its support to the establishment of an International Council on Archives (ICA) as the best means of rebuilding collegiality among archivists throughout the world. Duplicate sets of the *American Archivist* were distributed to

---

14 W. G. Leland, "The Archivist in Times of Emergency," *American Archivist* 4 (January 1941): 1-12; 4 (July 1941): 210; 7 (January 1944): 52-54.

15 SAA Honorary Membership Certificate, 7 October 1941, PPF 7972, FDR Presidential Library; *American Archivist* 6 (January 1943): 17.

European and Asian archives destroyed by war. In spite of dislocations and inconveniences of the war, SAA never failed either to hold its regular annual meeting or to publish the *American Archivist*.[16]

The end of the war marked the end of the society's first decade, and Philip C. Brooks wrote a history of the period. No one more qualified for this task could have been found, for he not only kept the administrative routines going but he also led the efforts of the society to serve the whole profession. Brooks recalled being unexpectedly called on to record the minutes of the 1936 meeting and of subsequently holding the office of secretary for the next six years. After describing the birth and early years of SAA, he looked to the future when the restoration of peace would mean archivists would have to redouble their efforts to restore the documentary heritage of the nation and the world.[17]

Few historical periods end in neat decades. It should be noted, therefore, that on 29 December 1945, ten years and one day after the Conference of Archivists voted to consider establishing a national association of archivists, the SAA incorporated itself in the District of Columbia, declaring, as it had for a decade, that "The object of this corporation shall be to promote sound principles of archival economy and to facilitate cooperation among archivists and archival agencies."[18]

Coming of Age, 1946-57

As the society matured, the wide diversity of interests and viewpoints of the members became evident. Secretary Cappon reported in 1950 that "State archivists have crossed swords with national; the internationalists have been criticized by some of our more domestic-minded members. Some 99.44% pure archivists have looked askance at curators of historical manuscripts in the society even though they have archives in their custody. The practical archivist has vied with the theoretical and the historical for space in our magazine." Each of the conflicts and tensions listed by Cappon shaped the society during its second decade.[19]

American archivists did not adopt an isolationist stance at the conclusion of World War II; instead, through their national organization, they sought to reestablish contacts with their foreign colleagues. The SAA joined the effort to create an international association of archivists to assist the archival programs of nations shattered by the fighting.

---

16 *American Archivist* 8 (January 1945): 70; 9 (January 1946): 62; 10 (January 1947): 71-72; "Letter Sent to Archivists of Foreign Countries Concerning the Organization of an International Archival Council," *American Archivist* 10 (July 1947): 227-31.

17 P. C. Brooks, "The First Decade of the Society of American Archivists," *American Archivist* 10 (April 1947): 115-28.

18 Certification of Incorporation, 200/3/1, 3/1.

19 *American Archivist* 14 (January 1951): 65-66.

Resolutions giving strong support to the establishment of ICA and an archives for the United Nations were passed at the 1948 annual business meeting. Solon J. Buck, second Archivist of the United States, paved the way for support for the ICA with his 1946 presidential address to the SAA. In 1949 the society agreed to contribute $250 to ICA even though the SAA had suffered a budget deficit the previous year. Efforts to have individual members contribute an additional $250 fell short, but at the 1950 business meeting the membership agreed to join ICA and to contribute $50 annually in addition to the nominal dues. The outbreak of war in Korea aroused fears that archival repositories around the world would once again be destroyed. Unfortunately, concern with international archival matters among SAA members declined rapidly in the 1950s.[20]

Committees charged with domestic affairs began to take a strong leadership role, however. The committees on state archives and state and local records continued surveying and analyzing archival legislation and completed a directory of state archivists as well as surveys of salaries, microfilm programs, and records destruction policies. The advice of the Committee on Archival Buildings and Equipment was sought by repositories completing construction and remodeling plans. The Church Records Committee prepared a bibliography of archival writings in its field. Shortly after its creation in 1949, the College and University Archives Committee became one of the most active committees, with breakfast conferences at annual meetings and diligent surveys of institutions of higher learning regarding archival programs, which resulted in a number of new members for the society.[21]

Unfortunately, many other committees accomplished very little. A chairman of the Committee on Archival Research, charged with encouraging members to write papers for the *American Archivist,* lamented that while his committee had accomplished something, much remained to be done. He reported on the frustrations of trying to pry articles out of reluctant members, who would not write even when they had promised to do so.[22]

If their work was not always all that could be desired, the committees did make a considerable contribution to the activities of the society, enabling it to fight for proper recognition of the profession and to cooperate with other associations on an equal footing. The dispute with

20 Solon J. Buck, "The Archivist's One World," *American Archivist* 10 (January 1947): 9-24; 10 (January 1947): 71, 76-77, 82-86; 11 (January 1948): 56-57, 64-67; 12 (January 1949): 57; 13 (January 1950): 51, 57; 13 (July 1950): 269; 14 (January 1951): 58; 15 (January 1952): 84; 15 (April 1952): 182; Brooks to L. K. Born, 17 September 1951, 200/1/3, 3/42; Brooks to Dean Acheson, 3 October 1949, 200/1/3, 3/42, 200/1/3, 3/48; 200/3/1, 1/16; 200/3/2, 2/14-16.

21 200/3/1, 1/9-21 200/3/2, 1/26 and 30, 2/1-3 and 4/20-5/18; *American Archivist* 12 (January 1949): 62-67; 13 (January 1950): 56, 62; 17 (January 1954): 71-72; 18 (January 1955): 46-47.

22 *American Archivist* 10 (January 1947): 87.

librarians over the limits of their respective professions continued when the National Association of State Libraries asserted in a pamphlet in 1956 that "the preservation, administration, and servicing of the archives is a function of the State Library." Council passed a resolution reminding the library group that the two professions differed in the nature of materials handled and in the administration of those materials. In the resolution, SAA contended that librarians were not adequately trained for archival administration, denied "the library's exclusive right to jurisdiction in matters archival" and requested that the offending passage be removed from the pamphlet in future editions so that the archival profession and the majority of state archives not in state libraries would not be injured. The passage of this resolution did not, of course, end misunderstandings between librarians and archivists; but it did lead to a friendly meeting between Council and a committee from the NASL to discuss areas of mutual concern. A joint ALA-SAA committee eventually developed out of such meetings.[23]

Relations with another group were more cordial, perhaps because there was not the sharp professional conflict that existed with librarians.

For almost a decade after it was established in 1940, the American Association for State and Local History frequently met either concurrently with or just before or after the SAA's annual meeting. The AASLH made a very compatible companion for SAA, though some SAA members chafed at attending sessions not geared exclusively to professional archivists. A joint Committee on Historical Manuscripts, formed in 1948 to consider plans for a union list of manuscript collections, eventually led to the National Union Catalog of Manuscript Collections. Just as the AHA had nurtured the young SAA, so did the latter provide similar support for AASLH in its formative years.[24]

Now able to hold its own with other national organizations, the SAA became, in its second decade, a national voice for the archival profession. Two national issues that ring a familiar, modern note first arose in the 1950s: independence for the National Archives and Records Service and expansion of the programs of the National Historical Publications Commission (NHPC). The society passed a resolution urging Dwight D. Eisenhower to maintain the nonpolitical character of the position of the Archivist of the United States when rumors appeared that Senator Everett Dirksen of Illinois wanted a Republican appointed to replace Wayne C. Grover. Because of the opposition of both historians and archivists, nothing came of the idea to replace Grover. In 1957 Grover introduced, and Council unanimously passed, a resolution

23 200/3/2, 4/21; *American Archivist* 19 (October 1956): 371-72; 20 (January 1957): 59.

24 200/3/1, 1/10; *American Archivist* 12 (January 1949): 55-56; 13 (January 1950): 47, 68; 15 (January 1952): 88-89; 18 (July 1955): 277.

urging support for a U.S. Congressional resolution "To encourage and foster the cooperation of private and state historical commissions with the National Historical Publications Commission." As a result, the NHPC not only supported the publication of papers of famous Americans but also encouraged the collecting and maintaining of historical manuscripts.[25]

The SAA could make its voice heard on the national level because it had become a national organization. Though the membership still concentrated in the middle Atlantic states, the society had gained considerable strength in the entire country. It held its 1947 annual meeting west of the Mississippi for the first time, assembling in Glenwood Springs and Denver. Of the 12 annual meetings from 1946 through 1957, 5 were held in the East, 5 in the Midwest, and 1 each in the West and Canada. In 1950 the geographical distribution of the membership in the United States was approximately 54 percent on the East Coast, 19 percent in the South, 14 percent in the Mississippi Valley north of Oklahoma, 8 percent in the West, and 4 percent in New England. By 1954 the secretary reported that an analysis of 120 biographical data forms revealed that the percentage of the membership from the East Coast had declined by 10 percent.[26]

Growth in absolute numbers was more important than the geographical distribution of the membership. As a result of several membership drives, the SAA grew from 283 individual members (as distinguished from institutional members or subscribers) in 1945 to 648 members by 1957. The society lost four members in 1947-48; and Council realized that, without additional members to share both financial responsibilities and administrative duties, the society could never reach its full potential. This growth in membership was not accomplished without a very significant shift in the criteria for joining. As early as 1946 Council considered revising the constitution to admit all those sympathetic with the objectives of the organization in addition to those actually working in the profession. SAA president Christopher Crittenden argued in 1949 that more liberal qualifications for membership should be adopted to "bring in new blood and new ideas." Denying that the professional archivist need fear being swamped by a flood of nonprofessional members, he observed: "Indeed, experience has shown that it is difficult to persuade these people to join the Society at all." Six years passed before Crittenden could announce at the 1955 annual business meeting that Council had approved an amendment to accept members on the basis of interest, not vocation, and to discontinue requiring a Council vote to approve each application. These

---

25 *American Archivist* 16 (July 1953): 273-74; 20 (October 1957): 387; McCoy, *The National Archives*, 270-71, 266-68.

26 *American Archivist* 14 (January 1951): 65; 17 (January 1954): 87-88.

changes were approved unanimously and without discussion by the members.[27]

The membership did not always docilely accept the recommendations of the leadership. For the first 12 years the nominating committee's slate, consisting of a single nominee for each office, always won election without opposition. This tradition ended in 1949 when the archivist of Delaware nominated the archivist of Mississippi, William D. McCain, to run against Philip C. Brooks for president. On the first ballot both candidates received 22 votes. Brooks's supporters rallied and garnered 2 additional votes on the second ballot, while McCain again received only 22. In a conciliatory move, McCain's seconder successfully moved that the election be declared unanimous.[28]

This election struggle almost certainly resulted not from personal opposition to Brooks, but from a desire of state archivists to see the presidency continue in the hands of one of their own (the archivist of North Carolina was the incumbent) rather than return to the National Archives. Four years later Leon deValinger won a seat on Council in the society's second contested election. This 1953 election achieved a rough balance of power: National Archives personnel held the presidency, vice presidency, and one Council seat; the secretary and treasurer were from business archives; and state archivists held the remaining four Council seats. The only unrepresented segments were the relatively small and young groups of college and university and religious archivists. The latter group has consistently been underrepresented in the governance of SAA. Two other contested elections occurred during the first two decades. In both cases the nominating committee's slate prevailed over the floor nominee.[29]

The election disputes between employees of the national and state archives revealed the deep dividing tensions between these two groups. Concentrated both professionally and geographically, SAA members from the National Archives were often seen by some state archivists as dominating the affairs of the society while neglecting the traditional professional concerns of state archivists. Specifically, they charged the National Archives with largely ignoring the arrangement and description of manuscript collections to be used by historians in favor of the management of noncurrent records systematically generated by governmental agencies. President Brooks, anxious to bridge the gap with the state archivists, asked Margaret Norton, chairman of the 1950 Program Committee, to plan a session in which state and national archivists

---

27 *American Archivist* 13 (January 1950): 59, 65-67; 11 (January 1948): 47; 10 (January 1947): 73; 12 (October 1949): 366-68; 19 (January 1956): 80.

28 *American Archivist* 13 (January 1950): 52.

29 *American Archivist* 15 (January 1952): 84-85; 17 (January 1954): 84; 20 (April 1957): 171.

would present papers outlining what professional contributions and obligations each group expected of the other. Concerned about "the old accusation that the National Archives plays too dominant a role in the Society of American Archivists," Brooks hoped that such a session would lead to a system of better cooperation, through which the National Archives could provide more technical assistance to the states while state archivists could assist the National Archives in the appraisal and disposition of records of interest to both the federal and state governments. He added, "Between us, the National Archives and State archivists have the tremendously important task of determining the archival heritage of the American people, and there are many over-lapping fields which we should be discussing more than we do in our SAA meetings. . . ."[30]

Norton planned the session entitled "Areas of Cooperation Between the National Archives and State Archives," reflecting her concern with the cleavage between the two groups. While editor of the *American Archivist* in the mid-1940s, she had written to SAA president Solon Buck about the trend that "[seemed] to be aligning most state archivists and the Washington people in two more or less antagonistic factions in the Society." She wanted state archivists to give more attention to records management problems and, praising the role of the National Archives in the society, declared of the National Archives: "lest anyone think you were trying to dominate the Society . . . you lean so far backwards that I sometimes fear you will topple over."[31]

In retrospect, the society benefited from this tension. Certainly neither group could fairly say that its interests had been subjugated. Of the 12 presidents who served from 1937 to 1957, 5 were state archivists and 5 (if Ernst Posner is included) were from the National Archives. The National Archives staff did bring in new approaches and archival prin-ciples that benefited all archivists, and the state archivists preserved the historical heritage of their respective states with a wide variety of inno-vative programs. Despite the unhappiness of certain individuals, who felt that the other group dominated SAA, the society grew to maturity under the administrations of archival giants such as Newsome, Buck, Norton, and Brooks, who, through their professional association, served the entire profession. It must be admitted that the influence of state archivists was divided among a large group spread all over the nation while that of the National Archives was concentrated in one location and on a few administrators; but the National Archives did not abuse its position in the limelight. Rather, it strove to serve the profession

---

30 Brooks to Norton, 9 December 1949, 200/1/3, 3/40.

31 *American Archivist* 14 (July 1951): 223-28; Norton to Buck, 14 January 1947, and Buck to Norton, 20 February 1947, 200/3/1, 3/6.

SAA officers and Council, 1956. Standing, left to right: Father Henry Browne, secretary; Wayne Grover; Karl Trever, editor of the *American Archivist.* Seated, left to right: Ernst Posner, president; William Overman, treasurer; Alice Smith; Dolores Renze; Leon deValinger; Henry Edmunds, vice-president. Council member David Duniway was not present for the photograph.

and the society by doing work that others could not do. For example, in 1949 the editorship of the *American Archivist* moved from the Illinois State Archives to the National Archives and Karl L. Trever became editor. All successive editors have been employees of NARS until the beginning of the current decade, and most of its editorial departments have been headed by other employees of that agency, not because of a desire for control by NARS, but because it has been the only agency that would, or could, devote the necessary resources to the task. Without the support of the National Archives in the form of paying the salary of the editor, the society would have had a very difficult financial burden. When the SAA published the journal in the late 1940s without the annual $500 subsidy from the University of Illinois, it quickly ran a deficit of up to $400 in publishing costs. By the mid-1950s, however, the press run was more than 1,100 copies, and the editor reported modest success in attracting articles.[32]

---

32 200/7/3, 1/41; 200/7/2, 1/14; *American Archivist* 11 (January 1948): 60; 12 (January 1949): 61; 13 (April 1950): 177-80; 20 (April 1957): 173.

Tensions over governance of the society became more than just an election issue when attention turned to revisions of the constitution. In 1946–47 a committee, consisting largely of past presidents and current officials, considered revisions to the ten-year-old document. Most of the proposed changes were minor, but one called for elimination of a phrase that assured the membership a voice in governance. The Council rejected this proposed alteration on the grounds "that this clause guarantees democratic procedure if the Society desires to overrule an action of Council." This idea was tabled at the 1947 business meeting. At the same meeting, the editor became a full voting member of Council even though the position remained an appointive one. This change in status reflected the appointment of a former president to the editorship and made the editor a more active participant in the affairs of the society.[33]

At the 1951 annual business meeting a rather acrimonious debate developed over a petition by five members to amend the constitution. One amendment would have removed the editor from the Council, even in an *ex officio* and nonvoting capacity. Another would have forbidden the president and vice president to succeed themselves. Both efforts failed, though the latter proposal did clear Council. In 1957 both Council and the business meeting approved an amendment limiting the president to a single consecutive term with the added stipulation that the vice president would automatically succeed to the presidency after a one-year term. This latter provision did not win approval without a debate over parliamentary procedural matters, an entertainment for which our annual meetings have become justly renowned.[34]

The old question of where annual meetings should be held also came under scrutiny. At the 1951 meeting, Council and the membership rejected, after some debate, a proposed amendment requiring that Council "shall consult the latest available mailing list and choose of the available meeting places that place of meeting which shall seem to them to be nearest the places of residence of the largest number of members." Undoubtedly, such a place would have been on the East Coast near the District of Columbia. Without much doubt, this amendment in defense of eastern provincialism developed out of opposition to the location of the 1950 meeting in Madison, Wisconsin.[35]

Morris L. Radoff, archivist of Maryland, complained to Brooks that the SAA would never reach the goal of being "useful professionally to the younger people . . . if we continue to meet in Denver, Quebec or Madison." While the educational and cultural advantages of meeting in a wide variety of locations persuaded Brooks and the rest of Council of the

---

33 *American Archivist* 11 (January 1948): 50-51.

34 *American Archivist* 15 (January 1952): 82-85; 21 (January 1958): 99; 200/3/33, 4/17.

35 *American Archivist* 15 (January 1952): 82-85.

wisdom of the policy of meeting in cities throughout the nation, it cannot be denied that the East Coast meetings were usually much better attended than those held beyond the tidewater. Meetings in Denver, Quebec, and Madison attracted between 50 and 60 people each, while 165 attended the 1951 meeting in Annapolis. The 1953 meeting, however, proved that meetings did not have to be held on the East Coast to be well attended if the program and setting were imaginatively planned and selected. This meeting, which was centered around business archives and the opening of the archives of the Ford Motor Company, was the first ever to be devoted to a single topic. The attendance in Detroit equaled that of Annapolis.[36]

The most significant constitutional change proposed in the 1950s involved the effort to honor outstanding members. The Professional Standards and Training Committee considered the matter for several years before reporting to Council in 1956 that "a special class of members of the Society known as Fellows of the Society of American Archivists" should be established. Council endorsed the proposal, which provided for the election of no more than 15 percent of the members as fellows by the Professional Standards and Training Committee. The committee consisted of all the past presidents, all of whom would automatically be designated fellows to avoid any charge of favoritism. The constitutional amendment was approved 56 to 40 at the 1957 meeting after a lively discussion. The close vote revealed the resistance of those members who feared that such a separate class of honored members would be divisive or elitist. Those supporting the idea, however, were concerned not with empty honors for those adept at playing archival politics, but with honoring those who had made significant contributions to the theory and practice of archival administration, thereby encouraging others to improve the standards of the profession. While it may be that many fellows have had more of a personal than a professional impact, the society owes a debt to such supporters of the fellows concept as Dolores Renze, Morris Radoff, and Leon deValinger, who struggled so hard for so long to raise standards in a profession with few clear educational or career guidelines and benchmarks.[37]

While the members focused their attention on such matters as fellows, the respective roles of state and national archives, and a variety of changes in the association and its constitution, the mundane issues of finances and budgets arose. Not unlike the situation with other teenagers, the cost of supporting the society began to climb in the second

---

36 Radoff to Brooks, 18 October 1949, 200/1/3, 3/49; *American Archivist* 13 (January 1950): 54; 200/9/1, 1/33; *American Archivist* 16 (July 1953): 273.

37 *American Archivist* 16 (January 1953): 89; 19 (April 1956): 177; 20 (January 1957): 58-66; 20 (April 1957): 175; 20 (October 1957): 384-85; 21 (January 1958): 98-99; Radoff to Committee on Professional Standards and Training, 28 February 1956, 200/3/2, 3/30.

decade as SAA coped with both the inflation after the war and the rising expectations of the members regarding services and programs. Dues, which had always been $5 a year for both individual and institutional members, increased to $10 for institutional members in 1951, while those for foreign members, which had been reduced because of the war, were returned to the domestic rate. In 1954 dues for individual members rose to $6 annually, and in 1956 provision was made for institutional sustaining members with dues of $100 to $500 a year. Increased costs made increased dues a necessity. Cash on hand as of 30 June 1951 dropped to $160.97. For each of the three previous fiscal years, expenditures had exceeded revenues by several hundred dollars, or approximately 10 percent of the budget. These overages were caused largely by high publishing costs, but in 1952 the *American Archivist* began to run advertisements. This income helped provide the society with a small surplus. The journal represented the largest drain on the resources of SAA. Subscriptions and sales produced about 40 percent of income in 1953 and 1954, but publishing and mailing costs equaled 80 percent of the income. The annual meeting also began to produce a small income by the mid-1950s. By 1952 the society had returned to a sound financial footing, and over the next six years it accumulated a surplus of several thousand dollars on budgets ranging from $4,257 in 1952 to $6,088 in 1957. The cash balance in 1957 amounted to $7,495, including a savings account of $5,095.[38]

This surplus allowed the accumulation of additional reserves earmarked for the most ambitious project yet: the hiring of a paid secretariat. President Ernst Posner announced a three-year program to raise $10,000 in pledges to support the position. Unfortunately, only $2,583 was pledged by 77 members. Some 60 others indicated support of the idea but were unable to make a pledge. Only 12 members opposed the plan, but their views prevailed by default as the society was unable to secure from foundations the critical financial support needed for the secretariat.[39]

The dream of a paid secretariat would have to wait until the 1970s, but this 21st year of the society in 1957 did witness the achievement of another long-term goal. For the first time more than 1,000 members and subscribers had enrolled — 648 individual members, 100 institutional members, and 347 subscribers. Secretary Renze noted in her 1957 annual report: "This 21st annual meeting in many ways reflects the coming of

---

38 *American Archivist* 15 (January 1952): 82; 14 (January 1951): 48-50; 20 (April 1957): 172; 14 (January 1951): 61; 15 (January 1952): 92; 17 (January 1954): 85; 18 (January 1955): 51; 19 (January 1956): 82; 200/4/1, 1/1-20.

39 *American Archivist* 18 (July 1955): 278-79; 19 (October 1956): 371; 20 (January 1957): 62; 20 (October 1957): 385–87; 200/3/1, 3/39.

Fellows. Six new Fellows were honored at the 1962 annual meeting of the society. Julian Boyd and William J. Van Schreeven were not present at the conference. Pictured here, from left to right, are William Alderson, Harold Pinkett, Robert Brown, and Al Leisinger.

age of the Society — the membership, the approach to problems encountered, and the examination of trends for the future."[40]

The Professionalization of the Association, 1958-74

The period after the society reached the age of majority can be summarized, in a rather clumsy phrase, as the professionalization of the association. In the years from 1958 to 1974, the leadership of the society turned increasingly toward professional methods of conducting its affairs. Funds were sought, and eventually found internally, for a paid executive director. No longer content just to stumble into a job, members demanded the education necessary for a professional career as an archivist; and the society began to devote additional resources and personnel to professional and technical research. By the 1970s it was clear to the leadership that the society would have to be both more efficient and more responsive to the professional needs of its members in order to successfully meet these challenges.

The exciting days of forming a new association were far behind when the society celebrated its twenty-fifth anniversary in 1961. Solon Buck's vision of the one world of archives dimmed in the face of an indefinite future as the SAA grappled with the questions of its contribution to the profession and its role in documenting the history and

---

40 *American Archivist* 21 (January 1958): 101, 104. The number of subscribers also included exchanges with other associations but did not reduce the total of 1,095 below 1,000.

culture of the nation. Contending forces pushed from opposite directions. A much larger, younger membership, working in a bewildering variety of repositories, sought an increasingly complex level of services and threatened to form its own professional associations if such services were not provided. To have the income and personnel needed to support the organizational structure and to provide the services demanded by the various factions, it was essential to hold this amorphous body of members together. Faced with these pressures, the leadership became more introspective in the 1960s as it analyzed the society and its programs.

Officers concerned about the future of the SAA warned about the dangerous possibility of various segments of the profession forming separate associations. An early rift between archivists, concerned primarily with historical documentation and manuscript collections, and records managers, involved in the disposition of current records, contributed to the formation of the Association of Records Executives and Administrators (AREA). Efforts to hold a joint SAA-AREA meeting in 1964 broke down over registration fees, which the archivists thought were too high. While the two groups did meet in 1965, the unfortunate gap between their closely related disciplines continued to widen. By the end of the 1960s, not only had the oral historians and librarians working with manuscripts formed their own associations, but archivists themselves had begun to consider forming their own groups based on either professional specialization or geographical proximity.[41]

Groups in Michigan and Ohio led a movement that in a few years saw the entire country organized into local, state, and regional associations. While some SAA leaders viewed regional associations as increasing the grass roots support for the profession and, in the long run, for SAA, others saw in them a further fragmentation of the national organization. Rapid growth of regional associations forced Council in 1972 to form a committee to meet with regional representatives. At the meeting in the spring of 1973 it soon became clear to everyone that, while the regionals jealously guarded their independence, fears of conflict between them and SAA were groundless and that, in fact, the regionals could provide educational training and professional relationships for isolated and inexperienced archivists who were unable to participate actively in SAA. The regionals were formed to provide services at the grass roots level, but many of their active members have served with distinction in SAA.[42]

---

41 200/1/9, 1/9; 200/3/4/2, 2/8 and 15; *American Archivist* 27 (July 1964): 444; 28 (July 1965): 463-65.

42 *American Archivist* 31 (April 1968): 214; 31 (July 1968): 328; 31 (October 1968): 622; 31 (January 1968): 67; 32 (January 1969): 61-63; 36 (April 1973): 305, 313-14, 316; 200/1/10, 1/23; 200/5/1, 2/13.

With assistance from the regionals on local affairs, the society, in theory, should have had more time to devote to international archival matters; but, given the preoccupation with the structure of SAA, international issues received little attention beyond minimal participation in ICA. SAA did host a reception for ICA's Extraordinary Congress on "Archives for Scholarship — Encouraging Greater Ease of Access" in Washington in 1966. The society's financial contribution to ICA remained at a minimal level even when Council passed a resolution calling on UNESCO to "improve the precarious financial position of the Council." The only real involvement with foreign archivists, beyond a few members attending meetings at their own or their institution's expense, came in the form of a $500 contribution to the Committee to Rescue Italian Art to be used to restore archives and manuscripts destroyed by the 1966 floods in Italy.[43]

In the 1960s relations with foreign archivists became largely a matter of teaching them, not learning from them. Council accepted grants from the Asia Foundation to provide SAA memberships for archivists in the Orient and funds to attend the society's annual meetings. One exception to this fairly dismal picture of international archivy should be noted. The word *American* in the Society of American Archivists has always included Canadian colleagues, a considerable number of whom have been members of the society. During this period, two distinguished Dominion Archivists of the Public Archives of Canada, W. Kaye Lamb and Wilfred L. Smith, were elected president of SAA. To a much lesser extent, archivists from Mexico, the Caribbean, and Latin America have also participated in the affairs of the society.[44]

Unlike international matters, NARS received a great deal of attention. Fearing that the resignation letter of Wayne C. Grover, which called for an independent NARS, might lead to a political backlash by the General Services Administration and result in the appointment of a nonprofessional as Archivist of the United States, Council passed a resolution in 1965 calling for Robert H. Bahmer's appointment as acting archivist to be made permanent. Very shortly thereafter the GSA administrator did appoint Bahmer to the position, but he did nothing to resolve the independence issues raised by Grover. The SAA did not directly confront the issue of independence until 1967, when it joined AHA and OAH in forming a Joint Committee on the Status of the National Archives. H. G. Jones conducted a study that eventually resulted in an analytical history of NARS. The controversies surrounding that study are beyond the scope of

---

43 *American Archivist* 30 (January 1967): 212; 29 (January 1966): 121; 29 (July 1966): 433-44; 30 (January 1967): 212; 30 (July 1967): 507; 30 (October 1967). 620; 200/3/4/2, 3/10.

44 *American Archivist* 25 (January 1962): 109-10; 26 (January 1963): 112; 29 (January 1966): 121-122, 125; 200/1/1, 1/4; 200/3/3/3, 4/16; 200/3/4/2, 1/23, 2/9, and 53; 200/4/5, 1/18-19.

this report except to note the honored place of both Jones and the SAA in the struggle for the independence of NARS. This struggle continues at a critical point today.[45]

The struggle for an independent National Archives consumed much of the energy the society devoted to national concerns; but other issues also received attention. The most positive development concerned the National Historical Publications Commission. All archivists owe a great debt to the efforts of Charles E. Lee and others that resulted in 1974 in the NHPC being reestablished as the National Historical Publications and Records Commission with additional funding to support records preservation and description projects as well as the traditional editorial projects.[46] The other major development, the famous Loewenheim case, proved to be much less positive for archivists and their society, though it has resulted in a better mutual understanding between historians and archivists.[47] James B. Rhoads, who had borne the brunt of Loewenheim's attacks, proposed in Council that SAA approach AHA and OAH about setting up a joint committee to mediate future conflicts of this type. Rhoads's proposal won acceptance and led to the eventual establishment of the Joint Committee on Historians and Archives. This committee prepared guidelines for handling disputes, whether brought to their attention by historians or archivists; but several years would have to pass before the historians recognized the equal partnership with archivists to the extent of changing the name to the Committee of Historians and Archivists.[48]

Discussions of the relationship between historians and archivists had gone on since the SAA's founding; and if the twenty-fifth anniversary in 1961 passed without resolution of all areas of conflict, at least both sides

---

45 200/1/1, 1/5; *American Archivist* 29 (April 1966): 307; McCoy, *The National Archives*, pp. 345-47; see pp. 352-363 for an analysis of Jones's study; H. G. Jones, *The Records of a Nation* (New York: Atheneum, 1969); *American Archivist* 31 (January 1968): 108; 31 (April 1968): 213; 31 (July 1968): 325-28; 32 (April 1969): 181; 200/3/5/2, 4/45-46; 200/1/6, 1/43; 200/3/5/2, 2/8; 200/1/8, 1/8-11; 200/1/7, 1/10. [*Editor's note:* The National Archives gained independence from GSA in 1985, with a formal name change from National Archives and Records Service to National Archives and Records Administration.]

46 200/1/1, 1/29; *American Archivist* 35 (October 1972): 456; 36 (January 1973): 136; 36 (July 1973): 475-76.

47 R. R. Palmer to F. G. Ham, 30 January 1970, and D. E. Miller to Ham, 27 January 1970, 200/3/5/2, 3/3; *American Archivist* 33 (January 1970): 78, 125; 33 (April 1970): 225-26; 33 (October 1970): 434, 34 (April 1971): 216-17; Herman Kahn, "The Long-Range Implication for Historians and Archivists of the Charges Against the Franklin D. Roosevelt Library," and Richard Polenberg, "The Roosevelt Library Case: A Review Article," *American Archivist* 34 (July 1971): 265-75, 277-84; *Final Report of the Joint AHA-OAH Ad Hoc Committee to Investigate the Charges Against the Franklin D. Roosevelt Library and Related Matters*, 24 August 1970 (Washington: American Historical Association, 1970); 200/3/5/2, 3/1-3.

48 200/6/1/1, 2/1; *American Archivist* 34 (April 1971): 222; 34 (October 1971): 409-10; 35 (January 1972): 96-7; 35 (April 1972): 250; 35 (October 1972): 460-61; 36 (April 1973): 319-20; 36 (July 1973): 415; 36 (October 1973): 627; 37 (April 1974): 370.

could take pride in the growth of the archival association, which owed so much to the support of historians. Membership in SAA increased from 243 in 1937 to more than 900 by 1961, with an additional 400 subscribers. The annual budget had, likewise, grown from just over $2,000 to more than $12,000, with a reserve and cash balance of $10,000. A membership directory, prepared by Dolores C. Renze, containing historical data on the early years of the SAA, was the first society publication ever produced using machine-readable technology.[49]

Renze left the office of secretary in 1963 after seven years of hard, devoted service. Thanks largely to her efforts, the SAA had orderly procedures and operations. Most importantly, its tax status had been changed to allow SAA to function as a tax-exempt, nonprofit corporation structured to meet the needs of the members for educational programs. The association now functioned about as smoothly as could reasonably be expected given the vagaries and spotty work habits of volunteer, short-term, part-time elected officials and committee chairmen. Such organization, however, had been achieved at the cost of considerable personal animosity and abrasion.[50] In 1964 Renze returned to the fray as vice president and president-elect after winning the first SAA election in which the nominations committee proposed a dual slate for the vice president and the two Council seats. This more democratic procedure also reflected complicated, behind-the-scenes political infighting involving disgruntled officers and Council members; NARS officials jealously guarding their role in the society; and members, particularly some state archivists, who objected to the excessive influence, in their view, of Washington in the affairs of SAA. In 1966 society politics again led to a contested election in which the nominating committee's sole nominee for vice president lost to a nominee from the floor. Fortunately, the bitterness of such campaigns has been replaced by the memory of the dedicated service of officials such as secretaries Philip P. Mason, F. Gerald Ham, and Robert M. Warner, who, as successors to Renze, carried forward the work of professionalizing the association.[51]

Ham, archivist of Wisconsin, playing the role of an archival Janus, used his 1970 secretary's report to look back at the accomplishments of the decade and to consider the future needs of both the society and the profession. Membership and subscriptions had increased by almost 1,000, and the annual budget had risen to more than $50,000. Whereas the 1961 meeting only had 160 registrants, 511 attended the 1970 meeting;

---

49 *American Archivist* 25 (January 1962): 120-22; "Proceedings of the Society's Twenty-fifth Anniversary Luncheon," *American Archivist* 25 (April 1962): 227-40; 24 (July 1961): 365; *Society Directory: 25th Anniversary Edition*, 1961.

50 200/3/3/1, 1/1–8.

51 200/2/1, 1/42; 200/3/3/1, 1/8; 200/3/4/2, 1/26-27 and 2/1, 15-16 and 57-58; *American Archivist* 28 (January 1965): 136-37; 30 (January 1967): 210.

and the number of sessions on the annual program had increased from 5 to 20. Educational offerings, limited to 3 summer institutes at the beginning of the decade, could now be found at 12 institutions, including 3 at the graduate level. Ham urged his audience to use this new strength to solve some of the long-neglected problems facing archivists, particularly in the areas of archival theory and advocacy.[52]

The contributions of state archivists such as Mary Givens Bryan, deValinger, Ham, Jones, Lee, and Renze proved vital in this period. If the National Archives constituted the preeminent institutional component of the society in its early years, state archivists occupied that position in this third period. Six of the 16 presidents from 1958 to 1974 were state archivists, as were 3 of the 4 secretaries, 2 of the 3 treasurers, and a large number of Council members. The Committee on State and Local Records, which had published detailed studies of state archival programs in the 1950s, continued to be one of the most productive committees. In 1958 it played a leading role in having Council form a Committee on Federal-State Relationships to deal with tensions between the two groups as well as to facilitate cooperation and the sharing of information on archival programs.[53]

In 1963 the State and Local Records committee established the Distinguished Service Award (DSA). Three distinguished state archivists and fellows of the Society — Dolores Renze, Mary Givens Bryan, and Leon deValinger — provided the trophy to be awarded "for significant and aggressive leadership in archival documentation or administrative improvement and development." The society established other awards, such as the Gondos Memorial Award, the Waldo Gifford Leland Prize, and the Philip M. Hamer Award, to honor its outstanding members and to win public recognition for the society and the profession.[54]

The DSA was conceived in part as an effort to improve state archival programs then undergoing examination in a study conducted by the society under a grant from the Council on Library Resources. Ernst Posner, America's foremost archival educator and theoretician, demonstrated the critical contribution of state archival programs to the nation's historical record-keeping activities in his *American State Archives* (1964). Cooperation of state archivists in this study took courage as the weaknesses of many state archives were exposed along with the strengths of sound programs. The chapter on "Standards for State Archival Programs," however, provided guidelines that led to several improved programs. An

---

52 *American Archivist* 34 (January 1971): 92-100.

53 *American Archivist* 22 (April 1959): 253; 22 (July 1959): 353; 200/3/3/2, 3/22-4/8.

54 *American Archivist* 26 (October 1963): 534-35; 37 (July 1974): 513; 200/1/5, 2/68. Although he was never an archivist, it is impossible to overstate Leland's contributions to the profession, which extended beyond his death with generous bequests to fund an award for publications.

Leland Prize. Phillip Brooks, right, presents the Waldo Gifford Leland Prize to Phillip Hamer for *A Guide to Archives and Manuscripts in the United States*. The presentation took place at the 1962 SAA annual meeting in Rochester, New York.

update of Posner's study is now being considered, and it is essential that the society cooperate as fully with this update as it did in the original survey. It is essential that the SAA and state archivists work in closest harmony.[55]

The dominant leadership role of state archivists began to dwindle in the 1970s, not because of a decline in talent or abilities within the group, but rather because they fell victim to demographics. The salad days of colleges and universities in the 1960s and early 1970s provided both money to support and graduates to staff archival programs in institutions of higher learning. Perhaps two-thirds of the more than 900 college and university archives listed in the 1980 *Directory of College and University Archives in the United States & Canada* had been created in the two preced-

---

55 200/11/3, Box 7 especially.

ing decades, and many of the archivists employed by them became members of SAA. The number of archival repositories in religious and business organizations also grew rapidly. In the survey of "American Archivists and Their Society," conducted by Frank B. Evans and Robert M. Warner in 1970, it was reported that of the 423 respondents, exactly one-third worked for colleges and universities while only 13.5 percent came from state government. There were almost as many college and university archivists as federal and state government archivists combined and almost as many from the business and religious fields combined as from state archives.[56]

The old cliché about real estate being a good buy because God is not making any more of it applied to state archivists. The 50 states did not increase their numbers, nor did the staff of the state archives grow enough to compete successfully with the institutional archivists for society leadership positions. The answer to Ernst Posner's question in the title of his 1956 presidential address — "What, Then, Is the American Archivist, This New Man?"[57] — had become, by 1970, "Crevecoeur, he or she is an institutional archivist."

The growth in the membership in this period challenged the leaders' traditional methods of operating the volunteer-staffed association. Twenty-one years had been required to reach the first thousand members and subscribers, but it required only a decade to reach the second thousand. Four years later, in 1971, the society had 1,000 individual members. In 1974 the new executive director reported 1,308 individual members and a total membership of 2,710, in spite of a dues increase and the deletion of many former members for nonpayment of dues. Just keeping track of this large membership required many hours of the secretary's time, leaving little time for program development.[58]

Many of the new members enrolled in the membership drives of the 1960s and 1970s were interested in archival work as a permanent career, not just as a job. This trend increased as the number of teaching positions in history declined. They turned to the society for placement services as well as for the specialized professional training provided by college programs. In 1963 SAA president Everett O. Alldredge proposed, and Council accepted his offer, to join NARS in sponsoring a series of symposia on archival administration. These one-day training sessions,

---

56 Nicholas C. Burckel and J. Frank Cook, "A Profile of College and University Archives in the United States," *American Archivist* 45 (Fall 1982): 410-12; 34 (April 1971): 162.

57 *American Archivist* 20 (January 1957): 3.

58 *American Archivist* 23 (January 1960): 95; 31 (January 1968): 113-14; 34 (January 1971): 99; 38 (January 1975): 119. This rise in membership also meant a broader geographical distribution. By 1966 the 840 U.S. members represented every state. The SAA had become a truly national association enriched even further by 66 (7 percent of the total) individual members from other nations. *American Archivist* 30 (January 1967): 216-17.

conducted largely by NARS regional offices, provided low-cost educational opportunities for new archivists and their more experienced colleagues to discuss problems, hear papers, and participate in panel discussions at both the beginning and advanced levels.[59]

Not all the educational needs of the profession could be provided through such symposia, and the Education and Training Committee in 1965 arranged for a two-week archival training course at Columbia University. As other institutes were offered, Council took up the issues of society sponsorship and certification of courses. The profession considered the various facets of the training of archivists: formal academic courses, institutes, library school training, and archival apprenticeships. The lack of standards made it very difficult, then as well as now, to develop a sound, comprehensive program of archival education and training.[60]

Development of archival education and training programs depended, as did almost every society activity, on the efforts of committee members scattered over the country, unable to meet except at annual meetings, forced to conduct business by mail and telephone, and with no staff support except within their own institutions. Results were often less than satisfactory. Members appointed to committees heard nothing from their chairmen, and many energetic members soon learned that little was expected of them except advice on a session topic for the next annual meeting. By the end of the 1960s, the committee system had reached the point that F. Gerald Ham, as secretary, prepared a report on the strengths and weaknesses of the system. He found that some committees, especially those on institutional archives, had been very busy. The business archives and college and university archives committees had prepared directories, the church archives committee had completed "A Preliminary Guide to Religious Archives" and had begun work on a manual, and the Committee on Archival Buildings and Equipment was ready to bring out its reader on archives and records center buildings. Other committees with specific charges achieved results. The Committee on Paper Research actively sought and received a large amount of out-side funding for research by the National Bureau of Standards on the permanence of archival paper and related materials.[61] Ham found that many other committees had only vague areas of responsibility or charges that no longer fully met the needs of the membership. In 1969 Council

---

59 *American Archivist* 27 (April 1964): 339-40; 27 (July 1964): 442; 29 (January 1966): 113, 125-26; 30 (January 1967): 213-25; 30 (April 1967): 349-50; 31 (January 1968): 111-12; the *American Archivist* of April 1968 was devoted almost entirely to this topic.

60 *American Archivist* 28 (July 1965): 468-69; 30 (April 1967): 383; 31 (April 1968): 135-37.

61 *American Archivist* 31 (July 1968): 324-25; 32 (January 1969): 45, 60; 33 (October 1970): 436-37; 34 (April 1971): 219-20; 34 (October 1971): 407-08; 200/3/5/1, 2/14 and 3/1-3; 200/8/1, 7/13-19.

reorganized the committee structure, eliminating and consolidating several functions and established new committees on machine-readable records, oral history, and collecting personal papers and manuscripts. This reorganization did not solve the problem of how to get committees to work, but it did make the structure more responsive to the new interests of the members. In his 1970 report, Ham pronounced the new committee organization an improvement, particularly for giving "more representation to some underrepresented segments of our profession" and dealing "more effectively with the problems of archives-manuscript administration that had not been within the purview of any of the existing committees."[62]

Problems continued to plague the committees, however. President Charles Lee, faced with Ham's 1970-71 report that "few [committees] had anything to show in the way of real accomplishment," assigned each Council member as liaison with several committees in an effort to increase efficiency and give better administrative control. Council soon abandoned this effort, and the members continued to complain, not only about how little the committees did, but also about how hard it was to be assigned to a committee in the first place. In an effort to ease these problems, Council increased the funding available to support committee activities in 1971-72 and also expanded the number of members assigned to committees.[63] All these reforms did nothing, of course, to cope with the fundamental problem of inactive committees.

As the 1960s drew to a close, however, the ferment for change in the social structure, which had swept the nation for most of the decade, reached SAA as both leaders and the general membership sought ways to democratize the society and make it more responsive to the needs of its members. A group of professionally active and socially concerned archivists at the 1971 annual meeting formed ACT, an informal organization of activist archivists, to work for changes and reforms within the society as well as to encourage it to take a position on political and social issues. A strong desire for better communication between Council and the membership came out of the 1971 membership survey. Members wanted a newsletter and wanted the *American Archivist* to be more timely and more useful to both practitioners and scholars.[64]

President Philip P. Mason, who had long been concerned with such problems during his terms as secretary, appointed an ad hoc Committee for the 1970s to "study the organizational and program needs of the Society for the coming decade." The committee, with some of the best minds in the society as members, investigated eight areas: organizational

---

62 *American Archivist* 33 (April 1970): 229; 34 (January 1971): 106.
63 *American Archivist* 35 (January 1972): 97-98, 107-8, 115; 36 (April 1973): 318-19.
64 200/3/6/1, 1/6-8; 200/8/1, 1/1-8.

structure and operations; relations with other professional groups and organizations; the committee system; research and publications; membership relations and development; education and training; annual meetings, conferences, and symposia; and finances. A blitz of questionnaires in which members were queried about every facet of their professional lives led Ham to proclaim 1970 as "the year of the questionnaire in the Society's annals." Of all the many contributions of Mason and Ham to the society, few have been as fundamentally important as this committee. Failures of earlier long-range planning committees to produce a comprehensive plan were redeemed by this committee's report, which permanently altered the society and its operations.[65]

The Committee for the 1970s issued its final report in the spring of 1972. Among its major recommendations were: to hire an executive director and raise the dues and fees to pay for the post; to present a dual slate of nominees for elective office; to establish a close working relationship with the regional archival groups; to open up committee membership; to expand the publications program; to encourage the preparation of guidelines and standards for education and training; and to urge that the annual meeting programs include sessions for all levels of archivists and that provisions be made for younger, newer members to participate in program sessions. Finally, "social relevance" received attention when the committee suggested that "SAA should be actively committed to the social goals of racial justice, equal employment, and reasonable access to research materials. . . . To this end, the SAA has a moral obligation to take official positions on those contemporary public issues, however controversial, which affect the archival profession."[66]

Council made only minor modifications to the committee recommendations; and though their response was more moderate, perhaps reflecting their fiduciary responsibilities, the leadership was committed to the new order brought about by these reforms. President Wilfred I. Smith established a Committee on the Status of Women and urged the recruitment of minorities into both the profession and the society. The membership responded in 1973 with a hearty endorsement of a comprehensive resolution to eliminate discrimination within the society on the basis of "race, color, religion, national origin, sex, marital status, age, life style, or political affiliation." Also at that 1973 business meeting, the membership quickly and easily adjusted to the new democratic procedures in spite of the previous year's experience with runoff elections and interminable counting of ballots. Council responded favorably to a petition from 17 members that those attending the business meeting,

---

65 *American Archivist* 35 (January 1972): 106; 34 (January 1971): 89.

66 Philip P. Mason, "The Society of American Archivists in the Seventies: Report of the Committee for the 1970s," *American Archivist* 35 (April 1972): 193-217; 200/8/1, 172.

rather than Council itself, conduct the election for two vacant Council seats. One of those elected in that last election not conducted by mail, Ann Morgan Campbell, served just one year on Council before accepting another prominent position in the society.[67]

Of most importance to the future development of the society, the members in 1973 committed themselves to a dues structure that would finance the executive directorship. From the mid-1960s Council returned again and again to the question of whether or not funding could be found to support such a position. Foundations would not support an ongoing administrative expense, and requests for voluntary contributions from SAA members raised only a few thousand dollars. Though clerical assistance was eventually hired, a paid professional position continued to elude the society. The crushing nature of the secretary's job is demonstrated by the increasingly shorter terms served by Renze's successors. "The difficulty clearly and simply is one of resources. We are no longer small enough to operate the Society by volunteer help; we are not large enough to finance a paid staff from membership dues," warned Secretary Mason in 1968 and again as chair of the Committee for the 1970s. He placed prime importance on solving this financial problem. The society's income had increased tenfold from 1957 to 1973, but even a budget of $79,000 produced a surplus of only $3,000. Reserves had likewise increased to more than $100,000, but restrictions on the use of the principal of these funds made a paid secretariat a hopeless dream until the members agreed to tax themselves heavily enough to fund the position.[68]

After a year as secretary, Robert M. Warner agreed in 1972 to serve an additional year as the appointed (but unpaid) executive director, replacing the elected secretary under a new constitutional amendment. Council had not endorsed this amendment, proposed by the Committee for the 1970s, not because it did not desperately want such a position, but only because the resources to support it were not in sight. The membership gave its approval, however, by the required two-thirds vote in 1972 and voted the necessary dues a year later. Thus the way was finally clear to hire a professional executive director. Finances remained unstable. Judy Koucky was hired as acting secretary for a few months, and Council encountered difficulties in finding a suitable director. Finally, Ann Morgan Campbell was hired in July 1974 and an office was established on the Chicago Circle campus of the University of Illinois.[69]

---

67 *American Archivist* 36 (April 1973): 315-16, 321; 36 (October 1973): 627; 35 (July 1972): 359-66; 36 (January 1973): 133-35; 36 (April 1973): 305-6, 310-12.

68 *American Archivist* 28 (July 1965): 467; 30 (October 1967): 598; 30 (January 1967): 217-18; 31 (January 1968): 114-16; 33 (January 1970): 123; 29 (July 1966): 448; Mason quotation from *American Archivist* 32 (January 1969): 63; 21 (January 1958): 105-06; 38 (January 1974): 121-23.

69 *American Archivist* 36 (April 1973): 236; 36 (January 1973): 138-39; 37 (January 1974): 165-69.

That is another story for another time. This story ends in 1974 with the Society of American Archivists poised on the threshold of becoming a truly professional association. Problems such as inadequate archival education and training, few professional standards or guidelines, a less than comprehensive publications program, and tensions between the various segments of the profession did not disappear with the hiring of an executive director; but those active in the society in the early 1970s knew fundamental changes were being made. In the 1950s the Council of Learned Societies rejected our application for membership on the grounds that we were a custodial, rather than a learned, profession. That rejection hurt our pride; yet, if not a learned society in the view of some, we knew by 1974 that we had the capacity to be far more than mere custodians of dusty records. Our role in preserving, protecting, and providing access to all forms of information is vital to all professions, all peoples. We knew by the 1970s that we had to build the kind of professional association that would be equal to this task.[70]

SAA presidents addressed the challenge of the professionalization of the association in this period. Mason saw SAA "at the crossroads" in 1970, Smith pointed out the "broad horizons" and the "opportunities for archivists" in 1973; and Ham in 1974 saw us on "the archival edge" of a bright future if we would face this challenge. We have met this challenge, not perfectly and in many ways not adequately; but our profession has an association in which we can take much pride, not only in its past accomplishments, but also in the sure and certain hope of future contributions.[71]

I am compelled here to recall the words of A. R. Newsome, our first president, in his 1937 address. Thinking back to the organizational meeting in Providence, he concluded with the observation and prayer: "A hospitable Providence was the place of the Society's birth. May a kindly Providence bless and immortalize its career."[72]

---

70 Herman Kahn, "Some Comments on the Archival Vocation," *American Archivist* 34 (January 1971): 3-12.

71 Philip P. Mason, "The Society of American Archivists at the Crossroads," *American Archivist* 35 (January 1972): 5-11; Wilfred I. Smith, "Broad Horizons: Opportunities for Archivists," *American Archivist* 37 (January 1974): 3-14; F. Gerald Ham, "The Archival Edge," *American Archivist* 38 (January 1975): 5-13.

72 A. R. Newsome, "Objectives of the Society of American Archivists," *American Archivist* 26 (January 1963): 299-304; *Proceedings*, 64.

Part Three:
Selection and Documentation

One of the critical functions of archives is to determine which records are necessary to fulfill legal, administrative, and cultural requirements for documenting organizations and individuals. Within organizations this archival process is often closely related to records management. Given the nature of modern societies and the voluminous records they produce, archives can not save everything that might conceivably interest future researchers. The selection of records for archival preservation necessarily means that other records will not be preserved, and the documentation of certain aspects of society means that others will not be fully documented.

Timothy L. Ericson considers the implications of these concerns for archival selection in "At the 'rim of creative dissatisfaction': Archivists and Acquisition Development." He challenges archivists to consider fundamental changes in their acquisition processes — and in their thinking about selecting records for preservation.

One of the most creative approaches to archival acquisition has been the concept of documentation strategies, first proposed by Helen Willa Samuels, in "Who Controls the Past." Documentation strategies challenge archivists to move beyond their institutional walls and to examine the sources for documenting broad aspects of society that come from many institutions. In "The Documentation Strategy and Archival Appraisal Principles: A Different Perspective," Richard J. Cox, one of the early proponents of this approach, considers how the concept had evolved after nearly a decade and how it relates to archival appraisal. Although criticized as unworkable, the concept of documentation strategies provides an instructive challenge to archivists weighing decisions about records selection and documentation of society. At the very least it encourages us to consider archival records as one part of the larger universe of information.

8

At the "rim of creative dissatisfaction": Archivists and Acquisition Development

TIMOTHY L. ERICSON

Abstract: Archivists collecting private records have struggled, as traditional thinking about appraisal and acquisition development has confronted the extraordinary volume and increasing technological complexity of contemporary records. Archivists are accessioning too many records that, while they may fall within the repository's collecting parameters, simply do not contain important information. Too often archivists have equated preservation with possession, leading to competition, or have not adequately conceptualized why we are saving the records we have chosen to acquire. Acquisition policies must be reconsidered, to include more specific defini-tions of whatever phenomena we are hoping to document. Archival collecting policies must be both interdisciplinary and more cooperative, if they are to be effective. Cooperating with other archivists and with allied professionals, as well as users, will help us make better acquisition decisions, avoid unnecessary duplication, and enable others to use what we have selected.

In the prologue to his 1987 book of essays entitled *Hidden History: Exploring Our Secret Past*, historian Daniel Boorstin writes that in the New World, "creativity has flourished" on something he terms "the Fertile Verge." Boorstin defines a verge as simply "a place of encounter between something and something else." He explains:

> The long Atlantic Coast, where early colonial settlements flour-ished, was, of course, a verge between land and sea. Every move-ment inward into the continent was a verge between . . . European civilization and the . . . culture of the American Indians. As cities became sprinkled around the continent, each was a verge between the ways of the city and those of the countryside.[1]

Boorstin contends that each new verge in our history brought with it challenges and an array of "new mixtures, and new confusions." He

---

Reprinted with permission; from *Archivaria* 33 (Winter 1991-92): 66-77. Abstract added for this volume by the editor.

1 Daniel J. Boorstin, *Hidden History: Exploring Our Secret Past* (New York: Vintage Books, 1987), xiii.

concludes that it was these that brought European emigrants to the "rim of creative dissatisfaction" where creativity flourished, and gave them the ability to adopt new ideas, and solve old problems in new ways.[2]

Archivists whose responsibilities include collecting private records are struggling at a verge today. It is the place of encounter at which our traditional thinking regarding appraisal and acquisition development has confronted the extraordinary volume and increasing technological complexity of contemporary records. We have been stalled at this verge for many years, and only a heightened sense of creative dissatisfaction will enable us effectively to fulfill our mission of making records of enduring value available for use through acquisition, arrangement and description, and preservation.

More than a half century has passed since our first glimpse of how twentieth-century record-keeping practices were pushing us into a new era. In 1937, when Sir Hilary Jenkinson was revising his *Manual of Archive Administration,* he recalled that the original edition had raised "at least one new question in Archive Science; one which has been little considered prior to that time." The question was that of quantity; the harbinger that Jenkinson had seen in 1922 was the "impossibly bulky" holdings of records that had been amassed during the First World War. Fifteen years later, Jenkinson had become even more concerned with preserving the "archives of the future" than he had been in 1922, and he observed that "the post-War years have only served to emphasize [the problem of bulk]."[3] In the past, he wrote, "we have assumed that the Archivist had always space to house [records] and that consequently the question of whether or not Archives were to be preserved at all did not arise."[4] "There is a real danger," he concluded, "that the Historian of the future, not to mention the Archivist, may be buried under the mass of manuscript[s]"[5] and "that in the future research work [in] Archives may become a task hopelessly complicated by reason of their mere bulk."[6]

At the same time as Jenkinson was writing, others, on both sides of the Atlantic, were echoing similar concerns. H. G. T. Christopher, in his 1938 monograph *Paleography and Archives,* observed, "in recent years [records] have been bulky and generally no attempt has been made at selection, and the archive repository is faced with either taking over a collection which would use more space than its probable value merited,

---

2   Ibid., xiv, xxv.

3   Hilary Jenkinson, *A Manual of Archive Administration: New and Revised Edition* (London: Percy, Lund, Humphries and Co., 1937), 21.

4   Ibid., 136.

5   Ibid., 138.

6   Ibid., 148-49.

or of selecting material."[7] A manuscript curator in the United States, analysing local historical societies, noted how "the acceptance of what happened fortuitously to be available has . . . been one of the chief causes of the accumulation of disparate, disorganized, masses of manuscripts," and concluded, "There is little virtue in mere acquisition if it is divorced from intelligent purpose."[8]

Since Jenkinson's time, the archival profession has become more accustomed to the need for selection. Succeeding generations of archivists, such as Philip C. Brooks, Herman Kahn, and especially Theodore Schellenberg, articulated a series of values in an effort to guide archivists through the decision-making process.[9] However, much of the appraisal theory they developed was conceived within the context of a single institution seeking to preserve its own records. Their appraisal guidelines were designed to provide archivists with a yardstick against which to measure individual record groups and series. Nevertheless, their seminal work has proven beneficial to all archivists, whether we work in an institutional or a public archives. In either instance the fundamentals of appraisal drive our selection process; archivists try to make decisions on the basis of the archival values that Schellenberg and others have articulated. Yet there has always seemed to be a gap between pure appraisal theory and how this theory applies more broadly to acquisition development, even though the problem of bulk is present in both instances. It is relatively straightforward to apply evidential and informational values in the micro sense to a single fonds or records series; it is more complex to apply these same values at the macro level to a repository full of public and private archives. To do so, archivists must go beyond simply identifying venerable archival values; we need to define better the context in which we should apply them.

In his article on deaccessioning archival materials, Leonard Rapport stated the problem precisely when he observed that:

> Schellenberg did not advocate accessioning records just because they were evidential or informational. He was aware that there was not a record created that is totally devoid of such values, however minute. These values had to be important values, and it is against this adjective that we collide and sometimes founder.[10]

---

7 H. G. T. Christopher, *Palaeography and Archives* (London, 1938).

8 Julian P. Boyd, "The Function of State and Local Historical Societies with Respect to Manuscripts," *Archives & Libraries* (Chicago, 1940), 129.

9 Nancy E. Peace, "Deciding What to Save: Fifty Years of Theory and Practice," *Archival Choices: Managing the Historical Record in an Age of Abundance* (Lanham, Md.: Lexington Books, 1984), 1-18.

10 Leonard Rapport, "No Grandfather Clause: Deaccessioning Archival Materials," *American Archivist* 44 (Spring 1981): 147.

The fact that Schellenberg and the others chose to use the word *value* is unfortunate, because they were really talking about evidential and informational *content.* But by using the term *value,* they implied to succeeding generations of archivists that whatever was evidential or informational was valuable and should be saved. Done properly, appraisal comprises several activities, but conceptually it should always include two important steps. In determining whether or not to acquire a set of records, archivists should first decide whether or not the records themselves contain evidential or informational content. But having done so we must then pause to ask, "So what?" The final decision regarding whether to acquire an individual fonds must be made with an eye on the larger universe that is defined by broader acquisition development policies. Stated another way, the principles of appraisal help us to answer the question, "*Why* am I saving this?"— while acquisition policies force us to answer the equally important question, "Why am *I* saving this?"

Unfortunately, while appraisal theory has developed over the years, ideas regarding acquisition policies have lagged behind. Much of our early literature on acquisition development was written by manuscript curators, whose perspective was heavily influenced by the assumptions of the age of scarcity. Policies were based on a presumption of competition, wherein the few prizes worth collecting were worth fighting for. They were written for a world in which it was important to mark one's territory: a world in which, as the director of a midwestern state historical society once stated, "Cooperation in collecting is synonymous with abdication."[11]

Such literature has been thin gruel for those interested in developing acquisition policies equipped to serve the needs of contemporary archival repositories. We have all read about the importance of imposing linguistic, geographical or chronological constraints on our acquisitions.[12] Our literature reminds us to include a statement of the archives' legal authority, and its mission."[13] We have been told to consider the type of programs that our archives supports, and the clientele whom it serves. We know to include collecting levels, present strengths, and circumstances under which materials may be deaccessioned.[14] As a result, we can wax eloquent on the need for well-defined policies; we can articulate beautifully crafted statements of lofty purpose, mission and goals. In the same way, we have learned that acquisition policies are suitable occasions

---

11 F. Gerald Ham, "Documenting Our Times," unpublished paper read before the Midwest Archives Conference, Columbia, Missouri, 16 October 1987, 1.

12 Robert L. Clark, Jr., *Archive-Library Relations* (New York, 1976), 125.

13 Canadian Council of Archives, *Guidelines for Developing an Acquisition Policy* (Ottawa, 1990), 1-3.

14 Faye Phillips, "Developing Collecting Policies for Manuscript Collections," *American Archivist* 47, (Winter 1984): 31-42. This article also contains a useful review of American literature dealing with acquisition policies.

for self-congratulation on our past successes, such as "The Society is justly proud of its reputation as a nationally important research institution
[and] . . . [a]ny reconsideration of Society collecting must rest on [this]
secure foundation."[15] But these observations do not attack the root of the
problem, which is similar to that which Rapport described vis-à-vis
Schellenberg's values: we are accessioning too many fonds that, while
they may fall within our geographical, chronological, and linguistic
parameters, simply do not contain important information.

For many of us, such acquisition policies — written more to legitimize collecting activity than to focus it — have not been able to save us
from ourselves. Most such policies have been conceived in dual isolation —
as though archival records were the only source of information that
archivists need to consider, and by pretending that other archival repositories did not exist. The results of this predilection to "go it alone" have
been unfortunate. Because similar information can be found in many different formats, acquisition decisions that are based on what is contained
only in other archival records are inadequate. In the same way, acquisition policies that fail to consider what information may be contained in
other types of documentation leave themselves open to simply perpetuat-
ing the same frustrating gaps and wasteful duplication that now characterize many archival collections.

By ignoring other repositories — both archival and non-archival —
with similar missions, we have tended to equate preservation with possession; as one writer phrased it, "some institutions regard manuscript collecting as a branch of intercollegiate athletics and vigorously strive to
beat the competition."[16] Many of us cling to the notion that it is both
possible and desirable to bring together under one roof all the documentation dealing with a particular subject. The idea is not far removed from
our professional ancestors of the last century, who assumed that it was
possible to bring together all the important documentation on a given
topic between the covers of a series of books. We are trying to accomplish
the same type of goal as Ebenezer Hazard, whose ill-fated monographic
series, "American State Papers," was to have included "every important
paper relating to America, of which either the original, or authentic
copies can be obtained."[17] The goal was not viable during the age of
scarcity, and it is less so today both because of the quantity and what has
been termed the "integration of modern information."[18] Just as Hazard

---

15 "Manuscript Collecting Policy for the State Historical Society of Wisconsin," (c. 1974), 1. This
    policy was replaced in 1988.

16 Walter Rundell, Jr., "To Serve Scholarship," *American Archivist* 30 (October 1967): 56.

17 Donald R. McNeil, ed., *The American Collector* (Madison, Wisc.: University of Wisconsin Press,
    1955), 2.

18 Helen W. Samuels, "Who Controls the Past," *American Archivist* 46 (Spring 1986): 111-12.

failed in the previous century, so too shall we if we cling to our antiquated assumptions.

This was one of the points of conflict in the debate about "total archives," which has as one of its dimensions "total" defined in terms of medium.[19] Whether or not it is true, as some contend, that "the separation of archival records by medium caused archivists to lose their perspective on why they are saving the records in the first place," it is unfortunate that some archivists thought it was *they* who needed to be responsible for preserving those abstract paintings set in Mexico and Peru, or the "costume collection containing examples of Greek, Roman, and even primitive caveman's garb."[20] While it is important for the archivist to *know about* and appreciate such resources and the information they contain — it is not necessary for archivists to *possess* them.[21] In such instances, archivists would be best advised to develop better cooperative links with their colleagues in the museum and library communities than to shoulder the burden of preserving every medium of expression ourselves.

But our instinct is still to see ourselves in the role of a twentieth-century Horatius-at-the-Bridge: the last line of defense between preservation and oblivion. This causes us to make utterly ludicrous decisions regarding acquisition by cloaking ourselves in the virtue of maintaining culture: if I don't save it, who will? At a 1987 conference, one archivist explained proudly how he had been offered a collection of risqué comic books. Although neither he nor his repository had even the slightest previous interest in risqué comic books (at least none to which he would admit), he promptly added them to the holdings so that they would be saved. Apparently it never even occurred to him that he might look elsewhere before unwittingly opening another collecting area for his institution. But decisions such as his are being made by archivists every day. Our intentions are good, but we contribute to the problem rather than ameliorate it. We need, in other words, to ponder more fully those accounts that report poor Horatius's demise despite his heroics!

But our most serious failing is that we have not taken the time to conceptualize adequately why we are saving the records that we have chosen to acquire. At times our attitude toward acquisition development seems to have been drawn from that passage in *Alice's Adventures in Wonderland,* in which Alice asks the Cheshire Cat for directions:

> "Cheshire Puss," [Alice] began . . . "Would you tell me please which way I ought to walk from here?"

---

19 Terry Cook, "The Tyranny of the Medium: A Comment on 'Total Archives'," *Archivaria* 9 (Winter 1979-80): 141-42.

20 Ibid., 143.

21 Terry Cook, "Media Myopia," *Archivaria* 12 (Summer 1981): 146-56.

"That depends a good deal on where you want to get to," said the Cat. "But I don't much care — as long as I get somewhere," Alice added. "Oh you're sure to do that," said the Cat, "if only you walk long enough."[22]

We think we shall "get somewhere," as long as we collect enough. Archivists have yet to act meaningfully upon F. Gerald Ham's simple precept, from "The Archival Edge," that "conceptualization must precede collection."[23] We are still slaves to *form-based* rather than *information-based* methodologies that guide our efforts. In our minds we have been collecting records as *physical objects* when we ought to have been collecting records for the *information* they contain. We want to document religion, so we collect church records; we want to document organized labor, so we collect trade-union records. As a result, we have lulled ourselves into believing that we are documenting particular subjects well simply because we have many related objects to show for our efforts. Ours is not unlike the situation that a critic of museum collecting once described:

> every museum of any size possesses . . . great quantities, of material which it cannot hope to display and . . . duplicates of items already on exhibition. [One museum] has, for example, more than two hundred eighteenth-century pottery milk-jugs, in the form of a cow. They ranged side by side on a shelf . . . like some huge herd on a farm. This is investment banking, not museology.[24]

The archival community has its own cow-shaped milk jugs. In the United States, one state historical society conducted a detailed analysis of its manuscript holdings in 1986. When it examined the topic of religion — a supposed area of strength — there were many fonds of church records to count. But despite the large numbers that had been amassed, it quickly became clear that decades of labor had documented, in fact, only a narrow spectrum of sacramental activity in a few principal Protestant denominations. There was precious little to offer beyond the names and dates that the genealogists covet. This may not have been investment banking as the museum critic defined it, but neither was it the result of thoughtful acquisition decisions.

Is it any wonder that our collections have too much information about some aspects of these subjects and not enough about others? By reading our annual reports it will become clear that many still equate the *size* of a repository's holdings and the breadth of its collecting focus with the *quality* of its program. Many annual reports citing acquisitions habit-

---

22 Lewis Carroll, *Alice's Adventures in Wonderland* (London, n.d.), 89-90.

23 F. Gerald Ham, "The Archival Edge," *American Archivist* 38 (January 1975): 12.

24 Kenneth Hudson, *Museums for the 1980s: A Survey of World Trends* (New York: MacMillan, 1977), 25.

ually express themselves in terms of volume of information rather than in terms of knowledge.

We acquire donations of dubious value simply because we do not take the time to think carefully about why we are accepting them in the first place. We seem to have the same aversion to thoughtful or difficult decision making that Jenkinson saw in records creators who saved multiple copies of individual documents, simply because it was easier to do so than to make a decision based on the importance of the document![25] So it is with archivists and acquisitions. Because our acquisition policies lack sufficient specificity, we save records for the wrong reasons. One U.S. writer admitted that "it seems preferable to [retain] noncurrent records in the basement, attic, or elsewhere than to risk public outcry at the disposal of such records."[26] In other instances we manage to convince ourselves that some researcher, some day, somehow, might find the records useful in a "study" of some sort. *Whether* the studies we conjure up already have been done, *why* someone might do them in the first place, or *who* would care, are irrelevant. In either case we are hostages to perceived or imagined need; thus, it is easier to accept marginal records from the abundant harvest than it is simply to refuse them.

Those who have responded to the need for change find themselves immobilized by the traditions that have preceded them. They become stuck in the mire of generality when it comes time to indicate in meaningful terms what it is they want to document. Many acquisition policies of the past two decades announce a commitment to documenting the lives of "ordinary people" or the "common man," without ever bothering really to define what constitutes "common" or "ordinary." We speak in phrases such as "capturing the general fabric of experiences," or capturing a "microcosm or representative sample of human activity." We report how we are "documenting the . . . experience in the community." Such statements sound good, or are useful as constructs that differentiate past from present practice, but alone they are insufficient as guidelines.

The impact of our vagueness has been marked. Much conventional wisdom in regarding both appraisal and acquisition development exists in the form of lists naming the types of objects we want, rather than as a more thoughtful analysis describing the type of information we want from what we collect or how to identify this information in the records

---

25 Jenkinson, *A Manual of Archive Administration*, 137. Jenkinson noted: "to think whether a copy of a letter is worth making is a troublesome matter. In old days, to make the copy was even more trouble and therefore the thinking was done: but now when . . . it has become a mechanical, not an intellectual, task, the natural tendency is to avoid the painful process of thought; why exert oneself to decide whether four copies of a letter, or any copy at all, are necessary when the labour is only that of putting five sheets instead of one into a machine?"

26 Lisa B. Weber, ed., *Documenting America: Assessing the Condition of Historical Records in the States* (New York: National Association of State Archives and Administrators, 1984), 94.

that we collect. A typical acquisition policy begins by enumerating the types of objects (personal papers, letters, diaries, corporate records) we wish to collect. These are objects, not information. Even our descriptive practices have succumbed. We do not, as too many archival finding aids suggest, collect correspondence, annual reports, or photographs. We collect information that happens to be preserved in these particular forms. Too often the result is as one archivist wrote:

> There have been no stated and few apparent restrictions on . . . material[s] that are admitted except that they must relate to one of [24 ethnic] groups, be two-dimensional records rather than three-dimensional objects, and 'deal with the causes of emigration . . ., the actual processes of migration, or the experience of immigrants and their descendants.' Every kind of personal paper, organizational record, and imprint has been considered desirable so long as it meets these criteria.[27]

We also have been seduced by our own siren's song of uniqueness. We forget that while the actual *objects* that we collect — the diaries and the soldiers' letters — may be unique, the *information* they contain may be neither unique nor even important. We have convinced ourselves that "since everything [we] collect is, in theory at least, unique, there is no such thing as building a foundation on the basic classics." But the point is that we *do* need to build such a foundation — it must be one that is composed of information rather than lists of record types.[28] Furthermore, it is a foundation that is built upon a knowledge of the issues, functions, or events relating to the topic we wish to document.

We archivists have paid a high price for our actions and continue to do so every day. We waste precious resources. Every moment spent dealing with marginal or plainly inappropriate material prevents us from working around our troublesome verge. We must process and shelve those marginal fonds, and all the resources spent doing so are lost to other activities more worthwhile. In this way, our backlog becomes larger and our shelves fuller. Our preservation dollars do not go so far as they might. Whenever we accept fonds that might be better housed elsewhere, we isolate the documents both intellectually and physically by placing them in a locale where they will be less well known or used than elsewhere, such as the archives in Wisconsin that had as one of its holdings an inventory of a sixteenth-century Spanish Indian mission in Sonora, Mexico, the repository's only other holding that was even remotely associated with the mission being the records of the local university's Spanish Club!

---

27 Susan Grigg, "A World of Repositories, A World of Records: Redefining the Scope of a National Collection," *American Archivist* 48 (Summer 1985): 289.

28 Clark, *Archive-Library Relations*, 125.

But perhaps most regrettably we confuse those who would understand us, and thus remain aground on the shoals of our public image — as society's "attic" or "dusty shelves." Ultimately, we relegate research materials to an oblivion that is almost as final as destruction itself. What researchers frequently find reminds one of Arthur J. Balfour's comment on looking through Winston Churchill's voluminous scrapbooks: it was like "rummaging through a rubbish heap on the problematic chance of finding a cigar butt."[29]

We can do better. Allowing that much of our previous thinking about acquisition policies is a good beginning, it is time to move beyond our present verge by focusing the power of our creative dissatisfaction on drafting policies that will better serve our needs in the age of abundance.

As a first step, we must move beyond the unconscious assumptions of the age of scarcity that still distort our thinking. Most of our current acquisition policies are too broadly conceived to be realistic in the Information Age. In the age of scarcity, it may have been possible to cast a broader net with respect to geographical and topical coverage, but now we must look with a skeptical eye at the grandiose goals that such policies declared. We can no longer be satisfied with such things as "The Society's . . . collections encompass materials from [the state], the [region], and the nation — as well as Canada — and cover a time span from the eighteenth century to the present."[30] Just as our professional forebears began to use appraisal to help limit their intake of records at the fonds level, so must we begin to use acquisition policies to limit our intake at the repository level. Given that we are awash with records, it should be clear that those statements, written decades earlier, and the goals they reflected, need to be scaled down. In certain respects those old statements are like the "gas guzzler" automobiles we have been forced to abandon. Like cars that gave nine miles to the gallon, broadly based, all-inclusive collecting policies were designed for a different era and based on assumptions that are no longer true. It is no longer realistic, as one archival repository has done, to demarcate territory that encompasses the history and development of all ethnic groups in America. How can we even argue that it is possible for a regional archives to "document" comprehensively a particular geographical area — no matter how small — when one good-sized accession of business records would fill its shelves and occupy the attention of its staff into the next millennium? Archivists need to take a more realistic view of what we can actually hope to preserve.

Just as we must reduce our overall goals, we must learn to become more selective in choosing individual fonds to add to our holdings.

---

29 William Manchester, *The Last Lion: Winston Spencer Churchill; Visions of Glory:* 1874-1932 (New York: Little Brown Company, 1983), 375.

30 "Manuscripts Collecting Policy for the State Historical Society of Wisconsin," 1.

Acquisition policies can be the cornerstone of this effort. In certain respects, the role of an acquisition policy is not to tell us what to collect; its real function is to delineate what we shall *consider* acquiring — an important distinction that we can use to good advantage. Policies build upon the fundamental ideas of archival value that have guided archivists for decades, but they add another dimension to the decision-making process. They pick up where evidential and informational values leave off and should be used as frequently to refuse potential acquisitions, or refer them to a more appropriate repository, as to accept them.

To this end, our new acquisition policies should be written so that they can serve both an external and an internal purpose. Most of our earlier efforts, ordinarily compressed into a succinct page or two of brilliantly crafted prose, are useful only externally, as a brief introduction for laypersons and potential donors. But even though sweeping generalities such as, "It is the general policy of the . . . Society to interest itself in all material generated by or pertaining to the citizens of . . . [the] county"[31] may help in this way, they hinder us as well because, to the same potential donors, they seemingly exclude nothing. In an environment in which there are many records from which to choose, and so much duplication of information, they lack the precision we need in order to make intelligent decisions about acquiring a particular fonds.

Guidance in such decision making is the internal purpose of a contemporary acquisition policy. However, it can be served only if the policy takes us beyond the generalities that the layperson can easily digest. We must have specificity to guide us when we are considering whether or not to accept an individual fonds and this can be achieved only if we take the time to define the local parameters against which we measure our traditional archival values.

To accomplish this, an acquisition policy should define not only the geographical or linguistic limits of our collecting focus and all the rest, it must also include a more specific definition and analysis of whatever phenomena we are hoping to document. To "document society in all its multiplicity and to transmit to posterity a manageable amount of records" is a broad mandate more easily stated than accomplished — even if it is defined within a narrow geographical or chronological context.[32] For most archivists, more specific instructions will be helpful. Actually to *do* the conceptualizing required is a painstaking, slow, and difficult process; it is not something that can be done in an afternoon of spontaneous discussion. Still, it must be done.

---

31 "A Preliminary General Collecting Policy Statement of the Milwaukee County Historical Society," 15 May 1979.

32 Peace, "Deciding What to Save," 11. Richard J. Cox, "A Documentation Strategy Case Study: Western New York," *American Archivist* 52 (Spring 1989): 195.

There are several models available to help with various aspects of this work. The SAMDOK project, wherein a group of Swedish museums initiated a cooperative program better to document contemporary life in that country, is frequently cited as a premier example of inter-institutional cooperation. But in many respects its real significance, indeed that which is probably responsible for whatever success it enjoyed, is that the participants first took the time to conceptualize what it was they wanted to document in contemporary Swedish life in any case.[33] In a similar way, oral historians have long accepted the need for extensive research — including a "careful examination of [their] institution's existing holdings" — prior to conducting an interview.[34] Because they recognize this, oral historians are comparatively skilled at articulating the issues about which they want to collect information.[35] If oral historians can undertake exhaustive research for a single interview, then so can archivists before they agree to accept another 100 cubic metres of records.

There is also the documentation strategy framework. Whether or not one accepts fully this construct, its emphasis upon cooperation should be reflected in any acquisition policy. For example, the documentation strategy recognizes that, for a variety of reasons, all information pertaining to a specific topic cannot be housed within a single institution. It actively involves archivists, museum curators, librarians, and records managers, along with records users and records creators (or depositors), to ensure that important documentation is not lost. In attempting to arrive at a strategy for documenting a particular topic, it considers the entire range of informational resources, rather than only those that are archival. It demands that we associate more closely the information we want with the records we propose to acquire.[36]

Having achieved a better overall understanding of the important issues or phenomena we want to document, we must then consider which archival sources will provide the information we need. It is tempting to oversimplify this process by simply posing the question, "What shall we collect?" But in looking at records creators, we should consider what portion of the information contained in the archival record is actually

---

33 *Museums for a New Century*, 37. See also "Collecting for Tomorrow: Sweden's Contemporary Documentation Program," 55-60.

34 "Filling the Gap," 151.

35 The following exemplifies the care with which one interviewer formulated documentation objectives for an interview dealing with labor history: "What were the worker's relationships to authority and how did this change? What was the role of leadership and to what extent did the leaders act or seem to act independently of their followers? How did the various groups of workers [understand] their struggle for power, and what impact did that struggle have upon their personal lives and personal outlooks?" David K. Dunaway and Willa K. Baum, *Oral History: An Interdisciplinary Approach* (Nashville, Tenn.: American Association for State and Local History, 1968), 133.

36 Samuels, "Who Controls the Past," 116-17.

unique and necessary, and what portion duplicates information that can be found in published and other types of sources. In an age when the boundaries between archival, museum, and library holdings are growing increasingly blurred, it only makes sense to build alliances with our colleagues in related professions instead of being overconcerned with marking our territory. Archivists need to base their own decisions in part on what museum curators and librarians are preserving. Archival collecting policies must be both interdisciplinary and more cooperative, if they are to be effective. In many respects we need to be more like the immigrants whom Boorstin describes in his essay, who "created new verges between their imported ways and the imported ways of their neighbours and the new-grown ways of the New World."[37] Or as a colleague working on a common descriptive cataloguing system recently wrote, "When the culture wants integrated cultural information systems, neither archives, nor museums [nor libraries] can afford to be information isolationists."[38]

Another facet of this effort to move away from information isolationism involves developing a fuller acceptance, integration, and knowledge of the non-textual media of archival documentation, such as sound/moving image and electronic records that comprise an important segment in our universe of information. Unfortunately, for many the current state of knowledge is not unlike appraising documents of which we can read only one of every five words. In the past, archivists have been unduly influenced by researchers such as the historian who wrote, "I place the highest priority on the written word as an historical source . . . nothing matches the authenticity of a letter, or the minutes of a meeting, or a page from a diary conveying 'the past.'"[39] Notwithstanding such bias on the part of some users against non-textual records, our ideas about how to document topics should be based upon the full utilization of the entire spectrum of resources that are available to us. We must better learn how to extract from non-textual records more of the information they contain rather than simply continue using them in a secondary or supporting role. We must not perpetuate the practice of some who operate with two acquisition policies: one for textual and another for non-textual (normally [photo]graphic) records. In other words, we must do what our researchers have been doing all along: bring together traditional textual archival records with audiovisual and artefactual documentation, using the mix of information thus gained to satisfy our enquiries.

Finally, we need to do what our colleagues in allied professions have been doing for decades: our acquisition policies should provide for the

---

37 Boorstin, *Hidden History: Exploring Our Secret Past*, xiv.

38 Marion Matters, "The Development of Common Descriptive Standards: Lessons from the Archival Community," *Spectra* (Summer 1990): 11.

39 Rudolph J. Vecoli, "'Diamonds in Your Own Backyard': Developing Documentation on European Immigrants to North America," *Ethnic Forum* 1 (September 1981): 2.

inter-institutional communication of holdings. The idea of lending materials is not new in the library community, and museums have been lending extremely valuable, unique works of art for years. But archivists have not moved beyond occasionally lending individual documents for exhibition purposes. For some reason, the concept of expanding this idea of lending entire fonds for *research* purposes remains revolutionary and controversial — some would even say heretical.

Nevertheless, the profession's limited experience with this concept shows that it can be used to good effect. Since 1962, the State Historical Society of Wisconsin has administered a statewide Area Research Center (ARC) network of regional archival repositories that permits the temporary transfer of original public and private archival fonds among network centres.[40] The benefits have been considerable. During the past 30 years, more than 10,000 inter-archives loan transactions have taken place within the network, for the benefit of thousands of researchers who otherwise would not have had the opportunity to use archival materials. No holdings have been lost due to transfer, and the possibility of borrowing archival materials from other network repositories has decreased competition among centres dramatically. Given the fact that there is far too much to collect, it has served everyone's purpose to carve out a smaller piece of the pie. Although, as archivists have recognized for decades, cooperation will not solve every dispute that arises from competing collecting interests, in Wisconsin, sharing has alleviated the need for archivists in the ARC network to feel as though they must collect everything themselves.[41]

In concluding "The Fertile Verge," Boorstin attributes to North Americans "three characteristic ways of thinking and feeling" that historically have helped to solve old problems in new ways. First has been a certain "self-awareness" that caused us to "notice more poignantly who we are, how we are thinking, and what we are doing."[42] Just as our ancestors needed to adapt the customs and beliefs of the Old World to the realities of the North American frontier, so too must we as archivists adapt our current professional practice to the realities of the Information Age. It is no longer possible to document the same breadth of topics by saving the same records in the same way as our professional forebears did at the time of the First World War. Self-awareness should extend broadly to understanding the full implications of changes that have taken place both in the nature and the extent of the documentary record. Within individual repositories,

---

40 For further information, see Richard A. Erney and F. Gerald Ham, "Wisconsin's Area Research Centers," *American Libraries* 3 (February 1972): 135-40; "Survey of Archival Networks," *Midwestern Archivist* VI, no. 2 (1982): 120-23; Timothy L. Ericson, "Sharing the Wealth," *MRRC News* 2 (May 1980): 1-4.

41 W. Kaye Lamb et al., "Acquisitions Policy: Competition or Cooperation?" *Canadian Archivist* 2, no. 1 (1970): 21-22.

42 Boorstin, *Hidden History: Exploring Our Secret Past*, xv.

self-awareness should also include achieving clearer understanding of the phenomena that the archives is attempting to document.

The second characteristic Boorstin ascribes to North Americans is a "special openness to novelty and change" that has enabled us to accept new ideas and whetted our appetite "for novelty and its charms."[43] Archivists must adjust to the changes brought about by new documentary media and develop the skills necessary in order better to utilize audiovisual and electronic records. We need to consider narrowing our self-expectations to reflect new realities, rather than simply pursuing the elusive prize of more space, more money, and more staff that we think will ensure success. We must remain open to innovative approaches, such as circulating material among repositories and assisting records creators to take responsibility for their own records, as alternatives to simply collecting everything ourselves.

The third characteristic Boorstin saw in our immigrant ancestors was a "strong community-consciousness" that makes "we, the similars, lean on one another when we confront the different and the unfamiliar," and encouraged newcomers to depend upon one another as they wrestled with common problems.[44] As "newcomers" to the Information Age, we must develop this same sense of community. Archivists need to build better bridges to the other information professions — especially our colleagues in museums and libraries — with whom we share many common problems and goals. The need for these bridges should be apparent in our acquisition policies. Cooperating with other archivists and with allied professionals will reduce our ultimate workload and the range of our self-inflicted responsibility. It will help us to make better acquisition decisions that fill gaps and avoid unnecessary duplication. Cooperation will help us to ensure that records with evidential and informational value, but which are out of scope topically or geographically, end up in more appropriate repositories. In a similar way, we need to cooperate with our users by remembering that we do not collect or preserve records as an end in itself; we do so in order that others may use what we have selected, whether by viewing it in an exhibit, by conducting personal research, or by reading the scholarship of someone else who has conducted research in our holdings. Acquiring records that are out of reasonable scope, of dubious value, or needlessly duplicative serves these researchers poorly by increasing our workload and inevitable backlog. It also increases the clutter through which researchers must struggle in their search for information. By keeping in the backs of our minds the researchers who (it is to be hoped) will use the records we collect, we must be able better to resist the temptation to acquire material such as that sixteenth-century Spanish Indian Mission fonds, or the two hundredth cow-shaped pottery jug.

---

43 Ibid.
44 Ibid.

Archivists will be able to move beyond the troublesome verge only if we are prepared to make some fundamental changes in the way we go about our work. Confronting the problem on an individual basis, or simply continuing to amass documentation on a broadly defined topic while deferring hard decisions, is no longer a sufficient response. We must approach the rim of creative dissatisfaction with an eye towards finally solving our problems, rather than merely postponing them.

9

Who Controls the Past

HELEN WILLA SAMUELS

Abstract: A modern, complex, information-rich society requires that archivists reexamine their role as selectors. The changing structure of modern institutions and the use of sophisticated technologies have altered the nature of records, and only a small portion of the vast documentation can be kept. Archivists are challenged to select a lasting record, but they lack techniques to support this decision making. Documentation strategies are proposed to respond to these problems.

Who controls the past, controls the future; who controls the present, controls the past. . . . The mutability of the past is the central tenet of Ingsoc. Past events, it is argued, have no objective existence, but survive only in written records and in human memories. The past is whatever the records and the memories agree upon. And since the Party is in full control of all records, and in equally full control of the minds of its members, it follows that the past is whatever the Party chooses to make it.
George Orwell, *1984*

Since the first satellites had been orbited, almost fifty years earlier, trillions and quadrillions of pulses of information had been pouring down from space, to be stored against the day when they might contribute to the advance of knowledge. Only a minute fraction of all this raw material would ever be processed; but there was no way of telling what observation some scientist might wish to consult, ten, or fifty, or a hundred years from now. So everything had to be kept on file, stacked in endless air-conditioned galleries, triplicated at the [data] centers against the possibility of accidental loss. It was part of the real treasure of mankind, more valuable than all the gold locked uselessly away in bank vaults.
Arthur C. Clarke, *2001: A Space Odyssey*

Reprinted with permission from the *American Archivist* 49 (Spring 1986): 109-24. This article was prepared with support from the National Science Foundation and the Andrew W. Mellon Foundation.

A vision of scarcity; a vision of abundance. Which will it be? Though once perceived as keepers, American archivists, having accepted appraisal responsibilities, perceive themselves as selectors.[1] Our modern, complex, information-rich society requires that archivists reexamine their role as selectors. The changing structure of modern institutions and the use of sophisticated technologies have altered the nature of records, and only a small portion of the vast documentation can be kept. Archivists are challenged to select a lasting record, but they lack techniques to support this decision making. Documentation strategies are proposed to respond to these problems. Before discussing documentation strategies more fully, this article will analyze the factors that have affected the nature of modern records and suggest why these changes require archivists to rethink the way they assemble their collections.[2]

The Integration of Modern Institutions

Traditional archival principles prescribed by Theodore Schellenberg and others emphasize the need to understand the bureaucratic structure of the institutions being documented. Archivists study the position and functions of each office in the administrative hierarchy.[3] Recently, more systematic studies of bureaucracies and decision making have been proposed as a method to strengthen archival theory and practice. Frank Burke suggested that archivists should examine "the nature of the decision-making process in the management and operation of a corporate body" and the effect of this process on records retention.[4] In separate studies, Michael Lutzker and JoAnne Yates have responded to Burke's challenge by analyzing the impact of particular bureaucracies on records creation.[5]

---

1 This fact is discussed in Thornton W. Mitchell's useful article, "New Viewpoints on Establishing Permanent Values of State Archives," *American Archivist* 33 (April 1970): 163-74.

2 Technically, archivists receive rather than collect archival material. Archivists have retention rather than collecting or acquisition policies. Since this article argues that both archivists and manuscript curators must rethink assumptions about the way they gather material, however, collecting will refer to both the transfer of archives and the acquisition of manuscripts, and archivists will refer also to manuscript curators. Terry Eastwood and others have argued that archivists should use the term acquisition rather than collection. I have continued to use the latter, but would welcome a change if the profession could agree on terminology. Finally, modern refers primarily to the post-World War II period.

3 T. R. Schellenberg, *Modern Archives: Principles and Techniques* (Chicago: University of Chicago Press, 1956), 152.

4 Frank G. Burke, "The Future Course of Archival Theory in the United States," *American Archivist* 44 (Winter 1981): 42-43.

5 Michael A. Lutzker, "Max Weber and the Analysis of Modern Bureaucratic Organization: Notes Toward a Theory of Appraisal," *American Archivist* 45 (Spring 1982): 119-30; JoAnne Yates, "Internal Communication System in American Business Structures: A Framework to Aid Appraisal," *American Archivist* 48 (Spring 1985): 141-58.

The analysis of single institutions, however, is insufficient to support the decisions archivists face. Individuals and institutions do not exist independently. Examination reveals the complex relationships between institutions and individuals. Government, industry, and academia — the private and public sectors — are integrated through patterns of funding and regulations. Governments award contracts to academic institutions and private companies to develop space shuttles and run hospitals, while they control the privacy of student records and the testing of new drugs. As federal funds to state and local governments diminish, municipalities are consolidating and contracting with private firms to provide public services. Academic institutions have responded to reduced federal funding by turning to industry and private foundations to support teaching and research activities.

Archivists solicit and receive collections from individuals, but multiple hands have created the "individual's" papers. Although seen most clearly in the evolution of science and technology from an individual to a team activity, this phenomenon is common throughout other sectors of society. For example, Patricia Aronsson's analysis of congressional records describes the team of personnel — aides, assistants, and secretaries — that creates the congressman's papers.[6]

These complex patterns exist in any modern institution. MIT receives research funds from the National Science Foundation, the Andrew W. Mellon Foundation, Exxon, and individual donors. Newark, New Jersey, receives federal funds for housing and road construction while it contracts out to a private firm for refuse collection. Farmers receive federal funds to control crop production. Records mirror the society that creates them. Integrated functions affect where and how the records of these activities are created and where they should be retained.

The Integration of Modern Information

As the integration of institutions has affected modern records, so too has the integration of modern information. The body of information that archivists "control" is part of a much larger universe that exists in many forms and is "controlled" by many specialists. While archival records may still provide fundamental documentation of institutions and activities, their form and substance have been altered by changing technologies and communication patterns. Archival repositories now gather information in many formats: visual, published, aural, artifactual, and machine-readable. Each form of documentation offers a different type of

---

6   Patricia Aronsson, "Appraisal of Twentieth-Century Congressional Collections," in *Archival Choices: Managing the Historical Record in an Age of Abundance,* ed. Nancy Peace (Lanham, Md.: Lexington Books, 1984), 81-104. Aronsson uses this understanding most effectively to formulate her appraisal recommendations.

evidence, and researchers generally use many forms of documentation in an integrated fashion. Appraisal techniques, however, generally support the analysis of specific forms of evidence (appraisal of machine-readable or photographic records, for example). The emphasis is placed on the form rather than the substance of the record.

Archivists lack techniques to appraise an integrated multi-format body of information. The historical record of the Congress, for example, includes not only the papers of individual senators, congressmen, and committees, but also the *Congressional Record,* reports in the *New York Times* and *Washington Post,* autobiographies of senators and congressmen, and visual and oral histories of the members. The invention and development of the transistor are documented not only in the laboratory notebooks and correspondence of the laboratory and its members, but also in published technical reports and scientific articles. Analysis of a total documentary record will enable archivists to determine the specific contribution made by each form of evidence and thereby support integrated appraisal decisions.

Effects of Integration of Institutions and Information

Thus the integrated nature of society's institutions and its recorded documentation must be reflected in archivists' efforts to document those institutions. Institutions do not stand alone, nor can their archives. Archivists must rethink their strategies and even redefine the very notion of an institutional collection.

An institutional archives' responsibility is to gather and preserve the historic records of that institution. As the activities in one institution are linked to those in another, so too the records of those activities are linked. The records of an institution's functions — the archival collection — can be dispersed in several archives. For example, how many archival repositories does it take to document the complexities of the moon shot?[7] President Kennedy committed the nation to the task, and the National Aeronautics and Space Administration (NASA) had the responsibility to oversee and coordinate the work. Where was the work done? Martin Marietta built the craft. MIT's Instrumentation Laboratory built the inertial guidance system. Astronomers, mathematicians, engineers, and physicists at numerous academic and industrial sites solved specific problems for the flight. Where is "the collection" documenting the moon shot? It exists as a unit only in the mind; physically it does not exist in one place. To gather the records together in one place — at the Kennedy Library, the National Archives, or NASA — would be artificial. As a totality the records document

---

7 Frank Burke used this as an example in his commentary on the report of the Joint Committee on Archives of Science and Technology (JCAST) presented at the 47th annual meeting of the Society of American Archivists, 5-8 October 1983, Minneapolis, Minnesota.

the efforts of the United States to place a man on the moon, but the individual parts of "the collection" document activities in the history of each participating institution — Martin Marietta, MIT, NASA, and others.

Although this discussion has focused on archival collections, the same arguments also apply to personal papers. Archivists are encouraged not to disperse the papers of individuals but to gather them in one institution, even though the individuals may have many institutional affiliations throughout their careers. In the scientific world it is not uncommon for scientists to move from laboratory to laboratory, often working with teams at several institutions at one time.[8] Administrators and politicians hold many positions throughout their careers. Although a biographer would benefit if the papers were housed together in one site, institutions would lose portions of their records.

The dispersal of related records at several institutions is not alien to archivists. What is alien is the concept of deliberately shaping collecting decisions based on the inevitable and appropriate dispersal of related records. This is not proposed as a method to eliminate competition, but as a strategy to build coherent collections cooperatively, minimizing duplication. It requires, however, that archivists' concept of their "collection" not end at their own doors.

Collection Development Versus Collection Management

Archivists and librarians traditionally articulate their collecting objectives in acquisition or collecting policies. The formulation of an archival collecting policy is most clearly presented by Mary Lynn McCree. Archivists are encouraged to prepare written policies after weighing scholarly, economic, physical, and political factors. McCree suggests that "it is wise for institutions to cooperate with one another, especially if they are located in the same geographic area."[9] This advice, however, is offered in the context of minimizing competition and placing papers at the most appropriate institution.

Librarians have traditionally used a similar form of analysis. In recent years, however, fiscal constraints and the proliferation of information has shifted their focus from collection development to collection management. "Collection development focuses on the building of collections and implies a process of continuing growth. It relates more to our earlier periods of affluence in the 1960s. Collection management, on the other hand, is a response to the economic retrenchment and decline of the 1970s. It is a systematic, planned, documented process of building, maintaining,

---

8 Joan N. Warnow, associate manager, Center for History of Physics, American Institute of Physics, argues this point persuasively for contemporary physicists.

9 Mary Lynn McCree, "Defining Collections and Collecting," *Drexel Library Quarterly* 11 (January 1975): 27.

and preserving collections."[10] Critical to the success of collection management are defined collection strategies, active selection, and coordinated cooperative plans among libraries.

In 1980 the Research Libraries Group (RLG)[11] initiated a collection management effort through its Conspectus project, an effort to facilitate coordinated collecting through the use of collection evaluation activities. Conspectus is an analysis of "existing collection strengths and future collecting intensities of the RLG" member libraries. Using subject and classification descriptors, member libraries describe their collecting levels on a scale of zero to five, with zero indicating no collection and five indicating a comprehensive research collection.[12] The project is built on the understanding that each library has a core collection molded by the needs, interests, and resources of the individual institution. This core collection is judged against local needs, not national standards. In the areas outside the core collection, the member libraries build linkages based on their individual strengths. Judged against national standards, the libraries determine which has the strongest collection in specific topical areas, and they agree to support the continuing growth and preservation of these collections.

The RLG program depends on the availability of the Conspectus information in the RLIN data base and the loan or photocopying of materials for other member libraries. The Association of Research Libraries (ARL)[13] has now initiated the North American Collections Inventory Project (NCIP) to investigate the wider uses of Conspectus for its membership, including selection, retention, and preservation activities.

As Jutta Reed-Scott has noted, however, ". . . archives and manuscripts, because of their qualities of uniqueness, present problems that differ from those relating to printed material." Indeed, the library model might have limited use for archivists because the archival universe of information is much larger than that of the library.[14] Archivists can profit nonetheless from studying the cooperative library projects, most specifically the concept of the core collection and its relationship to the larger collection. This concept is comparable to an archival collection — the official records retained by an institution for its legal, administrative, fiscal,

---

10 Jutta Reed-Scott, "Collection Management Strategies for Archivists," *American Archivist* 47 (Winter 1984): 24.

11 RLG is a membership organization with four main programs: a bibliographic utility entitled the Research Libraries Information Network (RLIN), shared resources, cooperative collection development, and preservation. In 1980 the RLG members were Columbia, Stanford, Yale, Cornell, and Temple Universities, the University of Minnesota, and the New York Public Library.

12 Nancy E. Gwinn and Paul Mosher, "Coordinating Collection Development," *College and Research Libraries* 44 (March 1983): 128-40.

13 ARL is composed of 117 university and independent research libraries in the United States and Canada.

14 Conversation with Jutta Reed-Scott, 5 January 1984.

and historical needs. The size and the scope of the collection should be judged by local needs and constraints, not national norms. Archivists' legal obligations to their institutions are fulfilled by gathering the core collection. With the legal mission assured, archivists can examine their collections as sources of information, seek ties with other institutions, and develop new strategies to build and manage collections. They will then be challenged to select material "within a much different environment, one in which each archive and library is not a self-contained entity, but a component of an undefined whole."[15]

Defining Collecting Strategies

Challenged by the abundance of materials, the scarcity of the resources to care for them, and the decentralized nature of contemporary society and its records, archivists must develop new intellectual frameworks to guide them.[16] Three levels of collecting strategies can be defined. The first two, collecting policies for individual institutions, and collecting projects, are familiar to archivists. The third, documentation strategies, is a new, untested idea that is proposed to respond to the challenges of modern documentation. It is hoped that the following discussion will stimulate debate and experiments.[17]

A *collecting/acquisition policy* is a written statement prepared by a specific repository to define the scope of its collection and to specify the subjects and formats of materials to be collected. A collection policy is developed in light of other repositories' policies and is implemented in part through cooperative collecting plans and documentation strategies.

A *collecting project* is a plan formulated to assure the documentation of a specific issue or event. In general, the issue or event is historic, not ongoing (e.g., development of the transistor, Harry Truman's presidency); more than one repository is involved in the identification and retention of the material; and existing records are gathered rather than new records created. A collecting project is of limited duration; it is not an ongoing activity.

A *documentation strategy* is a plan formulated to assure the documentation of an ongoing issue, activity, or geographic area (e.g., the operation

---

15 Patricia Battin quoted in Reed-Scott, "Collection Management Strategies," 26.

16 Any study of collecting activities must first reconsider F. Gerald Ham's three seminal articles on this topic: "The Archival Edge," *American Archivist* 38 (January 1975): 5-13; "Archival Strategies for the Post-Custodial Era," *American Archivist* 44 (Summer 1981): 207-16; and "Archival Choices: Managing the Historical Record in an Age of Abundance," *American Archivist* 47 (Winter 1984): 11-22.

17 My ideas about documentation strategies were formed while working with Larry Hackman on the 1982 SAA Program Committee and the Goals and Priorities Task Force. I thank him for his endless patience and inspiration. The fruits of his own investigation will be published in a forthcoming article.

of the government of the state of New York, labor unions in the United States, the impact of technology on the environment). The strategy is ordinarily designed, promoted, and in part implemented by an ongoing mechanism involving records creators, administrators (including archivists), and users. The documentation strategy is carried out through the mutual efforts of many institutions and individuals influencing both the creation of the records and the archival retention of a portion of them. The strategy is refined in response to changing conditions and viewpoints.[18]

Documentation strategies present many difficult questions. How are the topics to be documented chosen? Who chooses them? Where should these activities be based? These are not only intellectual but also political issues. An examination of existing models suggests some answers and provides direction.

Existing Models — The Discipline History Centers

The scientific and technological discipline-based history centers are among the most useful models to study. Though the American Institute of Physics's Center for History of Physics is the oldest and best known of the discipline-based centers, others exist for electrical engineering, chemistry, information processing, public works, psychology, geophysics, and botany.[19] Most have been initiated by concerned members of a professional society and are funded in part by them. Such centers are based at the professional societies (e.g., American Institute of Physics [AIP], Institute of Electrical and Electronics Engineers) or at academic institutions where they are supported by both a professional society and a university (e.g., Center for History of Chemistry, University of Pennsylvania; Charles Babbage Institute for the History of Information Processing, University of Minnesota). The centers gather printed and oral history materials, conduct historical research, and promote a concern for the history of their discipline. All of the centers have engaged in archival activities, predominantly identifying and placing collections at appropriate institutions and compiling directories of manuscript and archival collections. Archivists at numerous institutions benefit from the centers' services when they seek appraisal guidance, background on historical issues, or support for oral history projects. The centers, in turn, seek the cooperation of archival institutions when they place manuscript and archival collections.

The report of the Joint Committee on Archives of Science and Technology encouraged the history centers to expand their archival endeavors,

---

18 These definitions were prepared by Patricia Aronsson, Larry Hackman, and the author for a session on documentation strategies, presented at the 49th annual meeting of the Society of American Archivists, 30 August–3 September 1984, Washington, D.C.

19 See Joan K. Haas, Helen Willa Samuels, and Barbara Trippel Simmons, *Appraising the Records of Modern Science and Technology: A Guide* (Cambridge, Mass.: MIT, 1985; distributed by the Society of American Archivists), 84-90 for an extensive list of the centers.

as they have available to them the expertise of the creators and users of records that is required for appraisal and documentation studies.[20] Some centers, especially the Center for History of Physics, have achieved such an expanded archival program. Indeed, the AIP's entire program could be viewed as a documentation strategy.[21] The purpose of the program is to gather and preserve a record of modern physics and to encourage the use of these materials. The program is defined and monitored by archivists, historians, and physicists. The staff and advisors locate and place collections of papers of individual physicists, assess the available documentation of modern physics, and when necessary create documents to complete the historical record. The overall strategy has been carried out through a series of projects aimed at documenting specific topics: astrophysics, solid-state physics, and nuclear physics. In each case, historical research guides a search for sources and the creation of oral history interviews to supplement the available record. The AIP's study of records-keeping practices in four U.S. Department of Energy laboratories focused specifically on questions of archival documentation. The findings have been used to improve the records systems in the laboratories and have enhanced AIP's knowledge of the adequate documentation of a modern laboratory.[22]

History centers such as the AIP's have each been shaped by a specific discipline. While their activities provide a useful model, archivists must determine other ways of organizing documentation activities.

Documentation Strategies

A documentation strategy consists of four activities: (1) choosing and defining the topic to be documented, (2) selecting the advisors and establishing the site for the strategy, (3) structuring the inquiry and examining the form and substance of the available documentation, and (4) selecting and placing the documentation.

Choosing and Defining the Topic to Be Documented

Coordinated library acquisition activities are supported by common vocabularies of subject descriptors and classifications systems (for example,

20 *Understanding Progress as Process: Documentation of the History of Post-war Science and Technology in the United States: Final Report of the Joint Committee on Archives of Science and Technology* (HSS-SHOT-SAA-ARMA), ed. Clark A. Elliott (Chicago: Society of American Archivists, 1983).

21 A forthcoming article by Joan K. Warnow describes the center's activities as a documentation strategy.

22 Joan K. Warnow, *Guidelines for Records Appraisal at Major Research Facilities: Selection of Permanent Records of DOE Laboratories* (New York: American Institute of Physics, 1985); Joan Warnow, with Allan Needell. Spencer R. Weart, and Jane Wolff, *A Study of Preservation of Documents at Department of Energy Laboratories* (New York: American Institute of Physics, 1982).

Library of Congress subject headings and the Library of Congress classification system). Appropriate classification numbers are used by librarians to delineate specific topical responsibilities in cooperative collecting projects. Archivists have no equivalent universal vocabulary. Archival acquisitions are delineated by the responsibilities and activities of the institutions being documented, rather than by specified subject areas. Documentation strategies can build upon the fact that archival collections provide both a record of a specific institution and information on the subjects reflected in the activities of that institution. The Institute Archives at MIT, for example, provides a record of the administration, teaching, and research activities of the institute and thereby provides information about the history of computers, the economy of Massachusetts, and the contributions of women in science and technology. Documentation strategies do not foster subject collections. Rather, subject, functional, or geographic analysis permits archivists to look across institutions and plan for the appropriate retention of material in its appropriate setting.

Lacking an agreed-upon vocabulary, archivists must experiment with various constructs to define specific documentation strategies. The two most obvious choices are topical and geographic. The history centers provide a model of a topical definition, while some coordinated collecting activities by the state networks (Wisconsin and Ohio, for example) suggest how a geographic focus can be used. Whatever the construct, it must be defined specifically and its geographic and chronological boundaries delineated. A documentation strategy for the history of computers, for example, must specify the dates of the earliest machines to be included; whether both analog and digital computers will be documented; whether the strategy will focus on activities in the United States and/or other countries; and if the social, economic, and cultural impact as well as the technological aspects will be addressed. As documentation strategies begin to be implemented, archivists will learn more about how to choose and define appropriate and manageable topics. They will also develop techniques to blend topical and geographic approaches.

An additional problem associated with the selection of topics to be documented is that, of necessity, topics are chosen based upon current historical understanding. Though archivists are asked to consider future uses of records, they cannot anticipate research trends or the specific questions researchers will bring to the records. Selection must be based on current understanding and today's values. "The archivist's job is to document society in all its multiplicity and to transmit to posterity a manageable amount of records."[23]

---

23 Hans Booms, cited in Nancy Peace, "Deciding What to Save," *Archival Choices*, 11. The work of
    Hans Booms, a West-German archivist, has very interesting implications for the debate on the

Site for the Documentation Strategy

Once the topic for the strategy has been chosen, a permanent base for the activity must be identified and a group of advisors, representing the interests of the creators and users, selected to guide the project. The advisory board and the administrative structure established at the permanent base will develop, direct, and monitor the documentation strategy.

Again, archivists can look to the library community, which has established adminstrative structures for their cooperative activities. A national machine-readable data base of cataloging information serves as a basis for descriptive and collecting activities. The Library of Congress supports the data base by providing cataloging information on the LC MARC (Machine-Readable Catalog) tapes. This information is made available by computer networks (OCLC, RLG) to their member libraries, which then contribute additional cataloging and location information about their own holdings. The computer networks link libraries and promote shared cataloging and resources. The cooperative acquisition programs of state library systems, city library consortia, and networks of specialized libraries all build upon and contribute to this central data base. Major organizations, such as the Association of Research Libraries, supplement these activities by developing projects to respond to the particular needs of their members.[24]

Until very recently the archival community has not used automated networks because they failed to respond to archivists' needs. The new machine-readable AMC (Archival and Manuscripts Control) format provides a communications and management system that supports the contribution of information to these networks while also enhancing archivists' ability to describe, manage, and share information about holdings.[25] The increasing use of the AMC format and the growing number of archival and manuscript repositories that are contributing information to automated networks indicate a dramatic change in the archival profession and a new potential for cooperation.[26] In 1985 the National Historical Publications and Records Commission (NHPRC) funded a

---

archivist's role as an honest broker and the ability of archivists to appraise in light of future research trends. These are stimulating topics that deserve a separate article. A great service could be rendered by translating and publishing more of Booms's work in English. Peace has offered a tantalizing glimpse of his thought.

24 ARL's accomplishments include the Farmington Plan, the Foreign Newspaper Microfilm Project, the establishment of the Office of Education's Title IIC program to strengthen library resources, and the promotion of preservation and coordinated retrospective conversion activities.

25 See Nancy Sahli, *MARC for Archives and Manuscripts: The AMC Format* (Chicago: Society of American Archivists, 1985).

26 Yale and Cornell universities, among other RLG members, have contributed many records of manuscnpt and archival holdings to the data base.

project to enter descriptive records of seven state archives in the RLIN data base and to share appraisal information.[27] This project is one of many that will demonstrate how archivists can adapt and use the automated networks to support and coordinate their activities.

The archival community as yet lacks both the umbrella structure of a national bibliographic network and a clear understanding of how such a body of information can be used to support documentation activities. The NHPRC project and other similar efforts will begin to provide answers. In the meantime, other bases for cooperative activities must be established and tested. Eventually, a multi-level structure will exist in which documentation activities will be carried out at many institutions and, most likely, coordinated and integrated through automated databases.

Appropriate sites for documentation strategies must provide resources to sustain the effort, access to the required expertise, and a long-term commitment to the activity. These activities need not be based at an archives, since a documentation strategy involves examining the documentation and planning for its retention but does not require assembling it in one location. Among the most logical bases for these activities are state or city archives for geographical documentation strategies, and discipline history centers or specialized repositories for subject-based strategies.

At present, state archives and state historical societies are perhaps the most logical settings for these activities. Although their statutory authority, structures, and scope of responsibility differ, state archives and historical societies tend to have the resources and mandate that a documentation strategy requires. The state networks and statewide surveys of sources suggest structures that can support strategies and provide information about available documentation,[28] but these are only preliminary efforts. Networks clarify the location and responsibility for material, but not which material should be preserved. Survey results tell what exists, but not what archivists want to exist.

During 1982-1985 the NHPRC supported state assessment studies in forty-three states. In each case the states assessed the effectiveness of their state and local records programs, the other archival activities in their state, and the cooperative programs linking these activities. These efforts produced a vast amount of information about archival programs in the United States and stimulated plans to improve archival activities

---

27 "The Seven State Archives RLIN Project," NHPRC Grant #85-147. The seven states are Alabama, California, Minnesota, New York, Pennsylvania, Utah, and Wisconsin.

28 See *Midwestern Archivist* 6, no.2 (1982) for a very useful survey and analysis of the archival networks.

throughout the country.[29] Though the studies assessed administrative, financial, and legal problems, less attention was given to the quality of the collections and their ability to provide sufficient evidence about the history of each state. Documentation strategies could be initiated by extending assessment studies to this area. Do the collections in the state archives and other repositories in each state adequately document that state? If not, what topics and what areas are being neglected? What are the barriers to the preservation of the neglected materials? Is new legislation or are additional repositories needed? Should the state archives or another institution initiate a specific strategy to improve the documentation of a neglected area? For example, though the performing arts and the high-technology industry are extremely important to the history of the Commonwealth of Massachusetts, both areas are inadequately reflected in archival holdings in the state. Solutions for documenting the two areas will be quite different, but the Massachusetts Archives can play a key role by identifying the problems and coordinating the solutions.

Statewide documentation strategies must begin, as discussed above, with the appointment of advisors[30] and the clarification of the scope and purpose of the activity. In most cases the strategy will be carried out through a series of projects focused on specific topics or geographic areas: farming in Iowa, the labor movement in New York state, the coal industry in southeast Ohio. Each strategy must assess how the cities, counties, and institutions involved in each topic will contribute to the analytic process and collecting activities. Another major problem that must be addressed is the coordination of the strategies in each state and across state lines. Margaret Child's report on the NHPRC state assessment projects indicates the problems that arise when the states confine their analysis within their own borders.[31] As documentation strategy projects evolve, techniques must be developed to support statewide and nationwide coordination.

Thus the analysis and coordination necessary to develop documentation strategies will improve the effectiveness of state archives. A documentation strategy will reveal the decision-making process by which

---

29 Lisa Weber, ed., *Documenting America: Assessing the Condition of Historical Records in the States* (New York: National Association of State Archives and Administrators, 1984). The state assessment reports are available upon request from the individual state coordinators.

30 The State Historical Advisory Boards could assume this role. The boards are now used by NHPRC to oversee the records program in each state. Larry Hackman and F. Gerald Ham have proposed that the boards take on enlarged planning responsibilities. Larry J. Hackman, "The Historical Records Program: The States and the Nation," *American Archivist* 43 (Winter 1980): 17-32; F. Gerald Ham, "NHPRC's Records Program and the Development of Statewide Planning," *American Archivist* 43 (Winter 1980): 33-42.

31 Margaret Child, "Consultant Report: Statewide Functions and Savices," in *Documenting America*, 47-57.

material is chosen. Such activities will diminish the image of the archives as an endless warehouse and establish a justification for the resources that are required to house and administer the collections.

Structuring the Inquiry and Assessing the Documentation

At first, documentation strategies appear to be similar to traditional collecting activities. Topics are chosen, the turf defined, and then survey and collecting activities begin. Documentation strategies, however, do not start with surveys of available material. They begin with detailed investigations of the topic to be documented and the information required. The concern is less what does exist than what should exist.

Documentation strategies are designed to respond to abundance — an abundance of institutions and information. The intent is to design an analytic process that guides selection and assures retention of adequate information about a topic or locale. Historical research and discussion at the beginning of a project will clarify the goals and identify the specific issues to be documented. This process, though, encompasses more than constructing a wish list. Hard questions must be asked about what will and what will not be documented. How many institutions or events must be documented and what will be left undocumented? How much information is enough? In the past, appraisal and collecting activities have focused on the selection of records produced by an institution or individual. Now documentation strategies must help archivists select those institutions and events to be documented and examine the ramifications of leaving others undocumented. For example, a strategy to document digital computers might recommend that each first-generation machine be documented, but only specific key or prototypical second-, third-, and fourth-generation machines. Such a strategy recognizes that for some machines little or no documentation will be sought or preserved.[32]

One of the most difficult problems posed by these activities is the need to respect the archival requirements of institutions while shaping multi-institutional collecting efforts. If the state of Ohio is shaping a strategy to document its cities, how many towns and municipalities have to be included to accomplish this goal? Concurrently, what information does each city require to fulfill its legal and archival responsibilities to its citizens? Can these goals be integrated? Documentation strategies must be fashioned in sympathy with an institution's archival obligations.[33]

---

32 A machine can be designated to be documented either because it was a success or a failure.

33 In 1971 when Sam Bass Warner proposed that archivists establish sampling procedures to assure the preservation of the records of American cities, he was regarded as naive and foolhardy. Now he appears to have been more courageous and forward-thinking than his archival colleagues. See Sam Bass Warner, Jr., "The Shame of the Cities: Public Records of the Metropolis," *Midwestern Archivist* 2, no. 2 (1977): 27-34.

In recent years, archivists have grappled with the problems of abundance posed by labor union and railroad records. Specialized repositories have cooperated to identify, appraise, and place collections.[34] A documentation strategy builds upon this type of cooperation, but additional questions need to be answered. Is it necessary to preserve the records of every labor union and every railroad? If not, will any evidence remain of the labor unions and railroads whose records are not preserved? Is it an all-or-nothing question? Twentieth-century institutions are documented in a variety of published sources: annual reports, bylaws and rules, directories, newspaper accounts, and histories. Can archivists evaluate these published sources and then recommend a minimum archival record that should be preserved for each union and railroad? Railroads affect their employees and the cities through which they pass; unions affect their members and the companies that employ their members. If a strategy documents some unions and railroads more fully than others, can this documentation meet the information needs of the employees, individual union members, cities, and companies? The answer is probably no, but a strategy that fulfills everyone's needs returns archivists to the practice of saving everything.

Documentation strategies also help archivists manage modern records by acknowledging that they handle only part of the total documentary record. Archival and manuscript sources are not the only, or often the best, source of information. Information exists in many forms (published, visual, aural, artifactual, machine-readable) and is managed by many curators (librarians, museum curators, data archivists). Adequate information about a specific activity or topic can exist in forms not traditionally managed by archival institutions. Documentation strategies must examine all available forms of documentation and assess their ability to provide the desired information. For example, the conceptualization, development, and marketing of a computer are documented in laboratory notebooks, funding records, policy memoranda, technical reports, machine-readable tapes, manuals, photographs, advertisements, and the machine itself. While the adequate documentation of the pioneering and prototype machines may require the retention of all of this information, many computers can be adequately documented by retaining only the technical reports and manuals.

Currently, archivists lack well-developed techniques to evaluate records as a source of information in light of the information available in other forms. At the same time, librarians and other curators are also selecting materials without reference to all forms of available information.

---

34 An example is the NHPRC-funded Pennsylvania Railroad historical records project in which seven repositories participated in the appraisal and retention of the records.

Automated linked databases will support coordinated decision making. Current studies of descriptive practices, including authority controls and functional analysis, could provide a common language that is required to support these coordinated activities.[35]

While archivists acknowledge the overabundance of information, they also recognize that modern communication patterns and records-keeping practices leave gaps in the documentary record. Documentation strategies, however, are ongoing activities and provide the opportunity to intervene in the records creation process and assure the creation and retention of required information.

Documentation strategies, then, require two levels of analysis: first, an analysis of the history and scope of a topic so that the purpose of the strategy and the issues to be documented can be defined; and second, an analysis of the available sources of information so that an adequate record can be gathered for each issue. In *Appraising the Records of Modern Science and Technology: A Guide,* the authors address the second type of analysis by studying the documentation of a specific enterprise.[36] This appraisal guide examines the component activities in science and technology (establishing research priorities, funding, staffing, designing and running experiments, data gathering and analysis, and dissemination). Following an explanation of each activity, the information created and used during that activity is described and the relative potential for the reuse of that information evaluated. The authors argue, for instance, that the body of published scientific and technical reports is the most pervasive form of evidence. Though archivists need not read or comprehend the published record, they must understand its purpose and general content. Nonpublished sources, laboratory records, correspondence, minutes, and data will then be selected to supplement the published literature and more adequately document scientific and technological research activities. The authors also explore the role of artifacts, in this case scientific instruments, in contributing to the documentation of science and technology and advise museum curators and archivists to coordinate their acquisition activities.

Once the scientific or technological topics to be documented have been defined, archivists can use this publication to guide appraisal activities. For example, the guide will recommend the selection of an adequate record for each machine chosen by a documentation strategy for

---

35 Max Evans, "Authority Control: An Alternative to the Record Group Concept," *American Archivist* 49 (Summer 1986): 249-61; David Bearman, "Who About What, or from Whence, Why and How: Intellectual Access Approaches to Archives and Their Implications for National Archival Systems," paper presented at a conference on archives, automation and access, University of Victoria, British Columbia, 1-2 March 1985.

36 Haas, Samuels, and Simmons, *Appraising the Records of Modern Science and Technology: A Guide* (Cambridge, Mass.: MIT Press, 1985): passim.

computers. Appraisal guides, patterned after the science and technology appraisal volume, can be created for other areas (e.g., banking, court administration, labor unions) and used to support documentation strategies.[37]

Selection and Placement of the Documentation

The investigation and planning by the strategy team will guide the search for and placement of the documentation. Though the collecting objectives may have to be modified by the availability of records and repositories, the collecting activities will be altered, based on the rationale and goals laid down by the advisors during the initial investigation. The documentation strategy for computers, for example, will have named specific machines that should be documented. If records of those machines do not exist, other machines meeting the same basic criteria will be substituted.

The major problem that will be encountered during this process is the availability of sufficient repositories to care for the records. Specialized repositories (e.g., Social Welfare History Archives, University of Minnesota; Archives of Business and Labor, Wayne State University; The Arthur and Elizabeth Schlesinger Library on the History of Women in America, Radcliffe College) will be able to accept some homeless collections in their topical areas. The state historical societies and state archives should be able to accept some material from their geographic areas. Nonetheless, documentation strategies should build upon the ongoing archival responsibility of an institution for its own records. The massive records created by IBM or the Digital Equipment Corporation are the companies' responsibility. Their administrative, legal, and historical needs require these organizations to establish and maintain archival programs. Where programs do not exist, the archival community must provide education and encouragement. Documentation strategies can assist by demonstrating the role and contribution an institution can make to a larger body of documentation. A better understanding of and respect for the role of records and information in the management of institutions will foster and support archival activities.

Conclusions

Documentation strategies will not create subject collections or force any individual institution to assume more than its own institutional responsibilities. Rather, documentation strategies are a form of analysis that promotes the coordination of the activities of many separate

---

37 With funding provided by the Andrew W. Mellon Foundation, MIT will commence a study of the records of colleges and universities in the spring of 1986. The final product will be an appraisal guide for these records.

archives. A documentation strategy for Berkshire County in western Massachusetts, for example, will delineate the role of the cities, towns, and institutions in the county in preserving the needed documentation. The strategy must also take into account the crucial role of a number of institutions that are not based in Berkshire County but which have had a major social and economic impact on the area, such as the Boston Symphony Orchestra (BSO), General Electric, and the New York Central Railroad. In each case the documentation strategy team will work with and encourage these institutions to save specific material. The BSO will be asked to preserve documentation of land acquisition and development and information on the number and salaries of staff hired from the county.

An ideal documentation plan will be continually modified based on the availability of records and repositories. Each topical area will present different problems. At this point archivists lack the experience to suggest solutions. Experiments with documentation strategies, even the most modest ones, will begin to build a body of experience that will guide future efforts.

Are documentation strategies to be implemented only by large institutions, or will all archivists and institutions have roles to play? Any institution can initiate and carry out these activities. Any archivist can identify a topic to be documented and gather the required personnel to accomplish the program. In addition, when their holdings relate to specific documentation activities, archival repositories will participate as analysts of records and recipients of selected documentation. Future meetings of archival associations and archival publications will report on the progress of strategies and elicit the cooperation of archivists and their institutions.

Collecting is the most important and demanding task archivists perform. Cut off from one another, archivists view their collections as self-sufficient, but this is an illusion. Automated networks and improved descriptive information about holdings draw institutions together and thereby support the communication and coordination that will be vital to collecting strategy activities. In this environment, each collection and each repository becomes a part of a larger collection — our nation's collection. Archival collections may have roots in one institution, but their limbs reach out and touch others. A common soil and water source enriches and binds collections together. Archivists should offer the future not individual trees, but a forest.

10

The Documentation Strategy and Archival Appraisal Principles: A Different Perspective

RICHARD J. COX

Abstract: North American archivists have recently witnessed an upsurge in writings about appraisal theory. This essay takes a different approach to this topic. It attempts to describe a set of basic principles, derived from the archival literature, that relate to the practice of appraising records. These principles bridge the gap between theory and practice, but they represent — in the author's view — something more than just methodology. The essay also seeks to relate the decade-old discussion to the archival documentation strategy, showing how the strategy both emanates from such principles and is consistent with them.

Introduction

For the past few years, the readers of *Archivaria* and the *American Archivist* (and other archival journals) have had access to a steady stream of writings on archival appraisal theory, much of it in reaction to or encompassing the documentation strategy.[1] The theoretical concepts

---

Reprinted with permission from *Archivaria* 38 (Fall 1994): 11-36.

1 See, for example, the following essays: Helen W. Samuels, "Who Controls the Past," *American Archivist* 49 (Spring 1986): 109-24; Larry J. Hackman and Joan Warnow-Blewett "The Documentation Strategy Process: A Model and A Case Study," *American Archivist* 50 (Winter 1987): 12-47; Hans Booms, "Society and the Formation of a Documentary Heritage," *Archivaria* 24 (Summer 1987): 69-107; Judith E. Endelman, "Looking Backward to Plan for the Future: Collection Analysis for Manuscript Repositories," *American Archivist* 50 (Summer 1987): 340-55; Philip Alexander and Helen W. Samuels, "The Roots of 128: A Hypothetical Documentation Strategy," *American Archivist* 50 (Fall 1987): 518-31; Richard J. Cox and Helen W. Samuels, "The Archivist's First Responsibility: A Research Agenda for the Identification and Retention of Records of Enduring Value," *American Archivist* 51 (Winter/Spring 1988): 28-42; Margaret Hedstrom, "New Appraisal Techniques: The Effect of Theory on Practice," *Provenance* 7 (Fall 1989): 1-21; Terry Abraham, "Collection Policy or Documentation Strategy: Theory and Practice," *American Archivist* 54 (Winter 1991): 44-52; Terry Cook, "Many Are Called But Few Are Chosen: Appraisal Guidelines for Sampling and Selecting Case Files," *Archivaria* 32 (Summer 1991): 25-50; Hans Booms, "Überlieferungsbildung: Keeping Archives as a Social and Political Activity," *Archivaria* 33 (Winter 1991-92): 25-33; Helen W. Samuels, "Improving Our Disposition: Documentation Strategy," *Archivaria* 33 (Winter 1991-92): 125-40; Richard Brown, "Records Acquisition

range from immutable laws to a view that theory is no more than a codification of practice and principles; there is also the argument that there is
no theory at all. Much of both ends of this spectrum of views have also
swirled about basic archival concepts of evidence and information.[2] Some
may have taken too seriously Schellenberg's idea that "ascertaining values
in records cannot be reduced to exact standards" but can be "little more
than general principles."[3] More importantly, archivists have used the
terms *art* and *science* too loosely.[4] Some of the debate has also bogged
down on different conceptions of the archival mission, ranging from the

---

Strategy and Its Theoretical Foundation: The Case for a Concept of Archival Hermeneutics,"
Archivaria 33 (Winter 1991-92): 34-56; Terry Cook, "Documentation Strategy," *Archivaria* 34
(Summer 1992): 181-91; Thomas J. Ruller, "Dissimilar Appraisal Documentations as an
Impediment to Sharing Appraisal Data: A Survey of Appraisal Documentation in Government
Archival Repositories," *Archival Issues* 17, no. 1 (1992): 65-73; and Terry Eastwood, "How Goes It
with Appraisal?" *Archivaria* 36 (Autumn 1993): 111-21.

2 The professional debate on archival knowledge and theory that I refer to is typified by the discussion that began with Frank Burke's 1981 essay, "The Future Course of Archival Theory in the
United States," *American Archivist* 44 (Winter 1981): 40-46. This debate is worth a side trip in
this consideration of archival appraisal theory and the documentation strategy. Burke, in his
essay, argued that archivists must define their theory, separate it from and then relate it to practice, and that this theory will not be developed until there are archivists working full time as
educators who have the time to enunciate and test this theory. Burke was immediately rejoined
by Lester Cappon, who questioned his definition of theory and the practicality of developing
such theory, in his article "What, Then, Is There to Theorize About?" *American Archivist* 45 (Winter
1982): 19-25, and Michael Lutzker, who turned to look at other disciplines (in this case, sociology
and Max Weber) that "offer constructs that can deepen our understanding of how institutions
function" (and hence their records) in "Max Weber and the Analysis of Modern Bureaucratic
Organization: Notes Toward a Theory of Appraisal," *American Archivist* 45 (Spring 1982): 119. Gregg
D. Kimball, a Burke student, contributed to the debate in 1985 and also urged the empirical process
of developing archival theory instead of "law-like theorizing" that Burke seemed disposed to in his
original contribution; see "The Burke-Cappon Debate: Some Further Criticisms and Considerations
for Archival Theory," *American Archivist* 48 (Fall 1985): 371. While Kimball summarized and criticized earlier contributions to the debate, John W. Roberts, in 1987 and 1990, presented the
most extreme views when he defined the concern with archival theory as merely evidence of
the archivist's "emotional need for greater professional acceptance." Roberts saw little that is
unique to archival work, arguing that a "knowledge of historical scholarship and of the content of
particular collections become the essential components in making informed, professional decisions
about appraisal, description, and reference." Archives, states Roberts, is a "fairly straightforward,
down to earth service occupation" in his "Archival Theory: Much Ado About Shelving," *American
Archivist* 50 (Winter 1987): 67, 69, 74, and his later treatment, "Archival Theory: Myth or Banality,"
American Archivist 53 (Winter 1990): 110-20.

3 T. R. Schellenberg, "The Appraisal of Modern Public Records," *National Archives Bulletin* 8
(1956): 44.

4 Bronowksi has, for example, more precisely tried to characterize these differences. He wrote that
"in one way scientific knowledge is wholly different . . . from the knowledge which I shall
characterize as being carried by the arts. Science offers explanation. I hold that the work of art
carries a kind of knowledge which is not explanatory," but which is more experimental in the
sense that the "work of art is an experiment in which, if we enter the life of other people, we
experience the conflict of values which faces them." Archivists are, of course, in their quest for
documentation searching for explanations of institutional and societal development through
evidence and information. J. Bronowski, *The Visionary Eye: Essays in the Arts, Literature, and
Science* (Cambridge, Mass.: MIT Press, 1978), 60, 169.

preservation of evidence, through the creation of a representative documentation, to the broad quest to document all of society.

My aim in this essay is to describe a consistent set of archival appraisal principles, considering what the documentation strategy has to say about each. I view these principles as the raw material for an appraisal theory, not as the fully developed theory itself. Yet, I also believe these principles provide more specificity than the normal writings on the concepts of record, evidence, and information. Holding as I do to the notion of archival theory as patterns and codification of practice,[5] I believe that doing such analysis of practice as reflected in our fairly substantial (if uneven) literature will move us to a solid foundation of archival theory. I also believe that they show the contribution of the documentation strategy to appraisal theory and how it is generally consistent with the existing principles and practices.

A Brief Review of the Archival Documentation Strategy Concept

The archival documentation strategy was introduced in the mid-1980s. In the first of the published articles on this topic, Helen W. Samuels defined a documentation strategy,[6] but since then the definition has been refined, most recently in the Society of American Archivists's 1992 glossary, as

> an on-going analytic, cooperative approach designed, promoted, and implemented by creators, administrators (including archivists), and users to ensure the archival retention of appropriate documentation in some area of human endeavor through the application of archival techniques, the creation of institutional archives and refined acquisition policies, and the development of sufficient resources. The key elements in this approach are an analysis of the universe to be documented, an understanding of the inherent documentary problems, and the formulation of a plan to assure the adequate documentation of an issue, activity, or geographic area.[7]

---

5 Terry Eastwood stated that "it is not a question of creating rigid laws, which in any event do not exist even in the physical sciences, to explain reality, but rather a question of recognizing patterns in the generation and management of archives in any given legal and social reality and in any time": "Nurturing Archival Education in the University," *American Archivist* 51 (Summer 1988): 235. Frederick Stielow attempted to construct a foundation for archival theory by first defining a realistic notion for theory itself: "The concept of theory does not demand fustian exposition. It is simply the codification of rational and systematic thinking, the conscious development of general principles or guides to explain or analyze": "Archival Theory Redux and Redeemed: Definition and Context Toward a General Theory," *American Archivist* 54 (Winter 1991): 17.

6 Samuels, "Who Controls the Past," 115.

7 Lewis J. Bellardo and Lynn Lady Bellardo, comps., *A Glossary for Archivists, Manuscript Curators, and Records Managers* (Chicago: Society of American Archivists, 1992), 12.

The documentation strategy can be viewed as a conceptually simple mechanism to be added to the archivist's arsenal of appraisal approaches.[8] In reality, however, it was developed in response to the nature of modern documentation and perceived weaknesses in archival appraisal approaches. As a result, the documentation strategy must be considered as a part of archival appraisal theory, even though some have simply preferred to describe it as a *new* discussion about *old* concerns.[9]

The archival documentation strategy has stimulated considerable discussion in the archival profession since the concept was introduced. Some of this discussion has occurred due to misconceptions about the documentation strategy concept and because of varying notions of what constitutes archival appraisal theory (or whether there is such theory or not).[10] Many archivists think that the concept is meant to replace or supersede other archival appraisal principles and techniques; rather, the strategy is intended only to provide another needed procedure and to add a missing perspective to the archival appraisal process and theoretical foundations of appraisal. Others confuse the concept with other appraisal tools such as surveys, which are quite different. Finally, a smaller group of archivists believes that the documentation strategy concept violates basic archival appraisal theory, although what constitutes this theory or the violation has never clearly been indicated.

Building a Set of Archival Appraisal Principles

As a result of such preconceptions of knowledge and practice, archivists have not made many efforts at systematizing the principles

---

8 Hackman and Warnow-Blewett, "The Documentation Strategy Process," 20.

9 Abraham, "Collection Policy or Documentation Strategy," 44-52.

10 This can be seen most clearly and recently in Roberts, "Archival Theory: Myth or Banality," which views archival appraisal as an archival function that requires little theoretical knowledge. I suspect that many of Roberts's ideas are shared widely by archivists in the United States, the implications of which are that you do the best you can within your own institutional setting and do not worry about the consequences. Everything is subjective, and there is no real sense of common archival principles or any knowledge base. Roberts's attitudes, a confusion between archival theory and professionalism (which are related but quite different), work against any need to consider carefully the selection process except that you try to satisfy your own needs and the needs of your time as far as the preservation of information is concerned. He is right that archival theory is underdeveloped, but he refuses to see any value in or need for a knowledge of archival work. Roberts can only see the documentation strategy as a plea for the "indivisibility of archives, and a structure for increased consultation in the documentation process through the use of committees" (p. 114). Roberts cannot see how the documentation strategy relates to other archival appraisal approaches and principles. (It is interesting that he ignores the more theoretical writing on the topic by Helen W. Samuels that relates the strategy as a response to a fundamental shift in the very nature of documentation.) His essay is more a reflection, perhaps, of personal frustration (although about what, I am not sure) about the profession. But his totally utilitarian approach to archives is widely shared, primarily because most practicing archivists in the United States have no formal education in archival science except for a few workshops and what in-service training they might have been able to acquire.

into a theoretical foundation. Perhaps the main reason for this lies in how archivists have viewed theory in general, as characterized by the debate set off by Frank Burke's 1981 essay, a debate ranging from "universal truths and laws"[11] through Cappon's overarching "principles" that "emerged empirically"[12] to rejections of theory altogether. These views come from the fact that many archivists perceive theory as akin to the kinds of theorems that constitute mathematical or abstract knowledge rather than as a more straightforward "systematic statement of rules or principles to be followed," or a "scheme or system of ideas or statements held as an explanation or account of a group of facts or phenomena."[13]

Appraisal has been defined through a delineation of values such as evidential and informational, as well as through the development of techniques such as sampling and institutional collection analysis. Such views remain common, especially, or so it seems, at the United States National Archives,[14] formerly the home of pioneer archival theorists such as Philip Brooks and T. R. Schellenberg, who built the foundation for an epistemological basis for appraisal. The diminution of this institution's role in archival theory in the past generation or so may be one very important reason for the flaws in archival appraisal theory and methodologies in the United States. Most of the recent original work has occurred outside of the National Archives.

The scope of archival appraisal has been transformed from a process that is institutionally bound to one that is perceived to be a multi-institutional function, primarily as characterized in the documentation strategy model. This multi-institutional aspect is an effort to deal with the nature of modern documentation. As one archivist has stated, no matter how effective the appraisal approaches have been, "both the theory and methods are inadequate and inflexible for appraising contemporary records."[15] This results from the problem of trying to decide whether appraisal should be defined on the basis of some set of common processes, functions, and principles or whether it should be identified through the roles that archivists take on in their institutions when they do appraisal.

The scope of archival appraisal as evidence of the need for archivists to expand their basic practices and cooperative endeavors is a topic that has only recently been re-analyzed via the formulation of the documentation

---

11 Burke, "Future Course," 42.

12 Cappon, "What, Then, Is There to Theorize About?" 21.

13 These various definitions are from the Oxford English Dictionary.

14 See, for example, Elizabeth Lockwood, "'Imponderable Matters': The Influence of New Trends in History on Appraisal at the National Archives," *American Archivist* 53 (Summer 1990): 394-405, in which an archivist's historical knowledge and training is seen to be more of a determinant of appraisal practice than anything else.

15 Hedstrom, "New Appraisal Techniques," 2.

strategy. Archival appraisal was originally seen as the process of ascertaining whether a specific document, records series, or even record group or manuscript collection possessed sufficient informational and evidential content for the archivist to invest additional resources in preservation, arrangement and description, and other basic archival work. The traditional view has been to focus on archives as evidence; the American contribution has been to add the informational dimension.[16] But it is evident that many archivists now view their role to be a selector of recorded information leading to a documentation of society based on some fundamental principles of archival appraisal. This view is a result of the archivist's recognition of the immense volume of records, the interrelatedness of records — even those produced by diverse institutions and organizations — and the increasing diversity of recorded information forms.[17] It may also be the result of the influence of manuscript curators (who intend to collect and through their collecting to document something) over archivists (who normally have been institutionally based, serving the needs of their employers). The blending of the two is, however, most appropriate and essential given the nature of modern documentation, which, in effect, brings together the public archives and manuscripts traditions that the U.S. archivists have long described.

However, two basic problems persist here. First, the archivist relies on archival approaches to select, although these principles increasingly have been shaped or influenced by library collection development and other fields. Second, the archivist has restricted his or her activity to the traditional documentary forms, whether in paper or electronic media. The questions that must be asked are whether the archivist can document society with such a restricted set of sources, and, just as importantly, whether the archivist plays a role in selecting beyond the traditional documentary sources. The archival documentation strategy concept has much to contribute to both of these and other like concerns, provided that archivists and their institutions are willing to experiment with the process and embed it in their basic modus operandi. Whether they do or not depends on their view of appraisal and archival theory, as well as their definition of the archivist's mission (is it to document society, or to preserve institutional evidence, or something else?).

---

16 This latter dimension has caused many non-Americans to criticize the U.S. archivists as documentalists rather than archivists. This is obviously meant to be a criticism. However, I would contend that 1) the archivist needs to take on some of the additional roles of the documentalist given the changing nature of documentation; 2) archival theory is not static, which the anti-documentalists seem to suggest; and 3) archivists can, at the least, cooperate with documentalists and others of a similar ilk to ensure that the documentary heritage is maintained (this can be achieved, of course, through the documentation strategy).

17 Hedstrom, "New, Appraisal Techniques," 3-7. See also Chapter Two in F. Gerald Ham, *Selecting and Acquiring Archives and Manuscripts* (Chicago: Society of American Archivists, 1992), which provides an excellent brief summary of the half-dozen prevailing models of archival appraisal.

Archival Appraisal Principles

There are a number of ways in which we can construct an archival appraisal theory. The manner that I selected is to work through a series of broad statements, made by archivists through the past century; at the same time, I have drawn on other appropriate fields relating to the nature of records and information, as well as related archival principles that may not be at the same level of theory but are still broad enough to be applicable across archival institutions and types of records. The approach is in line with a general notion of theory: "*Theories* are logically interconnected statements about the world that describe, explain, and predict the occurrence of phenomena. They are based on *empirical generalizations* about the world, which are in turn based upon analysis of our direct observations."[18] In what I consider a tour de force in library science, Michael Buckland has emphasized that theory is a body of generalizations and principles that are formed in their association with practice leading to the intellectual content of a discipline. Theory requires that there be the possibility of a coherent set of hypothetical, conceptual, and pragmatic principles that form a general frame of reference for a field of inquiry. This allows for defining principles, formulating hypotheses, and considering actions.[19]

Theoretical Foundations: A Preliminary Proposal Based on Twelve Appraisal Principles

The basis of an archival appraisal theory can be limited in its scope. It starts with the notion that all recorded information has some continuing value, if not to the creator of that information, then to society. The quantity of information is so great, however, that it must be reduced in order to be useful. This reduction requires careful and tested criteria, built upon the notion of evidential and informational values. These criteria, moreover, are not determined solely by the institutional creators of this information;

---

18 Judith A. Perrolle, *Computers and Social Change: Information, Property, and Power* (Belmont, Calif.: Wadsworth Pub. Co., 1987), 30. Another approach, which is beyond the scope of this article, is to study the manner in which records are created, used by their creators, and reused by their creators and others. The reason why this is beyond this study is because archivists and others have not analyzed this issue as effectively as they probably should have done. Hugh Taylor stated that "it is very curious and perhaps significant that, despite all the massive corpus of writing about management and administration, so little attention has been given to the impact of the various records" ("'My Very Act and Deed': Some Reflections on the Role of Textual Records in the Conduct of Affairs," *American Archivist* 51 [Fall 1988]: 461). Clark Elliott has stated the same matter more bluntly: "Documents are at the center of the concern of historians and archivists, and yet neither profession has directed very great attention to a consideration of writing as social communication and to the functional relationship of documents to historical events" ("Communication and Events in History: Toward a Theory for Documenting the Past," *American Archivist* 48 [Fall 1985]: 358). All this extends back to the fundamental conception of theories.

19 Michael K. Buckland, *Library Services in Theory and Context*, 2nd. ed. (New York: Pergamon Press, 1988), Chapter Five.

there are some generic characteristics of recorded information that suggest some common or universal appraisal criteria and processes. The selection of this information is not for some undetermined future research but for the present needs of the records creators and based upon the present knowledge of the record-generating institutions and society. Archivists must also be cognizant of other, non-textual, information sources that either complement or complete gaps in the traditional textual records. To ensure that the proper records are preserved, the archivist must be involved with the records creator as far up the life cycle of records as is possible. This also requires that archivists have as an appraisal mission the documentation of society, and that they participate in a team-oriented, multi-disciplinary appraisal process. Archivists must also acknowledge that, because of past failures in appraisal, certain records must be automatically kept because of their age or form. Archivists can also use, in a selective manner, some methods for reducing the volume of records already determined to have archival value. All of these elements of an appraisal theory are discussed below in relation to the documentation strategy concept.

Principle One: All recorded information has some continuing value to the records creators and to society. This is why archival appraisal is so difficult and so important. It is also difficult because archivists, having largely come from the humanities (history primarily), are prone to find value in virtually anything.[20] Allan Pratt has noted, for example, that while the scientist sees nothing wrong in discarding old scientific papers because these papers can be obsolete, the humanist is reluctant to destroy anything.[21] Archivist Maynard Brichford supported this humanistic perspective, indicating that "all records have some research value"[22] as have other archivists such as Luciana Duranti.[23]

This is probably the main reason why many archivists have determined that appraisal is a subjective process and why many have determined to define its parameters from single institutional or individual perspectives. It is also probably the reason why many archivists have criticized the process and results of archival appraisal. F. Gerald Ham's

---

20 The historical literature is full of studies that have essentially drawn upon surviving scraps of documentary evidence to develop broad interpretations of past societies. The increasing use by historians, for example, of material culture and archaeological evidence is indicative of this approach. My comments are not intended to disparage such efforts but are rather meant to suggest that these approaches should not be used by archivists to recommend that such uses guide appraisal decisions in documenting localities or any other systematic appraisal of modern documentation.

21 Allan Pratt, *The Information of the Image* (Norwood, N.J.: Ablex Publishing Corp., 1982), 48.

22 Maynard Brichford, *Archives & Manuscripts: Appraisal & Accessioning.* (Chicago: Society of American Archivists, 1977), 7.

23 Luciana Duranti, "So? What Else Is New?: The Ideology of Appraisal Yesterday and Today," in Christopher Hives, ed., *Archival Appraisal: Theory and Practice* (Vancouver: University of British Columbia, 1990), 2.

assessment was that "archivists waste time and space preserving random bits and pieces, as well as large accessions, of the most dubious value";[24] if so, it is probably because archivists give in to their sense that all recorded information has some continuing value to the records creators and to society.

Ironically, however, the notion that all records have some value is peculiarly that of the archivist and some researchers, primarily scholarly historians. It is not shared by organizational records creators. Judging by the writings of records managers and information resources managers, institutions are less interested in preserving their recorded documentation and more likely to define the length of time they maintain records through legal and fiscal obligations — which leads to maintaining very few records for any long-term uses. This point of view is counter to traditional views of archivists working in the Jenkinsonian tradition, in which the records creator determines the archival value and the archivist maintains the records.

Principle Two: The immense quantity of recorded information is an impediment to the information's continuing value, leading to the need for the reduction of this quantity. Six decades ago, Sir Hilary Jenkinson stated that the bulk of modern archives is a "new and serious matter" requiring the archivist's attention. This bulk is caused, according to Jenkinson, by easier duplication and other methods of modern technology.[25] He also noted that "there is . . . a real danger that in the future research work upon Archives may become a task hopelessly complicated by reason of their mere bulk."[26] Margaret Cross Norton, writing at about the same time and from her vantage point in the United States, also stated that the growing quantity of government records has meant that the "emphasis of archives work has shifted from preservation of records to selection of records for preservation." In her situation she advocated a process whereby the archivist worked also as a records manager, so that the quantity of records could be reduced by selection and through the application of photographic processes and the prevention of creation of unnecessary accumulation at the point of records origination.[27] Norton affirmed the fact that all government records have some value for historians and other researchers; she also noted, however, that "even the historian realizes the impracticality of working from such an avalanche of records as would result from keeping everything."[28] Schellenberg continued this theme:

---

24 F. Gerald Ham, "The Archival Edge," *American Archivist* 38 (January 1975): 6.

25 Sir Hilary Jenkinson. *A Manual of Archive Administration*, rev. 2nd ed. (London: Percy, Lund, Humphries and Co., 1966), 137-38.

26 Ibid., 148-49.

27 Thornton W. Mitchell, ed., *Norton on Archives: The Writings of Margaret Cross Norton on Archival & Records Management* (Carbondale, Ill.: Southern Illinois University Press, 1975), 232-33.

28 Ibid., 239.

the first sentence of his seminal writing on the appraisal of public records was "Modern public records are very voluminous."[29]

More recently, other archivists have continued to make this record characteristic an issue that they must contend with in their appraisal work. German archivist Hans Booms, for example, stated similar sentiments and presaged some of the concerns expressed by the architects of the American documentation strategy approach.[30] It is obvious that the quantity of modern documentation is a particular concern of archivists with mandates to document geographical regions or topics. The concern for volume drives the asking of the right questions, leading to a proper surviving documentary heritage; dealing with one of the most salient aspects of modern documentation, it is an approach that is very important in the modern information technology era.[31] The volume of information is bound to continue to increase through the growing sophistication and pervasiveness of information technology.

Principle Three: This reduction of documentary sources may occur through accident and natural events, resulting in a random or, at the least, partial aggregation of documentation that may harm the records creators and society. Archivists have not confronted this matter as they should have. Is this accidental accumulation better or worse than planned archival selection? In a perceptive essay on this matter, Daniel Boorstin has laid out a philosophy of the durable and the least used. He notes "how partial is the remaining evidence of the whole human past, how casual and how accidental is the survival of its relics."[32] One reason for this, he writes, is the fact that "there is a natural and perhaps inevitable tendency toward the destruction and disappearance of the documents most widely used. . . ."[33]

Individuals in many other disciplines and perspectives have echoed this concern. According to Kenneth Dowlin, an advocate of the modern high-tech library, "information has reached the stage where a significant proportion of what is produced is throw-away."[34] Historian and material culture specialist Thomas Schlereth has supported this: "Evidence comes

---

29 Schellenberg, "The Appraisal of Modern Public Records," 5.

30 Booms, "Society and the Formation of a Documentary Heritage," 77.

31 One commentator on the use of online information systems and hypermedia has suggested that the premise underlying the use of such systems is to provide as much information as possible, but that this "can simply offer someone, who is already under stress, more information to process, whether or not that information relates directly to the tasks at hand." Philip Rubens, "Online Information, Hypermedia, and the Idea of Literacy," in Edward Barrett, ed., *The Society of Text: Hypertext, Hypermedia, and the Social Construction of Information* (Cambridge: MIT Press, 1989), 17.

32 Daniel Boorstin, "A Wrestler with the Angel," *Hidden History* (New York: Harper & Row, 1988), 4.

33 Ibid., 5.

34 Kenneth Dowlin, *The Electronic Library: The Promise and the Process* (New York: Neal-Schuman Publishers, 1984), 14.

to us . . . often seriously flawed by the fecklessness of historical survival and the penchant of most collectors to save only those objects . . . that once had the highest monetary value and now do likewise as antiques. Frequently only the best or the most expensive of past craftwork has survived to be enshrined in museums and ensconced in private antique collections."[35] Historian J. R. Pole has contributed a different perspective to this concern, noting that the "records that survive are themselves the direct *consequences* of past social and political decisions. . . . They present the present mind with a choice that is vast and variable but never merely random."[36] This opens up the possibility for archivists to think and act more creatively in the documentation of regions, at least in examining the causes of the present survivals of documentation.

   This characteristic of accidental or natural survival of records poses, of course, some very fundamental questions for the archivist engaged in appraisal. Following Boorstin's lead, if the most important records tend to be those that were the most often referred to while still in the hands of their creator, there is the greater likelihood of their loss, weakening, or misplacement in the files, thus minimizing the contextual knowledge that is so important to the archivist understanding and evaluating the record. This conclusion argues against the more traditional view of the archivist waiting for relatively long periods of time *before* receiving the records from the creator; it also poses some interesting questions about allowing the creator to determine what should be preserved, as the Jenkinsonians contend.[37] We are led, instead, to a more activist stance of archivist interacting with records creator. Hugh Taylor, in his study of diplomatics, has said as much: "If the record is to be of maximum value to the administrator and where appropriate, to the general public as user, then archivists must be far closer to the point of creation and original use."[38]

   One can make a strong case for the development of solid criteria and some planned selection. The chance of natural selection will not necessarily result in documentation that provides clues to the most important aspects of an institution, an individual, or society — or that provides, if

---

35 Thomas Schlereth, *Cultural History and Material Culture: Everyday Life, Landscapes, Museums* (Ann Arbor: University of Michigan, 1990), 121-22.

36 J. R. Pole, *Paths to the American Past* (New York: Oxford University Press, 1979), xii-xiii.

37 The famous Grigg Report (the basis of public archives in Great Britain), based upon the Jenkinson approach, advocated that appraisal was the responsibility of the records creator and should not reflect the interests or biases of academic researchers. The first review of any records would be made 5 years after the records are closed by the departmental officer, not the archivist. Records passing this review would be analyzed again 25 years later to identify research value; this is the point where the archivist first becomes involved.

38 Taylor, "'My Very Act and Deed,'" 467.

desired, a representative record (as others in other disciplines have suggested).[39] What should be the desired end of archival appraisal? Should it be what the records creator determines is important, as the Jenkinsonians want? Is it what Ham calls for when he states that our "most important and intellectually demanding task as archivists is to make an informed selection of information that will provide the future with a representative record of human experience in our time?"[40] Or, is it some other paradigm, such as the notion of adequacy of documentation?[41]

Even those involved with the documentation strategy approach have not completely resolved this intellectual debate. They see the strategy as a concept allowing an approach that either can build a representative record or can answer the best formulated questions of what is needed to be preserved based upon the best present knowledge of what is important. This seems better than allowing institutional records creators to determine what should be saved — since their perspectives are often quite faulty in their own right[42] — or allowing individual decisions to occur about records without any real input by archivists and others as to why these documents might be worth saving.

Some might contend that a truly random process of survival is an alternative method of identifying what records should be saved. How could such a true random process be achieved in archival appraisal?[43] While such concerns are real, relying on a true random process instead of a deliberative appraisal process seems to be a dangerous move. Obviously, this is yet another area that requires more serious reflection and research.

Principle Four: Even a faulty archival appraisal decision or decision process is better than records surviving haphazardly or not surviving at all. Because all recorded information has some continuing value to the records creators and to society, each decision must be, by necessity, equivocal. As Margaret Cross Norton indicated, "it is comparatively easy to select records of permanent value, relatively easy to decide on those of no value. The great bulk of records are borderline."[44]

---

39 See, for example, J. Geraint Jenkins, "The Collection of Material Objects and Their Interpretation," in Susan M. Pearce, ed., *Museum Studies in Material Culture* (New York: Leicester University Press, 1989), 119-24.

40 Ham, "The Archival Edge," 5.

41 Edward F. Barrese, "Adequacy of Documentation in-the Federal Government," *Information Management Review* 5 (Spring 1990): 53-58.

42 Consider, for example, that most corporations lack any institutional archives or any other provision for the identification, preservation, and use of their archival records. They often fail to see the importance of their own records.

43 David Bearman, *Archival Methods, Archives & Museum Informatics Technical Report* 3 (Spring 1989): 2.

44 Mitchell, *Norton on Archives*, 240.

This nature has led, perhaps, to somewhat circular statements by pioneer archival theorists. Schellenberg's statement that "in the long run the effectiveness of a record reduction program must be judged according to the correctness of its determination" suggests far more questions than it answers.[45] On the other hand, there is considerable evidence that the researchers, at least the scholarly historians among the users of archival records, will make use of what they can find. Boorstin posed the matter very well when he noted that "the historian-creator refuses to be defeated by the biases of survival. For he chooses, defines, and shapes his subject to provide a reasonably truthful account from miscellaneous remains."[46]

This suggests some need for reflection by all archivists, but especially those engaged in appraisal, and even more so for those doing appraisal for institutions with mandates to document geographic regions or topics. Archivists should feel freer to experiment, evaluate, develop, and refine their appraisal theory, principles, and practices — something that archivists have done too little of — since mistakes made may tell us something about the needed criteria and not seriously harm the final documentary record left from a particular period. It should also indicate the need for archivists to work with their researchers in developing better criteria and understanding of their use. Despite the fact that use has long been defined as a fundamental reason for their existence, archivists have done a woeful job in systematically evaluating the nature and implications of such use. The user's perspective is extremely important since a satisfactory set of output measures for any archives ought to be its ability to meet its users' needs, a crucial aspect of an archival program's effectiveness.[47] If the wrong records are held by the archives, in the opinion of its potential researchers, then there is little hope for meeting their needs. As Brichford commented, "the surest proof of sound records appraisal lies in the quality of use of the archives and the growth of its reputation among the administrators and scholars it serves."[48]

Archivists have also been loath to admit mistakes in appraisal, falling back on the fact that a mistake in accessioning original materials, even if those materials are hardly ever used, is somehow acceptable because they are unique and irreplaceable. Libraries can make two kinds of errors in

---

45 Schellenberg, "Appraisal," 5.

46 Boorstin, "A Wrestler," 23.

47 Such a definition of effectiveness is based upon the definitions of library effectiveness and output devices used to measure that effectiveness. See, for example, Nancy A. Van House, Beth T. Weil, and Charles R. McClure, *Measuring Academic Library Performance: A Practical Approach* (Chicago: 1990).

48 Brichford, *Appraisal & Accessioning*, 1.

their selection: they can fail to acquire books that would have been used or they can purchase printed materials that are little or never used.[49] While there have been exceptions, archivists in general seem reluctant to consider such issues. Jenkinson did state that archivists should not criticize past archival selection decisions if they were made according to the standards of their time.[50] Luciana Duranti, from a different vantage point, has stated that she does not know of one situation in which "appraisal decisions have destroyed documents that we needed to have for our protection, development, and intellectual growth. When serious losses have occurred, they may have been caused by accidental circumstances in more recent times, by the voluntary destruction of records creators of compromising documents, abducted while they were still active, and sometimes in the initial phase of creation. . . ."[51]

This returns to the issue of the archivist needing to confer with the user, to maintain adequate records, and to conduct sufficient research to answer such concerns. There are some rare instances when the researcher speaks directly to the archivist about this, as did historian JoAnn Yates when she questioned whether archival appraisal approaches were not so inadequate for documenting businesses that it might be better to preserve comprehensively the records of a few representative corporations.[52] The issue of representativeness rears its problematic head here again. This is certainly one reason why the documentation strategy concept and approach is built through the archival records user and creator working *with* the archivist in determining appropriate questions to be asked and selection strategies to be formulated and carried out.

Principle Five: Because of the immensity of this documentation and the importance of recorded information to its creators and society, a well-developed set of universal or common archival appraisal criteria is one of the most important elements for appraisal. This is a long-held view of the archivist — although the actual development of criteria has been less than successful. Maynard Brichford, on the first page of his appraisal manual, declared that the "most significant archival function is the appraisal or evaluation of the mass of source material and the selection of that portion that will be kept."[53] What should be the basis for these criteria? They should first of all rest on a theoretical foundation representing how organizations, people, and society function and be cognizant of archival appraisal practice that has proved successful in achieving this representation. Part of this

---

49 Malcolm Getz, *Public Libraries: An Economic View* (Baltimore: Johns Hopkins University Press, 1980), 107.

50 Jenkinson, *Manual of Archive Administration*, 139-40.

51 Duranti, "So? What Else Is New?," 12.

52 JoAnne Yates, "Internal Communication Systems in American Business Structures: A Framework to Aid Appraisal," *American Archivist* 48 (Spring 1985): 141-48.

53 Brichford, *Appraisal & Accessioning*, 1.

representative record should be the preservation of all records that serve as vital evidence for the organization; it is the remainder, the informational, that is so elusive. Some archivists have demonstrated that the practice and theory of other disciplines that affect the nature of recordkeeping to a certain degree must be used for developing effective archival appraisal criteria. This can be seen in David Klassen's view that records going into a social welfare archives should be derived from the documentation that is largely produced by that discipline's self-concious professional activity.[54]

The criteria should also facilitate effective decision making about the documentation that possesses archival value. In the field of management, Maier developed a formula characterizing an effective decision as equaling quality times acceptance. Quality is the feasibility of a decision arrived at by the use of data, facts, and analysis; it is the result of the cognitive or intellectual process. Acceptance is more subjective, suggesting the personal aspects of a problem that has been determined by those affected by the decision; it is the emotional and nonintellectual aspect of the human decision making process.[55] This notion clearly suggests that the archivist, in conducting appraisal, must know the objective of the appraisal process and determine the reactions of the records creators and users to the selection. Some archivists have suggested that this is at the heart of the archival appraisal dilemma: "I also contend," wrote David Bearman, "that we will only be able effectively to appraise larger volumes of records if we focus our appraisal methods on selecting what should be documented rather than what documentation should be kept, and develop tactics for requiring offices to keep adequate documentation, rather than trying to review what they have kept to locate an adequate record."[56] This is also affirmed by less theoretical notions of decision making. According to Charles McClure, a leading student of library and information professional effectiveness, "if one defines decision making as that process whereby information is converted into action, then decision making has largely to do with the process of acquiring, controlling, and utilizing information to accomplish some objective."[57] In this sense, the archivist conducting appraisal must do everything necessary in order to determine the desired ends of appraisal, consider the universe of documentation, and reflect on the users' and creators' interest in the appraisal decision. This also takes us back to the user, of course: standard systems approaches set forth classic input-output measures, with output being the effectiveness of use.

---

54 David Klassen, "The Provenance of Social Work Case Records: Implications for Archival Appraisal and Access," *Provenance* 1 (Spring 1983): 5-26.

55 John R. Rizzo, *Management for Librarians* (Westport, Conn.: Greenwood Press, 1980), 202-3.

56 Bearman, *Archival Methods*, 14-15.

57 Charles McClure, "Planning for Library Effectiveness: The Role of Information Resources Management," *Journal of Library Administration* 1 (Fall 1980): 4.

The reason for the significance of selection criteria is that the appraisal process is fundamental to the mission of any archival institution. Peter Drucker has noted that "profit is not a cause but a result — the result of the performance of the business in marketing, innovation, and productivity."[58] Archivists must ask what the equivalent of "profit" is for their organizations. Most would state that it is the successful use of their archival holdings by researchers. This successful use is dependent on appropriate and wise appraisal decisions. Akin to what Drucker stated about business organizations, use — if equal to profit — is dependent on appraisal; appraisal is likewise dependent on knowledge of researchers' needs, specified aims for appraisal, and the appropriate ability to perform these.

Is there a framework or other basis for such criteria? Even without a framework, are there suitable criteria for guiding appraisal? Most archivists would immediately point to the classic statements on evidential and informational values as the criteria to be followed. There have been detractors, such as Norton, who argued that "records are created for one purpose and for one purpose only, namely, to fulfill an administrative need; and if the records fulfill that need, the archivist considers them adequate. . . . If, as often happens in the case of government records, the documents tend to take on value for purposes of historical or other research, that is so much 'velvet.'"[59] Moreover, the concepts of evidential and informational value, as other specific criteria, have not been all that well defined. Schellenberg himself noted that "the distinction between evidential and informational values is made solely for purposes of discussion. The two types of values are not mutually exclusive."[60]

Other archivists have tried to refine these criteria by providing more specificity. Brichford describes uniqueness, credibility, understandability, time span, accessibility, frequency of use, type and quality of use as more specific criteria for selection for preservation.[61] Many archivists fall back upon these criteria as if they are precisely defined and use them as the explanation for most of their decisions. It is not difficult to see them devising checklists or weighted evaluation scales based on such records characteristics. In many cases, the use of the terms seems ill-advised and certainly lacking in methodological rigor.[62]

---

58 Peter Drucker, *Management: Tasks, Responsibilities, Practices* (New York: Harper & Row, 1974), 71.

59 Mitchell, *Norton on Archives,* 250-51.

60 Schellenberg, "Appraisal of Modern Public Records," 7.

61 Brichford, *Appraisal & Accessioning.* Such criteria have also been extended to museum artifacts, another factor suggesting connections between the archivists and museum curators: see *20th Century Collecting: Guidelines and Case Studies,* Special Report, *History News* 47 (May/June 1991).

62 Lockwood, "'Imponderable Matters,'" discusses this but does not seem to be particularly concerned about it.

The classic case of this is the notion of intrinsic value. This value is a very specific criterion possessing a lengthy set of terms used to define its parameters. A close reading of these terms, however, reveals a lack of precision itself. Terms as value-laden as "aesthetic or artistic" are used. Ironically, the only publication defining the concept of intrinsic value states clearly that its use is relative: "opinions concerning whether records have intrinsic value may vary from archivist to archivist and from one generation of archivists to another." Yet the same publication states, in one of the most obvious contradictions in the profession, that the "archivist is responsible for determining which records have intrinsic value," refuting the notion that archivists probably seek outside assistance in this.[63] Nevertheless, intrinsic value is seen by some as one of the major recent contributions to archival theory. [64] Some of this may be due to the fact, as lexicographers have found, that the precise or ultimate meaning of any word is impossible to determine. Archivists need interaction with individuals at either end of the spectrum, from institutional records creator to records user. It is this function that the documentation strategy makes an effort to provide.

Principle Six: The criteria that provide the basis for archival appraisal decisions are independent of records creators and their institutions and are generic to recorded information. Malcolm Getz, in his economic study of public libraries, suggested that "each library is molded at its birth by the needs that existed at that time."[65] What he meant was that these needs establish an institution's mission — which remains the continuing formative influences on libraries. If this is also true for archives (and I think it is true for all organizations), it means that appraisal practices, collection policies, and missions will be dictated by the institution's long-standing aims and traditions — rather than by the changing nature of society and its information systems and needs. It suggests that archival programs founded before the computer may continue to exercise older notions of how to carry out their mission rather than adapt to dealing with newer systems — partially explaining, in fact, why it has been so difficult for the archival profession to cope with electronic records.[66] Kevin Lynch, looking at this matter from the perspective of city planning and architecture, has suggested that urban preservation has been the "work of established middle- and upper-class citizens. The history

---

63 *Intrinsic Value in Archival Material,* Staff Information Paper 21 (Washington, D.C., 1982), 1, 3.

64 Trudy Huskamp Peterson, "The National Archives and the Archival Theorist Revisited, 1954-1984," *American Archivist* 49 (Spring 1986): 129-30.

65 Getz, *Public Libraries,* 45.

66 The standard explanation has been, of course, that electronic records pose severe technical problems that have been outside the scope of the archival profession's traditional training or that these records violate certain basic tenets of archival theory. These explanations are not totally satisfactory.

enshrined in museums is chosen and interpreted by those who gave the dollars."[67] Some of this is clearly dependent upon the filiopietistic origins of most historical societies and museums. Archivists have to make an effort to break away from such mindsets to provide a more even documentation of modern society.

There is little question that the need to understand how records originated in their environmental setting is important. Schellenberg noted that the "archivist must know how records came into being if he is to judge their value for any purpose."[68] This is clearly seen in Yates's study of internal communication systems in business organizations.[69] It can also be seen in an analysis of individual documents. Maps, for example, are "unique systems of signs. . . . Through both their content and their modes of representation, the making and using of maps has been pervaded by ideology. Yet these mechanisms can only be understood in specific historical situations."[70] The nature of modern documentation poses a number of interesting problems. Samuels has concluded that the "analysis of single institutions . . . is insufficient to support the [appraisal] decisions archivists face." "Institutions do not stand alone," Samuels contends, "nor do their archives."[71] Michael Lutzker has noted that "all working archivists recognize . . . that the records we receive, no matter how voluminous, contain something less than the full administrative history of our institutions."[72] Ham has also made this point: "in spite of the bulk and redundancy of modern records, there is also a problem of missing data."[73]

Yet the consensus among archival practitioners seems to run counter to this assessment. Frank Boles and Julia Young have stated that the "analysis of this element takes place within a universe defined by the archivist's experience and knowledge." That experience and knowledge is defined by their institutional setting. "Repository policies . . . and acquisition policies in particular, should guide the archivist in establishing the relative weights that should be assigned to the components and their elements."[74] In an article penned solely by himself, Boles carried

---

67 Kevin Lynch, *What Time Is This Place?* (Cambridge: MIT Press, 1972), 30.

68 Schellenberg, "Appraisal of Modern Public Records," 8.

69 Yates, "Internal Communication."

70 J. B. Harley, "Maps, Knowledge, and Power," in Denis Cosgrove and Stephen Daniels, eds., *The Iconography of Landscape: Essays on the Symbolic Representation, Design and Use of Past Environments* (Cambridge, England: Cambridge University Press, 1988), 300.

71 Samuels, "Who Controls the Past," 111, 112.

72 Lutzker, "Max Weber," 129.

73 F. Gerald Ham, "Archival Choices: Managing the Historical Record in an Age of Abundance," in Nancy E. Peace, ed., *Archival Choices* (Lanham, Md.: Lexington Books, 1984), 133.

74 Frank Boles and Julia Young, "Exploring the Black Box: The Appraisal of University Administrative Records," *American Archivist* 48 (Spring 1985): 129, 131.

this thinking to its natural conclusion, suggesting that "appraisal can be understood to be a three-part activity, involving first the application of institutional interest evaluation, second the implementation of record evaluation criteria, and third . . ., the interaction of institutional interest evaluation and record evaluation."[75] While this kind of thinking perhaps represents a very practical approach to appraisal, it potentially ignores the need to understand recordkeeping, information systems, and the nature of modern documentation. It is a denial of the empirical foundation of archival theory. Here, of course, the archivist must make a choice: the dependence on a single institutional perspective or expansion to multi-institutional approaches and various other interests as provided for in the documentation strategy.

Principle Seven: The most fundamental aspect of appraisal is the consideration of records as part of an organic whole related to institutional purpose and function. In their famous late-nineteenth-century manual, Muller, Feith, and Fruin stated that "an archival collection is an organic whole, a living organism, which grows, takes shape, and undergoes changes in accordance with fixed rules."[76] They also noted the fundamental archival truth that documents are often difficult to understand if removed from their context, since "the various documents of an archival collection throw light upon one another."[77]

This contextual aspect is reflected in many other documentary (and, even nondocumentary) fields. Lynch, in historic preservation, noted that "under the banner of historical preservation, we have saved many isolated buildings of doubtful significance or present quality, which are out of context with their surroundings and without a means of supporting their use or maintenance or of communicating their meaning to the public."[78] In archaeology "a find's context consists of its immediate *matrix* (the material surrounding it, usually some sort of sediment such as gravel, sand, or clay), its *provenience* (horizontal and vertical position within the matrix), and its *association* with other finds (occurrence together with matrix)."[79] Field archaeology is "based on the theory that the historical value of an object depends not so much on the nature of the object itself as on its associations."[80] Schlereth, looking at material culture and museum

---

75 Frank Boles, "Mix Two Parts Interest to One Part Information and Appraise Until Done: Understanding Contemporary Record Selection Processes," *American Archivist* 50 (Summer 1987): 358-59.

76 Samuel Muller, J. A. Feith, and R. Fruin, *Manual for the Arrangement and Description of Archives* (New York: H. W. Wilson, 1968), 19.

77 Ibid., 36.

78 Lynch, *What Time Is This Place?*, 37.

79 Colin Renfrew and Paul Balm, *Archaeology: Theories, Methods and Practice* (New York: Thames and Hudson, 1991), 42.

80 Leonard Woolley, *Digging Up the Past* (Baltimore: Rowman and Littlefield, 1973; orig. pub., 1930), 18.

collections, has considered the same problem: "Without a documented context, many artifacts remain little more than historical souvenirs."[81] Another museological rumination stated that the "universal language spoken by curators about these artefacts is contextual."[82] Stephen Jay Gould, writing from the perspective of a paleontologist, expressed the same concept in his treatise on the Burgess Shale: "What do scientists 'do' with something like the Burgess Shale, once they have been fortunate enough to make such an outstanding discovery? They must first perform some basic chores to establish context — geological setting (age, environment, geography), mode of preservation, inventory of control."[83]

This principle, perhaps a universal law, requires the archivist to look at records in their institutional context and to not consider them piecemeal — a fault pertaining more to the manuscript curator operating under a collecting policy than to the institutional archivist serving the needs of an organization. Jenkinson also suggested this same principle, noting that destruction had to be done on the large scale; otherwise it is too expensive to perform.[84] Schellenberg likewise argued that "appraisals of evidential values should be made on the basis of a knowledge of the entire documentation of an agency; they should not be made on a piecemeal basis."[85] More recently, Booms has shown the international hold on this idea: "The value of a particular item only becomes apparent when it is set in relation to something else and compared with that other item."[86] In general, archivists have interpreted this solely within an institutional environment, when in fact the changing nature of modern documentation demands a multi-institutional approach, as seen in the documentation strategy model.

Principle Eight: The quantity of recorded information should be reduced in a planned manner, based upon carefully determined and tested selection criteria. Planning has become a fundamental aspect of archival practice. Faye Phillips, in the best statement of archival acquisition policies, noted that "policies must precede active collecting rather than be developed as an afterthought." Why? Because "sporadic, unplanned, competitive, and overlapping manuscript collecting has led to the growth of poor collections of marginal value."[87] Judith Endelman also has shown how

---

81 Schlereth, *Cultural History and Material Culture,* 382.

82 Peter Gathercole, "The Fetishism of Artifacts," in Susan M. Pearce, ed., *Museum Studies in Material Culture:* (New York: Leicester University Press, 1989), 76.

83 Stephen Jay Gould, *Wonderful Life: The Burgess Shale and the Nature of History* (New York: W. W. Norton, 1989), 97.

84 Jenkinson, *Manual of Archive Administration,* 141-43.

85 Schellenberg, "Appraisal of Modern Public Records," 11.

86 Booms, "Society and the Formation of a Documentary Heritage," 82.

87 Faye Phillips, "Developing Collecting Policies for Manuscript Collections," *American Archivist* 47 (Winter 1984): 31, 36.

planning in reverse, using the notion of institutional collection analysis, is so essential to the refinement of acquisitions policies.[88] It is the matter of comparison between what we think we have been doing with what we have actually done. Careful planning is also important because appraisal dictates so much of what we do in all our activities: the use of our resources, the service to society, and whether we have been successful at all. As Ham has stated, "in a profound way we are also a product of our decisions."[89]

It is possible to detect these kinds of problems in other fields concerned with documentation. In Sweden, and other nations, history museum professionals have turned to careful planning because "it was clear that unless plans were made to document contemporary life, museums would be leaving behind the same kind of fragmented collections of their time that they inherited from past generations of curators."[90]

The planned archival appraisal process is especially important because a decision to save records is also a decision to destroy some other records. Due to the preservation requirements of recorded information and the limited resources of the archival repositories, not all of this information can be saved. Planned selection is often the result of both the peeling away of documentation that does not have value and the focus on documentation that is the most important. There is some universality in the combination of preservation-destruction; field archaeology has noted that "all excavation is destruction" in order to identify evidence of past settlement.[91]

Planning can conjure up numerous specters for archivists and other information professions, especially when it comes to a function such as appraisal. One librarian noted that the benefits of planning (minimizing risk, facilitating control, etc.) were counterbalanced by loss of communication, drop in motivation, lack of an opportunistic stance, and, most importantly, loss of creativity.[92]

The concept of planning as it is used in the archival documentation strategy must be clarified, in order to prevent undue confusion. Planning is careful research, evaluation, and reflection relative to the aspects of society and its people and institutions that are sought to be documented. Planning is also the mechanism by which various groups are brought

---

88 Endelman, "Looking Backward," 342.

89 F. Gerald Ham, "Archival Strategies for the Post-Custodial Era," *American Archivist* 44 (Summer 1981): 216.

90 Harry R. Rubenstein, "Collecting for Tomorrow: Sweden's Contemporary Documentation Program," *Museum News* 63 (August 1995): 56.

91 Woolley, *Digging Up the Past*, 40-41.

92 Dorothy J. Anderson, "The High Cost of Planning," *Journal of Library Administration* 6 (Spring 1985): 9-16.

together to enable such reflection to take place. The development of a documentation strategy should enable greater creativity to occur in the appraisal process, thus ensuring a better documentary heritage.

*Principle Nine: The archival appraisal selection criteria should rest not on unpredictable **future** research practices and trends but upon the more predictable sense of determining what are the salient and important features of contemporary institutions and society.* There have been numerous suggestions made by archivists through the years that their selection and preservation of archival records is for future researchers. Technically, this is true. Records brought into the archives will not be used until *some* point in the future, but many archivists have also suggested either that they must be able to predict future use and acquire records for it, or that they must be in the business of collecting to encourage new kinds of research. While encouraging use is a legitimate role for the archivist, any kind of prediction is an unreliable and inadequate basis for appraisal decisions. Andrea Hinding speculated that "outguessing the future by more than a few years is a game that no one, by definition, can win."[93] A more valid statement of this is that of Luciana Duranti: "*permanent value* is the capacity of consigning to the future the essence of a society's culture; it is the power of making permanent a society by making its culture a vital part of any future culture."[94] Jenkinson commented that archives acquired from the past should not be destroyed because it is impossible to predict their future use and unwise to superimpose the values of the present day on past decisions that led to the formation of those archives.[95]

This concept of Jenkinson's, which is contrary to more recently formulated notions such as reappraisal, sampling, and weeding, questions the basis of a relevant archival appraisal theory; certainly Jenkinson's advice must be used with caution, since he also stipulated that "destruction is an operation which can only be practiced with undoubted safety in one case — that of word-for-word duplicates."[96] Such a notion must be moved aside in the light of the vast bulk of modern archives and the increasing complexity of modern documentation and information systems. Other information specialists have also struggled with this concern. Benjamin Bates, for example, has suggested that the "value of information comes from its use at some future point, and is influenced by the circumstances of that use." However, he noted that the problem is that "information goods cannot be given a definitive or concrete value prior

---

93 Andrea Hinding, "Toward Documentation: New Collecting Strategies in the 1980s," *Options for the 80s: Proceedings of the Second National Conference of the Association of College and Research Libraries* (Greenwich, Conn.: JAI Press, 1981), 535.

94 Duranti, "So? What Else Is New?," 12.

95 Jenkinson, *Manual of Archive Administration,* 144-45.

96 Ibid., 147.

to their use, and that information goods may be used more than once."[97] This suggests that archivists need to rethink the basis for their appraisal decisions, fixing such decisions to a more concrete foundation than something as indeterminate as future use.

Characterizing the archival appraisal process in this manner brings up the old bugaboo of "objectivity." As soon as one raises the matter of trying to conduct appraisal in a manner that is planned, in order to capture the important issues of any institution, period, locality, or aspect of society, the questions of who decides what is important enters into the discussion and the notion of objectivity becomes the prime concern. We know that we are inadequate to the task. In an impressive analysis of our knowledge of the past, David Loewenthal concluded that the "past as we know it is partly a product of the present; we continually reshape memory, rewrite history, refashion relics."[98] Characterizing the work of history museums and historical societies, Thomas Schlereth observed that "there is bias in every method of collecting" and that the major method of dealing with this bias is to be aware of it.[99] Archivists could say the same.

How does objectivity fit here? Where do archivists' concerns with this matter really originate? For American archivists, at least, the concept derived from their origins as a profession in the old framework constructed by the scientific historians of the late nineteenth and early twentieth centuries. We have since learned that the concept of objectivity was a misreading of the intentions of the German historical school of Leopold von Ranke. As Peter Novick eloquently states, von Ranke and his followers did not intend history to be a nomothetic (law-generating) activity, but rather an ideographic (particular-describing) one; Americans took it as the former. Even if this were not the problem, the American archivist would still be required to reconsider the matter of objectivity. Archivists continually return to the argument about the centrality of historical study in their education and the need to understand their researchers' research methods and trends — yet the past 20 or 30 years has found the history profession in disarray over such concerns as objectivity and disinclined to stress method over subject content or political relevancy of their research in its published form. "By the seventies and eighties," according to Novick, "American professional historians' attitudes on the objectivity question were so heterogeneous that it was

---

97 Benjamin Bates, "Information as an Economic Good: Sources of Individual and Social Value," in Vincent Mosco and Janet Wasko, eds., *The Political Economy of Information* (Madison, Wisc.: University of Wisconsin Press, 1988), 77-79.

98 David Loewenthal, *The Past Is a Foreign Country* (Cambridge, 1985), 26.

99 Thomas Schlereth, "Contemporary Collecting for Future Recollecting," *Museum Studies Journal* 113 (Spring 1984): 26.

impossible to identify anything resembling a dominant sensibility." In addition, as he poignantly pointed out, the "evolution of historians' attitudes on the objectivity question has always been closely tied to changing social, political, cultural, and professional contexts."[100]

Objectivity in archival appraisal should always be a concern: it was, in fact, one of the concerns that led archivists to worry about the underdocumented elements of society in the 1960s and 1970s. Now objectivity needs to be seen as a goal in guiding appraisal decisions, not as something that hamstrings the appraisal process aimed at developing a reasonable documentary heritage that will be welcomed by both records creators and researchers wanting the kinds of information found in archival records. What are the options? Should the archivist allow the records creator to decide? Should the element of random survival dictate? Should the researcher, not considering objectivity but certainly deciding relevant information for his or her own specific slant and interest, make the appraisal decision? Or should the archivist, in tandem with and cognizant of researchers' needs and the records creators' desires, be the guiding force in determining what records will be selected and re-selected for preservation and other special treatment in order to ensure long-term use?

Some archivists have become preoccupied with the time distance they require (or think they require) from the records they are appraising. Their concern is that it is difficult to know what features of an institution or society will be important in the future. James R. Beniger, in his work on the origins of the "information society," addressed this problem directly: "one tragedy of the human condition is that each of us lives and dies with little hint of even the most profound transformations of our society and our species that play themselves out in some small part through our own existence." Reflecting on the reasons for this, the problems with it, and its results, Beniger offered a different lesson for the archivist: "Because the failures of past generations bespeak the difficulties of overcoming this problem, the temptation is great not to try." Instead, he suggests it is possible to be sensitive to this. "This reluctance might be overcome if we recognize that understanding ourselves in our own particular moment in history will enable us to shape and guide that history."[101]

Principle Ten: Archival appraisal is an incomplete process if it is done without consideration of the information found in non-textual records that archivists often do not take responsibility for in their work. Archivists talk about their mission to document society and then proceed to concentrate all their energies and resources on only one aspect of "documentation."

---

100 Peter Novick, *That Noble Dream: The "Objectivity Question" and the American Historical Profession* (Cambridge, England: Cambridge University Press, 1988), 593, 628.

101 James R. Beniger, *The Control Revolution: Technological and Economic Origins of the Information Society* (Cambridge: Harvard University Press, 1986), 1-6.

George Lipsitz, in an analysis of American popular culture, noted that "historical memoirs and historical evidence can no longer be found solely in archives and libraries; they pervade popular culture and public discourse as well."[102] Information valuable or essential to understanding any topic, geographic area, event, movement, an individual's life, a family's development, or a society can be found in a tremendous number of "sources." Artifacts, archaeological remains, popular culture, oral tradition, folklore, publications, movies and television, and archives and manuscripts are all essential for documenting society. What are the relative importance of these sources? Is there a hierarchy of values attached to them? How do, or should, they relate to each other? Can archivists, concerned with documenting the culture of their institution or society, really afford to ignore such materials as come from popular culture and other sources?

Popular culture is the group of perspectives that people develop in their everyday existence as they interact with societal norms, authorities, and institutions. John Fiske, in his provocative writings on this topic, has noted that the "people make popular culture at the interface between everyday life and the consumption of the products of the cultural industries" and that "popular culture is made by various formations of subordinated or disempowered people out of the resources, both discursive and material, that are provided by the social system that disempowers them."[103] The results of these interfaces are texts that outsiders can use to interpret the people's activities and life-styles and that the people themselves use to give meaning to their own existence. These texts are far different from traditional archival sources. For John Fiske, then, a text is a beach, a mall, or the image of the popular singer-actress Madonna. In other words, as George Lipsitz has found, television, music, film, and literature have become a significant source of providing a collective memory for people, giving structure to their lives and helping to provide them with a sense of meaning. The same case can be made for material culture, the remains of buildings, everyday objects, and other artifacts. In an essay on documenting the built environment, Nancy Carlson Schrock has suggested that the "best sources for information about the built environment are the buildings or landscapes themselves," although their destruction and alteration have made other sources especially important.[104]

The potential meaning of material culture and the importance and difficulty of its selection for preservation can be seen in how a museum

---

102 George Lipsitz, *Time Passages: Collective Memory and American Popular Culture* (Minneapolis, Minn.: University of Minnesota Press, 1990), 36.

103 John Fiske, *Reading the Popular* (Boston: Unwin Hyman, 1989), 1-2, 6.

104 Nancy Carlson Schrock, "Images of New England: Documenting the Built Environment," *American Archivist* 50 (Fall 1987): 476.

seeks to use material culture remains (and, of course, other more traditional textual sources) to interpret the past for the public. An excellent
glimpse into this process was seen in the Historical Society of Pennsylvania's recent exhibition, "Finding Philadelphia's Past." The exhibition
sought not only to interpret the history of Philadelphia, but also to provide understanding about the role of collecting artifacts and archives.
The exhibition showed that one institution cannot gather all the important relics and information sources of the past and that items collected
for one purpose often take on different meanings as time passes. The
symbol of the exhibition became Benjamin Franklin's bifocals, "to remind
museum-goers of the need to look at the exhibition with dual vision —
with one eye to what is there, one to what is missing; one eye to earlier
interpretations of an object, one to more recent interpretations; one eye
to what an artifact meant to its prosperous owner, one to what it meant
to less privileged members of the society."[105]

Archivists need Franklin's bifocals and a better working relationship
with colleagues such as history museum curators. A discussion of the
Swedish documentation effort noted, for example, that the "program was
originally conceived as a means to strengthen the collections through the
acquisition of contemporary artifacts. As the actual work began, however,
collecting became secondary to the overall objectives of documenting
society."[106] In another of Thomas Schlereth's essays, he noted that the
"principal task of material culture studies is an epistemological one; it is
an attempt to know what can be known about and from the past and
present conditions of mankind." The use of material culture remains adds
to our documentary evidence: "Such [material culture] data can provide
the historian with an opportunity to explore a facet of the past," Schlereth
suggests, "first-hand as it were, not as translated by someone in the past,
writing down experience or orally transcribing what he encountered."
Archivists sometimes suggest that the evidence from the transactional textual record is somehow superior to other evidence. Schlereth states otherwise: "Material culture is consequently seen as one type of historical evidence that might mitigate some of the biases of verbal data that (in the
American historical experience) are largely the literary record of a small
group of mostly white, mostly upper or middle class, mostly male, mostly
urban, and mostly Protestant cadre of writers."[107]

---

105 Barbara Clark Smith, "The Authority of History: The Changing Public Face of the Historical
     Society of Pennsylvania," *Pennsylvania Magazine of History and Biography* 114 (January
     1990): 64. Other essays in this volume about the exhibition are by Gary B. Nash, Emma J.
     Lapsansky, and Cynthia Jeffress Little and provide, as a group, an illuminating exploration of
     the use of material culture and other historical records in public exhibitions.

106 Rubenstein, "Collecting for Tomorrow," 57.

107 Thomas J. Schlereth, ed., *Material Culture: A Research Guide* (Lawrence, Kan.: University Press of
     Kansas, 1985), 7, 10, 12.

Connecting all of this is the sense of collective memory. Kenneth Foote wrote that "consideration of the collective, independent nature of institutional memory . . . implies that the cultural role of the archivist is hard to isolate from the contributions of other institutions and traditions."[108] In fact, some archivists have identified such connections in a manner that should cause us to wonder why as a profession we have not done better in this regard. Clark Elliott argued that "we have chiefly the remains of one form of communication (written documents) from which must be inferred other forms of communication (oral) that have left no artifactual remains. We must also use the written documents to infer the relations of both these communication modes to larger events in history."[109] In other words, archivists have long been concerned with the role of records in documenting events, institutions, and society. It is a natural extension to include artifacts, as Hugh Taylor suggested when he wrote that

> we need to give a great deal more study to the cultural impact of our media of record to the ways in which they "work us over" as we communicate with them, and to develop a kind of meta-diplomatics as we come to understand how maps, photos, film, sound recordings and fine arts are to be "read" if they are to be interpreted accurately and their impact on us and society in general assessed. This is essential for effective appraisal, since we may have to recognize the most appropriate medium out of many to preserve an event.[110]

The documentation strategy approach provides the needed bridge between archivists and other disciplines — as well as to the records creators — to resolve such problems.

A more pervasive notion of documentation is essential in considering the nature of and processes for documenting society. Museums have recently come to realize the complexities of their roles in interpreting local public culture, as well as being a part of this culture, causing them to develop more energetic activities in dealing with the community.[111] Such concerns have been expressed by information scientists in the matter of information retrieval and use. Michael Buckland, reviewing the

---

108 Kenneth Foote, "To Remember and Forget: Archives, Memory, and Culture," *American Archivist* 53 (Summer 1990): 380.

109 Elliott, "Communication and Events in History," 359.

110 Hugh A. Taylor, "The Totemic Universe: Appraising the Documentary Future," in Christopher Hives, ed., *Archival Appraisal,* 24.

111 See, especially, Ivan Karp, Christine Mullen Kreamer, and Steven D. Levine, eds., *Museums and Communities: The Politics of Public Culture* (Washington, D.C.: Smithsonian Institution Press, 1992).

work of European information scientists, has noted their emphasis on
documents as being "any expression of human thought" and as evidence.
As Buckland notes, "if you claim to be interested in information science,
then you have to go beyond dealing with text and records of communication and include those other undoubtedly informative phenomena
[such as "material objects, objects having traces of human activity . . .,
explanatory models and educational games, and works of art"]."[112] As
the symbolic nature of archival sources is more important than is often
readily acknowledged,[113] proponents of documenting society have to see
that architectural remnants, industrial sites, artifacts, and other material
manifestations of the past have to be accounted for and may say something far more important than — or at least substantially different from
— archival sources. The best way to determine this may be to develop
more systematic documentation projects, with the documentation strategy as a conceptual guide.

   *Principle Eleven: The nature of archival appraisal planning requires the
archivist to be involved actively in the selection process, operating with the
assistance of the archivist's selection criteria and theory.* This activism includes
being as close to the beginning of the records life cycle as is possible, likewise not a new concept. Margaret Cross Norton stated that the "archivist
as the ultimate custodian is also interested in the creation of records.
After the records have been transferred to the archives, it is difficult to
weed the files and too late to supply gaps where necessary records have
not been properly made."[114] Norton, in considering the archivist's relationship to the records manager, went even further in the archivist's
connection to the creation process: "The archivist's training in research
methods, his intimate knowledge of the history of his government, and
his experience with the various ways in which records are used for purposes other than administration qualify him to take an active part in the
creation of government records."[115] It is especially important for this kind
of activity to be followed in working with modern electronic records, in
which the systems are fragile and quickly replaced; without intervention,
documentation in electronic form will be lost long before the archivist
ever has a chance to identify and save the record. For some archivists,
this concern has been expanded to include the need to assist selectively
in the creation of documentation.

---

112 Michael Buckland, "Information Retrieval of More Than Text," *Journal of the American Society
     for Information Science* 42 (September 1991): 586.

113 James M. O'Toole, "The Symbolic Significance of Archives," *American Archivist* 56 (Spring
     1993): 234-55.

114 Mitchell, *Norton on Archives*, 234.

115 Ibid., 248.

An interesting idea to consider might be whether the records life cycle can be extended to include the kinds of documentation created outside of institutions with regularized archival and records management operations. Some study needs to be done on the extent to which the papers of individuals, families, and small organizations such as civic associations and family-owned businesses may have specific times when they fall prey to destruction. Could we discover, for example, regular patterns in the cycles of existence of small businesses that would indicate to archivists when they should be most concerned with the safeguarding of their records (provided it has been determined that these records will contribute sufficiently to the greater objective of documenting society)?

Principle Twelve: The main purposes of planned archival appraisal are to document institutions, people, and society. Part of this planned documentation is to be sensitive to the underdocumented and often powerless elements of society. Archivists, influenced by the work of social historians, have been especially concerned about the documentation of certain aspects of society. This concern led to a number of efforts to develop special subject archives that collect with the intention of filling in gaps. These efforts have not led to the development of any new archival appraisal theory, although there is certainly a basic principle here. Danielle Laberge has stated that archivists must be cognizant of all elements of society and to the fact that some of these elements may not be well represented in or protected by the kinds of archival documentation most often preserved. This led her to articulate a specific principle that "archivists . . . must remember in designing selection and sampling criteria to protect as far as possible representative slices and samples of case file information in order to document the basic rights of groups and individuals in society."[116] Others have observed how a society's collective memory tends to be connected to that society's nature of power.[117] Representative documentation is again an important postulate of archival appraisal. Who is to say that this should not be viewed as an aspect of every institutional archival program's work — since most institutions are responsible for or accountable to society?

This notion of representativeness probably extends to other organizations such as museums; "useful and representative collections for the study and presentation of American social history" is, for example, a task of American history museums.[118] A librarian, looking at the criteria for preservation selection, has also noted that one purpose of preservation is

---

116 Danielle Laberge, "Information, Knowledge, and Rights: The Preservation of Archives as a Political and Social Issue," *Archivaria* 25 (Winter 1987-88): 49.

117 Paul Connerton, *How Societies Remember* (Cambridge: Cambridge University Press, 1989). See also David Thelen, ed., *Memory and American History* (Bloomington: Indiana University Press, 1989).

118 Rubenstein, "Collecting for Tomorrow," 55. See also *20th Century Collecting*, 4.

to "provide scholars of the future with access to some kind of representative collection of documentation."[119] Archivists have expressed major interest in appraisal for evidential purposes to serve their organizations; but these organizations have great social responsibilities as well.

There is some legitimate question, however, about the degree of consensus among archivists concerning this issue of representativeness. David Bearman has suggested that the "profession does not agree whether this record is intended to be 'representative' of all of recorded memory, or 'representative' of the activities of members of the society, or 'representative' of those aspects of social activity perceived by members of the society at the time as important to the understanding of the culture. Most archivists apply appraisal criteria to records, not to activities or social policy processes, and therefore assume that the goal is not to skew the record as received."[120] These are good points. Terry Cook has begun to articulate an appraisal theory that encompasses the notion of public interest, suggesting that any other approaches to appraisal must be open to modification by the greater interests of the public.[121]

The documentation strategy affords a perspective that will resolve where archival appraisal ought to be going, especially as such issues as being sensitive to various groups and interests becomes ever more important in a society concerned with such matters as multiculturalism and political correctness.

Conclusion

The archival documentation strategy is a planning mechanism for the archivist to use in working through the landmines represented by the fact that all recorded information has some continuing value. The documentation strategy provides a mechanism for a careful and systematic reduction in the bulk of documentation. The strategy adds to a solid set of selection criteria. It takes into account the specific nature of modern recorded information. It is built on the best possible understanding, that of present — not uncertain future — concerns and needs. The documentation strategy opens up the means for understanding how to document all of society, using textual, graphical, and artifactual information. All of these attributes are built upon a solid archival appraisal theory and other archival theory.

---

119 Ross W. Atkinson, "Selection for Preservation: A Materialistic Approach," *Library Resources & Technical Services* (October/December 1996): 349.

120 Bearman, *Archival Methods*, 12-13.

121 Terry Cook, "Many Are Called But Few Are Chosen: Appraisal Guidelines for Sampling and Selecting Case Files," *Archivaria* 32 (Summer 1991): 25-50 and "Mind over Matter: Towards a New Theory of Archival Appraisal," in Barbara L. Craig, ed., *The Archival Imagination: Essays in Honour of Hugh A. Taylor* (Ottawa, 1992): 38-70.

Leonard Rapport, in his article on archival reappraisal, noted that, in his opinion, "appraising is at best an inexact science, perhaps more an art; and a conscientious appraiser, particularly an imaginative one with an awareness of research interests and trends, is apt to know nights of troubled soul searching."[122] The documentation strategy is one way of improving the nights of all archivists. And it supports the fact that, as Terry Cook has stated it, "appraisal is a work of careful analysis and of archival scholarship, not a mere procedure."[123] The archival documentation strategy is a mechanism intended to aid such analysis and scholarship.

---

122 Leonard Rapport, "No Grandfather Clause: Reappraising Accessioned Records," *American Archivist* 44 (Spring 1981): 149.

123 Cook, "Mind over Matter," 47.

Part Four:
Appraisal

Once records have been selected and accessioned into an archives the evaluation of their ongoing significance continues. Appraisal is the process of determining which records should be preserved in the archives. As Maynard Brichford wrote in 1977:

> Appraisal is the area of the greatest professional challenge to the archivist. In an existential context, the archivist bears responsibility for deciding which aspects of society and which specific activities shall be documented in the records retained for future use. Research may be paralyzed either by unwitting destruction or by preserving too much.*

One of the central tenets of archival appraisal has been that archival records are unique and therefore have significance that must be considered in making appraisal decisions. James M. O'Toole offers a thoughtful analysis of this concept in "On the Idea of Uniqueness." O'Toole shows the different attributes of archives encompassed by the concept of uniqueness and suggests how a reconsideration of this idea can lead to reevaluation of other archival concepts.

As a central aspect of archival theory and practice, appraisal has generated a great deal of thought and analysis. This conceptual thinking has not always been translated into specific appraisal methodology. In "Exploring the Black Box: The Appraisal of University Administrative Records," Frank Boles and Julia Marks Young offer a model encompassing a wide range of criteria that archivists use in making appraisal decisions. The article illustrates the results of efforts to apply social science methodology to resolving archival challenges, with the goal of making appraisal a more rigorous and less subjective process.

Appraisal requires archivists to determine their fundamental conceptions about the nature of archives and the purposes served by archival

---

* Maynard Brichford, *Archives and Manuscripts: Appraisal and Accessioning,* Basic Manual Series (Chicago: Society of American Archivists, 1977), 1.

institutions. If archives serve only to document business transactions, then legal requirements and administrative needs will shape appraisal — as they do for retention scheduling as part of records management. Mark Greene takes a different approach in "'The Surest Proof': A Utilitarian Approach to Appraisal," arguing that the social and cultural purposes served by archives suggest the importance of considering use of the archives as an important appraisal criterion. In this article, Greene reveals the struggle of an American archivist seeking to incorporate various strands of archival theory into a particularly American approach to appraisal. This approach combines a contextual emphasis on evidential value with concern for informational content and the usefulness of records in making appraisal decisions.

11

On the Idea of Uniqueness

JAMES M. O'TOOLE

Abstract: *Archivists have generally described the records in their care as unique. While this description seems straightforward and absolute, it has in fact been used to denote several different attributes of archives: the uniqueness of records; the uniqueness of information in records; the uniqueness of the processes that produce records; and the uniqueness of the aggregations of documents into files. This essay explores how the idea of uniqueness has evolved, especially in relation to the changing technologies of record making, and it speculates on the future usefulness of the idea for archival theory and practice.*

'No one to talk with,
All by myself;
No one to walk with,
But I'm happy on the shelf. . . .'
    —Fats Waller

Archivists' understanding of what they do, how they do it, and why it is important all turn on a core group of concepts or ideas. Most of these derive from the particular nature of archival materials. Because records and manuscripts have certain characteristics, because they differ from other forms of recorded information, archives are perceived to require certain methods and techniques, and not others. Throughout their professional education and subsequent practice, archivists come to take these fundamental characteristics of archival records for granted, ticking them off readily if asked to do so. Archives are permanent records: they therefore deserve more protection and care than materials with only temporary usefulness. Archives are original: they are the best and most direct form of evidence available, because they are generally set down in immediate circumstances by the primary participants in human events.

Reprinted with permission from the *American Archivist* 57 (Fall 1994): 632-58. This article was written as a product of the author's participation in the 1993 Research Fellowship Program for the Study of Modern Archives administered by the Bentley Historical Library, University of Michigan, and funded by the Andrew W. Mellon Foundation and the University of Michigan.

Archives are organic: they grow, largely unobserved, out of individual and corporate activity, and they must therefore be understood in the context of that activity. Archives, particularly in the modern era, are potentially quite voluminous, and their meaning is thus collective: large accumulations of records are more significant than individual items. Archives are useful, not just to their original creators for their original purposes but also to other people later on, for entirely different purposes.

In daily professional practice, archivists seldom have either the need or the leisure to analyze the content of these ideas, but a periodic examination of them illuminates the nature of the archival enterprise and affects the way archivists actually do their work. What do we mean by these characteristics of archival materials? What have we meant by them in the past, and how have those meanings, which we encounter as fixed absolutes, evolved through time? Are these ideas as clear and unambiguous as we think they are? What might these archival ideas mean in the future, as technology and other factors change both the nature of records and the role they play in human society? The present study is part of the author's ongoing examination of these fundamental archival ideas, an attempt to articulate a kind of "systematic theology" (to borrow the now-common metaphor) of archives.

Of all the core archival concepts, none has been more central or more frequently identified than the idea of uniqueness. Archival records are thought above all to be unique, and much of their value is seen as a consequence of this inescapable circumstance. Unlike other forms of information, especially library materials, archival records are one of a kind. In professional practice, archivists rest secure in the knowledge that the uniqueness of the materials in their care justifies their efforts and makes their collections valuable. Users can find in archives information they can find nowhere else. The importance of preserving those unique records thus seems morally unassailable, even if programs to accomplish that preservation are not as widely recognized or as fully supported as they deserve to be.

From the point of view of day-to-day archives work, the presumption of uniqueness may be unavoidable. Unfortunately, however, the idea of uniqueness has never been as clear in professional thinking as we may assume; changing forms of archival records have subjected it to serious challenges, and new challenges continue today. Thus, it is worthwhile to explore the idea of uniqueness. What do archivists mean when they say that archival records are unique? What have archivists meant in the past by this uniqueness? Does the idea have a future?

Uniqueness in Archival Thinking

"Modern archives are unique in character," said T. R. Schellenberg in his 1956 work, *Modern Archives*, which became the basic textbook for more than one generation of archivists. The statement had a directness that was difficult to assail or doubt. Archives "do not exist in large and widespread editions as is often the case with publications of various kinds," he went on. "While many copies of particular records may be made, the archivist is usually concerned only with the unique files in which they may be embodied."[1] Defining archives in this way, by an explicit contrast with other sources of information, Schellenberg found uniqueness at the heart of the distinction. "Records are unique," he said again a decade later in a book exploring the similarities and differences of archival and library practice. "Publications usually exist in multiple copies. The content of one record repository, for this reason, varies almost completely from that of another; but the content of various libraries is more or less approximately alike."[2] Even when there had been "prodigality" in the production of "numbers of copies of individual documents," archival records retained their uniqueness, and everything archivists did with them flowed from that characteristic.[3] Schellenberg's contemporary, Margaret Cross Norton, expressed a like sentiment, highlighting the same comparison between archives and libraries: "The quality which distinguishes an archive [sic] from a library is its uniqueness," she said.[4]

By stating the case in this way, Norton and Schellenberg, whose professional outlook was framed by their work in the management of public records and who were leaders of the "founding generation" of the American archival profession, were making explicit an attribute of archives that had remained largely implicit in the work of the earlier English-language archival theorist Hilary Jenkinson. Jenkinson was reluctant to speak of "uniqueness" as such, but the idea was not very far beneath the surface of his "moral defense" of archives and his emphasis on the importance of preserving the sanctity of their original order. An unbroken chain of custody of records was critical to Jenkinson, who thought their protection from subsequent, outside contamination the most important task the archivist could perform. Precisely because the information in archives was unavailable elsewhere, Jenkinson believed, "the person or persons responsible" for creating them had to maintain them inviolate from other influences "for their own information" and that of "their legitimate successors." Any archival record might someday

---

1 T. R. Schellenberg, *Modern Archives: Principles and Techniques* (Chicago: University of Chicago Press, 1956), 114.

2 T. R. Schellenberg, *The Management of Archives* (New York: Columbia University Press, 1965), 68-69.

3 Schellenberg, *Modern Archives*, 50.

4 Margaret Cross Norton, *Norton on Archives: The Writings of Margaret Cross Norton on Archival and Records Management*, ed. Thornton W. Mitchell (Carbondale: Southern Illinois University Press, 1975), 87.

be required in legal proceedings, for example, and the preservation of its pristine character, and therefore its validity as evidence, was essential. Jenkinson did acknowledge the problem of duplicate copies of individual documents; he even distinguished between "word-for-word duplicates" and "sense duplicates." Even so, he thought both might be useful if they provided evidence that was otherwise unavailable.[5] The careful preservation and guarding of information that could be found nowhere else was the archivist's first responsibility.

For Schellenberg and subsequent archival theorists, however, the uniqueness of archives assumed a greater importance, and the meaning of uniqueness became most apparent in the difficult problem of appraisal. Jenkinson had thought that making decisions on which records to keep and which to discard was best left to administrators, but Schellenberg argued that this was the archivist's duty, and he offered a set of criteria for shaping the surviving documentary record. In determining what he called the informational value of records, uniqueness was the first and most important of three tests Schellenberg proposed. Writing in a National Archives staff bulletin, later expanded into his general archival textbook, he defined what he meant by the uniqueness of records and why it was important. Uniqueness might be seen in records themselves or in the information they contained, but in either case the appraising archivist was enjoined to "apply the test of uniqueness . . . with great severity." In an age of easy duplication, absolute uniqueness was probably rare, but if records and information "cannot be found elsewhere" or if they constituted "the sole adequate source of information," they had a legitimate claim on archival preservation. Thus, the value of records was directly proportional to their uniqueness. As rarity increased toward complete singularity, archival value similarly increased; as records became more plentiful and duplicative, their importance for archives was vitiated.[6]

Schellenberg's discussion of uniqueness deserves careful attention, however, because, even though he stated his case in the language of absolutes — being unique was apparently like being pregnant or dead: one either was or was not, with no in-between — he in fact saw the matter as a comparative or relative one. Unique information, he said, was that which could "not be found *in* other documentary sources in as *complete*

---

5 Hilary Jenkinson, *A Manual of Archive Administration*, rev. 2nd ed. (London: Lund Humphries, 1965; originally published 1922), 11. His discussion of the role of duplicates is at pages 140-55. My own opinion is that Jenkinson did not stress the idea of uniqueness as such because it related too closely to the value of archives for historical research. Since he sought to deemphasize the idea of archives as useful primarily for scholarship and to emphasize instead their role in ongoing administration, he was less concerned than other writers with characteristics that made archives useful in outside research.

6 T. R. Schellenberg, *The Appraisal of Modern Public Records*, Bulletin of the National Archives, no. 8 (Washington, D.C.: National Archives and Records Service, 1956): 22-24.

and as usable a form" (emphasis added): if relative levels of completeness or usability were admitted into consideration, varying gradations of the quality were apparently available. Absolute uniqueness was untypical, since information in certain records was often "similar or approximately similar" to that available elsewhere. The demand to preserve unique information in some records might even be satisfied if it could not be located "as fully or as conveniently" in others.[7] If mere "convenience" and records that were "approximately similar" could be accommodated, the precise assessment of uniqueness was even more slippery. This seemingly ironclad test of informational value had some very large loopholes.

Most writers on archival theory after Schellenberg echoed his stress on the uniqueness of archives, though they did not always seem to appreciate the tension he had introduced between the absolute and the relative. James Gregory Bradsher and Fredric Miller, for example, grounded their discussion of the nature of archives on the distinction between archival records and published books, and they traced the development of several characteristic archival practices to this distinction. Archives, Bradsher wrote, were "unlike books," which could almost always be replaced if lost, while Miller asserted that archival collections were wholly unique, unlike the materials "duplicated and collected in thousands of libraries."[8] Writers on appraisal in particular followed Schellenberg's lead in making the test of uniqueness essential in deciding whether to keep or destroy records. In one of the first single-volume treatments of appraisal, published in 1977, Maynard Brichford maintained that "unique records are unequalled in kind or excellence," while Frank Boles, writing 15 years later declared it "a truism that archives seek and preserve information that is unique."[9] Writers on physical conservation also stressed this quality of archival materials. Original records "possess unique and desirable characteristics lost in copying," wrote William Barrow, a pioneer in conservation technique, and these characteristics justified the expense and bother of restoring records that had deteriorated rather than simply microfilming or reproducing them.[10] Researchers, too, treasured the uniqueness of archival records for their own reasons. In what was a methodological guide for a generation of American graduate students in history, Philip Brooks told prospective researchers that, of

---

7 Ibid., 22, 23.

8 James Gregory Bradsher, "An Introduction to Archives," in *Managing Archives and Archival Institutions*, edited by James Gregory Bradsher (Chicago: University of Chicago Press, 1988), 7; Fredric M. Miller, *Arranging and Describing Archives and Manuscripts* (Chicago: Society of American Archivists, 1990), 4-5.

9 Maynard J. Brichford, *Archives and Manuscripts: Appraisal and Accessioning* (Chicago: Society of American Archivists, 1977), 8; Frank Boles, *Archival Appraisal* (New York: Neal-Schuman, 1991), 41.

10 William J. Barrow, "Deacidification and Lamination of Deteriorated Documents, 1938-63," *American Archivist* 28 (April 1965): 285.

all the characteristics of original source materials, "uniqueness is the most significant": copies, even if precise duplicates, were "not quite the same." Scholars thus had to be especially assiduous in identifying the information that was "not duplicated" in other sources.[11]

This uniqueness of archival holdings was taken as the foundation for many of the distinctive archival methods for ensuring the organization and accessibility of information. Appraisal continued to be the area where identifying the unique record seemed most critical. In the most recent summary of the subject, F. Gerald Ham proposed a series of questions for archivists to ask themselves in appraisal, including the blunt, if grammatically somewhat suspect, "How unique is the physical record?" and "How unique is the information in the record?"[12] Archival arrangement and description, too, took the form they did because of the uniqueness of records, many writers said. Norton had sounded this theme early on, maintaining that the singular nature of archives meant that archivists could not rely on "a preconceived [cataloging] scheme" as librarians did; rather, archivists had to "construct [their] classification scheme anew to fit the different types of records kept by each department." In the same way, Miller argued that, without "the impetus of common holdings" among repositories, shared cataloging and other cooperative descriptive programs had been slow to develop among archives. Uniqueness also remained essential for successful preservation programs. Mary Lynn Ritzenthaler emphasized the measurement of uniqueness in deciding which of the available conservation treatments might be appropriate in any particular case, though she did allow that uniqueness could be affected by "how many items of a comparable nature (such as Civil War diaries)" were also available.[13]

The treatment of records in special formats also seemed to require attention to their unique character. Not even changing physical forms could diminish the importance of this trait for archives. In fact, archivists might themselves alter the format of records in their collections through various reprographic techniques in the interest of sound management of their holdings. Audiovisual records were, of course, generally made with

---

11 Philip C. Brooks, *Research in Archives: The Use of Unpublished Primary Sources* (Chicago: University of Chicago Press, 1969), 11. Brooks's vague assertion that copies were "not quite the same" echoed Barrow's belief that originals had unspecified "desirable characteristics" absent from mere copies. Both, I think, were alluding to the emotional and evocative impact of original documents, especially old ones. I have tried to explore some of these issues in "The Symbolic Significance of Archives," *American Archivist* 56 (Spring 1993): 234-55.

12 F. Gerald Ham, *Selecting and Appraising Archives and Manuscripts* (Chicago: Society of American Archivists, 1993), 54.

13 *Norton on Archives*, 92; Miller, *Arranging and Describing Archives*, 5; Mary Lynn Ritzenthaler, *Preserving Archives and Manuscripts* (Chicago: Society of American Archivists, 1993), 12.

the intention that they would be duplicated, but the idea of uniqueness still applied to them; in fact, the traditional standard of uniqueness might be more important for such material, not less. One recent author cautioned photographic archivists to look always for "camera originals or magnetic masters" in order to "avoid the unknowing acquisition of materials that are duplicated at other institutions." Another warned that maps and architectural drawings have "less and less value with each duplication." Archivists should therefore concentrate only on "blueprints and similar photocopies that bear manuscript annotations," since "each is a unique document that must be considered on the merits of the annotations," not on those of the duplicated information. Still another maintained that electronic records, perhaps the most easily replicable of all, made archivists' judgments about uniqueness more important, rather than less.[14]

Uniqueness of Records. The apparent unanimity of archival opinion is deceptive, however, for while most writers have identified uniqueness as an essential characteristic of archives, a closer reading indicates that they have not at all agreed on what the idea really means or where the uniqueness of archives resides. In fact, when they have applied the word *unique* to archival records, archivists have been designating four very different things. For some, the term meant the uniqueness of *records themselves.* The actual physical items, individually and collectively, which archivists encountered were unique, Ham said, even if the information in them was duplicated or approximated elsewhere. It was this artifactual uniqueness that accounted, perhaps, for Barrow's slightly mystical reference to the "unique and desirable characteristics lost in copying." Unique records were, Brichford said, "the opposite of duplicated records" and the more valuable for it. A library might occasionally acquire one-of-a-kind items, such as rare books, Bradsher acknowledged, but archives necessarily consisted of "unique documents, created in the course of specific transactions."[15] In its most direct sense, the uniqueness of archives applied to the physical documentary objects themselves.

Uniqueness of Information. For other archivists, the form of uniqueness in records that really mattered was found not in the actual items but rather in *the information* they contained. Schellenberg had, after all, originally introduced the idea of uniqueness in his discussion of the

---

14 William H. Leary, "Managing Audio-Visual Archives," in *Managing Archives,* 108; John A. Dwyer, "Managing Cartographic and Architectural Archives," in *Managing Archives,* 95; Bruce L. Ambacher, "Managing Machine-Readable Archives," *Managing Archives,* 129. For a concise statement of archival uses of copying, see Carolyn Hoover Sung, *Archives and Manuscripts: Reprography* (Chicago: Society of American Archivists, 1982).

15 Ham, *Selecting and Appraising Archives,* 54; Barrow, "Deacidification and Lamination," 285; Brichford, *Appraisal and Accessioning,* 8; Bradsher, "Introduction to Archives," 8.

informational content of records, and most subsequent writers similarly
emphasized the unique information one could find in records, regardless
of whether the physical objects were or were not duplicated. The proper
goal of an archival program, said Boles, was to "seek and preserve information that is unique"; the "absolute uniqueness of the records" themselves was secondary. Given Schellenberg's observation on the "profligacy"
of modern duplication, Boles noted approvingly that contemporary
archivists were coming to acknowledge a genuine "interest in limiting
the number of individually unique yet collectively similar documents
that are the product of modern society." Scarce resources were thus
focused more properly on "truly unique information" than on unique
items. Maygene Daniels agreed, summarizing the common view by saying that, in order to qualify for archival preservation, "records should
contain information that is not available elsewhere." If they contained
duplicate or published information, she said, "they are probably relatively
unimportant."[16] Though applied somewhat loosely to particular documents, the idea of uniqueness applied more importantly, these archivists
said, to the information documents contained.

Uniqueness of Processes and Functions.   Other writers
emphasized neither the physical record nor its information content. For
them, what mattered was the uniqueness of *the processes and functions*
that produced records. Archival records were "the product of specific
and unique activities," Miller wrote, and this explained why no two
repositories had identical holdings. Bradsher's reference to the "specific
processes" that created "unique documents" echoed this belief that
whatever uniqueness there might be in records or information was an
effect of something else. Luciana Duranti, making a case for the application to modern records of the "old science" of diplomatics, maintained that every record was inescapably "linked by a unique bond to
the activity . . . producing it." Understanding that bond had to precede understanding the records. Helen Samuels, among others, argued
that only by analyzing the functions of contemporary institutions
would archivists be able to cope with the massive amounts of documentation they produced. Identification of the functions that generated
records, rather than detailed analysis of their contents, she said, was
the essential starting point in archival appraisal. Terry Cook maintained
that, in an archival world in which "the very notion of an original,
physical record" had become increasingly rare, shifting concentration
to the larger functions and activities of which records are the by-product
was the only systematic way for archivists to proceed. "Macro-appraisal"
of functional and procedural forms was more likely to succeed than

---

16 Boles, *Archival Appraisal*, 41, 105; Maygene F. Daniels, "Records Appraisal and Disposition," in
    Managing Archives, 62.

"micro-appraisal" of particular records or isolated bits of information, no matter how unique or informative.[17] Writers who approach uniqueness in this way have taken a step back from both the documents themselves and the information in them, emphasizing instead the processes that generate both.

Uniqueness of Aggregations of Records.   Finally, when still other archivists spoke of uniqueness they meant neither documents nor information nor processes but *aggregations of records*. Uniqueness derived from the way individual items had been assembled into files; it was those assemblages — and the fact that they had been put together in that way and not some other — that gave them the uniqueness archivists should care about. Individual documents and even the same bits of information might be widely duplicated in the files of many different offices or people, but each of those files was at least slightly different from the others, and this gave them their uniqueness. It was the "unique aggregations of records" produced by daily activity that archivists were interested in, Mary Jo Pugh wrote, and these had to be understood "in the context of other documents created by the same activity over time." Archives were "file units created or accumulated in connection with a specific business or administrative transaction," Bradsher said, and that accumulation gave them their uniqueness. Other kinds of information might be assembled, but these were random and unofficial, and they were not "unique, at least in the sense archives are."[18]

Not only have recent archival writers identified these varying connotations of the idea of uniqueness, but all of them have also agreed, tacitly or aloud, with Schellenberg that uniqueness is best understood in relative rather than absolute terms. This qualifying of uniqueness is practically universal in the archival literature. Ham's formulation of the appraisal question as "How unique is it?" apparently indicates that the "uniqueness-switch" has more settings than just "on" and "off"; the characteristic can admit of degrees. Daniels's conclusion that information lacking uniqueness is "probably relatively" unimportant indicates a double-barreled qualification of the finality that would come from a simple declaration that some records are unique and others are not. Boles's contention that the "virtue" of archival collections was "not the absolute uniqueness of the

---

17 Miller, *Arranging and Describing Archives*, 5; Bradsher, "Introduction to Archives," 8; Luciana Duranti, "Diplomatics: New Uses for an Old Science," *Archivaria* 29 (Winter 1989-1990): 15; Helen W. Samuels, *Varsity Letters: Documenting Modern Colleges and Universities* (Metuchen, N. J.: Scarecrow Press and the Society of American Archivists, 1992), 1-18; Terry Cook, "Mind Over Matter: Toward a New Theory of Archival Appraisal," in *The Archival Imagination: Essays in Honour of Hugh A. Taylor*, ed. Barbara Craig (Ottawa: Association of Canadian Archivists, 1992), 38-70 (esp. 46-47).

18 Mary Jo Pugh, *Providing Reference Services for Archives and Manuscripts* (Chicago: Society of American Archivists, 1992), 3; Bradsher, "Introduction to Archives," 7.

records" but rather "the web of interrelated information" is indicative of what may be a larger movement away from the statement of any archival principle in universal, absolute terms.[19]

Such diversity of opinion in specifying what the idea of uniqueness really means may indicate that, like many other archival ideas, this one is clearest if one has in mind a very narrow range of archival materials. In particular, uniqueness may be most clearly defined if one primarily has in mind manuscripts, in the literal, etymological meaning of the word: things written by hand. An original letter John Adams wrote to Thomas Jefferson — but perhaps not, as we shall see, a letter that Jefferson wrote Adams — may be readily understood as a unique item: there are no other copies of it. Moreover, such a letter also satisfies the other kinds of uniqueness archivists have written about: the information it contains and the particular formulation are probably not duplicated elsewhere in precisely that way; the process that produced it was singular; and the compilation of that letter with others Jefferson received is also not replicated somewhere else. In the same way, the Declaration of Independence and the Constitution are unarguably unique documents on all four grounds, even though precursors and drafts of both exist. The items themselves are unique — indeed, they are venerated as such; the information in them is likewise unique; the processes that produced them were original at the time and have since been imitated but never repeated; their compilation (or lack of it) with related records and their subsequent treatment as unique items sets them apart from the rest of the nation's documentary heritage.

But what of everything else? If uniqueness applies to exceptional archival documents, which constitute only a very small fraction of the recorded information in existence, does it also apply to bulky collections of modern records? How do the four kinds of uniqueness — of records themselves; of information in records; of processes that produce records; of aggregations of records — apply to the materials archivists encounter more frequently? Does uniqueness still have meaning for changing record formats and technologies — and not just those of the present day, like electronic records, but to all the innovations in recordmaking technology in the last five hundred years, including even the printing press and the typewriter? How does the existence of archival records in such formats affect the idea of uniqueness? Is that idea still a useful one for archivists?

---

19 Ham, *Selecting and Appraising Archives*, 54; Daniels, "Records Appraisal and Disposition," 62; Boles, *Archival Appraisal*, 41. I have argued elsewhere that other apparently absolute ideas about archives are under similar challenge; see my "On the Idea of Permanence," *American Archivist* 52 (Winter 1989): 23-24.

Originals and Copies

In a culture just learning to use literacy and the skills associated with it, the act of writing something down is an unusual one, far less common than it is in a literate-minded society like our own. The cost of the materials needed to produce a written record and, even more important, the cost of the skilled personnel able to write are sufficiently high that comparatively few documents are created. One medieval historian, for example, has estimated that a book of laws, compiled from other sources in ninth-century Italy, cost the equivalent of 96 two-pound loaves of bread, a staggering sum for the time.[20] When the world of documents is populated only by handmade originals that require so much effort to create, the uniqueness of each one remains largely undiminished.

Moreover, in newly literate cultures, documents once made may be reproduced only with similar difficulty. Copies, themselves handmade, certainly may be needed for a variety of reasons, but they can be created only by means that, like those for making originals, are slow and cumbersome, and these factors inhibit "profligate" copying. It is also difficult to make such copies without some corruptions, whether accidental or deliberate, creeping into the text. Thus, the distinction between an original and a copy remains reasonably clear. Indeed, societies undergoing a transition to literacy find it necessary to establish procedures for differentiating originals from copies and genuine documents from suspect ones. These range from such simple techniques as reliable means for dating documents to more elaborate procedures such as diplomatics. Traditional diplomatics is at some pains to specify the various kinds of copies that may be made: simple copies, containing a mere transcription of the contents of the original; imitative copies, which reproduce not only the contents but also the forms of originals (in layout, script, and medium, for example); copies in the form of originals, identical to the original but sent separately, often for security purposes; authentic copies, those which are officially authorized as substitutes for the originals; and pseudo-originals, produced in an effort to deceive.[21] Copies have many uses, but traditionally they were rare and generally recognizable as copies rather than unique originals.

---

20 Rosamund McKitterick, *The Carolingians and the Written Word* (Cambridge: Cambridge University Press, 1989), 136-37; see also M. T. Clanchy's discussion of the costs of document production in Norman England, *From Memory to Written Record*, 2nd. ed. (Cambridge, Mass.: Blackwell, 1993), 121-123.

21 Duranti, "Diplomatics," *Archivaria* 28 (Summer 1989): 19-22. In specifying these various types of copies, Duranti says (page 22) that the diplomatic analysis of copies is most useful when applied specifically to medieval documents. To attempt a genealogy of modern copies, she maintains, would be "extremely difficult and probably a sterile exercise." See also the discussion of the various means, including signatures and reliable dating, for authenticating and therefore trusting documents in Clanchy, *From Memory to Written Record*, 294-327.

In the West, the copying techniques of the classical and medieval eras demonstrate the comparatively neat distinction it was possible to make between originals and copies. Professional copyists were available in the ancient world, and the circulation of literary texts in particular depended on them to no small degree, with authors generally arranging for their own works to be copied. The literate orders of society in the Middle Ages developed more regular means for the making and copying of important texts. Royal chanceries relied on formularies for the replication of routine administrative documents, and even the process of signing these became "automated" through the use of seals. An official edict was often distributed like a kind of chain letter, each recipient making a certain number of additional copies and sending them on to other people, who repeated the process. Monastic religious orders prescribed that a certain amount of time be set aside each day for intellectual activity, including copying. To be sure, the survival of a particular text was therefore subject to a certain amount of chance: why was this document copied rather than that one, and who decided?[22] Still, the number of reliable copies could grow, if at a slow pace.

In university towns, professional "stationers" made their living by lending texts to students for individual reproduction. Such texts, known as exemplars, were lent out (usually quire by quire), copied by the borrower, and then returned so the stationer could lend them to someone else. This practice and the fees associated with it were highly regulated: university officials were empowered to scrutinize exemplars before they were borrowed to ensure their conformity with the originals, and errors were subject to heavy fines. As late as the Renaissance, authors were still for the most part acting as their own publishers, circulating as many copies of their work as they could afford to patrons and friends, who would in turn make and distribute new copies. Indeed, such writers as Boccaccio and Petrarch seem to have chosen noble patrons as dedicatees of their works precisely in the hope that they would arrange for copying and distribution.[23] In all such cases, the

---

22 On copying in the ancient world, see William V. Harris, *Ancient Literacy* (Cambridge, Mass.: Harvard University Press, 1989), 14 and 298. See also Clanchy's discussion of the origins of bureaucratic document production and copying, *From Memory to Written Record,* 62-68. On the chance copying of particular texts, see Elizabeth L. Eisenstein, *The Printing Press as an Agent of Change* (Cambridge: Cambridge University Press, 1979), 1:46; the chain letter practice is also described there (1:46, n. 9).

23 For these methods of copying, see Marcel Thomas, "Manuscripts," in Lucien Febvre and Henri-Jean Martin, *The Coming of the Book: The Impact of Printing, 1450-1800,* translated by David Gerard (London: NLB, 1976), 18-21; C. H. Talbot, "The Universities and the Medieval Library," in *The English Library Before 1700: Studies in Its History,* ed. Francis Wormald and C. E. Wright (London: Athlone Press, 1958), 67-80; and Robert K. Root, "Publication Before Printing," *Publications of the Modern Language Association* 28 (1913): 417-31.

uniqueness of individual documentary items might be partially compromised (though with difficulty) by the making of copies, but no
small effort went into guaranteeing the uniqueness and integrity of
their information content nonetheless. Copies usually identified themselves as copies, distinct from the originals.

Forgeries always remained a special problem, of course. Since errors
and corruptions could appear in texts unintentionally at any time, it can
be difficult to say exactly when the word *forgery*, in the sense of a deliberately falsified document, applies. In the Middle Ages, some forgeries
became quite famous, none more so than the eighth-century Donation of
Constantine, which purported to show that the first Christian emperor
had granted the pope permanent political jurisdiction over Italy and the
western Empire four hundred years before. The document, which
appeared conveniently enough just as popes were struggling with secular
rulers for power, was like many later medieval forgeries in that it was produced less for personal motives than in support of some cause or perceived higher purpose. In the modern era, forgeries are understood to be
purposefully misleading documents made, as often as not, with a view
toward financial gain, but the line between copies, reproductions, facsimiles, and outright falsifications may still be a thin one.[24] Even so, a
unique original is still acknowledged (in theory, if not always in practice)
as the authoritative version of particular information.

The introduction of movable type printing changed the relationship
between unique originals on the one hand and copies on the other.
Producing uniform and accurate copies purely by manuscript means is
always a risky proposition, as anyone who has tried to copy even a short
passage of text by hand knows. Copying highly technical matter —
diagrams, drawings, or tables of numbers, for instance — with as much
accuracy as they usually demand is extremely difficult. Printing made
the production and distribution of faithful copies much easier, and at
the same time it also helped fix a distinction between handwritten originals and printed copies, a distinction that for a long time was taken as
the essential difference between archival and library materials. In addition to making possible the distribution of information on a wider scale,
printing also promoted a uniformity and standardization previously
unavailable. Illustrations of all kinds, both decorative and technical,
could be reproduced exactly by means of woodcuts and engravings.
Printed text was also easier to read than manuscript, since it minimized
the variations of different hands or even within a single hand; this in

---

24 For a good discussion of this entire question, see Giles Constable, "Forgery and Plagiarism in
the Middle Ages," *Archiv für Diplomatik* 29 (1983): 1-41; see also Clanchy, *From Memory to
Written Record*, esp. 318-27. An interesting perspective on this problem from the art world is
offered in Rudolf Arnheim, "On Duplication," *New Essays on the Psychology of Art* (Berkeley:
University of California Press, 1986), 274-84.

turn may have helped speed the transition from oral reading to silent reading.[25]

Printing did not completely solve the problem of corrupt texts, of course. The so-called Wicked Bible of 1631, for example, omitted the crucial word "not" from the commandment pertaining to adultery — to the relief, no doubt, of many readers. Still, the idea of "standard editions" of a given text, as contrasted with "errata," took on a clearer meaning with printing than was possible in a purely manuscript culture. Print also had a significant preservative effect, assisting the survival and transmission of documents simply by multiplying the number of copies in existence: even if only a few of them managed to survive physically, the information would not be lost. The comparative ease of production and distribution meant that selection of texts for reproduction could be more liberal with printing than it had been with manuscripts. Most important, however, printing made the distinction between originals and copies increasingly sharp.[26]

The clear line between the two began to erode at the end of the eighteenth century with the appearance of the first of many technologies that made multiple copying easier and more common. In 1780, James Watt perfected a kind of ink that could be used to produce copies of handwritten original documents by putting them through a press. The U.S. State Department was using a Watt press for routine business a decade later, and many prominent individuals, including George Washington and Benjamin Franklin, also acquired them for personal use. More significant, however, were the "multiple writing" machines that made their appearance at about the same time. Just after the turn of the nineteenth century, the American painter Charles Willson Peale patented and sold a device originally called a "pentagraph." Perfecting earlier English and German models of the same basic idea, Peale's machine was constructed so that, as the writer moved one pen along a sheet of paper, another pen, attached to it by wooden arms, wrote the identical words on a second sheet. "It is, in fact, writing two original letters at once," an early advertisement for the contraption boasted. Peale's device attracted its partisans, including Thomas Jefferson and Benjamin Henry Latrobe. "It is so superior to the copying press of Bolton and Watt," Latrobe said in 1805, "that no comparison can exist between them." Jefferson had acquired such a "polygraph" (literally, "many writing") a year earlier, and he used it enthusiastically for the bulk

---

25 See Eisenstein's discussion of the "features" of printing and print culture in *Printing Press*, 1: 71-159. Note also her telling analysis of printing's impact on the ability to reproduce illustrations and technical material (1:52-53). The importance of the transition from manuscript to printing is also considered in J. David Bolter, *Turing's Man: Western Civilization in the Computer Age* (Chapel Hill: University of North Carolina Press, 1984), 139-40.

26 Eisenstein, *Printing Press*, 1:80, describes the Wicked Bible and the heavy fine its producers incurred. On the importance of selection for reproduction through printing, see Febvre and Martin, *Coming of the Book*, 260.

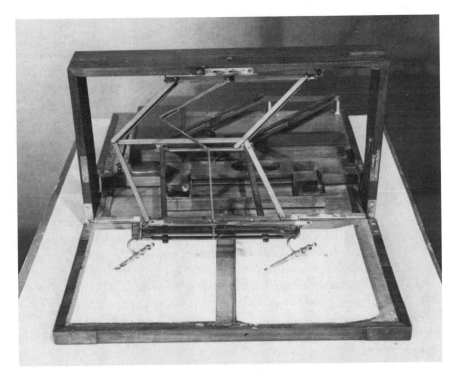

A "multiple writing machine." (Source: Thomas Jefferson's Copy Machine, Manuscript, Print Collection, Special Collections Department, University of Virginia Library)

of his personal and official correspondence. He even tried to improve on the idea by working, never successfully, on a portable model.[27]

Multiple writing machines proved to be a dead-end technology: never a commercial success, they went out of production shortly after their introduction. Their significance for the distinction between unique originals and duplicate copies, however, cannot be overstated. The newspaper advertisement had made the point precisely: the machine made two originals — not one original and one copy — at the same time. Strictly speaking, both could not be "unique," and yet they were. Here were two identical handwritten items, made simultaneously by the same person, not a handwritten original and a printed or even handwritten copy produced afterward. It

---

27 The brief life and early death of this technology is told in Silvio A. Bedini, *Thomas Jefferson and His Copying Machines* (Charlottesville: University of Virginia Press, 1984); the quotations are at pages 152 and 122. On the State Department's use of a Watt press, see Schellenberg, *Modern Archives,* 82. Jefferson's enthusiasm for the "polygraph" has led many writers (myself included in *Understanding Archives and Manuscripts* [Chicago: Society of American Archivists, 1990], 17) to assert incorrectly that Jefferson invented the machine; Bedini has demonstrated conclusively that he did not.

was as if one could write the same message legibly with a pen in each hand. Some might want to argue that, with the polygraph, the original was the document produced by the pen actually held by the writer, while the copy was the one produced by the pen in the mechanism. On the face of things, such a distinction has a certain common-sense logic about it. But why should that be the case rather than the opposite? Is physical contact between the writer and the writing implement really essential to the definition of "original"? If so, dictated works would properly be considered the product of the scribe rather than the author. Just as important, in documents produced by the polygraph, there was no opportunity for subsequent corruptions of the text since both had been created together. Both were unique originals, were they not? Presuming the writer could develop some skill at manipulating the machine, not even a trained eye would be able to tell which document had come into contact with the writer's hand and which had been produced mechanically; nor would it matter.

Later in the nineteenth century and on into the twentieth, other copying technologies continued to obscure the clear line between the ideas of "original" and "copy." The press copying process developed by Watt, for example, proved much more popular than Peale's polygraph. In administrative offices of government and business, the press became the most common means for copying outgoing correspondence. Letters were written with a special copying ink, the original was then placed between the onionskin pages of a copybook, the surface was moistened, and the book put in a screw press. With pressure, enough of the ink blotted into the copy paper to produce a facsimile while leaving the original legible enough to be sent. Skilled operators could produce copies nearly identical to the original, though it was clear which was which, as it was not with the polygraph, if only because the copy was on a different kind of paper.

Press copying had its problems, however. Copies had to be made quickly, while the ink of the original was still fresh, and at most only one or two copies could be made of a given original. In unskilled hands, it was easy to make a mess of the whole business. Filing and indexing the correspondence were also difficult: at a most basic level, it was necessary to file incoming and outgoing letters separately, since the former were loose sheets and the latter were pages of a bound copybook. Finally, the deliberate intention to make a copy had to be present at the time of making the original. If you decided several days later that you wanted another copy, it was too late: writing out a new longhand version was the only alternative.[28]

---

28 JoAnne Yates, *Control Through Communication: The Rise of System in American Management* (Baltimore: Johns Hopkins University Press, 1989), 25-39, discusses this and other copying techniques. I have seen (most notably in the collections of the Archives of the Roman Catholic Archdiocese of Boston, where I was once employed) instances in which, after the press copy was made, that sheet was cut out of the copybook and then filed with the incoming letter in filing folders and cabinets. This remained the standard office procedure in the archdiocese well into the 1920s.

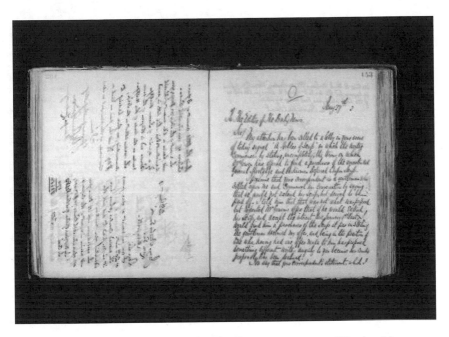

Pennsylvania Railroad letter press book. (Source: courtesy of Hagley Museum and Library, Wilmington, Delaware)

The Watt press and its successors produced copies that looked something like originals but could still be distinguished from them.

The development of the typewriter in the 1880s made it possible to produce neat documents that looked something like printing, but more significant was the concurrent development of carbon paper. This represented an improvement on press copying, but in the process the line between original and copy shifted back and forth. The first commercially available carbon paper was coated with ink on both sides. Writers sandwiched it between a piece of stationery on the bottom and a thin tissue paper on the top, writing on the tissue paper with a stylus. In that procedure, the "original" was the bottom sheet, its visible text produced by the underside of the carbon paper; the "copy" was the top sheet, with the ink from the top of the carbon paper visible through from its underside. As single-sided carbon paper developed, the designations were reversed: now the "original" was the top sheet, with ink from the pen or typewriter on its surface, and the "copy" was the bottom sheet, produced by the carbon paper. In either case the copy approximated the original in appearance, though it was still easy enough to tell them apart. Other copying techniques of the nineteenth and twentieth centuries — including various processes for mass duplication of copies from original masters, blueprinting, and other "wet" photocopying procedures — had the same

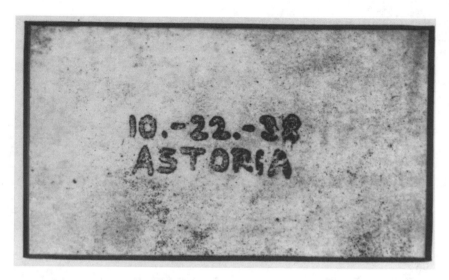

The first successful xerographic copy. (Source: courtesy of Xerox Corporation)

effect: the copy looked more or less like the original, but one was readily distinguishable from the other.[29]

The movement in all these forms of copying was in the direction of producing more copies of single originals at a steadily declining cost, but they still left the idea of the uniqueness of documentary records reasonably intact. Only with the multiple writing machines of the early nineteenth century and the later two-sided carbon paper was the distinction between original and copy so hazy as to challenge seriously the meaning and applicability of uniqueness. If anything, the others supported the notion that there was and always had to be a unique original version of a document; copies of it, "profligate" or not, were copies. Anyone (administrator, scholar, or archivist) interested in preserving information could still usefully employ the common understandings of uniqueness. Generally speaking, a particular physical item could still be identified as the unique original record; unique information was also recognizable in the limited number of copies it was possible to make; the processes that produced documents were still few in number and character; unique sets of files containing documents were similarly identifiable. All these were aspects of copying "B.C." — that is, "Before

---

29 On carbon paper and some of the other duplicating processes, see Yates, *Control Through Communication*, 46-56; see also Bedini, *Jefferson and His Copying Machines*, 191-99. There is no good, recent history of the typewriter, but see two classics: Bruce Bliven, Jr., *The Wonderful Writing Machine* (New York: Random House, 1954), and Richard N. Current, *The Typewriter and the Men Who Made It* (Urbana: University of Illinois Press, 1954).

Carlson": Chester Carlson, the inventor of xerography. With the appearance of that technology, the problem of unique originals and their copies became far more complex.

Xerography

The first successfully photocopied message was not as inspiring as Samuel F. B. Morse's "What hath God wrought"; it was more on a par with Alexander Graham Bell's frantic "Watson, come here; I want you." It said simply, "10.-22.-38. Astoria," thereby identifying the date and place of its creation. Chester Carlson, an underemployed engineer working for a patent attorney, had recognized a need to produce many copies of individual documents, copies that could be made cheaply whenever one wanted them in the course of transacting business. Photography was an expensive and time-consuming option, and so was the traditional resort to hand copying, with all the attendant risk of errors. Neither was entirely satisfactory. Accordingly, Carlson began to experiment with processes that would reproduce documents by exposing them to static electricity and light. The experiments proved successful, and by 1940 Carlson had received patents for what he called an "electrophotography" machine; later, it came to be known as "xerography," a neologism formed by combining the Greek words for "dry writing." In 1948, coincidentally on the tenth anniversary of his making the first copy, he announced his discovery at a meeting of the Optical Society of America.[30]

At first, no established business was interested in manufacturing Carlson's machine, forcing him to form his own company, eventually known as Xerox Corporation. Copying machines would always be a convenience and luxury in business offices, the conventional wisdom concluded, not a necessity. Carbon copies worked well enough for most purposes, experience seemed to show, and in any case they were familiar. Thus, it was to almost everyone's surprise when the appearance in 1958 of the Xerox 914 copier (so named because it could reproduce documents on sheets of paper with dimensions up to 9 by 14 inches) ushered in a revolution. Now it was possible, cheaply and quickly, to make many more copies than ever before, and the making of copies itself came to seem necessary and entirely normal. The first machines were slow by later standards, yielding only seven copies per minute; today, some can make up to one hundred copies per minute. Initial projections envisaged the sale of only 3,000 of the 914s over the entire lifetime of the product; in fact, more than 200,000 were sold. The company estimated that xero-

---

30 Chester F. Carlson, "History of Electrostatic Recording," in *Xerography and Related Processes*, eds. John H. Dessawer and Harold E. Clark (London: Focal Press, 1965), 15-491; for a technical description, see also in that volume M. Levy and Lewis E. Walkup, "Introduction to the Xerographic Process," 51-63.

graphic copies were being made at a rate of 50 million per month in
1961; by 1966, they estimated the monthly copying total at 490 million;
in 1986, they guessed that the number of copies made annually was in
the neighborhood of 2.5 trillion.[31] Contrary to all the established rules of
economics, the supply of this technology succeeded in creating the
demand for it.

The most obvious change wrought by xerography was surely this vast
increase in the number of copies of documents in circulation, but more
subtle changes were also at work. The very nature and meaning of copies
and their role in documentary processes were shifting. Both quantitatively
and qualitatively, the world of records and information was now very different from what it had been. Perhaps most significantly, the new copying
technology severed more sharply than ever before the temporal and intentional links between original and copy. In contrast to press copying or
mimeographic reproduction, xerography did not require the intent to ·
make a copy at the time one made an original. One no longer had to make
that original in a particular way, using specific materials (special inks, for
example) in order to be able to make a copy of it. Copies of virtually anything could now be made at any time, even long after the fact. Indeed,
documents written centuries ago could now be successfully copied. Because
it was so easy and so cheap, this "unplanned copying after the point of creation"[32] made copying random and unpredictable, done without a second
thought in response to constantly changing circumstances.

The nature and appearance of xerographic copies also represented an
important change. Copies could now look more or less the same as the
original, and they could be produced on the same kind of paper. The
"imitative copy" of diplomatics could be generated with a fidelity that
had been at best difficult in the past. In fact, copy quality improved to
such a degree that governments everywhere became concerned that the
criminally inclined would produce passable counterfeit money, and they
moved to take countermeasures. Copies could be made of copies, introducing more of a direct generational effect than had been evident with
earlier techniques. Because the xerographic process was at base a photographic one, copies of handwritten items showed the same penmanship
as the original. Early photocopies were readily recognized as such: the
paper was shiny and felt strange, the ink could rub or wash off easily. As
time went on, however, the quality of the copies improved to the point
where one might be unable to tell whether one was holding an original

---

31 See the history of the development of office copiers in J. Mort, *The Anatomy of Xerography: Its
    Invention and Evolution* (Jefferson, N.C.: McFarland, 1989), 53-69. For a broader cultural view of
    this whole subject, see Hillel Schwartz, *Striking Likenesses: The Culture of the Copy in the Modern
    World* (New York: Knopf, forthcoming).

32 Yates, *Control Through Communication*, 54.

or a subsequent copy. In such a circumstance, did the traditional distinction between the two even matter any more?

All these changes, which derived from the perfecting of xerography, served to undermine the traditional ideas of uniqueness. Individual items might still be identified as unique, though the technology was purposely making this difficult: copies that looked exactly like the original, including even the replication of color, were achievable. As copies could be made more and more indistinguishable from originals, the uniqueness of the latter was less clearly defined. Records creators made several copies of an original in the first place, and the designation of any one of these as the "first among equals" was problematic: a form letter could now be made to look less like a form and more like a personal, individualized letter.

Inexpensive and widespread copying likewise compromised the uniqueness of information in documents. With so many copies, the same information was in many different places at the same time. A prodigious duplication of information in records and files became the daily fact of life for records managers and archivists. In the average university, for instance, how many copies of course registration forms were created and circulated? Similarly, information on an organization's personnel — resumes, correspondence, appointment and discharge records, evaluative materials — exists in several places at once. The files of department supervisors, personnel officers, and others in the organizational hierarchy all have the same records on individual employees. That information is not uniquely recorded anywhere. Financial and purchasing records are likewise duplicated on a massive scale. If copying has made the identification of unique record items difficult, it has also served to vitiate the meaning, the significance, and even the existence of unique information.

The uniqueness of the processes that produce records has fared slightly better in the face of these changes, but even so its significance is diminished. Copying allows greater standardization of the processes that generate records: all personnel matters are now handled in the same way, all purchase orders conform to the same specifications, and so on. Thus, the information recorded and retained in these processes may diminish in variety, moving toward a smaller number of unique types. At the same time, however, information in organizations can be more easily shared across departmental lines, and information gathered for one purpose can be used for others. The same records pertaining to college students are found in the admissions office, the bursar's office, the various academic offices, and elsewhere. The connection between the information and the particular process that creates it is no longer singular and neccessary, and the uniqueness of that process therefore simply matters less. There may still be unique processes that produce records, but they are less significant.

Unique aggregations of documents also suffer a mixed fate from truly profligate copying. On the face of things, the uniqueness of record aggregates seems to be multiplied toward infinity. Hundreds of offices produce collections of files, each slightly different from the others in its contents and structure, even though the documents and the information they contain is largely duplicated elsewhere. In the 1980s, for instance, the records pertaining to one function of the Canadian national government (that of promoting employment) were being produced by 50 distinct programs operating out of 1,000 offices, generating about 3 million case files every year.[33] Though they contained much duplication, each of those files was at least partially different from each of the others and, thus, in its own way unique. The uniqueness of the aggregations of records was apparently unassailable. The significance of that uniqueness, however, was lessened. Even if each of the files was unique, did that matter to the archivist? The Schellenbergian notion of appraisal — that one preserves records if they contain unique information — is of little use in dealing with such files. The Canadian employment records, surely unique aggregations of documents, were accumulating at the rate of 100,000 linear feet every year. Where is the archives big enough to accommodate those unique files even if it wanted to? Thus, as the uniqueness of collections of records increases, a corresponding decrease occurs in the meaning of that uniqueness for what archivists actually do with these collections.

The copying that has become so characteristic of the modem era challenges all four of our traditional understandings of the idea of uniqueness. As uniqueness comes to mean both more and less, its usefulness in analyzing archival records is more and more problematic. Similar challenges come from other changes in the way modern records, in contrast to their ancient, medieval, and early modern predecessors, are produced.

Photography and Sound Recording

The last century and a half has been the age of the photograph and the sound recording. More directly than we could before, these technologies have allowed us to capture and reproduce what the eye can see and the ear can hear. By transforming the way information is recorded and transmitted, they have changed the way we perceive the world around us. To some degree, of course, all recorded information offers a transcendence of time and space: we can read the manuscript of the Declaration of Independence, just as Jefferson (or his amanuensis) wrote it out longhand, and the words still touch us across the years. Photography reaches through time even more clearly: we know, through photographs, precisely what Lincoln looked like, as we do not with

---

33 Cook, "Mind Over Matter," *Archival Imagination*, 42-43.

Jefferson, whose image comes to us only as interpreted through portraiture. Recorded sound, too, gives an immediacy to the past: we can hear the familiar cadences of Franklin Roosevelt or John Kennedy, just as they sounded to contemporaries, whereas we can only reconstruct and guess at Lincoln's accent or intonation.

Photography in particular enhances our hold on unique information. Individuals, objects, events, and the natural world can all be recorded, apparently just as they are. The camera, says one student of its impact and meaning, has been generally understood as a means "to record supremely accurate traces of the objects before them." Human intervention seemed minimal; the camera was "automatic, physically determined, and therefore presumably objective."[34] The historian's desire to know the past "as it actually happened" seemed never more easily within reach. Unique photographic records — " supremely accurate" ones, at that — could be created on unique occasions, capturing unique information otherwise unavailable, information never quite put together in that same way again.

The uniqueness of photographic records was clearest at the beginning, with the daguerreotype. In 1834 Louis Daguerre succeeded in making images on metal plates and, more important, in fixing those images so as to stabilize and thus prevent them from continuing to develop into complete illegibility. Daguerreotypes were images that were made directly. In contrast to the later and ultimately more successful photographic processes, there was no intervening negative: each image was printed directly onto the plate that was the finished product of the process. This gave daguerreotypes a clarity that has been difficult to equal since, and it also made each one quite literally unique. The daguerreotype could not itself be reproduced: if one wanted more than one copy (of a portrait, for instance) one had to take that many originals. This directness gave it an apparent objectivity and reality for, as one historian of photography has written, it offered the "magical verisimilitude and mirror-like presence of an astonishingly new kind of image." More broadly, the "mirror-like" daguerreotype helped form our earliest understanding of what photography was and what it could do: here was a singularly real and accurate reflection of the world.[35]

---

34 William J. Mitchell, *The Reconfigured Eye: Visual Truth in the Post-Photographic Era* (Cambridge, Mass.: MIT Press, 1992), 27-28.

35 Alan Trachtenberg, "Photography: The Emergence of Keyword," *Photography in Nineteenth-Century America*, ed. Martha A. Sandweiss (Fort Worth, Tex.: Amon Carter Museum, 1991), 20, 25. There are many general histories of photography, beginning with the daguerreotype; see, for example, Joel Snyder, "Inventing Photography," in Sarah Greenough, et al., *On the Art of Fixing a Shadow: One Hundred and Fifty Years of Photography* (Washington, D.C.: National Gallery of Art, 1989), 3-38, and the introductory chapters of Mary Lynn Ritzenthaler, et al., *Archives and Manuscripts: Adminstration of Photographic Collections* (Chicago: Society of American Archivists, 1984). See also Susan Sontag's nontechnical meditation, *On Photography* (New York: Farrar, Straus and Giroux, 1977).

The daguerreotype enjoyed only a short-lived popularity before it was supplanted in the middle of the nineteenth century by a succession of processes that produced photographic images on paper. These worked by first taking a negative image and then printing positive copies from it. This represented a fundamental change from the directness of the daguerreotype. Instead of being a singular item, each photograph was now created precisely for the purpose of being reproduced. The image had already been reproduced at least once before most people encountered it, and the reproduction might continue indefinitely. The economic and other advantages of the newer methods were many.

Within only a short time of its invention, photography was popular with and readily accessible to almost everyone; creating their own markets, its promoters made this the most democratic of art forms. Photography never entirely replaced the traditional arts of painting and sculpture, as some of its more enthusiastic early partisans asserted it would, but it did nonetheless challenge the monopolization of originality and did make widely available some of the talents once restricted to the artistically gifted and their patrons. It also altered the relationship between the image and the person who perceived it, as Oliver Wendell Holmes, Sr., noted in an essay in the *Atlantic Monthly* in 1859. The daguerreotype had been a one-of-a-kind object, experienced privately in a personal and individual way. By contrast, mass-produced photographic images (such as stereographic travel scenes) were multipliable, presenting the same image over and over to thousands of potential viewers. In fact, that was the whole point: when one owned a photograph, what mattered was ownership of the image (the "information," if you like); ownership of the thing itself was far less important.[36]

Photographic images thus affected the idea of uniqueness in conflicting ways. On the one hand, each image retained its unique quality: the subject or event being photographed looked just that way only at the instant the photograph was taken, and it never looked precisely that way again. The camera captured the unique moment and the unique information present in that moment. On the other hand, because that unique image could subsequently be reproduced, perhaps infinitely — often, the very deliberate intention of the photographer was to do exactly that — neither the photographic record nor the information it presented were ever really unique. Both would be multiplied. The distinction between originals and copies lost much of its meaning. What was the "original" in a photograph: the negative or the positive print? If the latter, which print was the original, the first one or the technically best one? Are

---

36 Trachtenberg, "Photography," 43. On the significance of the reproducibility of photographs, see also Estelle Jussim's essay, "The Reflexive Camera," in her collection, *The Eternal Moment: Essays on the Photographic Image* (New York: Aperture, 1989), 3-13.

photographs produced by so-called instant cameras (the famous Polaroid, for example) originals in a way that negative-to-positive photographs are not?[37] The difficulty of answering such questions suggests that, with photography, the traditional understanding of originals and copies is largely beside the point. Photographs thus had a paradoxical effect, both preserving and dissipating uniqueness at the same time.

More problematic still is the recent advent of the digital manipulation of photographic images. Until the last few decades, when we encountered a photograph we could take as given that the image we saw corresponded to some objective reality. What we could see in the photograph had actually been there at some point, and the camera had recorded it, "mirror-like"; its reality was or at least seemed, as one writer has said, "unequivocal."[38] To be sure, it was possible to doctor photographs, retouching them to make them seem to represent something they did not. The most famous example of this capability may be a photograph of Lenin and Trotsky standing together at some Soviet event, later altered on Stalin's orders to remove Trotsky's image after he had fallen from power. Such retouching was awkward and difficult to accomplish, however, and in most circumstances it was relatively easy to detect. Accordingly, we generally took for granted the veracity of the information presented to us in photographs. After all, "pictures don't lie."

We now know that they do. The ability to reduce photographic images to digital information has severed the apparently necessary connection between photography and reality. From its origins in the American space program in the 1960s, where it was first used to enhance the quality of pictures sent back from the moon, the digital manipulation of photographs has become progressively common. Indeed, while earlier retouching had required considerable skill and hours of work, the new means for altering photographs can be accomplished easily: they may now be done by almost anyone with a personal computer.

The skillful can create deceptions that are extremely difficult to detect, and examples of this technology have begun to appear with distressing regularity. National Geographic magazine suffered no small embarrassment — the editors were forced to apologize publicly — when, in its February 1982 cover photograph, it pushed two of the pyramids at Giza closer together so they would fit the available space better. In early 1994, the popular television and radio reporter Cokie Roberts and her crew were scolded by network officials after they had digitally spliced a scene of the U.S. Capitol building behind her to make it look as if she were really there, when in fact she was standing in a studio a couple of miles away:

---

37 Some of these questions are posed forcefully in Mitchell, *Reconfigured Eye*, 49.

38 Snyder, "Inventing Photography," 4; see also Estelle Jussim, "The Eternal Moment: Photography and Time," in *Eternal Moment*, 49-60.

she had even put on an overcoat to enhance the deception. *Scientific American*, featuring a story that explained the technology of digital doctoring, ran on its cover an apparently flawless photograph of a dour Abraham Lincoln with a laughing Marilyn Monroe on his arm.[39] Popular assumptions about photographic reality die hard, but photography is apparently in the process of transforming itself from a singularly trustworthy means of recordmaking into a distinctly untrustworthy one.

The implications of this development for the idea of uniqueness are at best ironic. As images are manipulated to produce scenes that do not exist in reality and never did, their uniqueness may be said to be increasing. Abraham Lincoln and Marilyn Monroe photographed together: yes, that is undoubtedly unique. If so, however, uniqueness has lost its value, and it ceases to be a reliable guide to anything. Its presence or absence becomes at best irrelevant and at worst misleading to our assessment and use of information. In appraising the Lincoln-Monroe match, of course, an archivist might well decide that this was an image worth preserving, but the decision would probably be made on grounds other than the uniqueness of either the item itself or the information it contained. The image might be considered evidence of a unique process that produced it, but it is not even that: as the technology spreads, the process is by no means unique. With tongues deep in their cheeks, archivists might try to assert that this represented a unique assemblage of information, but as an image constructed deliberately to lie, to misinform ("disinform," perhaps), does it have value? The assumption that uniqueness is a positive quality in records — keep the information that is unique and disregard that which is not — is thus under serious attack.

By the end of the nineteenth century, shortly after the development of practical photography, perfection of the ability to record sound worked on the same principles and had much the same effect. Sounds had originally been the only means for the transmission of information, but they were necessarily fleeting. Spoken words existed only as they were, in the process of going out of existence, and they were then gone forever unless someone could remember and repeat them. Sound recordings offered the possibility that, like the visual information in photographs, aural information, too, could be captured and preserved more immediately. In recording sound, an original "master," comparable to the

---

39 *National Geographic* 162 (February 1982): cover; *Washington Post*, February 15, 1994, page E4; William J. Mitchell, "When Is Seeing Believing?" *Scientific American* 270 (February 1994): 68-73, especially Mitchell's suggestions for how to detect digital forgery (71-73). For a good summary of this technology and the issues it raises, see Fred Ritchin, *In Our Own Image: The Coming Revolution in Photography; How Computer Technology Is Changing Our View of the World* (New York: Aperture, 1990). An interesting discussion of the ethical implications of this technology for the news business in the wake of the Roberts incident is in the *Chicago Tribune*, February 20, 1994, page 6.

photographic negative, was made first. This might itself become the archival record — such as the tape recording of a meeting or of a political speech — with no other copies made. An original recording could also be easily duplicated, however, multiplied in any number of copies. Recordings of musical performances, for example, reproduced and sold commercially, were created in just this way. Thousands, sometimes millions, of copies were made from the original, created so they could be distributed far and wide, just as millions of copies of a photograph might be seen around the world.[40] Thus, comparatively few sound recordings may be identified as unique items.

Moreover, the capacity to record and re-record sound, especially in digital formats, is the functional equivalent of the "computerized airbrushing" of photographs. In fact, with the exception of recordings specifically identified as having been made from live performances, most commercially available recordings of music are the result of extensive editing, reworking, and re-recording. A phonograph record or compact disc of a piece by a symphony orchestra, for example, does not contain music that the orchestra simply sat down and played straight through from beginning to end, with no break, even though we hear the piece that way when we listen. Rather, the music is the product of countless takes and retakes, during which portions are played again and again until just the desired effect is achieved. The results are then put together and smoothed into a whole that seems to have been continuous but was not. The result is as much the product of the sound engineers as of the conductor and the musicians. Such a recording may well represent a unique assemblage of scattered bits of aural information but, as with the computer-altered photographs, this kind of uniqueness is unconnected to any preexisting reality. A new, artificial reality has been constructed instead.[41] Thus are the traditional understandings of uniqueness undermined by technological change.

Electronic Records

Today, technological change is most clearly apparent in the area of electronic records — everything from the now-common word processor

---

40 For a historical overview of this entire subject, see Peter Copeland, *Sound Recordings* (London: British Library, 1993).

41 Helpful in sorting out these issues are Ken C. Pohlmann, *Principles of Digital Audio* (Indianapolis: Sams, 1985), and Dietrich Schuller, "The Ethics of Preservation, Restoration, and Re-Issues of Historical Sound Recordings," *Journal of the Audio Engineering Society* 39 (December 1991): 1014-17. The ability to manipulate the final product of sound recording and to create multiple unique performances has now extended to the listener. In 1994 the Boston Symphony Orchestra recorded two different endings for Bela Bartok's Concerto for Orchestra, in order to incorporate both the version usually heard and a manuscript alternative Bartok wrote but never published. Listeners may program their CD players to hear whichever one they choose.

to more sophisticated systems for recording, storing, and manipulating information. In just the last 30 years, computer technology has led a revolution that many observers justifiably rank as comparable to that of the printing press.[42] For archivists and other managers of information, the challenge is particularly acute, with many professionals believing that the skills and habits of mind suitable for the manuscript and printed record are inapplicable or even misleading for the electronic record. The challenge the computer represents to our preconceived ideas of uniqueness is serious.

Several attributes of computerized information bear particularly on this question. The first is the essential intangibility of information in electronic formats. Unlike manuscripts, printed documents, photographs, and other traditional forms of records, electronic records have no material existence — at least none that can be perceived without the intervention of both hardware and software. Though mechanical, computers are at the same time nonmechanical, operating only by invisible, fast-moving electrical impulses. In contrast to some of the early machines that could "compute," such as Charles Babbage's eighteenth-century "difference engine" or even the abacus, modern computers depend not on gears or moving parts but rather on a regulated flow of electricity the user cannot see. This immateriality makes largely irrelevant any attempt to identify a particular, unique record. What is the record in a computerized format: the invisible electromagnetic bumps on the plastic disk or the "virtual" document the software assembles for us on the screen? Does it matter? As Hugh Taylor has noted more than once, finding and "securing" the original becomes "increasingly elusive": both the act that creates a record and the record itself "occur simultaneously with little or no media delay or survival."[43]

Deriving from this intangibility is a more significant feature of electronic information: its mutability. Recording information by hand, printing, or other process requires deliberate and time-consuming effort; when that effort ceases the record is fixed and finished. Documents produced in this way may go through a succession of draft stages, but eventually the text and the information in it stop evolving and "stand still," at least for a while. Information recorded in an electronic format, by contrast,

---

42 Documenting the impact of the computer is a bit like documenting the impact of the sun coming up in the east. Studies fall behind the times technically almost before they are published, but among the most useful approaches to the entire phenomenon and its meaning are Bolter, *Turing's Man*, and Tom Forester, *High-Tech Society: The Story of the Information Technology Revolution* (Cambridge, Mass.: MIT Press, 1987).

43 Hugh A. Taylor, "'My Very Act and Deed': Some Reflections on the Role of Textual Records in the Conduct of Affairs," *American Archivist* 51 (Fall 1988): 468; see also Hugh A. Taylor, "Transformation in the Archives: Technological Adjustment or Paradigm Shift?" *Archivaria* 25 (Winter 1987-88): 12-28. On the intangibility of electronic records, see also Bolter, *Turing's Man*, 38.

may be changed so easily, quickly, and generally undetectably that change is the rule and stability the exception. Anyone who has written on a word processor knows firsthand that mutation is the norm. Texts are always flexible and tentative, always subject to alteration, both subtle and substantial. The idea of such malleability has even entered the language itself. In 1984, U.S. treasury secretary Donald Regan, signaling his willingness to negotiate with Congress over an administration tax proposal, said, "It was written on a word processor. That means it can be changed."[44] One wonders what George Orwell would have made of the coincidence in the date of Regan's metaphor.

The instability of electronic information is even more apparent in hypertext and hypermedia possibilities. It may be true that most archivists have yet to encounter this technology personally, but it seems only a matter of time before they will. As early as 1945, the computer pioneer Vannevar Bush had proposed but never built a "memex" in which the reader could display two texts on a screen simultaneously, creating linkages between them and storing the connections on microfilm. With hypermedia, readers of one text can today open a window on particular words or ideas, call up detailed notes, texts, or images related to them, repeating the process almost indefinitely wherever their own inclinations lead them. More than two thousand paintings from London's National Gallery, for instance, together with detailed artistic, cultural, and historical notes, are now available on a CD-ROM for less than $100 and operable on a personal computer.[45] This technical capability means that texts and other recorded information are now so fluid and unstable that no two readers will read them in precisely the same way. Users of information can reconfigure and reassemble it in as many different ways as they like. Formerly, several different readers could discuss a work of literature, an original letter, or even a table of statistical data on the assumption that they had all encountered the same information, the same formulation, and the same presentation of it. That assumption may no longer be warranted. Readers as much as writers can now make texts; users of information as much as recorders can form that information.

As yet more common than hypermedia, networks of all kinds provide a glimpse of the ease with which linkages can be made with electronic information. This connectability of electronic information is

---

44 Regan is quoted in Michael Heim, *Electric Language: A Philosophical Study of Word Processing* (New Haven: Yale University Press, 1987), 212. On this subject generally, see also Bolter, *Turing's Man*, 162-63; J. David Bolter, *Writing Space: The Computer, Hypertext, and the History of Writing* (Hillside, N. J.: Lawrence Erlbaum Associates, 1991), 5 and 31; and Phil Mullins, "The Fluid Word: Word Processing and Its Mental Habits," *Thought* 63 (December 1988): 413-28.

45 Bolter, *Writing Space*, 23-24, contains a brief history of hypertext and a discussion of the impact of these capabilities on the decline of the idea of the "author as authority," 153-56. *The Microsoft Art Gallery: The Collection of the National Gallery, London* (Redmond, Wash.: Microsoft Corporation, 1994) was reviewed in *New York Times Book Review,* 6 March 1994.

another of its central characteristics. In a purely manual world of information, the cross-referencing and linking of data from different sources are always cumbersome procedures, but technology opens new possibilities. The advent 30 years ago of even primitive computerized methods allowed social historians, for example, to attempt analyses undreamed of by their predecessors. The many studies of colonial New England towns were founded in no small measure on the ability to connect large amounts of data from a variety of sources, including church records, land deeds, wills and probate inventories, genealogies and family Bible records, and tax and census data. In an automated world, these linkages can now be interactive, themselves subject to constant change, allowing the user to say over and over, in effect, "What would this subject look like if we put the data together in this way?" Today, fully automated networks — everything from the ubiquitous Internet terminal to the "information superhighway" politicians promise to build us — provide the ability for users of information to make ever-new connections among disparate and apparently unconnected sources.[46]

All these developments have been generally bad news for the idea of uniqueness. The traditional understanding of physically unique records is difficult to sustain in a world of intangible, constantly changing, interconnected bits of data. The computer manipulation of information is so easy that, from one perspective, all documents may be said to approach an absolute uniqueness. Every version of a word-processed text, every hypertext "reading" of a shifting body of information, every electronic linkage along a network is unique: each differs from all the others, and each can at any time be changed into yet another different version. If everything is unique, however, how useful is that idea? If complete singularity is multiplied without end, does uniqueness offer any help in understanding or managing the information? In appraisal, for instance, where we have thought the uniqueness of records most meaningful, the category ceases to provide the archivist much guidance. Everything is unique, and the quality's usefulness in making appraisal decisions thus disappears: it no longer permits the archivist to distinguish one kind of record (the unique) from another (the not-unique). Gilbert and Sullivan said it best: "When everyone is somebody, then no one's anybody."

The other forms of archival uniqueness are also undermined. If unique documents may be multiplied infinitely, so may the unique information in them. No one source of text or raw data is likely to be any less singular than any other. In fact, as networks and other linkages prolifer-

46 For a discussion of the significance of linking and network possibilities, see Heim, *Electric Language*, 160-64. For a good summary of the New England town studies and what they do (and do not) add up to, see Douglas Greenberg, "Our Town," *Reviews in American History* 9 (October 1981): 454-58.

ate, it is likely that the same information will be even more widely replicated, distributed, and available. Indeed, that is the point. Duplication on
a massive scale, more readily accomplished and more open-ended even
than that of the Xerox machine, becomes commonplace. The information in archival records becomes available in countless other places and
ways; the encouragement that archivists search for the "truly unique"[47] as
the only fit candidates for archival preservation is therefore fruitless.

Unique aggregations of records will also have little meaning, if only
because they, too, are constantly multiplying. A particular assemblage of
information put together this morning will be changed by this afternoon,
and maybe sooner. Similarly, the unique processes that produce records
are multiplied past the point of meaning. Whereas archivists could formerly take these characteristics as proof of archival value, using them as
justifications for the maintenance of provenance and original order, the
fluidity of electronic information yields what might be thought of as
"too many" unique processes. Neither aggregations nor processes are
stable, and trying to document them all proves impossible.

Conclusion: The Future of Uniqueness

With this possibly frightening vision of the nature of the modern
records, what does the idea of uniqueness finally mean? Can archivists
continue to apply it to the materials in their care? Is it still useful for us
to speak of archival records as unique? While I am reluctant to spell out
too precisely the immediate implications of these challenges for day-to-
day archival practice — the ongoing professional dialogue must attend to
that — I will hazard a few general conclusions.

We must begin with an acknowledgment that uniqueness has always
been and remains a complicated and relative idea. To say that our collections are unique has offered us all the comforts of an absolute, identifying characteristic for which substitutes seem not readily available. In fact,
however, archivists have consistently used this absolute in relative or
comparative terms. "How unique" are records? we have wondered.
Grammatical precision has not troubled us and, in this instance, it probably need not: we have always seen uniqueness as a quality that is shaded
and measured by degrees. If we were to insist on uniqueness as an
absolute, it would prove entirely useless. In the end, everything differs
from everything else, and the presence or absence of uniqueness thus
permits us to draw no meaningful distinctions.

If we are to continue to think about archival uniqueness, however, it
will help us to restrict its application to certain kinds of archival records
where it is still meaningful. Original, handwritten manuscripts, for

---

47 Boles, *Archival Appraisal*, 105.

instance, may still be usefully characterized as unique, and a range of
appropriate archival actions — in appraisal, arrangement, description, and
preservation — may be derived logically from that condition. When dealing with such materials, we shall probably want, for example, to save the
unique original, while being less concerned for subsequent copies.
Increasingly, however, such documents are a smaller portion of the total
archival record, and the usefulness of this notion of uniqueness is thus
either limited or beside the point. As a result, before offhandedly applying
the characteristic of uniqueness and the implied values that accompany it,
archivists should try to sort out those circumstances in which uniqueness
is a helpful mental category and those in which it is not. The complica-
tions surrounding uniqueness and its meaning should serve as a caution
against archivists' applying the notion too loosely to their collections.

When archivists do think of uniqueness, the four different varieties of
that attribute which archival writers have unintentionally identified over
the years remain useful. We should continue to distinguish among them
but should do so more carefully. The uniqueness of records themselves;
the uniqueness of information in the records; the uniqueness of processes
that produce records; and the uniqueness of aggregations of records —
these are still important distinctions. Not all records will have an identifiable uniqueness, but for those that do, these four aspects still encompass
the phenomenon. Archivists will help crystalize their analysis of the materials in their care by attending to these differences, differences that are
sharp even though they have all gone familiarly by the same name. If we
are to identify uniqueness in some archival records, we must be precise
about which of the four distinct characteristics we mean and why, in any
particular case, one particular kind of uniqueness is important. The simple
and often unspoken assumption that archival records are unique and that
unique records are archival is insufficiently nuanced. Rather, in examining
any body of records, we must inquire how they are unique (if they are)
and, just as important, whether and why that matters.

In archival practice, more careful use of the idea of uniqueness can
lead to a more thoughtful approach to our holdings and to the actions
we take in managing them. In the area of appraisal, the various tests for
uniqueness demand that we be clear about the uniqueness we can identify
in records. Having taken that step, we can be more explicit about why
such uniqueness imparts enough value to the records to warrant their
archival preservation. Making such determinations conscious and explicit,
rather than leaving them adrift in a vague, generalized assertion of
uniqueness, will itself be a step toward better, more considered appraisal.
In arrangement and description, archivists have already begun to overcome their long-held assumption that unique documents demand unique
procedures for their effective organization. If the value of uniqueness
continues to erode in the face of technological change, movements in
the direction of standardized description will be all the more necessary.

In preservation, the unique individual document is a rarity. As a consequence, lavishing time and treasure on maintaining it in a pristine physical condition or on restoring it to some near-ideal original state becomes
less and less justifiable. A return to the older notion of "multiplying the
copies" may make more sense: such copies will not, by definition, be
unique, but will that make any difference?

Beyond these considerations, a reexamination of the idea of uniqueness should lead us to a similar rethinking of other central archival ideas.
The goal should not be revisionism for revisionism's sake, either as an
effort to knock down perceived archival notions simply because they are
tempting targets or as a means for demonstrating that we are smarter
than our professional forebears. Rather, thinking about archival ideas
and their implicit and explicit values for us can reinvigorate our
approaches to problems both old and new. The increased self-awareness
that may result from that process is essential to the continued intellectual
vitality of the profession.

12

Exploring the Black Box: The Appraisal of University Administrative Records

FRANK BOLES AND JULIA MARKS YOUNG

Abstract: *Although acknowledged as an essential archival function, appraisal is a complex process that is not fully understood. The authors examine the premises from which T. R. Schellenberg derived many of the practices used to appraise modern records and identify some problems in the widespread use of his approach. As an alternative, they offer a model comprised of the elements that should be considered when making an appraisal decision. Three interrelated categories of elements are discussed: value-of-information, costs-of-retention, and implications-of-the-appraisal-recommendations. While the focus is upon the appraisal of university administrative records, this model represents another step toward the development of a more systematic understanding of the entire appraisal process.*

The appraisal of modern records sometimes seems to be derived from a black box. Archivists mix together a variety of values and record characteristics and pull from the box a determination of the records' value. Many archivists find existing explanations of appraisal inadequate. They want a more integrated explanation of appraisal. This article analyzes the appraisal of university administrative records, both theoretically and through an example, and offers a model of appraisal that may, with modifications, be applicable to the appraisal of other types of records in diverse settings.[1]

Many of the roots of modern records appraisal are found in the work of the National Archives and Records Service (NARS). As one of the first

Reprinted with permission from *American Archivist* 48 (Spring 1985): 121-40. This article was originally written as a product of the authors' participation in the 1983 Research Seminar on Modern Historical Documentation held at the Bentley Historical Library, University of Michigan, and funded by the Andrew W. Mellon Foundation. The authors gratefully acknowledge the assistance, encouragement, and suggestions of the other Mellon Fellows — Paul Chestnut, Leonard Rapport, and JoAnne Yates — as well as Francis X. Blouin, Jr., and William K. Wallach of the Bentley staff, Gerald Munoff, and Thomas E. Powers.

1 This article is based upon the appraisal of paper records. While the relationship between paper records and those in other formats is occasionally mentioned, we do not systematically consider the application of appraisal guidelines developed for other record formats.

archival agencies to appraise modern administrative records, NARS developed guidelines that were widely distributed and often copied by other archivists. T. R. Schellenberg's "Appraisal of Modern Public Records" remains an influential work on the subject.[2] His principal contribution was a sharp distinction between evidential and informational values of records; this dichotomy remains a cornerstone of appraisal.[3] The most impressive subsequent writing on appraisal is Maynard J. Brichford's *Archives & Manuscripts: Appraisal and Accessioning.*[4] Brichford combined the Schellenberg framework with the experiences of the subsequent 21 years. He provided a thorough compendium of ideas and practices; however, his lists of criteria and their explanations, while valuable, were not integrated into an overall system.

Despite the usefulness of Schellenberg's dichotomy and Brichford's compendium, archivists continue to search for better explanations of appraisal.[5] In order to think about this topic, it is helpful to examine the premises of Schellenberg's discussion of appraisal. There are two points in his discussion that are troublesome. The first revolves around his explanation of the focus of an institutional acquisitions mandate.[6] The second involves Schellenberg's assumptions regarding the required completeness of documentation.

When he discussed the mandate and appraisal procedures of NARS, Schellenberg employed the statutory provisions defining the authority of the National Archives and certain American and European assumptions about the responsibilities of both government and archivists. He defined his appraisal criteria, evidential value and informational value, using the terms of the 1943 Records Disposal Act, which described the universe of federal records subject to inspection by the National Archives. Records with evidential value were those "containing evidence of the 'organization, functions, policies, decisions, procedures, operations or other activities of the Government.'" Records with informational value were those

---

2 T. R. Schellenberg, "The Appraisal of Modern Public Records," *Bulletins of the National Archives* 8 (October 1956).

3 Schellenberg also discusses this subject in *Modern Archives: Principles and Techniques* (Chicago: The University of Chicago Press, 1956), 133-60.

4 Maynard J. Brichford, *Archives & Manuscripts: Appraisal and Accessioning,* SAA Basic Manual Series (Chicago: Society of American Archivists, 1977). As subsequent notes indicate, many of our appraisal components and elements are discussed in this manual.

5 See, for example, Richard C. Berner, *Archival Theory and Practice in the United States: A Historical Analysis* (Seattle: University of Washington Press, 1983), 117-19, 178-80; and Frank G. Burke, "The Future Course of Archival Theory in the United States," *American Archivist* 44 (Winter 1981): 40-46.

6 All archival repositories define the kinds of records they accept. *Acquisitions* is the generic term used throughout this article to include all materials received, purchased, or transferred to a repository. All types and formats of material are included. Both manuscript and archival materials are considered to be acquisitions.

that "contain essential information on matters with which an agency dealt . . . the 'research' records, which contain information useful for studies in a variety of subject fields."[7] Schellenberg's definitions were obviously formed by their governmental context.[8]

Schellenberg also incorporated certain assumptions in his recommendations. To justify the retention of records with evidential value, regardless of their informational value, he asserted as self-evident that "an accountable government should certainly preserve some minimum evidence of how it was organized and how it functioned, in all its numerous and complex parts."[9] This assertion, however, is not self-evident. Although it is perhaps desirable that a government document itself, documentation of government activities is a matter of public policy as defined by law. The long political struggle to establish and support archival agencies at all governmental levels demonstrates that governments assume no inherent responsibility to document their actions.[10] Similarly, governing bodies of private organizations must decide to document their activities and to establish an archives. They must also determine the primary areas of responsibility of the repository. While records of administrative value to the parent institution may be part of a repository's mandate, these are not automatically archival responsibilities.

Given the potential diversity of institutional policies and responsibilities, Schellenberg's dichotomy between evidential and informational values and his recommendations regarding the level of documentation to be retained provide limited assistance to archivists. His thoughts reflect the legal priorities of the National Archives that require the archivist to consider first the evidential and then the informational values of the records. These priorities, however, are not universal. There are, for example, repositories that serve as institutional archives but whose primary goal is to document other organizations or subject areas. Retention of records of evidential value to the parent organization is not the principal concern. In fact, under these circumstances, the automatic classification of information into the two categories of evidential and informational is not always helpful. The evidential value of records is only information about the parent

---

7 Schellenberg, "Appraisal of Modern Public Records," 6.

8 Schellenberg, *Modern Archives*, 139-40.

9 Schellenberg, "Appraisal of Modern Public Records," 8.

10 Victor Gondos, Jr., *J. Franklin Jameson and the Birth of the National Archives, 1906-1926* (Philadelphia: University of Pennsylvania Press, 1981), and Donald R. McCoy, *The National Archives: America's Ministry of Documents, 1934-1968* (Chapel Hill: University of North Carolina Press, 1978) document the struggle to establish and define the role of an archives within the federal government. Ernst Posner, *American State Archives* (Chicago: University of Chicago Press, 1964), and the reports by Edwin C. Bridges and Richard Cox in, *Documenting America: Assessing the Condition of Historical Records in the States*, ed. Lisa B. Weber (Atlanta: National Association of State Archives and Records Administrators, 1984), document the same issues at the state and local levels.

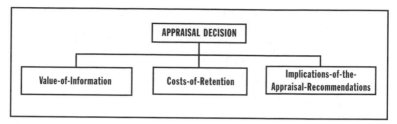

Figure 1. Appraisal Model for Institutional Records

organization. While it is useful for administrative history, this is only one informational topic that can be addressed through the use of the records.

There are also problems with Schellenberg's recommendations regarding the completeness of documentation required. It may be important, as he suggested, for the federal government to document all the numerous functions of its complex parts; but other government or private institutions may determine that it is either unnecessary or impossible to document their activities as fully and comprehensively. Again, the constraints imposed by the legislative mandate of NARS limit the applicability of Schellenberg's appraisal advice. Unfortunately, however, archivists have often stretched Schellenberg's definitions and recommendations beyond their intended context, limiting legitimate alternative choices that can be made by nonfederal organizations and archivists.

An appraisal model for institutional records that allows for diverse acquisition mandates and institutional settings is needed. To be realistic this model should include the three general categories of decisions evaluated when appraising records: (1) the value of the information, (2) the costs of retention, and (3) the political and procedural implications of the appraisal recommendations. These three modules are shown in Figure 1.

As diagrammed in Figures 2, 3, and 4, each of these modules consists of several levels of characteristics that are considered during appraisal. The first level will be called components. For example, in the Value-of-Information module (Figure 2) there are three components: circumstances of creation, analysis of content, and use of the records. The final level of considerations will be called elements. The elements comprising circumstance of creation are position in organization, unit activities, and record function. In some instances the complexity of the component requires that an intervening level of subcomponents be placed between the elements and the component. In the analysis of content, the subcomponents are practical limitations, duplication, and topical analysis.

All of the components and their elements should be considered when making an appraisal decision. They are not, however, of equal value. The relative weight of each component or element in a particular appraisal decision is determined by individual repository policies, most notably those relating to record acquisition and disposition. Moreover, the modules, components, and elements are dynamic and interactive. The process by which they are considered is dependent upon repository policies, the circumstances of the appraisal, and the record level at which the appraisal decision is made. Because of the complex interplay of the entire system, the diagrams do not adequately reflect the dynamics of the appraisal process. An examination of each module's elements and an explanation of how they could have been used in appraising specific records show more clearly the major relationships and dynamics of the model.

Value-of-Information (see Figure 2) is the first module that should be evaluated.[11] It assesses the potential of records for use after their active administrative life is concluded. Three components comprise Value-of-Information: circumstances of creation, analysis of content, and use of the records.

Circumstances of creation includes three elements: (1) the position in the organization of the generating office, (2) the principal activities of the unit or individual generating the records, and (3) the significance and function of the records in the unit's activities.

A belief in the intrinsic relationship between records and the activities generating them is basic to archival practice. Because of this relationship, archivists should look at the location of a unit within its organizational hierarchy and the activities of the unit. Organizational charts are a good starting point since they indicate official communication and decision-making positions; informal positions of influence are also significant. Regardless of hierarchical position, specific unit activities may vary widely. For example, in the office of a university dean, where policy making is a primary activity, there are also nonpolicy, "housekeeping" activities. Similarly, record function within a given unit may vary widely, sometimes related to the unit's principal activity, sometimes documenting supplemental or tangential activities. Thus, within a unit, the unit's activities and the function of the records in documenting specific activities should be determined.

The archivist should also examine the circumstances of creation for those documents received by the unit. The authors' principal activities and the functions of the records within these activities should be assessed. Understanding the circumstances of creation of the records, both individually and as a group, is the first step in evaluating the value of the information that they contain.

Analysis of content is an evaluation of the quality of the information contained in the records as a whole and as it relates to specific identifiable topics. There are three subcomponents: (1) practical limitations, (2) duplication of information, and (3) topical analysis.

---

11 Many of the components cited in the Value-of-Information module appear in Brichford, *Archives & Manuscripts: Appraisal and Accessioning.*

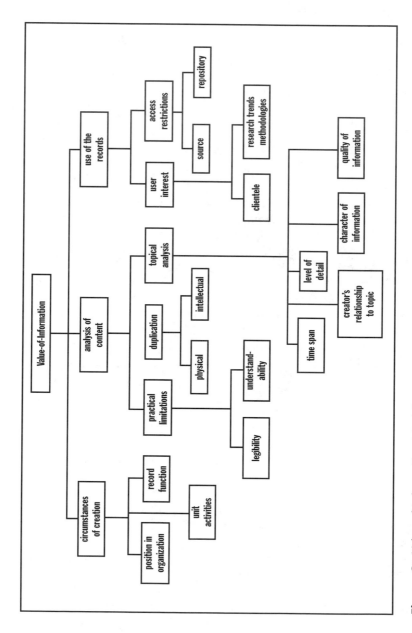

Figure 2. Value-of-Information Module

Practical limitations that would impede use of the records are an obvious concern. Severe problems, such as illegible handwriting or incomprehensible prose, may make the records useless. While these are rarely found in twentieth-century administrative records, if they are present the significance of the other elements should be evaluated with these limitations in mind.

Duplication can only be evaluated within the context of a designated universe of known documentation. Realistically this universe should be defined as those materials held by the archives, those the archivist has seen, and those scheduled through a records management program. It should include all formats and types of records. The content of this universe will vary based upon the experience and memory of the archivist and the repository.

There are two elements within duplication that should be evaluated: physical and intellectual duplication. Physical duplication is the exact reproduction of the information, regardless of format. The worth of the information is not increased by repetition and therefore archivists have generally eliminated physical duplicates. For example, many university archives establish a central file of widely distributed records, such as university publications and faculty minutes, and destroy all other copies. Intellectual duplication should also be considered. This is the reproduction of related information, in different records or formats. Summaries, for example, partially duplicate information contained in other records and should be assessed for their completeness. Annotated versions of widely distributed records represent an extension of the information contained in the basic document and should be evaluated in terms of their additional content.

Topical analysis is the evaluation of the information contained in the records relating to specific topics. Analysis can be done at either gross or more refined levels. At its simplest, the archivist should assess the records in comparison to the largest subject of interest. If desirable, this very general analysis can be supplemented by more refined topical analysis in which the archivist investigates the important themes found within the records.

For each topic identified, whether it is one or many, the archivist should evaluate the records in terms of five elements: (1) time span, (2) the creator's relationship to the topic, (3) level of detail, (4) character of the information, and (5) quality of the information. Time span evaluates both the inclusive dates of the records and the distribution of the records over the relevant chronological period of the topic, including significant gaps in the coverage. When thinking about dates, many archivists assume that older documents are inherently more valuable. This assumption is not valid. While scarcity of information may enhance the value of a record's content, simple age does not. The relationship of the record's creator to the topic is the second element that should be examined. For example, a participant's commentary is likely to be of more value than a secondhand account. The third element, level of detail, asks if the amount of information relating to the topic is superficial or thorough. While a particular group of records may touch upon many topics, often the information about many of them is quite tangential. Character of information, the fourth element, evaluates the kinds of questions answered by the records: why, how, what, where, and who. For example, a memo from a department chair may explain a routine procedure, such as the emergency evacuation of the building, or it may answer fundamental questions about the department, such as why a faculty member was denied tenure.

The final element evaluated in topical analysis is quality of the information. This measures the relationship of the records' information to the broader universe of information relating to the topic. The archivist should determine whether the records offer new information, verify existing information, or supplement the existing body of routine information. Like duplication, the analysis of this element takes place within a universe defined by the archivist's experience and knowledge. While quality of information and intellectual duplication appear superficially similar, they differ from one another in an important way. Intellectual duplication examines specific documents containing specific information. Quality of information looks at a broader information universe and assesses the information in terms of the topic. For example, intellectual duplication is an issue when an archivist considers marginal notes made on widely distributed minutes of a particular faculty meeting. Quality of information is at issue when an archivist considers the general similarity of faculty meeting minutes of various university departments.

Use of the records is the third component in the Value-of-Information module. It consists of two subcomponents: user interest and access restrictions. User interest is divided into two elements: repository clientele and contemporary research trends and methodologies. Both the circumstances of creation and the analysis of content may suggest members of the repository's clientele who have used similar records. Evaluation of current research trends and methodologies may also suggest potential users. As it is possible to imagine a use for almost every record, it is also possible to imagine a clientele for virtually any document. The relative importance of these clienteles should be consciously determined by repository policies. A strictly institutional archives, for example, may primarily serve administrators, while other archives may primarily serve scholars in a particular discipline. Appraisal should reflect the needs of a repository's primary clienteles.

Records may contain information that necessitates the restriction of their use. Such restrictions may be established for legal, ethical, or administrative reasons by either the source of the records or the repository, in order to protect the records' creator or other affected parties. Whatever the scope of the restrictions, access limitations affect the use of the records and thus the worth of the information they contain. To cite the most extreme example, the decision to retain permanently closed records is suspect.

The Value-of-Information module, then, is composed of three components: circumstances of creation, analysis of content, and use of the records. Before moving to a discussion of the next two modules, it is helpful to consider the general interaction of the Value-of-Information components and elements and their application to specific records.

The record level at which the archivist performs the appraisal affects the use of the components and their elements. Initial identification of potentially valuable records, the first decision in the appraisal process, often is best made at the record group or series level. The archivist primarily should employ the circumstances of creation elements to indicate units likely to generate significant records. For example, to document institutional policy making the archivist should use position in the organization to identify units near the top of the hierarchy. In contrast, to document institutional research, unit activities are a better indicator of potentially valuable records. The archivist then transfers those records of the most functional significance to the activities of interest.

Subsequent examinations should seek to refine initial judgments. In a process of search and confirmation, the archivist scans file folder headings, examining a sample of files and a few documents. If the contents confirm the archivist's expectations about the records, the inspection process ends. If expectations are not confirmed, additional folders should be selected and examined. This is a sampling procedure. As with any sampling procedure, the more carefully the goals and methodologies of the selection and examination process are articulated, the better the sample will reflect the overall quality of the documents.[12]

Appraisal at the series, file unit, or document level may involve detailed analysis of content. Careful examination of records for practical limitations or topical analysis can be time-consuming. An archivist, therefore, should choose the level at which records will be appraised. Just as many repositories choose not to arrange and describe records below the series level, so too they can decide not to appraise below the series level. Appraisal should be a continuous process, beginning with the

---

12   While the sampling technique employed in choosing records for appraisal is usually quite primitive, some very complex projects have been undertaken. The best documented involve the records of the Massachusetts Superior Court and the Federal Bureau of Investigation. For more information, see Michael Stephen Hindus, Theodore M. Hammett, and Barbara M. Hobson, *The Files of the Massachusetts Superior Court, 1859-1959: An Analysis and a Plan for Action* (Boston: G. K. Hall, 1979); and the National Archives and Records Service, *Appraisal of the Records of the Federal Bureau of Investigation: A Report to Hon. Harold H. Greene, U.S. District Court for the District of Columbia* (Washington, D.C.: National Archives and Records Service, 1981).

identification of record holders possessing potentially valuable records and continuing during on-site and post-transfer examination and processing at the various record levels.

The relative significance of each component within the Value-of-Information module is difficult to determine because it requires that the archivist compare abstract qualities such as the elements of analysis of content and use. Repository policies, however, and acquisition policies in particular, should guide the archivist in establishing the relative weights that should be assigned to the components and their elements. A repository whose acquisition policies sharply emphasize institutional administrative history would focus on significant administrative records. Topics other than administration and nonadministrative clienteles would be of minimal interest.

The Value-of-Information module can be better understood by applying it to the appraisal of a group of records from a specific repository. The Bentley Historical Library at the University of Michigan collects material relating to the history of the state of Michigan and serves as the university's archives. One of its major goals as the institutional archives is to document university policy and program formulation in order to facilitate scholarly research on higher education. To carry out this goal, the archivist surveyed 44 linear feet of administrative records from the university's medical school. Two hundred sixty feet of records were transferred to the repository for more detailed appraisal. Included in this project was a series of 92 linear feet of dean's correspondence, dating from 1915 to 1959. While the application of the model will be explained using these records, the model was developed after the records were appraised and processed. The examples, therefore, are illustrative.

Initially the circumstances of creation were studied. University organizational charts and histories of the medical school confirmed the expectations that the dean's office ranked high in the university's structure and was engaged in policy formulation. The school's departments, however, exercised great autonomy, indicating that the dean's office did not make all important policy decisions. A quick examination of the correspondence to confirm record function supported the conclusion that policy information, written both by the dean and by faculty correspondents in the departments, was located in the series. The examination also revealed that the series contained several other nonpolicy records.

Warned by the analysis of the circumstances of creation component that the series was not as simple as it might be, the archivist undertook a careful analysis of content. Two subcomponents, practical limitations and duplication, posed no problems. There was minimal physical duplication, and most of the material was typewritten. Topical analysis proved more complex because documentation for some anticipated topics was poor, and unanticipated topics emerged.

Initially the series was thought to document three topics: administrative history, the history of medical education, and the career of an early and prominent dean. Topical analysis confirmed that administrative history and the history of medical education were reasonably well documented. The records' distribution over the relevant time spans was generally adequate; the relationship between the records' creators and the topic was direct; the level of detail was well focused on the topics; and the records' character of information answered interesting questions about how and why things happened. The expected biographical material, however, proved a disappointment. The time span, already known to be shorter than desired since the records did not cover the individual's full tenure at the school, was even more disappointing. A three-year gap in the records, which did not strongly detract from the overall 44-year time span of the series, occurred in the years most critical for a biographer. Furthermore, the character of the information was poor. Of the four deans who were represented in the series, the one of most biographical interest was the poorest correspondent. He generally did not comment about his opinions and motivations nor those of others. In the traditional phrase of the archivist, his correspondence lacked substance.

A fourth unexpected topic, local medical practices and characteristics in Michigan, emerged in the series. From at least 1915 to about 1939 the dean was a frequent recipient of letters from physicians selling their practices or community leaders attempting to attract a physician to their areas. These letters covered a long time span and were obviously written by individuals familiar with the topic. This correspondence revealed a surprising amount of focused detail and offered a unique description of medical practices in small communities. These letters represented an unexpected but valuable discovery within the series.

For all of the topics, however, the quality of the information was lessened by certain overall characteristics of the series. Careful examination led to the conclusion that the series had served not only as the file for the dean's correspondence, but also as a general office file. From one-half to two-thirds of the series consisted of routine program implementation and housekeeping records. Three groups of routine, transactional records were defined. First, there was miscellaneous correspondence relating to students, including requests for application forms or school catalogs, clarification of admission criteria, announcements of postgraduate opportunities, and letters informing students of changes made in other records, such as a grade change on a transcript. Second, there was a large body of administrative forms, including voucher approvals, notices of staff vacations and travel plans, and temporary vacancies. Finally, minor papers of the various deans, documenting travel plans, invitations, regrets, and acknowledgements made up the third group. Thus, because the series documented several of the unit's activities, both policy making and transactional, the overall quality of the policy information was diminished. Policy documents were lost in a large body of transactional paper that merely supplemented an already existing and generally uninteresting body of routine information. The problem created by the quality of information significantly lowered the value established through the other four elements of topical analysis: time span, creator's relationship to topic, level of detail, and character of information.

Use of the records was apparent early in the appraisal process. Several categories of researchers, such as university faculty and alumni, medical scholars, and individuals interested in local history, would find the records valuable. Given the age of the records, neither the current administration of the medical school nor the repository staff questioned unlimited researcher access to the records. The application of the Value-of-Information module indicated, therefore, that the dean's correspondence series contained information of great value, documenting several topics of interest to users. This value, however, was diminished by the large amount of routine information also present.

Costs-of-Retention (see Figure 3) is the second module in the appraisal process.[13] This is an estimate of the potential costs to the repository of the appraisal recommendations. Four costs, both actual and deferred, should be evaluated: storage, processing, conservation, and reference.

Storage costs are determined by the amount and type of space required. Some record sizes and formats may require special storage facilities and thus create special costs. Since all records must be housed, storage costs are the minimum expense a repository assumes if records are retained.

Processing costs are the expenses necessary to appraise, arrange, and describe the records. They are determined by the level of archival expertise, quantity of work, and cost of supplies. Processing costs should be estimated by comparing the existing organization of the records to the arrangement and description that is desired. At a minimum, processing should make records usable, although circumstances may make it desirable to process records beyond this point. The comparison between the existing and the desired arrangement determines the skills, time, and supplies needed to perform the work.

Conservation costs are all those expenses necessary either to retard or to arrest record deterioration. The same three elements should be evaluated: level of expertise, quantity of work, and cost of supplies. Likewise, comparison between the existing and the desired condition of the records

---

13   Again, many of the components cited in the Costs-of-Retention module appear in Brichford, *Archives & Manuscripts: Appraisal and Accessioning.* The idea of including costs as a factor in appraisal was first presented by G. Philip Bauer, "The Appraisal of Current and Recent Records," *Staff Information Circulars* 13 (June 1946): 2.

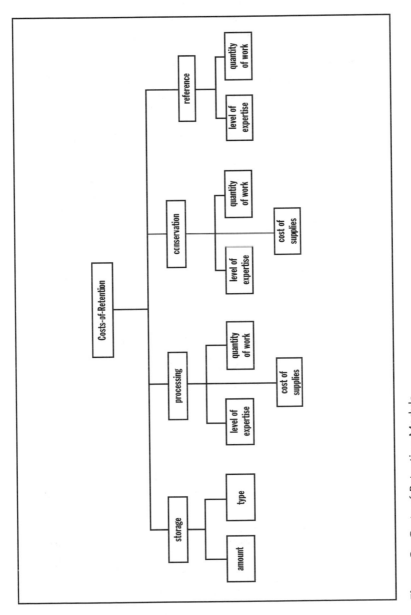

Figure 3. Costs-of-Retention Module

determines the necessary conservation measures and the costs. Overhead expenses related to specific environmental storage standards, such as the maintenance of constant temperature and humidity, and processing costs incurred for conservation measures, such as acid-free folders or the removal of metal fasteners, should be considered as conservation costs.

Reference costs, those expenditures necessary to facilitate the use of processed records, should be determined by the level of expertise and the quantity of work necessary to provide physical and intellectual access to the records. When estimating reference costs, the archivist should take into account the anticipated use by both repository clientele and staff.[14] Outreach programs should be considered part of reference costs. Although reference is often seen as an obligatory service, the archivist must nevertheless estimate the costs of providing such service.

Similar to the analysis of Value-of-Information, the four components of the Costs-of-Retention become more apparent at different records levels. The easiest to calculate, storage costs can be estimated at the record group level. Determination of processing and conservation costs involves a more detailed analysis at the series, folder, or even item level. Based on anticipated use and the level of processing, reference costs are the most difficult to estimate.[15] While dollar estimates of the Costs-of-Retention elements are the most precise, the archivist more frequently measures costs by comparing the costs of the repository's customary procedures with the potential costs of the records being appraised.[16] When the records pose unusual storage, processing, conservation, or reference requirements, the archivist recognizes that particularly high costs will be incurred should the appraisal recommendations be carried out.

Many costs are deferrable and adjustable. If projected costs exceed a repository's customary level, it does not necessarily mean that a group of

---

14 Archivists are often the single largest group of users of the records within an institution. In an unpublished paper entitled "The Value of Finding Aids in the Archives: A Quantitative Analysis" (presented at the spring 1983 meeting of the Mid-Atlantic Regional Archives Conference), James W. Oberly pointed out that at the archives of the College of William and Mary the staff was the largest user of their university collections.

15 Oberly also tested the hypothesis that improved finding aids reduce the amount of staff time spent in searching records for information. For a five-year period (1 July 1976 to 30 June 1982) he examined a randomly drawn 30 percent sample from a total of 1,512 forms filled out by staff performing a reference work. His conclusion was that as a result of improved finding aids the mean staff time spent researching questions dropped from 77 minutes (one hour and 17 minutes) in 1976 to 47 minutes in 1982. The size and distribution of the decline within the sample indicated that the result is statistically significant at the .05 level of confidence and cannot be attributed to sampling error or chance.

16 Two recent articles have discussed the calculation of processing costs; both have includcd actual cost figures. Thomas Wilsted, "Computing the Total Cost of Archival Processing," *MARAC's Dear Archivist . . . Practical Solutions to Archival Dilemmas* 1 (Summer 1982): 2-3, offers advice on how to calculate costs with a single example. William J. Maher, "Measurement and Analysis of Processing Costs in an Academic Archives," *College & Research Libraries* 43 (January 1982): 59-67, is a more extensive treatment of the same tropic, offering a much larger base from which average costs are calculated.

records will be rejected. It is more likely that costs will be adjusted. The proposed levels of processing, conservation, and reference may be lowered or deferred. Such decisions, however, should be carefully considered.

Applying the Costs-of-Retention module to the correspondence series of the dean of the medical school is helpful even though exact cost estimates are unavailable. As discussed, however, a comparison can be made between the university archives' customary expectations regarding storage, processing, conservation, and reference costs for similar records and those projected for the series. Storage requirements were typical and of little concern. Likewise, the usual difficulties created by aging, acidic paper could be dealt with through customary procedures, primarily storing the records in an environmentally controlled area in acid-free containers and folders.

Decisions regarding the processing of the series involved the relationship between description and arrangement and reference costs as well as an effort to resolve difficulties discovered through the evaluation of the Value-of-Information module. The large quantity of routine information and the arrangement of the series would lead to unusually intensive reference assistance. The series was arranged in an annual chronology, with each year's correspondence organized alphabetically by the correspondents' last names. Routine and significant correspondence was scattered throughout the series, making topical searches very difficult and requiring searching virtually at the item level. The size of the series also suggested high retrieval and reshelving costs unless very detailed finding aids were prepared. Although perhaps acceptable for a rarely used series, the identification of multiple clienteles indicated high use of the series.

Eliminating the routine material during processing, therefore, would ensure more typical reference costs, by reducing the time required to locate documents, and would significantly improve the worth of the information the records contained. Removing routine material would also reduce storage and conservation costs. Because of the character of the original order, however, item-level weeding would be necessary to achieve these results. After much discussion it was decided that the potential savings in the storage, reference, and conservation components, as well as the enhancement of the Value-of-Information, justified the high costs of processing. To minimize the expense of weeding the three previously identified categories of routine material, paraprofessional graduate student assistants performed most of the work, under the direction of a professional archivist.

Implications-of-the-Appraisal-Recommendations (see Figure 4) is the third module. The decision to retain or not retain particular records may affect the repository either positively or negatively. Before reaching a final appraisal decision, the archivist should consider the impact of the proposed recommendations, evaluating two components: political considerations and procedural precedents.

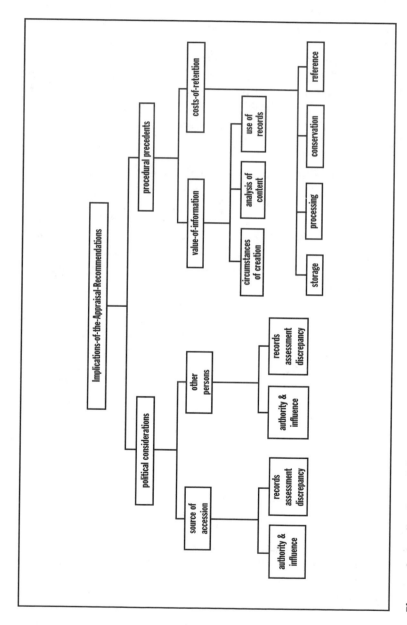

Figure 4. Implications-of-the-Appraisal-Recommendations Module

Political considerations are the implications of the appraisal decision for the repository's relationships with the source of the records and other persons, such as researchers, other donors, or persons mentioned in the records.[17] For both of these subcomponents, the archivist should decide if their authority or influence indicates that records should or should not be retained, regardless of the Value-of-Information or the Costs-of-Retention, in order to gain favor or avoid offense. This authority/ influence element is particularly important when a disagreement over the appraisal recommendations of the archivist is anticipated. The greater the archivist's estimate of the authority/influence element, the more critical the disagreement becomes. Such a discrepancy in the assessment of records can be caused by a difference of opinion relating to the worth of the information contained in the records. For example, a repository may automatically retain all records of a university vice president, regardless of their quantity, because the political benefits outweigh the Costs-of-Retention. Likewise, the influence of a frequent scholarly researcher may be so significant that records are retained because the scholar has expressed an interest in them. Records' assessment discrepancy also can be based on an emotional attachment to the records. This is more troublesome because it is difficult to refute rationally. For example, a retired administrator who has established and nurtured a program may feel very proprietary about the related records, not understanding an appraisal recommendation that suggests destroying several series of housekeeping records. The archivist may, however, determine that, given the administrator's limited influence, implementation of the appraisal recommendation will not adversely affect the repository.

Procedural precedents are the repository procedures relating to the components of the Value-of-Information and the Costs-of-Retention modules that are initiated, reinforced, or modified by implementation of the appraisal recommendations. For example, documenting a particular unit function may establish a precedent useful when later seeking similar records. Likewise, having established the precedent of rejecting certain categories of records may be helpful. The implementation of an appraisal decision sets standards for the future analysis of content, such as the amount of duplication or quantity of routine records that will be acceptable. Precedents relating to use are equally significant. An appraisal decision may continue previous practices favoring certain clienteles. On the other hand, by deciding to retain records that are beyond its established acquisition policies, a repository may commit itself to serve new clienteles. There are also precedents for the Costs-of-Retention module relating to storage, processing, conservation, and reference. For example, the

---

17 "Other persons" could also include organizations or institutions such as university units or businesses.

decision not to process a dean's records below the series level establishes a precedent for the processing of records of other deans. A repository that, for conservation reasons, has routinely removed metal fasteners from the records of nineteenth-century administrators must determine if it is able to support the cost of continuing this practice when dealing with the more voluminous records of their successors.

The procedural precedents and political considerations relating to appraisal decisions have long-term implications for a repository. When dealing with university administrative records, a repository cannot be all things to all people. It must make hard choices. These choices should be articulated in the repository's policies. Before deciding to implement an appraisal recommendation, the archivist should evaluate the associated political considerations and procedural precedents, for it is through implementation of individual decisions that repository policies and procedures evolve and develop.

To understand the Implications module it is again helpful to turn to the medical school records. The school was politically influential in the university. Its dean was cooperative and personally interested in the project. While the school considered its records to be important, it did not consider them to be sacred. The archivist had the authority to determine what would be retained.

Several traditional clienteles would be pleased to see the records made available. While these clienteles had no immediate authority, their influence might prove politically beneficial. There was, however, the possibility of angering some politically influential members of the university's medical community. In addition to the dean's correspondence series, the administrative records of the school included minutes of the faculty and numerous advisory committees, which contained candid discussions of faculty and other medical educators. The potential political problems posed by these records, however, could be resolved by temporarily restricting access to them.

Given the school's influence and cooperation, procedural precedents for several components of the Value-of-Information module could be set that would be useful when dealing with other university units. The precedent of depositing in the repository administratively significant records, such as faculty minutes and search committee records, would be strengthened. In addition, the access policies adopted would be valuable models. The vast majority of the school's records were immediately made available for scholarly research. In an effort to resolve the conflict between the desirability of open access and the privacy rights of third parties, confidential records such as the faculty minutes and search committee records were temporarily closed but would be open to all users 20 years after their creation. This precedent would be valuable in dealing with other university units that might want more stringent restrictions, based upon a different interpretation of relevant state law.

Several existing procedures relating to the costs of retention would be reinforced. Most importantly, the precedent of large-scale reduction of administrative records would be maintained. While the high costs incurred through item-level processing would be a burdensome precedent if other units requested similar treatment for their records, this was considered unlikely because detailed information about processing was not common knowledge outside of the repository.

Overall, the political and procedural implications of the appraisal recommendations relating to the medical school records were favorable. These implications supported the recommendation to item-weed the dean's correspondence series. As a result, 70 feet of records were weeded at the item level and 21 feet at the file unit level. In all, 50 of the original 92 feet of correspondence were removed from the series.

A few final points should be made regarding this model of the appraisal process. First, the components of the model are cumulative; none stands alone. Nor can one module operate without the other two. Rather, each interacts with the others and must be evaluated with them in mind. This interaction of the elements and components means that the collective value of the records is greater than the sum of their parts. This interaction also means that the model's components and elements should not be reduced to a simple checklist or flowchart. Such simplification would not adequately reflect the complexities of appraisal.

Second, while the model is cumulative, its components and elements are not directly additive. The application of a well-articulated repository acquisition policy to the model should cause some components and/or elements to be considered more important than others. Simple addition of the elements cannot reflect these important variations among repositories.

The model offers many advantages and solves many problems with existing explanations of appraisal. It is both flexible and comprehensive. It is flexible in that it can be applied to various types of administrative records at various levels of record analysis. It is comprehensive in that it tries to incorporate in a logical form all the significant parts of appraisal, both those traditionally acknowledged by archivists and those that are often unarticulated. Because of its flexibility and comprehensiveness, the model reflects appraisal in a number of situations: as part of a records management program, in traditional appraisal situations, and during reappraisal. In addition the model is viable for repositories of various ages and sizes with different political environments and acquisition mandates.

Although acknowledged as an essential archival function, appraisal is a complex process that is not fully understood. The model proposed here is an attempt to pull apart the elements and components of the process, to establish more precise definitions for them, and to analyze their interaction. Although developed primarily with administrative records in mind, it should have broader applications to the appraisal of other types of records in numerous institutional settings.

The exploration of the black box is not complete, however. Two areas in particular warrant further examination. The first involves implementing the model and assigning values to its components and elements. We must develop and test methods through which the qualitative assessments of the Value-of-Information and the Implications-of-the-Appraisal-Recommendation modules can be measured. If a simple checklist is not valid, perhaps some type of scales or continuums are more adequate measures of the components and elements. A second area of exploration to which the model points is the development and implementation of repository acquisition policies. As they now generally exist, acquisition policies are often open-ended statements designed primarily to grant a repository a perpetual hunting license for records. The way in which a repository defines, expands upon, and implements this very broad statement is the foundation of the appraisal process. As the model suggests, acquisition policies must be clear, focused, and refined in order for the archivist to reach sound appraisal decisions.

APPENDIX

To facilitate an understanding of the various elements discussed in this article, the elements and short-question definitions are provided in this appendix. The purpose of the appendix is to gather together the various elements in one place. It is not intended to serve as a checklist.

Value-of-Information Module

A. *Circumstances of Creation*
   1. Position in organization: What is the position of the generating office in the institutional hierarchy?
   2. Unit activities: In a given office, what are the principal functions of the particular unit (or individual) that generated the records?
   3. Records' function: In the context of the unit activities, what is the significance of the records? How directly are the records linked to the unit's principal activities?

B. *Analysis of Content*
   1. Practical limitations
      a. Legibility: Are the records decipherable?
      b. Understandability: Are the records coherent and clear?
   2. Duplication of information
      a. Physical duplication: Is the information in the document exactly reproduced elsewhere?
      b. Intellectual duplication: Is the information in the records approximately duplicated or expanded upon in related records (e.g., summaries, annotated versions)?

3. Topical analysis
   a. Time span: For a given topic, how well do the records cover the relevant chronological period? Are there significant gaps?
   b. Creator's relationship to the topic: Does the creator of the records have a direct or indirect relationship to the topic? Was the creator a participant or an observer, or does he or she provide a second-hand account?
   c. Level of detail: Is the information about the topic superficial or thorough?
   d. Character of information: What kinds of questions about the topic do the records answer (e.g., why, how, what, where, or who)?
   e. Quality of information: What is the relationship between this information and the broader universe of information on this topic? Is it new, does it verify assumptions already documented, or does it supplement an existing body of information?

C. *Use of the Records*
   1. Researcher interest
      a. Clientele: Are there members of the repository's clientele who are currently using or have used such records?
      b. Research trends and methodologies: What additional users of the records exist, given current research trends and methodologies?
   2. Access restrictions
      a. Source-imposed access restrictions: Has the source of the records identified legitimate administrative, legal, or ethical concerns that would affect the use of the records?
      b. Repository-imposed access restrictions: Has the archivist identified administrative, legal, or ethical concerns that would affect the use of the records?

Costs-of-Retention Module

A. *Storage*
   1. Amount: How much space will the records require?
   2. Type: What kind of storage will be required, given the nature, type, and format of the records?

B. *Processing*
   1. Level of expertise: Given the nature and existing organization of the records, what level of archival expertise and experience will be required to arrange and describe the records?
   2. Quantity of work: How much work will be necessary to process the records to the chosen level of arrangement and description?
   3. Cost of supplies: What is the cost of the supplies required to process the records?

C. *Conservation*
1. Level of expertise: Given the nature of the conservation problems, what level of skill and experience will be required to implement the recommended solutions?
2. Quantity of work: How much work will be needed to carry out proposed measures?
3. Cost of supplies: What is the cost of the supplies required to carry out the proposed conservation measures?

D. *Reference*
1. Level of expertise: What experience or knowledge will be required to provide physical and intellectual access to the processed records?
2. Quantity of work: How much work will be necessary to provide physical and intellectual access to the processed records?

Implications-of-the-Appraisal-Recommendation Module

A. *Political Considerations*
1. Source of the records
   a. Authority/influence: Is the authority or influence of the records' source such that the appraisal recommendations should be reconsidered?
   b. Records assessment discrepancy: Is there a disagreement over the worth of the records' information, based on a factual dispute or due to an emotional attachment to the records?
2. Other persons
   a. Authority/influence: Is the authority or influence of individuals other than the source (e.g., users, affected third parties) such that the appraisal recommendations should be reconsidered?
   b. Records assessment discrepancy: Is there the potential for a disagreement over the content of the records with individuals other than the source, based on a factual dispute or due to an emotional attachment to the records?

B. *Procedural Precedents*
1. Value-of-Information: If the appraisal recommendations are implemented, what precedents will be established, reaffirmed, or changed regarding the components, subcomponents, and elements of this module?

13

"The Surest Proof": A Utilitarian Approach to Appraisal

MARK GREENE

Abstract: *What follows is an analysis of the role of research use in making appraisal and reappraisal decisions at the series level. Building on the "Minnesota Method" approach to selection and appraisal of modern business records as described in a paper published in* The Records of American Business, *this article analyzes and assesses application of the Minnesota Method's appraisal criteria, using three studies of rates of use of business records by scholars and the general public. Ultimately, the validity of use as an appraisal criteria comes down to the fundamental question: What are archives? If archives are objectively identifiable evidence of business transactions then use is irrelevant as an appraisal consideration. However, if (as Terry Eastwood has said), "archives are social creations for social purposes" that have no validity aside from the value that an institution or society places on them, then use is the only measurement we have of that value (and of the success of archives operations as a whole). After examining the pros and cons of use as an appraisal criterion and the results of the three studies, the author concludes that "use of the archives and the growth of its reputation" is the "surest proof of sound records appraisal."*

This article is an analysis of the role that information about patterns of research use can and should have as criteria in making appraisal and reappraisal decisions at the series level, in particular as these choices apply to business records. In 1994 the manuscripts acquisition staff at the Minnesota Historical Society initiated a project to rationalize and describe acquisition and appraisal of twentieth-century Minnesota business records.[1] In 1996 the results of that project were presented to attendees of a symposium in St. Paul, sponsored by the National Endowment for the Humanities, on "The Records of American Business." In 1997 a

---

Reprinted with permission from *Archivaria* 45 (Spring 1998): 127-69.

1 Despite the vigorous (though to my mind not convincing) case being made by those who believe that the word "records" must or does refer only to "evidence of business transactions," the word is used here and throughout this article, except when placed in quotes or part of a direct quotation, in its more common understanding: "documentary materials . . . regardless of physical format" (U.S.C. 3301). If placed in quotes, "records" (or the quality of "record") will refer to the narrower definition of documentation of a business transaction. The most notable and accessible writing urging this narrower definition of "record" can be found at the University of Pittsburgh, School of Information Sciences, Functional Requirements for Evidence in Recordkeeping website at http://www.lis.pitt.edu/~nhprc/

refined version of the symposium paper was published by the Society of American Archivists in an essay collection of the same name. The approach to the selection and appraisal of business records presented in the symposium and book was dubbed the Minnesota Method (because, as was said then, "all the good names were taken"). The Minnesota Method encompassed a process for identifying, prioritizing, and ranking records creators, as well as suggesting various "levels" of documentation appropriate for records creators of different "rank." Analysis considered which types of series should be acquired at each level and, in general, which business functions should be documented. The weakest part of the Minnesota Method, however, was the rationale for defining and applying the different types and levels of documentation. This article presents an amplification, analysis, and justification of these appraisal criteria and of the value of research use as a primary criterion in records evaluation. Three studies of the use of business records by scholars and the general public serve as supporting evidence. It is hoped that this discussion will stimulate similar analyses of archival records in other subject areas — for example, culture, politics, and ethnicity.

A decade ago in *Archival Methods,* David Bearman pointed out that "the record of modern society is vast. It is created as a consequence of virtually every human activity and resides in every institution and with every individual. . . . At ratios of 1 person year to 10,000 cubic feet of records appraised, it would require 450,000 man years to review the 4.5 billion feet of paper records created annually in the United States, to say nothing of the machine readable data, images, sound records, video tape and other media." [2] More recently, Tim Ericson lamented "unconscious assumptions" stemming from the past "age of scarcity," when collections were relatively hard to acquire. These assumptions, he said,

> still distort our thinking. Most of our current acquisition policies are too broadly conceived to be realistic in the Information Age . . . . How can we even argue that it is possible for a regional archives to "document" comprehensively a particular geographical area — no matter how small — when one good accession of business records would fill its shelves and occupy the attention of its staff into the next millennium? Archivists need to take a more realistic view of what we can actually hope to preserve.[3]

Despite lip service to having breached the transition to "an age of abundance, " we as a profession have not devised or embraced a practical

---

2 David Bearman, *Archival Methods: Archives & Museum Informatics Technical Report 9* (1991): 7, 11. Let me note at the outset that while I applaud Bearman for targeting many real and important weaknesses in archival methodology, I disagree with virtually every solution he has proposed.

3 Timothy L. Ericson, "At the 'rim of creative dissatisfaction': Archivists and Acquisition Development," *Archivaria* 33 (Winter 1991-92): 72.

means of refining our acquisition and appraisal approaches to fit our goals and resources.

Perhaps the answer is as simple as becoming more realistic about our mission statements, which are often unrealistically broad. (Ours, for instance, proclaims its goal to "collect and preserve the materials and records of human culture relating to Minnesota and Minnesotans":[4] politics, culture, society, business — in short, everything.) But, while it may be possible to narrow mission statements at some repositories dramatically, for others it is wishful thinking: the requisite authority is not vested with persons equipped to formulate realistic goals. Mission statements, and even collecting policies, will for many repositories remain unreasonably broad so long as governing boards rather than archivists have the authority to define missions and policies. What archivists generally *do* have is authority to *implement* collecting policies — or decide *how* they are applied, which is more to the point. This authority includes deciding which records creators to solicit; which not to solicit (whether an active or passive decision); whether to accept records when unsolicited offers are made; and determining how many of the records are taken when a collection is acquired. But here, as in the creation of collecting policies and mission statements, we continue to be hindered by unexamined traditions and assumptions.

We have carried a conviction with us from the former age of scarcity that there are certain universals to appraisal and acquisition. To one extent or another, virtually all American archivists were taught that there are certain types of records that were inherently archival. Board minutes, executive correspondence, and annual reports would probably lead most lists. They also learned that certain types of records were inherently non-archival. Canceled checks and bank statements spring most immediately to mind.[5]

---

4 From the Mission Statement of the Minnesota Historical Society's "Collections Management Policy," 1994.

5 The most enduring and influential testament of this conviction is the original SAA basic manual on appraisal and accessioning, which listed in an appendix those categories of records that were "usually valuable," "often valuable," "occasionally valuable," and "usually without value." Maynard J. Brichford, *Archives and Manuscripts: Appraisal and Accessioning* (Chicago: Society of American Archivists, 1977), 22-23. Brichford's manual was only the most influential expression of this, a very common approach to evaluating records. For other examples relating to appraisal of business records see Maynard J. Brichford, "Preservation of Business Records," *History News* 11, no. 10 (August 1956): 77; Ralph W. Hidy, "Business Archives: Introductory Remarks," *American Archivist* 29 (January 1966): 33-35; Ralph M. Hower, *The Preservation of Business Records* (Boston: The Business Historical Society Inc., 1941); Arthur M. Johnson, "Identification of Business Records for Permanent Preservation," *American Archivist* 24 (July 1961): 329-32; Jack King, "Collecting Business Records," *American Archivist* 27 (July 1964): 387-90; David Lewis, "Appraisal Criteria for Retention and Disposal of Business Records," *American Archivist* 32 (January 1960): 21-24; Robert W. Lovett, "Of Manuscripts and Archives," *Special Libraries* (October 1973): 415-18. In looking at business records from the less traditional perspective of a labor historian, John C. Rumm ("Working Through the Records: Using Business Records to Study Workers and the Management of Labour," *Archivaria* 27 [Winter 1988-89]: 67-96) does not so much disagree with the records preservation demands of business historians as wish to add payrolls, discipline records, time and attendance sheets, and other employee records to their list.

The resulting mind-set means that we virtually predefine what an "archival" collection is, and consequently how big it will be — basing decisions on an abstract, objective ideal rather than a concrete and subjective assessment of what we want from the collection and what our resources will accommodate.[6]

There is, moreover, a tendency to assume that some sort of universal criteria exist defining what constitutes records creators whose holdings are "important" or "historically valuable." The most common criteria are, of course, antiquity and claims to some form of organizational primacy. Archivists frequently pursue — or accept — records of an organization or company because the newspapers have reported that it has reached its centenary (in the eastern United States, its bicentennial), or because it is the "first" in something (as in "first manufacturer of marble monuments in St. Paul").[7] We tend to do this even if the particular old or first institution or person is not as important or useful to our mission or clientele as other sources, and without giving much consideration, if any, to the cost in lost opportunities of pursuing or accepting such a collection. If an institution accepts, processes, and stores a 100-cubic-foot collection for the state's first video store, it cannot give that staff time and shelf space to, say, acquiring

---

6 To be sure, writing on functional analysis urges archivists to assess functions rather than records, but in the end merely substitutes one set of rigid assumptions for another: the literature of functional analysis implies, on the one hand, that it is necessary to document all functions of an institution, and on the other hand often resorts in the end to listing record types that contain documentation of the functions — lists that are remarkably similar to those in the old SAA manual. For expositions of functional analysis, see Bruce Bruemmer and Sheldon Hochheiser, *The High-Technology Company: An Historical Research and Archival Guide* (Minneapolis: Charles Babbage Institute, 1989); Helen W. Samuels, "Improving Our Disposition: Documentation Strategy," *Archivaria* 33 (Winter 1991-92): 125-40; Samuels, *Varsity Letters: Documenting Modern Colleges and Universities* (Chicago: Society of American Archivists and Scarecrow Press, 1992); Joan D. Krizack, "Hospital Documentation Planning: The Concept and the Context," *American Archivist* 56 (Winter 1993): 16-34; Krizack, ed., *Documentation Planning for the U.S. Health Care System* (Baltimore: The Johns Hopkins University Press, 1994). Krizack ("Introduction" and "Documentation Planning and Case Study" in *Documentation Planning for the U.S. Health Care System*) coins the phrase "documentation plan" to suggest a middle ground between functional analysis and documentation strategy. She does make an important contribution by insisting that even institutional archivists ask hard questions about the place their institution holds in the larger universe of similar institutions, and she is cognizant of the fact that the level of available resources will shape the actual size and content of a specific archives (xv). However, Krizack defines extensive "core documentation" for a hospital — I count 61 series in her list (pp. 213-14) — and refers to this as "the minimum documentation that should be preserved" (pp. 211-18). She thereby implies the existence of a universal objective criterion for defining archival value. Samuels (*Varsity Letters*), too, claims that she is presenting "guidelines" rather than "directives" (p. 24), but expects that every function of an institution must be documented (though not to the same level). Her many sections on the "Documentation" of various functions use the adverb "must" with remarkable frequency. Bruemmer and Hochheiser's *High Technology Company* does a better job of distinguishing between observations on types of documentation and recommendations for retention and does apply functional analysis in the setting of a collections repository.

7 This is different than the alacrity with which we pursue the papers of an organization favored by our governing board chair, because the need to please board members is practical and objective (though not necessarily palatable or a source of pride) while the necessity of documenting long-lived persons or institutions because of their age is quite suspect.

100 cubic feet of records documenting 50 years of a younger, but potentially more important state- or province-wide social service agency. The problem is not that the video store or social agency is necessarily more important, but that too often we do not consider what we are discarding for posterity through acting on traditional notions of objective value.[8]

Background: "The Minnesota Method" for Documenting Twentieth-Century Business

At the Minnesota Historical Society (MHS), vague anxieties over acquisition practices were coupled with a very real problem. The MHS is the state's largest historical repository. It holds 35,000 cubic feet of manuscripts, 48,000 cubic feet of state and local government records, as well as large library, photo, map, art, and museum collections. The ground breaking for a massive new building for the historical society in 1990 and the accompanying campaign for capital support dramatically increased the society's visibility and unsolicited donations of collections.[9] Nevertheless, staff resources remained static. To staff, it seemed inescapably clear that something had to change. What helped convince our administration was that, ironically, space concerns also became more acute. The new building contained about 50 percent more storage space than our previous facility, but it was evident that at our past rate of acquisitions they would fill the capacity in less than half the time it took to outgrow our previous building.

Concurrently, the society was committed to using the occasion of the new building to dramatically broaden and expand its already diverse clientele. While genealogists and amateur historians have always formed a large percentage of the MHS's clientele, a publicly funded building in a prominent location would bring new users with new needs and demands. Yet our past acquisition and appraisal approach was shaped largely by what we perceived to be the needs of our smallest group of users — academic historians. For many reasons, then, we could not continue to select and appraise records in the same way as we had in the past. A new method was required.

---

8 There is a similar issue created when we accept our billionth set of Civil War letters, caring little whether they tell society anything truly new or unique about the war, rather than spending the time trying to convince a potential donor to give us our first collection documenting a Latino businessperson. This is what Tim Ericson has labeled the "cow-shaped milk jugs" syndrome. As an example of archivists' tendency to thoughtlessly acquire endless sets of similar, though not strictly duplicate records, Ericson quoted a critic of museum collecting policies who referred to an institution with 200 eighteenth-century cow-shaped milk jugs "'ranged side by side on a shelf . . . like some huge herd on a farm.'" When paper records were scarce, and the possibilities for collecting were few, such choices were not perhaps as critical as they are now in the age of abundance (Ericson, "At the 'rim of creative dissatisfaction,'" 70).

9 For example, we received inquiries about donations from three Fortune 500 companies in the space of one year.

Any new method for manuscripts collections would naturally have
to focus on the institution's two largest bodies of records: its "congressional collections" (the papers of U.S. senators and members of Congress)
and its business collections. With both projects we adopted a similar
approach to ensuring that the work got done, which entailed creating
an internal team with two team leaders, and occasional contact with
outside experts.[10] We confronted congressional papers first,[11] then more
recently, the business records. Strategies for grappling with the acquisition and appraisal of business records have had similarities to our
approach to congressional papers, but have been broader and far more
complex. Minnesota has only eight congressional representatives in
addition to its two senators, so we could realistically acquire the entire
delegation's papers and concentrate our deliberations largely on deciding which series within congressional offices had the most historical
value. Decisions relating to business records have been more complicated. All congressional offices generate essentially the same records
(though they do not each organize them alike), so we could apply what
was essentially a single blueprint in appraising series in each and every
office. But the universe of businesses in Minnesota is far too vast for
the society to ever hope to acquire records from all companies; and different types of businesses (not to mention different size businesses)
generate very different types and quantities of records. Thus, for the
business records project we initially gave less detailed attention to series
appraisal than to appraisal at the records creator level.

As with public affairs, the MHS has traditionally documented business aggressively. It is one of the two largest repositories of business
records in the United States: we hold 21,000 cubic feet of business
records, covering 520 separate collections. The business landscape in
Minnesota is diverse. Minnesota boasts more Fortune 500 companies per
capita than any state save Illinois. Minnesota was the seat of milling,
lumber, and railroad empires in the nineteenth century and is home to
major concentrations of banking, supercomputing, and medical technology in the twentieth century. Currently, there are 120,000 business establishments in the state[12] and untold numbers of business leaders and

---

10 It is important to note at the outset that neither the congressional project nor the business project was supported by grants or other external resources. The one minor exception was the first
phase in implementing the reappraisal of congressional collections (consisting of reappraising
two of an eventual total of six collections), which was undertaken by an NHPRC/Mellon Fellow
during the summer of 1995.

11 Some details of the congressional papers project are discussed just before this article's concluding section. For a complete account of that project, see Mark A. Greene, "Appraisal of
Congressional Records at the Minnesota Historical Society: A Case Study," *Archival Issues* 19
(1994): 31-43; Todd J. Daniels-Howell, "Reappraisal of Congressional Records at the Minnesota
Historical Society: A Case Study," *Archival Issues* (forthcoming).

12 Bureau of the Census, "Minnesota," *County Business Patterns* (Washington, D.C., 1992), 3.

trade associations. To address this rich documentary universe — and the documentation of all other aspects of human culture in Minnesota — the MHS employs two manuscripts acquisitions curators![13]

The choices we faced, therefore, were those of most collection repositories:[14] balancing one set of documentation needs (in our case, business records) against competing documentary needs, then deciding which organizations can and should be documented — and to what degree. As we set about to establish an approach for the MHS, we wound up defining an acquisition strategy — dubbed the "Minnesota Method. " This is the topic of the essay in the book *The Records of American Business* — a 70-page analysis here summarized in a few paragraphs.[15]

As a basic stance the MHS decided that acquisition priorities exist and that choices necessarily get made either implicitly or explicitly. Ultimately, the collection of one business's records necessarily means that the records belonging to some other business will not be solicited or acquired — or that the papers of an equally important social service organization will be forfeited to the shredder. Unless thoughtful, conscious priorities are set, priorities will be completely dictated by chance (what business went bankrupt this week, which business's chief executive officer sits on the repository's board). Equally, restricting choices merely to which records should be acquired amidst the mass of records held by a business — micro-appraisal — will not address the larger need for improved documentation of business sectors now dominating the state's economy. Therefore — to an extent following Canadian concepts of macro-appraisal — we decided that series appraisal was the last thing that should happen in an overall appraisal process and should follow a prior assessment of records creators and their relative value as documentary sources.[16]

---

13 One of the two curators is the author of this essay, two of seven professionals who staff the society's Acquisition and Curatorial Department. Of the other five, only the Sound and Visual Curator (Bonnie Wilson) and the Department Head (James Fogerty) are involved in any way with business records or any other major manuscripts collections. (The other curators are responsible for art, maps, and books.) In addition, the staff of five curators in the society's Museum Collections Department are involved in appraising three-dimensional artifacts of various types, including business products, packaging, and advertising. The MHS also employs four manuscripts processors.

14 For the sake of convenience, we use the term "collecting repository" to denote those institutions that acquire archives and manuscripts collections through deed of gift, as opposed to "institutional archives" which are subunits of the creating agency and acquire fonds and series either through administrative directive or statutory authority.

15 Most of what follows is drawn directly or indirectly from Mark A. Greene and Todd J. Daniels-Howell, "Appraisal with an Attitude: A Pragmatist's Guide to the Selection and Acquisition of Modern Business Records," *The Records of American Business*, ed. James M. O' Toole (Chicago: Society of American Archivists, 1997), 161-229.

16 Terry Cook, "Mind Over Matter: Toward a New Theory of Archival Appraisal," *The Archival Imagination: Essays in Honour of Hugh A. Taylor*, ed. Barbara L. Craig (Ottawa, 1992), 53 (bold in original). On the other hand, macro-appraisal presumes that a deep analysis of all individual records-creating entities will emerge before prioritization takes place. In the Minnesota Method,

Our appraisal of records creators occurred only after extensively analyzing our current holdings, studying the twentieth-century evolution of the state's economy, and consulting with scholars in several of the most interested disciplines. But we also did our best to take account of our current and predicted future resources in both staff and space; the needs of our nonacademic users (who form the vast majority of our researchers); and our other documentary goals, priorities, and competing institutional program needs. In the end we wound up categorizing Minnesota businesses by industry, and then grouping the industries into 18 sectors.[17] We ranked these into four tiers based on economic impact (using revenues and numbers of employees within the state), extant documentation, identification with the state, and the degree to which the industry was unique to Minnesota.[18] Still, each sector contained far more businesses (with far more records) than we could realistically acquire. So to further

---

preceding prioritization with such creator-by-creator analysis of the hundreds, thousands, and tens of thousands of businesses in a county, state, or region is impossible. A more plausible approach would be an intense analysis of every business sector or subsector, but this is likely a practical possibility only for special subject repositories. A repository dedicated to documenting the history of computing, for instance, would probably be able to insist that its staff develop a formidable understanding of the computer industry. But most regional, state, and local repositories, charged with documenting most or all the social, political, economic, and cultural facets of their geographic region, would not have staff expertise on any facet of business history. Staff within these repositories are jacks-of-all-trades, masters of none. Again, this is not to say that a certain level of research and understanding is not absolutely necessary — only that the level of research and understanding envisioned by macro-appraisal is not assumed by our method.

17 We consulted several internal and external sources, including the Standard Industrial Code (SIC), and finally settled on a hybrid based in large part on the SIC. We could not adopt the SIC sectors directly, because many sectors prominent in the Minnesota economy get grouped together in ways that are not meaningful to the MHS. For example, health care, hospitality and tourism, entertainment, and advertising were all grouped under the Services sector. Therefore, we chose to break out and rearrange some of these sectors to more appropriately define the Minnesota economy as we understood it from our sources. The internal sources used included the 1980 and 1993 MHS collection analyses and an early 1993 Manuscript section draft list of business collection priorities. Other external sources included the St. Paul *Pioneer Press BTC (Business Twin Cities) 100* from 1994 and *Corporate Report Minnesota* from 1993. The final breakdown into 18 sectors — each one further broken down into its various subsections as indicated by the SIC — does not claim to be scientific and made little or no reference to economic theory, but was tailored to the practical problems we faced in our state at this time.

18 The top priority sectors (what we now call "tier I sectors") are Agriculture/Food Products, Health Care, and Medical Technology. Not only the particular results, but the very basis of the prioritization itself was peculiar to the MHS. This should be understood. Many different specific approaches to prioritization are not only possible but sensible. Florence Lathrop, in her article "Toward a National Collecting Policy for Business History: The View from Baker Library," *Business History Review* 62 (Spring 1988): 142, has stated quite presciently that: "A number of criteria can be used to select industries [as the focus for a repository's collecting]: the centrality of an industry to the local or national economy in a particular time period; the size of an industry, measured in a variety of ways — its contribution to gross national (or regional) product, the number of firms involved, or the number of employees; the significance of an industry with respect to organizational structure, labor relations, technological innovation or transfer; the extent of an industry's impact on other components of American social and political history, such as ethnicity, family structure, or foreign relations."

guide appraisal we identified and defined several additional factors reflecting institutional concerns and priorities. Along with tier ranking, these were intended to influence decisions about whether to seek documentation from an individual business and, if so, what.[19]

In our model the size of any single firm is less significant than the ranking given the firm's business sector. For example, our tier I sectors are agriculture, medical technology, and health care — but only one of Minnesota's top 30 employers is a medical technology firm and only two are agricultural, while eight are health care companies. When a sector becomes a top priority *all* businesses within that sector, regardless of size, become stronger, more attractive sources of extensive acquisition. Of firms in low priority sectors, only those firms that are among the largest employers in the state are, similarly, candidates for thorough documentation. As we discovered 50 years ago, when the records of virtually every lumber company in Minnesota were sought out and, if possible, acquired, there is a definite value to documenting an entire industry, both large firms and small — a value that exceeds that of the sum of the parts. While there are no sectors in the modern economy that have so few firms that we could hope to be that comprehensive, we do see a value to identifying a small number of sectors to document in breadth as well as depth. For those sectors, the smaller as well as the largest companies should be targeted to provide a better overall picture of the sector.

Nevertheless, more was needed. Deciding which sectors and which businesses to give high or low priority was difficult enough, but meant little if we could not go one step farther and define how these priorities would translate into the actual materials that would be acquired from any particular business. To do this we created five documentation levels ("*Do Not Collect,*" and levels D through A) in ascending order of comprehensiveness.

Do Not Collect

We start with the lowest level. "*Do Not Collect*" means just what it says: no records relating to the company will be accepted by the manuscripts section of the society.[20] This decision will not necessarily

---

19 Proceeding from the first to last question we ask about a firm, the "decision points" are: 1) Is it one of the state's top 25 employers? 2) Is it one of the five largest employers in its geographic region of the state? 3) Is it considered a leader in its particular industry (an industry being a subset of a sector such as health insurers and hospitals within the Health Care sector)? 4) Does it have a high degree of state or regional identification? (One obvious example would be the late, lamented Hamm's brewery.); 5) Can the particular firm serve as an illustrative example of a genre of businesses that we otherwise would not want to document fully? 6) Is the business "politically" important (for example, does its owner sit on the society's executive board, or is she the sister of the chair of the state senate's appropriation committee)? In addition, at any one of these decision points, our interest increases if the company is minority owned or has a particularly good set of records.

20 This decision does not necessarily bind other collecting units, such as sound and visual, or the museum.

bind other collecting units, such as the sound and visual unit and the society museum.

Level D

D level documentation is an attempt to preserve minimal evidence of the existence and purpose of a company. Typically, the only records sought for level D documentation are annual reports, some product information (such as catalogs), company histories in print, film or video, and if no such histories exist, one or more photos of the main or best-known company building. Depending upon the quantities of catalogs produced, only a sample may be sought and acquired. *MHS staff do not actively approach D level businesses for records.*

Level C

At level C, more records are acquired, including records documenting internal facets of corporate history as well as its more public, or externally oriented documents. Unlike practices at level D, internal features and functions of the company, such as planning, decision making, and employee culture, are documented — though at a much more summary level than at level B. But most attention focuses on documenting the basic chronology of the company (for example, through board minutes and annual reports) and its products and services — for instance, through complete sets of catalogs (one example of public documents). The types of corporate "archives" or "history files" often maintained by the public relations department as ready reference material may also be acquired if they exist. *Like level D businesses, businesses at level C are not actively solicited by society staff.*

Level B

Level B records acquisitions seek to document the internal life of a company (planning, decision making, legal matters, product production, internal communications, facilities, employee training, staff culture, research and development, summary financial accounts, and so on) as well as external facets of its existence (marketing, community relations, products, stockholders, financing, and so on). But typically, documentation will occur only at the highest administrative rung so that subject files, project files, and correspondence belonging to the board and chief executive officer are sought and retained if of any substance. Little, if any documentation is pursued below that level. Moreover, personal and family papers are typically neither sought nor accepted for purposes of documenting the business (although they may be acquired if they warrant preservation as social history). *As normal practice, businesses at level B are still not actively solicited by society staff.*

Level A

At the highest level of documentation, level A, acquisition activities seek to document both the internal and external facets of a company thoroughly. Documentation of internal communications, typically through such materials as letters and memoranda, is one of the most important distinctions between level A and level B. A second major distinction is that level A acquisitions typically include documentation of those individuals who most shape the evolution of a company; hence, extensive accessions of the papers of the founding families are sought and accepted. *Businesses at level A are actively solicited by society staff, as resources permit.*

Level D documentation is an attempt to address situations where some documentation may be justified, but only minimal evidence of the existence and purpose of a company — again, obtained through limited acquisitions restricted to such materials as annual reports, some product information such as catalogs, and company histories, and again, involving no use of active solicitation. Basically, this level was designed to give us a way of responding to companies that we might otherwise choose to ignore totally but for the existence of mitigating circumstances — for example, political pressure from board members. At the highest level of documentation, level A, we seek to see both the internal and external functions of a company thoroughly documented. This justifies active solicitation by society staff, unless prevented by lack of resources.

Documentation levels C and D, where the society will only seek and accept fairly minimal levels of material from a particular business, may seem contrary to traditional curatorial practice of acquiring the best documentation possible of any entity documented. This latter practice is not feasible because it presupposes that there are virtually no limits to facility space and staff time and that, as a result, time and space devoted to appraising, processing, and storing "complete" archives or the records of a low priority business will not prevent the repository from acquiring higher priority records from another source. To repeat what will increasingly be a familiar theme: in practical terms, archivists need to consider who will be using the records they acquire. The question for lower priority sources should be: which series will satisfy the most needs and users within the least space and with the least effort on the part of the repository?

In fact, it turns out that when we pay attention to what researchers actually use in studying modern business, we find that traditional company records are far down the list. At the MHS our documentation practices attempt to strike a balance between the demonstrable needs of a relatively few scholars for detailed documentation across a broad range of functions at certain companies, and the increasingly well-documented use of well-organized summary data by the majority of academics and amateur historians.

Shelves Crammed with Unused Material: Three Studies of Business Records Use

Published studies of the use of archives — what materials are actually requested or referenced by researchers — are few. All but two have been citation analyses. These have had the drawbacks of looking only at use made by academics, a small portion of archival users, and secondly, focusing exclusively on material receiving a formal citation rather than the larger body of material consulted by researchers in reading rooms.[21] Nevertheless, without exception, these studies paint a sobering picture of how frequently and how intensively archival collections are used. As the MHS approached the task of defining appraisal criteria for business records, we set out to gather specific data on the use of such collections.

During the period 1994-96, the MHS and the Hagley Museum and Library in Delaware were participants in the Records of American Business Project funded by the National Endowment for the Humanities. The principal product of the project was the book of essays *The Records of American Business*. In addition, the project stimulated or funded the creation of three separate studies on the use of business history sources. In the most ambitious of these, the Hagley Museum and Library sponsored an extensive analysis of scholarly citations; this provided substantive information about the types of businesses researched and records employed over the past 25 years in scholarly writing. The study's participants reviewed and categorized 79,000 footnotes. The Hagley study found a clear indication that, compared to internal and external publications, archival sources are not used heavily by business historians. Within the 79,000 footnotes, each of the following categories of material — trade publications, oral histories, company publications (annual reports, newsletters, and catalogs), government records, and published monographs — were cited far more frequently than all series of unpublished business records combined. The one exception was executive correspondence. Less than 1 percent of cita-

---

21 The published citation analyses of which I am aware are Jacqueline Goggin, "The Indirect Approach: A Study of Scholarly Users of Black and Women's Organizational Records in the Library of Congress Manuscript Division," *Midwestern Archivist* 11, no. 1 (1986): 57-67; Frederic Miller, "Use, Appraisal, and Research: A Case Study of Social History," *American Archivist* 49, no. 4 (Fall 1986): 371-92; Diane L. Beattie, "An Archival User Study: Researchers in the Field of Women's History," *Archivaria* 29 (Summer 1989): 33-50. There have been two studies looking at what material was consulted in the reading room. One, examining the relative use of series within congressional collections, was published in *The Documentation of Congress*, ed. Karen Dawley Paul (Washington, D.C.: U.S.G.P.O., 1992): 131-43. This describes a model worth following. Its drawbacks are that, though it ran for a year and covered 19 repositories, the study included only 75 users, mostly academics. The other reading room study tested a library science research approach to archival collection use. Though it has some methodological rough edges, William J. Jackson in "The 80/20 Archives: A Study of Use and Its Implications," *Archival Issues* 22, no. 2 (1997): 133-45 presents evidence that in archives, just as in libraries, 20 percent of the collections receive 80 percent of use.

tions were to financial records, and less than 2 percent to company minutes. Figure 1 illustrates these findings.[22]

A more limited study of the much more diverse set of users in the Minnesota Historical Society's reading room yielded the surprising result that nonacademic researchers (who make up the vast bulk of MHS users) use unpublished primary sources more than do their scholarly counterparts — at least within the realm of business and economic history. Assuming that a box of manuscript material and a single printed volume both equal one "source" (the best comparison possible for the moment), 83 percent of business-related material used by these researchers consisted of manuscript as opposed to printed sources.[23] This may be compared to the Hagley citation study of academic users, where only 30.5 percent of material cited was manuscript rather than printed. (Note how radically this differs from the long-held assumption among archivists that academics are the most prominent and appreciative, if not the most numerous users of archives and manuscript sources.) Overall, the most frequently requested sources in the MHS call slip analysis were (in order): executive correspondence, published monographs, executive-level subject files, and audio-visual material. Because we thought it likely that the use of the railroads records would be significantly different than that of other business records, we analyzed the two groups separately. In fact, the results were similar, especially at the top of the rankings. Figure 2 shows (in its first two columns) the relative ranking of series and material type by use taken from the MHS call slip analysis and divided between railroad and nonrailroad business records.

---

22 The citation analysis is summarized in Michael Nash, "Business History and Archival Practice: Shifts in Sources and Paradigms," *The Records of American Business* (Chicago: Society of American Archivists, 1997): 34-36. The Hagley was gracious enough to share the raw data from the study — done by Julie Kimmel and Christopher McKenna — with the MHS. The study used four journals — *Journal of American History, Business History Review, Labor History*, and *Technology & Culture* — looking through every issue within a year every five years starting in 1945 and running through to 1990. These accounted for over 12,000 citations. The study also analyzed 41 monographs published between 1962 and 1994; these accounted for more than 67,000 citations.

For additional evidence of the extensive use made of nontraditional sources by scholars, see Martha Lightwood, "Corporation Documents—Sources of Business History," *Special Libraries* (May-June 1966), 336-37. Also see James M. O'Toole, "On the Idea of Permanence," *American Archivist* 52, no. I (Winter 1989). O'Toole argues that "refocusing [archivists'] attention on the permanence of the information in records rather than on the documents themselves will restore a broader view and will reemphasize the possibilities and the usefulness of preserving information in formats other than the original" (p. 24).

23 The study was undertaken by a volunteer, Don Gipple, under the direction of Mark Greene and Todd Daniels-Howell. Don reviewed all the reading room call slips for the months of April and July 1995. During those months, there were a total of 2,012 boxes of manuscripts retrieved, of which 784 were business related (that is, records donated by businesses, papers of business people, and records of trade organizations); there were a total of 5,515 books retrieved, of which 159 were business related, Unfortunately, this study could not include requests for photos or for newspaper articles, which the Hagley citation study did include, and does not account for the fact that some published material is found in manuscript collections.

Figure 1. Hagley Citation Study Summary

	Journals % of Citations 12,336 total	Books % of Citations 67,235 total	Books & Journals % of Citations 79,571 total
PRINTED PRIMARY			
Annual Reports	2.0	2.0	2.0
Internal Publications	<1.0	1.5	1.5
Contemporary Articles	1.5	2.0	2.0
Contemporary Books	6.0	5.5	5.5
Instructional Material	<1.0	<1.0	<1.0
Trade Catalogs	<1.0	<1.0	<1.0
Trade Journals	11.0	10.5	10.5
Industrial Directories	<1.0	<1.0	<1.0
Government Documents	11.0	7.0	7.5
External Reports	<1.0	<1.0	<1.0
Newspapers	9.0	7.0	7.0
PRINTED SECONDARY			
Books	22.0	22.0	22.0
Articles	7.0	3.5	4.0
Unpublished Dissertations	1.0	2.0	1.5
Unpublished Papers	<1.0	1.0	1.0
ARCHIVAL: RECORD TYPES			
Minutes	1.5	1.0	1.0
Collected Papers/Misc.	1.0	1.0	1.0
Reports	1.5	1.5	1.5
Correspondence	14.0	17.0	17.0
Diaries/Memoirs	<1.0	1.0	1.0
Speeches/Addresses	<1.0	<1.0	<1.0
Audio-Visual	<1.0	<1.0	<1.0
Account Books	<1.0	<1.0	<1.0
ARCHIVAL: DEPARTMENTAL RECORDS			
Financial	<1.0	<1.0	<1.0
Advertising/PR	<1.0	<1.0	<1.0
Personnel	<1.0	<1.0	<1.0
Research & Development	<1.0	<1.0	<1.0
Operations/Production	<1.0	<1.0	<1.0
Legal	<1.0	<1.0	<1.0
Engineering	<1.0	<1.0	<1.0
Executive	<1.0	<1.0	<1.0
Board of Directors	<1.0	<1.0	<1.0
Sales	<1.0	<1.0	<1.0
OTHER RECORDS			
Trade Association Records	<1.0	2.0	1.5
Other Orgs (Unions, etc.)	<1.0	1.0	<1.0
Personal Papers	1.0	<1.0	<1.0
Oral Histories	1.5	2.0	2.0
Court Cases	2.0	1.0	1.0

The third study took the form of a survey sent to business archives across the United States asking them (among other things) to rank the sources used most frequently at their institutions by internal clients and visiting researchers.[24] The rankings are presented in Figure 2 (columns four and five). For internal clients those sources were (in order): audio-visual material, annual reports, internal publications, advertising and public relations material, personnel and biographical files, legal records (which were tied with research and development material), product catalogs, board meeting packets (excluding minutes), annual financial reports (which were tied with the board meeting materials), and board, committee, and other minutes. For external researchers the most frequently used sources were the same, but in a slightly different order: audiovisual material, annual reports, advertising and public relations material, internal publications, personnel and biographical files, product catalogs, and research and development files. For ease of comparison, Figure 2 also shows the relative ranking of sources in the Hagley citation study in addition to results from the business archives survey and the MHS call slip analysis.

If we instead look only at use of *unpublished* material and the relative distribution of use across series, we can learn something about the comparative utility of certain types of unpublished archival records. Figure 3 shows a comparison of the relative use made of different series of archival records according to the three studies. (While Figure 2 compares the use of both archival and published material, Figure 3 is restricted to archival records.) In the MHS call slip analysis, correspondence, audio-

---

24 Forty-seven corporate archives responded to a survey created by the MHS and distributed under the auspices of the society and the Hagley as part of the Records of American Business Project. Respondents were asked to select from a list of 39 record types and rank those used most heavily by both internal clients and external researchers. The record types were not identical to those used in the Hagley citation study, but have been correlated to the Hagley categories for ease of comparison. It should be noted that there were some variations in the ranking of most-used sources by type of business, but though ranked differently, the top five sources were the same across all business types. Work remains to be done in analyzing how (if at all), use by internal clients changes depending upon the administrative placement of the archives.

The corporate archives who responded to the survey were: Aetna Life and Casualty, Aid Association for Lutherans, Alabama Power Co., American Express, Ameritech Corporation, Amgen Inc., Aramco Services Co., Augsberg Fortress Publishers, Boston Edison Co., Cargill Inc., Chicago Mercantile Exchange, CIGNA Corp., Corning Inc., Deere and Co., Digital Equipment Corp., Duke Power Co., Equitable Life Assurance Society of the U.S., Ford Motor Co., Frito-Lay Inc., H.B. Fuller Co., Hallmark Cards Inc., King Ranch Inc., Kraft Foods, Inc., Lilly (Eli) and Co., Little Caesar Enterprises Inc., Merck and Co., MITRE Corp., Motorola, Nalco Chemical Co., New England Mutual Life Insurance Co., Northwestern Memorial Hospital, Nynex Corp., Pleasant Co., Procter and Gamble Co., Quaker Chemical Corp., Schlossberg (Edwin) Inc., Schwab (Charles), Sporting News, Stamford Hospital, State Farm Insurance Co., Texas Instruments, TIAA-CREF, Wells Fargo Bank NA, Weyerhaeuser, WGBH Educational Foundation, WIL Research Labs Inc., Wrigley (William, Jr.) Co. We are greatly indebted to the archivist at these companies for putting the time into answering the questionnaires. We are grateful, too, to MHS volunteer Don Gipple for doing the tallies.

Figure 2. Relative Use of Printed and Unpublished Sources

	MHS User Study/ Ranked Requests of:		Hagley Citation Study/ Ranked Use of Sources	Business Archives Survey/ Ranking of "Most Used" Sources by:	
	Business Sources	Non-Railroad Business Sources		Internal Clients	External Clients
PRINTED PRIMARY					
Annual Reports				2	2
Internal Publications		7		3	4
Contemporary Articles					
Contemporary Books	10	6	6		
Instructional Material					
Trade Catalogs	9	5		7	
Trade Journals			3		
Industrial Directories					
Government Documents		7	4		
External Reports					
Newspapers			5		
PRINTED SECONDARY					
Books	2	1	1		
Articles			7		
Unpublished Dissertations					
Unpublished Papers					
ARCHIVAL: RECORD TYPES					
Minutes				9	
Collected Papers/Misc.					
Reports					
Correspondence	1	2	2		
Diaries/Memoirs					
Speeches/Addresses					
Audio-Visual	4	3		1	1
Account Books		7*			
ARCHIVAL: DEPARTMENTAL RECORDS					
Financial				8**	
Advertising/PR				4	3
Personnel	6			5	5
Research & Development				6	6
Operations/Production					
Legal	7	6		6	
Engineering	5***				
Executive	3				
Board of Directors				8	
Sales					
Personal Papers	8	4			

*Represents a single researcher's use of eighteenth-century fur trade ledgers and journals.
**Represents annual financial records.
***Represents railroad technical drawings for rolling stock, capital facilities, and track.

visual records, and family papers drew 50 percent of the requests combined from researchers using nonrailroad business records. Legal records — particularly contracts and patents — eked their way into the double digits. So did financial records, due entirely to one researcher's intensive study of the account books of an 1830s Indian agent. Minute books received less than 1 percent of requests, and not one request was received for daily financial records dating from after 1850. Within the railroad records, patterns of use were slightly different due to substantial interest among railroad "buffs" in engineering records and among genealogists in the extensive personnel records of the Northern Pacific Railroad. Even so, correspondence files, executive department files (which are primarily correspondence), audio-visual materials, and legal records were far more heavily used by researchers than minutes (less than 1 percent), financial records and accounting books (less than 1 percent), and operational records (which were never used). Notably, in the Hagley citation analysis correspondence was also popular, cited 10 times more frequently than the next most cited archival source (55 percent to 5.5 percent). The third study, the business archives survey, reported that audio-visual, public relations, advertising, and personnel files (mostly biographical) were the most heavily used (in that order), notably by both internal and external clients. As a next, less-frequent set of choices, internal clients also made use of annual financial reports, minutes, and legal files, while external clients went next to building plans and blueprints (which the table categorizes as engineering files for lack of alternatives) and to research and development files. Summing up, executive correspondence, audio-visual material, and personnel files were the most consistently popular materials, with respectable showings by legal records, engineering documents, and personal papers.

The question that logically follows any analysis of use is: do rates of use correspond at all to rates of resource expenditure within repositories? The easiest resource to measure, collection for collection and series for series, is space. So, does use correspond to bulk? Data here is even more limited than that for use. The Hagley citation study had no means of measuring the size of the holdings cited. The survey of business archives did not ask for numbers of cubic feet within series.[25] But we certainly know that a book (or even 30 years of an employee publication) is less bulky than a box of records. The three projects appear to confirm conclusions already suggested in citation analyses studies: that unpublished sources are not consulted in even remote proportion to their bulk when compared to published sources. We can, moreover, make direct comparisons, albeit limited, about use versus bulk at the MHS.

We can, for example, compare use of business collections to the percentage of space these collections occupy within our total manuscript holdings. Business manuscripts at the MHS comprise 21,000 cubic feet, which is nearly 60 percent of the repository's total manuscript holdings.

---

25 Our advisors on the project were adamant that these questions would be useless to ask because most business archives would not know these figures and would be reluctant to spend the time to calculate them. For a moment we thought this was overly pessimistic, but we realized that at the MHS we had no easy means of reporting such figures for more than two of our business collections.

Figure 3. Relative Use Made of Different Series Among Archival Sources Consulted

	MHS User Survey/ Ranked Use of Record Types Within:		Hagley Citation Survey/ Ranked Use of Record Types	Business Archives Survey Ranking of Record Types Most Used by:	
	Railroad Collections	Other Collections		Internal Clients	External Clients
RECORD TYPES					
Minutes			4	4	5
Collected Papers/Misc			6	5	
Reports			3		
Correspondence	2	1	1*	6	
Diaries/Memoirs			5		
Speeches/Addresses					
Audio-Visual	5	2	1	1	
Account Books		5**			
DEPARTMENTAL RECORDS					
Financial					4***
Advertisement/PR		5	7	2	2
Personnel	4	5		3	3
R&D				6	5
Operations/Production					
Legal	6	4	8	5	
Engineering	2****				4†
Executive	1				
Board of Directors					
Sales					
OTHER RECORDS					
Trade Association Records			2		
Other Orgs (Unions, etc).			7		
Personal Papers		3			
Oral Histories					
Court Cases					

*In the Hagley citation analysis, the number one ranking accounted for 55 percent of the citations from archival sources, the number two ranking accounted for 5.5 percent; in this sense the rankings are misleading, and it could be argued that correspondence was the only unpublished material cited to a significant degree.

**Represents a single researcher's use of eighteenth-century fur trade ledgers and journals.

***Represents annual financial records.

****Represents railroad technical drawing for rolling stock, capital facilities, and track.

†Represents blueprints and plans for capital facilities.

Of these 21,000 feet, 14,000 are the records of the Great Northern and Northern Pacific Railroad, which therefore comprise almost 40 percent of the repository's manuscripts holdings, with the rest of the business records accounting for about 20 percent. The call slip study indicated that business collections represented 39 percent of all requests for manuscripts, as did railroad business collections. Thus, 60 percent of our holdings received, in this limited study, only 39 percent of retrieval requests.

The ratio is only very slightly better for the railroad collections (26.5 percent of use versus 40 percent of holdings) than for the rest of our business collections (12.5 percent use versus 20 percent of the holdings). This is true despite the fact that, in addition to traditional scholarly and local history research, the railroad records — more than any other business collections — also draw use from railroad enthusiasts and genealogists. At least one other unrelated study, completed at the University of Wisconsin, indicated that a mere 20 percent of manuscript collections there account for 80 percent of use.[26]

As well as comparing use to bulk at the collection level, we can also compare use to volume at the series level, although at present we can do this for the railroad collections only — where the space occupied by major series can be estimated. What we found is that the percentage of use for correspondence, audio-visual material, executive department subject files, and engineering records is proportionately much higher than the percentage of space these series occupy within the total body of railroad records. Conversely, use of accounting records, other financial records, board of directors' files (basically the records of the corporate secretary), and land records was proportionately much lower in relation to their volume (Figure 4). To be sure, the study covered two months only, and the percentages of space the respective series occupied within the holdings were merely estimated,[27] but this is the first time we have been able to go beyond conjecture and anecdote in analyzing use of MHS holdings.

Having done all this work, what conclusions can be drawn? It is probably a surprise to no one that unpublished sources are used in relatively low proportion to their bulk, though we now have hard evidence. So, given this new information, can we apply it in appraisal and reappraisal decisions? We can and must. However, no matter how desirable, it is simply not possible to declare that appraisal should be based on use and expect archivists to follow that advice. Over the years, archivists have advanced various arguments *against* making use a basis for appraisal. While in the end none of these are completely persuasive, they are substantial enough to ensure that use-based appraisal has been pursued with what might be termed true deliberate caution. This caution is reinforced by failed attempts by proponents of use-based appraisal to make their case: principal efforts to date have not entirely succeeded. Still — while blanket pronouncements both for or against can be found wanting — the placement of use at the center of what

---

26 Jackson, "The 80/20 Archives."

27 Figures for the size of each record series and type were drawn from the "Grant Request to Burlington Northern Inc, for Great Northern and Northern Pacific Railroad Historical Records Project," May 1976, stored in the Grants folder of the Burlington Northern accession file at the MHS.

Figure 4. Comparison of Use Versus Bulk in Railroad Records at the MHS

	Great Northern Railroad		Northern Pacific Railroad		Combined Figures*	
	% of Use	% of Record Group	% of Use	% of Record Group	% of Use	% of Record Group
RECORD TYPES						
Minutes	0	5	4	2	2	3
Correspondence	7	3	28	1	20	2
Audio-Visual	15	<1	4	<1	8	<1
Account Books	0	58	0	11	0	19
DEPARTMENTAL RECORDS						
Financial	2	7	0	5	<1	6
Advertisement/PR	3.5	5	0	<1	1	1
Personnel	<1	2	19	19	12	13
Operations/Production	0	7	0	<1	0	2
Legal	0	2	10	12	6	9
Engineering	22	<1	19	6	20	4
Executive	47	30	13	13	27	18
Board of Directors	0	<1	2.5	12	1	8
Sales [land records]	0	<1	0	10	0	7

*The GN records as a whole are about one-third smaller than the NP records, and the mix of record types and series is very different.

will necessarily always remain an unscientific process is a pragmatic, utilitarian step.

The Arguments Against Use as a Primary Appraisal Tool, and Why They Are Unsatisfactory

There are basically three arguments against making use an appraisal criterion. These are that

- archivists shouldn't do appraisal, period;
- use is a secondary and contingent characteristic of archival records, neither essential nor necessary, or "so much velvet" in Margaret Cross Norton's phrase;[28]
- practical value is characteristic of archives, but cannot be applied to appraisal.

Hilary Jenkinson's earlier formulation of the argument that appraisal is "unarchival," which had been buried by the weight of archival writing

---

28 Norton, *Norton on Archives*, 251.

since 1945, has recently been resurrected from the grave by Luciana Duranti.[29] Frank Boles and I have responded at length to Duranti.[30] Nothing more will be said here. Most archivists view appraisal as one of our primary functions, but there is much debate over the criteria we use to make appraisal decisions.

Those who believe that use of archival records is highly desirable but has no business serving as an appraisal criterion define other more or less objective qualities that make records "archival." They argue that these — not whether anyone ever consults the records — are the only proper criteria in determining whether something should be preserved. This stream has two branches. One defines certain types of records as archival by simple virtue of falling within certain records genres. The 1977 basic manual of the Society of American Archivists on appraisal concluded by ranking material from "usually valuable" to "usually without value," basing this ranking purely on record type. (Minutes and surveys were among the 65 types in the "usually valuable" category.)[31] In this, the SAA manual summed up a long tradition[32] — one that finds distinct echoes today in some writing on documentation planning.[33] Basically, this is the "minutes must always be kept" approach to appraisal. That is, it truly does not matter what minutes are about, whether they tell us anything, or whether anyone is ever going to use them. They are minutes, and therefore they are presumed to be archival.

The second stream defines "archivalness" solely on the probative value of material — its function in providing evidence of business trans-

---

29 Luciana Duranti, "The Concept of Appraisal and Archival Theory," *American Archivist* 57 (Spring 1994); Hilary Jenkinson, *A Manual of Archive Administration* (London, 1937), 123-28, 152-53.

30 Frank Boles and Mark Greene, "Et tu, Schellenberg? Thoughts on the Dagger of American Appraisal Theory," *American Archivist* 56 (Summer 1996): 176-88.

31 Maynard Brichford, *Archives and Manuscripts: Appraisal and Accessioning*, (Chicago: Society of American Archivists, 1977), 22-23. The implication that inherent value was based on record type came only after the manual first went to great lengths to explain the many criteria other than record type (administrative, research, and archival "values," including prospective use) that should be factors in appraisal. Unfortunately, it is the list at the end that seems to have become the most popular legacy of the manual.

32 For examples relating to the assignment of archival value to business records, see Maynard J. Brichford, "Preservation of Business Records," *History News* 11, no. 10 (August 1956): 77; Ralph W. Hidy, "Business Archives: Introductory Remarks," *American Archivist* 29 (January 1966): 33–35; Ralph M. Hower, *The Preservation of Business Records* (Boston, 1941); Arthur M. Johnson, "Identification of Business Records for Permanent Preservation," *American Archivist* 24 (July 1961): 329-32; Jack King, "Collecting Business Records," *The American Archivist* 27 (July 1964): 387-90; David Lewis, "Appraisal Criteria for Retention and Disposal of Business Records," *American Archivist* 32 (January 1960): 21-24; Robert W. Lovett, "Of Manuscripts and Archives," *Special Libraries* (October 1973): 415-18.

33 See Joan D. Krizack, "Hospital Documentation Planning: The Concept and the Context," *American Archivist* 56 (Winter 1993): 16-34. In *Documentation Planning for the U.S. Health Care System*, ed. Joan D. Krizack (Baltimore, 1994), she defines extensive "core documentation" for a hospital: there are 61 series in her list (pp. 213-14). She refers to this as "the minimum documentation that should be preserved" (pp. 211-18) and thereby implies a universal objective criterion for defining archival value, linked to record type.

actions or of the context of creation — those characteristics which, in this view, define its status as a *record*. Essentially, to be archival, material must constitute a record in this narrow sense. To quote Terry Eastwood, "the purpose . . . of archival institutions is to preserve the integrity of archival documents as faithful and trustworthy evidence of the actions from which they originated."[34] Or, in Terry Cook's words (though Eastwood and Cook differ in other respects), archivists must "reorient ourselves from the content to the context, and from the artefact (the actual record) to the creating processes behind it."[35]

Both perspectives — one emphasizing here, in particular, analysis of context, and the other, a record's value in documenting transactions — assume an objective definition of "archivalness" that has nothing to do with the potential or actual utility of the material. Moreover, even with a clear, evidence-based definition of value established, much difficult discretionary analysis is left to be done. The hard part remains of deciding which records creators and which of their actions, transactions, or functions are most significant from either an institutional or socio-cultural perspective.[36] Of course, archivists who focus appraisal on records' evidential value are not blind to practical considerations. All welcome, even encourage, active use of archival records by researchers. But neither evidence of past use nor assumptions about future use, they say, should

---

34 Terry Eastwood, "Nailing a Little Jelly to the Wall of Archival Studies," *Archivaria* 35 (Spring 1993): 237. See also Richard Cox, "The Record: Is It Evolving? A Study in the Importance of the Long-View for Records Managers and Archivists," 11 November 1995, and Wendy Duff, "Defining Transactions: To Identify Records and Assess Risk," 6 December 1994, both at the University of Pittsburgh, School of Information Sciences, Functional Requirements for Evidence in Recordkeeping Web site, at http://www.lis.pitt.edu/~nhprc; Luciana Duranti, posting to the Archives and Archivists listserv, 24 May 1993.

35 Terry Cook, "Electronic Records, Paper Minds: The Revolution in Information Management and Archives in the Post-Custodial and Post-Modernist Era," *Archives and Manuscripts* 22, no. 2 (November 1994): 304. Also see Terry Cook, "Documentation Strategy," *Archivaria* 34 (Summer 1992): 184; Terry Cook, "Archives in the Post-Custodial World: Interaction of Archival Theory and Practice since the Publication of the Dutch Manual in 1989 [*sic*]," *XIII International Congress on Archives: Third Plenary Session Principal Paper* (Beijing, 1996): 10.

36 Macro-appraisal is undergoing vigorous and thoughtful evolution, but seems to be based on a belief that evidence of certain government functions is essential and must be preserved, without asking whether or not anyone actually has recourse to that evidence. See Terry Cook, "Mind Over Matter," 38-70; Bruce Wilson, "Systematic Appraisal of the Records of the Government of Canada at the National Archives of Canada," *Archivaria* 38 (Fall 1994): 218-31; Richard Brown, "Macro-Appraisal Theory and the Context of the Public Records Creator," *Archivaria* 40 (Fall 1995): 121-72. There seems to be a great deal of macro-appraisal in the approach sketched by Hans Boom, "Überlieferungsbildung: Keeping Archives as a Social and Political Activity," *Archivaria* 33 (Winter 1991-92): 31-33.

   For expositions of functional analysis, see Helen W. Samuels, "Improving Our Disposition: Documentation Strategy," *Archivaria* 33 (Winter 1991-92): 125-40; and her *Varsity Letters: Documenting Modern Colleges and Universities* (Chicago, 1992). Samuels seems to expect that every function of an institution must be documented (though not all to the same level). She apparently considers documenting functions (rather than selecting material for use) to be the purpose of archives.

influence appraisal: "archives should not be appraised and acquired to support use," period.[37]

The third objection to use in appraisal is not that it is antithetical to archival values, but that use cannot be measured or applied in analytical judgment in such a way as to make it a reliable criterion. One objection is that use measures *present day* values only. In 1975 F. Gerald Ham penned the most succinct critique of use in appraisal method when he lamented that "narrow research interests" had created a selection process that was random and fragmented — with the archivist "nothing more than a weather vane moved by the changing winds of historiography."[38] However, the most precise argument has been put forward by Karen Benedict as part of a 1984 critique of reappraisal. Her indictment of use is threefold. First, she writes, frequency of past use is no predictor of future use, because researchers' interests change so much over time: "There are records that will be of great value to future generations, regardless of how much current use we make of them." Second, she says, "lack of use by researchers may be due to poor finding aids or a lack of knowledge of the records on the part of the reference staff rather than the intrinsic value of the records." Third, Benedict contends that archives' value to society is much less concrete and measurable than simple tallies of how many times a box gets used.[39]

Ultimately, some arguments against applying use in appraisal come down to first principles — what *is* an archives and what is the role of the archivist? If, given the one objection, all appraisal is unarchival, so, too, clearly are use-based considerations. Moreover, use is equally irrelevant if, given the second interpretation, archives are objectively identifiable according to record type or evidential importance: if an archivist's first duty is to identify and preserve the probative purity of the objective record then he or she can give no thought — at least at the point of appraisal — to the uses to which anyone might put that record.

---

37 Cook, "Archives in the Post-Custodial World," n. 43. Cook goes on to allow that "once acquired, however, their [archives'] description, reference, and diffusion should of course reflect client needs as far as possible." I would suggest that acquiring archives that are not useful and then describing them in user-friendly ways is of arguable assistance.

38 F. Gerald Ham, "The Archival Edge," *American Archivist* (January 1975): 8.

39 Karen Benedict, "Invitation to a Bonfire: Reappraisal and Deaccessioning of Records as Collection Management Tools in an Archives — A Reply to Leonard Rapport," *American Archivist* 47, no. 1 (Winter 1984): 47-48. See also, Roy C. Turnbaugh: "Archival Mission and User Studies," *Midwestern Archivist* 11, no. 1 (1986): 27-33, and "Plowing the Sea: Appraising Public Records in an Ahistorical Culture," *American Archivist* 53 (Fall 1990): 562-65. Margaret Cross Norton, who argued against use primarily on the grounds that certain records were inherently archival, also insisted that lack of use in the past was no predictor of future use: "The fact that a document may not have been consulted for a century does not rule out the possibility of the fact that tomorrow some attorney may attach great significance to it," Norton, *Norton on Archives*, 26.

There is an alternative conception — a different set of first postu-
lates. This is to accept, as Eastwood says, that "archives are social creations
for social purposes," and that "they be appraised on the basis of an analysis of the use to which they are put by the society that created them."[40]
Which conception of archives is right cannot be demonstrated in any
objective, empirical, or wholly final manner, this being the inherent
quality of first principles. Measuring use is empirical, but if use is not a
completely trustworthy criterion for creating or assessing archives then, in
some interpretations, measurement must remain moot. At the same time,
alternative stances cannot lay claim to purity. After all, it is subjective
human choice, rather than some objective scientific law, that determines
that the recorded evidence of actions performed by juridical entities
constitutes "records" and that, by light of further decisions, certain of
these "records" are archival.

Distinctions have pragmatic consequences because the two conceptions of archives are fundamentally incompatible in practice as well
as theory. For example, in an article in the *Midwestern Archivist* articulating the notion that records may be archival regardless of their utility, Roy
Turnbaugh contends that "it is entirely conceivable that a record in the
custody of an archives is rarely, if ever, used, and yet the clear responsibility of the archives is to preserve that record without regard for the
occurrence of use."[41] The logic of "recordness" (material is archival only
if it provides evidence of transactions or context of creation) leads both
to the retention of vast amounts of unused material by archives and their
failure to acquire and preserve much that could be truly useful. One obvious example of "nonrecord" material of high utility being rejected for
archival preservation is provided by the Federal Bureau of Investigation
case file contretemps in the United States, in which the FBI decided that
only certain types of files would be preserved by the National Archives
and Records Administration. The FBI and as well, the National Archives,
by acquiescing in this decision, applied appraisal criteria very similar to
those advocated by Terry Cook in his recent study on case files. That is, if
the purpose of archives is to preserve evidence of functions then case files
are largely superfluous except where they document divergence from the
norm. But society's interest in the FBI case files had at least as much to
do with the information they contained as the functions they documented

---

40 Terry Eastwood, "Towards a Social Theory of Appraisal," in *The Archival Imagination: Essays in
    Honor of Hugh A. Taylor*, ed. Barbara L. Craig (Ottawa, 1992): 78, 83. Eastwood presents two very
    similar forms of the same argument in "Towards a Social Theory of Appraisal," 71-89, and "How
    Goes it with Appraisal?" *Archivaria* 36 (Autumn 1993): 111-21. The quotes and analysis that fol-
    low are drawn equally from the two essays.

41 Roy Turnbaugh, "Archival Mission and User Studies," 28. Anyone who has worked in an insti-
    tutional archives (government or private) will acknowledge this truth, though it applies to most
    collecting repositories as well.

or divergences they recorded; users successfully demanded that more files be saved.[42]

This, I believe, is precisely the logic of the social theory of archives: that "recordness" *not* be the sole determinant of archives. Measured by use, "informational" content is as important as evidential value. When business archivists queried each other about company use of archives to support decision making, one of the few examples that could be cited was a project by the Kraft Corporation to analyze the comparative advantages of building their business through acquisition versus "new product development." In support of the study, participants "conducted an extensive investigation into Kraft's history of growth strategies." "Our best resource turned out to be our oral history collection," they reported[43] — not records having a stronger claim to intrinsic value as evidence.

Clearly, arguments that in order to safeguard archival values no appraisal should take place or that appraisal should be based on assessing inherent qualities as "records" have no more objective claims on validity than arguments for appraisal based on use. Yet there are still more obstacles to be met before use can be safely declared a credible principal criterion for appraisal. Arguments that use is an *unreliable* measurement are not easily set aside, even if use-based appraisal could or can be assumed to be valid in principle. The basic indictments by Ham and Benedict of use-driven appraisal are, indeed, to some degree true. These are that

- appraisal based only on what is academically in vogue at a given moment will lead to preservation of an inconsistent and fragmentary record;
- we cannot predict whether records unused for 100 years might suddenly be useful as new needs emerge;

---

42 Susan Steinwall, "Appraisal and the FBI Files Case: For Whom do Archivists Retain Records?," *American Archivist* 49, no. 1 (Winter 1986): 52-63; Terry Cook, "'Many are Called but Few are Chosen': Appraisal Guidelines for Sampling and Selecting Case Files," *Archivaria* 32 (Summer 1991): 25-50. Also see Richard Cox, who insists that "If these records are properly identified and managed, there will be more than enough documentation for the records creators, concerned parties, and other researchers." ("Putting the Puzzle Together: The Recordkeeping Functional Requirements Project at the University of Pittsburgh; A Second Progress Report," at the University of Pittsburgh, School of Information Sciences, Functional Requirements for Evidence in Recordkeeping Web site, at http://www.lis.pitt.edu/~nhprc). As well, see Luciana Duranti, who rejects as unarchival oral histories and everything else that is not a "record," relegating such nonrecords to the purview of "documentalists" and "historians" (posting to the Archives and Archivists listserv, 22 and 24 May 1993, 3-6 October 1993, 4-6 September 1996).

43 Elizabeth Adkins's posting to the Busarch listserv (busarch@gla.ac.uk), 11 June 1998. The business archivists on this list also seem fairly united in the belief that the "stuff" of archives is and must be a combination of records, library material, and other "historical material" — just so long as it is "needed" by the company in some way. (See the postings on 1 and 2 July 1998.) Additional testimony to the importance and utility of "nonrecord" information and data will be found in most of the essays comprising Seamus Ross and Edward Higgs, eds., *Electronic Information Resources and Historians: European Perspectives* (St. Katherinen, 1993).

- records may have an unquantifiable importance above and beyond their use in research (for, according to Benedict, society places abstract values on "the maintenance of the records of its institutions");

- there are factors, over and above lack of interest or utility, that may prevent use of records and thereby distort conclusions as to their true value.

All of these issues are plausible and must be addressed in considering any use-based approach to appraisal. However, in the final analysis, none of them constitutes a sufficiently persuasive argument that use should not be adopted as an appraisal criterion.

Ham's objection to archivists being weathervanes of historiography is sound only up to a point. First of all, errors in historiographical prediction have a limited impact. Historians are not archives' sole clients; genealogical research, for example, is not particularly affected by changes in academic historiography and in the collecting patterns that result. Secondly, Ham implies that a ruthless intellectual consistency exists among all archivists that would lead all archives to make rigidly identical choices in acquisition. In fact, collecting is likely to be much more eclectic: there are too many dissimilarities between archives in terms of their missions and resources (not to mention in archivists' intellectual perspectives) for the weathervane analogy to hold up as anything more than appealing rhetoric. Thirdly, in the same article Ham champions the goal of an archival record that will be a true and complete "mirror for mankind."[44] That is something that no mortal formulation of archival appraisal can ever hope to do. Appraisal of any kind is, by definition, a matter of making choices and choices mean that the archival record will be incomplete and biased. The real question before us is, how do we make the choices?

Similarly, Benedict's contention that past use cannot predict future use is ultimately a rationale for not discarding *anything* — not doing appraisal — because much the same logic applies there as well: demanding that all records be kept for the sake of ensuring that no important records are lost. Admittedly, Benedict is undoubtedly correct to argue that archives have symbolic importance. But an argument that this importance will be undermined or destroyed by judicious choice does not logically follow. Certainly, some of the symbolic weight of archives is carried by their presumed "permanence," but as we should all know by now, the concept of permanence is and always has been an illusion.[45] She is on firmer ground

---

44 Benedict, "Invitation to a Bonfire," 49; Ham, "Archival Edge," 13.

45 James M. O'Toole, "The Symbolic Significance of Archives," *American Archivist* 56, no. 2 (Spring 1993): 234-55; James M. O'Toole, "On the Idea of Permanence," *American Archivist* 52, no. 1 (Winter 1989): 10-25; Kenneth E. Foote, "To Remember and Forget: Archives, Memory, and Culture," *American Archivist* 53, no. 3 (Summer 1990): 378-92.

when she notes that there may be obstacles to the use of records that make it difficult to judge researchers' demands for them accurately.

In fact, there *are* a number of impediments to use that have possibly influenced *which* records have been used. Each of these might lead one to question whether past use can serve as an accurate measure of potential value; the resulting findings could perhaps be skewed. It is worth dwelling briefly on some of the factors that can reduce access to records, possibly affecting rates of use.

Over the last 10 years many archivists have raised fundamental questions about how well we as a profession provide current and potential users access to our collections. The Society of American Archivists' manual on reference service identifies three conditions that must be met before use of archival records can occur, stating that "to use archives, users need *intellectual, legal and physical* access."[46] In the absence of any of these conditions, barriers to use can be created. For example, *legal* — and one might add moral or ethical — issues regarding user access have been the focus of vigorous, if unresolved, discussion of late. There seems to be a movement within the profession to become increasingly protective of vaguely defined third-party "privacy rights" and restrict access to otherwise unrestricted collections.[47] The more restrictions that archivists impose, the more difficult it will be for patrons to use collections.

There is also the even more pertinent issue of users' *physical* access. Much of the literature has so far focused on consistent hours of operation and accessibility to handicapped patrons.[48] Such discussions presuppose that researchers are able to visit the repository in the first place. It is well worth noting, however, that the Historical Documents Study report of 1992, *Using the Nation's Documentary Heritage,* suggests that inability to travel to archives is far and away the most significant factor preventing researchers' access to records. Sixty percent of respondents surveyed — historians, legal scholars, public school teachers, and genealogists — gave inability to travel to the site as the primary obstacle to their using specific historical material.[49] This is unlikely to disappear as a barrier to records use.

---

46 Mary Jo Pugh, *Archival Fundamentals Series: Providing Reference Services for Archives and Manuscripts* (Chicago: Society of American Archivists, 1992): 56, 6 (emphasis added).

47 See Mark A. Greene, "Moderation in Everything, Access in Nothing? Opinions About Access Restrictions on Personal Papers," in *Archival Issues* 18, no. 1 (1993): 31-41, for a summary of the literature to that point. Since then there has been at least one session at every SAA meeting devoted to legal and ethical access issues.

48 Pugh, *Providing Reference Services*, 65-74.

49 Ann D. Gordon, *Using the Nation's Documentary Heritage: The Report of the Historical Documents Study* (Washington, D.C., 1992), 39-41, 46. Some archivists do recognize this fact. Former SAA President Anne Kenney has written that "Archives are harder to use than other sources and not just because of their bulk. A researcher cannot check material out and take it home, cannot order it through interlibrary loan, and must use it during fairly limited office hours. The most meaningful distinction between library and archives may not be physical form or 'method and purpose of creation,' . . . but access." (Anne R. Kenney, "Commentary" on Lawrence Dowler's

Moreover, despite all the attention archivists have paid to *intellectual* access — particularly through standardized descriptive practices and on-line availability of records descriptions — we have done a poor job of monitoring whether this has truly improved intellectual access to archival holdings. Although now six years old, *Using the Nation's Documentary Heritage* has suggested that the vast resources we have put into online cat-aloging formats, standards, and systems may not be achieving the goal of greater intellectual access. The report notes that "only 9 percent of respondents to the survey selected computer databases as an important way to find sources."[50] Will the same be true with Encoded Archival Description (EAD)? The evidence to date suggests that our current paper

---

"The Role of Use in Defining Archival Practice and Principles: A Research Agenda for the Availability and Use of Records," *American Archivist* 51, nos. 1-2 [Winter and Spring 1988]: 94-95.) For an academic researcher's similar perspective, see Robin Kolodny (Temple University), "Archival Research: A New Look at an Old Tool," a focus paper presented for a roundtable at the 1992 meeting of the American Political Science Association, 5-6.

While the possibilities of providing remote access to archival resources through digitized presentation on the Internet have begun to command a great deal of archival attention, much less expensive and resource intensive options have been ignored for years. As Tim Ericson has noted, "For some reason, the concept of . . . lending entire fonds for research purposes remains revolutionary and controversial — some would even say heretical." The intrastate loan program practiced by the State Historical Society of Wisconsin with its Area Research Centers since 1962 has seen the successful completion of 10,000 loan transactions, "for the benefit of thousands of researchers who otherwise would not have had the opportunity to use archival materials. And we are in the habit of loaning precious documents for months at a time to insti-tutions not only across the continent but across the world, for exhibits." Yet the profession has never given serious consideration to the development of loan protocols (much less made it a professional priority of the archival community), and so far as I know only one institution has undertaken interstate loans of original archival material for research purposes. This took place from Cornell to University of California, Santa Barbara, under recent RBMS guidelines for loan-ing rare and unique material (statement by Thomas H. Hickerson, Cornell University, during session entitled "Neither a Borrower Nor a Lender Be . . ." at the 1993 meeting of the Society of American Archivists.) The quotation is from Timothy L. Ericson, "At the 'rim of creative dissatisfaction': Archivists and Acquisition Development," *Archivaria* 33 (Winter 1991-92): 74-75. Researchers using collections of congressional papers expressed remarkably similar sugges-tions. See Paul, *The Documentation of Congress*, 143. The Society of American Archivists study, *Planning for the Archival Profession* (Chicago, 1986), also urges "expanding the availability of archival records beyond the confines of an institution's reading room" (28, 29).

Inability to travel to collections is challenged for first rank as an obstacle to access by one of the archival profession's dirtiest little secrets: the extent of our backlogs. As Gordon, writing in *Using the Nation's Documentary Heritage*, discovered, "about 30 percent of respondents had been barred from collections because repository staff had not yet described or arranged the records, and another 20 percent or more had been barred because records were in poor physical condi-tion" (46). See also *Documentation of Congress*, 6, 143, where a survey respondent is quoted as saying "there are too many unprocessed collections," and Bruce W. Dearstyne, "What is the Use of Archives? A Challenge for the Profession," *American Archivist* 50, no. 1 (Winter 87): 82, who cites laments about unprocessed collections found in the state assessment reports of California, Kentucky, North Carolina, and New York.

50 Gordon, *Using the Nation's Documentary Heritage*, 59. See also Jill Tatem, "Beyond USMARC AMC: The Context of a Data Exchange Format," *Midwestern Archivist* 14, no. 1 (1989): 43, 45: "If . . .

finding aids are no more geared to user needs than our catalog standards.[51] If this is true for hard copy finding aids, it will not likely be different for automated finding aids. Add to this the fact that access to the Internet is still a minority privilege. Despite the spread of computer technology, by the end of 1997 only 43 percent of U.S. households even owned a personal computer, and only 57 million out of the 200 million people in the United States over the age of 13 used the Internet the minimum of once a month—in itself a low rate of usage).[52] The likelihood that demonstrable improvements in intellectual access will come with EAD is at least debatable.

Clearly, impediments to use are likely to remain. Nevertheless, while access problems must be addressed in any use-based approach to appraisal, perfect access in an imperfect world cannot be required, in all fairness, as a precondition for appraisal based on use. Benedict's insistence that barriers to access be considered when employing past use to reappraise records does not negate the rationale for use-based appraisal. It suggests instead that corrective, compensatory steps be considered.

The Arguments for Use as a Primary Appraisal Tool, and Why They Are Unsatisfactory

Though the arguments against use as a primary appraisal tool are not conclusive, at the same time the writings of use-based appraisal proponents have generally been neither complete nor completely persuasive. Even Eastwood, though he has established a *conceptual* foundation for

---

archivists are going to embark on the expensive process of developing online catalogs, in order to assist end-users in discovering archival materials it is imperative to discover what users want to know." Otherwise, "the USMARC AMC format will be both an irrelevance and a failed opportunity." David Bearman's 1989 article on "Authority Control Issues and Prospects" did ask how researchers really use an online catalog to gain intellectual access, but few authors have followed his example. David Bearman, "Authority Control Issues and Prospects," *American Archivist* 52, no. 3 (Summer 1989): 286-99.

51 Elsie Freeman has charged that, "generally speaking, the archivists we produce believe that their clientele must be content with the product they offer — the body of records in the box accompanied by the standardized description, for example — not that they must have the skills to learn what the client needs and how to satisfy that need." Elsie T. Freeman, "Soap and Education: Archival Training, Public Service and the Profession — an Essay," *Midwestern Archivist* 16, no. 2 (1991): 89-90. John Roberts, "Archival Theory: Myth or Banality," *American Archivist* 53, no. 1 (Winter 1990): 120, also rails against archivists "talking to ourselves about ourselves" rather than paying attention to what the public needs and wants from us. Also see Hugh Taylor, "Chip Monks at the Gate: The Impact of Technology on Archives, Libraries, and the User," *Archivaria* 33 (Winter 1991-92): 174-75, 178. Taylor suggests, further, that overreliance on automated finding aids and "expert systems" presents the "danger of diminishing both ourselves and the user in a lonely deadlock if our technologies become inappropriate and lacking in a human context" (177). See, too, Beattie, "An Archival User Study," 47: " archivists . . . tend to be too passive and bureaucratic when writing inventories." As well, Beattie comments that, "to date, very few studies have focused on the information seeking behavior of researchers in archives."

52 These statistics were gathered from three sources: Reuters story posted on ZDNet News Channel, http://www.zdnet.com/zdnn/content/reut/1211/262406.html; RelevantKnowledge at http://www.relevantknowledge.com/Press/release/05_04_98.html; U.S. Census data, at http://govinfo.library.orst.edu/cgi-bin/buildit?la-state.usa.

use-based appraisal, has provided us with no serviceable methodology through which implementation can occur.

Sadly, published discussions of the role of use in appraisal seem to have gone downhill after its first and best articulation in the 1940s. G. Philip Bauer, who is most known as an early proponent of cost-benefit analysis in appraisal, can also be credited with developing the most detailed and closely reasoned justification for use as the principal indicator of "benefit" in determining archival value. "Public value in records," he asserted, "is purely utilitarian." In a staff information paper for the U.S. National Archives, Bauer explained how an evaluation of users and records uses could be employed to guide appraisal. Here he presented a more nuanced and prescient approach to assessing utility than either Schellenberg, Dowler, Rapport, or Eastwood have provided in subsequent decades. Bauer was clear in observing that assessments of use required appreciation of gradations that exist in kinds of use and types of users. He noted, as well, that the volume of the records in question cannot be ignored as a factor in appraisal and that, ultimately, assessments are defined largely by the particular mission and clientele of an individual archives. Bauer seems to have understood all the right questions (regardless of whether one agrees with all his more specific conclusions). Unfortunately, his presentation was weakened by lack of data substantiating what he surmised about who uses what records for which purposes.[53]

Other analyses followed. According to Theodore Schellenberg, "the end of all archival effort is to preserve valuable records and make them available for use. Everything an archivist does is concentrated on this dual objective."[54] However, Schellenberg knew that predicting future use was a gamble, and suggested that, while archivists should solicit the opinions of potential users when appraising records, *potential* use could not serve as the sole or primary basis for a decision. Schellenberg contended that, "since the records that are useful for studies of broad questions usually consist of large series that are costly to preserve because of their volume, the archivist should actively explore the interest of groups of scholars in them. He should act as a catalyst to precipitate decisions on the fate of such records." But at the same time Schellenberg emphasized that in addition to considering "the extent to which it has already been exploited," documentary "appraisals should take into account the form in which the information is available in the public records . . . and the extent to which it is available elsewhere."[55] Schellenberg provided little detail on how this process should work; nor did he provide examples of the types of records that might be appropriate targets for consultation.

---

53 G. Philip Bauer, *The Appraisal of Current and Recent Records*, Staff Information Paper 13 (Washington, D.C.: National Archives and Records Service, 1946).

54 Theodore Schellenberg, *Modern Archives: Principles and Techniques* (Chicago: University of Chicago Press, 1956), 224.

55 Ibid., 151.

Thirty years later, new viewpoints appeared. The SAA's *Planning for the Archival Profession* called "the use of archival records . . . the ultimate purpose of identification and administration."[56] Lawrence Dowler took up that challenge and proposed "collection use as the basis for archival practice." He realized that "all uses of archives . . . are not the same, and archival policies and procedures ideally should recognize these differences." Dowler called for studies of who our users are, of "what information in archives gets used, and how . . . the quantity of materials used and the intensity of use . . . [can] be more accurately measured." Dowler also noted the influences that outreach, description, and reference activities have on use of archival material. However, like Eastwood after him, Dowler did not develop a specific appraisal methodology or cite specific examples of its application. And where Eastwood would abjure reappraisal — an apparent inconsistency — Dowler was also inconsistent. His approach placed great stress on including predictions of "potential" use and users which were not based on evidence of past use, but on a comprehensive intellectual understanding of the various types of "questions asked [and] . . . methods used" by researchers within existing fields of archival research. Although equivalent to divining what users might one day decide to access, for Dowler this was "as important as knowing what actually gets used." However, this way of focusing on potential use ultimately provides untenable criteria.[57] As Bauer noted in the 1940s, "if we are to let our visions of possible use prevail, we may as well give up the idea of selection entirely. Anything is possible."[58]

Even one of the most recent analyses contains flaws. In " Towards a Social Theory of Appraisal," Terry Eastwood terms his emphasis on use in evaluating records a "scientific theory," arguing in turn that their value as records lies in "the objective facts of archives" — their status as evidence of transactions. Eastwood suggests that, in appraisal, the "scientific analysis of the archivist" consists of assembling "evidence that any particular transactions endure in importance in society through continued recourse to evidence in them." Yet Eastwood's claim that his approach is "scientific" raises questions. For a theory to be scientific, its validity must be subject to testing and measurement. While one can measure records use, this is a far cry from making the leap and assessing the much larger, theoretical implications inherent in claiming the validity of use as an appraisal criterion. One cannot thereby deduce the validity of use as an appraisal criterion.

The tension between appraising use and assessing evidence results in seeming paradoxes (if not contradictions) in the social theory. Eastwood acknowledges that evidential records can be used for informational

---

56 Society of American Archivists, *Planning for the Archival Profession*, 22.

57 Unless otherwise noted, all quotes in this paragraph are from Dowler, "The Role of Use."

58 Bauer, *The Appraisal of Current and Recent Records*, 6.

purposes, but rejects informational content as a consideration in appraisal. "The real thing being valued is evidence of transactions," he insists. He makes use the basis for appraisal, but, paradoxically, rejects its application to reappraisal, averring that this would compromise objectivity. Choices would be "prey to the relative value judgments of each succeeding age."

Moreover, Eastwood's argument begs the question of how to *evaluate* use and if, indeed, it should even be done. Do we simply count the number of times a piece of evidence is requested, or do we try to determine the number of times it actually proves "useful" to the researcher? Is the *quality* of use to be weighed along with the quantity? Are some *users* more important than others? Such questions must have precise answers if current and past use are to provide "empirical grounds on which to rest our projections" of future use, and thus provide the basic foundation for appraisal.[59] However, Eastwood is not alone in ignoring the issues. In his article on use as a foundation for reappraisal at the U.S. National Archives, Leonard Rapport overlooks many of the same questions, although at least giving specific examples of the types of records he thinks should be destroyed due to lack of use.[60]

The Case for Use as a Principal Appraisal Criteria

Use can, should, and must be a principal appraisal tool. If we acknowledge that archives do not have validity aside from the value that an institution or society places on them, then use is the only empirical measurement we have of that value, and significantly, of the overall success of an archives' various programs. This includes not only records appraisal decisions, but also arrangement and description, public access, and so on. The Minnesota Method, which focused on appraising records creators, was deliberately pragmatic, worried less about theory than about whether it was an effective way of getting necessary work done. In moving from appraisal of *records creators* to appraisal of *records,* the proposal is that we now embrace pragmatism's first cousin, utilitarianism, taking actions that result in the greatest good for the greatest number. That is, in appraising and reappraising records, what should be acquired from any source is that body of material that will provide the most use for the widest variety of users through preservation of the smallest quantity of records possible.

To be sure the utilitarian approach is neither precise nor scientific. This approach rests, admittedly, on a debatable and unverifiable premise: that (as suggested above) archives are social creations valued for social purposes. But this premise is no more or less true than any other "first principle" of archives. A mechanistic or formulaic application of the

---

59 Eastwood, "Towards a Social Theory of Appraisal," 80, 84-85.

60 Leonard Rapport, "No Grandfather Clause: Reappraising Accessioned Records," *American Archivist* 44 (Spring 1981): 143-50.

approach is not only unwise but impractical because, while use can be measured in certain ways, these measurements are not exhaustive and are open to multiple valuations. Society may not value all forms of use equally. A simple example is provided by asking whether the utilization of archival material that results in a citation in a book read by 1,000 people might not be considered more socially valuable than use made by a hobbyist, say, to construct a model railroad for his or her sole enjoyment. This same example points to another difficulty: use cannot probably be defined solely on the basis of how many times a box is requested. Not only might a single use communicate archival material to many other users through publication, but also exhibits must be considered, as well as access to materials in digital settings like the Internet. Hits on documents mounted on a Web site, in turn, remind us that lack of use may not in fact be evidence of lack of utility so much as lack of accessibility. If we digitize two collections and put them on the Web and they each get 1,000 hits, can we logically conclude that the contents of all our less-frequently accessed hard copy collections are therefore intrinsically less useful?

If use is not free from subjective judgments and problems of measurement, neither is it free of at least one inherent bias. Utilitarianism can quickly morph into simple majoritarianism, leaving the documentation of powerless minority classes begging while we hasten off to collect more material relating to middle- and upper-class educated whites, who are our most numerous users.[61] A good case can also be made that there are also a very narrow range of truly vital records, which must be preserved whether or not they are ever directly consulted. These might include original copies of materials critical to documenting our basic rights as citizens. A couple of examples are immigration records and birth records — records that are rarely accessed in their original condition. Other examples might be, for an institutional archives, minute books forming the primary legal record of decisions taken, and for a college archives, student records that document grades. For all these reasons use-based criteria should not be applied mechanically or with foolhardy rigidity, resulting in rules like "All correspondence files will be kept; no accounting records will be saved." I have always agreed with F. Gerald Ham that appraisal is ultimately more an art than a science, but also with

---

61 Hans Booms, in his "Society and the Formation of the Documentary Heritage: Issues in the Appraisal of Archival Sources," (translated by Hermina Joldersma and Richard Klumpenhouwer) found in *Archivaria* 24 (Summer 1987): 69-107, leaned toward exactly this danger in proposing that public opinion should both legitimize and dictate archival appraisal. One can agree that archivists have some obligation to be utilitarian without turning appraisal into a pure popularity contest.

There are two things, in fact, that can mitigate against this majoritarian danger. One is that "minority" constituencies are not only the fastest growing segments of the U.S. population, but for most of us the fastest growing segment of our user populations — hence utilitarianism insists we not ignore these communities. The other is that at the level of collection development (that is,

Virginia Stewart's caveat that "even an art form demands rigor, attention to detail, and some rationale for the technique."[62] A utilitarian approach to appraisal is a step toward making more rational and thoughtful choices — though neither wholly scientific nor completely objective.

Moreover, even if use could be applied scientifically and with pure objectivity, it could not stand completely alone as an appraisal criterion. Institutional mission, some assessment of records content and of the completeness of the series in question, an evaluation of the relative importance of a particular creator (and hence of their records), and of course, political considerations (such as a board member's particular interest in records being assessed) may all have a bearing. To be sure, several approaches to appraisal have already made either use or input from users a significant component, though one among many, in appraisal decisions. These approaches are those most notably described in Maynard Brichford's 1977 *Appraisal and Accessioning* manual, the "black box" taxonomy developed by Frank Boles and Julia Young, and the documentation strategy defined and popularized by Larry Hackman and Joan Warnow-Blewett.[63] Yet, even if reliance on use is not the autonomous and completely determinative scientific methodology Eastwood wishes to make it, the pragmatic and utilitarian approach introduced here raises it to far more than just one "module" among the many equivalent appraisal criteria identified, for example, by Boles and Young.

In the utilitarian approach, use becomes the presumptive determinant in appraisal or reappraisal. A basic assumption is, for example, that large series with low use will not be retained. The burden of proof, so to speak, falls on arguments for retention. Or, to borrow a phrase from the computer software industry (which has itself adopted language from archives), calculations of benefits versus cost — that is, the benefits of use versus the costs of appraisal, processing, space, and conservation — should form the "default" setting in series appraisal and reappraisal. Instead of assuming a universal set of values applicable to all specific measurements of use, it takes individual repositories' missions and clients into account. If adopted widely, this approach would give the profession a practical means to dramatically reduce the vast universe of records we are faced with cataloging and preserving, while increasing the usefulness and value of archives to those who support us.

---

deciding what records creators are going to be approached or whose records accepted into a repository), rather than at the level of appraisal (what materials will actually be preserved from each of those creators), there is more room to assert archivists' notion of what "ought" to be documented.

62 Terry Cook, "'Another Brick in the Wall': Terry Eastwood's Masonry and Archival Walls, History, and Archival Appraisal," *Archivaria* 37 (Spring 1994): 102; Ham, *Selecting and Appraising Archives and Manuscripts*, 72; Stewart, "A Primer on Manuscript Field Work," *Midwestern Archivist* 1, no. 2 (1976): 4.

63 Brichford, *Appraisal and Accessioning*, pp. 9-10; Frank Boles and Julia Marks Young, "Exploring the Black Box: The Appraisal of University Administrative Records," *American Archivist* 48 (Spring 1985): 121–40. Larry J. Hackman and Joan Warnow-Blewett, "The Documentation Strategy Process: A Model and a Case Study," *American Archivist* 50 (Winter 1987): 12-47.

Practical Application

With all these caveats, how would we apply a utilitarian method of appraisal in the real world? For this we can return to the studies made of business records use. A first observation is that with the exception of audio-visual material, the material in the MHS and Hagley studies found to be most frequently used does not overlap with that material similarly identified through the survey of business archives (Figure 2). This comparison strongly suggests that different groups of users have very different priorities. Albeit, if we shift from looking at the use made of *all* sources to use only of unpublished sources, some similarities appear among user groups (Figure 3). Nevertheless, this discovery does little to answer appraisal questions. *The conclusion must be that proper application of appraisal criteria can come only by considering the intersection of use, repository mission, and repository resources.* Based on these considerations, a repository that purposely serves a primarily scholarly clientele and has limited staff and space (and whose institution does not?) would choose pragmatically to save a different, and smaller set of materials from a given business than would a business archives or a repository serving a broad public clientele.

The materials having the greatest utility for the greatest number and variety of users seem to be found among company-produced material, annual reports, internal publications, trade catalogs and other advertising and public relations material, correspondence and executive-level subject files (so grouped because they are often difficult to differentiate), audio-visual material, and personnel records. With the exception of correspondence files and personnel files, these are generally small series.[64] What this suggests for the MHS, for example, is that that we can serve scholars, lay researchers, and our donors (these last constituents corresponding roughly to the internal users at business archives) by acquiring and preserving all the series each group most uses — and *still* acquire smaller collections than we have traditionally accepted. Similarly, if a county historical society has room either for a company's minute books or for their annual reports and employee publications, analyses of use should incline them to the reports and publications. If a business archives has just enough budget to either microfilm deteriorating ledgers or hire someone to index company publications, studies of use should point them to the latter. Use should similarly inform reappraisal.

If comparisons of use versus bulk for the railroad records can be sustained for other business collections, it would be extraordinarily difficult to justify acquiring or retaining accounting records or any but the most summary financial records for business enterprises of the late nineteenth century and beyond: use is extremely low and bulk is very high. These records have long been avidly collected by archivists and their acquisition

---

64 Legal and engineering files might warrant preservation depending on the type of company.

vigorously defended, even in the face of a widely acknowledged lack of use.[65] The Hagley citation study clearly shows that historians scarcely use accounting records from any twentieth-century business. The MHS call slip analysis confirms that lay researchers are just as uninterested. At the MHS, a full 10 percent of our entire manuscript collection consists of the accounting records of two railroads. These records are *not* used. The questions arise: why should we keep those records and why would we take more accounting records from more firms?

And what of minutes, that most traditionally archival of all record types? Their utility as *historical sources* seems slim, and for that reason the MHS has decided that they will not automatically be acquired from a business from which other records may be accepted.[66] While there may be reasons for accepting minutes in specific instances,[67] studies of use provide us with the basis for changing our "default" decision from "accept" to "question."

However, the institutional context within which a use-centered appraisal of records should take place leaves room for the MHS to acquire large, and what would be traditionally called "complete" sets of records from some select firms. The decision to do so is not be made [sic] on the basis of a neo-Jenkinsonian argument for preserving complete records, hence records in their full context. From a utilitarian perspective, the provision of extensive knowledge and evidence of context is at best a secondary responsibility; it matters only to some users some of the time and should therefore be the exception rather than the rule. To relate this to the Minnesota Method documentary level A, where context becomes a definite goal, it should be adopted only for those records creators at the pinnacle of a repository's priority list. Even then, the acquisition of such a complete body of records should be justified as much on the basis of our knowing that some users will need a full knowledge of context as on the basis of what archival theory dictates. For most businesses that a repository documents, more users will be served in more

---

65 See, for example, Henrik Fode and Jorgen Fink, "The Business Records of a Nation: The Case of Denmark," *American Archivist* 60, no. 1 (Winter 1997): 84-85, in which they acknowledge the lack of use of accounting records but insist that the answer is not to reappraise and destroy them but to convince historians to use them. See also the series of exchanges on the ARCHIVES list on just this topic, 5-8 May 1997. One has to wonder just how long archivists will feel compelled to wait for historians or other researchers to find utility in accounting records. Ledgers and journals prior to the late nineteenth century are sometimes used by researchers because there are few other sources for economic information in that era. Yet, as noted elsewhere, in the MHS call slip analysis the only accounting records to receive use were from a mid-nineteenth-century fur trader. The Baker Library at Harvard also reports use of textile company accounting records from the same period. See Laura Linard and Brent M. Sverdloff, "Not Just Business as Usual: Evolving Trends in Historical Research at Baker Library," *American Archivist* 60, no. 1 (Winter 1997): 91-92.

66 See Greene and Daniels-Howell, "Appraisal with an Attitude," 185-93.

67 These include the issues of whether the minutes contain more than preemptory reporting of decisions taken, the relationship of the minutes to other series, and the ever-present "political considerations."

ways by making appraisal decisions based on use rather than on preservation of context.

By definition, the application of use in appraisal must be based on assessment of the utilitarian value of extant holdings. Therefore, the most direct, safest application of the data is to the collections used to generate that information — that is, in reappraisal. Nevertheless, this is certainly not to say that this information should not be used to assess new acquisitions. *Statistics of use for late twentieth-century business records already in a repository can and should be used to define appraisal criteria for additional late twentieth-century business collections when a repository considers acquiring them.* Indeed, as a purely practical matter it is likely that a repository will employ use-based data more for appraisal than for reappraisal since (with the possible exception of massive series such as the railroad accounting records at the MHS) it would be hard to justify the staff time expended in terms of the space gained through a major reappraisal project. But simply saying that reappraisal may not be cost effective is not to say that it is unwise or unworkable. Eastwood's rejection of the application of use studies to reappraisal is impractical because it ignores the limits that past appraisal decisions place on current and future acquisitions. It is not only storage space that will not expand indefinitely: neither will conservation or media-conversion budgets. Hard choices must be made that include reassessing appraisal decisions made before anyone did use studies and before the democratization of access to collections made their practical value to the public a more pressing concern.

A justification for declining or deaccessioning minutes, financial accounts, or anything else does not depend on *no one* ever having used or being likely to use such records — only on the recognition that we cannot do or save everything and on the utilitarian argument that deciding what we *will* do and save should be based on providing the most benefit to the most people at the least cost. Nor is it suggested that a few hobbyists' *probable* use of bulky railroad purchase orders is in itself less valuable than the many uses demonstrably made of correspondence files. The argument is simply that preserving correspondence files is of more benefit to more people and that secondly, by not saving the purchase orders we can instead preserve other materials that will serve more people. Hobbyists' use is not considered in any way illegitimate; indeed, it is exactly this user group's overwhelming use of the (also much smaller) set of railroad engineering records that defines the utility of saving those records. Needs are simply weighed against both the costs required to meet these needs and the likelihood of meeting more requirements at less cost by making other appraisal and retention choices.[68]

---

68 It may be added, moreover, that the cost-benefit ratio may encompass more than the direct costs of storing and administering a series of records versus a valuation of use activity. A user group may provide other benefits to the repository that offset the direct costs of preserving a particular set of records despite the use of the records being too infrequent to justify retention: genealogists' well-deserved reputation as lobbyists and willingness to lobby funding sources on behalf of repositories is one example.

Indeed, a utilitarian approach must accept that accumulating traditional company files is not the only, or even necessarily the best means
of documenting business. Four of the chapters in *The Records of American
Business* look at nontraditional means of documentation. Timothy L.
Ericson looks at "external" records — that is, materials such as government
records, independent business publications, labor records, and the records
of industry trade associations that are not generated by companies. James
E. Fogerty examines the role of oral history in the documentation of business. Ernest J. Dick focuses on sound and visual records as business documents. And John A. Fleckner touches on the importance of artifacts, graphic images, and sound and visual material as sources for nonacademic history.[69] All of these sources have long been accepted as *supplements* to traditional business records. What a utilitarian approach to appraisal suggests is
that these sources — or collections of corporate publications such as annual reports and employee newsletters — should be frequently sought and
accepted as *substitutes* for minutes, ledgers, and payrolls.

There is one final thought about use-based appraisal: it carries with
it the implication that other aspects of archives administration —
particularly processing and reference — should also be more user-driven.
Some archivists have already begun to argue this position, suggesting
modest to radical changes in reference procedures and records processing
to make archival material more intellectually accessible to the majority of
our users.[70] It is possible to accept a utilitarian approach to appraisal while
rejecting similar approaches to processing (and vice versa), but they may
well be two sides of the same coin. It would be inconsistent to do one but
not the other. At the bottom of this issue is a set of fundamental questions about what archives are and who and what they are intended for.

Application to Other Record Types

Business records are not the only category of material to which we at
the MHS have begun to apply utilitarian approaches in appraisal and

---

69 Timothy L. Ericson, "Beyond Business: External Documentation and Corporate Records,"
    297-326; James E. Fogerty, "Facing Reality: Oral History, Corporate Culture, and the
    Documentation of Business," 251-74; Ernest J. Dick, "Corporate Memory in Sound and Visual
    Records," 275-96; John A. Fleckner, "Reaching the Mass Audience: Business History as Popular
    History," 327-48; all in *The Records of American Business*, ed. James O' Toole (Chicago: Society of
    American Archivists, 1997).

70 The most vocal advocate for a user-centered revision of archives administration has been Elsie
    Freeman Finch. See especially, Elsie Freeman, "Buying Quarter Inch Holes: Public Support
    Through Results," *Midwestern Archivist* 10 (1985): 89-97; Elsie Freeman, "In the Eye of the
    Beholder: Archives Administration from the User's Point of View," *American Archivist* 47 (Spring
    1984): 111-23; "Soap and Education: Archival Training, Public Service, and the Profession —An
    Essay," *Midwestern Archivist* 16 (1991): 87-94. Terry Cook has criticized this view, most sharply in
    "Viewing the World Upside Down: Reflections on the Theoretical Underpinnings of Archival
    Public Programming," *Archivaria* 31 (Winter 1990-91): 123-34.

reappraisal. As noted earlier, the MHS approach to business records was preceded by a roughly similar project to redefine our approach to appraising congressional collections. However, this did not include an evaluation of records creators as sources. The congressional appraisal guidelines focused almost entirely on series and function-level appraisal, since the society has reaffirmed its commitment to attempt to collect material from the state's entire congressional delegation. As with the business collections, our congressional collections were, and still are huge and were not receiving a proportionate share of use. In 1990 they totaled nearly 6,200 cubic feet, or approximately 16 percent of the society's total manuscript collection.[71] A full 95 percent of this 6,200 feet documents congressional activity since World War 11, 82 percent (5,000 cubic feet) since 1960 alone.

Historians and other users of congressional papers have admitted, often against their will, that the size of modern congressional collections and, in particular, the ever-diminishing ratio between content and quantity, make them difficult and frustrating to use. At the same time, many researchers are becoming increasingly adept at using the wide range of other, less voluminous sources that also document Congress. In the words of one scholar, "congressional collections are far larger than they need to be in order to reflect the important issues and activities that they document." "Only by paring down these collections to their unique elements," she said, "will archivists succeed in making them useful to researchers and manageable for archives."[72] Results of a study in 1992 of patterns of use in 19 repositories, including the MHS, found that case files and constituent correspondence files, which accounted for between 40 to 80 percent of each of our post-1960 congressional collections, received approximately 15 percent of total use.[73] These figures are even more approximate than those accumulated through the railroad record study because MHS fonds were not analyzed separately and because the figures for the use of constituent mail included the use of indexes and summaries. We have anecdotal evidence that indexes and summaries are used much more often than correspondence itself.

By 1993 we had developed new appraisal guidelines and began to implement them in evaluations of both new and existing accessions. The guidelines we developed took account not only of our holdings analysis and the rough statistics on use, but also of as much previous

---

71 This accounting of the congressional collections does not include the vice presidential portions of the papers of Walter Mondale and Hubert Humphrey; broader public affairs collections such as the papers of U.S. ambassadors, state governors, and state legislators; the records of political parties and interest groups; or the official records of the state government in the state archives.

72 Patricia Aronsson, "Appraisal of Twentieth-Century Congressional Collections," in *Archival Choices*, ed. Nancy Peace (Lanham, Md.: Lexington Books, 1984), 82-83.

73 Paul, *The Documentation of Congress*, 136

writing and discussion on the subject as we could gather.[74] Because
there is much duplication among members of the delegation in terms
of the issues and projects with which they deal[75] (as well as with constituents helped or heard from), and because the evidence was that the
largest series receive the least use, our main conclusion was that the
guidelines should reduce overlap by treating senators' records in a different manner from records acquired from congressional representatives. Several large series that had been traditionally considered archival
would no longer be retained.

The most important step we took in reducing the bulk and complexity of collections was to reject *in toto* acquisitions of casework and
constituent correspondence files from representatives, and to accept
these series from senators only if they were microfilmed or could be
sensibly sampled. As of the summer of 1999 we have applied these
guidelines to five new collections (two from senators and three from
representatives) and retrospectively to nine of our post-1960 collections
of representatives' papers. This reappraisal has resulted in the destruction of over 1,200 cubic feet, with an average reduction of 65 percent of
a collection's original size.[76] There are, therefore, now 1,200 cubic feet
of shelf space available for more useful material. Moreover, field staff
have many fewer boxes to handle, sort, and appraise when new congressional collections arrive. All this creates time that can be usefully
employed pursuing leads or appraising other collections.

Our decisions about congressional collections have been vigorously
debated by our colleagues (less in print than through the mail and dur-

---

74 In addition to Aronsson and *Documentation of Congress*, cited above, we used Richard A. Baker,
    ed., *Proceedings of the Conference on Research Use and Disposition of Senators' Papers* (Washington,
    1978); Frank Mackaman, ed., *Congressional Papers Project Report* (Washington, D.C.: National
    Historical Publications and Records Commission, 1986); Eleanor McKay, "Random Sampling
    Techniques: A Method of Reducing Large, Homogeneous Series in Congressional Papers,"
    American Archivist 41 (July 1978): 281-88; Lydia Lucas, "Managing Congressional Papers: A
    Repository View," *American Archivist* 41 (July 1978): 275-80. The most specific set of appraisal
    recommendations to date was Karen Dawley Paul, *Records Management Handbook for United
    States Senators and Their Repositories* (Washington, D.C.: U.S. Senate, 1991). Paul's handbook was
    indispensable in identifying and defining records series, but in several instances her retention
    guidelines give disproportionate weight to the individual senator rather than to documenting
    the office, the delegation, or the institution. The less formal House retention guidelines —
    "Recommended Disposition: Papers of Members of U.S. House of Representatives," (1993),
    unpublished handout available from the Office of the Clerk, U.S. House of Representatives — are
    more realistic about space constraints and researcher interest. Our discussions also benefited from
    discussions with, or papers by Richard Pifer (State Historical Society of Wisconsin), Herb Hartsook
    (University of South Carolina), Rebecca Johnson (University of Delaware), Karen Paul (Senate
    Historian's Office), Cynthia Pease Miller (Office of the House Historian). Finally, and in many
    instances most importantly, the guidelines have benefited from conversations with the staffs of
    several members of the Minnesota congressional delegation.

75 Aronsson, "Appraisal of Twentieth-Century Congressional Collections," 83.

76 An additional result of the reappraisal has been the creation of a better finding aid for the
    remaining collection.

ing the annual meetings of the SAA Congressional Papers Roundtable). As of the summer of 1998 we have still had no complaints from our past or present congressional delegation or researchers,[77] and a growing number of repositories have adopted these or similar guidelines. They have done so precisely because these guidelines reflect a more realistic understanding of repository resources and priorities than practices formerly employed.[78]

Conclusion

At least three things are glaringly obvious about the utilitarian approach to records appraisal. The first is that it is not perfect. Of course, if no archival theory or practice were allowed unless it was perfect, none would exist. Ultimately, the question becomes whether appraisal based on use is, granted its many imperfections, better or worse than the proposed practical alternatives. The second point is that its practicality and broad applicability depend upon an increasing number of use studies. Because every repository serves a somewhat different clientele, has a different mandate from its resource allocators, and must deploy different resources, in an ideal world every repository would do its own detailed use studies for every segment of its collections. These could be as simple as the MHS call slip analysis, as complex as a process of user interviews, or as intensive as a citation analysis. The world not being perfect, most repositories will have to extrapolate from studies done by similar institutions regarding similar records. The third caveat is that use-based utilitarian appraisal is not a magic bullet. Utilitarian appraisal does not equal "easy" appraisal. Unless we abandon appraisal as an archival responsibility, we will never make appraisal simple because we can never make it mechanically exact or scientific. If the situation were otherwise, there would be no reason for archivists to exist. But a utilitarian method will provide a better rigor and rationale for appraisal decisions.

---

77 When necessary (under the terms of our donor agreements), we sought and in all cases received permission from the donors to destroy the reappraised material. Moreover, the staffs of our sitting delegation members are pleased to have clear and detailed guidelines from us that help them manage, store, and transfer records.

78 While our guidelines have encountered no resistance from our congressional delegation or — to date — from our researchers, they have had a decidedly mixed response from our archival colleagues. There is nothing close to an archival consensus that case files and issue-related mail are not worth their bulk to preserve. Some archivists at repositories that exclusively collect congressional papers have been concerned that our guidelines will be seen as a universal standard. Not only have we not promulgated our guidelines as a broad standard, we specifically eschew such a goal. Each repository has its own mission and clientele, its own set of resources, and thus its own individual appraisal criteria. For more complete details of the congressional records project, see Greene, "Appraisal of Congressional Records at the Minnesota Historical Society: A Case Study," 31-43.

In the end, it is likely that making use a principal appraisal and reappraisal criterion will result in a broader rather than narrower historical record. It allows us to spend X amount of staff time and Y amount of stack space to save trade catalogs and correspondence from fifteen companies (or five companies, five civic organizations, and five churches) rather than the same resources to save the trade catalogs, correspondence, *and* accounting records and minutes for only two or three.[79] A utilitarian approach seeks not only to maximize service to our constituents, but also — and not coincidentally — to strengthen our case with the sponsors from whom we receive our resources. ("Look," we can say, "we have increased use statistics while reducing our storage needs.") Otherwise, we wind up arguing that we need more space, and more staff, to store more and more dross that nobody actually uses. To use my favorite quote from all archival literature: "Society," Gerry Ham once wrote, "must regard such broadness of spirit as profligacy, if not outright idiocy."[80]

Certainly we do not want to be viewed as profligates or idiots. Nor, I think, do we want to be seen as technocrats obsessing about the "record-ness" of material about which nobody truly cares in the long run. The utilitarian alternative, admittedly, is not flawless, but I think it is better. Churchill is reputed to have remarked that "democracy is the worst form of government except all the others that have been tried." It may be this is all that can be said similarly of a use-based approach to appraisal. If, as it seems, it is demonstrably true that some archives are much better supported by institutions or society than others,[81] we might ask why — then seek the reason. Personally, I think Maynard Brichford had it right 20 years ago when he suggested that "use of the archives and the growth of its reputation" was "the surest proof of sound records appraisal."[82] Ultimately, it is not a bad foundation upon which to rest our profession.

---

79 Distinguished historian Arthur Cole asked 50 years ago whether it really made sense for the Baker Library to devote 324 feet of stack space to records of the Slater textile company that had been used nine times in fourteen years, as opposed to filling that space with books or other types of sources that would undoubtedly be used more frequently. Arthur H. Cole, "Business Manuscripts: A Pressing Problem," *Journal of Economic History* 5 (May 1945): 50.

80 F. Gerald Ham, "Archival Choices: Managing the Historical Record in an Age of Abundance," *American Archivist* 47, no. 1 (Winter 1984): 12.

81 Ian E. Wilson, "Commentary: Reflections on Archival Strategies," *American Archivist* 58, no. 4 (Fall 1995): 418–19, has made this point most recently. As he notes, there have been no studies undertaken specifically to explain the evident disparity in the support enjoyed by different archival institutions in the same nation.

82 Brichford, *Appraisal and Accessioning:* 1.

Part Five:
Arrangement and Description

A rchival arrangement and description establish physical and intellectual control over records, enabling users to find the records they need. The fundamental archival principles of provenance and original order govern arrangement and description, dictating that archival records are organized by office of origin or records creator and that the original filing order should be maintained whenever possible. Because these functions are central to archival services, they have received extensive treatment in the archival literature and are the topics most frequently covered in archival writings.

Provenance has long been recognized as the essential principle of archival arrangement and description, but archivists have also sought to organize records in ways that facilitate research. This has sometimes led to efforts to establish subject or content based control over records. In "The Power of the Principle of Provenance," David A. Bearman and Richard H. Lytle argue that provenance should be recognized as the central organizing concept of archival information systems. Recommending discarding the record group concept, they argue that provenance, form of material, and function provide the best means of retrieval access for archival records. Significantly, after a "lukewarm reception by American editors,"* Bearman and Lytle published the article in *Archivaria,* the journal of the Association of Canadian Archivists, where it won the 1986 W. Kaye Lamb prize for the best article of the year. American archivists were not initially receptive to their emphasis on a contextual approach to archives, but the article has since been recognized as a seminal contribution.

Since the 1970s archivists have focused attention on automated techniques for archival description, seeking to harness the power of computers and the networking capabilities of national database systems. The

---

* Tom Nesmith, "Archival Studies in English-speaking Canada and the North American Rediscovery of Provenance," in Nesmith, ed., *Canadian Archival Studies and the Rediscovery of Provenance* (Metuchen, N.J.: Scarecrow Press, 1993), 8, 16.

emergence of the Machine Readable Cataloging (MARC) format for Archival and Manuscript Control (AMC) in the early 1980s led archivists to focus on learning a new system for cataloging records. This adaptation of library bibliographic systems did not always mesh well with archival approaches to collective description, hierarchical levels of control, and access methods. Avra Michelson concludes, in "Description and Reference in the Age of Automation," that archives exhibit significant inconsistency in establishing cataloging headings and authority controls. She recommends steps to correct such inconsistencies and to improve archival use of the MARC format.

The growing prominence of electronic records challenges traditional approaches to archival description as well as other archival functions. Margaret Hedstrom, one of the leading researchers focusing on electronic records, outlines some of these concerns in "Descriptive Practices for Electronic Records: Deciding What Is Essential and Imagining What Is Possible." This article, which also won *Archivaria*'s W. Kaye Lamb prize, emphasizes the management of metadata as an alternative to traditional archival descriptive practices for electronic records.

By the 1990s archivists sought to harness the power of the Internet for archival description and access. Beginning with Gopher sites to provide World Wide Web access to archival information, they eventually developed procedures for placing archival finding aids on Web sites using Standardized General Markup Language (SGML). Daniel V. Pitti, one of the leaders in this process, recounts the principles and procedures by which archivists established new archival standards in "Encoded Archival Description: The Development of an Encoding Standard for Archival Finding Aids." Encoded Archival Description (EAD) presents traditional archival inventories and collection registers, complementing the cataloging procedures developed using the MARC format. Currently, both standards are best used together, providing dual means of archival description and access.

14

The Power of the Principle of Provenance

DAVID A. BEARMAN AND RICHARD H. LYTLE

Abstract: Archivists can contribute to information management through their unique perspective provided by the principle of provenance as it concerns organizational activity, especially how organizations create, use, and discard information. Despite the insights provided by provenance, however, archivists have not exploited its potential for retrieval in traditional archival applications and have not even attempted its wider application to the management of all information within their organizations. The invaluable insight of the principle of provenance is the relationship it reveals between creating activity and information created by organizations. If the archivist's use of provenance in arrangement and description — which establishes links backwards from records to creating activities — is reversed, a potential exists for a practical and powerful means of gaining access to and managing information. The authors advocate a much more aggressive leadership role for archivists in the wider management of information resources.

The task of managing information in organizations is becoming more challenging as the organizations become larger and more complex, and as information technologics and general societal developments increase the volume and sophistication of available information. This task can best be met by the careful study of how these organizations create, use, and discard information. A *practical* understanding must be gained of organizations as living cultures or organisms that create and use information; upon this foundation, sound information management can be developed.

How many archivists will recognize the preceding comments as relevant to them and the archival profession? Do archivists have much to contribute to the management of information in large organizations? Will archivists bring their knowledge of how organizations create and use information to bear on modern information management problems? Will the archival profession consequently make a transition to the modern information culture, or will it remain behind as a keeper of paper and electronic relics?

The key to the archivists' contribution to information management lies in their unique perspective provided by the principle of provenance as

Reprinted with permission from *Archivaria* 21 (Winter 1985-86): 14-27. Abstract added for this volume by the editor.

it concerns organizational activity, especially how organizations create, use, and discard information. Despite the insights provided by provenance, however, archivists have not exploited its potential for retrieval in traditional archival applications and have not even attempted its wider application to the management of all information within their organizations.

This article offers a critique of the application of the principle of provenance in traditional archival environments and proposes its expansion in a more powerful application to information management. The article also advocates a much more aggressive leadership role for archivists in the wider management of information resources.[1]

Theoretical Background

In work over the past several years, the authors have noted increasingly persistent problems about the distinctive value of provenance for the retrieval of archival materials. Lytle, comparing the power of provenance as a retrieval tool with library-oriented content-indexing techniques, described weaknesses in provenance as archivists use it in retrieval, while pointing out its greater potential if more rigorously applied.[2] Bearman has been systematically defining data elements and information flows in archival information systems and has found that some of the problems in archival retrieval systems result from a failure to distinguish between provenance information about organizations and descriptive data about the records themselves.[3] In the course of writing and distributing several drafts of this paper to archival colleagues, it became apparent that problems with traditional provenance-based arrangement and description as a tool for retrieval were widely perceived, but that neither the sources of the problems nor solutions had emerged.

---

1 During this paper's lengthy gestation period, many people helped by commenting on it. Alice Prochaska, Eddy Higgs, and John Watford of the Public Records Office provided comments back in 1982. Several interested staff of the U.S. National Archives helped about the same time, at least once in a luncheon session called for the purpose. More recently, Terry Eastwood at the University of British Columbia; Tom Nesmith, general editor of *Archivaria*; and Terry Cook, former general editor of *Archivaria* provided very useful critique. Fred Stielow, University of Maryland, provided some very useful comments on a late draft. We are especially appreciative of the interest shown by our Canadian colleagues. Their encouragement motivated us to complete the paper.

2 Richard H. Lytle, "Subject Retrieval in Archives: A Comparison of the Provenance and Content-Indexing Methods," (Ph.D. diss., University of Maryland, 1979); "Intellectual Access to Archives: I. Provenance and Content-Indexing Methods of Subject Retrieval," *American Archivist* 43 (Winter 1980): 64-75; "Intellectual Access to Archives: II. Report of an Experiment Comparing Provenance and Content-Indexing Methods of Subject Retrieval," *American Archivist* 43 (Spring 1990): 191-207.

3 NISTF Working Group on Data Elements and Formats for Archival Information Exchange, "Data Elements for Archives and Manuscript Repositories: A Dictionary, Thesaurus and Format for Information Interchange," Society of American Archivists, National Information Systems Task Force, Washington, D.C. (February 1982); "Data Elements Used in Archives, Manuscript and Records Information Systems: A Dictionary of Standard Terminology," SAA, NISTF (October 1982).

Exploration of provenance as the predominant means of archival retrieval reveals it as much more than a principle for the arrangement and description of archival materials. The more aggressive application of provenance to retrieval is apparent in Lytle's earlier definition:

> The Provenance or P Method is the traditional method of archival retrieval, based on principles of archives administration and reference practices of archivists. Subject retrieval in the P Method proceeds by linking subject queries with provenance information contained in administrative histories or biographies, thereby producing leads to files which are searched by using their internal structures. Information in the pure or theoretically defined P Method derives only from what is known about the file — the activities of the creating person or organization and the structure or organizing principles of the file itself.[4]

The process of provenance-based retrieval requires expansion beyond previously published explanations. It is familiar to most archivists who perform reference service for the archives of large organizations. A user poses a subject question that the archivist (assuming no previous knowledge of relevant records) retrieves by relating the subject to the activities of the organization. That is, the archivist translates a user's subject query into the terms of organizational activity. Then either the records or their inventories are searched for information pertinent to the subject query, using the file classification structures created by the originating office and recorded by the archivist in container lists or the like. An example reference question at the Smithsonian Archives might be the following: "What do you have on the design and construction of large telescopes?" Based on research into the administrative history and functional mandates of the organization, the archivist knows that only the Astrophysical Observatory has such projects in its charge, but the records of the observatory are voluminous; the scope of records to be searched can be reduced, however, by further careful selection of organizational subunits that might have created the desired information. But the archivist also knows that the assistant secretary for science has staff assistants who sometimes get deeply involved in such projects, and so those records are identified as well for searching. Conversely, the records of top Smithsonian officials would not be good candidates for review unless the searcher was interested in the internal or external politics of scientific construction projects. As inventories and records are examined, further information is found about observatory activities as well as information directly pertinent to the query.

---

4 Lytle, "Intellectual Access to Archives: I," 64-65. The definition of the content-indexing method, the second method in Lytle's 1979 study, has been omitted here, since the emphasis of this paper is on the provenance method.

Lytle has argued that the transformation of subject queries into organizational activity statements is an *inferential* process, in that the archivist
infers from provenance information which organizational units might
have undertaken relevant activities and therefore might have produced
documentation pertinent to the subject query at hand.[5]

Provenance Beyond Hierarchy: Expanding the Archival View of Organizations

The provenance method of retrieval obviously rests on a detailed
understanding of both the structure and processes of the organizations
that created the records in question. The most important question, then, is
how adequate is the North American archival view of organizations?

Archival theory has been strongly influenced by the nineteenth-century
view of organizations.[6] Classical organizational theory assumes that the
typical organization is autonomous and sovereign. At the highest levels,
the organization's actions and the structures it produces are assumed to
be the result solely of internally formulated policy. Even if this view were
valid for a simpler time, it is far too simplistic for modern organizations
operating in a world of multinational corporations, intergovernmental
units, regulatory organizations, and federal programs administered by
state, provincial, and local governments. Other assumptions of classical
bureaucracies are also violated as the internal workings of modern organizations are explored. In the ideal organization, decisions were supposedly
made at one level, implemented at the next. In the modern world of task
forces and committees, staff roles and subcontracting, this seemingly
simple structural relationship is in reality immensely complex. On organization charts this complexity is indicated by dotted lines, influence arrows
and circles, two-way authority links, and other shorthands that represent a
host of nonhierarchical relationships. Management by consensus, collegial relationships, professional boundaries and rights, job responsibilities limited by union contracts, independent ombudsmen, or central
agency arbiters further complicate these relationships.

In short, the classical view of organizations emphasizes the importance of hierarchy, in a theoretical world where a given bureaucratic unit
is directly subordinate to no more than one higher unit. That kind of
hierarchy is called a *mono-hierarchical* structure by information scientists,

---

5 The inferential process is implied in Lytle's publications cited above, and Lytle has been explicit
with colleagues about the notion of inference (correspondence available). Despite its provocative
presentation and potential importance for archival practice, the inferential provenance method
process has never been studied. Some information scientists have shown interest in it, but
archivists have not.

6 Max Weber, "Essentials of Bureaucratic Organization: An Ideal Type Construction," in, *Reader in
Bureaucracy*, ed. R. K. Merton (Glencoe, Ill.: Free Press, 1952); Michael A. Lutzker, "Max Weber
and the Analysis of Bureaucratic Organization: Notes Toward a Theory of Appraisal," *American
Archivist* 45 (Spring 1982): 119-30.

and its application to organizations emphasizes the chain-of-command
dimension of organizations. Mono-hierarchy is thus a poor model for
understanding modern organizations.

The inability of mono-hierarchical systems to capture the complexity
of large organizations can be illustrated by organization tables in *The United
States Government Manual*.[7] The example reproduced here (see chart) is one
of the federal government's most traditional organizations, the Department
of the Army; the reader should note that it requires six footnotes to clarify
distinctions between reporting authority, supervision, advisory roles, and
policy roles. Two other example organizations, for which charts are not
provided, also defy representation in traditional organization charts. The
Smithsonian Institution identifies no fewer than eighteen advisory boards
and commissions and three separate boards of trustees with undefined
relationships to the Smithsonian Board of Regents and the secretary of the
institution. The National Foundation on the Arts and Humanities exists
only as a theoretical construct surrounding three independent councils
with imprecise relationships to each other and undefined responsibility
to the president of the United States.

One striking characteristic of these examples is the virtual absence
of hierarchy at higher organizational levels. For example, the army
chart contains two levels with nine offices reporting to the office of the
secretary of the army and thirty-one offices reporting to the chief of
staff. The richness of provenance information has little to do with the
hierarchical structure of these organizations.

Hierarchical schemata might be useful if they had meaning across
organizations, but unfortunately they do not. Levels within one organization have totally different functions from the same levels in another
organization, and absolute positions are meaningless. Hierarchical
schemata cannot be used, for example, to identify where the personnel
hiring function or the new product testing function resides within one
organization or to locate this function across organizations. Indeed, in
one organization, these functions might be a small section; in other
organizations they are larger divisions or major branches.

Having used these examples to demonstrate the weakness of mono-
hierarchical schemas for explaining structure, processes, and activities in
modern organizations, two important points are apparent. First, there is a
richness of information about organizations that has been captured at
least in part by those who create and administer them. This information
may be found in a variety of organization charts, mission statements,
annual reports, parliamentary or congressional submissions, and the
like. Secondly, a better theoretical model that captures the complexity
of modern, living organizations begins to emerge. Insofar as hierarchical

---

7 *The United States Government Manual 1984-85* (Washington, D.C.: 1984).

Figure 1.

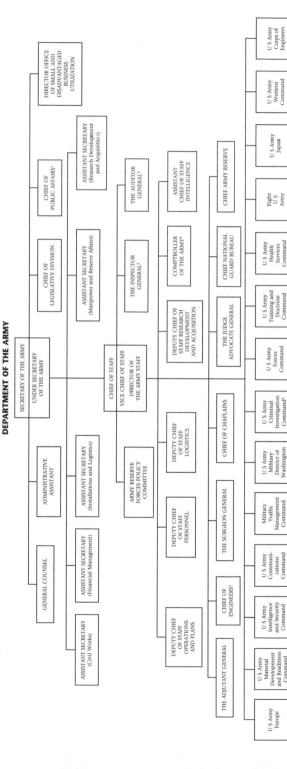

DEPARTMENT OF THE ARMY

[1] The Chief of Legislative Liaison and the Chief of Public Affairs report directly to the Secretary of the Army and are responsible to the Chief of Staff.

[2] The Inspector General serves as the confidential representative of and reports directly to the Secretary of the Army and to the Chief of Staff upon the morale, discipline, efficiency, and economy of the Army.

[3] The Auditor General reports directly to the Chief of Staff with concurrent responsibility to the Secretary of the Army.

[4] The Comptroller of the Army is under the direction and supervision of, and is directly responsible to the Assistant Secretary of the Army (Installations, Logistics and Financial Management), with concurrent responsibility to the Chief of Staff.

[5] The Chief of Engineers reports through the Assistant Secretary of the Army (Civil Works) to the Secretary of the Army on civil works matters and commands the U.S. Army Corps of Engineers.

[6] Commander, U.S. Army Criminal Investigation Command reports directly and concurrently to the Secretary of the Army and the Chief of Staff on criminal investigation matters.

Source: *The United States Government Manual 1984-85* (Washington, D.C.: U.S.G.P.O., 1984), Appendix C, 827.

structure is concerned, the model is *poly-hierarchical* because it captures traditional hierarchical relationships *across time* as organizations re-form themselves, and because it captures relationships that are not within the scope of superior/subordinate relationships. Some of the most important relationships are not hierarchical at all. All of these relationships can be encompassed by the concept of networking — capturing significant formal and informal relationships in an organization that together explain its mission, structure, and activities.

Unfortunately, North American archival theory has accepted the nineteenth-century view of organizations, probably more than most archivists realize. Intellectual limitations imposed by these assumptions, and consequent defects in archival practice, must be overcome before the power of provenance can be realized.

Identifying Defects in Current Application of Provenance

Consequences of the Received View of Organizations.
Current archival practice overemphasizes the importance of hierarchy. The placement of records-generating activities in organizational hierarchies has become almost an archival obsession. Provenance of archival records is indicated in archival information systems by terms that identify offices of origin and subsequent custodians (including offices responsible for the records); these terms are then linked in archival retrieval systems in a hierarchical schema that serves as a proxy for relationships between the actual offices of origin.

This distortion translates directly into records-keeping practices. In classical bureaucratic organizations, records were kept by and for the offices that used them. In the modern age of central management information systems, records retention and reporting regulations, and vigilant corporate legal staffs, these assumptions are rapidly becoming unwarranted. Offices that generate records frequently do not maintain them. When entire agencies are created or abolished, the connection with a hierarchical schema is difficult enough, but when changes take place within an agency, creating and abolishing divisions, departments, bureaus, and offices, or transferring them to other agencies, merging or dividing existing units, then a mono-hierarchical representation of these changes is impossible. Even more difficult to cope with are subtle shifts and changes over time in missions, functions, responsibilities, and reporting relationships. Yet all these changes take place within real organizations. The problem is that the current archival model does not fit such living organizations.

Dysfunctions Resulting from the Record Group Concept.
The record group concept, developed and applied at the National Archives of the United States and adopted widely by Canadian and American archives, is the central implementation of the principle of provenance in the arrangement and description of archives. In fact, the principle of

provenance and the record group have become so closely identified that, when drafts of this paper were circulated, archivists often equated criticism of the record group with a rejection of the principle of provenance. Given the identification of "record group" and "principle of provenance" in the minds of many North American archivists, it is important to emphasize that this critique aims at strengthening the application of the principle of provenance by pointing out serious limitations of the record group concept. Far from a rejection of the principle of provenance, the purpose is to strengthen its application to archival theory and practice.

Limitations of the record group concept are severe. It has debilitated archival theory and has limited effective development of provenance-based retrieval in North American repositories. There are two causes of its defects. One is the assumed importance of linking documentation with the hierarchical placement of the creating unit, a ramification of the classical view of superior/subordinate mono-hierarchical organizations which has been discussed. A second is that the record group, like traditional library classification schemes, is essentially a shelf-order system; since a record unit can go only one place on a shelf, a mono-hierarchical structure results.[8] Supporters of the record group concept point out that, in its implementation at the National Archives and other large repositories, it is not treated as a shelf-order classification. That rebuttal is beside the point. The record group imposes the *intellectual* constraints of a *physical* shelf-order classification; and in fact, many archivists act as though its purpose is to guide shelf-order arrangement. Despite its limited validity as a snapshot of one aspect of an organization, the record group concept has become an albatross.

Consequent Confusion Caused by the Record Group Concept. In case the reader doubts the reality of the record group albatross, some examples can be given of consequent practical and intellectual problems, quite beyond those already noted concerning its immediate implementation in repositories.

Early in its deliberations, the National Information Systems Task Force (NISTF) set out to identify descriptive elements (date, title, etc.) that had been applied to archival materials. This effort met with the insistence that the data elements be keyed to "hierarchical level," presumably to hierarchical level of record units. A thorough empirical study of the descriptive practices of archival repositories[9] demonstrated no connection

---

8 For a devastating criticism of the record group, see Peter J. Scott, "The Record Group Concept: A Case for Abandonment," *American Archivist* 29 (October 1966): 493-504, and in a subsequent exchange of letters between Scott and Meyer Fishbein. Unfortunately, Mr. Scott's advice has not been heeded.

9 Elaine Engst, *Report on Archival Practices for the National Information Systems Task Force* (unpublished paper, Society of American Archivists, October 1980).

between "hierarchical level" and descriptive elements, but the conviction continued, even within the NISTF, that such a relationship existed.

The importance of hierarchy has even been carried over to the design of computerized databases about archives. It was widely held that the SPINDEX software system was ideally suited to archives because its database structure reflected the "hierarchical" structure of archives. Thus the influence of the hierarchy assumption is apparent: a machine-readable database is structured to mimic hierarchical characteristics presumed to inhere in archival units. Some readers of this paper commented that the dependence on hierarchy was overemphasized in the SPINDEX example, or that it was certainly no longer considered crucial to the design of automated archival information systems. To that comment, a quotation from a recent *Computerworld* article on the American Presidential Libraries automation project follows: "[the project is now at the point of] designing a nine-level hierarchical data base that will index the vast collections, many of which are quite detailed."[10]

These examples illustrate that numerous archivists have come to operate as though archives (i.e., the records themselves) exhibit hierarchical relationships to each other.[11] Whether many archivists would agree with the proposition "archives are hierarchical" is not known, but many operate as though they believed it. The intellectual lineage of this misconception is clearly tied to the implementation of the record group concept in archival institutions, specifically the attempt to arrange records on shelves to reflect the hierarchical structure of organizations.

Absence of an Authority Record Approach. Arrangement and description practices add to the confusion caused by the record group because information about organizations and information about records are all mixed up in administrative histories, prefaces to inventories, and the like. These problems should be addressed by a disciplined approach to authorities, the primary authority being information about creating organizations.

An authority record is a formal means by which the creators and users of an information system maintain a common "language" between them to support information retrieval. An example is a geographical authority record maintained by scientists to support uniform description of where natural history specimens were collected. Good authority records maintain communications and support retrieval, and therefore must change over time. Archivists should not reject the use of authority records because they can point to problems with rigid library authority records such as the Library of Congress Subject Headings. A proposal for implementation of authority records is included in the following section.

---

10 *Computerworld* 18 (24 December 1984).

11 Of course, records do have some hierarchical characteristics, such as item/folder/box; these are not relevant here because they pertain to whole/part physical relationships rather than record-to-organization relationships.

Expanding the Power of Provenance-based Retrieval for Traditional Archival Environments

If dysfunctional aspects of record group systems are discarded, the path is cleared for a substantial improvement in provenance-based retrieval effectiveness for traditional archival repositories. The major areas of improvement discussed here indicate how progress can be made, without attempting a comprehensive description of a provenance-retrieval environment.

View Provenance Information as Retrieval Access Points. Archivists have traditionally viewed the principle of provenance — along with respect for the original order of records — as the basis for the arrangement and description of records. Although the presumed purpose of arrangement and description is enhanced retrieval, the practical result more closely approximates mere preservation. Significant strides can be made by taking a more aggressive approach to the application of the principle of provenance to retrieval.

Provenance information should be thought of as a means for providing access points to records in archival custody. In that respect, provenance information access points are the same in function as other kinds of access points such as chronological or geographical or subject information. To retrieve anything, a handle is required. The handle, or access point, is a characteristic that can be used in conjunction with other characteristics to identify a set of objects for examination. This applies equally whether the objects of retrieval are items in a grocery store, books in a library, or records in an archives. What differs is the appropriate characteristics — or, more precisely, which characteristics will prove most discriminating and most useful to searchers.

Lytle has made the largely unexplored assertion that provenance-related information will be a discriminating selector in the retrieval of archives. If provenance-related information will provide a powerful tool for retrieval, it must provide useful access points.

Specific Recommendations for Provenance-Related Access Points: Emphasize Form and Function. What elements of information concerning the provenance of records might serve as access points for a retrieval system oriented toward exploiting the power of provenance? Bearman has argued strongly for the discriminating power of function and form of material.[12]

---

12 David A. Bearman, "Implications of the Work of the NISTF for National Cooperation Among Folklife Archives" (unpublished paper, April 1984); "Towards National Information Systems for Archives and Manuscript Repositories: Problems, Policies, and Prospects" (paper presented at the Society of American Archivists National Information Systems Task Force Conference on Archival Information Interchange, Hoover Institution, Palo Alto, Calif. 14-15 March 1983); "Toward National Archival Policies: Assessment and Planning on a National Scale" (paper presented at the Society of American Archivists Annual Meeting, September 1984); "Who About What or From Whence, Why and How: Intellectual Access Approaches to Archives and Their Implication for National Archival Information Systems" (paper presented at the Conference on Archives, Automation, and Access, University of Victoria, British Columbia, 1-2 March 1985).

Whether the responsibility resides with the local magistrate, sheriff, county medical officer, parish priest, or census bureau, the governmental function "to record" births will generate predictable records, as will the function "to license" professions or "to authorize" expenditures. Functions are independent of organizational structures, more closely related to the significance of documentation than organizational structures, and both finite in number and linguistically simple.[13] Because archival records are the consequences of activities defined by organizational functions, such a vocabulary can be a powerful indexing language to point to the content of archival holdings, without need for actual examination of the materials themselves or for detailed subject indexing.

Function is not, however, adequate by itself to point to the intellectual content of archival materials. "Form of material" works with "function." "Form of material" is the name given to a particular type of record by cultural contemporaries who generate such records. "Forms of material" are known by contemporaries not from a detailed reading of their contents nor from the physical medium upon which they are written, but from commonalities in their structure.[14] The terms archivists have in the past uselessly assigned in construction of series titles (correspondence, day books, applications, surveyor field books, central registry files, etc.) are "forms of material" and are available to provenance-retrieval systems as intellectual content descriptors. For, if correctly defined by the archivist, such record "type" designations capture in cultural shorthand a description of the informational content of records. The distinction between a diary, a journal, and a day book in the nineteenth century represents a distinction between the categories of information each will contain and the perspective represented by their creator. Archivists know the differences between these "forms" and what information each contains without having to read each example; again archivists can thus know from provenance rather than from subject indexing certain elements of the intellectual contents of records. Across time, the logs, registers, and inmate case files of public institutions, for example, represent different contents and a careful designation of these historical changes is sufficient to denote that fact to researchers (a single form of material will also change across time, a fact that historical researchers know and use). In

---

13 In a recent think piece circulated to colleagues, Bearman has advanced a list of less than 500 transitive verbs which he suggests incorporate all functions of governmental, religious, and commercial organizations. Together with a relatively small number of nouns that serve as objects to these verbs, organizational functions are fully defined. David Bearman, "A Proposal for a Functions Vocabulary: Terms, Formats and Rules for Cooperative Development of an Authority File" (5 November 1985).

14 A bank check, written on a watermelon, is nonetheless a check and even negotiable! Less extreme, but equally interesting to the authors, is the fact that memoranda are recognizably memoranda even when circulated as electronic mail. Electronic letters are also recognizable as letters. Who knows what new forms of material might arise because of electronic media, but today's electronic exchange systems are still transporting pre-electronic "forms" of mail.

definitions of "forms of material," archivists will move to universal series
descriptions which can become the basis for records schedules and for
intrajurisdictional comparisons of holdings.[15]

**Establish Provenance Authority Records and Rigorously
Separate Authorities from Description of Records.** Authority records
can provide consistency in the use of name, subject, geographical, or other
access points. Libraries have established authority records for subject headings and for names of authors, for example. Archival practice regarding
authority files is highly variable, but attention to authority questions is
much less common in archives than in many other information services.

The purpose of an authority record is to maintain a common "language" between the community of users of an information system, and
in complex environments they are essential to effective system use. But
authority records must not become an end in themselves, where maintenance of ossified practices becomes enshrined in the rules and procedures
promulgated by self-appointed guardians. The fact that such bizarre
systems exist in library practice should not lead archivists to discard the
authority record altogether. Archivists should identify where they need
authority records and then proceed to implement them by the best
modern standards of the information services community.

The unique and most powerful archival authority is the provenance
authority record. For each organizational function and significant organizational event embodied in a department, committee, task force, working
group, planning meeting, or other activity, an authority record should be
created. Authority records would include as data elements and access
points, at least the name of the entity, the source of its authority, its mission, its functions, the entity to which it reported or was otherwise related,
and its active dates. Provenance authorities would be expanded and
enriched by the ongoing results of provenance-based retrieval. To this
peculiarly archival dimension should be added authority records from relevant information services; for example, an archives with natural history
data might wish to adopt a standard scientific geographical authority.

Provenance authority data (as described above) and data about actual
records must be rigorously segregated. For the latter, an archival control
record should be created for every archival series, or for any smaller unit
of records to which administrators and other clients might wish access.[16]

---

15 Bearman initiated discussions of how to implement such authority controls with the state
archives in Utah, Alabama, and Kentucky. Recent work by these archives and the National
Archives suggests that agreement on these authorities can be reached and should have the theoretically projected value.

16 In a recent paper following up on some of these ideas, Max Evans has argued that the series should
be accorded a privileged position in information systems because he feels it is a "natural" organizational unit of documentary materials. While we agree that nothing except administrative convenience in one period in the history of the National Archives recommends the record group, we see
no need for such a privileged status for series. Max Evans, "Authority Control: An Alternative to
the Record Group Concept" (paper presented at the SAA Annual Meeting, 1 November 1985).

Provisions should be made to indicate relationships between archival control records in the control system. The relationships to be represented would be limited to those that were about the records themselves: horizontal (media transformation for example), vertical (whole/part), and chronological (versions or records of successor series).

Relationships between offices of origin should be captured in the intellectual content of provenance authority records and such linkages would therefore be exploited through searching the indexes. These authority files would be linked, however, to the archival control records.

The entire system should preserve a clear distinction between four categories of information that archivists and records managers employ in establishing control over their holdings: 1) information about actions performed by the archival repositories and maintained in archival control records; 2) physical description (record "form") and related access data; 3) content descriptions (agency "functions") and related access data; and 4) authority data, including the authority data unique to archival organizations: information about the history, structures, processes, and activities of records-creating organizations.[17]

Integrate Archival Processes. The present practice of most archival repositories segregates the information that the archives may accumulate about the current status of the records-creating organizations and their activities and records (for example, the National Archives' *Federal Register,* the Canadian *Access to Information Register, Privacy Index,* and the *Canada Gazette*); the information gathered in the course of the management of that organization's current records; and the information gathered as its archives are appraised, arranged, and described. The intellectual aspects of these segregated efforts have much in common. For example, the provenance authority record should be systematically constructed as the earliest information is available before it is lost, and then all subsequent steps should enrich and verify that record. The process works the other way too. Once a full provenance authority record is available at the archival repository, the information it contains should be very useful to information specialists in the originating organization. In short, by integrating these three sources or systems of information,

---

17 Bearman has written a design model for a Collections Information System for the Smithsonian Institution's holdings (which range from paintings to beetles, from buttons to minerals) based on these same four categories of data. *Request for Comment, Smithsonian Institution Collections Information System — A Plan for the Acquisition of an Integrated, Generalized Collections Management Information System* (Office of Information Resource Management, Smithsonian Institution, April 1984), 28 pp. and three appendices. Most recently, Bearman coauthored a generic model for any action-based systems using heuristic models drawn from artificial intelligence research which further illustrates the fact that it is the "collectedness" rather than the "objectiveness" of items in archives, museums, zoos, and botanical gardens that makes it possible to define fundamental structures for information systems designed to support the management of such holdings. *CMASS: Statement of Problem* (Office of Information Resource Management, Smithsonian Institution, September 1985), 48 pp.

records management and records appraisal will be better supported as well as improved archival retrieval.

Proposal for a Provenance-based Universal Information Access System

The invaluable insight of the principle of provenance is the relationship it reveals between creating activity and information created by organizations. If the archivist's use of provenance in arrangement and description — which establishes links backwards from records to creating activities — is reversed, a potential exists for a practical and powerful means of gaining access to and managing information.

The suggestions made in the last section for improving traditional archival information systems can be greatly expanded. The ingredients of such a system, and the means for automating it, can be stated, although the practicality of fully implementing such a system is unknown.

The system concept is quite simple. The objective is to capture the full richness of provenance information — the structures, processes, and activities of organizations — and to make routine the inferential process that permits one to locate information that has been or is being created by organizational activities. The power of the system will be its ability to retrieve present as well as past information created by organizations; in fact, extrapolations to information yet to be created could be made within certain constraints.

Much of the necessary provenance data is presently being collected. For example, the American National Archives is the publisher of the *United States Government Manual,* the authoritative guide to the structure and mission of the American government, and of the *Federal Register* in which official actions of government agencies and public documents are announced. It could be involved with the Federal Information Locator System which the Office of Management and Budget now maintains. It could also be tied into the General Accounting Office information system on agency/bureau missions. These systems already contain much of the content of the projected provenance authority record, albeit in very primitive form, as it relates to current organizations. (Where such information is not readily available for older or defunct institutions, archivists would have to research the usual historical sources to uncover it.)

This proposal anticipates greatly enhanced techniques for dealing with provenance authority data. For example, it would be necessary to create dynamic, interrelated databases from presently static systems that capture organization structures, functions, missions, activities, and relationships. That new system could serve as the principal access tool for all documentation/information created by organizations. Such enhanced authority control would incorporate poly-hierarchical structural relationships and non-hierarchical relationships in a complex networking model, which would permit tracking of particular functions or activities over time and across jurisdictions. In addition to locating information, the system would serve as a first order institutional memory with independent value for current policy-making processes as well as for location, use, and management of information. As organizations grow larger, more complex, and less hierarchical, their management officials have need of an analysis tool as powerful as the one envisioned for day-to-day administration. The personnel office has an organization table, the budget office has a picture of some ongoing projects, the public relations office knows of other projects, the archives has inventories of records series generated by various activities, the planning office has statements of functions and missions —but no one has an overview of what the organization was, how it became what it is today, and where it is headed tomorrow. Archivists are ideally situated to provide such a view through the information systems that they ought to be creating to provide intellectual control for historical materials.

The second component of the ideal information system is the inference process that supports two-way translation between subject questions and provenance/organizational activity terms. This inference process can be observed whenever a reference archivist translates a user inquiry for information first into a question about what kinds of records hold that information and then into a question about what functions generate such forms of material and from there into a question about institutional history so as to locate the record series that is most likely to answer the user query. More rigorous study of the precise manner in which this inference process functions would be required to develop rules by which the process could be automated.

A fully automated archival retrieval system for naive users would have two components. The first would be a computerized information system containing complete knowledge of an organization's administrative history — one full complement of provenance information — in a very flexible database environment that supports the complex relationships involved in modern organizations. The second would be an "inference engine," a software system that executes the provenance-inference process in place of the reference archivist.[18] The inference engine will have the ability to make inferences from user's questions to provenance information and hence to the desired documentation or information.

Clearly, the ultimate system is not in our immediate future. But the preceding discussion — and the notion of a vastly expanded and automated provenance system — has its applications for archivists today and will support enhanced automated applications tomorrow.

---

18 Archival readers may be uncomfortable with the notion of an inference engine. For some years, information and computer scientists have been exploring the potential of automated systems to perform "human-like" reasoning. Very primitive prototypes are in existence. See *Computerworld* 19 (19 August 1985).

Conclusion

Immediate steps for archivists to take in order to improve archival information systems have been suggested. In summary, they are as follows: view provenance information as a provider of retrieval access points; emphasize form of material and function in retrieval systems; establish provenance authority records; rigorously separate authorities from description or control of records; and integrate archival processes from records creation through records appraisal to records description. Two immediate steps should be taken to enhance present retrieval systems and to take advantage of imminent new automated capabilities.

Improvements presently within our grasp could use "form of material" and "function," in addition to more traditional archival descriptive access points, to support detailed content inquiries and permit reference archivists to retrieve with greater precision and recall than they can using currently existing approaches. Most of these new capabilities could be supported by appropriately designed manual systems. Immediate work is needed, however, to elaborate and standardize a "form of material" and "function" vocabulary for archival retrieval systems, for they are the critical components of the data architecture of the automated system. While these immediately realizable results are being achieved, improvements can also be made that will capitalize on the inference engine and other vastly more powerful information technologies when they become commercially available.

The second step pertains to the inferential process itself that archivists use to proceed from subject queries to location of pertinent documentation. Archivists should study the application of the reference archivist's inferential process discussed at some length in this paper. At best, this process will be the engine that drives vastly enhanced information retrieval systems. At a minimum, archivists could achieve considerable improvement simply by understanding the process more completely.

In these and other efforts, archivists should keep in mind that the need for more effective management of information and other resources in modern organizations can be exploited by archivists to gain additional staff and money for their work. Perhaps the best way to attract such new resources is to exploit the power of existing provenance information by better structuring current systems around authority controlled access points. Archivists hold the key to provenance information becoming a major tool for management of all resources in modern organizations.

15

Description and Reference in the Age of Automation

AVRA MICHELSON

Abstract: This article is a report of the results of a survey conducted in 1986 to determine the effects of descriptive practice on retrieval capabilities of archive and manuscript materials described in bibliographic utilities. Forty repositories inputting into RLIN AMC were surveyed on (1) standardization in the choice and construction of headings, (2) levels of authority control, and (3) treatment of out-of-scope materials. Massive inconsistency in descriptive practice was found. The author makes five recommendations to correct inconsistency in the file and the retrieval difficulties that result.

During the past decade, the desire to share information on archival holdings in an automated environment emerged near the top of the archival profession's agenda. Although there was a variety of options, many repositories determined participation in bibliographic utilities to be the most viable method for information exchange. David Bearman's 1981 report on the work of the National Information Systems Task Force (NISTF) outlined more than a dozen possible prototypes for information sharing.[1] The choice to automate through bibliographic utilities represented merely one option that offered the archival community distinct benefits. First, it provided a way to integrate archival and manuscript collections with other types of material in library catalogs, offering repositories whose mother institutions were RLIN or OCLC members both a vehicle

Reprinted with permission of *American Archivist* 50 (Spring 1987): 192-208. This article was written as a product of the author's participation in the 1986 Research Fellowship Program for Study of Modern Archives administered by the Bentley Historical Library, University of Michigan, and funded by the Andrew W. Mellon Foundation and the Research Division of the National Endowment for the Humanities. The author thanks Francis X. Blouin and William Wallach for assistance beyond the call of duty, Paul Conway, Lisa Weber, and members of the RLG Task Force on Archives and Special Collections for comments on methodology and research design; David Blair and Frank Boles for assistance in research analysis; and David Bearman for patience, support, and careful readings of countless drafts.

1 David Bearman, "Towards National Information Systems for Archives and Manuscript Repositories: Alternative Models; First Working Paper on Scenarios for Multi-Institutional Exchange and their Implications for the Profession" (unpublished, 20 August 1981).

for greater local visibility and the promise of wider use. Second, participation in bibliographic utilities offered improved local and networkwide subject access to holdings. Third, and not incidentally, bibliographic utilities rapidly introduced many archives to automation. Information sharing through bibliographic networks, thus, allowed archivists to mainstream materials into library catalogs, exchange information on holdings with other archives, and begin the automation process within repositories.

Information sharing through bibliographic utilities involved trade-offs, however; joining these systems meant adopting system standards, which led to some fairly predictable problems for archival repositories. For example, because there were few archival descriptive standards suitable for an automated environment, repositories, in order to automate quickly, had little recourse but to accept the library conventions used by bibliographic utilities — such as *Anglo-American Cataloging Rules,* second edition (AACR2); Library of Congress Subject Headings (LCSH); and the Library of Congress Name Authority File (LCNAF). As a result, library cataloging largely supplanted customary archival description in preparing the automated record at this early stage of archivists' work. Resolving tensions between existing local practice, the needs of a system, and the requirements of a group of users is a complicated matter. Because a number of archives have participated in bibliographic utilities for several years, a body of data exists that permits evaluation of the status of information sharing within the profession, the implications of the use of library standards for archival retrieval, and the steps that can be taken to improve network access to descriptions of archival collections.

The actual performance of national networks in providing access to archival and manuscript holdings has never been tested. Various elements influence searching and systemwide retrieval capabilities in automated bibliographic networks, including format design, system architecture, the application of standards, and the compatibility of standards with particular formats of material. The research discussed below examined the variant descriptive practices of the 40 repositories inputting into the Research Libraries Group's (RLG) Research Library Information Network (RLIN) Archival and Manuscript Control (AMC) file in 1986. By surveying these repositories, it was possible to evaluate the extent to which lack of uniform descriptive practices complicates accessing information within a database. The survey included questions on three types of practices: (1) standardization in the choice and construction of headings, (2) levels of authority control, and (3) treatment of out-of-scope materials (i.e., holdings that are outside a repository's topical, geographical, or chronological collecting policy guidelines). Of the 40 repositories actively inputting into RLIN AMC, 36 responded to the survey, representing 88 percent of the records in the database.

Network environments rely on the use of standard conventions to facilitate information retrieval. Because computers are unforgivingly literal, the degree to which cooperating repositories can agree or "converge" on what they put into the system directly affects what they can get out of it. Although standard conventions guide their work, archivists are far from achieving standard practice. Extreme inconsistency in describing materials is the key problem facing archival reference in the age of automation. Archivists are inconsistent in both *how* they describe and in *what* they describe. Resolving these discrepancies will profoundly affect the ability of the reference archivist to respond to user queries. This article will report inconsistencies found in the RLIN AMC database, examine the implications of these inconsistencies, and suggest methods for improving retrieval in automated bibliographic networks.

The first area of inconsistency appears in the assignment of topical index terms. Previous information retrieval studies have shown a positive relationship between interindexer consistency and retrieval effectiveness; that is, the more convergence in cooperating repositories' choices of index terms, the greater the likelihood of retrieving relevant materials from the database.[2] In this study, interindexer consistency among those inputting into RLIN AMC was measured by asking all repositories to assign topical index terms to the same three descriptions of collections, using their own descriptive procedures (see Appendix A). Consistency was calculated by determining the total number of different terms selected to describe each collection in ratio to the number of terms selected by all repositories. An unrealistically high level of convergence might be expected, because survey respondents performed this exercise with the equivalent of an identical card catalog description in hand, preventing many of the opportunities for divergence that arise in drafting descriptions from the beginning.

The findings, however, contradicted initial expectations. In the first of three descriptions, the Carter family of Indiana, 21 indexing repositories assigned 162 different access points to this collection (see Appendix A).[3] No term was assigned by all indexers, resulting in an indexing consistency rate of zero. Even when terms were reduced through truncation to their most global representation, such as WOM#N or INDIANA# (which would result in an unwieldly number of hits if searched as such), interindexer consistency still equaled zero; there was not one term, collapsed to its most generic root, that was chosen by all repositories to describe this collection.

The other two collections included an even more extreme bias toward interindexer convergence. Each repository was asked to describe one collection — either record group or a manuscript collection — that represented its predominant holdings (see Appendix A). This self-selection

---

2 William S. Cooper, "Is Interindexer Consistency a Hobgoblin?" *American Documentation*, no. 20 (July 1969): 276.

3 Although 36 repositories responded to the survey, not all repositories answered every survey question. When less than 36 repositories responded to a particular question, the number of responses has been supplied in the text.

should have resulted in overrepresented consistency, because convergence depended on the agreement of a few repositories indexing familiar materials. Again, however, there was no consistency. The extreme lack of consistency in the assignment of topical index terms constitutes the major finding of this study.

Survey analysis reveals that repositories avoid certain kinds of topical terms, further complicating networkwide access. Terms identifying "occupations" and "conferences or meetings" tend to be used significantly less often than other points of entry. Respondents indicate that 19 percent of records are not assigned occupation index terms even when appropriate. Twenty-two percent of records are not assigned conference or meetings index terms. Although the percentage is slightly higher for the latter, the absence of occupation terms poses the more serious problem because occupation terms permit searches related to a particular activity (e.g., teaching, nursing, publishing). The ability to search by activity-related terms is central to archival retrieval, yet survey reports indicate that search queries using occupation terms will result in a significant number of misses.

Considerable nonconformity also appears in the preferred level of specificity in choosing topical terms. For example, some respondents described a trip by rail to Florida as "Voyages and travel," while others termed it "Railroad travel — United States." Records documenting the sale of public lands in Indiana might be "Indiana — Government property" or "Land titles — Registration and transfer — Indiana." The 18 repositories that entered 61 percent of the records surveyed favored narrow terms. Seven respondents, representing 13 percent of the records surveyed, favored broad terms. The other seven repositories, representing 25 percent of the records surveyed, used both types of terms. Although survey responses indicate that repositories are much more apt to assign specific terms rather than broad terms when creating records, irregular practice in this area creates further retrieval difficulties.

Lack of uniformity in the choice and construction of topical index terms is compounded by a second inconsistency, inadequacies in RLIN's syndetic structure. Syndetic structure is the linking mechanisms used with groups of words or phrases in an information system.[4] An authority file that uses "see" and "see also" references is the most commonly found syndetic structure in library catalogs. Authority control files are the key mechanism for ensuring consistency within bibliographic catalogs by distinguishing names, showing relationships (among variant forms of names, parent bodies, and earlier to later names), and documenting decisions.

---

4 Ritvars Bregzis, "The Syndetic Structure of the Catalog," in *Authority Control: The Key to Tomorrow's Catalog*, proceedings of the 1979 Library and Information Technology Association Institutes, ed. Mary W. Ghikas (Phoenix, Ariz.: Oryx Press, 1982), 26.

Such files thereby promote consistency in the subsequent determination of relationships and identification of headings.[5]

RLIN AMC users use the Library of Congress Name Authority File (LCNAF) for systemwide authority control for personal names and corporate entries. The respondents reported searching from 0 to 100 percent of their personal and corporate name terms in the LCNAF, with an overall average of 90 percent. Although most RLIN AMC users regularly search the LCNAF, their terms are not apt to appear in the file because it contains names associated with published works. Only 36 percent of the index terms entered into RLIN AMC have been searched and found in the LCNAF; as a result, approximately two-thirds of respondents' personal and corporate name index terms have been entered into the system with no networkwide authority control. This lack of rigorous systemwide authority control significantly compromises access capabilities.

The survey results likewise indicate an alarming lack of authority control on the local level. Nearly one-half of the records input by surveyed repositories relied exclusively on the LCNAF and/or the RLIN AMC file for authority control of personal and corporate names. These repositories maintained no separate local authority file, but instead used RLIN AMC in that capacity. For many repositories, using RLIN AMC in this way appears a reasonable accommodation to the costs of automation. Maintaining an authority file is extremely labor intensive.[6] RLIN AMC, however, is a catalog, not an authority file. It is not designed nor intended to alleviate inconsistency and provides no comprehensive mechanism for linking variant forms of headings, distinguishing names, and documenting decisions. Reliance on a catalog for authority control ultimately harms retrieval. If two-thirds of the names entered are not screened for systemwide consistency and there is inadequate control of one-half of the respondents' RLIN AMC records, inconsistency is surely epidemic.

The third area of inconsistency concerns the descriptive treatment of out-of-scope material. The extent to which such materials are assigned access points is significant because the ability to share information on these holdings constitutes a key benefit of national networks. Network members, however, stand divided in their willingness to make out-of-scope materials accessible through the AMC file. Nine repositories,

---

5 David R. McDonald, "Data Dictionaries, Authority Control, and Online Catalogs: A New Perspective," *Journal of Academic Librarianship* 11, no. 4 (1985): 219. An authority file distinguishes two persons with the same name who were alive at approximately the same time by indicating that one was a biologist and one a molecular scientist, or by providing place of birth, names of publications, or other differentiating information. Similarly, an authority file leads one from Samuel Clemens to Mark Twain or indicates that the Atomic Bomb Casualty Commission has been known by at least five other names.

6 One Library of Congress cataloger estimates that 50 percent of LC's descriptive catalogers' staff time is spent exclusively on name authorities. See Lucia J. Rather, "Authority Systems at the Library of Congress," in *Authority Control: The Key to Tomorrow's Catalog*, 158.

representing one-half of the records surveyed, reported that their index-ing of out-of-scope materials was inferior to their indexing of core hold-ings. In many cases, these materials are insufficiently described in finding aids and thus must be reprocessed to permit better access, tremendously taxing a repository's available resources. Determining the appropriate bal-ance between local priorities and network demands is automation's key challenge for the profession. With respect to out-of-scope materials, sur-vey results indicate that RLIN AMC repositories currently tend to favor local priorities.

Providing networkwide access to information in bibliographic utili-ties is complicated, because the use of standard conventions has not yet produced a standard practice. But to achieve effective retrieval, databases require convergence on what is entered. Determining the most cost-effective use of a file characterized by massive inconsistency in subject headings, authority control, and description of holdings presents formi-dable challenges for the reference archivist. There is, however, reason to persevere, as bibliographic automation offers archivists a significant tool and an extraordinary catalyst for professional growth and development. The strategies adopted to improve data input and retrieval must be well researched and wisely selected. Based on this study, five corrective approaches are recommended, some quickly accomplished and others long-term in nature.

First, measures should be taken to upgrade indexing. This is not to sug-gest that all archivists require basic instruction in subject cataloging. Indeed, repositories usually chose very appropriate, although different, terms in completing the survey. Although the zero consistency among this survey's respondents is extreme, all studies on retrieval have found some inconsistency.[7] Retrieval experiments report considerable disparity even when the same indexer performs an identical exercise at two different times.[8] Thus, information retrieval scientists have concluded that substan-tial interindexer inconsistency forms the rule rather than the exception.[9]

Information scientists hesitate to generalize about rates of consis-tency that can be reasonably attained. They do, however, point to factors such as the degree of vocabulary control, the subject of materials indexed, and the conditions under which indexing is performed, as

7 David C. Blair, "Indeterminacy in the Subject Access to Documentation," *Information Processing and Management* 22, no. 2 (1986): 230.

8 Frances I. Hurwitz, "A Study of Indexer Consistency," *American Documentation*, no. 20 (January 1969): 92-93.

9 See for instance Cooper, "Is Interindexer Consistency a Hobgoblin?" 268; Pranas Zunde and Margaret E. Dexter, "Indexing Consistency and Quality," *American Documentation*, no. 20 (July 1969): 259; Blair, "Indeterminacy in the Subject Access to Documentation," 220; and Michael R. Middleton, "A Comparison of Indexing Consistency and Coverage in the AEI, ERIC and APAIS Databases," *Behavioral and Social Sciences Librarian* 3 (Summer 1984): 140.

elements that affect indexing quality.[10] A consistency rate of zero is unacceptable, however, regardless of limitations. Yet concentrating the profession's efforts exclusively on upgrading indexing is no solution. Archivists can best address this problem by creating network users' groups whose purpose is to determine common use, promote adherence to conventions, provide needed training, and monitor participants' practice. Agreeing to agree is the prerequisite to achieving consistency.

As a second step, the inconsistency related to the use of LCSH, an orderless controlled vocabulary, must be reduced. The library community has criticized LC Subject Headings for many years, citing problems with terminology, form and structure, complexity and size, currency and prejudices, and the use of Cutter's rule of specific entry.[11] Despite its adoption of rules to guide subject term selection, Library of Congress practice has wavered seriously on adherence to established principles.[12] LCSH were adopted for use with automated systems in spite of a lack of consensus within the library community. As one observer remarked, using LC Subject Headings for computer access with MARC makes MARC "rather like a modern jet plane powered by a late nineteenth-century model of a steam engine; the thing might possibly move or even fly, but it will soon be prone to accidents, unreliable, and above all, the streamlined features of the fuselage will be wasted because of the slow speed attained."[13]

Both economic and political realities, however, make serious consideration of revamping LC Subject Headings unfeasible. Thesaurus construction is prohibitively expensive. Development time for a small specialized thesaurus can require up to three years. Studies estimate that a small-scale thesaurus of only 2,500 terms would require two full-time staff six months to complete.[14] The creation of a subject-controlled vocabulary or thesaurus designed for use with bibliographic utilities and appropriate to archival and manuscript materials would entail thousands of terms and call for the input of countless subject specialists as well as the development of a sophisticated mechanism for continual administration, update, and change. Further, nearly all national, academic, and

---

10 Middleton, "Comparison of Indexing Consistency and Coverage," 140.

11 Pauline A. Cochrane, *Critical Views of Library of Congress Subject Headings: A Bibliographic and Bibliometric Essay, and an Analysis of Vocabulary Control in the Library of Congress List of Subject Headings* (Syracuse, N.Y.: Eric Clearinghouse on Information Resources, Syracuse University, 1981).

12 See Richard S. Angell, "Library of Congress Subject Headings — Review and Forecast," in *Subject Retrieval in the Seventies: New Directions*, proceedings of an International Symposium held at the Center of Adult Education, University of Maryland, College Park, 14-15 May 1971, ed. Hans Wellisch and Thomas D. Wilson (Westport, Conn.: Greenwood Publishing, 1972), 148-49 and 153; and Cochrane, *Critical Views*.

13 Hans Wellisch, "Subject Retrieval in the Seventies — Methods, Problems, Prospects," in *Subject Retrieval in the Seventies: New Directions*, 15.

14 State Historical Society of Wisconsin Archives Division MSAGP Subject Access position paper (unpublished, c. 1980), 5.

public libraries in the United States and many such libraries abroad use LCSH.[15] The overhaul of LCSH would require either complete archival detachment from the library community or a commitment from innumerable archivists, librarians, administrators, resource allocators, and the bibliographic utilities to transform LCSH. Archivists are not in a position to inaugurate either change.

Topical term selection, while currently inconsistent, is nevertheless not random; some terms are chosen more than others. Providing online access to LC Subject Headings with a running count of each heading's use within AMC would promote greater consistency in term selection. Archivists could use this file when creating index terms and, where choices exist, select the heading most often used in the database. Because archival term selection is original and seldom derivative, archivists have a greater need than librarians to know the extent to which headings are used within a system. Incorporating information on heading-use patterns into the term selection process ultimately should lead to greater convergence. RLG plans to provide online access to LCSH in RLIN, but current plans do not include provision for reporting on the use of terms.[16]

Augmenting the syndetic support available on RLIN AMC offers a third way to improve access. The authority file provides the foundation of the automated library system.[17] It is the primary tool used throughout the data-processing industry to maintain consistency within databases.[18] The need for authority control when automating in a cooperative network has been firmly documented. While archivists might argue about the high costs of implementing authority control, they cannot ignore the greater costs associated with excessive searching or failed retrieval.

Archival participation in the Library of Congress's Name Authority Cooperative (NACO) offers a beginning. Qualified RLIN AMC users will soon be able to contribute to the LC Name Authority File through NACO, which permits libraries throughout the country "to provide their own local name authority data to be included in the LC automated name authority file and made available as a whole."[19] Attention also must be devoted to developing local authority files. In the age of automation,

---

15 Wellisch, "Subject Retrieval in the Seventies," 16.

16 Conversation with Ed Glazier of RLG, 28 July 1986.

17 *Initial Considerations for a Nationwide Database*, prepared by Edwin J. Buchinski, ed. and revd. Henriette D. Avram and Sally McCallum, Network Planning Paper (Washington, D.C.: Library of Congress, 1978), 1.

18 McDonald, "Data Dictionaries," 222.

19 Suzanne L. Liggett, "The Name Authority Co-op Project at the Library of Congress," in *Crossroads*, proceedings of the First National Conference of the Library and Information Science Association, 17-21 September 1983, Baltimore, Md., ed. Michael Gorman (Chicago: American Library Association, c. 1984), 121.

providing access to materials necessarily includes the cost of developing substantial syndetic systems.[20]

As a fourth route to greater access, archivists should direct resources to developing an archival science of searching. Some may consider the term "science of searching" an overstatement. Results of this survey suggest, however, that successful retrieval of primary source materials from bibliographic utilities requires systematic data gathering, analysis, and testing. Additional research especially is needed because the process of providing access in RLIN AMC to primary materials differs in three ways from that of providing access to books.

First, archival records describe heterogeneous collections that require many more index terms than those used to describe monographs. The average number of index terms assigned to records by the survey respondents was thirteen; the average number assigned to books by the Library of Congress is three.[21] Retrieval specialists have discovered that "information systems do not scale up. That is, retrieval strategies that work well on small systems do not necessarily work well on larger systems."[22] The greater number of access points created for archival and manuscript collections, therefore, significantly affects retrieval. Second, archival retrieval is complicated by less-adequate authority control and the tendency toward less convergence of terms because archival cataloging is primarily original and seldom derivative. Consequently, greater inconsistency characterizes the file.

Third, the expectations of library and archival users differ, which creates conflicting demands on the system. The retrieval of *some* relevant citations, either books or journal articles, normally satisfies most library patrons. Scholars using primary source materials, however, are more likely to expect an exhaustive listing of the relevant collections. Complete information on their topic then allows them to develop a research strategy. Two different kinds of retrieval are involved: the library patron needs precision retrieval; the scholar, recall retrieval. Precision and recall are the most widely used measures of retrieval effectiveness. Precision assesses how well a system retrieves *only* relevant documents, or the

---

20 Little has been written on archival authority systems. The works of David Bearman, Max Evans, and Richard Szary comprise current thinking and deserve wide reading within the profession. See Richard V. Szary, "Expanding the Role of Authority Files in the Archival Context," paper presented at the annual meeting of the Society of American Archivists, Austin, Texas, 1 November 1985; Max J. Evans, "Authority Control: An Alternative to the Record Group Concept," *American Archivist* 49 (Summer 1986): 249-61; David Bearman and Richard Szary, "Beyond Authorized Headings: Authorities as Reference Files in a Multi-Disciplinary Setting," paper delivered at ARLIS/NA Conference on Authority Control, 10 February 1986. An online archival authority system is currently under development for the archives catalog of the Smithsonian Institution Bibliographic Information System.

21 Sally McCallum, "Evolution of Authority Control for a National Network," in *Authority Control: The Key to Tomorrow's Catalog*, 56.

22 David C. Blair and M. E. Maron, "An Evaluation of Retrieval Effectiveness for a Full-Test Document-Retrieval System," *Computing Practices* 28 (March 1985): 298.

probability that a retrieved document will prove relevant. Users who want a few relevant citations are served best by high-precision retrieval. Recall, on the other hand, measures how well a system retrieves all relevant documents, or the probability that a document relevant in any degree will be retrieved. An inverse relationship exists between a system's ability to be precise and its ability to be exhaustive. This only known "law" of information retrieval performance presents the key stumbling block archivists will encounter when transferring library retrieval methods to an archival setting.[23] Searching strategies devised for libraries cannot necessarily serve as models for archives. Instead, concentrated research leading to the development of search strategies for primary source materials is needed.

As a beginning, RLIN AMC users might maintain a record of research questions searched in AMC, the nature of each query (precision or recall), the search strategies employed, the search query statements, and the search results. The goal would be to collect sufficient data in order to identify successful patterns that might guide the searching of archival databases. Precision requests probably will be quite perfunctory; the system can readily provide some relevant items for most searches. Recall retrieval, however, is apt to be more complicated. To retrieve all relevant network material, archivists must conduct repeated searches, using all related and synonymous terms in countless combinations until relevant records are no longer retrieved. Recall searches, therefore, inevitably entail considerable computer time and retrieve many irrelevant items.[24] Consequently, archivists should not hold unrealistic expectations of the system. They must compare the most effective types of search strategies with different types of inquiries to provide cost-effective, efficient service to users. Retrieval research should result in a set of model searches or prototypes that are particularly effective for archival materials. By identifying searching as essential to enhancing retrieval, archivists will build on the existing strength of the reference archivist as expert intermediary between users and materials.

Fifth, to improve access to archival and manuscript collections in bibliographic utilities, archivists must come to terms with the treatment of out-of-scope materials. Research has shown that RLIN AMC members usually did not adequately describe these holdings. The benefits of participation in a national network will only increase through cooperation in this area. Network participants should agree to share full information on out-of-scope materials processed in the future, and they should seek

---

23 See Karen Sparck Jones, ed., *Information Retrieval Experiment* (London: Butterworth and Co., 1981), 2; M. H. Heine, "The Inverse Relationship of Recall and Precision in Terms of the Swets' Model," *Journal of Documentation*, no. 29 (1973): 81; and Cyril W. Cleverdon, "On the Inverse Relationship of Recall and Precision," *Journal of Documentation*, no. 28 (1972): 199.

24 Elizabeth D. Barraclough, "Opportunities for Testing with Online Systems," *Information Retrieval Experiment*, 129.

outside funding to upgrade access to those out-of-scope materials already entered into the database in order to correct the existing file.

In conclusion, the research discussed above has shown (1) that the use of standard conventions has not yet produced a standard practice among archivists; (2) that the lack of consistency in archival practice impedes the ability to access information; (3) that attaining consistency within bibliographic utilities will be difficult to achieve; and (4) that the resolution of these problems requires research, allocation of resources, and a willingness to balance local priorities with those of the network.

Automating through bibliographic utilities entails numerous compromises for archival and manuscript repositories. An awareness of the intrinsic limitations should temper unrealistic expectations of these systems. Adopting library standards used with bibliographic utilities creates problems in providing access to archival holdings. But automating through this route also offers advantages. In addition to mainstreaming primary source materials into the library research community and enhancing access to archival holdings, this process can provide an effective way to gain needed education in information systems, challenge archivists to begin transforming internal practices, and encourage the development of a body of users expert in archival automation. The knowledge gained from participation in this process will prepare archivists to undertake the tasks needed to create a new generation of information systems more authentic to archival retrieval.

Appendix A: Questionnaire and terms selected by surveyed repositories to describe collections

Below you will find three hypothetical descriptions of collections. Assuming the information is complete, please create RLIN AMC records, on paper, for two of these collections, *following the internal conventions of your repository.* Please send me descriptions formatted on your own worksheets or whatever your repository normally uses to create a record. For the purposes of this exercise, complete only the bibliographic fixed and variable fields, not the archival control segment, and do not conduct any authority work on personal or corporate names (the information supplied is assumed to be correct). Be sure to create index terms (6XX & 7XX fields) *in accordance with standard practice within your repository.* Assume, however, that your repository is located in the state of Indiana and has state history as its collecting theme.

Question: To be Completed by all Repositories

1. Carter family of Indiana
   3 linear feet

Papers, 1815-1950 and 1967, of the Carter family of Muncie and South
Bend, Indiana. Contain papers of Mark Carter, Muncie businessman and
postmaster, concerning banking, milling, and railroads, and includes letters from his son Leonard, concerning his studies in the 1840s at
Indiana University and Brown University, travels in Europe, and his participation in the Dred Scott slavery case; papers of his wife, Rose Vaill
Carter, local teacher and woman's rights advocate, relating in part to the
Civil War, her interest in the cause of coeducation and suffrage for
women, and her involvement in the First Presbyterian Church of Muncie;
papers of their son, Leonard, attorney and regent of Indiana University,
1883-1884, concerning business matters, family affairs, post–Civil War
politics in Virginia, his campaign for Indiana state supreme court justice
in 1885, and his work on the board of regents, particularly as relates to
the School of Medicine at Indiana University; papers of Leonard's son,
Mark Carter, South Bend attorney and Grand Master of the Knights of
Templar in the United States, largely concerning freemasonry activities,
but also including Indiana University student notebook, 1877, of course
taught by Charles K. Mathews, and scrapbook, 1875-1876, of university
life; papers, 1916-1932 of Leonard's daughter, Maria Carter Murray,
South Bend physician, concerning her work as a settlement house
reformer and on behalf of the reproductive rights of women; papers of
Mark's son, Abbott Carter, concerning his interest in political issues,
1936-1946, as reflected in correspondence with the state's congressional
delegation, and letters, 1967, from his grandson, Allan, concerning
opposition to the Vietnam War and the draft at Indiana University; and
related papers of other family members, notably the Halsey family of
Missouri.

Charles K. Mathews, 1835-1902
Abbott Carter, 1887-1968
Leonard Carter, 1823-1894
Maria Carter Murray, 1856-1938
Mark Carter, 1796-1882
Mark Carter, 1857-1943
Rose Vaill Carter, 1797-1876
Allan Carter, 1949-

Terms assigned by repositories for the Carter family of Indiana:

Abortion—Moral and ethical aspects (1)
Banks and banking (3)
Banks and banking—Indiana (1)
Banks and banking—Indiana-Muncie (2)
Banks and banking—Muncie (Ind.) (1)
Banks and banking—19th century (1)

Birth control (2)
Birth control—Indiana—South Bend (1)
Birth control—Moral and ethical aspects (1)
Birth control—Law and legislation (1)
Business (1)
Business records (2)
Businessmen (3)
Businessmen—Indiana (2)
Businessmen—Indiana—Muncie (1)
Churches—Indiana—Muncie (1)
Coeducation (4)
Coeducation—Indiana (1)
Coeducation—19th century (1)
College students (1)
College students—Indiana (1)
College students—Indiana—Political activity (1)
Correspondence (2)
Education (1)
Education, Higher—Providence (R.I.) (1)
Electioneering—Indiana (1)
Elections — Indiana—1885 (1)
Elections and election campaigns—Indiana (1)
Essays (1)
Europe (2)
Europe—Description and travel (5)
Europe—Description and travel—1800-1918 (2)
Family—Indiana (1)
Family—Missouri (1)
Family papers (1)
Family records (1)
Feminists (1)
Flour and feed trade (1)
Freemasonry (3)
Freemasonry—United States (1)
Freemasons (2)
Freemasons—United States (1)
Indiana (2)
Indiana—Commerce (1)
Indiana—History (4)
Indiana—History—Civil War, 1861-1865 (3)
Indiana—History, local (1)
Indiana—Industries (1)
Indiana—Muncie (2)
Indiana—Politics and government (7)
Indiana—Politics and government—19th century (1)

Indiana—Politics and government—1865-1950 (1)
Indiana—Politics and government—1929-1938 (1)
Indiana—Politics and government—1939-1945 (1)
Indiana—Social conditions (1)
Indiana—South Bend (2)
Lawyers (4)
Lawyers—Indiana (3)
Letters (2)
Letters—19th century—Indiana (1)
Letters—20th century—Indiana. (1)
Medicine (1)
Medicine—Indiana—South Bend (1)
Medicine—Study and teaching (1)
Military service, compulsory (1)
Military service, compulsory—Draft resisters (1)
Military service, compulsory—Public opinion (1)
Military service, compulsory—United States—Draft resisters (1)
Milling—19th century (1)
Mills and millwork (1)
Mills and millwork—Indiana—Muncie (1)
Mills and millwork—Muncie (Ind.) (1)
Missouri (2)
Missouri—History—Sources (1)
Muncie (Ind.) (8)
Muncie (Ind.)—Churches (1)
Muncie (Ind.)—Commerce (1)
Muncie (Ind.)—History (2)
Muncie (Ind.)—Industries (1)
Muncie (Ind.)—Manufactures (1)
Muncie (Ind.)—Social life and customs (1)
Notebooks (4)
Notebooks—19th century (1)
Physicians (4)
Physicians—Indiana—South Bend (1)
Political letter writing—20th century—Indiana (1)
Politicians (1)
Politics, Practical (1)
Postal service—Indiana—Postmasters (1)
Postal service—Muncie (Ind.) (1)
Railroads (1)
Railroads—Indiana (5)
Railroads—Muncie (Ind.) (1)
Railroads—19th century (1)
Reconstruction—Virginia(1)
Reformers (1)

Scrapbooks (8)
Scrapbooks—19th century (1)
Settlement houses—Reform (1)
Settlements, social (1)
Slavery (2)
Slavery—Antislavery movements (1)
Slavery—Law and legislation—United States (1)
Slavery—Legal status, laws, etc. (1)
Slavery—United States (3)
Slavery—United States—Law and legislation (1)
Slavery—United States—Legal Status of slaves in free states (3)
Slavery in the United States—Indiana (1)
Slavery in the United States—Law and legislation (1)
Slavery in the United States—Legal Status of slaves in free states (1)
Social reformers (1)
Social reformers—History—Indiana (1)
Social reformers—Indiana—Muncie (1)
Social science (1)
Social settlements (4)
Social settlements—Indiana—South Bend (2)
South Bend—(Ind.) (6)
South Bend (Ind.)—Benevolent and moral institutions and societies (1)
South Bend (Ind.)—History (2)
South Bend (Ind.)—Social life and customs (1)
South Bend—Social conditions (1)
Student movements (1)
Students—Indiana—Political activity (1)
Teachers (2)
Teachers—Indiana—Muncie (1)
Travel (1)
Travel—Europe (1)
United States (1)
United States—History—1849-1877 (1)
United States—History—Civil War, 1861-1865 (9)
United States—History—Civil War, 1861-1865—Women's work (1)
United States—History—Vietnamese conflict—1961-1975—Public opinion (1)
Universities and colleges—Indiana (2)
Universities and colleges—19th century (1)
Universities and colleges—Rhode Island (1)
Vietnamese conflict—1961-1975 (4)
Vietnamese conflict, 1961-1975—Draft resisters—Indiana (2)
Vietnamese conflict, 1961-1975—Protest movements (7)
Vietnamese conflict, 1961-1975—Public opinion (1)
Virginia (1)
Virginia—History—1865-1950 (1)

Virginia—Politics and government (4)
Virginia—Politics and government—1865-1950 (3)
Voyages and travel—Europe—19th century (1)
Woman—Rights of women (1)
Woman—Suffrage (2)
Women—Education (2)
Women—Suffrage (8)
Women—Suffrage—19th century (1)
Women—Suffrage—United States (1)
Women in church work (1)
Women physicians (3)
Women physicians—Indiana (2)
Women social reformers (1)
Women teachers (1)
Women's rights (10)
Women's rights—Indiana (3)
Women's rights—19th century (2)
Women's rights—20th century (1)
Women's rights—United States (1)

Question: Create a record for either #2 or #3 below (use whichever description most closely resembles the collections found in your repository).

2. Indiana. State Land Office
    207 volumes and 3 linear feet.

Records, ca. 1818-1924 and 1944-1946, of the Indiana State Land Office; contain plat and tract books containing the record of the survey and sale of public lands in Indiana, 1818-1920; surveys of lumber on state-owned land, 1890-1919; records of lands owned by the Indiana Harbor Belt Railroad, including taxes paid on these lands, 1879-1915; and record of plats and notes on the surveying of the state road between Muncie and South Bend; also, records pertaining to the policy concerning suburban development and the sale of state lands.

Terms assigned by repositories for the Indiana State Land Office:

Administrative agencies—Indiana (1)
Cities and towns—Indiana—Growth (1)
Forests and forestry—Indiana—Mensuration (1)
Indiana (1)
Indiana—Forest policy (1)
Indiana—Government property (1)

Indiana—History (1)
Indiana—Public lands (4)
Indiana—Surveys (1)
Land grants—Indiana (2)
Land—Indiana—Taxation (1)
Land subdivision—Indiana (1)
Land titles—Registration and transfer—Indiana (1)
Land use (1)
Land use—Indiana (1)
Land use—Planning (1)
Maps (1)
Notes (1)
Patents (1)
Plats (3)
Plats—19th century (1)
Plats—20th century (1)
Public lands (1)
Public records—Indiana—State Land Office (1)
Real estate development (1)
Real property (1)
Real property, exchange of (1)
Real property—Indiana (1)
Real property—Indiana—Maps (1)
Real property—Maps (1)
Real property tax—Indiana (1)
Roads—Indiana—Surveying (2)
Surveying—Public lands (1)
Surveying—Public lands—Indiana (1)
Surveys (Land) (2)
Surveys—19th century (1)
Surveys—20th century (1)
Tracts (1)

3. Philip Slater diaries, 1840-1847, 1854-1858, 1885, and 1887-1888. 5 volumes

Farmer in Vernal Township, Monroe County, Indiana. Description of farm life in New York and his settlement in Monroe County, Indiana; also diary of his son Edwin, 1887-1888, recording farm and church activities, local affairs, the gubernatorial election of 1888, and weather; and diary of his daughter Grace describing a trip by rail to Florida.

Philip Slater, 1828-1902
Edwin Slater, 1852-1935
Grace Slater, 1877-1956

Terms assigned by repositories to the Slater diaries:

Agriculture (1)
Agriculture—Indiana (1)
Agriculture—Indiana—Monroe County (1)
Agriculture—New York (State) (2)
Agriculture—Social aspects—Indiana—Monroe County (1)
Agriculture—Social aspects—New York (State) (1)
Churches—Indiana—Vernal (1)
Churches—Monroe County (Ind.) (1)
Diaries (6)
Diaries—19th century (1)
Elections—Indiana (1)
Elections—Indiana—1888 (1)
Family records (1)
Farm life (1)
Farm life—Indiana (6)
Farm life—Indiana—Monroe County (1)
Farm life—Monroe County—Indiana (1)
Farm life—New York (State) (7)
Farmers (3)
Farmers—Indiana—Monroe County (2)
Farmers—New York (1)
Farms—Indiana—Monroe County (1)
Farms—New York (State) (1)
Florida—Description and travel (4)
Florida—Description and travel—1865-1950 (1)
Governors—Indiana (1)
Indiana (1)
Indiana—Governors—Election (1)
Indiana—Governors—Election, 1888 (1)
Indiana—History (2)
Indiana—Monroe County (1)
Indiana—Politics and government (3)
Indiana—Politics and government—19th century (1)
Indiana—Politics and government—1865-1950 (1)
Indiana—Religious life and customs (1)
Indiana—Social life and customs (1)
Journals (1)
Monroe County (Ind.) (3)
Monroe County (Ind.)—Climate (1)
Monroe County (Ind.)—History (3)
Monroe County (Ind.)—Social conditions (1)
Monroe County (Ind.)—Social life and customs (2)
Monroe County (Ind.)—Vernal Township—History (1)

New York (1)
New York (State) (1)
New York (State)—History—1865—Indiana—History (1)
Railroad travel (1)
Railroad travel—United States (5)
Rural families (1)
United States (1)
United States—Description and travel (1)
United States—Description and travel—1865-1900 (1)
Vernal (Ind.)—Social life and customs (2)
Voyages and travel (1)
Weather (1)
Weather—Monroe County (Ind.) (1)
Women—Diaries (1)

16

Descriptive Practices for Electronic Records: Deciding What Is Essential and Imagining What Is Possible

MARGARET HEDSTROM

Abstract: The challenges raised by electronic records present an opportunity to define the essential purposes for description: to reassess its objectives, agents, and timing; and to imagine new approaches that harness the power of information technology while respecting archival principles. This article discusses how archival description must support the need to identify, gain access, understand the meaning, interpret the content, determine authenticity, and manage electronic records to ensure continuing access. Management of metadata is proposed as an alternative strategy to current descriptive practices.

Archivists are increasingly aware of the need for descriptive practices that encompass all formats of records and all forms of material. Nevertheless, electronic records archivists question whether any of the approaches to description promulgated or proposed by archivists are adequate, relevant, and effective for description of electronic records.[1] David Bearman has challenged the concept of description, especially as presented in the ICA "Principles," because of its focus on records, rather than the activity of records-generating institutions or persons, as the object of description.[2] Charles Dollar has suggested that the ICA "Principles" and the Canadian *Rules for Archival Description* (*RAD*) require clarification and refinement before they are workable for description of electronic records from systems that do not create analogues

---

Reprinted with permission from *Archivaria* 36 (Fall 1993): 53-63. The author thanks David Bearman, Terry Cook, John McDonald, Tom Ruller, and Lisa Weber for comments on earlier versions of this article.

1 International Council on Archives, "Statement of Principles Regarding Archival Description," *Archivaria* 34 (Summer 1992): 8-16; International Council on Archives, "ISAD(G): General International Standard Archival Description," *Archivaria* 34 (Summer 1992): 17-32; Bureau of Canadian Archivists, Planning Committee on Descriptive Standards, *Rules for Archival Description* (Ottawa, 1990); and "Report of the Working Group on Standards for Archival Description," *American Archivist* 52 (Fall 1989): 400-57.

2 David Bearman, "Documenting Documentation," *Archivaria* 34 (Summer 1992): 33-49.

of paper records, such as geographic information systems, multimedia systems, and complex distributed databases.[3] Terry Cook recognizes that theoretically sound and effective descriptive practices for electronic records must account for multiple creators and multiple custodians of records that are not limited to a single arrangement.[4]

The purpose of this article is to explore further these concerns by defining basic requirements for description of electronic records and by assessing the potential to exploit descriptive information (metadata) in automated systems in order to achieve archival objectives.[5] Archivists only recently turned their attention to description of electronic records, while only a few archivists acknowledge that the requirements for description of electronic records may expose the need to transform descriptive practice for all formats of archival records.[6] As long as description is viewed as a process directed toward the holdings of archives, which begins after records have been accessioned and arranged, archival descriptive practices will remain ineffective for electronic records.[7] The challenges raised by electronic records present an opportunity to define the essential purposes for description; to reassess the objects, agents, and timing of description; and to imagine new approaches that harness the power of information technology while respecting archival principles. This process may ultimately lead archivists to descriptive practices that are more theoretically sound, more cost-effective and practical to implement, and that yield far more satisfactory results for the end user.

---

3 Charles M. Dollar, *Archival Theory and Information Technologies: The Impact of Information Technologies on Archival Principles and Methods,* ed. Oddo Bucci (Ancona, Italy: University of Macerata, 1992): 60-62.

4 Terry Cook, "The Concept of the Archival Fonds: Theory, Description, and Provenance in the Post-Custodial Era," in *The Archival Fonds: from Theory to Practice,* ed. Terry Eastwood, (Ottawa, 1992): 62-74.

5 For a detailed discussion of metadata, see David A. Wallace, "Metadata and the Archival Management of Electronic Records: A Review," *Archivaria* 36 (Autumn 1993).

6 David Bearman, "Description Standards: A Framework for Action," *American Archivist* 52 (Fall 1989): 515-16; and Victoria Irons Walch, "The Role of Standards in the Archival Management of Electronic Records," *American Archivist* 53 (Winter 1990): 30-43. Both Bearman and Walch point out that descriptive practices for electronic records may present models that can be applied to other types of archival records.

7 Wendy M. Duff and Kent M. Haworth, "The Reclamation of Archival Description: The Canadian Perspective," *Archivaria* 31 (Winter 1990–91): 31. The ICA Ad Hoc Commission on Archival Descriptive Standards recognized that description may occur at any stage of the life cycle, but focused its attention on description "at a point after the archival material has been selected for permanent preservation and arranged": International Council on Archives, "Statement of Principles," 10. The SAA Working Group on Descriptive Standards defined description somewhat more broadly as "the process of capturing, collating, analyzing, and organizing any information that serves to identify, manage, locate, and interpret the holdings of archival institutions and explain the context and records systems from which those holdings were selected": "Report of the Working Group on Standards for Archival Description," 442.

The Descriptive Needs and Requirements for Electronic Records

Electronic records will force archivists to clarify the distinction between records and all other types of recorded information. In the electronic environment, the physical manifestation of a record, if relevant at all, is secondary to its logical organization and its relationship to the context in which it was created and used. Physically, electronic records exist as streams of binary digits represented as electronic impulses that may or may not be captured on a storage device. There are no clues in the physical manifestation of electronic records to distinguish one record from another, or to distinguish records from electronic information that is not a record. Software provides a structure for data and imposes a basic level of organization on what would otherwise be an undifferentiated stream of bits, but this level of description and control alone is insufficient for interpreting the meaning of the electronic information or managing electronic records.

Description will play a critical role in helping the original creators of records, researchers, and others to identify, understand, and use electronic records. Descriptive practices, based on archival principles and designed to meet archival requirements, must distinguish electronic records from other computer-generated data structures that lack documentary characteristics. Such practices must be grounded in a recognition that electronic records result from corporate functions and activities, carried out by organizations or individuals. They are created to produce evidence of transactions and decisions and to hold individuals and organizations accountable.[8] The record is a byproduct of corporate activity, not a deliberate product of it.[9] Users need to know about the mandates, functions, and activities that gave rise to the creation of records, the circumstances surrounding their creation, and the organizational framework in which records were created and used in order to understand electronic records and derive meaning from them.

Descriptive practices originating in a computer systems environment, as well as the descriptive methods used by data archives, fall short of what

---

8 David Bearman, "Guidelines for the Management of Electronic Records: A Manual for Policy Development and Implementation," Chapter II, in *Electronic Records Management Guidelines: A Manual for Policy Development and Implementation* (New York: United Nations Advisory Committee for the Coordination of Information Systems, 1990), 19-20. See also Glenda Acland, "Managing the Record Rather Than the Relic," *Archives and Manuscripts* 20 (1992): 57-63.

9 This does not imply that organizations do not take deliberate measures to ensure that records are created. Organizations establish procedures and design systems in order to meet record-keeping requirements. In an electronic environment, it is essential for organizations to identify record-keeping requirements and ensure that systems are designed to meet them. Organizations do not create records for the sake of creating records, unless they are in the business of record making.

is needed because they focus on data structures and content with insufficient regard for the contextual information needed to define and understand electronic records. Computer systems specialists recognize many of the requirements for describing data structures, and they produce documentation that meets specific user and system requirements to define and control data in systems. Likewise, most data archives have adopted elaborate rules for description that assign authorship, delineate data structures, and provide access to the content of files.[10] Neither approach to documentation provides essential information about provenance of records, or the context of records creation, sufficient to support their interpretation or use as evidence, or to manage information in electronic form as records.

Electronic records, like all archival records, require sufficient descriptive data to render them available, understandable, and usable for as long as they have continuing value.[11] The types of information needed to describe electronic records will differ from, and may exceed, that needed to describe records in paper formats, but the basic purpose of description remains much the same. Electronic records must have sufficient descriptive information to permit a user to learn that the record exists, *identify* and locate it, and determine the conditions under which it may be used. Once the record is located, the user must have sufficient descriptive information to write a command or instruct a computer to *access* the record or retrieve information from it. The user must be supplied with descriptive information about the provenance of the record and the context in which it was created, sufficient to *understand* its meaning and significance. Users of electronic records also need descriptive information in order to *interpret the content* of the records, especially when abstract schemes are used to represent data values. Descriptive systems must provide sufficient information about the nature, timing, and circumstances under which transactions were recorded, in order to *establish authenticity* of the record. Finally, description must provide sufficient data to *manage* electronic records for continuing access.

The types of descriptive information needed to make electronic records available, and the methods used to disseminate information about archival electronic records, may differ from those employed for traditional formats of records. Traditional descriptive practices have satisfied

---

10 Sue A. Dodd, *Cataloging Machine-Readable Data Files: An Interpretive Manual* (Chicago: American Library Association, 1982). The responsible party, producer, and distributors are essential descriptive elements of bibliographic records for data files catalogued according to AACR2 and the USMARC Format for MRDF. The limitations of this approach lead some archivists working in traditional archives to reject descriptive guidelines for MRDF in favor of descriptive practices based on archival principles.

11 The basic requirements that electronic records remain available, understandable, and usable were articulated by the Information Standards and Practices Division, National Archives of Canada. See John McDonald, "Preservation of Corporate Memory," discussion document, June 1992.

this requirement for archival holdings by developing repository-level guides to archival materials and, more recently, by contributing bibliographic records to national and international databases such as RLIN, OCLC, and WLN. The desire to add descriptions of archival records to national databases was the fundamental impetus behind the establishment of the USMARC format for Archives and Manuscripts Control (AMC) as the United States standard for cataloging holdings of archival materials in repositories. Among social science data archives, a similar desire to share descriptive information about their holdings of numeric data files led to the development of a different standard, the USMARC Format for Machine-Readable Data Files (MRDF), for cataloging machine-readable records.[12] This approach satisfied the need to make holdings known, but it does not address the archival management of electronic records, many of which may never be transferred to the physical custody of an archives.[13]

Electronic records archivists have challenged the timing of description that occurs after records are selected for permanent preservation, transferred to an archival repository, and arranged. Electronic records require description earlier in their life cycle in order to address the descriptive needs for records that may never be transferred to the physical custody of an archives, and to ensure that the standards and procedures for describing electronic records are established when an automated system is designed. To address these concerns, some archivists have begun to explore use of information locator systems and other tools that identify records regardless of their physical location, and that may provide a means for disseminating description information about records earlier in their life cycle.[14] Locator systems generally identify information sources by originator and title, direct users to the custodian of the records, and indicate terms and conditions of access. Such systems have the advantage of describing records at all life cycle stages, including active records that are in frequent demand. Locator systems that point

---

12 Library of Congress, Network Development and MARC Standards Office, comp., *U.S. MARC Format for Bibliographic Data: Including Guidelines for Content Designation (UFBD)* (1989), with updates.

13 Some archivists are beginning to question, for both practical and conceptual reasons, the feasibility and the wisdom of transferring electronic records to the custody of archives. See David Bearman, "An Indefensible Bastion: Archives as a Repository in the Electronic Age," in *Archival Management of Electronic Records*, ed. David Bearman (Archives and Museum Informatics Technical Report, No. 13) (Pittsburgh: Archives & Museum Informatics, 1991), 14-24; and Charles Dollar, *The Impact of Information Technology on Archival Principles*, 53-55.

14 Charles R. McClure, et al., *Federal Information Inventory/Locator Systems: From Burden to Benefit*, Final Report to the General Services Administration, Regulatory Information Service Center and the Office of Management and Budget, Office of Information and Regulatory Affairs (17 July 1990); New York State Forum for Information Resource Management, *The New York State Sourcebook Pilot Project: A Metadata Approach to Information Management* (Albany, N.Y.: New York

users to information sources are prerequisites for responsible decentralized, noncustodial archives.

Simply locating electronic records will not satisfy user requirements, unless there is also sufficient information about each data structure to instruct a computer to access and retrieve the desired records, display or print them, or subject them to further computer processing. Even the most sophisticated retrieval software will not be able to recognize a data structure or retrieve records from it, without minimal description, such as its type, name, and address on a storage device. The exact requirements for access and retrieval vary by type of data structure, but may include the names of files, documents, or elements; descriptions of the directory system; addresses on a storage device; and technical specifications for the hardware and software necessary for retrieval. The descriptive requirements for access and retrieval of electronic records exceed those for paper files, because even the simplest machine-readable data structure by definition requires access and retrieval by a device.

Users need a detailed record or file layout in order to access records in a simple "flat file" of structured numeric data. In advanced software-dependent data structures, directory systems store this descriptive information in more readily accessible, computer-readable forms. Most database management systems require a rudimentary description of data content and values before users can build a database. Similarly, office automation systems for textual documents provide directory systems that contain, at a minimum, the name and creation date of each document. Some document tracking systems provide facilities to identify drafts and versions of documents, track transmittal and receipt, and search for content or structural attributes. Most advanced data structures include their own protocols for description of data values, physical layout, and entity relations. Software engineers and data administrators continue to produce more advanced data objects that integrate description of structures, values, and content into complex objects. The descriptive elements imbedded in these data objects are both essential for access and retrieval and rich sources of information about the data, but they rarely include the essential contextual information necessary to retrieve, interpret, and understand archival records.

Advanced software systems may be able to deliver desired electronic documents or data rapidly, yet users will not be able to understand the records without sufficient information about the provenance and the context of their creation. Electronic records share this requirement with

State Archives and Records Administration, 1992); and Charles Robb, "Information Resource Management in Kentucky State Government," *Archives & Museum Informatics Newsletter* 4, no. 4 (Winter 1991): 2-4. Although these systems seem promising, considerable conceptual and design work remains to be done to distinguish descriptions of information and records in locator systems.

other types of archival material, although the contextual information that is essential for the description of electronic records may not be captured at all, or may be structured differently from that of traditional textual records. Provenance and the relationship between context and the content of records have been long-standing pillars of archival theory and practice. In the electronic era they are vital to description, because they provide the key to distinguishing records from nonrecord material; to understanding why, when, and by whom a document was created; and to determining the context in which the record was created, and hence its value and meaning. Users need rich descriptive information about the record that explains who created it, why it was created, and how it was used to support or document the mission and functions of an organization, in order to understand and use electronic records as meaningful evidence of events, transactions, and activities.[15]

Users will also need sufficient information about the life cycle management of electronic records in order to establish the nature, timing, and authenticity of transactions. Because electronic records can be altered without physical evidence, they present records creators and archivists alike with new challenges for determining authenticity. Moreover, our society has not yet developed cultural habits and practices to authenticate electronic transactions intuitively.[16] Requirements for authentication will be application-specific and based on the degree of precision and security needed by the creating organization. At a minimum, however, users of electronic records need to be assured that security and access procedures were in place and followed, and that procedures for audit trails exist to test the integrity of the system.[17] The unbroken chain of custody, once a fundamental principle of archives, will assume greater significance, oriented toward a documented and unbroken chain of control, in the noncustodial electronic era.

The authenticity of electronic records as historical evidence will require more technical information about system characteristics and more contextual information about the use of computer systems by organizations and individuals. It will be important, for example, for a future user of electronic records to know whether the database that created the records supported the work of an individual analyst who used it to

---

15 Dollar, "The Impact of Information Technology on Archival Principles and Methods," 48-51. For the classic discussion of the application of the principle of provenance to archival description, see David A. Bearman and Richard Lytle, "The Power of the Principle of Provenance," *Archivaria* 21 (Winter 1985-86): 14-27.

16 For a discussion of the significance of the cultural practices surrounding information handling, see Margaret Hedstrom, "Understanding Electronic Incunabula: A Framework for Research on Electronic Records," *American Archivist* 53 (Summer 1991): 322-24.

17 Bearman, "Guidelines for the Management of Electronic Records," 29.

manipulate data and store results, or whether it served as the central records repository for an organization that stored the evidence of its decisions there. To understand the meaning and significance of electronic mail messages, future users will need contextual information about an e-mail system, such as who used e-mail and whether an organization considered the e-mail system a mode for official communications, in order to determine whether the electronic messages are authentic reflections of events and transactions.[18]

Descriptive information that identifies electronic records, permits users to retrieve them, and explains their provenance makes the records available and understandable. Electronic records may not be usable unless the description includes definitions of any codes that are used to represent data values. For simple numeric data files, the code-book serves as a catalog of the representation scheme, while more sophisticated data structures use directories, data dictionaries, or series of tables to store the codes and definitions. The need for linkage between content and representational schemes is not limited to files containing numeric data. The "code-book" for electronic textual records may include pointers or references to larger bodies of contextual information. Take, for example, an electronic record that tracks felony convictions, offenders, and the crimes they committed. Such a record would have as one "code-book" a reference to the penal code under which individuals were convicted, rather than a carefully designed, abstracted coding scheme. The descriptive information for a series of electronic documents might include a reference to the tables that automatically supplied the dates when documents were sent or received. This type of information once existed as an integral part of the document content or as separate documentation in paper form; however, increasingly it is part of an automated system — residing in a data dictionary, separate database tables, or as a set of pointers to different databases — and has a dynamic nature of its own.

These simple examples illustrate the extent to which description of electronic records challenges current archival descriptive practices. Creating or capturing sufficient descriptive information to permit users to identify, access, understand, authenticate, and interpret the meaning of electronic records requires an appreciation of the complexity of modern records systems.[19] Increasingly, descriptive practices must capture data on a web of relations between the creation and use of the records and their

---

18 Margaret Hedstrom, "Technology and the Historical Record's Transformation," *OAH Newsletter* (February 1992): 6-7.

19 David Bearman, "Records Systems as the Locus of Provenance: Implications for Automation and Archival Control and Management of Electronic Records," paper presented at the Ontario Association of Archivists, 13 May 1993, and published in *Archivaria* 36 (Autumn 1993).

content, context, and structure. These relations cannot be encompassed through a single, hierarchical path because electronic records can have multiple creators and multiple users at any single point in time, and indeed throughout their life cycle.[20] Lateral relations link data content to explanatory references, while a separate set of hierarchical relations describe the data structures independently of the contexts in which they are created and used.

A final requirement for description of electronic records is sufficient information to manage the records in order to ensure continuing access. The precise information requirements will vary depending on the structure of the records and who is responsible for their ongoing management. Control information includes technical specifications for the hardware and software needed to access the records, as well as information about maintenance and preservation of the physical medium. Information about the type, age, condition, storage history, and maintenance of the physical medium on which electronic records are stored is an essential descriptive element, whether the records are retained in their native software environment by the original creator or transferred to a repository operating a different hardware and software platform.

Neither the methods used today by systems designers to manage and control information in automated systems, nor the descriptive practices used by archivists to manage records in archives satisfy the requirements for archival description of electronic records. Systems management fails because its object is data, not records. Archival descriptive practices fail because the agent of description is the archivist applying descriptive methods after records have been accessioned and arranged. Successful descriptive practices for archival records must incorporate archival descriptive practices into the design of information systems, so that archival description can exploit the rich descriptive information that is an integral part of many electronic records systems. To accomplish this, the archival profession must articulate its requirements clearly and convincingly to records creators and the designers of record-keeping systems, or otherwise miss the opportunities for more effective descriptive practices that the electronic era offers.

Imagining What Is Possible

Stepping back from current descriptive practice forces archivists to return to fundamental questions about the purpose, objects, agents, and timing of archival description. Setting aside assumptions about who describes archival records, what is described, and when description

---

20 Cook, "The Concept of the Archival Fonds," 68-72.

should occur will help archivists to imagine possibilities for descriptive systems and practices that are far more effective than the descriptive practices that are in common use today. Archivists can learn much from the organizations and institutions that create electronic records, about the methods that they use to make data in systems available, understandable, and usable. At the same time, archivists can teach records creators about archival methods that will help organizations make the transition to electronic record keeping without sacrificing their corporate memory. Establishing such partnerships will ensure a more relevant and vital role for archivists in the organizations they serve.

In the electronic era, archivists will need to exploit the metadata (data about data) that organizations generate about their records in order to create inventory and locator systems, to obtain sufficient information about the provenance and context of records creation, and to achieve highly refined access to the contents of records. Increasingly, organizations create extensive directories and data dictionaries to document the data in their systems, because organizations need systematic description of data elements, relations, and systems in order to operate effective information systems for current needs. Information Resource Directory Systems (IRDS), which structure and manage descriptive information about databases; mark-up languages and document architectures, which utilize the structure and format of documents to carry descriptive information about their purpose and content; and message-handling systems, which include electronic "envelopes" for each message — all store rich descriptive information about electronic records.[21]

Archivists in the electronic era will have countless opportunities to capture descriptive information created and maintained by records creators. In "Archival Methods," David Bearman proposed that "archivists should find, not make, the information in their descriptive systems."[22]

---

21 United States National Archives and Records Administration, Archival Research and Evaluation Staff, *A National Archives Strategy for the Development of Standards for the Creation, Transfer, Access, and Long-Term Storage of Electronic Records of the Federal Government*, National Archives Technical Information Paper No. 8 (June 1990); Margaret H.. Law and Bruce K. Rosen, *Framework and Policy Recommendations for the Exchange and Preservation of Electronic Records*, report prepared by the National Computer Science Laboratory, National Institute of Standards and Technology, for the National Archives and Records Administration (March 1989); Canada Bureau of Management Consulting, *Data and Document Interchange Standards and the National Archives* [Project No. 1-6465] (Ottawa, June 1987); Protocols Standards and Communications, Inc., *The Application of ODA/ODIF Standards*, prepared for the National Archives of Canada (Ottawa, 1989); and Protocols Standards and Communications, Inc./National Archives of Canada, *Situation Report on the Information Resource Directory System (IRDS)* (March 1989); Charles Dollar and Ted Weir, "The Role of Standards in Integrated Systems Management: A Requirement of the 1990's," Chapter 3 in *Management of Electronic Records*, 71-86; and Walch, "The Role of Standards in the Archival Management of Electronic Records," 30-43.

22 David Bearman, "Archival Methods," *Archives & Museum Informatics Technical Report* 3, no. 1, (Spring 1989): 31.

Electronic records best illustrate the potential for exploiting the metadata that organizations create for archival description as well as the folly of describing electronic records using a separate set of tools and techniques. When archivists download data from databases and preserve electronic records in software-independent form, they lose or destroy the directories and descriptions of database relations that are essential for users to understand the records. An archivist must create a new set of metadata in order to make this data extract-accessible and usable. Likewise, when an archives attempts to save the content of e-mail messages or office documents, but destroys the directories, it must then invest in new descriptive systems to help users find their way through large bodies of textual information. What remains is a large body of text, the documentary character of which has been lost. No amount of arrangement or description can compensate for the loss of the directories and audit trails that provided the essential contextual information about records creation and use. For both practical and conceptual reasons, archivists need to focus attention on approaches and methods that find and capture the descriptive information that forms an integral part of all records systems, rather than attempting to create or re-create it. Such methods must recognize and respect the organic relation between the content of the records and the ways in which organizations structure and describe them.

Electronic records present archivists with the potential for much richer description. In the electronic era, the descriptive paradigm will shift from the current practice of augmenting scarce descriptive information to one of selecting from an abundance of metadata, which could form a complete audit trail of all actions taken to create, update, and modify a record, and of all its uses. Automated systems have the capacity to capture and record far more descriptive information than was technically possible or economically feasible with manual systems. An automated case-tracking system, for example, could include (in addition to the data about each case) definitions of the contents and relations in the database, a complete log of every transaction against the database ranging from substantive updates of the status of the case to error corrections, a "library" of routines to produce standard output reports, and a record of each special view of the database by each user. In a system such as this, the data about each case requires only a tiny portion of the storage and processing capacity of the system. Automated systems can capture not only information about the creator of the record and its content, but also a complete history of its creation and use.[23] Given both technical and resource limitations, archivists

---

23 This problem was presented as one of the key electronic research issues for the archival profession in a report of a recent conference. See *Research Issues in Electronic Records,* published for the National Historical Publications and Records Commission (St. Paul, 1991), 10-11.

must determine what we want systems to document and how much descriptive data is enough.[24] Management of metadata and capture of the contextual data about electronic records also require more advanced descriptive practices and more elaborate archival control systems. As descriptive practices shift from creating descriptive information to capturing description along with the records, archivists may discover that managing the metadata is a much greater challenge than managing the records themselves.

The electronic era will also alter the timing of description and reassign responsibility for carrying it out. Decisions made when systems are procured will determine whether a system has the capacity to record adequate documentation, including sufficient contextual information about provenance, data definitions, and use of the system, to permit secondary use for legal, audit, or research purposes. Decisions made during application development will determine whether and how a particular application utilizes these metadata facilities. Such decisions will be based on organizational needs and requirements for available, understandable, and usable records, with little or no consideration for secondary use of the records and, perhaps, without sufficient concern for long-term access and use by the original creators. End users of systems will be responsible for those aspects of description that are not captured automatically according to procedures and standards for adequate documentation. This approach to metadata creation and management leaves few opportunities for fruitful intervention by the archivist once systems are procured, applications developed, and procedures established.

Archivists will pay less attention to description of the content of electronic records, because detailed description of content will become unnecessary, irrelevant, or beyond the control of archivists. Information systems with sophisticated search and retrieval tools will permit rapid searching through the content of electronic records, while search tools such as "WAIS," "Gopher," and "Veronica," will locate information resources that are resident on large-scale networks.[25] Search and retrieval methods developed by information scientists, which harness the potential of

---

24 This is a new dilemma for archivists, not only because the electronic environment creates the potential for much richer description and much more precise access, but also because archivists have never defined criteria for sufficient arrangement and description. Archivists have rarely been satisfied that sets of traditional records have been adequately arranged and described, and the profession generally lacks any measures for the outcome of arrangement and description that would permit one to know definitively when the job is completed.

25 Brewster Kahle and Art Medlar, "An Information System for Corporate Users: Wide Area Information Servers," *Online* (September 1991), 56-60. Recent research on large-scale networks draws attention to the potential for using networks to distribute facsimiles of archival records, or their contents, in machine-readable form. For a discussion of the implications of network technology for archives, see Avra Michelson and Jeff Rothenberg, "Scholarly Communication and Information Technology: Exploring the Impact of Changes in the Research Process on Archives," *American Archivist* 55 (Spring 1992): 236-315.

computer processing, could provide users of archival records with access to the content of records on a far more detailed level than is currently feasible for traditional textual records. Organizations that need to share data across organizational boundaries will also develop standardized data definitions and thesauri to make the retrieval of information more predictable. Rather than attempting to create and impose external standards for data content on the creators of records, archivists will benefit from identifying data content standards used by records creators and exploiting them in archival descriptive systems.

In summary, the electronic era holds out the promise of richer, more detailed descriptive systems that are incorporated into the design of automated applications and implemented as records are created. Archivists' attention will shift from creating descriptive information to capturing metadata and managing it to promote access, use, and understanding of archival records. The arena for descriptive standards development will also change from developing internal standards and guidelines that are endorsed by the archival profession, to participation in the standards development process of others.

Conclusion: Realizing What Is Possible

Imagining what is possible is easy. Realizing the potential of new descriptive practices, on the other hand, presents formidable challenges to the archival profession. There is a large chasm between existing practice and the potential of the electronic era. Proposals for the capture and reuse of metadata in archival systems are predicated on the adoption of information technology standards for database structures, shared applications, document architectures, directory systems, and data interchange. Yet many of these standards are still under development, and vendors have been slow to produce standard-compliant products. In the absence of standards or products that facilitate information interchange, organizations continue to generate electronic records using a wide array of non-standard systems and software.[26] Although tools such as data dictionaries can support better documentation of electronic records, archivists should not ignore the long history of shoddy documentation practices in organizations and a culture that places primary emphasis on system design and application development.

There are also conceptual challenges for the archival profession. Current metadata systems do not account for the provenancial and contextual information needed to manage archival records. Archivists and records-generating organizations lack models, systems, and procedures for effective management of metadata about provenance and context.

---

26 Walch, "The Role of Standards in the Archival Management of Electronic Records," 41-42.

Organizations may not create or capture sufficient contextual information to render their electronic records understandable to users outside the
immediate functional group responsible for the records, or to their own
organizations over time. Archivists do not know whether the metadata
that is deemed *necessary* for description of records by the creating agency
is *sufficient* for archival description, because archivists have not clearly
defined requirements for the description of electronic records. As a consequence, archivists are not certain which descriptive elements support
basic record-keeping requirements and should therefore be part of any
record-keeping system, and which descriptive elements belong in archival
control systems. Finally, archivists have not tested empirically the retention and use of metadata to support the needs of archival description.[27]

Improving the description of records in the electronic era will
demand research into archival requirements for electronic records management, development of software and systems that satisfy those requirements, empirical testing of proposals and models for the preservation
and use of metadata, development of data interchange and interoperabil-
ity standards, and education of archivists in the issues and potential for
more powerful approaches to description. Such efforts should begin by
building on descriptive standards, practices, and systems that utilize
information about record-generating organizations and their mandates,
functions, and activities. Archivists can make a unique contribution to
the management of information, whether for current or future use, by
developing effective descriptive practices and systems that exploit the
principle of provenance in order to link the content of records to the
context in which they were created and used. Such systems show promise of providing models for descriptive practices that better support the
current needs of organizations and ensure that archival records are
understandable and usable by current and future users.

---

27 Two projects funded by the United States National Historical Publications and Records
Commission are examining various aspects of this problem. A project at the University of
Pittsburgh is developing a definition of the functional requirements for record-keeping systems.
Although the model will not specify how the requirements should be satisfied, it will provide a
necessary framework for distinguishing descriptive requirements for archival control systems
from functional requirements for record-keeping systems. The "Building Partnerships" project
at the New York State Archives and Records Administration is testing the feasibility of capturing
metadata and using it to describe electronic records in complex structures.

17

Encoded Archival Description: The Development of an Encoding Standard for Archival Finding Aids

DANIEL V. PITTI

Abstract: *Encoded Archival Description (EAD) attempts to overcome obstacles to intellectual access for geographically distributed primary resources by providing a standard encoding structure for archival finding aids. EAD is the most recent in a line of similar efforts to address universal intellectual access to such data, and like its predecessors, EAD applies emerging technology to the problem. The technology underlying EAD is Standard Generalized Markup Language (SGML) and Extensible Markup Language (XML). This article reviews the background of EAD and the contributions of archivists in both large and small repositories to its development.*

As Encoded Archival Description (EAD) nears completion and formal release as a standard, it seems useful to recall the long-standing problem that it seeks to address, to survey the technology that it employs, and to recount the process by which its nature and structure have been defined.

Successful innovation does not take place in a vacuum. The intellectual inspiration for innovation comes from tradition, even if at the same time the innovation seeks to transform past practice. The chief motivation for developing EAD was to provide a tool to help mitigate the fact that the geographic distribution of collections severely limits the ability of researchers, educators, and others to locate and use primary sources. Modern attempts to overcome the obstacles presented by the geographic distribution of resources date back to at least the middle of the nineteenth century,[1] and the library and archival communities have been trying in various ways since then to tackle this problem. EAD represents but the most recent and certainly not the last endeavor in this ongoing tradition.

Reprinted with permission from the *American Archivist* 60 (Summer 1997): 268-83.

1 Charles C. Jewett, *On the Construction of Catalogues of Libraries, and Their Publication by Means of Separate, Stereotyped Titles* (Washington, D.C.: The Smithsonian Institution, 1853).

Attempts to address the problem of the geographic distribution of materials have focused on providing universal *intellectual* access. Attempts to solve the problem of universal physical access to the materials themselves, or, more accurately, to their intellectual content, are in their infancy, as the technological means for doing so have only recently emerged. As we began to work toward a standard computer-based data structure for finding aids — the textual analytic guides that control and describe archival collections — we believed that such a standard would be an important contribution toward realizing the long-sought goal of universal intellectual access, but also would set the stage for providing access to the intellectual content of the physical materials themselves.

There is a close relationship between endeavors to overcome geographic obstacles and the emergence of technological innovations; all efforts to improve access have been inspired by new technologies that suggest promising new solutions.[2] EAD is not different from its predecessors in this regard. Emerging computer hardware and software technology, combined with advances in standards and network communications, have stimulated the imaginations of those involved in the development of EAD.

In addition to being an intellectual and technological undertaking, the development of a standard is also a political exercise; it is a community-defining and -building activity. A successful standard must reflect a community's interests, and the community must be directly involved in the standard's development if its interests are to be served. From the beginning of the development of EAD, we have sought to involve the archival community.

Universal Access via Printed Catalogs

The attempt to overcome the geographic distribution of primary sources places EAD development squarely in the mainstream of a major movement in both the library and archives communities that has been making its relentless way throughout most of the current century. Well before the emergence of international networked computing and online catalogs, the library community was working steadfastly to overcome the challenge presented by the geographic distribution of collections. Initially, these efforts were directed toward providing union access to published materials. In 1909 the Library of Congress began a catalog card exchange arrangement with several major libraries. Herbert Putnam, then librarian of Congress, described the plan and its purpose as follows:

---

2 Stereotype printing was the technological development behind Jewett's plan to develop a universal catalog. Instead of metal plates, however, Jewett intended to use clay. When the plan failed, it was derisively referred to as "Jewett's Mud Catalog."

The Library of Congress expects to place in each great center of research in the United States a copy of every card which it prints for its own catalogues; these will form there a statement of what the National Library contains. It hopes to receive a copy of every card printed by the New York Public Library, the Boston Library, the Harvard University Library, the John Crerar Library, and several others. These it will arrange and preserve in a card catalogue of great collections outside of Washington.[3]

This was the first tentative step toward what would eventually become the *National Union Catalog*. Other libraries joined the effort, and by 1926, the Library of Congress had compiled a file of nearly two million cards. In 1948 the file was officially named the *National Union Catalog (NUC)*, and the libraries that had been only selectively reporting acquisitions were asked to report comprehensively.

Gathering the titles together was only the beginning of the effort to create a useful union listing. In order for it to be universally useful, it needed to be universally accessible. It would take until 1956 for the library to develop a solution to this problem by reviving the book catalog, a format that had not been used by most libraries for 50 years. In 1946 the library published *A Catalog of Books Represented by Library of Congress Printed Cards Issued to July 31, 1942*. Ten years later, at the urging of the American Library Association, the Library of Congress applied this approach to the *National Union Catalog* and began issuing in book form the titles acquired by the reporting libraries. This eventually led to the publication of the more than 600 volumes of *The National Union Catalog Pre-1956 Imprints*, the largest single publication ever produced.[4] For the first time, the library world and the public it served had a system for building a national union catalog and making it universally available. But this union catalog, significant as it was, provided access only to published materials, and not to the nation's rich collections of primary source materials.

In 1951 the National Historical Publications and Records Commission (NHPRC)[5] began to compile a union register of archives and manuscript collections held by the nation's repositories. The objective was to provide central, intellectual access to the nation's primary source materials. The effort initially focused on collection-level summary description rather than on in-depth subcollection or item-level description. After gathering collection-level data from 1,300 repositories nationwide in the 1950s, the commission published *A Guide to Archives and*

---

3 *The National Union Catalog Pre-1956 Imprints*, vol. 1 (London: Mansell, 1968), vii.

4 Ibid., x.

5 At the time, the NHPRC was named the National Historical Publications Commission.

Manuscripts in the United States in 1961.[6] The commission decided to revise the directory in 1974, but, after assessing the situation, found that the number of repositories and records had increased so dramatically in the 13 years that had elapsed from the publication of the first directory that compiling collection-level descriptions would be prohibitively expensive. The commission decided to change the focus to repository-level information and thereby provide a coarser level of access. Despite this shift in focus, the commission continued to envision a "national collection-level database on archives and manuscripts."[7] For a variety of reasons, the idea was abandoned in 1982.

In 1951, the same year that NHPRC began planning the directory, the Library of Congress began actively to plan the *National Union Catalog of Manuscript Collections (NUCMC)*.[8] *NUCMC* was intended to be for manuscripts and manuscript collections what the *NUC* was for printed works. Winston Tabb at the Library of Congress has described a major factor in the decision to develop *NUCMC*:

> Scholars, particularly in the field of American history, were instrumental in urging the establishment of a center for locating, recording, and publicizing the holdings of manuscript collections available for research. They had long been frustrated by the difficulties of locating specific manuscripts and even of identifying repositories possibly containing primary-source materials.[9]

It was not until late in 1958 that the Library of Congress began to implement its plans with a grant from the Council on Library Resources. In 1959 the Manuscript Section was established in the library's Descriptive Cataloging Division and was given responsibility for initiating and maintaining the *NUCMC* program. The union manuscript catalog would provide collection-level description for collections held in U.S. repositories and, for particularly important manuscripts, item-level descriptions. Like the *NUC*, the catalog would consist of catalog cards and was to be published in book form, available by subscription. The first volume of *NUCMC* was published in 1962, one year after the NHPRC's *A Guide to Archives and Manuscripts in the United States*. After 32 successful years, the library announced in 1994 that volume 29 would be the last *print* publication of the *NUCMC*.

---

6 This account is based on Richard A. Noble's article "The NHPRC Database Project: Building the 'Interstate Highway System,'" *American Archivist* 51 (Winter/Spring 1988): 98-105.

7 Ibid., 99.

8 This account is based on the Foreword to the *Library of Congress National Union Catalog of Manuscript Collections: Catalog 1991* (Washington, D.C.: Cataloging Distribution Service, Library of Congress, 1993), vii-ix.

9 Ibid., vii.

The elimination of the *NUCMC* print publication in no way suggests that it is no longer important to build union catalogs to provide access to our intellectual and cultural resources. Instead, this change was the logical and prudent response to the realization that *NUCMC's* objective would be better served by using powerful networked computer technology instead of print technology.

Universal Access via Online Catalogs

The advent of machine-readable catalog records, coupled with the emergence of nationally networked computer databases, provided the archives and library communities with the means to build centralized union catalogs that would be available everywhere, all the time, and in doing so, set the stage for the development of standards such as EAD. For the first time, technology enabled archives and libraries to provide universal access that was not geographically and temporally constrained and thus was far more accessible and effective than printed catalogs. Technology also has greatly facilitated the compiling of union databases. Over the course of the 1980s and 1990s, the OCLC and RLG databases, by aggregating millions of machine-readable catalog records, emerged as *de facto* union catalogs to not only the nation's bibliographic holdings, but to a good share of the world's as well. Scholars, educators, and the general public, using networked computers in offices, homes, and libraries, could discover what published materials existed and where copies could be found.

As of 1983, the records in these national utilities almost exclusively represented published print materials; the primary source materials in the nation's archives and manuscript repositories were not represented. This was all to change with the work of the National Information Systems Task Force (NISTF) of the Society of American Archivists. From 1981 to 1984, NISTF paved the way, both intellectually and politically, for the development of the USMARC Archival and Manuscripts Control (MARC AMC) format.[10] The AMC format made it feasible for archives and manuscript repositories to provide brief, synoptic surrogates for collections in their care in bibliographic catalogs. The AMC format by itself, however, only specified content encoding standards; it did not provide standards for the actual content of the records themselves, and without such standards, the format was simply an empty vessel. The archives and manuscripts community found the *Anglo-American Cataloging Rules,* second edition *(AACR2)* inadequate because its chapter on manuscript cataloging abandoned long-standing archival descriptive principles. In response, Steven L. Hensen, then working at the Library of Congress, developed an

---

10 For a short history and evaluation of the work of NISTF, see David Bearman, *Towards National Information Systems for Archives and Manuscript Repositories: The National Information Systems Task Force (NISTF) Papers 1981-1984* (Chicago: Society of American Archivists, 1987).

alternative set of rules that was to complement the AMC encoding standard. These rules, entitled *Archives, Personal Papers, and Manuscripts (APPM)*, coupled with the AMC format, have enabled the archives and manuscripts community to contribute more than 475,000 records to the Research Libraries Group's RLIN database.[11] Through these utilities, scholars now have access to a growing accumulation of brief descriptions of the nation's archival and manuscript collections.

As important and revolutionary as these accomplishments have been, however, they represented only one major step toward enabling researchers to easily locate primary source materials. The generalized descriptions found in AMC records can only lead a researcher to a collection which *may* have individual relevant items. The researcher must next consult the assortment of inventories, registers, indexes, and guides, generally referred to as finding aids, with which libraries and archives have achieved administrative and intellectual control of archival materials in the form of in-depth, detailed descriptions of their collections. Finding aids provide hierarchically structured description, proceeding in defined stages from the general to the specific. At the most general level, they roughly correspond in scope to collection-level catalog records. At the most specific level, they briefly identify individual items. In between, in varying degrees of detail, they describe subsets or series of related items. Finding aids are the detailed maps that lead one from the main highway to the byways, and from those to one's ultimate destination, the item itself.

MARC AMC collection-level records and finding aids are intended to work together as parts of a hierarchical archival access and navigation model. At the top of the model, the AMC record represents a collection in the online catalog and leads, through a "finding aid available" note (field 555), to the more detailed information in the finding aid. The finding aid, in turn, leads to the materials in the collection.

In this three-tiered model, the descriptive information in the collection-level record is based on and derived from the collection's finding aid. Only a very small portion of the information contained in the registers and inventories finds it way into the bibliographic record. The summary nature of the collection-level record is dramatically illustrated by the finding aid and catalog record for the *National Municipal League Records, 1890-1991 (bulk 1929-1988)* in the Auraria Library in Denver, Colorado. The finding aid comprises more than 1,400 pages and 30,000 personal names. By comparison, the AMC record for this collection is approximately two pages long and has nine personal names as access points!

Thus, as positive a development as the AMC format has been, it was not the final step in the drive for universal access to primary sources.

---

11 RLIN database statistics were provided by Ann Van Camp at the Research Libraries Group and reflect the RLIN database as of August 25, 1997.

Nevertheless, AMC was an excellent prologue to the final act. AMC records whetted our appetite for more information and, almost immediately, made us aware of where we should look for it: in the detailed inventories and registers from which the collection-level catalog records had been derived in the first place. It was clear, then, almost as soon as AMC had triumphed, that the next logical step to facilitate scholars' easily locating relevant primary source materials without buying a plane ticket or putting the completion of a research project at the discretion of the U.S. Postal Service was the creation of yet another encoding standard to complement the AMC standard, a standard for the finding aids themselves. And it was equally clear that this standard would lead to the creation of union Internet access to the nation's finding aids for archives and manuscripts.

The Value of Standards

But why insist on the development of a standard? The success of AMC itself should obviate any need to argue the necessity of standards to the archival community, but recent experience has shown that the lure of simple techniques can lead us to ignore lessons already learned. In an era of tightening budgets, it can be difficult to remember that we exploit the new information frontier best if we bring enduring value to it. In the current atmosphere, it is critical to remind ourselves of the importance of standardizing our own time-honored practices rather than rushing to embrace ephemeral digital fashions that will not stand the test of time.

MARC has successfully demonstrated the value of a community-based standard in realizing the goal of universal access to primary resource materials. We are steadily and inexorably moving toward providing comprehensive, universal intellectual access to both primary and secondary resources. This remarkable effort would not be possible without the library community's pioneering work in developing content and structure standards. With the development of AMC, the archival community joined in recognizing the paramount importance of standards. Having grown accustomed to the benefits of well-designed, community-based descriptive standards, it was inconceivable that the archival community could accept proprietary, nonstandard, or worse, substandard approaches to providing universal access to finding aids and the resources they document.

Standards are the foundation upon which individuals sharing common interests form communities, enabling them not only to coexist but also to cooperatively build shared and enduring works. While many archivists were skeptical about the adaptation and use of bibliocentric library standards, the desire to make archival materials available to users more effectively motivated them to work with the library community. Archivists share with librarians the compelling objective of making information concerning the existence, availability, and nature of the materials in their care more readily available to users. Thus, when the means was found to create surrogates for archival collections in online public catalogs, enabling users to locate and identify relevant primary resources more easily, the archival community embraced it.

The Lessons of MARC

Many of the design features successfully demonstrated in MARC are also desirable in an encoding standard for finding aids, and the developers of EAD looked to MARC as a model from the very beginning.

An encoding scheme such as MARC, a computer-readable system for representing the unique, intellectual structure of cataloging data, was absolutely essential if we were ever to build large networked databases that could support sophisticated and effective control, searching, display, and navigation of library collections.[12] Merely transferring complex catalog records into networked computers as unstructured text would not in itself have enabled computers to exploit the complex distinctions and relationships among the elements of descriptive cataloging records.

Cataloging is an "order-making" activity by which complex rules are applied to a defiant, unruly information universe in order to "whip it into shape," making it appear orderly to the users of catalogs. [13] Catalogers determine the identities of authors, works, and items, and the relationships among them. To be usefully exploited by computers, all of this complex order-making data must be explicitly represented in a manner that allows machines to process it with intended, predictable results. Computers cannot reliably perform complex processing on flat, unstructured text, because programmers cannot instruct machines to process that which has not been identified. To take full advantage of network computer technology, it was thus necessary to have an encoding system for catalog data that rendered the boundaries of its intellectual components explicit to programmers and computers alike.

The original designers of MARC saw it primarily as a method for automating the production of printed catalog cards, but they wisely invented an encoding system that would support more than this one use. Given the many uses to which cataloging information would eventually be put, it was important that the encoding scheme developed be sufficiently flexible to support all potential uses. The best way to accomplish this objective was to make the scheme descriptive rather than procedural.

Procedural encoding tells the computer what to do with specified components of a text; by its very nature, it is dedicated to only one use of the information. But as we know, cataloging data is subjected to multiple forms of processing in order to provide effective control, searching, display, and navigation. To support application of multiple procedures,

---

12 "Control" is here intended to mean "knowing what we have and where it is."

13 David Levy, *Cataloging in the Digital Order*, <http://csdl.tamu.edu/DL95/papers/levy/levy.html>.

each component could be encoded with multiple processing instructions. This would be highly inefficient, however, because it involves a great deal of redundancy and also forecloses on new processes unforeseen at the time the encoding scheme was developed.

An alternative approach, and the one wisely chosen by the developers of MARC, is to descriptively encode the information. Descriptive encoding involves designating what each important component is: a catalog record, an author, a title, and so on. If we know what a data component is, then it is possible to apply different procedures to it based on explicit knowledge of its nature. The decision to make MARC a descriptive markup system ensured that information could be exploited in multiple ways, and it left the door open to apply procedures unforeseen in the early stages of development. In addition to faithfully representing cataloging data, MARC's developers also recognized that the system they were designing had to be a publicly owned standard to ensure that cataloging information would endure in an ever-changing computer environment. A standard must not be based on any specific hardware or software platform if it is to endure in our rapidly changing technological environment.

The descriptive nature of MARC encoding, in addition to supporting flexible processing, also supports MARC's long-term survival through means such as mapping MARC data into other computer representations. In fact, most existing MARC systems do not store and use MARC in its native form; to comply with the standard, they simply import and export MARC records. Mapping MARC into a successor standard, if and when one emerges, will be a simple export procedure. MARC's successful survival of the unbelievably rapid transformation of computing over the course of the last 30 years is a testament to the wisdom of its designers. These aspects of the design of MARC — the fact that it is descriptive markup and that it is publicly owned — strongly influenced the developers of EAD and determined the nature of EAD's design to a large extent.

Early in the development of EAD, we surveyed options for the encoding of finding aids. The primary selection criteria were (1) that the system chosen had to be a standard, which is to say, a formal set of conventions in the public domain, not owned by and thus not dependent on any hardware or software producer, and (2) that it had to be capable of faithfully representing the complex intellectual content and structure of finding aids in a manner that would enable sophisticated searching, navigation, and display.

Because of MARC's design qualities, its success in capturing the intellectual content of bibliographic description and the fact that it had been used successfully by archivists for providing collection-level summary access to collections, MARC immediately earned consideration as an option. It was a standard in the public domain. But was it capable of representing the complex intellectual content and structure of finding aids?

After careful study and deliberation, we decided that MARC was not the best available scheme for three principal reasons. First, MARC records are limited to a maximum length of 100,000 characters. This represents approximately thirty 8 1/2-by-11 pages of 10-pitch unformatted text stored in ASCII. Since many finding aids are longer than this, the size restriction was a prohibitive obstacle. Second, and even more significantly, MARC accommodates hierarchically structured information very poorly. Since finding aids are inherently hierarchical documents, the flat structure of MARC makes it unsatisfactory. As archivists are painfully aware, MARC was primarily designed to capture data describing a discrete bibliographic item; complex collections requiring descending levels of analysis quickly overburden the MARC structure. At most, a second level of analysis can be accommodated, but the kind of information supplied is limited.[14] The third reason for not using MARC for finding aids involves the marketplace. It is a gross understatement to say that libraries, archives, and museums are generally not resource-rich institutions. To put this into perspective, the cost of one B-2 bomber would fund the Library of Congress for well over three years.[15] Lacking large amounts of capital, MARC's user community has been incapable of driving state-of-the-art hardware and software development.

SGML, HTML, XML, and EAD

After determining that MARC would not provide an adequate representation of finding aid data, we shifted our attention to Standard Generalized Markup Language (SGML). SGML provides a promising framework or model for developing an encoding scheme for finding aids for a number of reasons. First, like MARC, SGML is a standard (ISO 8879). It comprises a formal set of conventions in the public domain, and thus is not owned by and thereby dependent on any hardware or software producer. Second, unlike MARC, SGML accommodates hierarchically interrelated information at as many levels as needed. Third, there are no inherent size restrictions on SGML-based documents. Finally, the SGML marketplace is much, much larger than MARC's.

While SGML is both standard and generalized, it does not provide an off-the-shelf markup language that one can simply take home and apply

---

14 One possible way around this problem is to employ multiple, hierarchically interrelated and interlinked MARC records at varying levels of analysis: collection-level, subunit, and item. The use of multiple records, though, introduces extremely difficult inter- and intra-system control problems that have never been adequately addressed in the format or by MARC-based software developers. Even if the control issues were adequately addressed in the format, the control required to make multiple record expression of hierarchy succeed would entail prohibitive human maintenance.

15 According to the United States Air Force Web page, the unit price for one B-2 bomber is $1.3 billion. Various other sources place the figure at closer to $2 billion. The 1997 Library of Congress budget is $360,896,000.

to a letter, novel, article, catalog record, or finding aid. Instead it is a markup language metastandard, or in simpler words, a standard for constructing markup languages. SGML provides conventions for naming the logical components or elements of documents, as well as a syntax and metalanguage for defining and expressing the logical structure of documents and relations between document components. It is a set of formal rules for defining specific markup languages for individual kinds of documents. Using these formal rules, members of a community sharing a particular type of document can work together to create a markup language specific to their shared document type.

The specific markup languages written in compliance with formal SGML requirements are called Document Type Definitions, or DTDs. For example, the Association of American Publishers has developed three DTDs: one for books, one for journals, and one for journal articles. A consortium of software developers and producers has developed a DTD for computer manuals. The Library of Congress currently is testing a draft USMARC DTD. The Text Encoding Initiative has developed a complex suite of DTDs for the representation of literary and linguistic materials. DTDs, when shared and followed by a community, are themselves standards.

While MARC is devoted to structuring a specific kind of data, namely cataloging data, SGML is very general and abstract. It exists formally over and above individual markup languages for specific document classes. Because SGML syntax and rules are formal and precise, it is possible to write software that can be adjusted with relative ease to work with any compliant DTD. Typically, an SGML software product has a toolkit that allows the user to adapt its functionality to a specific DTD. As a result, all SGML users, not just library and archival users, comprise the market that drives SGML software development.

Similar to MARC, SGML is intended to support descriptive rather than procedural markup of text.[16] As discussed above, procedural markup specifies a particular procedure to be applied to a document component, while descriptive markup defines each component, leaving the processing routines up to applications.

It is useful to distinguish two kinds of descriptive markup: structural and nominal. Descriptive structural markup identifies document components and their logical relationships. Structural elements generally are components that warrant distinct visual presentation: examples include chapter titles, paragraphs, lists, and block quotes. Descriptive nominal markup identifies named entities, both concrete and abstract; examples include corporate names, personal names, topical subjects, genres, and geographic names. While a specific visual presentation of them may be

---

16 For a detailed description of different types of markup, see James H. Coombs, Allen H. Renear, and Steven. J. DeRose, "Markup Systems and the Future of Scholarly Text Processing," *Communications of the Association for Computing Machinery* 30 (November 1987): 933-47.

desirable, such elements usually warrant being indexed in particular ways to provide access to some aspect of the document. It is also possible to SGML also supports referential markup. As its name suggests, referential markup refers to information that is not present; it is markup in the third person, so to speak. Referential markup is most commonly used for hypertext and hypermedia, providing the foundation for dynamic references or links to other text and to original digital or digital representations of manuscripts, photographs, audio and audiovisual materials, drawings, paintings, three-dimensional objects of all kinds, chemical formulae, printed pages, music, choreography, and anything else that can be digitally captured and rendered in some useful form. In addition to its many other benefits, using SGML for finding aids offers the exciting option of providing access to digital representations of the primary resources in our archival collections.

HyperText Markup Language (HTML) is an SGML DTD that has enjoyed enormous success as the encoding standard underpinning the World Wide Web. As a specific application of SGML, the HTML DTD limits itself to simple procedural encoding dedicated to online display and hypermedia linking. Because of HTML's relative ease of use and its ability to support online display of finding aids, many have suggested that it suffices for the encoding of finding aids. The EAD developers felt strongly, however, that HTML was inadequate because its procedural focus would not represent the complex intellectual content and structure of finding aids in a manner that would enable sophisticated searching, navigation, and display. Evidence of HTML's limited ability to support intelligent searching and document discovery, let alone complex display, navigation, and other processing, is not difficult to find. Many of us have used Web search engines to look for both known items and items relevant to a particular topic, and more often than not, we are overwhelmed by voluminous results. Our patience frequently is exhausted looking for an item or two that satisfies our need.[17]

The success of HTML as a display format for the Web brings into sharp relief the one major weakness in available SGML software, namely the limited options currently available for delivering native SGML over the Internet. SGML software developers have produced very good and affordable tools for SGML authoring and editing, data conversion, and database indexing and searching; they also have produced very good publishing tools for in-house and CD-ROM publishing. Though delivering SGML documents on the Web has been a serious obstacle, the prospects for this changing in the near future appear to be bright.

---

17 In response to this problem OCLC has led an international effort since 1995 to develop a simple, generic descriptive metadata scheme that would make it possible to more intelligently index and search HTML documents on the Web.

In 1996 the World Wide Web Consortium (W3C) founded the XML Working Group to build a set of specifications that would make it easier to use SGML on the Web.[18] The working group, in a short period of time, wrote a specification for a simplified subset of SGML named Extensible Markup Language (XML). Both Microsoft and Netscape have committed to fully implementing XML in their Internet browsers.

The motive behind the development of XML is the recognition that HTML will not support complex, community-based use of shared information on the Internet. HTML hardwires a small set of procedurally oriented tags. Constraining the set of tags has made it easy to build applications that make life relatively easy for authors and Web publishers, and ease of use has been a major factor in the Web's remarkable success. The small, closed tag set, however, has come at a price: HTML has extremely limited functionality. Jon Bosak has identified three areas in which HTML is wanting: extensibility, structure, and validation.[19] SGML is strong in all of these areas, but its strength, like HTML's weakness, comes at a price: SGML is complicated for both application developers and the users of the applications. The W3C's XML Working Group addressed this weakness by identifying and proscribing some features in SGML that are difficult to implement. The result of their work is XML, a simplified subset of SGML for use on the Web.

The ongoing development of XML and closely related standards promises to overcome the last major obstacle to the use of SGML for encoding finding aids: their easy delivery over the Internet.[20] Fortunately, most of the SGML features proscribed in XML were not used in the EAD DTD, and expressions used in EAD that do use proscribed features can easily be expressed in XML-compliant ways. Thus very little modification of the EAD DTD is required to take advantage of future Internet browsers produced and distributed by Microsoft, Netscape, and other vendors, and these changes will have been completed prior to the release of EAD version 1.0.

The decision to develop EAD as an SGML DTD still appears to have been propitious. It allowed us to incorporate MARC's strengths — descriptive markup and public ownership — and to overcome its weaknesses — limited record and field length, hierarchical poverty, and small market appeal. It was an article of faith when we began developing EAD that to become truly robust the Web would have to outgrow HTML, and that the

---

18 The original name was SGML Editorial Review Board. Jon Bosak of Sun Microsystems is chair of the Working Group. Other members include Jean Paoli, head of Microsoft's Internet Explorer development, and Tim Bray, representing both Textuality and Netscape.

19 Jon Bosak, *XML, Java, and the Future of the Web*, <http://sunsite.unc.edu/pub/sun-info/standards/xml/why/xmlapps.htm>.

20 XML includes three related initiatives: XML, Extensible Linking Language (XLL), and Extensible Stylesheet Language (XSL). For current information on the status of the development and the latest drafts of each, see <http://sil.org/sgml/xml.html>.

likely successor to HTML would be based on SGML. This was a calculated risk, but it appears to have been thoroughly justified.

EAD's foundation in the mainstream of library and archives efforts to achieve universal access coupled with the use of emerging powerful computing and network technologies, would appear to provide EAD with everything it would need to succeed. But the most important element of any standards process: the community that will use the standard — also had to be brought into play.

Overview of EAD Development

The success of any standard depends upon broad community participation in its development, followed by widespread recognition of the standard's utility. Standards are the products of communities, not of individuals working in splendid isolation, and the development process is as much a political exercise as it is an intellectual and technical undertaking. Thus, to be successful, an encoding standard for finding aids must reflect and further the shared interests of the archival community and of the agencies and institutions that support it.

From the very beginning of the effort to develop an encoding standard for finding aids, those involved realized it would be crucial to involve the archival community in the intellectual and technical design of the standard. In 1993, when the UC Berkeley library staff was first beginning to contemplate developing such a standard, Jackie Dooley and Steven Hensen both firmly emphasized the necessity of broad community involvement if the effort was to succeed.

The Berkeley Finding Aid Project (BFAP), funded with a grant from the Department of Education's Title IIA Program, began the process that has led to EAD. BFAP's objective was to demonstrate through development of a draft DTD (initially named FindAid), as well as an Internet-accessible database employing the DTD, that an SGML-based encoding standard was both feasible and desirable. To ensure that the prototype DTD reflected the content and structure of the community's finding aids, BFAP staff solicited representative examples of finding aids, regardless of quality, from scores of repositories.[21]

Early in 1995, two developments served to transfer ownership of BFAP's work to the national community. In April the Commission on

---

21 The response to this solicitation provides an interesting glimpse into the standards development process. Many repositories enthusiastically promised to send finding aids, but after several weeks, only a handful had arrived. BFAP staff began to approach each repository that had promised to send finding aids to request them once again. Over and over the response was that, while they wholeheartedly supported the effort, they were concerned about how their colleagues would view their finding aids. The finding aids they eventually submitted tended to be those in which they had the most confidence. Thus the community itself voluntarily began to normalize finding aid practice.

Preservation and Access (CPA) and the Berkeley library cosponsored a Finding Aid Conference at Berkeley attended by 70 representatives of special collections, archives, libraries, and museums. The purpose of the conference was to evaluate the results of BFAP and to make recommendations about what should be done next. Those gathered enthusiastically agreed that BFAP had succeeded in its limited goals and that the effort should continue, though with the active participation of archival descriptive experts.

The opportunity for engaging archival experts more closely in the project came with the author's successful application to the Bentley Library Research Fellowship Program at the University of Michigan for a team fellowship. The team, led by the author, included noted archival description experts [22] as well as distinguished SGML expert Steven J. DeRose of Electronic Book Technologies. The team met in Ann Arbor in July 1995 to evaluate formally the BFAP finding aid model and DTD and to develop a new model. The team reached early agreement on design principles, which were called the "Ann Arbor Accords," and spent the remainder of the week developing the model on which a new DTD would be based.[23] It was at this time that BFAP was renamed Encoded Archival Description (EAD).

A flurry of activity followed the Ann Arbor meeting. In the next two months, the author wrote the first draft of the EAD DTD. At the September 1995 annual meeting of SAA in Washington, D.C., members of the team began the process of determining appropriate mechanisms for profession-wide adoption and maintenance of an encoding standard for finding aids. The design principles and revised data model were presented to SAA's Committee on Archival Information Exchange (CAIE), and CAIE was invited to become formally involved in the development of EAD. CAIE agreed and created the EAD Working Group (EADWG) chaired by Kris Kiesling and including representatives from the Library of Congress (LC), RLG, OCLC, and SAA. EADWG was charged by CAIE with 1) assisting in developing and reviewing a data model for archival finding aids; 2) reviewing the EAD DTD; 3) testing and evaluating the EAD DTD; 4) reviewing application guidelines; and 5) initiating review of EAD by the SAA Standards Board and SAA Council. SAA also agreed to formally request that the LC Network Development/MARC Standards Office (ND/MSO) assume the maintenance of EAD once it had undergone thor-

---

22 Other members of the group were Jackie Dooley, University of California, Irvine; Michael J. Fox, Minnesota Historical Society; Steven Hensen, Duke University; Kris Kiesling, University of Texas, Austin; Janice Ruth, Library of Congress; Sharon Gibbs Thibodeau, National Archives and Records Administration; and Helena Zinkham, Library of Congress.

23 "Ann Arbor Accords: Principles and Criteria for an SGML Document Type Definition (DTD) for Finding Aids," *Archival Outlook* (January 1996): 12-13.

ough community review and was accepted as a standard. In October 1995 LC's National Digital Library (NDL) sponsored a meeting of the team in Washington, D.C., to review the model and draft DTD.

After the October meeting in Washington, ATLIS Consulting Group, under contract to LC and in consultation with the author, began revision of the DTD and creation of a tag library. In a letter to Susan Fox, SAA Executive Director, the ND/MSO formally agreed to be the maintenance agency for EAD, with SAA responsible for ongoing intellectual oversight and development of the standard.

In December 1995 SAA received funding from the Council on Library Resources to create application guidelines for EAD, and at a meeting at UCLA on January 4-6, 1996, the EAD project team met with Anne Gilliland-Swetland and Thomas LaPorte to review the draft DTD and tag library and to outline the content of the guidelines. Further changes were incorporated into the "alpha" version of the DTD, which was completed and released electronically by ND/MSO for use by early implementers in February 1996. On April 27-29, 1996 the EAD team met in Berkeley to discuss the draft guidelines drafted by Gilliland-Swetland and LaPorte and to review suggested changes to the alpha version of the DTD that had been suggested by team members and early implementers. Agreed-upon changes were incorporated into the "beta" version of the DTD, which was completed by the author on June 15, 1996, and after review by the development team, was released publicly that September. The draft guidelines, tag library, and encoded examples of a wide variety of finding aids were made publicly available on the Internet in December 1996.

During the course of the EAD development process, a variety of major research and demonstration projects began implementing EAD. From the earliest stages, UC Berkeley, Duke University, and LC's NDL began encoding finding aids using EAD to test its intellectual and technical soundness. Yale University began working with the alpha DTD as soon as it was released in early 1996, as did Harvard University. The University of California, San Diego, successfully began experimenting with exporting into EAD finding aids that had been created in a database. SOLINET decided to incorporate EAD into its Department of Commerce–funded Monticello Project, and the NEH-funded Dance Heritage Coalition also made the decision to employ EAD in its archival access project.

Since the EAD beta public release in September 1996, several repositories have initiated finding aid projects of varying sizes and complexities. The Public Record Office in London is currently developing a strategy for conversion of its repository guide. When completed, this guide will comprise hundreds of thousands of pages describing several centuries of British public records. Several universities in the United Kingdom, including Liverpool, Oxford, Durham, and Glasgow, have substantial EAD projects underway. In the United States, UC Berkeley, with funding from NEH, embarked on the California Heritage Digital Image Access Project.

The goal of this project was to demonstrate that USMARC collection-level records linked to EAD-encoded finding aids could provide effective, useful access to collections comprising more than 25,000 digital representations of pictorial materials documenting California history and culture selected from the Bancroft Library's vast pictorial collections. Significantly, the California Heritage Project's prototype access system is being used in an ambitious UC Berkeley K-12 outreach program called the Interactive University Project, which is funded by a Department of Commerce grant. In this project, a team of faculty and library staff are working with K-12 teachers and curriculum planners from the San Francisco and Oakland public school districts to create a teaching program and lesson plans that will use the digital archives to teach subjects related to California history and cultures during the 1997-98 school year and possibly beyond.

The California Heritage Project also has provided the foundation for two other projects, the NEH-funded American Heritage Virtual Archive Project and the University of California EAD Project (UCEAD)[24], the latter funded by UC's Office of the President as the first in a series of UC-wide digital library projects. In addition to building a UC-wide database of finding aids, a key goal of UCEAD was to train archivists at all nine UC campuses to efficiently implement EAD through the use of customized software "toolkits." The American Heritage Project involves a collaboration between Stanford University, the University of Virginia, Duke University, and UC Berkeley; its goal is to demonstrate that EAD can be uniformly applied to diverse existing finding aids for collections documenting American heritage and culture at the four collaborating repositories to enable building a combined virtual archives. The project is exploring the intellectual, political, and technical issues that need to be resolved to provide integrated access to finding aids from multiple institutions.[25] The centerpiece of this project is the development of "an acceptable range of uniform practice" in the application of EAD to existing finding aids. At a meeting in Berkeley in November 1996, representatives from the four collaborating institutions, building on the extensive work of a team of Berkeley technical and archival staff, debated and reached consensus. That consensus was codified in the first draft of the *EAD Retrospective Conversion Guidelines*. Soon thereafter, archivists representing the nine UC campuses met in Los Angeles to launch the UCEAD Project and to further refine the consensus represented by the *Guidelines*. The American Heritage and

---

24 The UCEAD Project later was renamed the Online Archive of California.

25 Given current technical limits, the project is integrating the finding aids into one centralized database. As technology improves for integrating access to distributed databases (a model much preferred for many practical reasons), the lessons learned from this project will inform migration to the new technology.

UCEAD participants, representing 12 university repositories, all agreed to follow these *Guidelines*. These repositories hope that the guidelines will serve as the basis for a discussion leading to a national consensus on "an acceptable range of uniform practice."[26]

The Research Libraries Group recognized that development of EAD training was critical to its community-wide acceptance and use. In the summer of 1996, in collaboration with UC Berkeley, RLG developed the Finding Aid SGML Training (FAST) workshop curriculum. Over the course of the following year, with grants from the Delmas Foundation and the Council on Library Resources, RLG held several workshops in the United Kingdom, Canada, and the United States. Taught by Michael Fox and Kris Kiesling, the FAST workshops have successfully provided initial training to scores of archivists. FAST and other EAD workshops have led to a number of other repositories, large and small, initiating their own finding aid encoding projects. The University of Iowa, University of Vermont, New York Public Library, North Carolina State University, and University of North Carolina, to name a few, all have projects underway. In August 1997 RLG turned the workshop over to the Society of American Archivists at the society's annual meeting in Chicago, and SAA has now integrated the workshop into its educational curriculum.

RLG and Chadwyck-Healey both are exploring incorporating EAD into their products and services. Following successful development of EAD training, RLG has formed an EAD advisory group to assist in planning and implementing new services. At this stage of planning, RLG intends to provide union access to finding aids worldwide, both those housed on local servers and those deposited on the RLG server by repositories lacking the resources or desire to mount their own findings aids. The advisory group has identified the need for participating repositories to apply EAD uniformly and, in this regard, has decided to use the *EAD Retrospective Conversion Guidelines* to initiate discussions leading to community-wide "best practice" guidelines. In addition, RLG is exploring the feasibility of hosting a retrospective conversion service that would make use of third-party vendors. Chadwyck-Healey is contemplating a similar service and is considering ways to enhance its *ArchivesUSA* product by incorporating EAD-encoded finding aids. In addition to the activities of RLG and Chadwyck-Healey, a number of software vendors have EAD products under development.

---

26 Citing a 1980 NHPRC report, Richard Noble reports that commission staff projected that 20,000 repositories and over 700,000 collection descriptions would be included in a national database. See Noble, "The NHPRC Database Project," 100. The finding aids in the Berkeley database average 27 pages in length. If this average is representative, then 700,000 finding aids would amount to nearly 19 million pages of text!! It is worth noting again that after only 11 years there are over 475,000 records for archival materials in the RLIN database. Since many of the nation's archival collections have never been processed, arranged, and described, 700,000 may be a conservative estimate.

In addition to the successful transfer of the FAST workshop to SAA, there were several other important developments at the 1997 SAA annual meeting. Jackie Dooley, chair of the SAA Publications Board, reported on discussions with LC concerning the publication of the EAD DTD, tag library, and application guidelines. Kris Kiesling, chair of the EADWG, announced that Meg Sweet of the Public Record Office in the United Kingdom had joined the Working Group and that the Delmas Foundation had funded a meeting of the Working Group in fall 1997 in Washington, D.C. At this meeting, the group reviewed revisions to EAD suggested by the international archival community and, after thorough discussion, decided which changes would be codified prior to EAD's public release as a standard in 1998. The Working Group also reviewed drafts of the tag library, publication of which will coincide with the formal release of the DTD.

Conclusion

Prior to the advent of MARC AMC and *APPM*, the archival community had little motivation to develop descriptive standards. The economic benefits of sharing cataloging that motivated libraries were not available to archivists, whose collections are mostly unique. Nevertheless, archivists wanted to make their materials more accessible, a professional objective they shared with their library colleagues. This desire provided the motivation to explore and eventually embrace MARC AMC and *APPM*, the success of which convinced the archival community of the value and importance of encoding and descriptive content standards. Further, archivists were inspired to want to go beyond summary descriptions and to find a way to provide access to the full, detailed finding aids that constitute the heart of all efforts to make archival collections accessible.

The emergence of the Internet, which has enabled the revolutionary transcending of the spatial and temporal boundaries of our information environment, awakened an abiding but dormant aspiration: to provide comprehensive universal access to the world's primary cultural and historical resources. For the first time in history, it is possible to render the absent present. Not only will archivists be able to better serve those we have traditionally served, but we will also, for the first time, have the means to make our collections accessible to educators and students at all levels and to the general public.

EAD and related standards have initiated the realization of an information future in which serious scholars and the casually curious alike will easily find the cultural treasures they seek. In this emerging future, information seekers will follow clearly marked paths from catalogs to finding aids, and from finding aids to a wealth of information in a multitude of digital and traditional formats. We are embarking on providing not only intellectual access to our collections, but also access to digital facsimiles, at least selectively, of the materials themselves.

While we have not yet fully realized this long-sought goal, and much work remains to be done, it is now possible to begin to envision a future even more promising — one which builds new and unprecedented collaborations between scholars, educators, publishers, archivists, and librarians. Over and above the structured database of catalog records, finding aids, and digital representations of primary source materials, it will be possible to create both private and public information spaces that interpret materials from a wide variety of perspectives and disciplines to serve an equally wide array of cultural needs. Archivists will play an essential role in building the networked digital information environment that promises to transform the intellectual community by admitting new groups of people who, prior to its advent, had never set foot in an archives.

Part Six:
Reference and Use of Archives

As American archivists increasingly focus on new technological means of description and access, the traditional roles of reference and outreach sometimes seem overshadowed. This has in turn led to a renewed emphasis on serving users of archives and a recognition that outdated assumptions about the nature of the research clientele needed to be reassessed. The articles included in this section represent three aspects of this process.

Elsie Freeman Finch has been one of the leading advocates for focusing attention on the needs of researchers and other archival users. "In the Eye of the Beholder: Archives Administration from the User's Point of View" articulates this concern for shifting from a materials-centered approach to archives to a client-centered approach. Her appeal for more systematic investigation of archival users found echoes in several other writers.

One of those who called for more user studies is Paul Conway, who devised a research model for such studies in "Facts and Frameworks: An Approach to Studying the Users of Archives." Conway later applied this model to a major user study he conducted at the National Archives and Records Administration.*

Another approach to examining the users of an institutional archives is presented in Elizabeth Yakel and Laura Bost Hensey, "Understanding Administrative Use and Users in University Archives." Yakel and Bost focus not on the traditional emphasis on historical research, but on the important but often overlooked uses of archives for administrative purposes within institutions. This reflects an increasing recognition by archivists that historians and other academic researchers are not the

---

* Paul Conway, *Partners in Research: Improving Access to the Nation's Archives* (Pittsburgh: Archives & Museum Informatics, 1994).

primary clientele for archival reference. Genealogists, local historians, land surveyors, legal researchers, administrators and others constitute the majority of archival users. This recognition is beginning to change the orientation of many reference archivists.

18

In the Eye of the Beholder: Archives Administration from the User's Point of View

ELSIE FREEMAN FINCH

Abstract: The author proposes that we learn systematically, not impressionistically, who our users are and might be, what kinds of projects they pursue, and, most important, how they approach records. We must begin to think of archives administration as being centered on our clients, not on materials. Freeman presents a series of misassumptions on which archivists operate and thereby render their work with users far less effective than it might be. The misassumptions are that as a profession we are oriented toward users; we know who these users are; we understand the nature of research; and we provide adequate help in doing it. She discusses three of these misassumptions at length and examines the changing nature of research, the problems inherent in our finding aids, and the likelihood of a useful connection between how the researcher approaches information and the development of realistic appraisal standards. She then proposes a series of national, regional, and local efforts intended to retrain our thinking about the place of users in archives administration. These include a nationally initiated study of usership, national recognition for exemplary outreach programs, local programs that will elicit information from users, a reexamination of our descriptive and reference practices, and a restructuring of our archival training programs.

My proposition is, on the surface, a simple one, but one which, if it were accepted, would turn our administrative, descriptive, reference, and training practices upside down. Or, more modestly, it would cause us to arrive at our desks each day with an entirely different set of imperatives from those now before us. That proposition is this: the identity and the research habits of our users — who they are, how they think, how they learn, how they assemble information, to what uses they put it — must become as familiar a part of our thinking as the rules of order and practice (sometimes called principles) that now govern the acquisition, processing, description, and servicing of records. We must begin to learn systematically, not impressionistically as is our present tendency, who our users are; what kinds of projects they pursue, in what time

Reprinted with permission from the *American Archivist* 47 (Spring 1984): 111-23.

frames, and under what sponsorship; and, most importantly, how they approach records. Put another way, we must begin to think of archives administration as client centered, not materials centered.

Is it the case that we do not, as we would like to think, put the user first? And, if we do not, why should we begin to now? First, and most importantly, we should alter our emphasis because we believe as history professionals that, in the analysis of problems, the history of the problem counts. As technologies for reaching current information make that information more accessible, competition between archivists and other suppliers of information will increase. Historical information delivered in bulk, as we now deliver it, will become increasingly less attractive to users who have neither the deep historical commitment nor the time or training to burrow for it. The kindest thing one can now say about our role in the larger world of information access is that we are a quiet, slowly flowing stream. Advanced technologies may very well make us a backwater, not because our material is irrelevant to current or retrospective questions but rather because of the difficulty users have in reaching the information hidden in the records we hold. The historical element in problem solving will diminish, and that diminution will be a loss to all that we represent.

Second, we should shift our emphasis from materials to users so that we can begin to identify, within some usable context, that mystical universe of documentation about which we have been talking for some time. Within the discretionary areas of acquisition and appraisal, beyond that which appears necessary to document the life of an institution, we should have at least one verifiable frame of reference. We must learn the uses to which our material is put and the methods of the clients who use it.

Finally, we need soon to shift our emphasis so that we do not become caught up in useless technologies or technologies that only make more quickly and expensively the mistakes we have made manually. Our romance with information technologies, evidenced by our increasing use of the phrase information resource managers to describe archivists, has hazards enough. It is already clear that we are well on the way to creating electronic systems that do not supply what users want or, far more important, what they will actually use. Richard Lytle, a central figure in archival information technology studies, puts it well:

> Archivists often operate as though they could construct archival access systems without reference to users. Identifying the users and potential users of archives and manuscript collections, and how these users approach the collections, are the most important considerations in constructing a national information system.[1]

---

1 Richard H. Lytle, "A National Information System for Archives and Manuscript Collections," *American Archivist* 43 (Summer 1980): 424.

I would add to that a local system, whether computer generated or manual, in any form, whether the still ubiquitous card catalog or the printed inventory.

That we do not put users first is evidenced by a series of misassumptions on which our administrative system is based. These misassumptions, which inevitably skew our thinking about users, also alienate us from current as well as potential users. This alienation makes the archival profession profoundly vulnerable, not only to budget cuts and immediate administrative punishments, but also to the dangers of antiquarianism. When it is pursued by an individual, antiquarianism can be charming. Pursued by a profession, it is potentially destructive.

Our first misassumption is that, because we like reference work, we are, as a profession, oriented to users. In fact, we have what can most kindly be called adversary relationships with genealogists, one of our largest clienteles, and with other avocationists. That one can do research for fun seems not to fall within our categories of acceptable use; thus we distinguish between the serious researcher and all the others. Yet, as we will see, the others comprise a significant, even major, part of our usership. Similarly, we tend to be cool to the user who is not professionally trained to do research. This category probably includes most of our clientele. We favor the researcher who understands, or at least does not question, our organization of the records; who is willing to do labor-intensive work to uncover the nugget sought; whose experience is such that he or she is able to use our categories of description; and who can spend time browsing, a research activity that is rapidly becoming a luxury for many. It matters very little to this argument whether the researcher is engaged in either academic or applied research, as William Joyce has distinguished between them, though that distinction may have great bearing on how we appraise, organize, and describe records in the future.[2] We favor the researcher who speaks our language; we tend to be less sympathetic to the researcher who doesn't. In neither instance do we appear to make a serious effort to discover how the user arrived at our material, either in the physical or intellectual sense; why he or she asks certain questions; or how the user will integrate the information obtained.

Second is our misassumption that we know who our users are. We want to think that they are historians, or at least scholars, though we know that within at least our public institutions the largest group of

---

2 William L. Joyce, "Archivists and Research Use," *American Archivist* 47 (Spring 1984): 124. Joyce distinguishes between academic and applied research. The first is likely to be "theoretical in nature and proceeds in the manner of an open-ended inquiry." Applied research, on the other hand, is characterized by "a very specific need and a deadline." Trudy Huskamp Peterson makes a similar distinction in conversation, referring to "researchers of the interpretation" and "researchers of the fact." The distinction is less important to this discussion than the fact that both interpretative and factual researchers who are trained historians are likely to approach information differently from those who are not historians.

users, undifferentiated in the statistics we irregularly keep, are avocationists. Otherwise, custodians of public institutions assume that they
work largely with bureaucrats like themselves, or with professionals —
lawyers, social planners, writers, developers, and the like — whose time
is either limited at the outset or, increasingly, monitored by the funding
agencies that pay for their projects. It is time to investigate in detail the
suspicion, held by many of us now, that the bulk of our clientele in
public archives, apart from avocationists, are professional people with
minimal historical training who are interested in information about the
past, that is, retrospective information, but not in history as we understand it. It is even more important to evaluate the clientele of manuscript collections, who are even more frequently assumed to be historians or other scholars but who, in fact, may often be amateur researchers
or researchers seeking information for other professional purposes. In
neither case, however, will these users pursue or integrate the information in records as would trained historians. If this suspicion proves to
be true, its implications are considerable for at least our descriptive and
reference services. It also has broad implications for archival training
programs and outreach services.

Stemming from this misassumption are two others: first, that we
understand how research is done, and, second, that we provide adequate
help in doing it. The last is reflected in litanies touching on the need for
the client to do the secondary reading and our obligation to do only reference, not the client's research. Both, in my view, evade collegial and
didactic responsibilities toward the client.

Of these four misassumptions — that we are oriented to users, that we
know who uses our material, that we understand the research process,
and that we provide practical, even sufficient, help in doing it — three are
worth discussing at length. At the very least we must consider who our
users are and what we have yet to learn about them.

Our information on who our users are is spotty because not much
statistical information appears to be kept, nor is it disseminated when it
is compiled. That is in itself stunning given our frequent references to the
historians/scholars who we say are our users. We can, however, gather
some information by inference. Margaret Steig surveyed 767 historians to
discover their attitudes toward, and use of, periodicals and other library
resources, including manuscripts, microcopies, maps, newspapers, theses,
dissertations, and films and other audiovisual documentation. One-half
of those queried responded. Predictably, books and periodicals were the
most frequently used items, with manuscripts running third. Other formats that we also consider to be primary sources, however, including
films, maps, photographs, microfilms, and computer printouts, ranked
anywhere from seventh to thirteenth place. Even more interesting, those
formats seen by historians as the least convenient to use were the least
used. Books and periodicals, which they viewed as the most convenient

formats, were also the most frequently used.[3] Steig also drew some interesting conclusions about the research habits of historians. They do not
have a "well-developed invisible college as do scientists, but depend primarily upon printed sources of information."[4]

Their research is essentially unsystematic but, more important,
uncritical. They rely as much upon book reviews as upon the books
themselves. They fail to use the abstracts and indexes provided them by
both librarians and archivists and tend to rely upon such bibliographic
sources as the *Reader's Guide to Periodical Literature,* seldom viewed as a
scholarly resource. In one telling comment, Steig noted that

> A number of historians went out of their way to say that they
> never used indexes or abstracts; many considered them irrelevant.
> Only one individual said that his nonuse was probably because
> he never learned how.[5]

Four years earlier, however, Michael Stevens had come to similar conclusions. Commenting on the research habits of 123 American historians
whom he had polled, one-half of whom responded, Stevens found that
historians most frequently use formal methods of learning the where-
abouts of documents and references found in secondary sources. Thus
the *National Union Catalog of Manuscript Collections* and Philip M. Hamer's
Guide to Archives and Manuscripts in the United States, precursor of the present National Historical Publications and Records Commission *Directory of
Archives and Manuscript Repositories,* fall at the bottom of six suggested
ways of finding information. This casts severe doubt on the utility of our
national finding aids. Overwhelmingly, Stevens' respondents reported
that other historians, either in their writing or by word of mouth, were
the principal sources of information.[6]

That creating a good guide is not adequate inducement to heavier
scholarly use is demonstrated by Roy Turnbaugh of the Illinois State
Archives. Hoping to alter their heavy use by genealogists and bureaucrats
to include more use by scholars, the Illinois State Archives produced a
Descriptive Inventory in 1978. The publication was well received among
professionals and was publicized widely. Illinois public, university, and
college libraries purchased 600 copies. Did the rush to scholarly use
begin? It did not, as Turnbaugh noted:

3   Margaret F. Steig, "The Information of [sic] Needs of Historians," *College and Research Libraries* 42 (November 1981): 551.

4   Ibid., 553.

5   Ibid., 554.

6   Michael E. Stevens, "The Historian and Archival Finding Aids," *Georgia Archive* 5 (Winter 1977): 68.

The hope was that shortly after publication, the archives would acquire a growing coterie of scholarly patrons. These expectations have not been realized. The state archives had some scholarly users before the guide appeared and continues to have about the same since it was published.[7]

More provocative is Turnbaugh's next comment. Noting that since 1933, about 30,000 doctorates in history have been awarded in the United States, he says:

Even if the Illinois State Archives received one reference request from each one of these historians, living and dead, in the course of a single year, it would still remain heavily dependent on . . . bureaucrats and genealogists to justify its continued existence.[8]

Based on the impressionistic experience of other archivists in public institutions, we would not be surprised to find that genealogists and bureaucrats appear to be the principal users of archives, with social scientists, publicists, filmmakers, lawyers, public policy planners, and other professionals probably following close behind. Surprising in their implications are the results of an informal survey taken by Arthur Breton, curator of manuscripts for the Archives of American Art. This repository is housed in the Smithsonian Institution and includes personal papers of American artists and craftsmen. Surveying 416 users, Breton found that only 13 percent were academic faculty, while 43 percent were students, including undergraduates. These two groups of academics comprised 56 percent of the clientele. Surprisingly, however, 31 percent — nearly one-third — of the archives' users were private individuals, that is, clients researching their own art holdings, doing genealogy, or simply looking. When Breton broke down the purposes of research into categories defined by the clients themselves, he found that half of the work being done was toward a book, article, coursework, or dissertation. Even in this esoteric collection, whose resources might have been thought to be the special province of scholars, 17 percent of the use of the material was toward such professional activities as filmmaking, development of catalogs, or exhibition production. Even more surprising, 27 percent of the use was personal: aimed at seeking information about personal art holdings, in pursuit of genealogy, or done out of curiosity.[9] In addition, using information contained in 190 interlibrary loan forms, Breton found

---

7   Roy Turnbaugh, "Living with a Guide," *American Archivist* 46 (Fall 1983): 451.

8   Ibid.

9   Arthur Breton compiled these figures from user statistics between January 1980 and November 1982. They are available from him at the Archives of American Art, Smithsonian Institution, Washington, DC 20560.

that nearly 30 percent of the archives' users were in disciplines other than art history, art, or fine arts. These included not only the humane studies but sociology, political science, medicine, kinesiology, architecture, film, education, and museology.[10]

From this scattered information, a number of conclusions seem inevitable. One is that historians are neither our principal nor our most significant users. Even with the little information we now have, we know this intuitively; it is the prejudice we find hard to let go. It follows from this that, if historians are not our principal users, we need not produce the elaborate bibliographic tools that they ask of us, particularly since the evidence is clear that they do not use such tools when they are produced. It is equally clear that, in spite of the difficulties inherent in working with records, we have a varied and astonishing number of users — some academic, others professional, still others simply avocational — who hold the promise of still more and varied categories of users. We owe them simplicity, elegance, and welcome.

In contrasting academic librarians with urban public librarians and special librarians, Margaret Steig made a comment that has meaning for archivists:

> What urban public and special librarians have in common is aggressiveness. Neither waits for the patron to come to the library. . . . They place a greater emphasis on finding out what the patron thinks he needs (and providing it) *regardless of library traditions* than do academic librarians. Both attach great importance to providing the information in the format most convenient to the user.[11]

It follows from Steig that archivists, whom I would equate with academic librarians, have a great deal to learn from urban public and special librarians. It is very likely, for example, that for all users, convenience of use is the issue, a fact on which we must reflect before we undertake one more traditional or computer-generated index, inventory, or guide. The model of Steig's study itself is perhaps most immediate. She seeks to know with accuracy and intentionality not only what users claim to want but what they actually do, how they think, and, most important, who they are. (In research as in life, want and need are separable categories.) Seeking this information of all users of archives should be first on our research agenda, not only as a profession but as archivists within our own institutions. Our failure to gather this information and apply it gives

---

10 Breton's conclusions are based on figures compiled in 1979-80 and are also available at the address given in note 9.

11 Steig, "The Information of [*sic*] Needs of Historians," 559. Italics added for emphasis.

credence to our prejudices, which, in turn, govern our practice. The National Archives, for example, has not done a study of its users since 1976. That study was informally done, and the information in it was taken entirely from registration information whose categories were defined by archivists and from interviews with archivists, not users. In one collection, well known to many of us, 30 percent of the users were characterized as "other." When no precedent exists for characterizing users more specifically, there is little wonder that one out of three users is relegated to such a meaningless category.

The fact is that we have never examined systematically who our users are, either on a national, regional, or institutional basis. Those unexamined users are undoubtedly changing. There is an unstudied "other" to whom we must address ourselves lest they forget what we know, that history has a method and that history counts. We can learn what questions to ask from other professional communities who have studied their clienteles and from the archival community, in which a few studies have been made. As a member of the Joint Committee on the Archives of Science and Technology, Helen Slotkin, archivist at the Massachusetts Institute of Technology, is interviewing users and prospective users of archives. She finds that they comprise a wider and more diverse group than we have ever supposed. Historians of science, it is worth noting, make up only a small portion of the users.

Whether we provide adequate help in doing research, either in print or during the reference process, and whether we understand the nature of research are open questions. They are certainly related questions. Mary Jo Pugh noted some of the assumptions that archivists make about the reference process, with particular reference to subject retrieval. Among them, she says, is that of continuous interaction between user and archivist, which, while requiring the user to have knowledge extrinsic to the records, nevertheless renders him or her dependent on the archivist. Another is that the user wants "high recall and does not care if he gets low precision."[12] In other words, according to the archivist, time and efficiency are not objects in the stately realms of research. Noting that standard reference practice is inadequate to user needs, that arrangement and description procedures in archival repositories fail to focus on user needs, and that archivists have not sought to analyze "the elements which comprise a successful reference interview and have not studied the process of question negotiation in the archival setting," Pugh pleads for more discriminating, intellectually involving description:

> Analysis of both provenance and content can and should be part of our daily work. Archivists tend to be too passive and

---

12   Mary Jo Pugh, "The Illusion of Omniscience: Subject Access and the Reference Archivist," *American Archivist* 45 (Winter 1982): 38.

bureaucratic when writing inventories and registers. Inventories, which should be the major intellectual accomplishment of our profession, are too often merely lists of container and file headings. . . . Preparing a sensitive, perceptive, provocative essay on the strengths and weaknesses of records for research use is difficult. It requires historical knowledge, imagination, and the ability to write clear prose. It is also difficult to assess records for current research interests and to anticipate other uses of the records. But if we are unable to assess and analyze the records, why are we saving them?[13]

To Pugh's plea for intellectual rigor in description, add imagination, appropriateness of format, and convenience of use. What we are pleased to call finding aids are at best intramural communications written by one archivist to be read by another, not by a user. Writing in the language of administration, authors of these documents address neither the expressed needs of the user nor the historical context of the records themselves. Authors of most finding aids assume an exquisite knowledge of chronology and context that the specialized nature of most research and the want of historical training of many users must belie, and they assume unlimited leisure on the user's part. Most finding aids are very difficult to locate.[14] When I was an undergraduate, it was a popular trick to put a penny under the bed to see if the cleaning staff would find it. Later, realizing the limitations of our vision, we raised the ante to a silver dollar. Even so, the prize lay under the bed from one semester to the next. The principle is simple: if it is not worth sweeping under the bed at the outset, one will not bother to do it. If our procedures do not encourage sweeping, how do we expect the silver dollars to be found?

The larger question of how we know what we know must be approached warily, particularly when one senses that the question is related to our assumptions about the acquisition and appraisal of records. Archivists want to think that, in documenting the life of an institution, they lend the institution a kind of paper immortality: Cerberus, guarding the metaphysical gates of the individual, the family, the corporation, or the organization. Two problems arise here. The first is that we may be

---

13 Ibid., 42.

14 On the basis of 441 microfilm requests for Archives of American Art materials, Arthur Breton has concluded that 37 percent of the respondents learned about the institution's holdings from reading a checklist, compiled by the curator of manuscripts, which had been widely distributed and was for sale for $6. Many respondents had bought a copy and keep it permanently on their desks, a testimony to the principle of convenience. The remainder of the respondents had learned about the archives' material from five other sources, ranging from conversations with colleagues to a published directory of sources. None mentioned any of the major national finding aids even though entries for the Archives of American Art have appeared in NUCMC since 1959.

confusing the wider and wider accumulation of records with research vitality, just as some mistakenly assume that a great number of articles published equals a healthy, critical profession. The second is one of epistemology. Records are not artifactual in the sense that they have the shape or physical properties of objects. They are not houses built of paper nor the jewels of the Medici, valuable in themselves as objects whether or not they are used. Records are inert until they are acted upon by the human mind. It can be argued that, like George Berkeley's tree falling in the forest, records do not exist until they are used.

Similarly, institutions do not exist, once they have disappeared in time, until they are re-created by the human mind. Research has characteristics that render incorrect our single-focused view that we, as archivists, are solely responsible for the lives of institutions and individuals as those lives appear in the records created around them, as if that re-creation were somehow a process inherent only in the records. Among these characteristics, we find that the researcher, whatever his or her training, is able to read only one document at a time and that, after each reading, the question may change. We find that in research, each step decides the next, and that no two inquiries, however similarly worded, are the same. If we also allow that our usership is, both in reality and potentially, very much broader than the small community of history professionals we now think of as our clientele, it follows that questions about how and by whom records are used take on considerably greater magnitude than we have heretofore given them. At the very least, the so-called universe of documentation is peopled; and, until we know the learning and thinking characteristics of those people, we acquire and appraise in a dangerous vacuum. Certainly a look at how and why users approach records will give us new criteria for appraising records. Interestingly, the Slotkin study is intended to establish appraisal criteria. Presumably Slotkin will develop recommendations for the appraisal of records in the sciences different from those we now have, since she is discovering users different from those we supposed we had. It is also worth noting that the task force recently created in the National Archives to examine appraisal and disposition has included in its study plan an extensive list of questions relating to use and users.

How, then, do we turn our own psychological and professional tables? How do we make users, rather than the records or their manipulation, the focus of our daily activity? We do so by developing at the national, regional, and institutional level an agenda that affects our professional meetings, our training programs, and our concepts of archives administration. Most important, this agenda will affect the choice we make as we walk into the office in the morning to make papers or people our first priority.

First, we must make a statistically sound examination of who we are serving, who our potential users are, and how they approach the material they use. The Society of American Archivists, for example, should seek funding to work with one or more regional organizations to study the information needs and methods of the users of representative institutions, compiling not only statistical but also anecdotal information about them, the material they use and to what purpose, how they approach the material, and how these approaches compare among disciplines. Models exist in the library profession and, as we have seen, in our own. Seeking information not only about users but directly from them, using their categories to describe their work, noting the product of their research as well as its subject matter, and acquiring narrative as well as numerical information should become part of the daily work plan of every institution. This is unlikely to happen until the concept has been vested at a high level. Such a survey is also possible on a regional level under the aegis of a regional organization.

In our local repositories, we can begin seeking information rather than only dispensing it. In addition to formal statistical surveys of usership, let me suggest one or two other means of learning about our clientele. The entrance interview, for example, is standard procedure and allows us to give information. Not so typical is the exit interview, in which the archivist seeks information about the client's approaches to the records, the success or failure of these approaches, and the ways in which the client's questions have changed. Conducted carefully, with consistently asked questions, accurately recorded answers, and meticulous attention to the client's language and content, these interviews can be invaluable in building a body of information we now lack.

Another variation on an old theme is the work group or conference, in which the archivist seeks information from the client rather than delivering it. Such exchanges need not be entirely in one direction, but the focus of the archivist should change from that of preceptor to student. Inevitably, in the best adult learning exchanges, all participants will both teach and learn. In such a work group, the archivist gathers a small group of users who may represent either a present or a potential community of users, then seeks specific information from them. How, for example, did they hear about the repository? What reference aids have they used? What are the research trends in their field? What are the time or budgetary constraints upon them? Who are their leaders and change agents? If, for example, these clients are faculty members, the archivist might ask what curricular or enrollment changes they foresee or what changes seem likely in research, employment, or other trends in their field. I have never run such a meeting; but I know, as a fact, that people like to talk about their work to someone clearly interested in it.

Once we accept the concept that we must reach out to clients for information about their work and find them where they are, ideas for doing so emerge readily. Just as doctors are once again making house calls and lawyers are advertising, archivists must move beyond the limited circles of the *National Union Catalog of Manuscript Collections* and national or regional historical journals to make their materials known. If the archivist's clientele occasionally includes a staff member for a local politician, for example, he or she would do well to be in touch with the offices of other political figures both before and after campaigns. If the city planning commission is preparing a study, the city archivist can remind its members that he or she is there to help them review where they have come from, with a view to their knowing where they are going. If a department in the local university is planning a curriculum review, the university archivist with appropriate records might well consider offering not only material for research papers — this is easily ignored — but the ingredients for a curriculum base. The principle is a simple one: uncover a need and then fill it conveniently.

In seeking to learn about the intellectual and working needs of our clientele and then filling those needs, we can profit from asking ourselves the questions that archivists in public programs regularly ask. These questions would illuminate all our administrative practices, not only those that result in conferences, workshops, exhibitions, or educational materials. These questions include: What is the mandate of my institution? How are the publics we serve comprised? Of these publics, on which should we focus our resources and for what reasons? Who are the members of that community, and what, specifically, do they need from an archives? How can we ascertain that need? Does that need take the form of research, publication, or program assistance? From which of these kinds of assistance can we get a maximum return on our archival resources? Do we define "maximum" in terms of numbers, short-term effect, or dollars? How can we best deliver these programs? How do we evaluate our efforts?

Our second requirement is to find ways to turn information out more quickly, imaginatively, and appropriately. Mary Jo Pugh's observations are useful here, suggesting as they do that we still expect users to spend enormous amounts of time panning for gold when their work schedule, in fact, requires a quick strike. We force them to work on our terms, not theirs. Let me offer a few observations about reference service and the creation of finding aids. First, not all users need traditional one-archivist-to-one-researcher reference service, which is the most expensive kind we offer. All users need equal access; they do not all need equal time or the same method of access. Second, it is possible to build a certain amount of cost return into some kinds of reference service. Third, there is more than one way to write a finding aid; every one should be literate, understandable to the clients, available easily outside the archives (preferably at low cost), and aimed at freeing the user from dependence upon the archivist. In short, finding aids should focus on the convenience of the user, not the archivist.

If, for example, we are dealing with a clientele, such as genealogists, family historians, legal researchers, or claimants, that seeks name identification, let that clientele pay to support the development of appropriate databases by private firms. Such support is certainly available in these communities, and industry has the technology. Or, as David Bearman suggests, let a commercial firm answer such questions for a price levied upon the user.[15] The Dutch genealogical society works with the national archives of the Netherlands as a self-supporting company providing just such a service for profit. If our clients are commercial publishers, let them build the cost of specialized reference service into the cost of publications. Most publishers already hire researchers who are not as efficient as archivists. We might, for example, hire archivists with an education background to search records for educational publishers or archivists with art backgrounds to provide illustrations. The reference needs of the educational community constitute another separable category that is a natural milieu for us. Production of educational material for growth industries in education — community college courses or occupational training programs, for example — is only one possibility. If, on the other hand, we deal with a clientele who would willingly use records if somehow our reference points resembled theirs, perhaps we should modify our finding aids. To do so, we may have to learn new languages. Is it not possible, for example, to write checklists aimed at users in specific disciplines from traditional finding aids or to provide précis of collections that point out their uses beyond the traditional historical ones? Staff representatives of other disciplines might well provide this information to their members as a service with help and cooperation from us. We might also begin to write descriptions of research procedures that will aid the large number of users with little or no training in, or complex knowledge of history, or with little experience in searching records. At the very simplest level, we can show drafts of new finding aids to the people we expect to use them and solicit their comments as editorial advice.

Regional and national possibilities suggest themselves. The Mid-Atlantic Regional Archives Conference has recently established a prize for the year's best finding aid. Criteria considered include readability, design, breadth of historical context, and availability.[16] The Society of American Archivists might consider establishing an award for the institution that is particularly active and innovative each year in reaching new audiences, in accommodating the needs of established audiences, or in finding imaginative and administratively sound ways to place the needs of users first on its list of institutional priorities.

Without a doubt, viewing our work as centered on our clients rather than on records would change significantly the way we appraise records, describe and publicize them, and provide reference service; but in no area would our revised view be so evident as in the training of archivists. At present, training is focused on the management of records, not on the

---

15 David Bearman, "The National Archives and Records Service: Policy Choices for the Next Five Years," paper delivered at the National Archives Assembly, Washington, D.C., 15 December 1981.

16 Criteria for this award are available from Jacqueline Goggin, Library of Congress, who chairs this committee.

needs of users. Archival trainees learn to appraise records with little serious consideration of their use; to organize and describe records according
to traditional rules that have little or no bearing on the ways in which
these records are actually used or by whom; and to provide reference
service to a public perceived monolithically. Toward the end of the typical training course, the trainee hears a lecture on public programs, in
which a smorgasbord of conferences, exhibits, workshops, and publications is described. The archivist can choose which ones to produce, but
nowhere is he or she given any indication of their apparent relation,
either to each other or to other administrative functions in the archives.
What would happen to this potpourri if we were to change our focus
from the administration of the records to the requirements of users?
What might such a training course include?

High in the syllabus would be a series of sessions designed to teach the
trainee a range of techniques for surveying use and users: how to discover
who one's clientele is and can be; how to seek information; how to structure an administrative program with users in mind. Second, such a course
would consider the problem of records processing in terms of alternatives,
keeping in mind, for example, that original order is not always useful to
users. Archivists would become accustomed to processing at different levels
within a collection and among collections as well as to making processing
decisions based on information about use rather than on questions of uniformity. Both the assumptions and the implications of provenance should
be examined at every turn. Appraisal standards and techniques would be
examined and reordered in the light of information from a wide variety of
users, including not only scholars, but professionals and avocationists.
Sessions on the reference process would be based on observation and
analysis of successful and unsuccessful reference interviews and would
emphasize techniques for gathering and integrating information, asking
and hearing questions, and developing sound research strategies with
the client. The trainee would move through a series of increasingly sophisticated reference negotiations. Both trainees and clients would participate in
reviews of the process. Description of records would focus first on the writing of literate, historically enlightening finding aids and then on the adaptation of this information to a variety of forms geared to various research
and educational uses. Ideally, planning for these descriptions would be
done by both trainee and user. At the least, any descriptions written by a
trainee would be reviewed by a user, then revised appropriately. Such an
exercise could not help but be a fascinating project in group interaction,
learning, and application. Public programs, often omitted entirely from
our training programs, would be integral to a revised course and would
focus on the administration of outreach and educational events. The
trainee would be required to weigh resources and choices in the light of
community needs, staff resources, and institutional objectives. Negotiation
and planning with the community as well as with archives staff would be

essential in this kind of instruction. Sessions on planning, budget, and general administration would include consideration of ways to alter traditional priorities in the archives so as to create the time and resources necessary to learn about the users; to ascertain the cost of greater and different service to users, particularly in archives whose holdings are increasingly machine generated, and where, therefore, the cost of service increases; and to analyze staff talents and resources in terms of a changed administrative focus. At no time in this training process would the archivist be isolated from the user as is uniformly the case in current archival training programs. Staff for such a course would include not only archivists but users, social scientists, and educators, the last of whom would teach skills for information gathering and negotiation. I recommend that the Society of American Archivists join with interested educators in the profession to seek funding soon to plan and present an experimental course of this kind.

As an alternative and more immediate start, the society might organize a series of workshops on reference and the administration of public programs based on the three excellent manuals it has published on these subjects. The principal objectives of these workshops would be to provide trainees with techniques for ascertaining what users need and supplying those needs. The society has thus far been reluctant to offer these specialized workshops, on the ground that archivists have not asked for them. Given archivists' attitudes toward users and their present priorities, it is unlikely that we will clamor for such training until society leadership understands the need for it and makes it available. Like a close examination of usership, training that changes our attitudes and priorities must be vested at a high level.

I am aware that the recommendations I make would change long-established relationships, control, and patterns of authority, not only between archivist and user but also among archivists. In short, they are unsettling; but they are worth beginning at home and supporting nationally. It is helpful to remind ourselves that in this nation a sense of the value of history does exist, often only for its personal and recreational uses but also for its use in shaping our sense of what constitutes the common good. That sense often lapses into nostalgia and can be dangerous, particularly when it is used to shape public policy. As the sources of history stir us, they stir the public, whether professional or avocational. Not only are archivists the custodians of these sources, but in a curious way we have become custodians of the process of history itself. That process is irresistible; and communicating and sharing it should be all the more possible in a society that believes that history has public value. It is possible for us to transmit daily our vision of the past and how that past is known: its rigor, its unrelentingness, its usability. To do so, we must know to whom we are delivering that vision and how it will be perceived. It is none too soon to begin actively reflecting upon how to do that and then placing our resources where those reflections lead us.

19

Facts and Frameworks: An Approach to Studying the Users of Archives

PAUL CONWAY

Abstract: *The continuing reluctance of the archival profession to develop a better understanding of users seems less a problem of will than a problem of method. The framework presented here is a first attempt to structure a comprehensive program of user studies. Built on definitions of users, information needs, and use, the framework combines the basic elements of information that should be recorded, analyzed, and shared among archivists with a scheme to gather this information. The author illustrates how parts of the framework can be implemented as an ongoing program through the use of a reference log and suggests applications of the framework at the personal, repository, and professional levels.*

> Science is built up with facts as a house is with stones. But a collection of facts is no more a science than a heap of stones is a house.
> Henri Poincaré, *Science and Hypothesis*

Frameworks are the structures that organize the "heap of stones" that is the world around us.[1] Varied in form and content, frameworks are simplifications of reality — ways of reducing complexities to a set of meaningful, manageable ideas. Their great use is to summarize old facts and lead to new ones. Central to the best frameworks is the possibility of action derived from practical and useful rules. As such they are interim steps on the way to a developed theory. Archivists can use analytical frameworks to understand complex issues in systematic ways and to share the knowledge gained in the process.[2]

Reprinted with permission from the *American Archivist* 49 (Fall 1986): 393-407. This article was written as a product of the author's participation in the 1985 Research Fellowship Program for Study of Modern Archives administered by the Bentley Historical Library, University of Michigan, and funded by the Andrew W. Mellon Foundation and the Earhart Foundation of Ann Arbor.

1 Henri Poincaré, *The Foundations of Science: Science and Hypothesis, The Value of Science, Science and Method*, trans. George Bruce Halsted (Lancaster, Pa.: Science Press, 1946), 127.

2 Charles Nordmann, "Henri Poincaré: His Scientific Work; His Philosophy," *Annual Report of the Board of Regents of The Smithsonian Institution* (Washington, D.C.: U.S. Government Printing Office, 1912), 741-63.

The framework for studying the users of archives presented here is a first attempt to structure a comprehensive, profession-wide program of user studies. Built on definitions of users, information needs, and use, the framework describes the basic elements of information that should be recorded, analyzed, and shared among archivists to assess programs and services. In addition, the framework illustrates a scheme to gather information on groups of users over time that takes advantage of accepted reference practices already in place in many repositories. The framework should be widely useful because it is not rooted in specific institutional procedures. If tested and applied, the framework has the potential to help archivists compare and assess the results of individual studies.

In recent years archivists have described why we need a more systematic approach to understanding users. Elsie Freeman Finch, Mary Jo Pugh, William Joyce, Bruce Dearstyne, and William Maher especially have been in the forefront urging the archival profession to develop a greater balance between archival materials and those who use them.[3] They argue that recognizing and responding to the information needs of users is central to the wider use of historical information in contemporary problem solving, central to the proper documentation of society, and central to the viability of a profession faced with rapid technological change. "Use of archival records is the ultimate purpose of identification and administration," declares the final report of the Society of American Archivists' Task Force on Goals and Priorities. Archivists are beginning to consider high-quality research on users an essential means toward this goal.[4]

Archivists are less sure about *how* to design useful user studies, especially who and what should be studied, when and where user studies should be conducted, and how to gather information systematically. Freeman, Pugh, and others have suggested that archivists make better use of orientation and exit interviews to query researchers.[5] But archivists have yet to develop a comprehensive approach that links the basic objectives of a user study program and a practical way for gathering and

---

3 Elsie T. Freeman Finch, "In the Eye of the Beholder: Archives Administration from the Users Point of View," *American Archivist* 47 (Spring 1984): 111-23; Mary Jo Pugh, "The Illusion of Omniscience: Subject Access and the Reference Archivist," *American Archivist* 45 (Winter 1982): 33-40; William L. Joyce, "Archivists and Research Use," *American Archivist* 47 (Spring 1984): 124-33; Bruce W. Dearstyne, "The Impact of Research in Archives," paper presented at the annual meeting of the Society of American Archivists, Washington, D.C., September 1984; William J. Maher, "The Use of User Studies," *Midwestern Archivist* 11, no. 1 (1986): 15-26.

4 *Planning for the Archival Profession: A Report of the SAA Task Force on Goals and Priorities* (Chicago: Society of American Archivists, 1986), 22. See also Karen Benedict, "Invitation to a Bonfire," *American Archivist* 47 (Winter 1984): 48; Maynard J. Brichford, *Archives and Manuscripts: Appraisal and Accessioning* (Chicago: Society of American Archivists, 1977): 9; Nancy Sahli, "National Information Systems and Strategies for Research Use," *Midwestern Archivist* 9, no. 1 (1984): 10-12.

5 Freeman, "Eye of the Beholder," 119; Pugh, "Illusion of Omniscience," 39; Carl M. Brauer, "Researcher Evaluation of Reference Services," *American Archivist* 43 (Winter 1980): 79.

recording valid, reliable information from users. In short, archivists' continuing reluctance to develop a better understanding of users seems not so much to be a problem of will as a problem of method.

Archivists are not alone in their concern that user studies be useful analytical tools. For initial guidance on building a comprehensive framework, they might turn to the perceptive literature describing and criticizing the many studies of library patrons. A 30-year tradition of research on national, regional, state, and local levels and in public, university, and special libraries has produced a backlog of over 1,000 studies.[6] Their topics run the gamut from in-house use of library materials and circulation patterns, to characteristics of users and nonusers, to the assessment of programs and services.[7] In general they have tended to describe programs in particular libraries, rather than take a multi-institutional approach. When they have focused on users in broader terms, library user studies often have described behavior of individuals rather than of groups.[8] Finally, library user studies have not shown how information gathered in the study process can be applied to designing and assessing programs for users beyond the clientele being studied.[9] Individually, library user studies are not very useful for archivists.

By considering them as a group, however, several perceptive critics of library user studies in the United States and the United Kingdom — including Geoffrey Ford, John Brittain, Colin Mick, and others — have identified patterns of findings. Some of the concepts underlying these patterns may be useful for archivists because, removed from their particular library settings and stripped of their specific library procedures, user studies have identified some of the components of the process of information transfer. This fundamental form of communication is the point of departure for building user-oriented services in both libraries and archives.[10] In an archives, information transfer occurs in many different ways, but most typically when a researcher with a specific information need interacts with archivists and finding aids and in the process acquires archival information of use in meeting some part of the need. For archivists, the three important parts of this equation are users, information need, and use.

6 Susan Crawford, "Information Needs and Uses," *Annual Review of Information Science and Technology* 13 (1978): 61-82.

7 Ronald Powell, "The Utilization of User Studies in the Development of Performance Measures," unpublished paper, University of Michigan School of Library Science, 1984, 2-13.

8 Colin Mick, Georg N. Lindsey, and Daniel Callahan, "Toward Usable User Studies," *Journal of the American Society for Information Science* 31 (1980): 347.

9 Geoffrey Ford, ed., *User Studies: An Introductory Guide and Select Bibliography* (Sheffield, U.K.: Centre for Research on User Studies, 1977), 70.

10 Ford, *User Studies*, 7-17; Mick, "Toward Usable User Studies," 347-56; John M. Brittain, *Information and Its Users* (Bath, U.K.: Bath University Press, 1970).

Users, in the most elementary sense, are people who seek information in archival materials. They may be researchers who visit repositories or who use items obtained from archives. Archivists are users when they extract information from a body of files and organize it in a finding aid, reference letter, or exhibition. More fundamentally, users are also people who may never visit an archives but utilize archival information indirectly, for example, as partners or clients in a law firm, students in a classroom, viewers of a documentary film, or editors of a newspaper. Users of archives are, therefore, all beneficiaries of historical information.

By this definition, it is unlikely there are many nonusers of archives. Critics of library user studies have described ways to think about grouping users into meaningful categories. Nearly all agree that researchers rarely act in isolation, but rather as members of networks with a variety of informal and formal ways of sharing information. Library studies have also shown that the functional nature of the groups to which the user belongs has a much greater impact than individual personal or professional characteristics on how that person perceives a need for information and goes about satisfying it.[11] In other words, the fact that a lawyer visited an archives on behalf of a client is more useful to know than either the specific name of the law firm or the lawyer's race, sex, or age.

Archivists should regularly question researchers who visit archives. The primary purpose of this questioning, however, is to identify the most immediate groups of beneficiaries of archival information and begin to understand the process of information transfer within and beyond the archives.

An *information need* is simply a question for which archival information may provide all or part of the answer. The concept is far easier to define than to explain. Geoffrey Ford has suggested that the purposes for which individuals seek particular forms of information are largely determined by their roles along a work/leisure continuum. Colin Mick has further refined this concept to distinguish between applicational needs (e.g., a specific document) and more abstract nutritional needs that increase general knowledge or competence.[12] An important goal of a broad user-study program is to contribute to a better understanding of the factors determining information needs that can be influenced by archival programs and services. Archivists need to know how individuals define particular information needs and why they seek their answers in archives.

Use of archival materials is comprised of two distinct activities. Use occurs in a physical sense in reference rooms when researchers scan collections, series, folders, or individual items in search of information relevant

---

11 William J. Paisley, "Information Needs and Uses," *Annual Review of Information Science and Technology* 3 (1968): 1-31; Ford, *User Studies,* 18-37.

12 Ford, *User Studies,* 38-44; Colin Mick, "Human Factors in Information Work," *Proceedings of the American Society for Information Science* 17 (1980): 21-23.

to their needs. This form of use is most frequently documented in annual or quarterly administrative reports. For example, X number of researchers made Y number of daily visits and in doing so consulted Z number of collections, series, or items. Archivists need to evaluate systematically such use not simply for basic reporting purposes but also to assess the impact of physical use on archival materials and to evaluate alternatives to physical use.

A second kind of use is more difficult to explain but as important to document — usefulness, or the use made of archival information to benefit individuals, groups, or society as a whole.[13] The impact of use beyond the repository is not documented through the ubiquitous lists of important research visitors and their important projects, but through a careful analysis of the dissemination of historical information within a wide variety of written and oral contexts. By identifying systematically both the physical use of archival materials and the impact of archival information beyond a single repository, archivists can better evaluate and plan archival programs and more clearly realize the value of the services they provide.

Elements of the Framework

Based on these working definitions of users, information needs, and use, the framework presented in Figure 1 depicts what archivists could learn from a comprehensive program of user studies and how they could build such a program. As a whole the framework is an alternative to the common view of reference service as one segment in a linear progression of processes for handling archival materials. From this perspective appraisal, acquisition, processing, description, reference, and outreach activities each flow one after the other and set the bounds for each successive process. Archival manuals breaking the sequence into its component parts reflect the conventional approach, as do archival management decisions that establish functional specializations.[14] At best, information on the needs of users is factored in if and when it is available.

The framework's structure presupposes that service to users is the foundation of archival programs, regardless of the administrative structure of an institution and regardless of how archivists choose to organize their work.[15] It envisions a reference program as both a direct service for researchers and a central evaluative mechanism for the repository. Information gathered in user studies provides essential raw data to help

---

13 Dearstyne, "The Impact of Research in Archives," 2.

14 Kenneth W. Duckett, *Modern Manuscripts: A Practical Manual for Their Management, Care and Use* (Nashville: American Association for State and Local History, 1975). See also SAA's Basic Manual Series 1, published in 1977.

15 Frank G. Burke, "Archival Cooperation," *American Archivist* 46 (Summer 1983): 295.

METHODOLOGY

OBJECTIVES	Stage 1 Registration (all users/always)	Stage 2 Orientation (all users at selected times)	Stage 3 Follow-Up (sample users/selected times)	Stage 4 Survey (random sample)	Stage 5 Experiments (special groups)
Quality	Nature of Task • definition in terms of subject, format, scope	Preparation of Researcher • experience • stage of defined problem • basic/applied Anticipated Service	Search Strategies and Mechanics • search order • pos/neg search • who recommended • time spent searching • time spent talking	Expectations and Satisfaction • styles of research • approaches to searching • levels of service	Access and Nonuse • frustration indexes • perceptions of use
Integrity	Identification • names • address • telephone Agree to Rules	Knowledge of Holdings and Services • written sources • verbal sources	Intensity and Frequency of Use • collections used • time spent with files	Alternative to Physical Use • value and use of microforms • value and use of databases	Format Independence • linkages with information creation • technology and information
Value	Membership in Networks • group affiliation Can We Contact You? Can We Tell Others?	Intended Use • purposes in terms of function and product	Significant Use Significant Info • importance of archives • other sources • valuable information • gaps in information	Impact of Use • increased use • citation patterns • decision making	Role of Historical Information in Society • total potential demand • community network analysis

Figure 1. Framework for Studying the Users of Archives

administrators evaluate reference programs, descriptive practices, outreach activities designed to increase use, processing priorities, and a
myriad of other programs traditionally considered beyond the domain of
the reference room. Information from users combined with the substantive knowledge that archivists acquire from archival materials are the two
keys to understanding fully these programs.

The framework's structure also emphasizes that archival program
objectives cannot be evaluated solely by researchers who visit. Past
researchers, potential users, and even the broad extra-institutional community served by an archives must sometimes be queried to gain a full
understanding of such complex issues. While the framework identifies
the basic elements of an ongoing user-study program, it is not a script for
directing the program itself or reference service activities in general.
Instead it enhances the traditional, passive custodial role of archivists by
helping them become active gatherers and consumers of information
about the services and programs they provide.

The core of the framework describes three complex objectives summarized by the words *Quality, Integrity,* and *Value.* Expressed as simple
questions, Quality is "How good are the services?"; Integrity is "How
good is the protection of archival information?"; and Value is "What
good do the services do?" Quality and Value may be considered more
meaningful substitutions for the information science jargon "effectiveness" and "benefit."[16] Integrity is derived from the essential responsibility
of archivists to preserve the integrity of archival materials.

The choice of terms with a certain fuzziness of meaning is intentional
for several reasons. First, there are no specific archival terms equivalent to
the three objectives. The intuitive nature of the words indicates that they
mean both something simple and something complex. Indeed, the
notion that an important problem may have layers of understanding is
fundamental to implementing the framework. Each objective consists of
five gradations, and information gathered in each stage clarifies the questions to be asked in each successive stage. In addition, such nontechnical
words have meaning simply because all of the concepts are not totally
measurable. The framework assumes that quantitative measures and qualitative assessments together provide a complete description of the issue. It
recognizes that the subjective judgments of archivists are valid assessment tools if checked against objective measures wherever possible.[17]

In the framework, the Quality of archival programs and services is
assessed in terms of how well archivists understand the information
needs of their users and how well the programs and services are able to

---

16   See R. H. Orr, "Measuring the Goodness of Library Services: A General Framework for
       Considering Quantitative Measures," *Journal of Documentation* 29 (1973): 315-32.

17   Ibid., 317-18.

meet those needs they are intended to serve. At the most basic stage, Quality involves understanding how researchers define their task in terms of the subject, format, and scope of information needed. At more complex levels, Quality involves understanding research capabilities and expectations for service (Stage 2); research strategies and problem-solving methods (Stage 3); and the nature and degree of satisfaction with the research process (Stage 4). Ultimately, one objective of archival programs and services is to recognize how users actually or potentially approach archival information, including why archives are not used, and to take every possible measure to enhance access to useful information (Stage 5).

In the framework, the Integrity of archival programs and services is assessed in terms of how well archivists balance their responsibilities to enhance use while preserving the information in archival materials. At the most basic stage, Integrity involves identifying researchers as a first step toward limiting theft and abuse of materials.[18] At more complex levels, Integrity expands to include how researchers become aware of available information (Stage 2); assessments of the impact of physical use on the preservation of materials (Stage 3); and assessments of the value of alternatives to physical use, including microforms and computerized databases (Stage 4). Ultimately another objective of archival programs and services is to understand and take action to assure that the information in archival materials is preserved and made available regardless of the format in which it is located (Stage 5).

In the framework, the Value of archival services and programs is assessed in terms of the effects of use on individuals, groups, and society as a whole. At the most basic stage, Value simply involves understanding the extent to which individual researchers are a part of groups with similar interests and activities. At more complex levels, Value expands to include understanding the intended uses of archival information (Stage 2); the relationship of archival information to other sources of information (Stage 3); and the impact of use beyond the repository (Stage 4). Ultimately, another objective of archival programs and services is to understand and increase the role of historical information in contemporary society.

Beyond identifying and describing three primary objectives of archival programs and services, the framework includes a scheme for gathering assessment information from users. The methodology combines two assumptions. First, archivists can gather information within a continuum of standard reference services, but at the most complex levels of understanding, rigorous surveys and even controlled experiments are needed. Second, archivists can benefit by understanding and using basic survey research techniques to limit the total population studied while increasing the reliability and validity of the findings.

---

18 Nancy Lankford, "Ethics and the Reference Archivist," *Midwestern Archivist* 7, no. 1 (1983): 7-13.

Sue Holbert has described researcher registration, orientation interviews, and exit interviews as standard elements of the reference continuum.[19] Robert Tissing and Carl A. Brauer, among others, have suggested how archivists can make special use of orientation and exit interviews to gather information.[20] The valuable opportunities of exit interviews often are lost through well-meaning procrastination on the part of reference archivists or unceremonious departures by researchers. As a partial solution, archivists could banish the term "exit interview" from their vocabularies and substitute instead "follow-up discussions." Less formal and more fluid than interviews, follow-up conversations may begin anytime after a researcher has settled into the research room.

In the framework, five increasingly more sophisticated research methods parallel the stages of the three objectives of Quality, Integrity, Value. Just as information from each stage of an objective serves as a base for the succeeding stage, the research methods at each stage help define or narrow the sample population of users studied at succeeding stages. To sample users effectively archivists must build a base of information about the universe of actual researchers.[21] Stage 1, Registration, may be the best place to accomplish this task. Registration forms can help ensure essential security and gather information on research problems and the circumstances of use. Archival repositories should always require every researcher to complete a registration form.

Stage 2, Orientation, and Stage 3, Follow-Up, allow archivists to select a specific time period during which to study researchers or to further limit the population by selecting a specific group of researchers for special emphasis. In both stages, the reference room serves as the principal location of user studies. Stage 4, Survey, and Stage 5, Experiments, recognize that the most complex aspects of a research problem are not necessarily best understood through routine repository procedures. Instead, sophisticated surveys of randomly sampled populations and controlled experiments with groups selected by a variety of criteria may be more appropriate. The last two methodological stages need not be confined to researchers who actually visit archives, but may tap a broader base of users. At all stages of the framework, archivists should choose the populations and method most appropriate to the problem being studied.

---

19 Sue E. Holbert, *Archives and Manuscripts: Reference and Access* (Chicago: Society of American Archivists, 1977), 12-13.

20 Robert W. Tissing, "The Orientation Interview in Archival Research," *American Archivist* 47 (Spring 1984): 173-78; Brauer, "Researcher Evaluation of Reference Services," 79; Freeman, "Eye of the Beholder," 119.

21 The best introduction to survey research is Charles Backstrom and Gerald Hursh-Cesar, *Survey Research*, 2nd ed. (New York: Wiley and Sons, 1981). Also useful is Maurice B. Line, *Library Surveys* (London: C. Bingley, 1982).

The framework is an integrated unit and presents a comprehensive approach to user studies. Reading an objective from left to right gives a sense of how each of the three objectives becomes more complexly defined in succeeding stages. Reading one of the stages from top to bottom indicates the most important elements of the three objectives that should be recorded at that stage. The elements in each cell of the framework are those aspects of an ongoing user-study program that should be shared among archivists and repositories to develop a profession-wide understanding of Quality, Integrity, and Value.

Implementing the Framework

Translating the framework into an ongoing research program at a repository does not necessarily involve massive questionnaires and sophisticated computer analysis. The "Reference Log" in Figure 2 is one example of how Stages 1, 2, and 3 of the framework could be made operational for daily use. It is called a log because it tracks and records researchers at different points along the reference service continuum. By linking activities and assessments across time, archivists can better understand the process of seeking and finding useful information. As such, the log would enhance, but not replace a sign-in register recording daily visits to the research room. The reference log in the example combines the two most basic survey research approaches — observation and questioning — but distributes the task of completion about equally between reference archivists and the researchers.

The sample reference log is designed as a two-sided form with four distinct parts. Except for the section labeled "Search Report," the questions on the log have been field tested for accuracy and usefulness.[22] Nevertheless, the specific wording of the questions and response categories may be tailored to the patrons of specific repositories. Given the log's level of inquiry and analysis, the underlying elements of a question are more important than the specific wording of the text or response categories.

Information requested within the blocked area of the log is based largely on the elements in Stage 1 of the framework. As a registration form, this section asks researchers to identify themselves, waive the confidentiality of their research activity, and agree to basic procedures. All these elements are standard features of many registration forms.[23] The most important parts of this section are the open-ended question on the nature of the research project and the multiple-choice question, "What

---

22 Paul Conway; "Research in Presidential Libraries: A User Study," *Midwestern Archivist* 11, no. 1 (1986): 35-36; Ina Berzins, et al., *The Methodologies Report on Research and Public Service Component Program Evaluation Study,* Volume III, report prepared for the Public Archives of Canada by Currie, Coopers and Lybrand, Ottawa, Canada, January 1985.

23 *The Archival Forms Manual* (Chicago: Society of American Archivists, 1982).

Figure 20. Reference Log

Information in this box is required to use the research room facilities. The principal purpose of this form is to identify and record individuals who use materials at the archives, to help us identify which materials may be most useful, and to permit later contact with researchers as part of more detailed studies of research use.

APPLICANT'S NAME (Last, First, Middle Initial)	PERMANENT PHONE NO.	OCCUPATION (please be as specific as possible)
PERMANENT ADDRESS (Street, City, State, ZIP)	INSTITUTION	WHAT WORK BROUGHT YOU TO THE ARCHIVES?
DESCRIPTION OF RESEARCH PROJECT (Include subject, dates, important names, type of material needed)		☐ ☐ ☐ ☐ ☐ ☐ ☐ ☐

MAY WE ADVISE OTHER INDIVIDUALS OF THE SUBJECT OF YOUR RESEARCH? ☐ YES ☐ NO	MAY WE ADVISE OTHER INDIVIDUALS WHICH ITEMS WERE SERVED TO YOU? ☐ YES ☐ NO
I HAVE READ "REGULATIONS FOR THE PUBLIC USE OF RECORDS" AND I WILL COMPLY WITH THE RULES. Applicant's Signature Date	MAY WE CONTACT YOU BY MAIL OR TELEPHONE AS PART OF A FUTURE USER STUDY? ☐ YES ☐ NO

Orientation

Your answers to questions in this section of the form will help the reference archivist orient you to using the archives' holdings. Together with answers from other researchers, the information you provide will enable archivists to assess the overall use of the archives.

What is the purpose of your current research project that involves using the archives' holdings or services? (Circle all that apply.)

1. Academic requirements
2. Genealogy
3. Publication (book, article)
4. Background information for newspaper, magazine article, advertising
5. Exhibition
6. Film, radio, television program
7. Government research
8. Professional research (for individual, group, association)
9. Personal interest/hobby
10. Other _____

Some researchers prefer to rely on their background preparation or the finding aid system in the research room. Others feel most comfortable if reference archivists guide their searches of the holdings.

Please mark the scale below to show your personal preference for doing archival research.

1	2	3	4	5
rely on finding aids		archivist and finding aids		rely on archivist

Before your first visit on this project, did you write or telephone to get information on holdings or services?

☐ YES ☐ NO ☐ DON'T KNOW

Excluding writing or telephoning the archives directly, which of the following sources did you *most* rely on to identify the holdings or services of use in your research? (Circle the *best* choice.)

1. References, citations in published works
2. Published guides to archives, primary sources, bibliographies
3. Teacher, professor, colleagues
4. Archivist/librarian at other institutions
5. Information from historical, professional, or genealogical organizations
6. Television, radio, newspaper
7. Presentation by archives staff
8. Visit to museum exhibition
9. General knowledge, assumptions
10. Other _____

If you have done archival research in the last five years, please write the name of the archives in which you have *most recently* worked.

_____

Figure 2. (continued)

Search Report

The reference archivist should note the first 10 collections consulted by the researcher, the source of recommendation, and whether the researcher located information of use in the research project. Data for this section is obtained from paging slips, photocopy request forms, observation, and if necessary, by questioning researcher.

RECOMMENDATION   COLLECTION NAME   SEARCH RESULTS

ARCHIVIST   USER   FINDING AID   POSITIVE NEGATIVE

Follow-Up

The information you provide in this section will assist archivists to understand how archival research is carried out and how archival information may be used.

Please provide an approximate breakdown of the total time you spent at the archives during this research project across each of the activities listed below. (Make sure the total equals 100%.)

Orienting yourself to the archives'
   services and facilities _____%

Searching through finding aids and
   collections to locate documents _____%

Actually reading/viewing/studying
   documents _____%

Discussing research project with
   archivists or other researchers _____%

                    TOTAL   100%

What portion of your research project will be based on archival materials located at this archives or other archives?

1. I hope to use primarily *archival sources* of information.

2. I hope to use archival sources and other sources *about equally.*

3. I hope to use *other sources* of information primarily.

4. I don't know yet.

On the line below, please write the name of the collection in which you located the most useful information.

☐ no useful information located

If you expect to share the information you find at the archives, please describe below in what ways the information will be used. Please use this opportunity to name the title of a proposed publication, describe the group that may benefit from your archival research, or describe the results of your research in more detail.

work brought you to the archives?" This form presents the prime opportunity for a researcher and the archivist to record an understanding of
the subject, scope, time frame, and function of the research question. In
combination with information on institutional affiliation, these questions form the basis for understanding a researcher's group identity and
approach to the archival record.

The log's second section, "Orientation," is a brief questionnaire for
researchers to complete during or immediately following the orientation
interview. The questions tap the elements from Stage 2 of the framework.
Included are inquiries on the intended use of information located, how a
researcher found out about holdings or services, the nature of the service
anticipated, and the existence of prior archival research experience. If a
sampling strategy is necessary to limit the population studied, this section
might only be completed by a selected group of researchers — for example,
undergraduate students — or during a selected time period — for example,
the first week of every month. The information in this section could also
help subdivide the full researcher population for further, more detailed
questioning.

The reverse side of the log contains the third and fourth sections,
labeled "Search Report" and "Follow-Up." Together these sections apply the
elements from Stage 3 of the framework. The Search Report, an untested
proposal at this point, is designed as a way to learn about the complex
problem of research strategies and the process of locating useful information. Like the Orientation section, it is not necessarily intended for all
researchers at all times, but for selected groups of researchers sampled during specific points in a year. Alternatively, this section may serve simply to
illustrate the varied ways collections are used by groups of researchers.

Reference archivists administer the search report by observing
researcher behavior, examining evidence such as call slips and photocopy
requests, and noting the names of the first 10 collections consulted.
Archivists would then check a box for each collection noted to indicate
whether the reference archivist, researcher, or in-house finding aids were
the principal source of the recommendation that the collection may contain useful information. Finally, the observer-archivist would indicate
whether the researcher located useful information. While this last information may be obtained through observation, some direct questioning
may be necessary.

The fourth section of the reference log, Follow-Up, draws on additional elements from Stage 3. Included are questions on how a researcher
spent time, the researcher's expected use of archival and nonarchival
sources of information, and the most significant collections used. A final
open-ended question enables the researcher to comment in more detail
on the results of work or how the obtained information will be used. As
with the Orientation section, the follow-up questions in the log represent
only the very basic pieces of information that should be obtained and

recorded from the groups of researchers chosen for study. The queries should be considered a point of departure for further discussions or a way of clarifying issues that could be addressed more completely in Stage 4 and 5 projects.

A reference log is not the only way to implement the research strategy explained in the framework's first three stages. Archivists could design separate survey instruments to collect information for each stage. A microcomputer at the reference desk, equipped with database management software, could substitute quite well for a whole range of survey questionnaires. It bears emphasizing that the fundamental goal in implementing the first three stages of the framework is to record information gathered so that it can be used to link groups of researchers with their evaluations of services and programs.

User surveys and special studies implementing Stages 4 and 5 should be built on information gathered in the earlier stages. They are opportunities to move beyond researchers in reference rooms, to tap the behavior and attitudes of past users, potential users, and the community of beneficiaries. Surveys and special studies are also more amenable to multi-institutional approaches. Examples of research topics of this nature might include factors that contribute to user satisfaction, the impacts of frustration and limited access on scholarly research, citation patterns in a given subject area, and the value and usefulness of nonpaper records. As archival research questions become more complexly defined, so too should research methods become more rigorous and sophisticated.

Applying the Framework

Putting to practical use information gathered in a user-study program begins with an analysis of the data. This does not require computing equipment. A reference log will yield a wealth of information from hand tabulation. Simply shuffling logs into piles with specific questions in mind can be enlightening. Take for instance the question, "This year, what portion of their time did genealogists spend in the research room becoming familiar with the repository's holdings and services?" Dividing the logs completed by genealogists into three groups according to the range of responses to the appropriate follow-up query will produce a simple answer. A closer inspection of other parts of the completed logs in each group will help archivists understand why some genealogists begin research more quickly than others. At this level of analysis, archivists equipped with microcomputers merely will find the data analysis more efficient and convenient than hand tabulation.

Both archivist and researcher should find an ongoing user-study program founded on a systematic framework a valuable learning process. Structured contacts actively demonstrate to researchers the concern archivists have for successful research efforts without adding substantially to the researchers' burdens. If widely implemented, researchers may even come to expect opportunities for orientation questionnaires and follow-up discussions. For the reference archivist, structured contacts transform a role that sometimes begins to resemble that of a traffic cop into a central evaluative mechanism for the entire repository. Routinely recording useful information on researchers is much less burdensome than recording routine production statistics — especially if the information gathered is an integral part of the design and evaluation of all archival programs.

Integrating the results of user studies into the administrative structure of a repository begins with more creative reporting to resource allocators, senior administrators, and user communities. Head counts and daily researcher visits can be augmented by reports on the wide variety of questions addressed through archival research. Reports based on vivid data from users of archival services may be far more powerful tools than those based on dry statistics. Archives administration from the users' point of view requires that archival programs be defended from the users' point of view.

Beyond its value in reporting, an ongoing user-study program can have a central role in the design and modification of archival programs only if archivists trust the guidance users provide. Data collected from users in an ongoing program, even at a very basic level, may be substantially more reliable, and hence more useful, than even sophisticated one-time surveys because of the program's capacity to reflect change. Evaluating the success of programs for users, such as an automated catalog or an outreach program designed to increase physical use, is far easier if user evaluations provide benchmarks over time. In short, without direct and continuous user evaluations, archivists can only suppose that their information needs are being met on a regular basis. For public institutions with a mandate to serve the research public, suppositions can only be stretched so far at budget time.

A general framework for understanding users can serve as an agenda for talking about the archival profession's progress toward the goal of user-responsive programs and services. But at some point the talk must take a back seat to cooperative study projects. Perhaps the classroom is an appropriate place to begin building a research tradition. Elsie Freeman has suggested that archival education should include training in survey research techniques.[24] Archival educators might consider transforming the practicum portion of a two-course sequence into a laboratory for teams of students to design, carry out, and evaluate archival research projects, including user studies.

Knowledge from user studies will have value beyond single repositories only if widely shared. Mechanisms for a cooperative effort need to be developed and supported. At the very least, an archival information clearinghouse, such as the one proposed by NAGARA, should be prepared to

---

24 Finch, "Eye of the Beholder," 122.

actively gather, evaluate, and disseminate the results of user studies.[25] A proactive clearinghouse can serve the same broad functions for archives that the perceptive critics of user studies served for libraries — to discover patterns in isolated studies, encourage further research, and develop strategies for integrating research findings into standards of practice.

Mathematician and philosopher of science Henri Poincaré was not the first scientist to explain in clear terms the fundamental need for structures to order random observations. But his pragmatic approach to scientific investigation seems particularly appropriate to a profession trying to find larger meaning in the details of history. Poincaré saw no dichotomy between theory and practice because any theory worth the name could only be judged in practical terms. Indeed, Poincaré saw in the problems the fledgling library profession was confronting in developing descriptive practices a proper metaphor for the problems of mathematical physics. Theories organize thought as a means of organizing action.

Archivists too are universalists of sorts. They are proud of their broad understanding of the process of historical research and their attention to the details of past experience. Given the profession's practical nature, archivists may never develop a scientific theory that meets Frank Burke's definition of universal and immutable laws.[26] But to avoid building a profession on a set of immutable platitudes, archivists' practice can and should be based on solid conceptual structures that transcend the limits of local precedent. Analytical frameworks encourage systematic problem solving, promote cooperation, and allow archivists to collect the information necessary to develop standards of practice benefiting the profession as a whole.

The framework for studying users and the reference log are offered as basic tools in such a process. Archivists should begin with the basics, coordinate research designs, collect data, share results widely, and revise their approaches based on these results. The specifics of the proposed system need to be tested and refined. Archivists can acquire the skills and insight necessary to design an ongoing evaluation program that includes users by studying library surveys and mastering sound survey research methods. But ultimately archivists must design their own methods and define their own goals, beginning with a commitment to develop a truly user-responsive archival profession. Making the reference room rather than the loading dock the hub of archival activity requires facts about users — recorded facts, shared facts, but most of all facts organized for clear objectives.

---

25 *Planning for the Archival Profession*, 31.

26 Frank G. Burke, "The Future Course of Archival Theory in the United States," *American Archivist* 44 (Winter 1981): 40.

20

Understanding Administrative Use and Users in University Archives

ELIZABETH YAKEL AND LAURA L. BOST HENSEY

Abstract: The users of institutional archives range from local and professional historians to lower- and upper-level administrators. In many cases, administrators are the primary user population. Past archival studies, however, have focused on users with principally a historical purpose. The lack of research is surprising since most archival programs rely on their parent institutions for funding. This study is an initial attempt to examine administrative use and users in a university archives setting. It raises some interesting questions concerning how administrators analyze primary sources, what types of finding aids are most appropriate, and how much interpretation archivists need to do. The research suggests that archivists should look at themselves less as the historical voice in an institution and more as part of the administrative team.

The primary mission of many archival programs is to manage the non-current records of their parent institutions. Institutions rely on archival records for a variety of reasons: to assist in consistent planning efforts, to understand the processes behind official positions, and to preserve materials related to the infrastructure. Despite the value of archival records for administrative purposes, archivists have been slow to study administrative use. Administrative use is any inquiry directed to the university archives to assist university administrators, clerical staff, or faculty carry out their official, job-related duties. For the purposes of this article, student organizations using archival records is considered an administrative use. Administrative use of archival records is an understudied aspect of archival administration. This lack of research is surprising since most archival programs rely on their parent institutions for funding. The analysis of administrative use patterns and the questions and concerns of administrative users begin to suggest ways in which college and university archivists can better serve this population.

Reprinted with permission from the *American Archivist* 57 (Fall 1994): 596-615. The authors wish to thank two people for their encouragement and suggestions on this paper. William K. Wallach of the Bentley Historical Library provided very astute comments that made the manuscript clearer. A version of this paper was originally written for a class taught by Miranda Pao; the authors also thank her for comments.

This is an exploratory study of administrative use of archival records in a university setting. It is hoped that the value of an in-depth case study concerning administrative use at a specific institution, at this point when virtually no research on administrative use in archives exists, will stimulate more research in this area and be theory generating. The study combines two research techniques: (1) an analysis of historical or existing statistics, and (2) interviews with administrative users.

Preliminary conclusions indicate that the archives is seen by administrative users as serving a vital function of preserving institutional memory. Furthermore, although time is always of the essence for administrative users, they use the archives when searching for specific items and researching more open-ended questions. However, administrators expect archivists to do much of the information search and analysis for them. Administrative users rarely use finding aids or other access tools and rarely question the reliability of the information they are given. Confidence in the archivist signifies reliability of the information provided. Other research findings highlight several problems with using reference statistics to understand users and the importance of major institutional events to generate new user groups for the archives.

Literature Review

Three fields contribute important background information and research to this study: organizational theory, archival administration, and library and information science. Although none of these fields explicitly discusses administrative use of archival records in depth, a literature review reveals how each bears on the topic at hand.

The organizational theory literature contains studies of decision making, organizational behavior, and organizational culture. Within this large body of literature is a relatively small number of works focusing specifically on universities. Among others, Karl Weick, Michael Cohen and James March, and Arthur Stinchcombe argue that institutions of higher education are unique.[1] The organizational dynamics, power bases, hierarchical structures, and decision-making practices in colleges and universities differ from all other types of organizations. Following this line of thought, one would assume that information-seeking behavior among administrators in a university setting would differ from that in other types of organizations. The present study attempts to contribute to the

---

1   Michael D. Cohen and James G. March, *Leadership and Ambiguity: The American College President,* 2nd. ed., (Boston: Harvard Business School Press, 1986); Karl Weick, "Educational Organizations as Loosely Coupled Systems," *Administrative Science Quarterly* 21, no. 1 (March 1976): 1-19; Arthur L. Stinchcombe, *Information in Organizations* (Berkeley: University of California Press, 1990). The pertinent section in Stinchcombe is Chapter 9, "University Administration of Research Space and Teaching Loads: Managers Who Do Not Know What Their Workers Are Doing," 312-40.

establishment of a baseline for administrative information-seeking behavior in universities, which eventually could be juxtaposed with administrative use of archives in corporate settings.

Cohen and March consider universities "organized anarchies," which have no shared goals, foster fluid participation, and maintain little understanding of their processes. They note that in many cases the "garbage can" model is at work: decisions and solutions find each other accidentally, depending on temporal and spatial coincidence.[2] For example, a person with a decision to make may encounter one solution (problem solver) one day and another solution (problem solver) another day. Solutions wait for decisions just as much as decisions wait for solutions. Extrapolating from this model, archival records (potential solutions) wait for administrative questions, and archivists need to get the records to the right place or to the right problem-generating administrator at the right time.

Cohen and March also characterize universities as having a weak administrative information base: "Information about past events or past decisions is often not retained. When retained, it is often difficult to retrieve. Information about current activities is scant."[3] They continue by stating that when information is provided, it

> need have no particular validity. Consider, for example, the common assertion in college decision-making processes about what some constituency . . . is "thinking." The assertions are rarely based on defensible evidence, but they tend to become organizational facts by virtue of the shortage of information. More generally, reality for a decision is specified by those willing to spend the time required to collect small amounts of information available, to retrieve the factual assertions of others, and to disseminate their findings.[4]

These findings — based on extensive interviews with college presidents, other highly placed officials in universities, and members of their support staffs — present the main challenges and opportunities for university archives. As a first step in better understanding the process of seeking archival information, the present study focuses solely on users. Of course, this does not mean that an examination of nonusers would fail to reveal equally interesting data concerning the dynamics of information seeking.

---

2 The garbage can model is a probabilistic computer simulation of the decision-making process, which manipulates the variables of problems and solutions. March, Cohen, and Olsen apply the garbage can model to many different types of organizations, not just to those in higher education. It was originally introduced by Michael D. Cohen, James G. March, and Johan P. Olsen, "Garbage Can Model of Organizational Choice," in *Administrative Science Quarterly* 17 (March 1972): 1-25.

3 Cohen and March, *Leadership and Ambiguity*, 207.

4 Cohen and March, *Leadership and Ambiguity*, 207-8.

Weick builds on the concept of educational institutions as organized anarchies. He sees universities as "loosely coupled" systems; events are related but "each event also preserves its own identity and some of the evidence of its physical or logical separateness."[5] Educational institutions are loosely coupled, according to Weick, because the two most prevalent mechanisms for coupling — a technical core and authority of office — are less relevant. Weick does not argue that tight couplings do not appear in universities, just that two of the significant populations, students and educators, generally fall outside the coupling mechanisms.

Technical couplings are task dependent, the task or process is the organizing element, and people must work together to accomplish the entire process. Examples of technical couplings might be the development of a specific unit's budget, strategic plan, or annual report. Authority couplings concern the mechanisms by which positions are filled, responsibilities are set, and people are evaluated. For example, disciplinary issues will be tightly coupled or more highly regulated in a university. Classroom content will be loosely coupled or left up to the individual professor. The implications for this study are that information is created in many different administrative entities and not shared because of their loose couplings. More to the point, entities may not be aware of exactly what information exists elsewhere. In an academic environment such as the one described by Weick, the archivist might be the first person to see the range of information produced and may be one of the few people able to link problems and solutions.

Stinchcombe demonstrates how the ideas of Cohen, March, and Weick translate into the real problem of space allocation in a university. He notes the importance of research at many universities in terms of prestige, money, and power. Yet, knowledge of the research is concentrated in departments different from those that deal with space allocation and needs. Therefore, administrators do not have sufficient information to compare research projects. Once space has been allocated to a certain department, it is virtually impossible to reclaim the space. Stinchcombe finds that this is because

> information needed [by administrators] to compare the space needs of different kinds of scientists is concentrated in the (separate) lowest units. . . . This deficiency of adequate information at higher levels also means that people at lower levels see higher-level attempts to manage space as an intervention by ignorant people into matters they do not understand. . . . Vice presidents for research see a lab empty and

---

5 Weick, "Loosely Coupled Systems," 3.

propose to reallocate that space without knowing that this lab is merely between projects.[6]

Formal information sharing concerning administrative matters in universities is not a traditional activity. In this organizational culture, archival activity involving administrative use of university records should be viewed as, at best, an anomalous activity, and at worst, a subversive activity.

While many articles in the archival literature relate tangentially to this topic, the ideas in two areas are of particular value to this study: the first is use and user studies, and the second is management of archival and records management programs in colleges and universities. The absence of concern regarding administrative use is prevalent in both of these areas. Even Lawrence Dowler's essay, which defines a research agenda for archival user and use studies, fails to specifically mention administrative use as an important factor for archivists to consider.[7]

Use and users studies are found in both the archival literature and the library and information science literature. The library literature looks at academic use of libraries and information centers by students and faculty or corporate use and users. The latter, however, is often geared toward professional affiliation (e.g., scientists or engineers) and not organizational identity. The archival literature has largely studied the same populations. One could consider the studies done by Colin Mick, Georg Lindsey, and Daniel Callahan, by David Ellis, or by Robert Taylor to be investigations of administrative use.[8] Yet, while these studies raise important issues for consideration in any use or user study, they fail to acknowledge the central place of organizational dynamics in information seeking. Mick, Lindsey, and Callahan study the information-seeking patterns of two disparate groups: scientists and engineers. Although the response rate to their questionnaire is low and the validity of the comparison between these two groups can be challenged, these authors at least acknowledge that organizational culture plays a significant role in information behaviors. Their article notes individual, environmental, and situational variables in the hope of finding means of better responding to information needs. However, they do not generate a usable construct for analyzing these variables.

Taylor and Ellis study individual search behaviors even though the individuals examined (engineers, legislators, and practicing physicians for

---

6 Stinchcombe, *Information in Organizations,* 323-24.

7 Lawrence Dowler, "The Role of Use in Defining Archival Practice and Principles: A Research Agenda," *American Archivist* 51 (Winter and Spring 1988): 74-86.

8 Colin K. Mick, Georg N. Lindsey, and Daniel Callahan, "Toward Usable User Studies," *Journal of the American Society for Information Science* 35 (September 1980): 347-56; David Ellis, "A Behavioral Approach to Information Retrieval System Design," *Journal of Documentation* 45 (September 1989): 171-212; Robert S. Taylor, "Information Use Environments," *Progress in Communication Sciences,* ed. Brenda Dervin, vol. 10 (Norwood, N.J.: Ablex, 1991), 217-53.

Taylor and social scientists in an academic setting for Ellis) are part of
larger environments. Furthermore, the culture of the setting and organizational structure are variables that neither considers. Research by
Patricia Fandt and Gerald Ferris, among others, has demonstrated how
information can be used for control or to assert power in organizational
settings.[9] Martha Feldman and James March also note that organizational
cultures can promote or discourage information seeking through unwrit-
ten cues and signals.[10] Administrative user studies must not only account
for the user and the reason for use, but also for the environment in
which the user works.

Archival user studies are similar to the library and information science
studies. Paul Conway carries out investigations and provides an overall
framework for archivists to employ while studying users.[11] Conway is
interested in information transfer and makes a distinction between the
use of records (quantity) and their usefulness (quality). He cites the need
to look at archival reference services differently and proposes a three-part
model encompassing quality (how researchers define their task in terms
of subject, format, and scope of information), integrity (how archivists
balance their responsibilities between making the information available
and protecting the materials), and value (evaluation of the services rendered). Conway states that better internal record keeping is necessary, as
are more surveys and experiments. His sample research form, however,
would not provide clear indications of who the administrative users are
or of what administrative use is occurring. William Maher also argues for
more user studies but sees a great problem in the fact that there "is a
great deal of variance in what is counted and what is done with the
data."[12] Although Maher calls for user studies of different types of use
(historical, administrative, genealogical), administrative use studies have
not been done.

Two good studies of historical users, one by Conway and another by
Jacqueline Goggin, provide a basis for the information needs of historical
researchers.[13] Both authors examine how scholarly researchers learn about
archival information and approach archival collections, how historians

---

9   Patricia M. Fandt and Gerald R. Ferris, "The Management of Information and Impressions:
    When Employees Behave Opportunistically," *Organizational Behavior and Human Decision
    Processes* 45 (February 1990): 140-58.

10 Martha S. Feldman and James G. March, "Information in Organizations as Signal and Symbol,"
    Administrative Science Quarterly 26, no. 2 (1981): 171-86.

11 Paul Conway, "Facts and Frameworks: An Approach to Studying the Users of Archives,"
    American Archivist 49 (Fall 1986): 393-408, and "Research in Presidential Libraries: A User
    Survey," *Midwestern Archivist* 11 (1986): 35-56.

12 William J. Maher, "The Use of User Studies," *Midwestern Archivist* 11 (1986): 17.

13 Conway, "Research in Presidential Libraries," and Jacqueline Goggin, "The Indirect Approach:
    A Study of Scholarly Users of Black and Women's Organizational Records in the Library of
    Congress Manuscript Division," *Midwestern Archivist* 11 (1986): 57-67.

define and refine their questions during the research process, and how they use the archival materials as evidence. Goggin accomplishes this through an examination of Library of Congress Manuscript Division call slips (1971-1981) that document the usage of their collections. She then takes a sample (unsystematic) of the resulting published works, citing the collections used and analyzing the quality of the use of sources. Goggin asserts that a majority of the researchers have little training in the location and evaluation of archival sources. If this is true, historical researchers may have more in common with administrative users than is traditionally thought.

Conway's study of presidential libraries indicates that reference archivists also perform a filtering function or mediated reference service for historical researchers. This indicates another similarity with administrative users in this study. In his survey, Conway finds that 35 percent of the researchers noted that the orientation interview with the archivist helped them to narrow or define their topic and that 68 percent stated that the orientation interview helped them to locate important collections.

A final user study of note is David Bearman's "day in the life of" archival reference study.[14] On 15 March 1989, eighteen archives in nine institutions of various types (corporate, college and university, manuscript repository) provided Bearman with data from all reference questions from all sources for that day. This totaled 1,559 inquiry forms. His purpose was to get a better understanding of the questions asked, the use to which the answers would be put, and the criteria for success. Bearman criticizes past studies: "They recorded profiles of users, but not the contents of their questions, thus leaving us with some knowledge of who users are, but only prejudice about what each category of user might want."[15] Administrative use is a low 3 percent. However, Bearman's categories are undefined, and several categories — including records creators, legal/professional, and general — could possibly encompass administrative use. This again points to the necessity for a common definition of *administrative use* in archives.

While Bearman's survey is unsystematic, his data do indicate areas in which more research is necessary. He questions the myth that archival users are not looking for a specific item. Bearman finds that 56 percent of the requests are for specific items. The present study also finds evidence, in both the existing statistics and the user interviews, indicating that a higher number of administrative users than previously mentioned in the archival literature are seeking specific items. Bearman also alludes to the difference between authenticity and reliability of archival information.

---

14 David Bearman, "User Presentation Language in Archives," *Archives & Museum Informatics* 3/4 (Winter 1989/90): 3-7.

15 Bearman, "User Presentation Language," 3.

Reliability is the correctness of the data. Authenticity is whether or not the creator had the authority to provide the data. For example, anyone can issue a birth certificate with the correct information included, but only a county clerk has the authority to issue a birth certificate that will be legal and "authentic." Although Bearman does not cite a percentage, he states that "many queries are for authority data."[16] The context in which records were created may matter to users.

Many works treat the administration of college and university archival and records management programs. The most recent is by Maher.[17] However, his section on use concentrates on the management of historical use. This is surprising, considering the fact that administrative use at his repository, the University of Illinois-Champaign/Urbana, averages 18 percent of the total use of that archives over a five-year period (1987-89 to 1991-92).[18] An even higher percentage of administrative use of academic archives is noted by Patrick Quinn in his impressionistic article.[19] Quinn finds increasing levels of administrative use in the repositories he contacted as well as in his own archives at Northwestern University. He observes that the difference between administrative users and historians is that "patrons seeking information expect instantaneous responses, while sustained researchers mine their own information."[20] The administrative constraints of time and the desire for quick responses are supported by the interviews in this study.

Records management is closely tied to administrative use because an effective records management program will bring larger amounts of administrative information into the archives in a more systematic manner. Marjorie Barritt and Don Skemer and Geoffrey Williams discuss records management programs in colleges and universities.[21] Barritt conducts a small, nonrandom survey of 12 university archives with records management programs and finds that many are hampered by a strong institutional tradition of collecting manuscripts:

> Among the institutions surveyed, college and university archivists do not adopt records management techniques to enhance administrative

---

16 Bearman, "User Presentation Language," 6.

17 William J. Maher, *The Management of College and University Archives* (Metuchen, N.J.: Society of American Archivists and Scarecrow, 1992).

18 University of Illinois, University Archives, *Twenty-Ninth Annual Report, July 1, 1991 to June 30, 1992,* 24.

19 Patrick M. Quinn, "Academic Archivists and Their Current Practice: Some Modest Suggestions," *Georgia Archive* 10 (Fall 1982): 14-24.

20 Ibid., 22.

21 Marjorie Rabe Barritt, "Adopting and Adapting Records Management to College and University Archives," *Midwestern Archivist* 14 (1989): 5-12; Don C. Skemer and Geoffrey P. Williams, "Managing the Records of Higher Education: The State of Records Management in American Colleges and Universities," *American Archivist* 53 (Fall 1990): 532-47.

service and reference or to provide space saving and cost effectiveness —
although these are important outcomes of such techniques. Rather
they adopt and adapt selected records management techniques that
will allow them to maintain more efficiently cultural facilities focussing
on the preservation of records for [historical] research use.[22]

Weick, Cohen and March, and Stinchcombe would also argue that this
phenomenon is linked to the organizational culture.

Skemer and Williams conducted a more systematic survey of 1,532
universities which generated 449 responses. They sought to answer three
basic questions: "Why have some institutions developed programs while
others have not? Why do some succeed and others fail? Are there any
valid operational models?"[23] The article provides comprehensive frequency
data on numbers of programs, records management services offered,
characteristics of records administrators, records retention and disposition schedules, and software used. However, the authors fail to examine
the amount of use and users in any detail. Use and users are aspects of a
records management program that would seem essential to answering all
three questions, particularly why some programs succeed and others fail.
If one can assume that the existence of a records management program
facilitates administrative use of noncurrent records, it is telling that
Skemer and Williams find over a third of the respondents said they had
no records management program.

Mary Jo Pugh points out that archivists act as intermediaries in the
reference process and that the traditional provenance-based system of
archival organization will succeed only if the user supplies information
extrinsic to the finding aids (e.g., names of people and organizations
with activities).[24] She asserts that archivists assume historians want high
recall and low precision. The interviews completed for this study indicate
that administrative users are more interested in high precision. This is a
decisive difference between these two groups that requires more study.

Although Pugh alludes to the need for archivists to become more
aware of the information-seeking processes of archival users, the library
and information science literature does a much better job of analyzing
different search processes. Brenda Dervin and Michael Nilan note three
major approaches to understanding users' information-seeking patterns.[25]

---

22 Barritt, "Adopting and Adapting Records Management Programs to College and University
    Archives," 10.

23 Skemer and Williams, "Managing the Records of Higher Education," 533.

24 Mary Jo Pugh, "The Illusion of Omniscience: Subject Access and the Reference Archivist,"
    American Archivist 45 (Winter 1982): 33-44.

25 Brenda Dervin and Michael Nilan, "Information Needs and Uses," *Annual Review of Information
    Science and Technology* (ARIST) 21 (1986): 3-33.

These three approaches are all more user oriented and user focused. The first is Dervin's "sensemaking" approach, which examines the conceptual and theoretical premises of how users make sense of their world and use information. This concept originated in and is prominent in Herbert Simon's work. Simon discusses how sensemaking applies in an organizational setting when culture, control, and power become central variables.[26] In fact, Robert Birnbaum asserts that sensemaking, not decision making, should be viewed as the main goal of colleges and universities.[27]

A second approach, termed the "anomalous states of knowledge approach," is attributed to Nicholas Belkin.[28] Belkin proposes that users approach systems with incomplete questions and needs that are constantly being refined. He argues that systems need to be more responsive to users' needs and should be designed to respond better to a user, helping him or her to define questions, rather than forcing the user's search process into a predetermined, automated direction.

The third approach is characterized by Susan MacMullin and Robert Taylor's user-values approach. The user-values approach concentrates on the dimensions of the user's problem and the information traits required to satisfy the user's need.[29] Each of these approaches can be applied to a study of the archival information needs of administrators in a university setting. Thus, in this study, an attempt is made to map the process by which users got to the archives. The investigators also seek to understand how users defined their questions or how those questions were defined for them by an archivist. Clearly, more research is needed on the information-seeking patterns of administrative users and nonusers.

Methodology

The first challenge is to define the limits of administrative use of university records. As stated, in this study, administrative use is any inquiry directed to the university archives to assist university administrators, clerical staff, or faculty carry out their official, job-related duties or to help student organizations verify their official status within the university. Within this study, research by faculty or students for class projects is not considered an "administrative" use. Faculty members seeking information in an official departmental capacity and students representing

26 Herbert A. Simon, *Administrative Behavior: A Study of Decision-Making Processes in Administrative Organizations* (New York: Free Press, 1976).

27 Robert Birnbaum, *How Colleges Work: The Cybernetics of Academic Organization and Leadership* (San Francisco: Jossey Bass, 1988), xvii, passim.

28 Nicholas J. Belkin, "Anomalous States of Knowledge as a Basis for Information Retrieval," *Canadian Journal of Information Science* 5 (May 1980): 133-43.

29 Susan E. MacMullin and Robert S. Taylor, "Problem Dimensions and Information Traits," *The Information Society* 3 (1984): 91-111.

student organizations or trying to maintain the official status of a student organization within the university are considered administrative users. And, in this study, administrative users are divided into four categories: (1) higher administration (e.g., offices of the president, vice president, provost); (2) support services (e.g., the bulk of administrative offices, research, public relations, library, development); (3) academic departments (faculty, administrative assistants, etc. working in a departmental capacity); and (4) students who had to perform some administrative function for a student organization.

The university considered in this study is a public institution in the Midwest with an enrollment of approximately 25,000 students. The university archives agreed to participate in the study and provided access to its user statistics. The academic schedule is four semesters or quarters per year: September to December; January to mid-March; late March to June; and July to August (when two five-week sessions and one ten-week session run concurrently). However, students and faculty are predominantly present during the former three semesters. The archival program is 23 years old and includes an active manuscripts program as well as a university records management program. The records management program gained significant authority after a decision and mandate by the institution's governing board in December 1992. The university records program employs three full-time equivalents (one professional, one clerical, and three students).

The university archives provided consistent user statistics for a five-year period. These longitudinal data are the basis for the statistical procedures. However, the problems associated with using existing statistics became readily apparent. For example, the reference process for administrative users begins with a telephone call to the archives with a request. The archivist responds to the caller by helping the requestor define the problem. Generally, it is the archivist who fills out the request form and who does the actual research for the administrative user. Therefore, the reference question, as it is defined on the forms, is the archivist's interpretation of the user's need. Likewise, the materials-requested section is usually the archivist's best estimate of where the answer to the question will be located, not a search suggestion by the administrator. This pattern has been identified by Richard Lytle, who notes the inferential process of translation from a topical request to an answer based on the context or provenance of the records.[30] This also

---

30 Richard H. Lytle, "Intellectual Access to Archives: I. Provenance and Content Indexing Methods of Subject Retrieval," *American Archivist* 43 (Winter 1980): 64-75 and "Intellectual Access to Archives: II. Report of an Experiment Comparing Provenance and Content Indexing Methods of Subject Retrieval," *American Archivist* 43 (Spring 1980): 191-205. These articles are derived from his dissertation, Richard H. Lytle, "Subject Retrieval in Archives: A Comparison of the Provenance and Content Indexing Methods," Ph.D. diss., University of Maryland, 1979.

provides further evidence to support Conway's contention that "the most complex aspects of a research problem are not necessarily best understood through routine repository procedures."[31] If this pattern holds for other institutions, it indicates that there is very little unfiltered information concerning actual user needs, the precise questions asked by administrative users, or their actual knowledge of the scope of the information available for later analysis and study. If archivists continue to be the only ones knowledgeable of the information available, this will reinforce and support Weick's theory of the university as a "loosely coupled" system.

Figures 1 and 2 show the original and revised forms, the two types of statistics sheets the university employed from 1988 to the present. Both forms ask users to identify their affiliation (e.g., administrator, faculty, student, etc.). Neither form, however, asks users to state if the primary purpose of use is administrative. The revised form (Figure 2) indicates whether administrative records (e.g., university records) are used, but not whether the use is actually administrative. Therefore, the investigators had to return to the actual statistics sheets to determine the extent of administrative use. At times, this required a qualitative judgment on the part of the investigators to determine whether a certain faculty member was requesting information for personal research or to fulfill his or her duties as department chair or representative. This finding supports Barritt's assertions concerning continuing emphasis on historical use and the lack of serious attention given to administrative concerns.

To supplement the existing statistics and to get a better understanding of administrative users without filtering, interviews were carried out at the university. Eight interviews were conducted with two different categories of administrative users: higher administration (3) and support services (5). Unfortunately, no convenient interview time could be scheduled with a faculty member or a student. Interviewees were purposefully selected after reviewing the request forms. Selection was designed to represent the different categories of administrative users and different rates of use (frequent and infrequent, longitudinal, and new users). The university archivist sent each potential interviewee a letter introducing the project. Attached to this letter was a letter from the investigators and an article on the project written for the library newsletter. Figure 3 is a list of the basic interview questions asked of all the interviewees. In fact, the questions were designed as discussion starters and, as hoped, the interviewees explored other issues as they arose during the interviews. Although the archivist knew who might be interviewed, the archivist was not told who agreed to be interviewed. Potential interviewees were assured that

---

31 Conway, "Facts and Frameworks," 400.

Figure 1. Original Form

REQUEST FOR USE OF MATERIALS
(Please print)

Name _____　Date __6/20/95__

Address __VP Business Affairs_____　I.D. No. _____

_____　Phone No. __2660__

Check One:

___ Undergraduate Student　　___ Faculty　　　　　　___ Other (Please specify):
___ Graduate Student　　　　✓ Administrator or Staff　_____
Major: _____　　___ Alumni　　　　　　_____

PURPOSE OF RESEARCH

___ Research Paper　　　　　　　___ Verification of Facts/Dates
　　Thesis/Dissertation　　　　　___ Personal Interest
___ Publication (Book, Article, Firm)　___ Other (please specify): _____
　　　　　　　　　　　　　　　　_____

Topic of Research: Board of Directors, Restricted Fund _____

INFORMATION REQUESTED

Rare Books:

Call No.　　　　　　　　　　　　Call No.
　Author _____　　　　Author _____
　Title _____　　　　　Title _____

Call No.　　　　　　　　　　　　Call No.
　Author _____　　　　Author _____
　Title _____　　　　　Title _____

Archives or Manuscripts:
Description of Information requested: _____
_____

← **READ THE REVERSE CAREFULLY AND SIGN WHERE INDICATED** →

FOR OFFICE USE ONLY. LIST MATERIALS USED. Treasurers Office,

Subject Files; Finance Office Inventory _____
_____

Visit _____　Phone ✓ Letter _____

Figure 2. Revised Form

SPECIAL COLLECTIONS REQUEST FORM

Date _____

Name _____

Address or university office

_____

_____

Phone number _____

❏ Undergraduate
❏ Graduate Student
  Major _____
  ID Number _____
❏ Faculty
❏ Administrator or Staff
❏ Alumnus
❏ Researcher
(Specify academic affiliation, if any)

PURPOSE OF RESEARCH

❏ Research paper/speech
❏ Thesis/dissertation
❏ Book/article

❏ Verification of facts/dates
❏ Personal interest
❏ Other _____

I have read and understand the rules regarding use of materials in the center and I acknowledge that failure to abide by these rules will result in my being prohibited from using center materials.

_____
(Patron's signature)

MATERIALS REQUESTED

Office Use Only				Call no. or Collec. no. & Box-Folder no.		Office Use Only (Initials)	
Date	R	A	Mss		Author and title	Out	In

Figure 3. Interview Questions Asked of All Interviewees

Could you summarize the functions of your office for me?

Think about a specific instance when you used the archives, and answer the questions in reference to that instance.

Instance remembered: _____

1. At what point in the research did you contact the archives?
2. Was it the first place you contacted for the information?
3. Was your question well defined?
4. Were you looking for a specific document?
5. Were you sure it existed?
6. Were you interested in materials your office sent to the archives?
7. Does your office regularly send materials to the archives? If not, why not?
8. Was authenticity a question?
9. Was reliability a question?
10. Did you do your own research, or did archives staff do the research for you?
11. Do you use the archival finding aids?
12. Was the specific incident you are describing typical of your questions for the archives?
13. How is the incident atypical? Which of the questions would you have answered differently?
14. If there was anything you could change about the archives service, what would it be?
15. Do you have anything to add?
16. Is your office affected by the academic schedule?
17. Do others in your office use the archives? If yes, why; if no, why not?

their remarks would be confidential and that none of their comments would be attributed to a specific person.

Results

Statistical information from the university provides sufficient data to test for use frequency. Total reference requests in 1990-91 numbered 650, and administrative use comprised 30 percent of these requests. In 1991-92, total reference requests numbered 557, and administrative use reached 41 percent.[32] Figure 4 indicates the frequency by month for the

---

32 Archives Annual Reports, 1990-91 and 1991-92.

Figure 4. Administrative Use by Month, 1988/89-1992/93

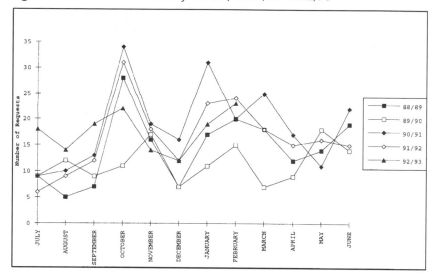

past five years and gives a visual representation of administrative use frequency by month. October and February are consistently the months with the greatest amount of administrative use. Both are midsemester periods at the university. Dips occur in December for the holidays and in July-August, a less popular quarter for both student enrollment and faculty teaching. Clearly, the traditional academic calendar influences the pace and need for administrative consultation of university records.

The differing amounts of administrative use by these four groups (higher administration, support services, departments, and student organizations) is shown in Figure 5. In the interviews, only the higher administrative interviewees indicated that their offices were not affected by the academic schedule. This is demonstrated by the data that indicate that archival reference questions from higher administrative offices are the most evenly distributed throughout the year and over the five-year period of the four groups studied.

A series of analyses of variance computations was done to determine if increased usage between the academic years 1988-89 and 1991-92 was within the range of statistical probability. In spite of the overall growth trend in the archival program, administrative requests were significantly lower in the 1989-90 academic year. The statistical comparisons indicate that administrative use in 1989-90 is lower than would be statistically probable than 1990-1991, and 1991-92, and 1992-93. No explanation could be found for this. Administrative use in 1990-91 is probabilistically higher than either the previous or subsequent years (although 1992-93 should come close when all the reference statistics have been counted). The high degree of administrative use in 1990-91 is possibly attributable to

Figure 5. Administrative Users by Category, 1988/89-1992/93

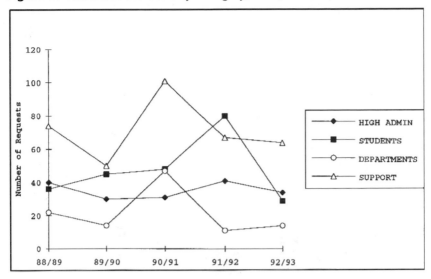

participation in a reaccreditation self-study, which was mentioned in several of the interviews and on the reference forms in the archives. The increased use may also be part of a general trend toward greater usage of the archives by administrators, which is evident by looking at the overall use frequencies for the five-year period. But the growth in this archives surpasses the level of use one would predict through statistical analyses. This is definitely a growing archival program, which is increasing use every year.[33]

The comparisons of usage between different categories of administrative users are also revealing. Support services are consistently the heaviest users of the archives. As previously noted, the numerical distribution over five years shows that use by higher administration has been the most consistent during the period in question. Departmental use peaked in 1990-91 during the pre-reaccreditation self-study. Otherwise, departmental use is also stable. The reaccreditation process was a significant event in both the life of the university and the archives. This demonstrates how a single event can bring many more reference requests to the archives and how important it is to respond to that event in a manner that brings the requestors back when they have an ordinary question. As was revealed in the interviews, administrative users who had successful

---

33 After examining the frequency data, a one-factor analysis of variance (AOV) was computed to test if any significant difference between the number of requests and the years (1988-89 to 1991-92). This was done for the four-year period for which complete data were available at the university. A statistically significant difference is found between yearly levels of use, $F(3,44) = 3.93$, the critical value at the .05 level is 2.76. As a next step, a Multiple F test indicates that critical differences exist between some of the sample means, $CD(1,44) = 4.42$, $p < .05$ — thus, identifying 1989-90 as an exceptionally low-use year and 1990-91 as an exceptionally high-use year.

Figure 6. Percentage of Use by Different Categories of Administrative Users, 1988/89-1992/93

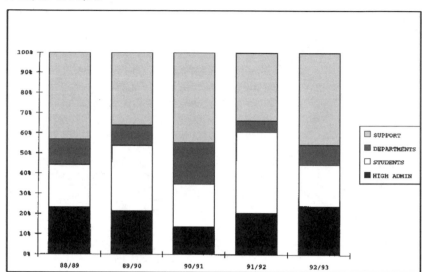

experiences (relevant retrieved information) in the archives were very likely to be repeat archival users.

Statistically significant differences exist between the various administrative groups of archives users. Support services use the archives reference services significantly more than all the other groups. There is also a wide discrepancy between student organizational and departmental use.[34] Figure 6 shows the percentage of use by each of the groups under study.

There is a consistent peak of archival reference requests by administrators in October over the five-year period. This is broken down in Figure 7, which illustrates the frequency of use in October 1988-89 to 1992-93, according to the different administrative use groups. Higher administration seems less prone to this tendency, and the interviewees from higher administration both stated that their offices are influenced little by the academic calendar. Student organizations, departments, and support services all show a rise in midsemester activity during the fall term. Student organizations must reregister themselves with the administration every few years to retain their status as official student organizations. This often entails a trip to the archives to find the organization's by-laws and other pertinent information, and it results in a statistically

---

34 A one-factor analysis of variance (*AOV*) was also completed to test for statistically significant use-frequency differences based on membership in the designated administrative use groups. This procedure confirmed that some statistically significant difference exists, $F (3,16) = 8.21, p < .05$, between rates of use by the different administrative groups over a five-year period (1988-89 to 1992-93).

Figure 7. Administrative Users in October, 1988-1992/93

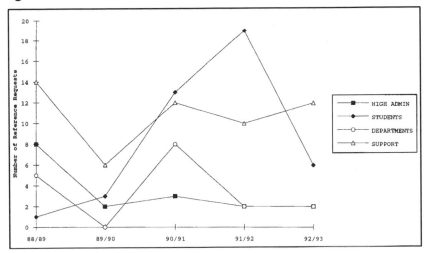

significant difference between student use and departmental and higher administrative use in the month of October.[35] Reasons for heavy support service use were not determined, but possible explanations are fall celebrations such as homecoming, which require a significant amount of public relations and alumni office activity.

Turning from the quantitative aspect of this study to the qualitative, the interviews at the university provide more evidence to support themes found in the literature and the statistical computations. Weick and Stinchcombe's observations concerning the lack of centrality of information in a loosely coupled system and the ensuing lack of a single organizational culture based on the collective memory of an institution is a major thrust of one of the interviews. For one of the interviewees, the archives' critical function is the preservation of the institutional memory. This interviewee attributes the institutional memory lapses to high turnover and the transitory nature of presidents, staff, faculty, and students.

The interviews also give evidence related to Quinn's assertion that time is of the essence for administrators. In four separate interviews, the interviewees said that they felt a tension between saving time by having the archives staff complete a research request and the interviewees' desires to do the research themselves. Interviewees thought they might

---

35 A significant difference also exists for October usage between groups, $F (3,16) = 8.38, p < .05$. A further multiple $F (1,16)$ test reveals a critical difference (4.82) between the means of use of support services (higher) and both higher administration and academic departments. There is also a critical difference in means (e.g., higher rate) between the rate of student use and higher administration and academic departments.

"see" something in the records that would be useful for their project but that had not specifically been requested of the archivist. In the interests of time, however, interviewees were willing to forgo these possible discoveries. Pugh notes that archivists assume historical researchers in archives want high recall. These administrators want high precision, but they realize there may be a high cost for this choice.

Pugh also expresses concerns that archival indexing systems are not serving historical users. The interviews revealed that none of the administrative users had ever used any of the archival inventories, the card catalog, or the finding aids. There are a combination of reasons for this phenomenon. First, much of the archival administrative reference is over the telephone and the "answer" is sent to the office. Even if users enter the archives, it is the archivist who translates the question and uses the inventory. As one interviewee stated, the archivist does the "dirty work." The question arises, for whom are the finding aids intended? If they are intended to aid the archivist, are they really designed for the archivist as audience?

This type of archival reference and research service places much of the question definition and the search strategy in the hands of the archivist. Ellis notes that scientific researchers benefit from backwards and forwards chaining, following citations, and pursuing additional works by favored authors. This pattern of reacting, following leads, and refining the search strategy is not an option for many administrative archival users who need the information yesterday and are very grateful to have an archivist do the work.

Two of the higher administrative interviewees regularly transferred files to the archives. Prior to sending the files, each interviewee prepares an inventory list. If these files are required in the future, the inventory list is used to select files. Neither administrator requests files that another office has transferred to the archives. One of the women said that if the files of another office were required, she would contact the secretary for that office and let the other secretary contact the archives. Exploring new archival territory is not popular among administrative users.

Two of the interviewees were employed by the university prior to the establishment of the archives, and another works in the same building with the archives. In these cases, existence of the archives was "always" known. The four other interviewees found out about the archives through other sources. One woman, now a full-time employee, discovered the archives when she was a student intern in her current office. Her boss told her to call the archives for the information she was seeking, and she found it "worked." She is now one of the archives' heaviest users. She works in an office that regularly transfers files to the archives. (As an aside, the former boss now teaches and has one class assignment requiring archival research.) One man found out about the archives after calling a frequent source of information, the documents librarian, who referred him to the archives. Although his work requires less archival research, since the initial contact he has been a repeat user. This makes one wonder if search behaviors are learned. If a behavior is fruitful, it will be repeated. If this is true, much of the increased usage since the self-study year prior to reaccreditation could be linked to good archives reference during that self-study.

As noted above, several of the administrative users who require archival materials the most are also in offices that regularly transfer materials to the archives. Records management at the university has not been systematically done in the past, and it was not mandatory for offices to participate. Records management at the university is similar to the programs described by Barritt, a program that adopts and adapts practices, rather than implementing mandatory policies. One of the occasional users expressed concern about his ability to regain records if they were transferred to the archives. This provides a small amount of evidence for the assertion that use and perceived ease of use affects compliance with records management programs. Although it requires more study, there does appear to be a logical, if unproven, link between higher use and larger amounts of records transferred to the archives. The effects of the recent approval of an official records management program by the board of trustees at this university will be interesting to follow.

One of the questions asked in the interviews concerned the degree to which administrators worried about the authenticity of the documentation or the reliability of the information. The biggest surprise in this study was that no interviewee had any major concerns. A couple of interviewees mentioned that they had confidence that the archival system would prevent any tampering that would affect authenticity (legality). One of the women commented that she probably should consider the reliability (accuracy) of the documents more carefully. Only one of the men stated that he had ever questioned information given by the archives, and this happened when a student assistant, not one of the professional archivists, provided the data. For these users, confidence in the information equals confidence in the professional archivist. There was considerable high praise for the archives director, and users wondered how the system would function without her.

Administrative users may approach archives with little experience in using archival records. Only one of the interviewees had specific training in research methods, where skepticism and criticism of sources might be acquired. More research is needed in how administrators interpret records. This is especially important when administrators are given "the answer" rather than records in context. Administrators view archivists as the protectors of the authenticity of records and see trust in the archivist as equivalent to the reliability of the answers they provide.

Bearman finds that 56 percent of the requests reported in his study were for specific items. A specific item is a need for a certain object, as opposed to a request for specific information that could come from a number of sources. This is somewhat supported by the data examined in this study and in the interviews. Interviewees were divided about how often they requested specific, known items. The two women who frequently request their own files are after specific items. The other interviewees are after specific items only a small portion of the time.

Conclusions

Better tracking of administrative users and administrative uses in university archives is necessary to provide a better basis for studying this important group of users. As Bearman, Maher, and Conway assert, archivists are better at tracking records used than at tracking users. A useful first step is revising the forms used for collecting statistics so that they will better reflect administrative use.

A second step is for archivists to pay greater attention to their unconscious filtering of information on the request forms. There are few questions on the forms analyzed for this study that do not reflect the archivist's understanding or even the answer to the question. A more user-oriented approach that would better represent the user's need is required. Mediated reference in archives is unlikely to change in the near future because of the organization of records according to provenance and the security under which collections must be housed. Reference archivists should note, however, that they are mediators in two ways. First they assist administrators in the question definition process, and then they themselves often filter sources during the search process. This aspect of administrative use needs further study.

By and large, the administrators were unaware of the scope of the archival holdings at the university. This lack of awareness of the entire holdings contributes to their feeling that by looking at the records themselves, they would see some other interesting item that they had not requested. This lack of awareness also ties into the nonuse of the archival inventories and finding aids. Do researchers not use finding aids because they are difficult to understand? Or do archivists unconsciously design finding aids to help archivists, who are aware of archival arrangement, can locate the materials better, and make the most use of the inventories? Clearly, if administrative users are not employing these devices to locate materials, the prioritization of the production of these devices and the emphasis placed on their production in archival education programs and archival workshops is questionable. This relates to Conway's notion of integrity — do archivists provide the most appropriate means of access to collections? Furthermore, how well does the administrative user's view of archivists as searchers and analyzers fit with archivists' perceptions of themselves? Pugh's concerns relating to drawbacks of mediated archival reference (e.g., an archivist's memory lapses or personality clashes between the archivist and the researcher) are exacerbated in a system where the administrator is entirely dependent on the archivist for access to information.

Another question arises concerning who needs training in research methods. Should better training be done with archival students on the graduate level so that they can better serve administrators? Or is it feasible to provide administrators with some orientation in the archives? Does this lack of knowledge concerning research methods and use of primary sources by administrative users result in a lax attitude toward authenticity and reliability of the documentation?

Administrative users, long the stepchildren in many archival programs, are now their primary constituency in many instances. Knowledge concerning the archival information needs, search strategies, and research skills of this group is small. This paper has presented some of the concerns and limited findings of a case study. More in-depth studies, as well as studies of administrative users in other college and university settings, are needed to refute or confirm the findings of this study. Administrative use studies in other types of institutional archives are also needed to better understand this phenomenon.

Part Seven:
Preservation

Sir Hilary Jenkinson identified the archivist's primary responsibility as the moral and physical defense of archives. It is thus natural that physical preservation of records has become an important priority for the archival profession. The three articles in this section consider preservation from a variety of perspectives.

James M. O'Toole addresses an important aspect of archival theory, in "On the Idea of Permanence." He delineates various ways that archivists have considered their responsibility to preserve records "permanently" or "in perpetuity," and how these concepts have been challenged by the physical impermanence of records media and by the scope of the problem of preserving vast quantities of modern records.

One of the means that archivists and librarians have used to determine the scope of these problems has been conducting surveys of preservation needs. In "Archival Preservation Practices in a Nationwide Context," Paul Conway presents the results of the first national survey of archival preservation practices in the United States. The article presents his methodology, findings, and recommendations, and is a useful example of the application of social science survey methodology to archival issues.

The methodology and practice of preservation has been an important segment of the preservation literature, covering a wide range of approaches to ensuring the longevity of records and their restoration. Archivists and librarians often focus attention on paper-based records and books, but other media face preservation challenges and often require even greater technical expertise. Christopher Ann Paton discusses the important preservation concerns for sound recordings, and offers technical advice, in "Preservation Re-recording of Audio Recordings in Archives." The rapid changes in preservation research and practice can be seen in the need to add a caveat and update to this article, only a few years after its initial publication. Although this update is needed, the article represents the value of practical advice given in the preservation literature.

21

On the Idea of Permanence

JAMES M. O'TOOLE

Abstract: This essay explores the changing understanding archivists have had of the idea of permanence as it applies to the records in their custody. Though it seems to be an absolute, archivists have in fact used this word to denote very different ideas and concepts, ranging from permanence of the information in documents to permanence of the physical objects themselves. Today, archivists are increasingly reluctant to employ the idea at all, and the essay concludes with some speculations about the future of archives without permanence.

> In time, the Rockies may crumble, Gibraltar may tumble; They're only made of clay. . . .
> Ira Gershwin

Like the practitioners of most other professions, archivists possess a vocabulary of their own, a set of words and phrases that hold special meaning for them and that help them structure and define what they do. Most of this vocabulary is perfectly recognizable to those outside the profession, but the peculiar meaning and significance of its elements are different for those within the field. Arrangement and description, for example, are words that both archivists and nonarchivists use, perhaps every day, but when an archivist uses them, they are intended to denote very specific activities and concepts that are generally absent when a layperson uses them. Professional vocabulary may degenerate into jargon, a term with a distinctly negative connotation, but regardless of that danger a

Reprinted with permission from the *American Archivist* 52 (Winter 1989): 10-25. This article was written as a product of the author's participation in the 1987 Research Fellowship Program for the Study of Modern Archives, administered by the Bentley Historical Library, University of Michigan, and funded by the Andrew W. Mellon Foundation, the Research Division of the National Endowment for the Humanities, and the University of Michigan. The author is grateful to a number of friends who read and commented on earlier versions of this essay, particularly his "fellow fellows," Dennis Rowley and Leon J. Stout.

particular set of terms and meanings is both inevitable and necessary for the development of any profession.[1]

Because the professional vocabulary of archivists is acquired and employed fairly readily, archivists generally do not reflect on the words they use or on how those words define and control the way they think and what they actually do. Just as no one can communicate at all by pausing to analyze every word that is uttered, so archivists cannot carry their glossaries with them at every moment and indeed have no need to. Too much reflection is paralyzing, but too little reflection risks obscuring distinctions that are rightly made, as well as blocking the consideration of new ideas and techniques that may be improvements over the accepted way of doing things. Periodically, therefore, it is useful to "pause in the day's occupations" to examine professional vocabulary, to understand how the words archivists use have changed over time and therefore how archival ideas have themselves developed. Such an exercise is more than just historical, tracing what ideas and words have meant at different times; it is also of benefit in present professional practice because it may open up new perspectives and possibilities.

One word in the archival lexicon used repeatedly without reflection is the word *permanent*. Archivists speak almost instinctively of their collections as being the permanent records of an individual or entity. The materials in archives are separated from the great mass of all the records ever created and are marked for special attention and treatment because they possess what is frequently identified as permanent value. Whether by accident or design — and the distinction is at the heart of the modern idea of appraisal — certain materials are selected by archives for preservation into the indefinite future. They are in that sense permanent. The word *permanent* does not appear in the standard glossary definition of *archives*, though the reverse is true: the entry for *permanent records* says simply, "*See* archives." The term has been employed in less formal sources and most archivists do indeed use it as a way of distinguishing archival records from those of lesser value.[2] Ironically, though archivists have not formally defined permanent records, the records managers have. The glossary of that profession specifies permanent records as those that are kept "indefinitely," often for legal reasons, and provided with "continuous preservation because of reference, historical or administrative significance."[3]

---

1 On the importance of precision in professional vocabulary, see Frank B. Evans, et al., "A Basic Glossary for Archivists, Manuscript Curators, and Records Managers," *American Archivist* 37 (1974): 415-16. On the general characteristics of professions, see Richard J. Cox, "Professionalism and Archivists in the United States," ibid., 49 (1986): 231-33.

2 Evans, "Basic Glossary," 417. No less an authority than Ernst Posner defined archives as "records considered worthy of permanent preservation," in *Collier's Encyclopedia*, 6th ed., s.v. "Archives."

3 Association of Records Managers and Administrators, *Glossary of Records Management Terms* (Prairie Village, Kans.: ARMA, 1985).

By judging some records to be permanent, archivists make a substantial commitment to them, a commitment of time and resources, a commitment that is intended to last well beyond the tenure or lifetime of any individual professional. From that judgment and that commitment, a whole range of specific activities seems logically to flow.

But what do archivists really mean when they talk about their holdings as permanent records? As Leonard Rapport has noted, permanent is "a convenient term for which no simple substitute comes to mind."[4] The timelessness of such a term is difficult to grasp, but the idea of permanence offers nonetheless all the comforts of any absolute. The word's meaning is so self-evident, why should it trouble us? To say that archival records are permanent seems to fix their nature beyond doubt and to establish beyond challenge the full extent of the archivist's responsibility to them. Permanence is like pregnancy: there is apparently no middle ground. In fact, however, *permanent* has always been a more complicated, even relative, term than it appears, and an examination of its shifting meaning and use over time may illuminate its current and future usefulness as a category in archival thinking.

Permanence in Oral and Written Cultures

Recording information and preserving it for long periods of time are very old problems, and human culture has found different ways of accomplishing these tasks. Before the invention of writing, a relatively late development for the species, all information had to be stored mentally and transmitted orally, and oral cultures evolved particular means of doing so efficiently and effectively.[5] By emphasizing certain characteristics that enhanced the memory — the use of formulaic language and rhythm; the embodiment in ritual of key stories, values, and pieces of information; the association of physical objects with certain events; the reliance on social and interpersonal communication of things to be remembered — all oral cultures, even those that survived into the twentieth century, achieved a degree of permanence in what they knew, preserved, and handed on to the indefinite future.[6] Some degree of

---

4 Leonard Rapport, "No Grandfather Clause: Reappraising Accessioned Records," *American Archivist* 44 (1981): 148.

5 For a general theory of the oral transmission of information, see Frederick J. Stielow, *The Management of Oral History Sound Archives* (New York: Greenwood Press, 1986), 11-33.

6 The literature on oral cultures is fascinating and extensive. For the best guide through the issues it raises, see Walter J. Ong, *Orality and Literacy: The Technologizing of the Word* (London: Methuen, 1982), esp. 31-57. On the use of formula and rhythm, see Eric A. Havelock, *The Literate Revolution in Greece and Its Aftermath* (Princeton: Princeton University Press, 1982), esp. 226, and Ananda E. Wood, *Knowledge Before Printing and After: The Indian Tradition in a Changing Kerala* (Delhi: Oxford University Press, 1985), 7-9. For ritual, see Jacob Neusner, *The Oral Torah: The Sacred Books of Judaism, An Introduction* (San Francisco: Harper & Row, 1986), 26-27, and Robert Goldenburg, "Talmud," in *Back to the Sources: Reading the Classic Jewish Texts*, ed. Barry

timelessness was achievable in such cultures: a kind of permanence was possible.

The advent of literacy, however, changed these mnemonic necessities and offered a more objective means of recording information and of preserving it intact for the indeterminate future. Specific texts, particular ways of expressing ideas, and not just the general thrust of a story or argument, could themselves be fixed and given permanence. *Accuracy* took on a new, more precise meaning based on continuity of text.[7] Since knowledge could now be written down and stored outside the brain, it would not be lost through forgetfulness, and it could be called back to life whenever necessary or desired. It could be more securely transmitted from one place to another or from one time to another. Permanence could be more reliably achieved through the preservation of writing. The ancient adage stated this advantage succinctly: *verba volent, littera scripta manet* — "words are fleeting, written letters remain." It was by remaining that writing could emerge as triumphant, even "pre-emptive," over oral means of preserving information.[8] Thus, the very act of writing something down would invest it with a permanence it would not otherwise have had. To be sure, not all writing was intended to be kept literally forever; indeed, early in literate cultures a distinction was drawn between writings created for posterity and those with only a limited effect or usefulness. St. Paul's letters to the Christian churches of the Mediterranean world, for example, were "near-oral" means of communication not necessarily intended to be enduring; in the Middle Ages, drafts of documents, meant to be transitional and impermanent, began to appear, writings produced on materials (such as wood blocks covered with wax) that were cheaper than those used for formal records.[9] Still, in comparison to purely oral systems, writing seemed a better, more reliable guarantee of permanence.

The distinction between the kind of permanence offered by oral cultures and that which was available to cultures with writing was most readily apparent at the times of transition from one system to the other.

W. Holtz (New York: Summit, 1984), 131, and Werner H. Kelber, *The Oral and Written Gospel: The Hermeneutics of Speaking and Writing in the Synoptic Tradition, Mark, Paul, and Q* (Philadelphia: Fortress Press, 1983), 168-177. For the use of objects as *aides-memoires*, see M. T. Clanchy, *From Memory to Written Record. England, 1066-1307* (Cambridge, Mass.: Harvard University Press, 1979), 21-24. For the social context of records, see Kelber, *Oral and Written Gospel*, 23-24 and 92-93, and Albert B. Lord, *The Singer of Tales* (Cambridge, Mass.: Harvard University Press, 1960).

7 Edward P. Dirringer, *The Book Before Printing: Ancient, Medieval, and Oriental* (New York: Dover, 1982), 15; Lord, *Singer of Tales*, 138.

8 Ong, *Orality and Literacy*, 11-12 ("pre-emptive," p. 12); Havelock, *Literate Revolution in Greece*, 87.

9 Kelber, *Oral and Written Gospel*, 168-69; Clanchy, *From Memory to Written Record*, 116-25; see also Ernst Posner, *Archives in the Ancient World* (Cambridge, Mass.: Harvard University Press, 1972), 4-5.

The history of writing is long and complex, but at least since the perfection of an alphabetic system by the Greeks (ca. 700 B.C.E.) writing has come to different cultures at different times, and the change has not always been smooth. Socrates, for example, was skeptical of writing, fearing that "it will implant forgetfulness" in the human mind, offering "no true wisdom, . . . but only its semblance." What is more, writing broke down the human links that were at the heart of the information storage and transfer process in the oral world. "Written words . . . seem to talk to you as though they were intelligent," the philosopher said, "but if you ask them anything about what they say, from a desire to be instructed, they go on telling you the same thing forever."[10] Writing could not be cross-examined as a speaker could, and Socrates found this a distinct disadvantage in the process of advancing understanding. Similarly, in ancient Jewish culture, both oral and written means of long-term storage of information coexisted for centuries, but social dislocation as well as religious and political turmoil led at different times to the encoding of certain basic tenets in written form. One such occasion was the emotionally powerful return to Zion (ca. 450 B.C.E.), which resulted in the codification of the Torah books known to Christians today as the Old Testament; another came after the destruction of the Jerusalem temple in 70 C.E. during the rise of Christianity, leading to the writing down of the teachings of the Talmud and the Mishnah, which had previously been available only in oral form.[11]

The key element in any such transition was not, as the historian M. T. Clanchy has pointed out with reference to Norman England, the mere fact of literacy itself (i.e., who can read and write and who cannot). Rather, the critical shift came with the reliance on written records rather than on individual recollection as the basis for society, by literates and nonliterates alike. Thus, the authors of the Christian Gospels, which had been transmitted orally for a generation or two before being written down, were deliberate in choosing language that emphasized the legal validity of the writing as an acceptable replacement for the actual eyewitness testimony of the members of the apostolic generation, whose stories they told.[12] By writing the Gospel narratives down, the authors hoped that they had thereby "guaranteed longevity, if not perpetuity."[13] Similarly, in medieval England transfers of land and other property, as

---

10 Plato, *Phaedrus*, 274C-275D. In this connection it is worthwhile to note that Socrates himself left no written account of his thinking, this task being performed for him by his next-generation, fully literate successor, Plato.

11 Neusner, *Oral Torah*, 26, 222.

12 Kelber, *Oral and Written Gospel*, 92–93; Birger Gerhardsson, *Memory and Manuscript: Oral Tradition and Written Transmission in Rabbinic Judaism and Early Christianity* (Uppsala, Sweden: Gleerup, 1961), 221-22.

13 Kelber, *Oral and Written Gospel*, 105.

well as other forms of agreements and contracts, came to be expressed in documents, and both the legal system and the language itself had to change as a result. Whereas in Edward I's time a nobleman could prove his title to a piece of land by displaying the rusty sword with which he had seized it years before, a generation later a charter was the only acceptable proof. At the same time, the word *deed* came to denote not only the act itself, but also the document that embodied and recorded the act and thus preserved the memory of it for future generations.[14] The results of this shift were both practical and symbolic, and it was the symbolic significance that underlined the greater degree of permanence that was available through writing. "A document could indeed make time stand still," Clanchy says of England (though the same could apply to other cultures in the process of accepting literacy); "it could pass on a record of an event to remote posterity."[15]

Permanence in American Archives

The seemingly inherent ability of written records to freeze time in this way, to make more reliably permanent what would remain fragile and evanescent if retained orally, meant that once records were preserved in archives they would attain a degree of permanence they might not otherwise have had. Because some records survived in archives while others did not, those that were preserved would naturally be valued more highly and therefore retained indefinitely. In eighteenth- and nineteenth-century America, as elsewhere and earlier, formal archival agencies readily accepted the responsibility to do just that. The subsequent discovery that archival records could be used for broad research as well as for administrative purposes reinforced this long-term view of the archives and their functions. As writing spread to all areas of American society and written records multiplied, not everything written down could be permanent, but everything gathered into an archives would be.

Most early American archival repositories, especially those founded with a specific commitment to research, stated this desire to ensure or enhance the permanence of their holdings. Though earlier preservation efforts had had similar motivations, the historical societies founded at the beginning of the nineteenth century took as their primary goal "the responsibility to safeguard their collections," and this responsibility was echoed by their many successors and imitators.[16] The American Antiquarian Society, established in 1812, proclaimed that "its immediate and peculiar design" was "to discover the antiquities of our own continent,

---

14 Clanchy, *From Memory to Written Record,* 2, 21-22, 36-37, 204.

15 Ibid., 20.

16 Leslie W. Dunlap, *American Historical Societies, 1790-1860* (Philadelphia: Porcupine Press, 1944), 79.

and, by providing a fixed and permanent place of deposit, to preserve such relicks of American antiquity as are portable." The society optimistically observed that "all things . . . are in their nature durable, if preserved from casualty and the ravages of time." Accordingly, "a depository like this may not only retard the ravages of time, but preserve from other causes of destruction many precious relicks of antiquity, . . . which once lost could never be restored."[17] Even the location of the repository was a deliberate choice in the desire to preserve records indefinitely. Given "the destruction so often experienced in large towns and cities by fire, as well as the ravages of an enemy . . . in times of war," the society decided that, "for a place of deposit for articles intended to be preserved for ages," an inland, out-of-the-way place (like Worcester, Massachusetts) was preferable.[18]

By offering a "fixed and permanent place of deposit" for "articles intended to last for [the] ages," other historical and archival collections likewise had permanence in mind as a rationale for their activities. One historical society in Ohio in the 1840s announced its intention "to preserve the manuscripts of the present day to the remotest ages of posterity," adding almost theologically, "or at least . . . as near forever as the power and sagacity of man will effect." To accomplish this it proposed to store its manuscript and archival holdings in "airtight metallic cases, regularly numbered and indexed, so that it may be known what is contained in each case without opening it."[19]

Preserving records in archival repositories was thus intended to ensure their permanence, but the promoters of such efforts recognized the potential dangers inherent in such an effort. Unusual circumstances could put carefully preserved records at risk. In 1814, for example, a committee of the New York Historical Society prepared to move that organization's collection out of the city in the event of a British attack; many smaller organizations, uncertain that they would be able to maintain the interest of a sufficient membership, provided for the relocation of their collections in the event of the organization's demise.[20] Fire was the most obvious hazard, and the destruction of some of the holdings of the Massachusetts Historical Society in 1825 and of most of the holdings of the Vermont Historical Society in 1857 provided sobering examples of how records that had been preserved and were intended to be permanent

---

17 *Archaeologia Americana: Transactions and Collections of the American Antiquarian Society* (Worcester, Mass., 1820), 1:18, 29, 30-31. The repeated association of documents with "relicks" is noteworthy.

18 Ibid., 31. This argument may simply have been an attempt to make a virtue of necessity, since the society's founders and benefactors were all located in Worcester already.

19 Quoted in Dunlap, *American Historical Societies*, 142. The organization in question is the Logan Historical Society of Cincinnati.

20 Ibid., 79.

could be lost. "By all manner of means," a colleague wrote Lyman C. Draper after one such disaster, "have a *fire-proof building*. Don't now look at size and splendor — but safety."[21]

Concern for the safety of archival materials led those responsible for them to consider other means of preserving them "as near forever as the power and sagacity of man will effect," and understandably they turned to whatever technology, the fruit of that sagacity, was available to them. The society that had proposed airtight containers with detailed descriptions on the outside apparently hoped to safeguard its holdings from the possible deleterious effects of the environment and from the wear and tear of handling — both of these concerns entirely recognizable to modern conservators. Even more common among these archives was the aim of preserving their collections by publishing them. "Repositories of every kind, however desirable, are exposed to . . . accidents, from the hand of time, from the power of the elements, and from the ravages of unprincipled men, as to render them unsafe," the Massachusetts Historical Society declared in 1806. "There is no sure way of preserving historical records and materials, but by *multiplying the copies*. The art of printing affords a mode of preservation more effectual than Corinthian brass or Egyptian marble."[22]

Permanence of Information

Among the many early archives and historical organizations that sought to preserve their materials by publishing and diffusing them, there developed a surprisingly modern distinction between the permanence of the archival documents themselves and the permanence of the information they contained. Initially, historical collections were valued principally for their information, information that testified to the "pastness of the past" and thereby certified "the reality of progress." Only later did repositories come to value their collections as things worthy in their own right and, later still, as sources for specialized study by professional scholars.[23] Preserving the documents was certainly worthwhile, but it was not ultimately as important as preserving the information. By relying on printing as a preservation technology, one repository hoped to "secure our treasures by means of the press from the corrosions of time and the power of accident," while another sought to "preserve and perpetuate by publication."[24] The same principle could be applied to public records as

---

21 Quoted ibid., 79-80.

22 *Collections of the Massachusetts Historical Society* (Boston, 1806), 1:3.

23 Henry D. Shapiro, "Putting the Past Under Glass: Preservation and the Idea of History in the Mid-Nineteenth Century," *Prospects: An Annual of American Cultural Studies* 10 (1985): 243-78, describes the evolving viewpoint of collecting organizations; the quotations are at 258.

24 Walter Muir Whitehill, *Independent Historical Societies* (Boston: Boston Athenaeum, 1962), 40; Dunlap, *American Historical Societies*, 177.

to the holdings of private historical organizations. "Let us save what remains," Thomas Jefferson wrote in 1792, endorsing Ebenezer Hazard's first compilation of *American State Papers*, "not by vaults and locks, which fence them from the public eye and use in consigning them to the waste of time, but by such a multiplication of copies as shall place them beyond the reach of accident."[25] There were enough examples of the permanent preservation of the information contained in records through printing before the loss of the originals to highlight the importance and the usefulness of achieving permanence through publication. The most famous of these was the original journal of Massachusetts's Puritan governor John Winthrop, a portion of which had been destroyed by fire in 1825 after the publication of a documentary edition.[26]

As technology advanced, archivists gained access to other means by which they could hope to safeguard their collections and preserve them "as near forever" as they desired. The development of practical microfilm technology, for example, seemed to offer a better means of reproducing documents than letterpress publication — better because it preserved actual images of the items themselves, not just the information they contained, thereby in some sense preserving both. This use of microfilm for storing records of permanent value had been suggested as early as 1853, and by the early 1870s it was actually being employed. In 1871 a French insurance company was regularly producing a microfilm copy of all its policies; three years later an enterprising Irishman received a patent to record property deeds in this way, using what seems to have been a lineal ancestor of the modern-day rotary camera.[27]

Permanence of Original Documents

In the twentieth century still newer technological developments focused on archival records and eventually worked a near-revolution in the way archivists looked at and cared for the permanent records they held. Concern for the information in records was still strong, but concern for better treatment of the originals themselves increased, in part because it now seemed possible to do something about them. At least since the mid-nineteenth century, archivists had worried about the physical deterioration of their collections, even those that were already published or microfilmed, and about how to preserve them permanently; now the advance of preservation theory and practice offered the possibility that the long-desired goal could in fact be achieved. Preservation

---

25 Quoted in Whitehill, *Independent Historical Societies*, 4.

26 *Winthrop's Journal: "History of New England," 1630-1649*, ed. James Kendall Hosmer (New York: Barnes and Noble, 1908), 1:17-18.

27 Frederic Luther, *Microfilm: A History, 1839-1900* (Annapolis, Md.: National Microfilm Association, 1959), 24-25, 84, 94-95.

technicians learned more about the physical properties of documentary materials and the forces that caused them to deteriorate, and they began experimenting with methods for retarding, stopping, and reversing that deterioration.[28] In the process, the technical distinction between extending the so-called usable lifetime of documents (a more modest and realistic goal) and preserving them literally forever was often blurred. The "ravages of time" that had for so long troubled those in charge of archives could at last be controlled: real, physical permanence seemed within reach.

There may well have been a significant psychological predisposition in favor of preserving and repairing the original documents, of not being satisfied with printed or micrographic substitutes that preserved the original information, but in a different form. "Copies are never totally satisfactory," said the pioneer preservation researcher William J. Barrow in explaining the motivation for his work at the Virginia State Library, "for the originals possess unique and desirable characteristics lost in copying."[29] Though he did not specify what those "unique and desirable characteristics" were, he probably did not have to. The desire to preserve unusual original papers was often what had attracted many archivists to their profession in the first place. In its earliest manifestations, the collection of manuscripts was closely associated with the collection of other interesting curiosities, including museum objects and specimens in the physical and natural sciences.[30] These efforts were reinforced by a broader cultural disposition that preferred to see even historic items in their pristine condition. Deterioration "symbolizes failure," the philosopher of history David Lowenthal has observed, serving perhaps as a reminder of our own transcience and mortality. Accordingly, "however venerated a relic, its decay is seldom admired"; indeed, "decay is more dreadful when it seems our fault."[31] With the advent and apparent perfection of preservation technology, archivists seemed capable of mastering decay; not to do so would only increase the "fault" of those whose responsibility it was to keep the permanent records of society.

As a result of the work of Barrow and others throughout the middle of the twentieth century, an active concern for the details and techniques of conservation developed and flourished among archivists. They learned more about the physical characteristics of their holdings, and they were increasingly disposed to act on the basis of that knowledge. Advancing

---

28 For some of the early history of preservation work and research, see James L. Gear, "The Repair of Documents — American Beginnings," *American Archivist* 26 (1963): 469-75.

29 William J. Barrow, "Deacidification and Lamination of Deteriorated Documents, 1938-1963," *American Archivist* 28 (1965): 285.

30 Shapiro, "Putting the Past Under Glass," 244-45.

31 David Lowenthal, *The Past is a Foreign Country* (Cambridge: Cambridge University Press, 1985), 143, 147, 175.

far beyond early methods of "silking," or backing documents with synthetic crepeline, Barrow had perfected a method for deacidifying archival materials by about 1940, later maintaining that such a procedure extended their life expectancy "by a factor of from 8 to 10."[32] Archivists reported happily that they were using these procedures to good effect, along with the eventually controversial process of lamination (also developed by Barrow): Leon deVallinger, state archivist of Delaware, endorsed Barrow's method, reporting that his state archives had treated 5,000 documents in its conservation laboratory's first year of operation.[33] A kind of technological imperative took hold in archival thinking. Archivists could actively preserve their holdings; they could approach more nearly the long-desired goal of physical permanence. In the process, they did not doubt either the wisdom or the efficacy of doing so. They could do it, and they naturally assumed that they should.

Concern for conservation was suddenly everywhere in the archival profession. The very first article published in the new journal, the *American Archivist*, in 1938, dealt with the subject of "manuscript repair," and it was followed in subsequent issues by a string of related papers, many of them describing preservation and restoration laboratory techniques in great detail.[34] The Historical Records Survey of the depression-era Works Progress Administration was actively concerned with preservation problems as it went about its business of surveying the documentary holdings of the various states.[35] Barrow appeared regularly on the programs of archival meetings, describing his own research and not unnaturally promoting his own methods and procedures. He and other preservation specialists found interested audiences among their archival colleagues. A session at the Society of American Archivists' second annual meeting in Springfield, Illinois, in 1938 dealt with "Fumigating, Cleaning, and Repairing Archival Material," and the large audience greeted the formal presentations with "an animated discussion."[36]

Throughout the 1940s and 1950s the number of program sessions and journal articles on preservation activities, most focusing on specific techniques and positive steps that archivists could take, continued to

---

32 William J. Barrow, *The Barrow Method of Restoring Deteriorated Documents* (Richmond: Virginia State Library, 1965), 7. On silking and other methods of document repair and reinforcement, see Gear, "Repair of Documents," 470-75.

33 Leon deVallinger, "Lamination of Manuscripts at the Delaware State Archives, 1938-64," *American Archivist* 28 (1965): 290-93.

34 L. H. Smith, "Manuscript Repair in European Archives: I. Great Britain," *American Archivist* 1 (1938): 1-22. See also Smith's "Manuscript Repair in European Archives: II. The Continent (France, Belgium, the Netherlands)," ibid., 51-77.

35 William F. McDonald, *Federal Relief Administration and the Arts: The Origins and Administrative History of the Arts Projects of the Works Progress Administration* (Columbus, Ohio: Ohio State University Press, 1969), 751-828.

36 *American Archivist* 1 (1938): 233; ibid., 2 (1939): 23.

grow.[37] At the same time, though the concern for microfilm techniques and applications remained strong, consideration of preserving archival records through publication virtually disappeared from professional discussion.[38] With so much attention focused on the care and treatment of documents in their original form, archivists were — perhaps unconsciously, perhaps deliberately — restricting their notion of permanence. Increasingly, *permanence* became a technical term, a term that was defined by conservators and accepted by archivists in a limited, specific sense. More and more, *permanence* meant the physical permanence of archival collections, a goal which, thanks to the forward march of archival science, seemed attainable. "Today, for the first time," one technical report said expansively in 1964, "the possibility of preserving mankind's most significant records — in their original form and almost indefinitely — is at hand."[39]

Conservation Consciousness

Other aspects of professional culture reinforced this growing conservation consciousness. In April 1950, Arthur Kimberly of the National Archives announced the results of a study on archival record containers, approving the use of pressboard boxes (not specifically identified as being acid-neutral) covered with foil to retard fire damage. Two years later, the Hollinger Corporation advertised such a box for sale, again without any reference to its acid content, but highlighting the box's "unique metal edge construction, . . . no paste or glue to attract vermin."[40] Hollinger introduced in 1961 an archival file folder, "tested and approved by leading authorities," that was "100% Rope Manila Paper; PH Neutral Guaranteed," and in 1963 the Milltex Paper Company produced archival quality paper "for document, map and picture folders and for other uses where permanence is essential."[41] The Council on Library Resources funded a project to

---

37 See, for example, Adelaide E. Minogue, "Some Observations on the Flattening of Folded Records," *American Archivist* 8 (1945): 115-21, and Minogue, "Treatment of Fire and Water Damaged Records," ibid., 9 (1946): 17-25; James D. Breckenridge, "Have you Looked at Your Pictures Lately?" ibid., 17 (1954): 25-36; Harry F. Lewis, "The Deterioration of Book Paper in Library Use," ibid., 22 (1959): 309-22.

38 The National Historical Publications Commission, revitalized in the early 1950s, did begin to promote documentary publishing during this period, but its main goals were scholarly use and wider dissemination of materials rather than preservation. See Mary A. Giunta, "The NHPRC: Its Influence on Documentary Editing," *American Archivist* 49 (1986): 134-41, and Lester J. Cappon, "A Rationale for Historical Editing Past and Present," *William and Mary Quarterly*, 3rd ser., 23 (1966): 56-75.

39 "'P' Stands for Permanent," *The Laboratory: Current Developments in Instrumentation and Technique* (1964): 101.

40 Arthur Kimberly, "New Developments in Record Containers," *American Archivist* 13 (1950): 233-36; Hollinger advertisement, ibid., 15 (1952): 46.

41 Hollinger advertisement, *American Archivist* 24 (1961): 131; Milltex advertisement, ibid., 26 (1963): 468.

develop a "safer" archival box at about this same time. The result was the birth of what quickly became an archival staple and cynosure: the acid-free box, first advertised in the *American Archivist* in July 1966.[42] That journal had added a regular section of "Technical Notes" in April 1963, the first of which centered on some newly available microfilm equipment and, more significantly, on a test of various ballpoint pens to determine their suitability for use in making "permanent" records. In the following year, the journal took the next logical step. Deciding to practice what it preached with regard to physical permanence, the principal periodical for the archival profession in the United States changed the paper on which it was printed to one defined as durable (i.e., able to withstand wear and tear) and permanent (i.e., sufficiently stable chemically to withstand internal deterioration).[43]

As concern for the physical permanence of their collections grew, archivists and conservators naturally began to study the deterioration and preservation of records more intensively. The results were both a greater understanding of the nature of the problem and a greater realization that active, ongoing programs were needed to address it. A number of national studies were commissioned, and the dimensions of the preservation challenge began to emerge. The Association of Research Libraries (ARL) surveyed the condition of deteriorating library and archival materials and, with an activism that was typical of the Great Society era in which it appeared (1964), proposed a central national agency to address the problem. Ten years later ARL was working on "detailed specifications for a national system for preservation of library materials," which resulted in the formation of a National Conservation Advisory Board. On the regional level, too, archivists and librarians were banding together to advance the preservation cause in the interests of ensuring the permanence of their holdings. The New England (later Northeast) Document Conservation Center (NEDCC) was organized in 1973 to provide preservation and restoration services for that part of the country; several studies later explored the idea of setting up similar organizations elsewhere, especially in the West. The founding director of the NEDCC, George M. Cunha, became a sort of traveling missionary for the conservation gospel, and his works quickly became standard reading and reference points for archivists concerned about preserving their collections. In 1976 the Library of Congress sponsored a conference to outline the scope of a "national preservation program"; by the early 1980s the Society of American Archivists (SAA) had embarked, with money from the National Endowment for the Humanities, on a basic conservation program that sought, through workshops and publications, to

---

42 Gladys T. Piez, "Archival Containers — A Search for Safer Materials," *American Archivist* 27 (1964): 433-38; Puhlig Brothers advertisement, ibid., 29 (1966): 393.

43 "Technical Notes," *American Archivist* 26 (1963): 263-66; announcement, ibid., 27 (1964): 562.

spread awareness of physical conservation issues even more widely through the archival profession.[44]

So much thinking and worrying about the physical permanence of records resulted in archivists' and conservators' beginning to appreciate just how massive the problem was. This recognition was only aggravated as the number of archives holding valuable records grew throughout the 1970s, with more and more bulky collections expanding at an alarming rate. The spread of new technologies, especially those that were computer-based (tapes and disks, for example), further complicated the problem by adding new media for storing information, media that had their own particular problems and required their own special treatments. The 5,000 manuscript documents treated by the Delaware State Archives in the late 1930s, impressive in its own day, were now seen as only the very small tip of a very large iceberg.

A kind of preservation apocalypticism set in, as archivists came to understand graphically not only what was needed to make their collections truly permanent, but also just how impossible it would be to do so with the time and resources that would ever conceivably be available. "The magnitude of the deterioration problem in American manuscript and printed records appears to be far greater than realized," William Barrow had said calmly enough in the 1960s, but in the following decades a steadily gloomier tone became the standard in any consideration of preservation and permanence. Cunha spoke of the "dire straits" the archival profession was in and estimated that as much as 80 percent of all materials in archives and library special collections was in need of some kind of treatment. Daniel Boorstin, the librarian of Congress, described the problem, which was of "cataclysmic proportions," as being "all the more serious because it [i.e., the slow deterioration of materials] is so undramatic."[45] Drama was not lacking from other quarters, however, as one report showed a conservator blowing on a handful of paper that scattered through the air like so much confetti. A film produced in 1987

---

44 Many of these developments are described in Carolyn Clark Morrow, "National Preservation Planning and Regional Conservation Efforts," *Conserving and Preserving Library Materials,* ed. Kathryn Luther Henderson and William T. Henderson (Urbana-Champaign: University of Illinois, 1983), 37-53. See also Ann Russell, "The Northeast Document Conservation Center: A Case Study of Cooperative Conservation," *American Archivist* 45 (1982): 45-52. ARL, *The Preservation of Deteriorating Books: An Examination of the Problem with Recommendations for a Solution* (Washington, D.C.: Library of Congress, 1980). Cunha's work is summarized in his *Conservation of Library Materials: A Manual and Bibliography on the Care, Repair and Restoration of Library Materials,* 2 vol. (Metuchen, N. J.: Scarecrow Press, 1971), and its updated version, *Library and Archives Conservation: 1980s and Beyond,* 2 vol. (Metuchen, N. J.: Scarecrow Press, 1983).

45 Barrow, *Barrow Method for Restoring Deteriorated Documents,* 3; Cunha, *Conservation of Library Materials,* 1:140, 233; *A National Preservation Program* (Washington, D.C.: Library of Congress, 1980), 11-12, 13. Boorstin painted a picture of documentary deterioration as a kind of "silent killer" of civilization that had to be checked.

and broadcast widely on public television showed a deputy librarian of
Congress performing the same trick and, while a funeral bell tolled a
steady peal of doom on the soundtrack, the narrator spoke sonorously of
"these precious volumes [that] are burning away with insidious slow fires,
. . . falling apart within their covers and within the very fortress meant
to preserve them."[46] A study prepared for the National Association of
Government Archives and Records Administrators (NAGARA) concluded
that no state even approached "the goal of providing adequate preservation" and estimated that a colossal $500 million would be needed to
remedy the situation and to provide satisfactorily for the "permanently
valuable government records [the state archives] need to preserve and
make accessible."[47] Having become convinced of how important it was to
preserve their physical holdings permanently, archivists began to realize
how impossible it would be to do precisely that.

Retreat from the Absolute

Virtually everywhere in the profession there was a subtle but steady
retreat from the idea of physical permanence as archivists had come to
understand it. The National Archives had recognized as early as 1950
that "a selective, rather than a comprehensive, rehabilitation of records"
was the only realistic choice, especially in large collections, though this
distinction was often lost in the conservation euphoria of the following
decades.[48] More to the point, archivists began to grow uncomfortable
with the apparently limitless commitment that adherence to a notion
of absolute permanence implied, and they began to view questions of
appraisal and preservation in much more relative terms. Maynard Brichford,
author of what became a standard manual on appraisal, felt constrained
in 1977 to put the word *permanent* in quotation marks while describing
how the value and usefulness of records changed over time, thereby
intimating that what was permanent about archives might not in fact
endure. "The documented past is represented by a static body of surviving records," he wrote, "but the human perception of the past is dynamic." Archivists erred, therefore, if they imputed too great a degree of
immutability to their collections.[49] Shortly thereafter, Brichford applied

---

46 *Slow Fires: On the Preservation of the Human Record* (Council on Library Resources, 1987). When
   the author showed this film to an introductory archives class recently, the students giggled
   through this melodramatic introduction to the problem.

47 National Materials Advisory Board, *Preservation of Historical Records* (Washington, D.C.: National
   Academy Press, 1986), 40; NAGARA, *Preservation Needs in State Archives* (Albany: NAGARA, 1986),
   2-3, 5, 13.

48 "The Rehabilitation of Paper Records," *National Archives Staff Information Paper No. 16* (December
   1950), 5.

49 Maynard J. Brichford, *Archives and Manuscripts: Appraisal and Accessioning* (Chicago: SAA, 1977), 5.

this belief specifically to the subject of preservation in archives, prompting a blunt "let it rot" philosophy. "Documents that need the conservator's attention, if they are to be preserved for posterity, may not be worth the cost of conservation," he argued before an SAA annual meeting. While acknowledging such an attitude as potentially "sinful," he added pointedly: "We have wasted a lot of money placing acid-laden documents in acid-neutral folders and boxes."[50]

A significant aspect of the retreat from the absolute of permanence was a renewed emphasis on the idea of the intrinsic value of records. T. R. Schellenberg had hinted at this idea in his discussion of the form and uniqueness of certain records, and the notion had been current in archival and preservation circles for some time. The archival glossary of 1974 included *intrinsic value,* prescribing its use to designate the worth of documents "dependent upon some unique factor," a not particularly helpful designation in singling out materials in collections the entirety of which claimed to be unique.[51] Concern over the possibility of throwing money into a bottomless conservation pit in the hope of achieving permanence led to a renewed consideration of intrinsic value. The National Archives formed a committee on the subject in 1979, which sought to outline the criteria for assessing the "qualities and characteristics that make the records in their original format the only archivally acceptable form for preservation." All records had such characteristics, of course, but some had them "to such a significant degree" that the originals had to be maintained and, if necessary, restored.[52] The report itemized nine standards by which to judge intrinsic value, including aesthetic value, exhibit potential, and cases where the physical form of the record might itself be a legitimate object of study. Far more tricky was the issue of "general and substantial public interest because of direct association with famous or historically significant" persons or events, a category that presumably covered items like the Declaration of Independence.[53] As with Justice Potter Stewart's supposed remark about pornography — "I can't define it, but I know it when I see it" — archivists were left with some guidelines for judging intrinsic value but with something less than a precise formula for evaluating it.

---

50 Maynard J. Brichford, "Seven Sinful Thoughts," *American Archivist* 43 (1980): 14. That Brichford felt compelled to label this notion "sinful" is an indication of how much archivists had come to accept the responsibility of at least attempting to ensure the physical permanence of their collections.

51 Evans, "Basic Glossary," *American Archivist* 37 (1974): 424. See also T. R. Schellenberg, *Modern Archives: Principles and Techniques* (Chicago: University of Chicago Press, 1956), 150-51, and Schellenberg's chapter on "Record Attributes" in *The Management of Archives* (New York: Columbia University Press, 1965), 119-43.

52 The committee's report, originally contained in *NARS Staff Information Paper No. 21* (September 1980), is reproduced in the *Report of the Committee on the Records of Government* (Washington, D.C.: Government Printing Office, 1985), 117-25; the quotations are at 118.

53 Ibid., 120-21.

The decision to subject any particular records to preservation treatment remained an involved process, one in which priorities and desires had to be balanced against available resources and potential benefits. For the first time, archivists began to examine and rethink the technological imperative that had previously governed much of their approach to preservation work. The National Archives, for example, determined that only 0.5 percent of its holdings — a far cry from Cunha's 80 percent — should ever receive preservation laboratory treatment, with the remainder receiving no treatment, "maintenance" through proper housing in a good environment, or copying.[54]

At the same time, the focusing of renewed attention on the subject of appraisal led archivists to rethink the triple meaning of the idea of "preserving" records: collecting and acquiring the original documents; intervening to conserve or restore their physical condition; and preserving the information in an alternative format. The implications for the idea of permanence were to reemphasize the relative at the expense of the absolute. Leonard Rapport presented the case for reappraising and destroying records that already were in archives, in what was a serious blow to the notion of archives as truly permanent records. Arguing that there should be "no grandfather clause" for records, Rapport raised the possibility that permanence was a quality that was subject to change or even outright revocation: records that were permanent today might not be so permanent tomorrow.[55] Though his argument was controversial and, in fact, few archives have as yet followed his advice on a large scale, Rapport's point of view helped underline a growing archival attitude in which permanence seemed an unrealistic and unattainable ideal.

Other examples of this reconsideration of the idea of permanence emerged in professional discussion. In the middle 1980s, the SAA Task Force on Goals and Priorities (GAP) in its monumental and comprehensive report, *Planning for the Archival Profession,* nowhere referred to archives as permanent records, preferring instead to speak of "records of enduring value."[56] This distinction, relying on the participial form, was more than semantic or purely stylistic: the implication was that once the enduring value stopped enduring, the permanence of the records was at an end. At about the same time, even a preservation group recognized the problem and spoke of the idea of "acceptable permanence," treating information in its original form or copying it into some other form so that it could survive and be useful to a certain degree.[57] If the GAP report implied that

---

54 National Archives and Records Service, *Twenty Year Records Preservation Plan* (Washington, D.C.: NARS, 1984), no pagination.

55 Rapport, "No Grandfather Clause," 143-50.

56 *Planning for the Archival Profession* (Chicago: Society of American Archivists, 1986), 8 and elsewhere.

57 Materials Advisory Board, *Preservation of Historical Records,* 6.

permanence could exist for a time and then come to an end, this group seemed to argue that a limited amount of permanence might be enough. In either case, the absolute had been dethroned, and archivists were left with the vague sense that permanence simply meant nothing any more. Whether consciously or not, the word *permanent* seemed to be disappearing from the archival lexicon, even as it was lingering in the archival mind.

Archives without Permanence

Thus, the idea of permanence as it is understood by archivists has changed considerably over time, passing from an unattainable desire to an absolute value within the realm of achievement to an extremely relative notion of little clarity. Today, the idea may be in the process of evolving out of usage altogether. This should not come as a surprise; the twentieth century is not a congenial climate for absolutes of any kind. At the same time, an information-rich society such as the modern one is inclined to accord any particular datum or document a lesser value than would an information-poor society. If this is the case, however, what are the implications for archival theory and practice? How should archivists think and what should they do in a professional world without the security of the traditional idea of permanence? As might be expected, there are more questions than answers.

First, do conservation decisions become simpler or more complex? The restriction of the idea of permanence to mean primarily physical permanence instilled in archivists a set of instinctive habits, the value of which seemed impossible to doubt. Would any archivist, given the choice, actually prefer to store records in acidic folders rather than acid-free ones? Is not Brichford's sinful thought precisely that, and even foolhardy as well? From one perspective the benefits of acid-free storage appear so self-evident as to defy challenge. From another, such an activity is at best an exercise in fighting a rear-guard battle that will only delay the inevitable for a brief time. Not even the most enthusiastic conservator can say with any certainty what the measurable benefits of acid-free storage are. At worst, therefore, archivists may indeed have simply wasted their money. At the same time, preservation activities become a slippery slope, leading inexorably to ever more elaborate and expensive procedures. In the way conservators have "sold" conservation consciousness and in the way archivists have been disposed to "buy" it, archivists have been lulled into a false sense of security about the permanence of their collections. As a result, they have lost sight of the larger purposes of their work — preserving over time information that is of benefit and use to society — and have restricted the available options for approaching that goal.

Refocusing their attention on the permanence of the information in records rather than on the documents themselves will restore a broader view and will reemphasize the possibilities and the usefulness of preserving information in formats other than the original. For larger archives, this will inevitably mean a better use of scanty resources: the National Archives found, for example, that physical conservation of one large group of heavily used records was more expensive by factors of two or three to one than transferring the information they contained to other media.[58] For smaller repositories, unable to provide or acquire sophisticated alternative technologies, the implications will be less dramatic but no less real: acid-free folders (which actually touch the documents) might still be a necessity, for example, but the money spent on acid-free boxes (which touch only the folders) might well be applied to other purposes. In repositories of whatever size, the intrinsic value of records might be assessed more rigorously, perhaps with the assistance of subject specialists, before materials are submitted to the conservation laboratory. A harsher, more demanding standard of what archivists wish to preserve — and why — might restrict even further the amount and nature of material that is submitted for conservation treatment.

Second, do appraisal and accessioning decisions become simpler or more complex in a world without physical permanence? Abandoning the implicit guarantee of permanence that archival preservation has come to entail, will certain repositories not have freer reign to define and redefine the scope and purpose of their collections, as well as greater flexibility in managing them? Will an active documentation strategy approach to assembling archival materials make constant redefinition of what is permanent and what is not more likely? Despite their reluctance to do so heretofore, will repositories not be in a better position to follow Rapport's advice and to cross the line between permanent and valuable on the one hand and impermanent and valueless on the other? Though no one would argue for archival collections that respond only to research fads (real or perceived), the result may be archives that are more regularly forced to reexamine their basic purposes and to respond more directly to the needs of their users and of society at large. At the same time, however, the ongoing reappraisal of collections will surely complicate the acquisition of material. Will records creators — whether private individuals seeking repositories for their papers (as traditionally defined) or officers of the parent organizations that archives serve — be reluctant to entrust their recorded memory to archivists without the assurance that it will be safeguarded as long as possible? The abandonment of permanence as an archival ideal may open new options in the management of historical records, but it may also lead the creators of those records to look elsewhere for assistance in preserving them.

---

58 NARS, *A Study of the Alternatives for the Preservation and Reference Handling of the Pension, Bounty-Land, and Compiled Military Service Records in the National Archives* (Washington, D.C.: NARS, 1984), esp. Table 6.2.

Third, what impact will new technologies have on the notion of permanence? By almost any standard, virtually all of the newer means of recording information, though more flexible, are less permanent than older ones. The contrast is most visible at the extremes: magnetic impulses on computer disks are certainly more unstable than baked clay tablets. The continued development of the technological means for recording information will therefore increase the options available to archivists for preserving information and for transferring it from one medium to another. Like physical conservation, however, such transfers are not without cost, and archivists will be forced to evaluate their options repeatedly, resisting the natural human temptation to rely on similar solutions to different problems. Choice is a fine thing and seems to possess inherent value. The availability of choice, however, does not make the choosing any easier.

Finally, does the decline of archival permanence shed any light on the fundamental motivations that cause creators to create records and archivists to keep them? Why do individuals or administrators not simply throw their records away once their immediate usefulness is passed? Why do they give them to archivists, and why do archivists lavish such attention on them? What are the intrinsic values of certain records, whether for individuals — diaries, love letters, records of significant life-events; for corporate bodies — the company's charter, the denomination's organizational minutes, the school's first enrollment register; or for whole societies — the Declaration of Independence? What is the basis for the human disposition to keep these records, to keep them in as near pristine condition as possible for as long as possible? Is it merely revulsion at even the smallest reminders of our own mortality, as Lowenthal maintains, or is there a larger, even quasi-religious meaning? What are the connections between records and relics? How do both attempt to ensure the continued presence of past events, persons, and things, and what ongoing meaning do they therefore have? To argue that permanence is devoid of meaning may be possible, but do certain basic human impulses thereby go unfulfilled?

Such larger questions are surely beyond the scope of the archivist's daily professional practice. They do, however, constitute appropriate subjects for future research and reflection. Questions about the meaning of archival vocabulary are always relevant because they lead to greater clarity in thinking about what archivists do and why they do it. In maintaining a healthy balance between theory and practice, the tension is helpful for any living and growing profession.

22

Archival Preservation Practice in a Nationwide Context

PAUL CONWAY

Abstract: The preservation of historical materials, in a variety of forms and formats, is both a cultural necessity and a central responsibility for professional archivists. Archivists need to define for themselves just what archival preservation entails and to assess the capacity of the thousands of archives, large and small, scattered and isolated from each other, to develop and administer sophisticated preservation programs. The author presents the results of the first nationwide study of archival preservation practices in the United States. He describes a model of archival preservation that partially shaped the research project, summarizes the research process involved, reports the major findings, and discusses the implications of the research for archivists and the archival profession.

The preservation of historical materials, in a variety of forms and formats, is both a cultural necessity and a central management responsibility for professional archivists. The findings and implications of a two-year research, evaluation, and planning project, the results of which are described in this article, make it clear now more than ever that archivists confront special challenges in preserving the unique archival materials in their custody. In responding to these challenges, archivists need to develop processes, within the context of a nationwide archival preservation strategy, that improve their capacity to undertake comprehensive preservation programs at the institutional, regional, state, and national levels. Meeting this need is as much an educational problem as a financial one.

Until a decade ago, it appeared possible that archivists could fulfill their responsibilities to the historical record, and therefore to society, merely by collecting and housing materials in secure environments and permitting access to those who asked. Today more and more archivists recognize that preservation is a specific set of technical and administrative processes that affect every archival function.[1]

Reprinted with permission from the *American Archivist* 53 (Spring 1990): 204-22.

1 Mary Lynn Ritzenthaler, *Archives and Manuscripts: Conservation* (Chicago: Society of American Archivists, 1983), 47.

The development and implementation of comprehensive, integrated preservation activities in archives can be an expensive proposition. Environmentally benign storage space, for example, comes at a premium price; many treatment activities are labor intensive and often require specialized equipment and supplies and highly skilled personnel. And yet, in the past few years archivists have seen a dramatic increase in popular support and funding from government and private sources for preservation projects.[2] The hypothetical question that confronts every person committed to the preservation of what Paul Banks calls our "movable culture" is: "If a windfall befell you, could you spend the money wisely?"[3]

Some preservation experts have believed for years that wisdom is learned, not bought. Pamela Darling, for instance, concludes that accurate information is crucial to successful administration, and that the real problem is the shortage, not of money, but of knowledge. "Financial constraints are serious and will become more so; but until the preservation field reaches the point at which most people know what ought to be done and how it should be done, the lack of money to do it on a scale appropriate to the need is not terribly significant."[4]

Archivists need to define for themselves just what archival preservation entails and assess the capacity of the thousands of archives, large and small, scattered and isolated from each other, to develop and administer sophisticated preservation programs. From this base of information, archivists will then be able to build a nationwide strategy for archival preservation that supports preservation programs instead of recommending how to pour money into flashy but limited projects.

It is with these issues in mind that the Society of American Archivists, with the assistance of the National Endowment for the Humanities (NEH), carried out the first nationwide study of archival preservation practices.[5] This article will describe a model of archival preservation that partially shaped the research project, summarize the research process involved, report the major findings of a nationwide survey, and discuss the implications of the overall project for archivists and the archival profession.

---

2 The popular acclaim accorded the film *Slow Fires: On the Preservation of the Human Record* (Council on Library Resources, 1987), and the recent major increases in funding for the NEH Office of Preservation are but two examples of the renewed public commitment to preserving cultural resources.

3 Paul Banks, unpublished keynote address to Latin American Archivists Conservation and Preservation Institute, Austin, Texas, 11 September 1989, 2.

4 Pamela W. Darling, "Creativity v. Despair: The Challenge of Preservation Administration," *Library Trends* 30 (Fall 1981): 185.

5 National Association of Government Archives and Records Administrators, *Preservation Needs in State Archives* (Albany: NAGARA, 1985). This is a national study, prepared by Howard Lowell, concerning the nation's 50 state archives.

Archival Preservation: A Proposed Definition

Archival preservation is the acquisition, organization, and distribution of resources (human, physical, monetary) to ensure adequate protection of historical information of enduring value for access by present and future generations.

Archival preservation encompasses planning and implementing policies, procedures, and processes that together prevent further deterioration or renew the usability of selected groups of materials.

Archival preservation management, when most effective, requires that planning precede implementation, and that prevention activities have priority over renewal activities.

What Is Archival Preservation?

One distinguishing characteristic of an evolving field of specialization, such as preservation, is disagreement on key definitions. Definition setting sometimes seems like a trivial exercise. At certain times, however, program development and research both become dependent on clear statements of principles and priorities. In the past decade, archivists and librarians have been approaching such clarity.[6] The following three-part working definition synthesizes an emerging consensus and serves as a structure for the research project.

First and foremost, the essence of archival preservation is resource allocation:

Archival preservation is the acquisition, organization, and distribution of resources (human, physical, monetary) to ensure adequate protection of historical information of enduring value for access by present and future generations.

Underlying this first part of the definition are a number of assumptions. First, as its ultimate goal, preservation is for use and not simply for its own sake. Second, preservation largely concerns information and knowledge, in a variety of forms and formats, that has been identified as

---

6 "Glossary of Selected Preservation Terms," *ALCTS Newsletter* 1 (1990): 14-15. The case for consensus is made in Pamela Darling and Sherelyn Ogden, "From Problems Perceived to Programs in Practice: The Preservation of Library Resources in the U.S.A., 1956-1980," *Library Resources & Technical Services* 25 (January/March 1981): 10. The best preservation bibliographies are published annually in *Library Resources & Technical Services* (*LRTS*). See Lisa Fox, "A Two Year Perspective on Library Preservation: An Annotated Bibliography," *LRTS* 30 (July/September 1986): 290-318; Carla J. Montori, "Library Preservation in 1986: An Annotated Bibliography," *LRTS* 31 (October/December 1987): 365-85; Carla J. Montori and Karl Eric Longstreth, "The Preservation of Library Materials, 1987: A Review of the Literature," *LRTS* 32 (July 1988): 235-47; and Karl E. Longstreth, "The Preservation of Library Materials in 1988: A Review of the Literature," *LRTS* 33 (July 1989): 217-26.

having long-term values, including historical, legal, evidential, informational, and monetary. Archivists have the primary responsibility for
identifying these values. Third, the word *adequate* in the definition
implies that there is no ultimate or perfect solution to the preservation
challenge and that there are many ways to approach solutions — probably
as many ways as there are archivists. Finally, the definition assumes that
responsibility for preservation ultimately rests with every person charged
with caring for historical materials and pervades every function of a
repository. Collection or repository level strategies take precedence over
activities directed toward individual items.[7]

Although these assumptions are echoed by nearly every author who
has written on managing preservation programs, a second level of definition is needed that organizes the wide variety of specific preservation
activities into a conceptual structure:

> *Archival preservation encompasses planning and implementing policies,*
> *procedures, and processes that together prevent further deterioration or*
> *renew the usability of selected groups of materials.*

The statement suggests a possible way to identify and organize in
two dimensions activities relating to the care and handling of archival
materials. The first dimension distinguishes between the two basic
aspects of the management function: planning and implementation.[8]
The second dimension reflects the distinction between activities that
prevent or significantly retard deterioration and those that address damage that has already occurred. Less than a decade ago, archivists used the
term *conservation* to describe all activities on archival materials, whether
preventive or corrective. Today the term *preservation* is widely considered
by conservators, preservation librarians, and archivists to be an umbrella
under which conservation treatments on items or groups of materials
are included.

Prevention involves identifying problems in the acquisition, storage,
and handling of materials; establishing repository-wide policies and
procedures that take a systems approach covering the entire life-cycle of
materials; and taking specific actions to retard deterioration or damage

---

7 Some of the most persuasive arguments on these points are contained in Pamela W. Darling,
  "Planning for the Future," in *The Library Preservation Program: Models, Priorities, Possibilities*, ed.
  Jan Merrill-Oldham and Merrily Smith (Chicago: American Library Association, 1985), 103-10;
  Ritzenthaler, *Archives and Manuscripts: Conservation;* Robert H. Patterson, "Conservation: What
  We Should Do Until the Conservator and the Twenty-First Century Arrive," in *Conserving and
  Preserving Library Materials*, ed. Kathryn Luther Henderson and William T. Henderson (Urbana-
  Champaign: University of Illinois, 1983), 12.

8 Paul H. McCarthy, "The Management of Archives: A Research Agenda," *American Archivist* 51
  (Winter/Spring 1988): 52-69.

to the entire collection.[9] There are four major planning activities in prevention:

- Survey the building and microenvironments for variation from standards on temperature, relative humidity, light, dust, gases, and pests.
- Prepare contingency plans for use in case of fire, flood, storms, and other natural or humanmade disasters.
- Establish policies on use of holdings by patrons and staff and on the public display of holdings.
- Conduct surveys assessing the scope and nature of deterioration within collections.

The model contains four corresponding implementation activities:

- Install equipment to monitor and stabilize environmental conditions.
- Maintain the physical facilities routinely.
- Enforce security procedures for staff, patrons, and others.
- Implement routine holdings maintenance actions, including rehousing and removing or replacing damaged or deteriorated items.[10]

Renewal involves policies, procedures, and processes that improve or otherwise enhance the usability of groups of archival materials. There are two principal planning activities in the renewal area:

- Develop a set of strategies to evaluate and select materials for physical and chemical treatments, for reformatting, and for replacement, as appropriate.
- Establish or review specific recovery procedures to be followed in the case of disaster.

The model contains four corresponding implementation activities:

- Treat batches of materials physically or chemically, including washing, deacidifying, drying or humidifying, resizing, dry cleaning, restoring, repairing, and rebinding.
- Reformat materials on microfilm, fiche, paper, optical, or magnetic media.
- Replace original items with duplicates, microform, or paper.
- Respond to emergencies and disasters in a timely fashion.

---

9 The specific activities noted in Figure 1 are adapted from "Standard Terminology for USMARC 583," recently developed by ALA's Preservation of Library Materials Section, with cooperation from the Library of Congress.

10 Mary Lynn Ritzenthaler, *Preservation of Archival Records: Holdings Maintenance at the National Archives,* Technical Information Paper Number 6 (Washington, D.C.: NARA, 1990).

Figure 1.

Archival Preservation

	Planning	Implementation
Prevention	Environmental survey Disaster planning Use policies Holdings survey	Environmental controls[1] Building maintenance Security procedures[2] Holdings maintenance[3] ---------------------------------- Staff and user education Outreach/community liaison Fundraising
Renewal	Strategy for treatment Strategy for reformatting Strategy for replacement Disaster procedures	Physical and chemical treatments[4] Reformat[5] Replace[6] Disaster response

[1] Temperature, relative humidity, light, dust, gas, pests

[2] Building, stacks, reference room

[3] Rehouse, remove, or replace damaging or deteriorating items

[4] Wash, deacidify, dry or humidify, resize, dry-clean, restore, repair, rebind

[5] Microfilm, fiche, paper, optical disk

[6] Microform, paper, duplicate copy

Figure 1 displays archival preservation activities graphically. Several observations are important here. First, the structure is not mediaspecific but includes prevention and renewal activities appropriate for all types and formats of materials found in an archives (indeed, even in the same box), including loose and bound paper-based materials, film, and magnetic and optical media. Second, in reality archival preservation is neither as static nor as two-dimensional as presented above. There should always be an ongoing interaction between planning and implementation that involves monitoring progress and making adjustments as necessary. Third, activities such as staff and user education, outreach and community liaison, and fund raising certainly have major impacts on the preservation of archival materials; and they should be considered in developing a preservation program.

The management of archival preservation in any institutional setting is largely incremental and involves making choices among options over a long period of time. Priorities are needed to guide these choices, giving rise to a third part of the definition:

Archival preservation management, when most effective, requires that planning precede implementation, and that prevention activities have priority over renewal activities.

This third element of the definition is particularly important for purposes of research, program development, and education. Without a statement of priorities and values, it would be difficult to assess individual efforts, more difficult still to compare the progress of archival programs, and nearly impossible to chart over time how the archival profession meets its central preservation mandate.[11]

How the Research Project Was Designed

The primary goal of the research project was to construct a meaningful portrait of current archival preservation activity as a point of departure for designing SAA's next decade of educational initiatives. The centerpiece of the research project was a nationwide survey of archival repositories supported by literature reviews, an assessment of the documentation on SAA's decade-long experience with preservation and conservation education, interviews with preservation experts, and on-site inspections of conservation laboratories. The working definitions described above guided the development of the research project.

Two current limitations of the archival community, however, complicated the design of the nationwide survey itself. First, no full listing of archival and manuscript repositories exists. The recently published *Directory of Archival Repositories in the United States* has serious coverage biases, especially in terms of the range of types of repositories covered.[12] In addition, a number of the 4,200 organizations included can most generously be described as "wanna be" archives, fundamentally lacking in holdings, staff, and services.

Possible alternatives to the *Directory* are the membership database of the Society of American Archivists and an assemblage of membership directories from over 50 regional and local archival associations. Neither the membership database nor the regional listings have been subjected to a systematic analysis to determine how representative they are of the archival profession as a whole. An unpublished study comparing joint membership in SAA with regional associations shows that overlap ranges from 11 percent to

---

11 For a discussion of the implications of the definition for archival education, see Paul Conway, "Archival Preservation: Definitions for Improving Education and Training," *Restaurator* 10, no. 2 (1989): 47-60.

12 *Directory of Archives and Manuscript Repositories in the United States*, 2nd ed. (Phoenix: Oryx Press, 1988); reviewed by Paul Conway in *American Archivist* 52 (Winter 1989): 102-3.

54 percent, depending in part on the age of the regional association.[13] For purposes of the current study, it was prohibitively expensive and time consuming to combine the SAA database with regional and local listings.

A second limitation that complicated the design of a nationwide study is the absence of accepted standards defining an archives. For example, unlike the fields of public or academic librarianship, the archival profession is largely defined in terms of the nature of the materials collected rather than in terms of the user populations served or the setting and functions of the repository. The ubiquitous nature of historical materials and the long history of small, isolated collecting programs makes it difficult, if not impossible, to define the archival universe. Even if an adequate list of archival repositories existed, selecting a sample would have required confronting serious definitional issues that were beyond the scope of the study.[14]

Considering these limitations, and the original charge by NEH to attempt to assess the impact of SAA's preservation education programs on participants, the research centered on a more limited study population: administrative units that enrolled one or more staff members in one of the 22 Basic Archival Conservation Workshops offered by SAA from 1981 to 1987. The total number of original participants in the program was 544. A count of discrete organizations in the full group of participants yielded 400 archival repositories. The study excluded four consultants without an institutional affiliation, three organizations from Canada, and the National Archives central office in Washington, D.C., which has vast resources and a unique mission.

Data for the study were gathered by means of a questionnaire sent by mail to the director or key contact person at each archival repository. The technique for administering the survey was based on the Dillman Total Design Method, which calls for a carefully constructed, pretested instrument and cover letter, and multiple follow-up contacts to encourage a high response rate.[15]

The questionnaire itself consisted of an eight-page booklet. Almost all questions were multiple choice, requiring only that respondents circle the appropriate response or fill in blank lines. Each questionnaire had a unique number, making it possible to administer the study effectively while giving respondents anonymity.

Four hundred questionnaires were sent on 28 March 1989 by first-class mail, accompanied by a personally addressed letter and a preprinted,

---

13 Timothy Ericson, then education officer of the Society of American Archivists, compiled these figures by matching membership lists from 30 regional archival associations with the SAA membership database.

14 Richard J. Cox, "Professionalism and Archivists in the United States," *American Archivist* 49 (Summer 1986): 229-48.

15 Don A. Dillman, *Mail and Telephone Surveys: The Total Design Method* (New York: Wiley, 1978), 160-99.

stamped return envelope. Six weeks after a postcard reminder and a second copy of the questionnaire were mailed in succession, 320 of 400 questionnaires had been returned, for a base response rate of 80 percent. An additional 20 individuals returned the questionnaire either too late for processing or uncompleted with sometimes lengthy explanations about how little time they had for questionnaires. These unusable questionnaires bring the overall response rate to a respectable 85 percent.[16]

Administrative Setting

The survey questionnaire was designed to yield a basic portrait of archival settings. The study's unit of analysis is the "administrative unit," rather than the individual survey respondent or the parent institution. An administrative unit is a separately identifiable organizational structure with a primary responsibility for acquiring, preserving, and making available to users archival resources in a variety of media. Examples of administrative units are a special collections department in an academic or public library; a state archives division or independent historical society; the archives-library of a corporation or nonprofit organization; the archives of a diocesan head-quarters; or a rare book and manuscript library administered separately.

When interpreting the findings, it is important to remember that the group of institutions studied is not necessarily representative of the archival community as a whole. The survey responses describe only one set of archival programs, a self-selected, yet very diverse group.[17]

Table 1 shows how the 320 responding archival units are distributed among eight types of parent organizations, compared with the distribution of respondents to the 1985 Census of Archival Institutions.[18] The *federal* category consists of archival units that are part of the federal government, including National Archives field units and National Park Service historic sites, but not including the National Archives in Washington, D.C. The *state* category consists of state archives and state historical societies. The *local* category primarily consists of municipal archives, local historical societies, and public libraries. *Corporate* refers both to profit and nonprofit organizations. The *religious* category

---

16 The approximate total cost for printing and mailing the original questionnaire, the postcard, and the follow-up letter was $1,400, or about $4.40 per usable response. More information on the design of the questionnaire and administration of the survey is available directly from the author.

17 Social scientists distinguish between research that is statistically generalizable to a large population from that which describes characteristics of a known population for purposes of developing a base of information for further research. The latter approach is taken in the current study. See Charles H. Backstrom and Gerald Hursh-Cesar, *Survey Research*, 2nd. ed. (New York: Wiley, 1981), 37.

18 Paul Conway, "Perspectives on Archival Resources: The 1985 Census of Archival Institutions," *American Archivist* 50 (Spring 1987): 174-91. The 1985 census population consisted of institutions represented in SAA's current membership database. Forty-four percent of those contacted returned the census questionnaire.

Table 1.

Administrative Setting				
	1989 Survey Respondents		1985 Census Respondents	
Academic	40%	(129)	38%	(206)
Local	16%	(50)	5%	(29)
Religious	12%	(37)	19%	(103)
Museum	8%	(26)	3%	(19)
State	8%	(26)	10%	(60)
Corporate	7%	(22)	6%	(33)
Federal	6%	(20)	5%	(26)
Special	3%	(10)	13%	(73)
Total	100%	(320)	100%	(549)

Note: *Figures in parentheses represent the actual numbers of respondents in each category. Percentages in this and the following tables have been rounded to whole numbers and thus do not always total 100 percent.*

excludes denominational colleges and universities, which are included in the academic category, along with the three prep school archives. The *special subject* category contains archives whose primary purpose is to collect in a focused subject area, even though technically they may be affiliated with another type of organization. Finally, the *museum* category contains archival units that document the activities or collections of a museum. In most cases, respondents' self-categorizations were accepted at face value, unless an obvious error was detected during data analysis.

The distribution among types of parent organizations is quite similar from 1985 to 1989. Proportionately greater numbers of religious institutions may have responded to the 1985 census because of targeted publicity at the time in a Catholic weekly magazine. In addition, it appears that relatively fewer local historical societies were represented in the 1985 census because the population studied consisted of institutions drawn from SAA's membership database. Only 54 percent of respondents to the 1989 survey were affiliated with SAA in any way.

Most archivists work in administrative units that are, in many cases, minor parts of their larger parent organizations. Only 17 percent of responding units can be characterized as independent organizations with ultimate responsibility for their unit's budget, organization, and activities. The remaining 83 percent are departments or divisions in organizations whose primary mission may have little to do with the care of historical materials.

The survey documents the intimate connection between archival units and libraries. A majority (56 percent) of all responding units are a part of a library. Special collections departments of academic libraries, local history collections in public libraries, and corporate archive departments in corporate libraries are the most typical examples of archival units in libraries.

Size of Archival Units

Archival units vary tremendously in size, regardless of how size is determined. One possible measure of size is a unit's total annual budget. Such information is difficult to obtain in a mail survey. Only half of the respondents to the 1985 census, for instance, were willing or able to report their total annual budget, and fewer still were able to break out the figure into predefined categories. Small administrative units often do not have any control over budgets and function on a "funds as needed" basis. In addition, archival administrators sometimes consider budgetary information to be highly confidential.

The 1985 census demonstrated that staff size, measured in full-time equivalents (FTEs), could serve as a somewhat reliable proxy measure of resources, since typically about 75 percent of a unit's resources are used to pay salaries and benefits. The preservation survey gathered information on the number of FTEs in each administrative unit involved with the administration and care of archival materials. Table 2 reports the figures by type of parent organization, ordered from largest to smallest median staff size. Included are full- and part-time employees, as well as student assistants and volunteers.

State-level archival units are significantly larger than any other group of archives, averaging more than 20 FTEs per unit. Howard Lowell's study of preservation needs in state archives yielded an average of 14.5 FTEs for

Table 2.

Size of Archival Unit in Number of Full-Time Equivalents (FTEs)								
	FTEs							
	0-1	1.1-3.0	3.1-10	11+	N	Mean	Min.	Max.	Median
State	0%	19%	31%	50%					
N	0	5	8	13	26	20.3	2.0	87	11.0
Federal	10%	25%	30%	35%					
N	2	5	6	7	20	8.1	1.0	19	7.0
Local	12%	44%	36%	8%					
N	6	22	18	4	50	5.4	0.13	50	2.9
Corporate	18%	50%	23%	9%					
N	4	11	5	2	22	5.7	0.38	36	2.3
Academic	23%	33%	30%	13%					
N	30	43	39	17	129	5.4	0.05	34	2.2
Museum	23%	39%	23%	15%					
N	6	10	6	4	26	6.5	0.6	60	2.0
Special	0%	70%	30%	0%					
N	0	7	3	0	10	3.2	1.1	8	1.8
Religious	43%	40%	19%	0%					
N	15	15	7	0	37	2.2	0.3	9	1.0
ALL	19%	37%	29%	15%					
N	63	118	92	47	320	6.5	0.05	87	2.7

Table 3.

Size of Archival Unit in Volume of Holdings (cubic or linear feet)									
	10–100 ft.	101–750 ft.	751–3,000 ft	3,001–7,500 ft	7,501 + ft.	N	Mean	Min.	Max.	Median
State	8%	4%	17%	13%	58%					
N	2	1	4	3	14	24	23,111	100	86,000	8,500
Federal	10%	20%	15%	25%	30%					
N	2	4	3	5	6	20	6,719	10	30,000	3,276
Academic	14%	24%	25%	18%	18%					
N	18	31	32	23	23	127	4,942	15	50,000	1,499
Corporate	0%	52%	33%	10%	5%					
N	0	11	7	2	1	21	1,829	200	13,000	635
Special	10%	40%	30%	10%	10%					
N	1	4	3	1	1	10	1,927	30	10,000	500
Local	22%	37%	20%	14%	6%					
N	11	18	10	7	3	49	2,187	18	21,000	413
Religious	11%	66%	17%	6%	0%					
N	4	23	6	2	0	35	800	25	4,500	332
Museum	27%	31%	27%	12%	4%					
N	7	8	7	3	1	26	1,886	12	16,900	263
ALL	14%	32%	23%	15%	16%					
N	45	100	72	46	49	312	5,070	10	86,000	987

42 state archives.[19] The breakout by size grouping shows the high concentration of one-person shops in religious, academic, and museum organizations.

Staff size alone, however, is not a sufficient base for judging the preservation challenges of archival units. Individual archives may vary considerably in terms of the volume of materials for which they have responsibility. Survey respondents were asked to report the total cubic or linear footage of paper-based holdings, as well as the number of reels of microfilm and sheets of microfiche in the collection. As a way of roughly comparing types of units, Table 3 reports the responses to the question of volume of paper-based holdings, ordered from greatest to least median volume of holdings in cubic or linear feet.

The variation between types of archival units is tremendous. An average state archives or state historical society has almost 30 times as much material as a typical religious archives. On slightly closer inspection, three clusters of archival programs emerge. Federal and state programs are much larger, at least in terms of holdings, than any other group. Local, corporate, religious, special subject, and museum archives typically are at the other end of the spectrum, with most of them falling well below 500

---

19 NAGARA, *Preservation Needs*, 16.

linear feet per organization. The typical academic archives falls somewhere in the middle in terms of volume. One implication of this variation is that there may not be a single approach that is appropriate for planning preservation activities and taking preservation action in all settings. Planning tools, educational programs, selection strategies, and perhaps even funding approaches may need to be tailored to archival units in specialized institutional settings.

Variation within any one type of archival unit is also large. In every type of organization except corporate, at least one archival unit reported having less than 100 linear feet of material, in some cases far less. At the other end of the spectrum, at least one archives in each category reported having custody of more than 10,000 feet of material. The largest state archives reported having 86,000 feet of paper-based records, which is consistent with Howard Lowell's findings. Lowell reported on the difficulty of getting archives to report accurate information uniformly, and the same caution applies with this study. Even if the figures are taken as approximate and used for general comparison only, it still is necessary to develop another way of comparing and contrasting archives with widely varying resources and staff.

Intensity of Care Index

Four hypothetical cases illustrate the extremes in the relationship of volume of holdings to size of staff. In the first case, a unit has custody of huge quantities of material but has limited staff to service the holdings. A records center operation with archival functions is a typical example. In this case, only the most rudimentary preservation actions may be possible beyond those necessary to protect the collection from fire and theft. In the second case, a unit also has custody of a large volume of material, but with a large staff, perhaps organized into functional departments. Many state archives and federal repositories fall into this category. In this case, if properly planned, preservation activities may begin to approach the preferred situation in which all departments and functions have a preservation component, overseen by one or more individuals with comprehensive responsibility.

In a third case, a unit has custody of a relatively small amount of material, but also has little or no staff to care for it. A significant portion of archival units, especially in college and university settings, are in this group. In this case, identifying a proper balance between holdings and resources, and identifying priorities for action are crucial to accomplishing systematic preservation activities. In the final case, a unit has custody of a small amount of material and has ample resources to care for it. A typical example of this case may be a museum whose archival holdings are an auxiliary responsibility compared to the care and conservation of works of art.

One possible approach to the problem of comparing archival programs is to build a measure of the preservation challenge that considers
both the quantity of historical materials needing care and the staff
resources available to do the job. Such a measure is needed, not only
because of variation among and between types of archival units, but also
because the extent to which an archival unit is capable of carrying out
systematic preservation activities, regardless of their costs, may be largely
dependent on achieving a balance between available resources and the
preservation needs of collections.

For purposes of this study, an Intensity of Care Index has been calculated by dividing the volume of holdings in linear feet for each archival
unit by the total FTEs in that unit. The index may be a more meaningful
way of measuring size of repositories and may indicate which types of
repositories face the greatest preservation challenges. Archival repositories
with the lowest intensity of care (high ratio of holdings to staff) face the
greatest pressure in balancing the demands of the collection with available resources. Units with the highest intensity of care (low ratio) may be
out of balance in the other extreme, with a middle group facing moderate, but perhaps manageable pressure.[20]

Table 4 displays the results of calculating the index ratio for each
survey respondent, ordered from highest to lowest median score. The
Intensity of Care Index flattens out the differences between types of
administrative units. With the exception of state archives (which always
seem to be the exception), both the averages and midpoints are much
more similar than either holdings or staff taken separately. Instead of a
factor of 28 separating the high and low figures, the factor is only eight,
with the median for all units in the middle.

When the Intensity of Care figures are collapsed into three categories, the preservation challenge faced by each type of archival unit
becomes clearer. State archives and archival units in academic environments have relatively larger proportions in the low-intensity category,
over 1,000 feet per FTE. On the other extreme, museum archives, special
subject collections, and many units in local settings care for holdings at a
higher intensity, having less than 250 linear feet of holdings per FTE. The
remaining types of organizations are clustered in the middle, around
300 linear feet per FTE.

The figures indicate that no single approach to preserving historical
materials will be satisfactory for all archival units. Those in the low-intensity
category need far more assistance in setting priorities and getting the
greatest benefit from limited resources. Those units in the high-intensity
category should be encouraged to resist the temptation to indulge in
excessive treatment activities. Archives with moderate intensity of care

---

20 See Conway, "Perspectives," 185, for an earlier use of the Intensity of Care Index.

Table 4.

	Intensity of Care (Volume of Holdings per FTE)							
	High (Less than 250 feet/ FTE)	Moderate (250- 1,000 feet/ FTE)	Low (More than 1,000 feet/ FTE)	N	Mean	Min.	Max.	Median
State	16%	36%	48%					
N	4	9	12	25	1,359.8	29.4	6,462	872
Academic	28%	40%	32%					
N	35	50	41	126	920.2	11.7	8,000	600
Corporate	38%	52%	10%					
N	8	11	2	21	505.3	12.3	2,500	337
Federal	35%	35%	30%					
N	7	7	6	20	829.8	10	3,846	337
Religious	46%	41%	14%					
N	17	15	5	37	526.5	25	3,920	300
Special	50%	20%	30%					
N	5	2	3	10	549.3	20.7	1,250	182
Local	60%	23%	17%					
N	29	11	8	48	465.7	1.2	3,068	160
Museum	65%	19%	15%					
N	17	5	4	26	618.5	3.6	8,325	105
ALL	39%	35%	26%					
N	122	110	81	313	768.6	1.2	8,325	405

may benefit most from tools and techniques that expand their capacity to plan comprehensive preservation programs. One implication of calculating an intensity of care measure is that continuing education workshops and institutes, publications and handbooks, and other tools designed to assist archivists in their preservation tasks should be targeted carefully to archival programs with different levels of need.

The boundaries between the three categories of the Intensity of Care Index are not hard and fast. Further research is needed to refine the index as a fully reliable measure. At this stage repositories with significant collections of nonpaper materials may not be assigned to the proper category. In addition, the index ignores variation in the value of any particular collection. It may be that a unit in the low-intensity category contains an extraordinarily valuable but small collection requiring intensive item-level treatment.

Conservation Expertise

Archivists need ready access to conservation expertise since preservation has a technical side to it that may seem daunting to archivists who are not also chemists, microbiologists, and mechanical engineers. The survey contained two simple questions designed to find out how available such expertise is to archivists. Respondents were asked first to indicate whether any staff members of the administrative unit had received training in conservation by graduate course work or formal apprenticeships, and then if conservators are readily available within the parent institution for consultation.

Thirty-eight percent (122) of the respondents claimed to have staff trained in conservation beyond the basic level. Twenty-five percent (79) of the respondents claimed to have access, either readily or with some effort, to a conservator in the parent institution. When combined, the answers to these two questions provide a rough estimate of the availability of conservation expertise.

Overall, about 12 percent (37) of responding institutions claimed to have both conservation expertise in the archival unit and access to a conservator. Fully 54 percent of the group (174) have access to neither staff trained in conservation nor an in-house conservation department. The remaining 34 percent of the respondents (109) have either conservation expertise on staff, or an in-house conservator. Seventy percent of this middle group claimed to have expertise on the staff but no ready access to in-house conservators. The claims of respondents should be judged carefully, since the true level of technical expertise in archival units may be significantly lower than claimed. Nevertheless, this group of archival repositories that participated in SAA's workshop program expresses a fairly high level of confidence that conservation expertise can be located easily when needed.

Budget

The existence of a specific line item for conservation treatments and supplies in the annual budget of an archival unit is an important indicator that archivists are institutionalizing preservation activities. SAA's basic conservation workshop emphasized the importance of targeting conservation funds directly in the budget. Throughout the history of the program, workshop applicants were asked to indicate if a line item for conservation existed, and if so, how much money was allocated per year. A nearly identical question was included in the 1989 survey of participating institutions. Table 5 shows the percentage of workshop participants who reported a specific budget line for supplies and services (excluding personnel), the percentage of respondents who had a budget line item in 1988, and the median annual conservation budgets in 1988 for eight types of institutions. Information on budgets derived from the original workshop application forms is not included in the table because of the poor quality of the data.

The table suggests that there has been a significant increase in the percentage of archival units that have a specific conservation budget.

Table 5.

Institutions with Specific Budgets for Conservation Supplies and Services				
	Workshop Participants 1981-87		1989 Survey Respondents	Median 1988 Budget
Museum	50%	(27)	61%	(15)	$1,950
Local	28%	(28)	60%	(40)	$1,500
Special	36%	(16)	60%	(5)	$1,300
Corporate	17%	(6)	55%	(12)	$750
Federal	19%	(7)	55%	(11)	$7,076
State	43%	(19)	54%	(14)	$6,100
Religious	22%	(11)	41%	(11)	$700
Academic	19%	(28)	28%	(32)	$2,687
ALL	28%	(142)	44%	(140)	$2,475

Publicly supported archives have the most generous budgets; federal government archives as a group seem to have made the greatest strides in incorporating conservation treatments into the annual budget. Museum archives have the best record overall. The two columns of figures are reported by the same population — participants in SAA's workshop program — suggesting that significant progress has been made in the past decade to make preservation a routine part of archival practice, even if the amount of money currently allocated to conservation supplies and services is small.

About one-third of the survey questionnaire was designed to discover the extent to which archival units are attempting to carry out preservation activities in the variety of areas described earlier in the model shown in Figure 1. For purposes of this article, the findings on environmental conditions, holdings maintenance, treatment activities, and microfilm production will be reported.

Environmental Care Index

The base of reliable information about preservation activities in archives is so limited that the current study could only develop a simple portrait of current conditions. A more sophisticated analysis would assess the capabilities of archivists to control environmental conditions in key storage areas, monitor the environment accurately and continuously, and protect their holdings from fire, pests, theft, and natural and human-made disasters.[21] A less complete picture of the scope of preventive activities, however, may be drawn by combining responses to a set of simple questions about essential activities.

---

21 Due to an oversight during the design process, the survey questionnaire neglected to probe in any systematic way the problems archivists confront with mold and pests.

Archivists' answers to those questions, in lieu of direct observation or measurement, form the basis for the four components of an Environmental Care Index (ECI) — temperature stability, monitoring equipment, fire protection, and disaster planning. The first component, temperature control, was assessed by simply asking respondents to state whether their storage areas were equipped to provide a controlled temperature plus or minus three degrees Fahrenheit. Fifty-six percent (179) of the survey respondents claimed to have such steady temperatures, while only 44 percent (141) claimed to be able to control relative humidity in the storage areas. Both figures should be greeted with a certain amount of skepticism.[22]

The second component of the index is the use of a recording hygrothermograph, which Mary Lynn Ritzenthaler considers to be an essential piece of equipment for archivists.[23] Again, it was not possible in the limited space of the questionnaire to inquire about the capabilities of archivists to calibrate and maintain such equipment, or even to place it in the proper location. Twenty-seven percent (86) of the survey respondents reported having at least one recording hygrothermograph in the storage area.

Protection of archival materials from fire and the capability to suppress fire are a third important indicator of the capabilities of archival units to carry out preventive preservation. The survey asked a multipart question to assess the level of fire protection in the storage area. Ten percent (32) of all respondents may indeed be violating fire codes in their community by having neither fire and smoke detection equipment in the stacks nor any capacity to put out fires that may start. It is important to note that respondents in this group either do not have basic fire detection equipment or do not know if they do, which is just as dangerous.

Fifty-two percent (166) of the group have fire and smoke detection equipment in place and fire extinguishers in the storage areas, but do not necessarily have the capacity to suppress fires after hours. The remaining 38 percent (162) of archival units have detection equipment in place and the capacity to suppress fires at any time, either by wet/dry sprinklers, halon gas, or carbon dioxide gas.

Finally, disaster planning is widely recognized as an essential part of a comprehensive preservation program. A well-crafted, up-to-date plan helps the staff of an archives prevent humanmade disasters, react to catastrophic events in a timely way, and limit damage to materials during recovery. Fifty-six percent (179) of the survey respondents claimed to have a disaster plan in place or in the planning stages.

---

22 The questionnaire contained a follow-up question intended to obtain information on the actual temperature in the storage area on the day the survey was completed. Data from this question proved to be unreliable when it became apparent during data entry that respondents sometimes listed the outside ambient air temperature. The actual question read "What is today's temperature in the area where the majority of your materials are stored?"

23 Ritzenthaler, *Archives and Manuscripts: Conservation*, 32-34.

Table 6.

		Environmental Care Index				
		Number of Index Elements Reported				
	None	1	2	3	All	Mean
Federal	0%	20%	15%	5%	60%	3.05
N	0	4	3	1	12	20
State	12%	19%	15%	35%	19%	2.30
N	3	5	4	9	5	26
Museum	15%	12%	31%	27%	15%	2.15
N	4	3	8	7	4	26
Corporate	9%	46%	14%	23%	9%	1.77
N	2	10	3	5	2	22
Local	18%	26%	34%	18%	4%	1.64
N	9	13	17	9	2	50
Academic	16%	35%	25%	20%	5%	1.63
N	20	45	32	26	6	129
Special	20%	30%	20%	30%	0%	1.60
N	2	3	2	3	0	10
Religious	43%	27%	14%	14%	3%	1.05
N	16	10	5	5	1	37
ALL	18%	28%	24%	20%	10%	1.76
N	56	93	74	65	32	320

Table 6 reports the results of combining the four components into an Environmental Care Index for each type of reporting organization, ordered by mean score. The first column displays the percentage of archival units that reported having no stable temperature controls, no monitoring devices, no fire protection, and no disaster plan. Overall, 18 percent (56) of the survey respondents fall into this category. In the fifth column, at the other end of the spectrum, are units that reported having all four components of the Environmental Care Index in place. Overall, 10 percent (32) of the units are in this category. In the middle columns are archives with either one, two, or three of the index components. The final column is the average score for each type of repository.

The Environmental Care Index is not designed for judging the efforts of any particular archives, but rather as a tool for comparing groups or types of archives. As a group, federal, state, and museum archives appear to have accomplished the most in providing minimal level environmental care for their collections. Religious archives, representing more than 10 percent of the respondents, are struggling to put in place the four basic components of the Environmental Care Index. Only one of the religious archives reported having all four components.

Care of Collections

Archivists have available a significant array of techniques to stabilize collections, prevent further deterioration, and address damage that has

Table 7.

Care of Collections			
	Mean Holdings Maintenance	Mean Treatment Actions	Percentage Microfilm Production
Academic N = 129	3.9 128	2.4 129	51% 66
Corporate N = 22	4.3 21	2.1 22	45% 10
Federal N = 20	4.1 20	1.7 20	45% 9
Local N = 50	3.8 50	2.4 50	44% 22
Museum N = 26	3.3 25	2.2 26	23% 6
Religious N = 37	3.6 37	1.6 37	19% 7
Special N = 10	3.4 10	1.7 10	40% 4
State N = 26	4.2 26	2.8 26	80% 21
ALL N = 320	3.8 317	2.2 320	45% 145

already occurred. Routine preventive, stabilizing activities together constitute holdings maintenance. The questionnaire asked respondents to indicate which of the following six actions are routinely carried out in the unit: rehousing in acid-free containers, segregating acidic paper, segregating photographic media, removing fasteners, copying deteriorated items, and "other" holdings maintenance actions.

The questionnaire also solicited information on a selected group of item-treatment activities, including deacidification of sheets of paper, dry cleaning surfaces of documents, mylar encapsulation, basic mending and repair, simple testing of inks and pH, and "other" conservation treatments. The list of preventive and treatment activities chosen for the study was based on the set of recommendations made to participants in the basic conservation workshop.

One important preservation strategy for archivists is reformatting deteriorated collections on microfilm. The questionnaire requested information on the production of microfilm in 1988, both by in-house technicians and through external vendor contracts. Respondents also indicated the primary purpose for which the materials were reproduced, including limiting the handling of originals and preserving the information content of holdings.

Table 7 is a summary of the responses to sets of questions on holdings maintenance, treatment actions, and the production of microfilm, broken out by type of repository. The first column is the average number of routine holdings maintenance activities carried out in the 12 months immediately prior to the survey; the second column is the average number of treatment activities carried out during the same period. The third column is the percentage of respondents who reported producing any microfilm for any reason in 1988.

At least two observations are evident from the information in the table. First, archivists from all types of organizations and from all sizes of repositories apparently are taking preventive action on their collections on a routine basis. The average number of holdings maintenance activities far exceeds the average number of treatment activities in all categories. Second, archivists are making solid use of microfilm technology for both preservation and enhanced access. While state archives and historical societies lead in this regard, all types of archival organizations show signs of a commitment to reformatting archival collections.

Implications of the Research

Describing the administrative context of archival preservation and the broad scope of preservation activities is only the first step in understanding the strengths and limitations of the archival profession's preservation practices. Data from the nationwide survey, when combined with secondary research and the informed opinions of leading preservation experts, lead to a series of conclusions about where the archival profession stands today, and where archivists ought to be heading in the near future. From these patterns, it may be possible to chart a path in the decade ahead to improve the care and handling of archival materials wherever they are housed.

Overall, the findings of two years of research and analysis suggest that although archivists now understand the significance of their preservation efforts and have absorbed information on basic prevention and treatment techniques, they have only partially integrated into their professional practice the set of innovative approaches that together have come to be defined as archival preservation management. Archivists are not yet accustomed to viewing preservation as a management umbrella under which many archival functions can be placed.

At least three professional issues should concern every archival institution that takes its preservation mandate seriously. First, preservation is preventive medicine, not emergency surgery. The analogy to public health is apt, since an ongoing planning approach to preservation often renders specialized, expensive conservation treatments unnecessary by identifying problems at the collection level, before they become more serious, and taking cost-effective remedial actions. The data from the study and supporting research demonstrate that archivists take a piecemeal approach to preservation, picking and choosing from among the possible activities, instead of working through a planning process that sets priorities for the unit and for the parent organization.

Second, appraisal of archival records does not stop at the receiving dock. Archival institutions need to develop and implement more systematic strategies both for selecting materials from among the holdings for preservation action and for using preservation methods appropriate to the value of selected materials. Archivists long ago recognized that their fundamental professional skill is their ability to assess the archival values of large volumes of records and manuscripts and to select the small portion with enduring value. Archivists can enhance their capacity to develop comprehensive preservation programs by acting on the essential relationship between appraisal and preservation strategies.

Third, archival units are isolated from the organizations of which they are a part, playing a far more limited role in supporting the institution's mission and purpose than they should. Archivists need to integrate their programs more fully into the institutions that support them. It is doubtful that significant progress on preserving archival collections can occur in many types of administrative settings until archivists succeed in functionally integrating the activities of their departments into those of their institutions. If undertaken systematically and comprehensively, archival preservation has the potential to become the primary impetus for improving the overall quality, value, and effectiveness of individual archival programs.

In looking toward the future, as the volume of archival information increases and as archival records appear in a constantly expanding variety of forms and formats, archivists are faced with difficult decisions. It is inappropriate and, in fact, impossible to make responsible preservation decisions without coordinating preservation efforts with other archival repositories on state, regional, and national levels.

Additionally, archivists should align themselves with other professionals already involved in developing and implementing nationwide strategies and in setting priorities. Librarians, in particular, have made unprecedented progress in this area over the past decade. It is critical that archivists strengthen and support ongoing nationwide preservation initiatives to ensure that archival concerns are integrated into the process.

To accomplish these tasks, the archival profession needs a framework that provides archivists, institutions, service organizations, funding agencies, and professional associations with a clear statement of archival preservation goals and objectives. An outline for action should reflect commonly accepted operating principles and should clearly focus the efforts of both the archival profession and individual archivists. Most important, a nationwide strategy should enhance the capacity of this country's archival facilities to build institutional and public support for comprehensive preservation programs.[24]

---

24 A draft nationwide strategy document is printed as an insert in the January 1990 *SAA Newsletter*. Review, revision, and dissemination of the document is the responsibility of the SAA Task Force on Preservation, established for a three-year period in October 1989.

In the decade ahead, preservation management must join appraisal and use as an equal partner in the archival enterprise. The development of comprehensive preservation programs may be the most important factor in the long-term health of the archival profession, simply because preservation provides to administrators a rationale for funding archival programs in institutional settings that is not provided by all the innovative research that has been done recently, and that will continue to be done, in appraisal and use. It is the professional responsibility of archivists to make the case for preservation programs in practical terms.

Archival programs must make sense to the people who pick up the tab, whether these people are taxpayers, legislators, or university presidents. Archivists should take the time to make sense out of the sometimes complicated challenge of archival preservation, translate possible solutions to specific institutional settings, and step back from the daily routine to see how preservation planning can solve more problems than it creates.

23

Preservation Re-Recording of Audio Recordings in Archives: Problems, Priorities, Technologies, and Recommendations

CHRISTOPHER ANN PATON

Abstract: *This article offers a context for examining archival audio holdings, determining preservation needs and priorities, and planning audio re-recording (reformatting) projects. It addresses such issues as identification of the most vulnerable recording types, the meaning of "preservation re-recording," and the skills, equipment, and personnel that are necessary for working with older recordings. The information provided is drawn in part from the experiences of archivists at Georgia State University during an in-house archival audio re-recording project funded by the National Historical Publications and Records Commission.*

Author's Note: *Due to developments in recording technology since this article was written, the cautions about digital formats for preservation purposes have begun to change and may be obsolete by the time this publication appears in print.*

In recent years, preservation of audio recordings has become a topic of increasing concern to archivists. Unfortunately, many archivists are discovering that their professional training has not prepared them for dealing with recording media and systems, and they find themselves at a loss when attempting to administer and preserve their audio collections.

This article is intended to offer a context for examining archival audio holdings, determining preservation needs and priorities, and planning audio re-recording projects. It will attempt to clarify several key issues relating to audio preservation, including the types of recordings that are most at risk of loss, the meaning of "preservation re-recording," and the skills, equipment, and personnel that are necessary for working with older recordings. It will not explore issues relating to cylinder, dictation, wire, or acoustical recordings; nor will it provide specific details

Reprinted with permission from the *American Archivist* 61 (Spring 1998): 188-219. The author wishes to thank Dave Wickstrom for his assistance with this article.

on selecting recording equipment or cleaning and restoring recordings. These topics are complex, and most are discussed at length in other publications.[1] The information provided here is drawn in part from the experiences of archivists at Georgia State University (GSU) during an in-house archival audio re-recording project funded by the National Historical Publications and Records Commission conducted from 1992 to 1994.

Prologue

Audio re-recording is expensive and time consuming. In order for any re-recording project to be both successful and efficient, its plan must be based on a clear understanding of the problems to be addressed, of the strengths and weaknesses of the available preservation options, and of the types of personnel, equipment, and administrative support necessary for success. Time invested, before a project is begun, in studying the institution's collections and learning about re-recording options will save money and reduce frustration as work progresses. While the various issues can be divided and presented in a number of ways, the presentation here will roughly follow the progression pursued by personnel at GSU in planning and implementing its preservation project:

Examining the collection:

- identifying vulnerable types of recordings
- identifying sizes, speeds, and formats
- setting priorities
- determining when to re-record

Understanding "preservation re-recording":

- how recording technology works
- defining "preservation re-recording"

---

1   See, for example, George Boston, ed., *A Guide to the Basic Technical Equipment Required by Audio, Film and Television Archives*, written by members of the Coordinating Committee for the Technical Commission of the International Organizations for Audio, Film and Television Archives (1990); *Archiving the Audio-Visual Heritage: A Joint Technical Symposium, Fédération Internationale des Archives du Film, Fédération Internationale des Archives de Télévision, International Association of Sound Archives*, published in 1984, 1988, 1991; Association for Recorded Sound Collections, Associated Audio Archives Committee, *Audio Preservation: A Planning Study — Final Performance Report* (Silver Spring, Md., 1988); Alan Ward, *A Manual of Sound Archive Administration* (Brookfield, Vt.: Gower Publishing Co., 1990); Gerald Gibson, "Decay and Degradation of Disk and Cylinder Recordings in Storage," in *Archiving the Audio-Visual Heritage*, ed. Eva Orbanz (Berlin: Stiftung Deutsche Kinemathek, 1988); Christopher Ann Paton, Stephanie E. Young, Harry P. Hopkins, and Robert B. Simmons, "A Review and Discussion of Selected Acetate Disc Cleaning Methods: Anecdotal, Experiential and Investigative Findings," *ARSC Journal* 28 (Spring 1997): 1-23; Marie P. Griffin, "Preservation of Rare and Unique Materials at the Institute for Jazz Studies," *ARSC Journal* 17, no. 1-3 (1985): 11-17.

Transfer technology options and recommendations:

- the importance of careful reproduction (playback)
- transfer technology: analog vs. digital; tape, disk, or other new media
- documenting the preservation process
- the audio technician
- current recommendations for preservation transfers

Final considerations:

- estimating cleaning and transfer time
- estimating costs (including in-house and out-of-house considerations)
- support staff needs
- space considerations

Examining the Collection

Identifying Vulnerable Types of Recordings

The first step toward starting an audio preservation re-recording project is determining which recordings are vulnerable to loss due to age, damage, or inherent vice. Although all sound recordings are subject to wear and tear during use and as a natural result of aging, only a few types are currently considered "at risk" and in need of prompt attention. Detailed descriptions of both historic and contemporary formats can be obtained from a number of sources;[2] what follows is a brief overview of some of the types of audio recordings commonly found in archives and the formats posing the greatest concern for archivists.

Grooved Phonodisc Types. The grooved phonodisc family includes the "78s," "45s," and "LPs" familiar to those born and raised prior to the advent of cassette tapes and compact discs, and also includes the less-familiar "instantaneous" recordings known variously as *acetates, lacquers,* and *direct-cut discs.*[3] Shellac-type 78s, and vinyl-type 45s and LPs are not presently considered especially vulnerable to

---

2 See, for example, Roland Gelatt, *The Fabulous Phonograph, 1877-1977,* 2d rev. ed. (New York: Macmillan Publishing Company, Inc., 1977); A. G. Pickett and M. M. Lemcoe, *Preservation and Storage of Sound Recordings* (Washington, D.C.: Library of Congress, 1959); John Van Bogart, *Magnetic Tape Storage and Handling: A Guide for Libraries and Archives* (Washington, D.C.: Commission on Preservation and Access, June 1995); and Gilles St.-Laurent, "Preservation of Recorded Sound Materials," *ARSC Journal* 23, no. 2 (1992): 144-56.

3 For more information, see Ward, *A Manual of Sound Archive Administration;* Gibson, "Decay and Degradation of Disk and Cylinder Recordings;" and Christopher Ann Paton, "Preservation of Acetate Disc Sound Recordings at Georgia State University," *Midwestern Archivist* 16, no. 1 (1991): 11-20.

age-related deterioration or inherent vice.[4] Instantaneous, or acetate, recordings, however, present serious preservation concerns.[5]

Acetate disc recordings came into common use in the 1930s. They were used for commercial, broadcast, and home recording purposes before magnetic tape technology was perfected. They also existed side-by-side with tape in regular use for a period of years (c. 1946-1960s), and are still used today in the production of long-play (LP) phonodiscs. Acetates consist of a soft plastic coating over a base disc of aluminum, glass, or cardboard; the grooves are cut into the surface of the blank disc by a disc recording machine, often referred to as a *cutter*, producing a grooved phonodisc that can be played like the commercially pressed discs with which many adults are familiar. Although their audio quality can be surprisingly good, they are inherently unstable and will inevitably deteriorate until they become unplayable. In most instances, it is the plastic coating (cellulose acetate or cellulose nitrate) that deteriorates; in other cases, the glass base breaks, the cardboard base is damaged (by exposure to water, for example), or the metal base is bent or dented. Deterioration of the plastic coating is marked by the appearance on the disc surface of a greasy white powder and eventually a shrinking, cracking, and peeling of the coating from the base material (see Figures 1 and 2). The white powder, which can be mistaken for mold by the uninitiated, is composed of byproducts (fatty acids, notably palmitic acid and stearic acid) produced as the coating's plasticizers deteriorate.[6] Although careful storage under cool, dry conditions will prolong disc life to the fullest possible extent, all acetate discs will eventually deteriorate and must be re-recorded if their audio content is to be preserved.

While acetate discs appear similar to other types of phonodiscs, and are often confused with them, they can be distinguished from other members of the phonodisc family in several ways. Most acetates have typed or handwritten labels instead of the formal, printed labels common to published, commercial sound recordings. Many discs also have, in addition to the center spindle hole, one or more additional holes near their center, sometimes hidden under the label. These fit over the pins that were provided on certain models of cutters, to keep the disc from slipping during recording; if the disc base material is metal or cardboard, the metal or

---

4 Pickett and Lemcoe, *Preservation and Storage of Sound Recordings,* 46; ARSC, "Recorded Sound Carrier Formats" chart, *Audio Preservation: A Planning Study,* 84.

5 See ARSC, *Audio Preservation: A Planning Study,* 84; Gibson, "Decay and Degradation of Disk and Cylinder Recordings," 49-50; Ward, *A Manual of Sound Archive Administration,* Chapter 6; Paton, "Preservation of Acetate Disc Sound Recordings;" and Paton et al., "A Review and Discussion of Selected Acetate Disc Cleaning Methods."

6 Paton et al., "A Review and Discussion of Selected Acetate Disc Cleaning Methods"; Gibson, "Decay and Degradation of Disk and Cylinder Recordings"; Ward, *A Manual of Sound Archive Administration;* 150-51 St.-Laurent, "Preservation of Recorded Sound Materials," 146-47, 153.

Figure 1. Detail of deteriorating instantaneous disc, showing both a heavy accumulation of plasticizer residue and the extra holes surrounding the spindle hole that are often found on these recordings.

Figure 2. Aluminum-based instantaneous disc with shrinking, peeling coating.

cardboard layer can often be seen inside these holes, as well as inside the spindle hole. Not all acetates will have such holes, as some types of cutters use a vacuum system to hold the discs firmly in place during recording. The base material may also show through at the rim of the disc, where the plastic coating is often thinner and somewhat transparent. Glass discs frequently bear labels identifying them as glass and when held (carefully) up to the light will usually prove translucent. The appearance on the surface of the disc of plasticizer residue (as opposed to mold) is a sign that a record is likely an acetate and not a regular LP or other commercial phonodisc; peeling plastic coating that exposes a metal, glass, or cardboard base material, is, of course, another good indicator. Archivists should be aware that some types of commercial discs, shellac 78s in particular, are also laminated products, featuring cardboard or paper sandwiched between layers of shellac-type substances. In addition, the surfaces of shellac discs that have been played very heavily can have a white appearance. Such discs are usually easily distinguishable from acetates, however, by an examination of the labels (which are usually printed with the record company name, issue number, and other key information) and also by the appearance and texture of the disc and its surface.

Magnetic Tape Types. Although magnetic tape has historically been considered fairly sturdy, it does deteriorate over time, sometimes catastrophically.[7] All tape consists of a flexible base (most commonly plastic of one sort or another), a binder, and minute magnetic particles (usually referred to as "oxide"), along with various lubricants and other ingredients that help improve tape functioning. Modern polyester-based tape also has a back-coating, which is applied to the underside, or back, of the tape to help control static electricity generated by the polyester and enable the tape to move through the tape deck mechanisms more easily. Deterioration of the tape can occur in the base, the binder, or the oxide, with base and binder problems being the most common causes of premature tape failure. In order to evaluate the condition, potential life expectancy, and preservation needs of audio tape in an archives, the archivist must know which types of tapes are present and how they age and deteriorate.

Some tapes made in the 1940s used paper as the base material. Paper tape can be identified by its pale appearance, sometimes with plain paper exposed beyond the oxide at the edges of the tape. Although paper-based tape is often found to be in surprisingly good shape, given its makeup and age, the paper base is both fragile and, frequently, nonstandard in width, and is easily torn during playback. Consequently, these tapes should be given high priority for copying to a modern medium.

During the 1940s and 1950s cellulose acetate was the most common tape base. Acetate tape becomes brittle with age and is subject to cupping,

---

7 See Van Bogart, *Magnetic Tape Storage and Handling,* 2-7, for a discussion of magnetic media structure and deterioration.

Figure 3. Two reels of magnetic tape, one holding acetate base tape (left) and the other containing polyester base tape (right), photographed on a light box. Note the translucent appearance of the acetate tape and the completely opaque appearance of the polyester tape.

curling, and other forms of physical distortion. In addition, it can suffer from the "vinegar syndrome" that afflicts acetate motion picture and photographic film.[8] To determine whether a tape base is cellulose acetate, hold the reel of tape up to a light source and look through the flat, circular surface of the tape pack (as if looking into a hand mirror); if the tape pack appears translucent it is most likely cellulose acetate (see Figure 3).[9] Another test for acetate base involves breaking a small piece off the end of the tape, being careful, of course, not to break off any of the tape that is recorded. Acetate-based tape will break easily across the width of the tape. It is wise to pay attention, when testing any tape, to whether the tape has a leader (length of blank tape, often clear, white, or some other color) attached to the end. Leader materials often differ from the main body of the tape, and testing the leader may give incorrect results.

Although the primary mode of failure for acetate tape is usually embrittlement or distortion of the tape base, failure of the binder, accompanied by shedding of the binder and oxide, is also possible. Reliable

---

8   See Van Bogart, *Magnetic Tape Storage and Handling*, 6; and Dietrich Schüller, "Sound Tapes and the 'Vinegar Syndrome,'" *Phonographic Bulletin* 54 (July 1989): 29-31.

9   Van Bogart, *Magnetic Tape Storage and Handling*, 6; Ward, *A Manual of Sound Archive Administration*, 173.

life-expectancy figures are not available for acetate tape (although such tapes frequently exceed all reasonable expectations for sturdiness and durability), but since virtually all cellulose acetate tapes are now at least 30 years old, and many are nearly 50 years old, they are considered a high priority for copying. Tapes exhibiting signs of vinegar syndrome (identified by an odor of vinegar about the tape) should receive particular attention. Paradoxically, acetate tapes that are in good condition may still outlast "preservation" copies made on newer polyester-based tape, much of which has a shorter life expectancy.

Polyester has been the standard tape base since the 1960s. Because polyester is much stronger and more stable than cellulose acetate, does not break easily, and is not greatly affected by changes in temperature and humidity, one might reasonably expect that tape made with this base would have a greater life expectancy, but this is not necessarily true. Shortly after the tape manufacturers changed the tape base, they also changed the type of binders used to hold the oxide to the base and added an antistatic "back-coating" to improve tape handling and reduce static electricity. The binders adopted throughout the tape manufacturing industry, and still in use today, employ polyurethane as a primary component. In the late 1980s archivists and recording engineers began to encounter tapes that squealed when played and shed oxide and binder that stuck to the playback heads. It is now understood that tape hydrolysis, or "sticky shed syndrome," as it is commonly known, is caused by absorption of moisture by the binder, resulting in binder failure.[10] When the tape is played, the binder sticks to the tape transport and begins to peel off, taking the magnetic particles with it. Although there are temporary fixes for this condition (notably baking the tapes at low temperatures for a period of time), in the long run, tapes afflicted with sticky shed syndrome must be copied if their content is to be preserved. Manufacturers have made an effort to improve the binder formulations, but life-expectancy predictions vary, and most tapes manufactured today carry only a 10-year warranty. Tapes made prior to the discovery of the problem (from the mid-1970s through the mid-1980s), or used and stored under humid conditions, may have shorter life expectancies. In most cases, the polyester base will almost certainly last longer than both the binder-oxide mixture that contains the recorded information and the back-coating.[11]

To identify polyester tape bases, hold the reel up to a light source and look through the flat, circular surface of the tape pack as if looking into a hand mirror. If the tape pack appears opaque, it is most likely polyester (see Figure 3). Acetate-based tape, as noted earlier, usually

---

10 Van Bogart, *Magnetic Tape Storage and Handling,* 3-5; Scott Kent, "Binder Break-Down in Back-Coated Tapes," *Recording Engineer/Producer* (July 1988): 80-81; Philip De Lancie, "Sticky Shed Syndrome," *Mix* (May 1990): 148-55.

11 Van Bogart, *Magnetic Tape Storage and Handling,* 6.

appears translucent when held to the light; it may be useful to perform a comparison test by viewing one reel of each type of tape.

The audio cassette deserves special attention here, if only in recognition of the great quantities of cassettes that reside in archives. In brief, the cassette is an inexpensive, short-lived format that should not be relied upon for long-term storage of historical information. Audio cassettes contain exceptionally thin and narrow tape which causes them to be more susceptible to damage and failure than reel-to-reel tape. These tapes are particularly prone to damage during playback. The tape in shorter cassettes, such as those running up to 60 minutes, is usually the sturdiest because it is the thickest, while longer-running cassettes, particularly the 120-minute varieties, contain thinner tape that poses an increased risk of damage through fouling (being "eaten" by the playback unit). Other common problems with cassettes include leaders that become disconnected from the tape hubs and a gradual degradation of both audio quality and playback ability.

Although there are no published figures available on the life expectancy of audio cassettes, some archivists feel that any cassette over two years old is suspect. In any case, cassettes should be considered likely candidates for preservation re-recording.

Identifying Sizes, Speeds, and Formats

It is important to note the sizes of recordings present in a collection while examining them for possible preservation action, because size is one factor used in calculating their cumulative playing time and determining the types of equipment needed to play them. It is also important to determine the speed of the recordings, which constitutes a separate factor in determining their playing time. Each "family" of recordings includes characteristic sizes and speeds with which the archivist should become familiar.

In addition to sizes and speeds, the archivist should become aware of the various formats associated with each type of recording. By "format" the author means whether the recording is monaural or stereo (or one of the many other, less common, formats), and the way in which the recorded information is captured on the recording (types and sizes of grooves, or, for tape recordings, track configurations—the number, size, placement, and orientation of the recorded tracks on the tape). The format of each recording can be an additional factor in determining playing time and will determine the types of equipment needed to play the recording.

Grooved Phonodisc Sizes and Speeds. Phonodiscs commonly range in size from about 7 inches in diameter (the size of a 45, or "single") to 16 inches (a size frequently used in broadcasting), although smaller and larger sizes are also possible. Most middle-aged adults today remember that commercial 12-inch LPs play at 33⅓ rpm (revolutions per minute) and 7-inch singles play at 45 rpm. Some still remember that 10-inch shellac discs play at 78 rpm. Speed is not related to disc size, however, except by custom, and the speed of a disc should not be assumed based on its size. A 7-inch disc can play at 33⅓, 16, or another speed besides the usual 45 rpm; 10-inch discs can be recorded at 33⅓ or other speeds (such as 80 or 66) instead of 78. Although certain sizes and speeds have dominated the *commercial* market over time (such as the 7-inch 45-rpm single, the 10-inch 78, and the 12-inch 33⅓-rpm LP), the possible size-and-speed combinations for *instantaneous* discs ("acetates") are potentially limitless, and it is not unheard of to find acetate discs that bear multiple "cuts" recorded at different speeds or that play at a different speed for each side. In practice, most tend to play at approximately 78 or 33⅓, but this can only be confirmed by playing the recordings.

Phonodisc Formats. Grooved phonodiscs recorded prior to 1948 are almost always monaural and recorded with what are called "coarse," or "standard," grooves (defined as measuring approximately 85 to 150 grooves per inch of recorded surface), using equalizations that differ from current standards. In addition, if they are instantaneous discs, they may play from the inside out rather than the outside in. In order to play the discs in a manner that accurately reproduces their recorded content, preservation project personnel, especially the audio technician, must have access to monaural styli of dimensions suitable for the larger grooves, and to an adjustable equalizer to re-create as nearly as possible the equalization of the original recording. *Equalization* refers to the practice of increasing and decreasing the level of various parts of the sound spectrum during recording and playback for the purpose of improving the overall sound of the recording. If the discs are larger than 12 inches in diameter, a turntable capable of playing the larger discs will also be necessary. The most common speeds for pre-1950s acetate discs are nominally 78 rpm and 33⅓ rpm; because speeds may vary slightly, a turntable with an adjustable speed control is recommended and is sometimes required. Sixteen-inch discs in this format (coarse groove, monaural) recorded at 33⅓ rpm ordinarily hold about 15 minutes of recording per side. The playing time of grooved disc recordings can be estimated by using the following formula:

$$T = \frac{NS}{rpm}$$

where T is the playing time in minutes, S is the recorded width in inches, N is the number of lines per inch, and rpm is the turntable speed in revolutions per minute.[12]

---

12 Howard M. Tremaine, *Audio Cyclopedia,* 2d ed. (Indianapolis: Howard M. Sams & Co., Inc., 1969), 670 (section 13.115).

Phonodiscs recorded after 1948 but before the mid-1950s are usually monaural, but may be "microgroove" in format rather than coarse groove, because the LP microgroove disc, whose longer playing time was made possible by fitting more grooves of a smaller size across the disc surface (200-300 grooves per inch), was introduced to the commercial market in 1948. Microgroove recordings gradually replaced the coarse-groove format and became the standard for 7-inch singles and 10- and 12-inch LPs. The monaural styli used during playback of microgroove recordings must, obviously, be substantially smaller than coarse groove styli in order to properly fit the grooves.

Phonodiscs recorded after the mid-1950s will often, but not always, be stereo in addition to being microgroove, and if they are stereo, they will require a stereo microgroove cartridge, stylus, and electronics for playback, as opposed to either a monaural or coarse/standard set-up. Such recordings are more likely to employ the Recording Industry Association of America (RIAA) equalization that became standard in the recording industry in the mid-1950s. Monaural and stereo microgroove technology, using RIAA equalization, co-existed in the recording industry for a number of years, while some broadcasters continued to use monaural, coarse-groove recording equipment and their own in-house equalization customs into the 1960s. Consequently, it is not wise to assume either that all post-recordings are microgroove, or that all recordings made after 1955 are stereo with RIAA equalization. Only examination of the discs and supporting documentation will clarify groove type. Confirmation of equalization, particularly for broadcast and home recordings, may not be possible until the recordings are played and examined by an audio technician. Even then, many discs remain mysterious in this regard, leaving the technician to make a "best guess" judgment on equalization.

Magnetic Tape Sizes and Speeds.   Reel-to-reel tapes are usually found on reels measuring from 2 or 3 inches to 10.5 inches in diameter (14-inch diameters are also possible), with 5, 7, and 10.5 inches being the most common sizes found in archives. Hub diameters (the diameter of the centermost part of the reel, around which the tape is wrapped) can be small, medium, or large; larger hubs allow the tape to wrap in a more gradual curve, as opposed to a very tight circle, and are therefore less stressful to the tape. The length of the tape on each reel can vary greatly, depending on the thickness of the tape and the size of the hub. The thickest and sturdiest tape has a base that measures about 1.5 mils thick and has superior recording and performance qualities. A full 7-inch reel of 1.5-mil tape contains 1,200 feet of tape; the same size reel will hold 1,800 feet of thinner (about 1.0 mil), "time and one-half" tape; and 2,400 feet of "double play" tape, which is the thinnest of all reel-to-tapes (about .5 mil).

Tape speeds can range from 15/16 ips (inches per second) to 30 ips. The speeds most often found in archives include 15/16, 1⅞, 3¾, and 7½ ips, along with lesser quantities of recordings at 15 and 30 ips, which are more likely to be found in performing arts collections. Modern audio cassette recorders are standardized at 1⅞ ips, although some recorders offer the recordist "slow speed" or "high speed" options. As with phonodiscs, the size of reels, lengths of tape, and tape speeds present in the collection are major factors in calculating the amount of material to be copied.

Magnetic Tape Formats. In addition to the size of the reel, tape length, and tape speed, the tape recording format is a factor to be considered when calculating the playing time of audio tapes. Magnetic recordings made prior to the mid-1950s are usually monaural, and many recordings of the types that frequently come to archives, such as conference and meeting recordings, were recorded in monaural format well beyond the advent of stereo technology, sometimes into the 1970s and 1980s.

On a ¼-inch wide audio tape, the size most commonly found in archives, a monaural signal can be recorded in a number of configurations. Common monaural formats include "full-track" (recorded the full width and length of one face of the tape in one direction only); "half-track" (down one side of one face of the tape and, if the tape is recorded on both sides, up the opposite side of the same face with a space between the two tracks, somewhat resembling a divided, two-lane highway); and "four-track" (up and down the face of the tape four times, with spaces between each track).

Stereo tape formats were developed in the mid-1950s. Common stereo formats include "two-track" or "half-track" configurations (two channels, one "left" and one "right," running the length of the tape in one direction with a space between them); and "four-track" versions (two pairs of tracks, one pair running the length of the tape in one direction, and the other running in the opposite direction, with spaces between each track, and sometimes with the tracks interleaved).[13] Archivists should note that other formats exist and that terminology for even the few formats mentioned here is not standardized: one audio technician's "half-track" can be another's "two-track" or "double-track."

The combined elements of format and speed can have a dramatic effect on playing time. The playing time for a 7-inch reel holding 1,200 feet of recorded tape will run about 30 minutes at 7.5 ips, full-track; approximately one hour when recorded at the same speed in a double sided two-track format; or about two hours using the same speed and a monaural four-track format. The same tape, recorded in monaural four-track at ¹⁵⁄₁₆ ips will play for approximately seven and a half hours. It is

---

13 In open reel four-track stereo formats, the pairs of tracks are interleaved, meaning that, if the tracks were numbered "1,2,3,4" from one edge of the tape to the opposite edge, tracks 1 and 3 would constitute one pair, running in one direction, and tracks 2 and 4 the other pair, running in the other direction. On cassette tapes, the four tracks are not interleaved; instead, one pair of tracks runs down one side of the tape, while the other pair runs in the opposite direction on the other side, with a space between each track and between the two sets of pairs.

Figure 4. This chart, showing estimated playing times in minutes and seconds of specific lengths of magnetic tape recorded in full-track format, is adapted from a similar chart distributed by the 3M Corporation.

Tape Length	Nominal Tape Thickness	Reel Size	$^{15}/_{16}$ ips	$1^7/_9$ ips	$3^3/_4$ ips	$7^1/_2$ ips	15 ips	30 ips
600	1.5	5″			:32	:16		
900	1.0	5″			:48	:24		
1200	1.5	7″			1:04	:32	:16	:08
1800	1.0	7″			1:36	:48	:24	:12
3600	1.0/1.5	10.5″	12:48	6:24	3:12	1:36	:48	:24

also common, of course, to find reels that are only partially recorded, or that contain multiple recordings that have been spliced together on one reel, sometimes recorded in different formats. In any case, knowledge of how tape sizes, speeds, and formats interrelate is essential in any attempt to estimate playing time. (See Figure 4 for a list of common tape recording speeds, tape lengths, and playing times for full-track recordings.)

When estimating playback time and determining the types of equipment required to play magnetic tapes, one must know the track configurations as described above, the tape width and length, and the recording speed. While size of reel and width of tape can be determined by visual inspection, it may be necessary to have help from an audio technician in determining speeds and track configurations, unless that information is documented elsewhere (perhaps on the box or reel label, or on the leader) in a reliable fashion. To estimate the playing time (in minutes) of a full-track recording, use the following formula: multiply the tape length (in feet) by 12 (to convert it to inches), then divide that number by the speed (expressed in inches per second) multiplied by 60 (to convert the speed into inches per minute). Longer playing times are achieved by recording at a lower speed, by using a longer tape, by using a format that fits more information on the tape (such as two or four tracks instead of one), or by a combination of these means. Longer playing time, naturally, equates to longer preservation transfer time, a calculation that is critical to formulating preservation project timelines and budgets. Many archives, particularly those holding large numbers of tapes of conferences and proceedings, will find that their recordings were made at slow speeds using two- or four-track configurations, producing long-playing tapes of relatively poor audio quality that can be difficult and expensive to copy.

Setting Priorities

Identifying the recordings in an archives' holdings that are either vulnerable to deterioration or that depend upon obsolete or nearly obsolete equipment (hardware) for use constitutes the first step toward setting priorities for audio preservation. As with all preservation projects, the prioritizing should not stop at this point. The content and quality of the recordings should be examined as well; if the content is not important, the recording probably does not warrant the effort audio preservation requires, and if the audio quality of the recording is exceedingly poor, the effort may be useless anyway. Another question to consider is whether the content of the recording merits retention in audio form, as opposed to a textual transcription. Some types of sounds (musical and theatrical performances, historic speeches and news events, and sounds of animals and nature, for instance) cannot be transcribed effectively. Proceedings of meetings and conferences, on the other hand, often can. If there is no inherent reason to maintain the recording in audio form, it may be more economical in the long run to invest time and money in producing good transcriptions, rather than continue to reformat the recordings generation after generation. This can allow the archives to focus its preservation effort on its most valuable audio recordings, those that are vulnerable and that also contain important audio content.

Determining When to Re-record

Archivists have hoped for years that someone would develop a test to predict the optimum time to re-record audio materials, a time before the recordings deteriorate significantly but not so early as to be foolish. Unfortunately, such a test does not presently exist and may never come to be. This leaves archivists to make their own best guesses as to when recordings should be transferred. Obviously, one wants to transfer tapes before they shrivel or become sticky, and acetate discs before they delaminate. The experience at GSU indicates that it is wise to transfer (re-record) acetate discs before significant deposits of plasticizer residue have formed on their surfaces. Doing so saves time that otherwise must be spent cleaning this substance off, and it helps ensure that the surface of the disc is in better condition, which leads to improved audio quality in the copy recording. During the GSU project, acetate disc recordings that were 40 years old or less were found to be in far better shape than those in the 45- to 50-year age bracket. At the same time, audio cassettes more than 20 years old were found to be significantly noisier and more difficult to handle than younger ones (under 10 years old), but the archivists questioned whether the increased noise was due largely to advanced age or, on the other hand, was mostly characteristic of the nature of the cassettes and cassette recording technology used during that period. Acetate tapes, even those that were nearly 40 years old, presented few problems as long as they had been recorded properly and stored well.

Understanding "Preservation Re-recording"

Having examined its holdings, identified vulnerable materials that merit preservation, and determined the approximate number of hours of recordings needing preservation, the archives must consider what is meant by the term "preservation re-recording." This is an important decision. For recordings that cannot be preserved for very long in their original form, longevity will be achieved only by regular and repeated copying, a process whose integrity will be shaped by the choices the archives makes as it structures its preservation procedures.

How Recording Technology Works

Before considering theories and goals of audio preservation, it is perhaps wise to review, in very simple terms, how the recording process works.

When an audio recording is made, sounds (of voices, music, birds, etc.) are converted by a microphone into electrical energy (called the "signal") which is captured on sound carriers (phonodiscs, tapes, etc.) in the form of grooves on phonodiscs, magnetic patterns on tape, or, in the digital realm, "pits" on laser discs. During reproduction (playback), a reading device (phono cartridge and stylus, tape playback head, or laser) recovers the signal from the sound carrier, converts it back into electrical energy, and sends it to the loudspeaker or headphones through an amplifier so that the recorded sounds can be heard again. The recorded sounds are referred to as the "signal," and it is the signal that archivists preserve when copying (transferring) the information from a failing sound carrier to a new medium.

The sound quality of all audio recordings, whether analog or digital, depends on a number of factors, including the use and placement of the microphone (when making "live" recordings), the quality of the recording equipment and tape used, and the skill of the technician. Poor techniques and equipment lead to poor-quality recordings; careful planning, skill, and adequate equipment combine to help create high-quality recordings. Anything that disrupts the signal during the recording or preservation transfer processes produces flaws that may be audible in the form of noise, missing portions of the sound ("drop-outs"), or distortion. In preservation work, such disruptions are commonly caused by damage to the original recording, by dirt and debris on the playback or recording equipment or on the recording itself, by poor cables or connections between the various pieces of equipment, by electrical fluctuations, and by use of inappropriate or malfunctioning equipment. Many of these problems are not discernible without special equipment coupled with experience and a thorough understanding of both the recording process and the nature of the recordings being transferred. Other transfer problems are caused primarily by human error or ignorance, such as incorrect reproduction of historic formats or misuse or overuse of technologies such as filtering, noise reduction, and signal processing.

In the end, the quality of an audio preservation project depends upon accurate reproduction of the original recordings and careful transfer of the signals to the new sound carrier. It is around such issues as "accuracy" that much of the discussion among audio archivists has circled in recent years.

Defining "Preservation Re-recording"

For many years now, at professional meetings and in professional literature, audio archivists have discussed what it means to "preserve" audio recordings.[14] Although considerable progress has been made toward building a consensus regarding the proper role of re-recording in audio preservation, standards for preservation re-recording remain elusive, and archivists are left to wonder what the term means. Obviously the intent is to preserve the recordings, or at least the content of the recordings, by transferring the information to a newer storage medium which will eventually stand in the place of the lost original. But recordings can be copied in many different ways, not all of which are suitable for preservation purposes. The audio information, or signal, can be enhanced or clarified; noise can be reduced; and old recordings can be modernized to make them sound more contemporary. Which methods and goals are appropriate for preservation work?

The Technical Coordinating Committee (TCC) of the International Organizations for Audio, Film, and Television Archives offers the following definition of preservation re-recording: "Re-recording serves a very specific function; it is a means to preserve the original sonic content of a recording. . . . The archivist's function is to preserve history, not to rewrite it. Given this precept, the archivist must always strive to maintain objectivity in the application of various retechniques."[15] The TCC goes on to identify several specific types of re-recording and to discuss which types have a place in archives.[16]

This definition of audio preservation, which is supported by sound archives in the United States and abroad, encourages archivists to transfer, or copy, the signal from the original source to the new medium as

---

14   See William D. Storm, "A Proposal for the Establishment of International Re-recording Standards," *ARSC Journal* 15, no. 2-3 (1983): 26-37; William Storm, "The Establishment of International Re-recording Standards," *Phonographic Bulletin* (July 1980): 5-12; Dietrich Schüller, "The Ethics of Preservation, Restoration, and Re-Issues of Historical Sound Recordings," *AES Journal* 39 (December 1991): 1014-17; Boston, *Guide to the Basic Technical Equipment*, section 4, "Audio Archives."

15   Boston, *Guide to the Basic Technical Equipment*, 39.

16   Boston, *Guide to the Basic Technical Equipment*, 39-41 and 64-65.

accurately as possible, neither "improving" the original nor allowing the introduction of new distortion or flaws. Under this definition, careful reproduction that respects the particular character of the historic recording is emphasized as a means of preventing or minimizing noise and distortion. Filtering, noise suppression, and other enhancements may be employed in producing service copies, if desired, but should be avoided except in extraordinary circumstances when creating the preservation copy. The transfer process should be carefully documented and there should be no "secret formulas" or practices employed during re-recording.

Archives that accept this definition of audio preservation transfer will not find that it answers all of their questions, but they will find that it provides them with at least four goals to help guide their preservation projects: (1) to make sure that the original recordings are reproduced (played) accurately during the transfer process; (2) to choose recording technologies and media for the preservation copy that will capture the quality of the original signal as faithfully as possible; (3) to employ, for audio preservation work, technicians who possess the knowledge and skills to work with aging and often obsolete recordings and the ability and willingness to employ technology and techniques that are appropriate to archival work; and (4) to document what is done with and to the recording during the preservation process.[17] These goals provide the archives with a framework to use in selecting personnel and equipment for the project, evaluating and choosing recording technology and media for the preservation copy, explaining and justifying these choices and decisions to administrators and funding agencies, and evaluating their work.

Transfer Technology Options and Recommendations

Having examined its collections and defined its goals for the project, the archives has three major steps remaining before it can finalize its budget, personnel needs, and timeline and begin the project. It must use the information it has collected regarding the audio recordings that need preservation to determine what is needed to ensure accurate reproduction of the original recording, select the recording technology and sound carrier it believes will serve most faithfully and reliably as a preservation medium, and choose an audio technician to carry out the work.

The Importance of Careful Reproduction (Playback)

Playing the original recording appropriately, using equipment that matches the format and engineering characteristics of the original and that is well maintained and skillfully operated, maximizes audio quality

---

17 Boston, *Guide to the Basic Technical Equipment*, section 4, "Audio Archives."

while minimizing noise and distortion. It will also minimize the wear that is unavoidable when playing recordings, enabling playback that neither destroys nor unnecessarily degrades the original recording. This is the first necessary technical step toward good audio transfer work.[18] A clean, carefully played "old" recording can sound amazingly good under the right circumstances. Accurate reproduction requires access to the equipment, or hardware, that matches the archives' recordings, or software, and knowing how to use it.

For tape recordings, this means having playback machines that can accommodate the size and track configurations of the original tape. For disc recordings, it means locating and acquiring appropriate modern phonograph equipment and then using it intelligently.[19] For all types of recordings, care must be taken to ensure that the equipment is installed, maintained, and used properly. If it is not functioning correctly or if the installation is poor, both the signal passing through the system, and, consequently, the preservation copy can be flawed. Malfunctioning equipment can also damage or destroy tapes and discs as they are played.

Acquiring the equipment for appropriate playback can be a challenge, particularly now that both grooved phonodisc and analog tape technology are becoming obsolete. For both tape and phonodisc playback, the purchase of modern equipment is recommended over the use of vintage equipment, largely because modern equipment is more reliable and easier to keep properly calibrated. It is still possible to purchase new equipment to play most older tape formats, but the cost of these machines is increasing at the same time that fewer vendors are willing to carry them. Professional tape equipment is available through local and regional dealers, as is some modern phonograph equipment. Specialized phonograph machines and supplies, suited for use with historic disc formats, can be obtained from a number of individuals and small companies. [Editor's note: A selected list of sources appended to the original article is not included here because the information is no longer current.]

Transfer Technology: Analog vs. Digital; Tape, Disk, or Other New Media

The next technical step toward accurate re-recording involves choosing an appropriate technology and storage medium to recapture the signal, or content, of the original recording. This is where the choices become more complicated. At the present time, archivists have two basic

---

18 Boston, *Guide to the Basic Technical Equipment,* 41, 44-58.

19 For a good discussion of the types of equipment required for both disc and tape reproduction, see Boston, *Guide to the Basic Technical Equipment,* 43-58. The equipment and procedures outlined with regard to commercial 78 rpm records are similar to the requirements for older (1930s-1940s) acetate discs.

forms of recording technology from which to choose: analog and digital. In addition there are several different types of analog and digital recording media from which to choose, including open-reel tape, various types of cassettes, recordable CDs, and computer disk. Which of these are appropriate for preservation work? What are the factors to consider in selecting a preservation medium? To resolve these questions, archivists must first decide whether to select analog or digital transfer technology, or perhaps a combination of the two. Rumors and opinions abound regarding the advantages and disadvantages of both technologies. The following discussion may help clarify the issues and provide a more balanced picture of present options.

Analog Technology: Pros and Cons. Analog technology has existed since the beginning of recorded sound. It works by recording a representation (an analog) of the original sound wave onto a storage medium (such as grooves on a phonodisc or magnetic tracks on a tape). When properly employed, analog recording technology produces clean, clear recordings with minimal distortion. While there is some loss of quality and fidelity from one analog generation to the next, the loss is gradual, and is minimized if the transfers are skillfully made. The usual recording medium for analog preservation work is open-reel magnetic tape in widths beginning at ¼ inch.

The primary advantages of analog technology are that it is fully mature; its formats are both standardized and well known; and it can capture and reproduce sounds with very good fidelity. In addition to its maturity and reliability, the major arguments in favor of analog technology have been that it has been expected to remain available for some time to come and that analog playback equipment can be re-created by skilled engineers, if necessary, after it becomes obsolete. As of this writing, however, it appears that vendors and manufacturers of analog recording media and equipment are hastening its obsolescence by withdrawing products from the market in spite of the enormous quantity of recordings and equipment still in use. While skilled engineers certainly can reproduce analog playback devices, the number of engineers capable of doing this is very small in comparison to the quantity of extant analog recordings, meaning that most archivists cannot expect to maintain analog equipment for very long after supplies and spare parts cease to be readily available from commercial sources.

One primary disadvantage of analog tape technology is "tape hiss," a form of noise that is inherent in analog tape recording. A second disadvantage is the gradual loss of quality and cumulative increase in tape hiss that occurs with each successive generation. Contrary to popular myth, however, the loss of quality from one generation to the next is not so dramatic and sudden as to be startling, unless something is greatly amiss with the transfer process; rather it is subtle and cumulative. "Analog ages gracefully," audio technicians say today, and while such aging may not be desirable, it is predictable and can be controlled to a certain extent by careful storage, use, and transfer of the recordings.

Digital Technology: Pros and Cons. Digital recording came into common use in the 1980s, and is both the current technology of choice for many audio technicians and recording studios and the technology that will eventually supplant analog recording. In digital recording, the sound wave is "sampled" and converted to binary code by use of an analog-to-digital converter (ADC). The code is then stored on a recording medium, usually magnetic tape or optical disk. During reproduction (playback), the code is converted back into analog form for listening purposes, by use of a digital-to-analog converter (DAC).

The quality of the sound produced by digital technology depends upon a number of factors, including the sampling rate and the quality of the converters and filters used, in addition to the concerns listed above under How Recording Technology Works (microphone placement, quality of the recording medium, and the skill of the technician).[20] Archivists must keep in mind that "digital recording" does not refer to just one type or format. There are presently several different digital storage media (including DAT/RDAT, ADAT, 4 mm, 8 mm, Beta, VHS, and other forms of cassettes, open-reel tape, and optical disk), a variety of types of recording equipment, and at least three different sampling rates, with new developments reaching the marketplace on a regular basis. It should also be understood that a digital copy of an analog source does not automatically mean a reduction of noise or improvement in sound quality; such changes are accomplished by use of filters, noise suppression, and signal processing techniques, not simply by copying a recording using digital technology.

Digital recordings offer certain specific advantages over analog recordings. Many technicians find them easier to edit, and the recording systems themselves are inherently less noisy than analog systems. In theory, at least, it should be possible to "clone" digital recordings, permitting the creation of many generations of identical copies. Many technicians believe that digital recordings are free of the distortion that is known to afflict analog recordings and count this as an advantage; other technicians take the more pragmatic position that all audio recording systems are subject to distortion and that the differences between analog and digital distortion are a matter of type and degree rather than presence and absence. This latter approach is finding support in articles appearing in audio engineering literature that discuss forms of distortion that are unique to digital recordings.[21]

---

20 See, for example, Bob Hodas and Paul Stubblebine, "Five Outboard A/D Convertors," *Mix* (May 1991): 82-88.

21 See, for example, Bill Foster, "The J-J-Jitter Bug," *Studio Sound* 36 (October 1994): 37-40.

There are several particular disadvantages associated with present-day digital technology. The technology is still evolving and improving at a very rapid rate, and, consequently, hardware obsolescence is a major concern, as it will require the migration of recordings to newer storage formats on a regular and frequent basis. As of this writing (summer 1996) there is no consensus on what constitutes an appropriate sampling rate or method for archival work. While many archivists believe that even the highest of the current rates is too low, others think that even the lowest is acceptable. The longevity of digital storage media, both tape and disc, is currently suspect. Technicians and archivists report sudden, unexplained failure of some digital tapes, and optical disk life expectancies are still under discussion.[22]

And, finally, the ability of digital recordings to be cloned indefinitely without loss of quality has been questioned by some technicians and archivists.[23] It is certainly true that digital processes include error detection and correction mechanisms that, theoretically, allow the generation of flawless copies; it is not true that this ability has been fully perfected, tested, and confirmed as reliable. Errors exist naturally in recording media, and if they are severe, or multiply from generation to generation to the point that they exceed the capability of the error correction system being used, the recordings suffer from "mutes" (drop-outs caused when the playback system cannot read or locate the information needed at that point in the recording) that cannot be corrected.

In short, many of the factors that make digital technology potentially so attractive for archival uses are still evolving and improving. Although digital technology offers great promise and will eventually become the standard recording technology, it is presently neither perfect nor a magic cure, and should be utilized cautiously and with a full understanding of the long-range implications of such a decision. In keeping with the long-standing tradition among archivists of using only proven, mature, trustworthy techniques for preservation purposes, analog technology is presently preferred over digital for audio preservation re-recording, although the making of simultaneous digital transfers is becoming more common. This preference for analog technology is likely to change soon, particularly if higher digital sampling rates come into common use, improved digital recording media become available, and analog equipment and media continue to be withdrawn from the market.

Recording Media.   Choices made regarding transfer technology will, to a certain extent, dictate the choice of recording media. For analog recordings, the medium of choice is open-reel tape. The tape should be

---

22 Sam Wise, "DAT Tape Tests," *Studio Sound* 35 (May 1993): 61-70 and "What's DAT Error," *Studio Sound* 35 (August 1993): 63-65.

23 Bob Hodas, "The Question of Digital Transfers," *Mix* (May 1991): 85.

new (not previously recorded on) and of high quality. At present, both of the major U.S. manufacturers of magnetic tape (Ampex and 3M) have withdrawn from the market altogether, and at least one of the best-known European manufacturers (BASF) has also discontinued its tape line. The Ampex and 3M product lines have been taken over by a new company (Quantegy), which will continue to manufacture recording tape domestically. Archivists will find that all of the remaining well-known manufacturers are foreign. Whether these changes mark the beginning of a sudden decline in quality and availability of tape, or simply one more step in the pending obsolescence of the medium will only become clear over time. Whatever the end result, in the interim the decades-old dance between archivists who seek reliable product information and manufac-turers who are pledged to protect proprietary interests is likely to become even more complicated.

For digital recordings, the medium will depend upon the type of digital hardware to be used. Some digital systems require magnetic tape, in open-reel or cassette form, while others use recordable CDs. Other types of media will undoubtedly appear soon, if they have not already. At pres-ent there are no easy answers, except for a general consensus among sound archivists that DAT cassettes are unsuitable. Some technicians point to the inherent minute flaws that inevitably exist in magnetic tape as evidence that tape is not a good digital recording medium, while many archivists question the life expectancy of recordable CDs, which, although highly touted by their manufacturers, remain a new and there-fore slightly suspect medium. It appears that tape will become outmoded in the near future, but the nature of its replacement cannot be reliably predicted at this time.

Documenting the Preservation Process

As recordings are reproduced and transferred in the course of a preservation project, details of the reproduction and transfer should be carefully documented so that future technicians and archivists will understand both the nature of the original recording and the techniques used to preserve it. "Documentation" means that the technician and the archivist keep a record of how the copies were made, including informa-tion on the original format, how the original recording was played dur-ing transfer (including the equalization used, in the case of phonodiscs), and how the transfer recording was made. Recording speeds, the presence of test tones, the track configuration, and any other information that will help archivists and technicians understand clearly what the new recording is and what the original recording was should also be noted. Documentation adds time, and therefore cost, to the process, but also leaves a trail of clues that future caretakers will appreciate.

The Audio Technician

Of course, as noted previously, equipment alone does not ensure the success of a preservation project. Of all of the components of a preservation project, the audio technician is the most important. No matter how good the equipment, how fine the recording medium, or how elaborate the studio, the entire effort will be wasted if these elements are not coordinated and employed skillfully and intelligently. Unfortunately, at the present time there are no formal training programs to teach audio technicians about archival work, and there is no consensus about what an archival audio technician should be or do. Only a handful of technicians in the U.S. who specialize in working with archival recordings are available to help with projects on a contract basis, yet, in recent years, the number of recording studios soliciting archival work and claiming to be expert in audio preservation has increased noticeably.

Archivists seeking an archival audio technician might begin by looking for a person with a good background in studio work coupled with experience working with archival and obsolete recordings. Word of mouth is always helpful in selecting a project technician or vendor, and colleagues who have undertaken audio preservation projects can often provide good leads and references. The technician should be willing to listen to the archives' desires regarding the handling and re-recording of the materials. He (most technicians presently doing this work are male) should be willing to openly and honestly discuss his usual procedures, including cleaning and preparation treatments. He should possess or have access to the equipment needed to play the older formats. He should not force the archives to accept recording technology that it does not want, or be secretive about how he handles and treats the recordings.

Technicians who have worked extensively with old recordings usually have their own preferred methods for handling, cleaning, and copying them. They should be willing to discuss their reasons for these preferences, which may be well founded; it is especially helpful if they are willing to consider altering their usual practices if the archives prefers. Most experienced technicians will admit that it is never possible, in this line of work, to have all the answers or to have "seen it all." Humility is sometimes a good sign; a technician who is aware of his limitations is less likely to proceed blithely with inappropriate treatment or techniques. Experienced technicians will be aware of the critical role of proper reproduction in the preservation process. A recording that has been carefully cleaned and played on appropriate equipment by a knowledgeable technician will be quieter, with less distortion than might otherwise be the case.[24] Such treatment requires patience in addition to knowledge and skill and a

---

24 Boston, *Guide to the Basic Technical Equipment*, 42.

willingness to forgo the simpler, quicker solutions of relying on filters and after-the-fact signal processing.

Technicians one might well avoid include those who promise a quick fix for aging recordings, who offer to digitize and enhance recordings as they "lock them in time," who are vague about what they do with the recordings, or who believe that they can handle everything without assistance or further discussion. By failing to understand and respect the unique qualities of older recording formats, such technicians may play them improperly, thereby introducing inaccuracies, or alter the sound significantly in a misguided attempt to "correct," "improve," or "modernize" the sound — actions that are not acceptable for preservation work.

Archives that wish to train their own staff members for audio preservation work will find the lack of educational opportunities especially frustrating. Two options for providing staff training are to send personnel for mini-training sessions at archives with existing preservation programs or to hire consultants to do in-house training. When training in-house personnel, it is important to designate the person or persons who will be trained and to keep their work focused on audio preservation as exclusively as possible until they are secure in their skills. Such training takes time and cannot be accomplished by half-way efforts or by dividing training among several different staff members. The temptation to employ cheaper labor for this purpose in the form of student assistants, work-study students, or interns is best avoided unless a truly knowledgeable and capable technician is available on-site to train and supervise the staff.

Once located, hired, and, if necessary, trained, the audio technician should be charged with ensuring that the technical portion of the project is handled as objectively and appropriately as possible. The technician should clearly communicate his or her plans and progress during the project and should understand and be willing to discuss all issues that arise relating to the playing and copying of the recordings.

Current Recommendations for Preservation Transfers

Although standards for audio preservation re-recording have not yet been developed and approved, the major sound archives in the United States and abroad, along with the recording media manufacturers, recommend the following guidelines for audio preservation transfer projects (as of summer 1996). Readers are cautioned that these recommendations may change by the time this work is published and are advised to check with other archivists for the most current information before proceeding with reformatting projects.

Recommendations:

- Use analog recording technology. [*Editor's note: See author's note at beginning of article.*]

- Use virgin (brand-new, unused) reel-to-reel tape with an overall thickness of 1.5 mils and a minimal base thickness of 1.2 mils.

- Record in full-track format for monaural original sources and half-track for stereo original sources at a speed of 15 ips. (Many archivists substitute 7.5 ips for spoken word recordings; preservation copies should not be made at speeds lower than 7.5 ips.)

- Store the tapes on metal NAB reels with unslotted hubs. (Standard professional quality tape can be purchased on appropriate reels, eliminating the need to purchase reels separately.)

- Avoid having splices in preservation tapes. (Splices create bumps in the tape pack which can lead to deformation of the tape during long-term storage, and their adhesives tend to bleed onto adjacent layers of tape, causing additional damage.)

- Include a series of test tones recorded at the head of each tape. (This helps future audio technicians and archivists understand how the tape is set up and recorded.)

- Never use preservation copies as service copies.

Note that standard analog audio cassettes are not suitable for preservation work under any circumstances. All analog cassettes held by archives should be copied to more robust formats, and suggestions that such formats are suitable for preservation work because they are cheaper, smaller, or easier to handle should be resisted at all costs. Most major sound archives also avoid using DAT/RDAT cassettes for preservation re-recording; the relative fragility of the tape and its high data density, combined with problems stemming from hardware that is frequently unreliable, do not recommend this medium for long-term storage of important information.

Final Considerations

As noted throughout this article, audio preservation re-recording is time consuming and costly, just how time consuming and costly is difficult to imagine without having carried out such a project.

Examining the collection, setting preservation priorities, hiring a contractor or setting up an in-house operation, preparing recordings for transfer, documenting the process, cataloging or indexing the recordings, and producing service copies — all of this takes time, and that time must be accounted for in project workplans and timelines. The flow of the work is important as well, requiring a steady supply of recordings provided to the audio technician at a pace that matches his or her pace of work.

Estimating Cleaning and Transfer Time

Estimating the time needed to prepare and clean recordings is difficult and depends greatly upon the condition of the recordings and the preferred cleaning and preparation methods. Transfer time (defined as the time it takes the technician to transfer the signal from the original recording to a new preservation medium), however, can be accurately estimated at three to five times the playing time of the original items for acetate discs, and about two or two-and-a-half times the original playing time for tapes. In some cases service copies can be generated as the preservation transfers are made; but if that is not feasible, additional time will be required. For making copies of analog preservation tapes that are in good condition, allow at least one-and-a-half times the playing time of the tapes.

Estimating Costs

The most costly single items in the budget for out-of-house projects will likely be the audio technician's time and a supply of new recording media for the transfers. As of this writing, studios regularly charge $50 to $85 per hour of work time, and high-quality tape can cost $18 per reel or more, even when purchased in bulk. In addition, cleaning supplies for acetate discs can also be costly, depending upon the method chosen. After investigating a number of cleaning methods and options, the GSU project chose Kodak Lens Cleaner as its cleaning fluid. If purchased off the shelf in small quantities, the cost would have been prohibitive (several dollars for a very small bottle). Even when purchased in bulk, the cost was not insignificant.

In-house projects incur these costs, plus costs relating to the outfitting of space for the transfer portion of the project. Ideally, this means outfitting a studio that has been designed specifically for audio preservation work. More commonly, space is set aside and modified to be minimally acceptable for preservation work. The space must be quiet, should have its own separate, well-grounded electrical supply to reduce the chance of electrical fluctuations that can produce audible flaws in the recordings, and must be outfitted with all the equipment needed to play and copy the recordings. If the recording equipment is to be maintained by qualified on-site personnel, test equipment such as oscilloscope, voltmeter, tone generator, and test tapes will be needed. If maintenance will be handled by outside contractors, funds will be required to pay the related fees.

Support Staff Needs

Audio preservation projects require staff to help clean and prepare the recordings, document the actions taken, and (for an in-house program) service the equipment regularly to keep it running properly. The amount of support staff time needed to clean, prepare, index, and rehouse recordings should not be underestimated, particularly if recordings need to be cleaned or, in the case of tapes, wound carefully to even and retension the tape pack prior to transfer. During the GSU project, many of the acetates with surface deposits of plasticizer residue required 45 minutes each to clean, more than double the time originally estimated. Winding tapes can also be time consuming, and routine cleaning, checking, and calibration of audio equipment (required of an in-house project) require both time and money; neither the technician nor the rest of the staff can use the equipment while it is being serviced (a cost of time), and qualified technicians must be hired and scheduled to perform some or all of the maintenance (a cost of money — sometimes a major one, since the supply of good repair technicians is nearly as small as the pool of competent archival audio technicians). Archivists planning an audio preservation project will do well to think carefully about all of the tasks involved and to avoid underestimating the amount of staff time that will be required.

Space Considerations

Original recordings should not be discarded unless they have completely deteriorated (and it should be noted that some engineers expect that improvements in imaging technology will enable "playback" of broken discs by this means in the future). This means that space and shelving will be needed to store the preservation copies, which should be kept in addition to, not in place of, the original recordings. If the project generates preservation reel tapes recorded at 15 ips, for example, this can mean a substantial amount of space if the project is large. One or two slender 16-inch discs can fill a reel of tape that takes up an inch of shelf space. One hundred such discs, when copied to tape, can require an additional six to eight feet of shelf space. Use copies, of course, require additional, separate, storage.

Epilogue

To summarize the issues outlined in this article, the production of preservation copies of aging audio recordings is much harder than it appears on the surface. Every aspect of the work is difficult (some prefer the term "challenging"), from acquiring appropriate equipment to finding knowledgeable audio technicians and developing in-house guidelines for the creation of preservation copies. Given all of the obstacles, relatively few archives will have both the energy and the resources to invest in pursuing preservation of their audio holdings, and those who do will find themselves making difficult compromises along the way.

Then why attempt preservation of audio recordings at all? Because we must, in some cases, because of institutional mandate or other obligations; but more importantly, because of the unique and sometimes startling or spectacular elements such recordings can add to the historical record. Recordings that contain "medium-specific" content, such as musical performances, stump speeches by key figures in politics, or the call of a bird or other species that is perhaps extinct; all of these inform us as the written word cannot, capturing, in addition to the "plain facts," the sound and flavor of a place, a creature, an event, or an era. The work, in short, can be tremendously rewarding, in spite of the enormous obstacles that archives must sometimes overcome.

In order to improve our ability to preserve important audio recordings, given the current, rather sorry, state of this particular art, archivists need to focus more on broader issues rather than strictly institutional or collection-specific ones. For example, the lack of any type of formal or informal educational opportunities for audio technicians who wish to work with archives recordings continues to retard research and development in transfer techniques, and the ongoing lack of research and development continues to contribute to the difficulty and high cost of preserving audio recordings. Where, when, or how this chicken-and-egg cycle will be broken, if it is broken, remains a mystery; in the meantime, the related lack of published standards for preservation copies simply serves as an additional stumbling block to archivists who try to implement audio preservation programs.

The archives community must mobilize to improve education about audio recordings and the means of preserving them; to participate in the development and promulgation of standards for archival audio technicians, for preservation re-recording and for recording media; to continue pressuring the tape and recording media manufacturers to produce media with an increased life expectancy; and to work with funding agencies to improve education, training, and preservation relating to audio recordings in archives. Continuing to wait for someone else to accomplish these things will reap the same lack of results so visible today and will contribute to massive losses of audio recordings in the near future.

Part Eight:
Electronic Records

One issue not specifically addressed in the SAA Archival Fundamentals Series is the nature of electronic records and archival approaches to meeting the challenges they present. Archivists have grappled with these problems — access, preservation, description, custody, and so on — in both theoretical and practical terms. Because of their seeming intangibility electronic records require creative solutions to these problems, which seem to overwhelm our resources. This has produced a literature about electronic records that is very much in flux, and that has produced some heated debates.

One of the major issues for consideration is whether electronic records pose challenges that require a basic rethinking and restructuring of archival theory and practice. A growing consensus seems to have emerged that electronic records confirm the essential validity of basic archival principles such as provenance; but how this should affect archival practice continues to stir controversy.

One of the early calls for a broad reconceptualization of archival practice in response to electronic records is "Reinventing Archives for Electronic Records: Alternative Service Delivery Options," by David Bearman and Margaret Hedstrom. Responding to recommendations for "reinventing government" made by David Osborne and Ted Gaebler, Bearman and Hedstrom suggest that archivists should consider a wide range of innovative options such as noncustodial archives, in which archivists would establish legal regulations for maintaining electronic records, but not assume physical custody.

Although presented as untested conceptual thoughts on meeting the challenges posed by electronic records, the recommendations made by Bearman and Hedstrom generated heated debates within the profession. Bearman, Hedstrom, and others have criticized the National Archives and Records Administration, among other archival agencies, for its handling of electronic records. In "Schellenberg in Cyberspace," Linda Henry of the NARA staff responds with a vigorous defense of traditional archival practices and a critique of Bearman, Hedstrom, and other advocates of a "new paradigm" for electronic records.

These two articles represent very different theoretical and method-ological approaches to managing electronic records. The conflicting views indicate how passionate the debate over archival identity sometimes becomes. Archivists need to be aware of these debates in order to deter-mine how they will approach the theoretical and practical issues relating to electronic records.

Another approach to these issues comes from Anne Gilliland-Swetland in "Digital Communications: Documentary Opportunities Not to be Missed." This article examines the important issue of applying archival expertise to preserving and accessing electronic records in collaboration with colleagues in related professions. She thus reasserts the value of archival principles and methods in meeting the challenges of the information age.

24

Reinventing Archives for Electronic Records: Alternative Service Delivery Options

DAVID BEARMAN AND MARGARET HEDSTROM

Abstract: Dramatic changes in electronic communications and data processing are transforming the business processes that archivists must document and overwhelming archives with new demands that few archivists feel competent to meet. Confronted with these challenges, it is time that archivists reexamined their program structures and methodologies. In a time of "re-inventing" government and organizations, archivists would be well served by thinking through alternatives to their current methods. The authors have selected some ideas with special relevance to electronic records management that hold out some chance of improving outcomes without increased resource allocations for archives. None of these ideas is fully tested and the authors do not recommend wholesale abandonment of traditional approaches in favor of them, but they urge pilot tests as a way of trying to break out of the cycle of failure in which archivists are now trapped. Electronic records can be a vehicle for archives to move from rowing to steering, toward more enterprising and customer-driven approaches to service delivery and toward empowering others to take action in a decentralized records management environment.

The Situation of Archives

Archives, public and private, large and small, are unable to cope with the volume of records for which they are responsible given the methods at their command.[1] The problem is not just one of degrees. It reflects a fundamental gap between the task that archivists have assumed for themselves — ensuring adequate documentation of our society — and the resources at their disposal to accomplish this task. In many cases several orders of magnitude separate the responsibilities of archivists from their current capacity to achieve them.

Dramatic changes in electronic communications and data processing are transforming the business processes that archivists must document

Reprinted with permission from *Electronic Records Management Program Strategies*, Archives and Museum Informatics Technical Report No. 18, ed. Margaret Hedstrom (Pittsburgh: Archives & Museum Informatics, 1993), 82-98. Abstract added for this volume by the editor.

1 David Bearman, *Archival Methods*, Archives and Museum Informatics Technical Report No. 9 (Pittsburgh: Archives & Museum Informatics, 1989).

and overwhelming archives with new demands that few archivists feel competent to meet. In a period of downsizing, right-sizing, and just plain cutting back, the impact of new information technologies is not the only challenge that archivists must confront. Organizations in the public, private, and third sectors are reexamining the way they do business, reengineering their business functions, and redistributing responsibility and resources for carrying out their mandates and operations.

Confronted with these challenges, it is time that archivists reexamined the program structures and methodologies that served them reasonably well up until a generation ago but within which they still largely practice their craft. In a time of "reinventing" government and organizations, archivists would be well served by thinking through alternatives to their current methods. In an age of measuring outcomes rather than outputs, archivists must demonstrate that they are achieving the ends for which archives are established — preserving access to records of continuing value — and not just increasing the volume of records accessioned, the numbers of researchers, or the percentage of holdings described in national networks.

The problem is that these actions are not sufficient to accomplish the fundamental purpose of archives, even though increasing accessions, researchers, or collections may be valuable (depending on the quality of accessions, the satisfaction of researchers, and the quality of description). If all these measures rise, year after year, but the evidence of important events and decisions in the organizations served by archives remains undocumented or inaccessible, then archives are failing to accomplish their purpose. If new recordkeeping systems are being implemented that increase the insecurity of records, rather than assure their security, then archives are failing to ensure the keeping of adequate documentation. And this is where many American archives find themselves in the 1990s.

In May 1993, the authors found themselves together at a conference on Archives and State Information Policy in Montgomery, Alabama, organized by the state archivist and the state director of information management who had decided to try to reinvigorate accountable information management across the state government. We found ourselves exploring with archivists and EDP directors of state agencies approaches to organizing their respective jobs that respected none of the traditional assumptions about organizing archives. We asked about turning each function of the archives over to private or other public interests. We explored merging archival documentation and EDP documentation tasks. We considered the possibility of completely noncustodial archives and examined the arguments for and against selling data and even selling records. Earlier in the month we met with the NAGARA Committee on Information Technology and the SAA Committee on Automated Records and Techniques at the session documented in *Electronic Records*

Management Strategies, Archives and Museum Informatics Technical Report No. 18, edited by Margaret Hedstrom (1993), and we heard archivists asking themselves how to envision alternative futures and program structures that might work better than those in place now.

Reinventing Archives

We found numerous principles and concepts from *Reinventing Government* especially useful for rethinking archives, whether they are located in the government, university, private, or nonprofit sector.[2] David Osborne and Ted Gaebler propose that governments rethink their service delivery options, define areas of strength, shift performance measures from outputs to outcomes, separate direction and oversight from service delivery (or steering from rowing — in their terms), and encourage entrepreneurship and action by others. They urge experiments with a host of new methods in order to create governments that are more effective, efficient, responsive, and equitable. We believe that many of their basic concepts can be applied to rethinking archives.

From our years of thinking about alternatives, and an initial exploration of how the ideas proposed by Osborne and Gaebler in their book *Reinventing Government* might be applied to archives, we compiled a list of dozens of blue sky ideas. Subsequently one of us (DB) conducted a workshop on electronic records management in Australia at which participants imagined additional options. From these we have selected some ideas with special relevance to electronic records management that hold out some chance of improving outcomes without increased resource allocations for archives. None of these ideas is fully tested and we are not recommending wholesale abandonment of traditional approaches in favor of them, but we are urging pilot tests with results reported back to the profession as a way of trying to break out of the cycle of failure in which we are now trapped.

The fundamental change in recordkeeping practices by the organizations that archives are designed to serve provides the catalyst for reexamining how archives define and accomplish their work. The flaws we have identified in existing archival programs are numerous. In order to present them we discuss them in relation to the life cycle of the archival record, although they are interrelated and reflect some larger problems with how archivists approach their work, which we discuss after the specifics. Two issues should be noted up front. First, neither archivists nor the public seem to know what kind of organizational entity archives are. This is reflected in the plethora of organizational locations to which the function is assigned and the inability of archivists to identify their customers

---

2 David Osborne and Ted Gaebler, *Reinventing Government: How the Entrepreneurial Spirit Is Transforming the Public Sector* (New York: Penguin, 1992).

Figure 1.

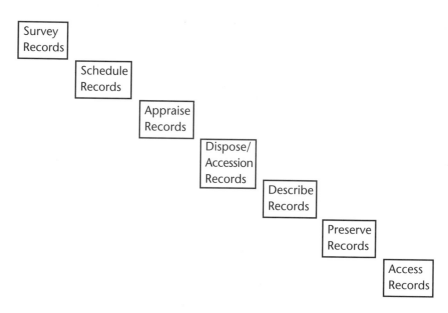

without accumulating new and equally important audiences. The entities to which archives report are usually not clear about what services archives perform or why they exist. In government, archives typically report to the executive branch which is appropriate if their function is to improve management. But it is noteworthy that the legislative branch wants the oversight facilitated by archival records and is willing to pay for accountability, yet no archives in a major U.S. political jurisdiction reports to the legislature or is an independent entity serving all three branches of government.

Second, we believe that these flaws are the result of several decades of unchallenged thinking in which it was assumed that archives were best designed as autonomous units with their own staffs, budgets, and methods, and with responsibility for carrying out, within those resource limitations, all activities associated with appraisal, accessioning, preservation, description, and access to records. Archivists' limited success in dealing with electronic records, more than any other single issue, has exposed the limitations of this approach. We believe that the problems discussed below result from the methods and systems used in archives, not the people who work in archives, and that archivists can do much to remedy this situation.

Why Current Methods Fail for Electronic Records

Our traditional model of what archivists do can be illustrated by the cascading task diagram in Figure 1. Unfortunately, this model is not very helpful in structuring programs for electronic records although most existing programs are still trying to structure themselves around it.

Survey Records. Electronic information systems are being designed and implemented so as not to make records, but to provide up-to-date information that is seen as better by being changed to reflect the latest circumstances and knowledge. Nevertheless, archivists continue to begin their work by surveying records holdings and conducting inventories. They have, until recently, not even been able to articulate what is wrong with the design premises of systems that do not create or capture a record of every business transaction. While the important activities of organizations are everywhere going undocumented as a consequence of information systems that are designed not to be adequate record systems, archivists forgo involvement in systems design and implementation required to assure the creation of adequate documentation. They cling to the assertion that they lack sufficient authority to require records creation, adhere to a dictum that causing records to be created would result in proliferation of records of unimportant transactions, fail to notice when critical information systems are being designed and implemented, and have little advice to offer on how to implement systems in organizations in a way that will satisfy recordkeeping requirements. Therefore archivists are not considered as potential allies even when management discovers that it cannot account for recent functions or activities. Managers implicitly realize that existing archival methods have as their object records that have been created rather than functions and activities that need to be documented.

Schedule Records. In order to identify the 1 to 3 percent of records that are archival, archivists traditionally have attempted to schedule all the records created by an institution. Even if electronic systems always created records, reviewing 100 percent of records created in order to select the less than 3 percent that should be saved beyond the time they are needed for ongoing operations is inefficient. By focusing on series, archivists have reduced the scheduling task, but electronic records are not filed in "series" unless archivists have been present in the systems design process. Scheduling approaches, therefore, fail to identify records of significant transactions because so much effort is involved in disposing of the routine material that there is no time to locate the documentation of more important, and less routine, activity. Few agencies ever complete the scheduling of all the records under their jurisdiction. Because archivists provide no criteria for what records to schedule and no sanctions are imposed for failing to develop schedules for the most important records, the tendency is to schedule large, routine series. When records retention involved significant space costs, archivists asserted the benefit of scheduling routine series for administrative efficiency, but in an electronic environment space is not an important criterion, and administrative efficiency is achieved by being able to locate records germane to particular types of transactions over time. Because archivists don't develop an independent knowledge of recordkeeping systems and organizational functions that would support asking why no schedules had been developed for historically significant materials, they tend to be fully occupied with trivial work. In focusing on scheduling records rather than on identifying the significant activity of the organization, archivists miss an opportunity to build a knowledge base on the structure and functions of the organization which is much needed by other divisions within the organization and by outside interests. Moreover, insisting on details of records disposal perpetuates the impression that archivists are bean counters rather than management partners. One effect of this perception is that senior managers do not take archival requests for documentary accountability as seriously as similar demands made by auditors that have explicit management consequences.

Appraise Records. In paper-based systems, archivists have generally attempted to appraise records when they are inactive or even after they have been received by the archives, at which point they are removed from both the record systems that created and maintained them and the organizational processes that they supported. Professional expertise is directed toward trying to reconstruct the context of creation of the records in order to understand their significance as evidence. Because of the limited number of ways that paper records are maintained and the visibility of these structures to the archivist, this reconstruction of the likely use of records is plausible for paper systems. The electronic record, however, is stored randomly, and the structures that support its use by the organization are documented only in software code not accessioned with systems, so appraisal of electronic records after accessioning is typically not reasonable. While the information the records contain can be discovered through external software functions such as full-text searches, the evidence they supply is based on their link to activity that will have been lost. The activity for which the records were created must be considered independently as the reason for retaining the records and must be rigorously identified in the appraisal process. Otherwise only those factors that data archivists have tended to call "technical," such as the ease of use of the records, their completeness, and their documentation, will be criteria for retention. Instead of keeping valuable evidence, we will be reduced to keeping easy-to-use information.

Dispose/Accession Records. Archivists insist on preserving the authority for records disposition, including disposal, but this assumes that an act of disposing is required in order to rid oneself of records. In the electronic environment most records will cease to be available, usable, and understandable as a consequence of lack of action rather than as a result of disposal. Thus the focus on disposal authority is misplaced in electronic records creating organizations, and emphasis must instead be placed on providing help to management to keep records useful.

In order to preserve records that are archival, archivists have traditionally accessioned them into archival repositories where they are physically controlled by archivists. But obtaining custody of electronic records in archives is no guarantee of better control. Indeed in the electronic age, custody of archives may require the ongoing maintenance of a range of hardware and software and continuing migration of both data and applications, both of which activities are never ending and very expensive. This puts records in archival custody at relatively greater risk than those whose ongoing management is regulated by archivists but which remain in the physical custody of agencies that created them. Also, as a consequence of serving in a custodial role, archivists are perceived as keepers of old records, become experienced in obsolete technologies, and are constantly involved in migrating data and systems, instead of becoming experts on the most recent technologies and how to control them.

Describe/Document Records. Traditionally archivists have described records after appraising them and accessioning them by examining their content and structure. Not only does this process miss the opportunity to use information collected about the structure and functions of the organization, and the link between transactions and records, it assumes that post-accessioning description will be possible. In electronic records systems, metadata about the records and the configuration of permissions, views, and functions is created and controlled in the active data environment. In principle, this metadata if correctly specified could fully describe and document the records without post-hoc activity by archivists. Archivists will need to specify what metadata must be kept and how it should be linked to records over time. The effect of such a proactive stance toward active information systems will put archivists in control of an information locator function that is needed by, will be used by, and could even be sold to, other divisions within the organization and outside interests. Privacy, security, vital records management, auditing, and archives all require the same metadata management program, so they could share the responsibility and/or the cost.

Preserve Records. The greatest expense in preserving records is associated with keeping their physical form rather than retaining their evidential value. The most expensive records to keep are those whose physical form is most fragile. Because there is no way to actually keep the original artifact in the case of electronic records, physical preservation becomes a nonissue. All records must be copied over time and retained in software independent formats or with appropriate software to read them. All copies have the same evidential value and there is no limit on the number of copies that can be made without degradation. Indeed, paper archives would not be in any way diminished as sources of evidence or information by selling original records with significant market value. Instead, archivists tend to resist disposing of originals even after adequate record copies are created, thus contributing to the perception that they are antiquarians.

Access Records. Archives provide reference services to the public at considerable cost in manpower and space, but traditionally they have had only one "outlet" per repository and provided substantially less documentation of their holdings than libraries. This has rendered archival records less available and less accessible than published information sources. Paper records are, of course, unique and difficult to reproduce or distribute remotely, as well as inherently difficult to describe in detail, so these limitations on access were not noticed or were considered necessary characteristics of archives. These same limitations need not affect access to electronic records. It is easy to provide copies of electronic records to numerous "outlets" at the same time and through metadata management to support item-level description of records without archivists engaging in item-level description. By employing networks we could greatly expand the ability of individual citizens to get information from archives. Distributed points of access could also be supported by a proactive reference service staffed by public librarians and other information providers rather than archivists.

Alternative Models/Program Options

What traditional archival methods have in common is that archivists take on the burden of doing the work. Archivists survey records and develop schedules. Employees in organizations are instructed in great detail about when to dispose of records and how to transfer records to the archives. Thereupon the archivists appraise and describe the records, preserve them, and make them accessible. The tasks are all envisioned as being the responsibility of archivists. It is presumed that archivists are required to assure they are done correctly. Resources to do them come from archival budgets, the work is conducted in centralized archives, and archivists are the gatekeepers for users whose needs they understand.

In *Reinventing Government,* Osborne and Gaebler explore some alternatives for the delivery of any governmental services that have applicability to archives, whether they are governmental or not. By allowing our minds to invent alternative program models, we hope to have exposed a few ideas that, when pursued further and refined, will help archives overcome the limitations of traditional practice.

Steering Rather Than Rowing

Osborne and Gaebler use the metaphor of steering rather than rowing to distinguish innovative governments from traditional organizations. Many of the governments that Osborne and Gaebler critique are caught in a cycle of taxing and spending to meet increasing demands for government services with declining revenues. They argue that governments should shift from a pattern of direct service delivery (rowing) to governance based on setting policy direction, fostering healthy social and economic institutions, and providing requirements and incentives for others to provide services. This approach empowers communities to solve their own problems, permits competition among service providers, and provides governments with maximum flexibility to respond to changing needs and opportunities. Shifting from rowing to steering means that governments replace their propensity to do everything with governance by directing. Steering organizations make more policy decisions, put more social and economic institutions into motion, and do more regulating.

We believe that archives can benefit from a similar shift from rowing to steering. Most archives today are typical "rowing" organizations, taking actions on records after they have been accessioned into an archival repository and providing services to users who visit research rooms in order to access and retrieve records. Traditional methods assume that records adequate to document transactions of the business are created in the first instance, and that archivists can take corrective actions (through arrangement, description, and preservation) to compensate for ineffective access systems or the poor physical state of records when they are taken into custody. Efforts to improve control earlier in the records life cycle focus on use of retention and disposition schedules, typically enforced only when regulated agencies wish to dispose of records they no longer want or need. Rather than providing overall policy direction for adequacy of documentation, archivists deliver services to records and to researchers that make up for poorly designed systems. Rather than steering records creators toward adequately documenting government business, archivists and records managers regulate the disposal of obsolete or unneeded records. Rather than directing organizations toward designing records systems that meet recordkeeping requirements and conform to access, description, retrieval, and preservation standards, archivists attempt to make records conform to standards after the fact.

What might archives look like as steering organizations? Drawing on the lessons from Reinventing Government, archivists might begin by defining desired outcomes, rather than focusing on outputs. An outcome-based definition for government archives might be that government creates and ensures continuing access to the evidence of its policies, decisions, activities, and transactions. A steering approach to achieving this outcome would increase monitoring and oversight by the archival agency while assigning responsibility to agencies for achieving adequately documented functions and programs. Strategies for steering rely on legal rules and sanctions, regulations, monitoring, and investigation. Examples of tactics archives might consider include creating legal rules and sanctions:

- An archival agency could define an outcome-oriented regulation: "documentable history" or "significant activities are evidenced."

Annual archival filings with the legislature, consisting of definitions of accountable record systems, would be required for appropriations.

- The "statute of limitations" for some types of activities could be changed so that organizations would have incentives in liability or risk management to keep records of them for appropriate lengths of time.
- New rules of evidence could require records creators to keep and locate records. New rules of evidence could place responsibility for being able to locate evidence on the party holding it, even if it has not been requested.
- Declassification laws could be revised to make everything open after 30 years unless an exception is filed by the creating agency with specified criteria acceptable to court or special tribunal.
- Loss of accountability for government information could be made a felony, or made grounds for dismissal of civil servants and political appointees and removal from office of elected officials. Civil remedies for loss of accountability could include punitive damages.
- Archivists, working with certified accountants and auditors, could make breaches of documentation requirements a new category of liability for all private and public organizations, thus rewarding private sector entities that keep adequate records and applying sanctions against those that don't.
- Archives and records management programs could publish compliance data and projections of future, unnecessarily incurred, records management costs as a sanction against agencies that lack plans or systems for managing their records.

Regulating and deregulating:

- Recipients of federal funding could be required to maintain adequate documentation, if this could be defined by outcomes.
- Archivists could set standards for storage and access to records and legalize alternatives to depositing with the archives.
- The number of agency employees allowed classified clearances could be dramatically reduced.
- An operating license could be required for archivists, which would carry with it the authority to see any records. Archivists could be insulated somewhat from agency/employer pressures by having careers depend on a separate board (a board of archival examiners) or on achieving outcome measures.
- Firms doing business with the government could be required to purchase documentation insurance with premiums based on adequacy of their existing records programs.

- Government agencies and organizations using government-subsidized networks could be required to post archival records in a network environment for automatic retirement by electronic archives.
- Agencies could be required to obtain a permit to produce paper documents similar to permits required for point source air and water pollution.
- Archives could require record-creating bodies to file a records or archival impact statement in which they iden-tify the resources necessary and consequences of record keeping associated with each new function.
- Determine a maximum percentage (.5 precent?) of each agency's records that can be considered archival. Require each agency to determine the contents of its archives and publish an index to them. Require new legislation to redefine the limit.

Monitoring and investigation:

- Like FOIA, archival responsibilities could be the subject of an annual report by the agency and an annual report by an "archival inspectorate" equivalent to an independent audit authority.
- A third party, such as management auditors, could be used to identify important record systems and accountability lapses and impose standards for compliance.
- Investigation could support quality control in a distributed archives system.
- Standards could be enforced through procurement processes that require open systems and an implementable plan for continuing access to archival records.

Empowering Others Rather Than Serving

Empowering communities to solve their own problems is another key element of reinventing government. Osborne and Gaebler contend that communities have more commitment to their members than service delivery systems have to their members. Often, communities understand their own problems better than service professionals, are more flexible than large service organizations in responding to problems, and may be more cost effective. Empowering others to solve problems often works because communities have a vested interest in the solution.

Applying this concept to reinventing archives opens the door for a dialogue between archivists and the communities they serve, including records creators, users, and professionals from related information disciplines. It would compel archivists to define their communities, acknowledge potential conflicts between the communities that archives serve, and provide leadership for conflict resolution. Archivists would provide tools, incentives, guidelines, and support to institutions holding archival records and involve users in problem solving and service delivery within a clearly articulated framework of principles and standards. In turn, institutions holding records and users of archival materials would make more day-to-day decisions, such as which records to retain or how to best provide user access. If archivists can engage their communities in solving archival problems, then they can rely more on their communities to achieve mutually desired ends.

Some of the tactics that archivists might pursue to put such an approach into action are listed here:

- Encouraging agencies and organizations to care for their own archives and empowering them through incentives and support to take on their own records. Encourage development of different approaches to appraisal, access, and preservation provided basic outcomes were defined in regulations.

- Private entities could be licensed as government archives and records management services, thus enabling government agencies to contract out, providing a potential source of income and supporting standards.

- The private sector could be given rights in data about federal functions, activities (*Federal Register*), and records (FOI Locator) in return for delivering the information to the government in a specified format.

- Civil servants could be rewarded with bounties for identifying records in their agencies that have archival value.

- Archives could provide vastly expanded technical assistance as a benefit to repositories that are willing to assume custodial and access responsibilities.

- Organizations could be encouraged to develop and test methods for electronic records administration and to release code in the public domain.

- To encourage ideas and competition, archivists could publish regular reports on experiments and finance data collection about outcomes through grants and contracts.

- License researchers to provide reference services.

- Have volunteers take over servicing information-based queries.

- Permit researchers, willing to undergo security clearance review, to access classified records and provide declassification services in return for that access.

- Permit universities to provide appraisal and access services for government records when the records relate to the academic strengths or regional focus of a university.
- Give genealogical data to genealogical societies to administer.
- Give ecological data to environmental groups.
- Archives could monitor and report on citizens' problems in acquiring access to government records and maintain a hotline that distributes information about successful strategies.
- Bring the press to bear. Develop methods that use the power and interest of the press in open governmental information, especially when important communities are mobilized.

Enterprising Archives

Enterprising government for Osborne and Gaebler means reexamining the ways that revenues are generated, costs are distributed, and investments are made to support government services. They endorse strategies that turn the profit motive to public use, raise money by charging fees for some services, and spend money to save money in the long run through investments that pay a return. Such an approach ultimately means identifying the true costs of delivering services. As Osborne and Gaebler point out, most governments have no idea how much it costs to deliver the services they offer. Neither do most archives. A critical challenge for "enterprising archives" would involve building a documentable case for the benefits to be gained through investments in archival information systems and in development of business systems that meet recordkeeping requirements. Other enterprising strategies for archives might include:

- Charging records creators for costs of future archiving based on extent of records creation.
- Adding fees to certain record-creating transactions for certain types of transactions and then use the revenue to care for records, as in New York State, Kentucky, Missouri and elsewhere.
- Publish images of large data sets that are interesting to the public. Provide copies for review and advertise widely.
- Permit FOIA documents to earn royalties if they are published. Develop a mechanism for FOIA offices to compete for earnings.
- Bring images and sounds in archives to the market. Use income to build the program to bring more to the market.
- Require R&D publications using goverznment funding to deposit data sets with publishers, universities, or other distributors.

Permit distributors to market data sets as they see fit, provided they also ensure preservation.

- At the time of creation, electronic records could be "sealed" in object-oriented envelopes with attributes that keep a record of their use and modification and report to the system on their location and access restrictions.

- Agencies could be assessed as they classify records to pay for subsequent declassification.

- Agencies could be given authority to contract out archives and records management to each other or to the private sector.

- One level of government could contract with another (federal-state, state-county, county-city, etc.) to administer its records.

- Archives could contract with libraries to provide reference service for records, with reimbursement set by level of use.

- Contractors could be provided with tax benefits for donating records in specified formats and with specified intellectual controls (previously required under regulation) to the archives of the granting agency.

- User fees could be placed on citizens using public records to support access and preservation.

- Commercial organizations could be given tax breaks for having archives.

- The size of the tax benefit for donating records could be tied to the restrictions placed on them. Make open records entitled to full benefit with others having lesser benefits based on how soon they will be open and the severity of other restrictions.

- Provide additional tax benefits to depositors of presidential advisory documentation based on when (how soon) they donate it and what restrictions apply (the fewer restrictions, the greater the tax benefit). Make it considerably greater than any tax benefit that could be obtained by other means.

- Private organizations willing to care for government records could be granted tax credits for servicing them. The government could underwrite loans to organizations willing to house and service government records.

- Services qualifying for repayment of student loans could include work in archives.

- Required overhead categories for grants could include payments for archival administration of grant-related records.

- Archives could franchise universities by giving them rights to hold and service government records for renewable periods of time.

- Design a new "copyright" that takes effect after records are released for a fixed period of years. Give these "copyrights" to those administering data with privacy, security, and archival values with the constraint that the copyright will not be protected from lawsuits if the copyright holder fails to administer the privacy, security, and archival values in an acceptable way. This would make disaggregated statistical information currently controlled for privacy available much more readily, while protecting privacy.

- Franchise the opportunity to respond to user queries. Sell rights to freelance researchers.

- States could be provided with incentives to manage records of federal programs. The federal government could contract with all 50 states to provide the service for them, thereby reducing redundancy.

- The private funding concept behind presidential libraries could be extended by joining with universities to provide federal historical research centers.

- Government could sell data from archives in value-added services — GIS data, legislative reference data, demographic data, etc.

- Contracts for information-recording media and devices could be surcharged to support life-cycle management of records.

- Pubic servants identifying cost savings and risk reduction in records systems design and operation could be made eligible for rewards or for a percentage of the savings.

- Archives could sell rights to "mine" holdings. Discoverers of material that can be reappraised as nonarchival could receive a reward based on first 10 years of cost savings.

- Archives could issue vouchers to agencies to be used for archiving records.

- Archives could sell records with intrinsic value, use income to capture information content of additional records with intrinsic value, and sell those.

- Archives could create market demand for information by investing in value-added activities and commercially marketing them.

- Tax deductions could be given for using licensed archival appraisers just as they are for accounting services. Tax deductions for donations to archives could be graduated based on the degree of access restriction imposed and tax rebates could be offered for donations satisfying specified description standards.

- Archives could subsidize pressure groups interested in access to records, enabling them to alert public opinion to the need for archival intervention.

- Underwrite loans or provide guarantees to businesses archiving records under franchises.

Customer-Driven Archives

In critiquing government programs, Osborne and Gaebler emphasize the need to give the customers for government services a greater say in the types of services offered and the direction of government programs. Administrators of contemporary government programs need to confront the fact that customers for government services have rising expectations, increasingly demand more choice in the services available, and cannot all be satisfied with a single, standard menu of services. One key strategy for rebuilding the credibility of government services and building support for government programs is developing more relevant and responsive services that are oriented to the needs of customers.

Reinventing Government describes a variety of methods that organizations can use to develop customer-driven programs, including use of focus groups, customer interviews, electronic mail, customer service training, ombudsmen, complaint tracking, and 800 numbers, which solicit input from the customers about their problems, needs, and perceptions. While we agree that most of these methods could be applied to reinventing archives, the problems and issues confronting the archival community are more fundamental. Few archives have defined their customers beyond the traditional user communities. In response to growing variety in the types of records available in archives and the uses of archival records, archives had added more user communities without assessing the impact of new user communities on the services provided or the methods used. Only a few archival program have made effective use of advisory committees and similar means to gain input from customers and increase awareness of the problems and challenges facing archives. Some of the strategies that archives might pursue toward a customer orientation include:

- Reward agencies based on the use of their records thereby encouraging them to advertise availability of records deposited in archives to relevant constituencies and to discover how best to describe them for use.
- Reward archivists based on use of records they appraise, document, or service.
- Give grants to potential users of archives to define ways in which records could be important to their constituencies and to develop use of archives along these lines; increase the level of support based on results.
- Require publication of information about records disposal and holdings of records for a period of time to enable customers to identify alternatives.

- Auction records being disposed to customers with a private interest in them.

Decentralized Archives

Another relevant theme from *Reinventing Government* is the notion of decentralized government. Decentralized institutions are more flexible and more receptive to innovation and change. They can be more effective and more productive and may generate a greater commitment from those who work in them. The concept of decentralized archives challenges many of the basic rationales used to support large centralized repositories with specialized centralized services. Such concepts as economies of scale, the convenience of a central repository, and the need to consolidate resources and expertise are challenged in the electronic era when distributed processing and networking eliminate the need to consolidate holdings in a central location or to visit a research room to gain access. This new potential presents archives with opportunities to reexamine centralization, not only from the perspective of centralized holdings, but also in the organization of programs and service delivery. Some of the strategies that archives could pursue to advance decentralization include:

- Provide grants to local governments for capital investments in archives in return for guarantees of local operating support.
- Authorize archives within agencies or departments if they satisfy criteria established for quality archival programs and report information on their holdings to a shared database.
- Increase the number of outlets for reference services to archival holdings by contracting with libraries, museums, professional associations, or other information providers to service them.
- Trivialize the significance of the location of the record by providing equal access over networks to an electronic version of the record regardless of its storage location.

Putting It All Together

Reinventing Government presents a menu of optional ways to reconsider program structures and delivery mechanisms, only a few of which we discuss in this essay. When rethinking and reinventing archives, archivists can select from many approaches and pursue those best suited to their jurisdiction, mandates, organization culture, and customers. Undoubtedly, most programs will seek a balance between regulations and market forces, between entrepreneurial endeavors and enforcement of standards, and between customer-driven approaches and achievement of predefined outcomes.

While different programs will adopt different structures in the future just as they have in the past, electronic records management requirements will tend to influence archives to adopt some dramatically different structures than those under which they currently operate. In reformulating program strategies, it will be helpful to consider not simply how the function can be reorganized, but also how the function can be "reinvented," steering rather than rowing, empowering others rather than serving, becoming enterprising and customer-driven, and decentralizing. The fundamental premises of what constitutes archival work could well be transformed by this kind of reinvention of the archival functions. Reinvented archives provide for much greater flexibility in methods and program options. At the same time, however, archivists need a model for practice that distinguishes archival work from other types of information management and delivery and that can be used to define the outcomes the archives should achieve and the customers for archival activity.

The older model of archival activity, around which archival manuals and education are structured, was presented earlier. It uses terms such as *survey, appraise, dispose, accession, describe, preserve,* and *access* to describe the work of archives and models the flow of information between sequential and chronological archival activities. A different model is suggested in Figure 2.[3] The object of the verbs in the traditional model is always records; all traditional archival activity focuses on records. The second model contains no verbs whose objects are records; all archival activity focuses on the business activity of organizations, the requirements they present for accountability, and the methods one might use to control information. The traditional model administers physical material while the second manages organizational behavior.

It is useful to carry the analysis of these divergent models further in order to understand their implications for electronic records management programs. If archivists shift their programmatic orientation in the way suggested by the second model, they will be acting in organizations before records are created and defining recordkeeping regimes for employees to follow but not deciding about specific records. This approach is particularly well suited to electronic records, although it may have relevance for paper-based archives as well. The advantages to electronic archives programs is that the focus on documentation of significant types of organizational transactions permits the archivist to use information developed by others within the organization for different purposes while becoming the repository of knowledge about how the

---

3 This model was first developed by David Bearman in a workshop with Australian archivists conducted at Monash University in May 1993. The contributions of all participants in that workshop are acknowledged.

Figure 2.

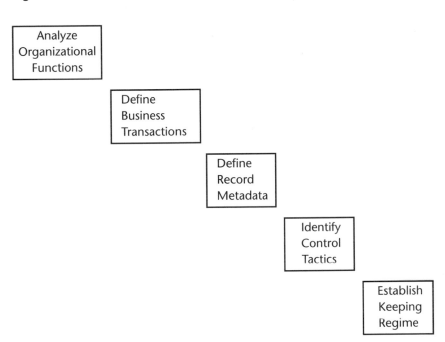

organization works. The focus on identifying metadata that is required to create records, before they are created, makes the archivist an ally of information systems managers, auditors, freedom of information act administrators, information security personnel, and program managers without placing the responsibility for documentation on the archivist. Archivists can serve as internal consultants, defining record keeping regimes and tactics, without being burdened by custody or by delivery of records requested through the information systems they maintain with agency provided metadata. In these and other ways, electronic records can be a vehicle for archives to move from rowing to steering, towards more enterprising and customer driven approaches to service delivery and towards empowering others to take action in a decentralized records management environment.

25

Schellenberg in Cyberspace

LINDA J. HENRY

Abstract: *In the last few years, advocates of the ideas of David Bearman have written that archivists need a "new paradigm" for electronic records. The new ideas would change or overturn traditional archival theory and practice, as represented by T. R. Schellenberg and the first writers about electronic records. This article discusses several of the new ideas and the differences between traditional archival writers and those who support a new paradigm for electronic records.*

For the last two decades, archivists have struggled with the challenges presented by electronic records. The first writers about electronic records believed that archivists could apply traditional archival theory and practice to records in electronic format. In the last few years, however, some writers have argued that the very nature of electronic records requires archivists to adopt new ideas that would change or overturn traditional archival principles. Archivists trained in and practicing traditional archival theory and practice, as represented by the writings of Theodore R. Schellenberg, can find the new ideas confusing and unsettling. They well may ask, whatever happened to Schellenberg and informational value? This article assesses the new ideas regarding electronic records with reference to Schellenberg and traditional archival theory, practice, and literature, but also draws on contemporary writings that oppose the adoption of new archival theory and practice specific to electronic records.

Background

As archival practitioner, theorist, and writer, Theodore R. Schellenberg (1903-1970) influenced and continues to influence generations of archivists, particularly in the United States. Schellenberg and colleagues at the

Reprinted with permission from the *American Archivist* 61 (Fall 1998): 309-27. This article is a revised and expanded version of a paper presented on August 28, 1997, at the SAA annual meeting in Chicago. The author thanks Bruce Ambacher especially, and Tom Brown, Mark Conrad, and other colleagues at the Center for Electronic Records for suggestions and support; Nancy Sahli for editing assistance; and Alan Kowlowitz for the title of the paper. This article does not necessarily represent their views or those of the National Archives and Records Administration.

National Archives, such as Philip C. Brooks and G. Philip Bauer, drew on European archival theories, but they found it necessary to revise and develop new archival concepts in order to manage great masses of records. In 1934 the newly created National Archives inherited an enormous backlog of records. The expansion of federal agencies in the 1930s and 1940s only exacerbated the problems of dealing with a large volume of records. Schellenberg's synthesis of concepts of appraisal — emphasizing the primary and secondary uses of records and evidential and informational values — offered an approach to managing voluminous amounts of records. One concept, imaginative for its time, shifted the focus of appraisal from records proposed for destruction to the identification of permanently valuable records. In urging that archivists work with creating agencies early in the life cycle of records, Schellenberg emphasized the importance of records management. He thus foreshadowed writings of 40 years later about electronic records. In addition, Schellenberg argued for the standardization of such archival functions as arrangement, description, and reference. Furthermore, he broke new ground in advocating that the principles and techniques for managing public records also could apply to private records and manuscript collections. For decades, Schellenberg's principles and techniques shaped the training of American archivists, while translations of his publications reached audiences beyond North America. His concepts formed what American archivists have long regarded as the "traditional" approach to archival work.[1]

In the second half of the twentieth century, the issue of voluminous modern records became an even greater problem than when Schellenberg first focused on it. The development of computers promised to reduce the physical bulk of records, given the great storage capacity of electronic media, but it also presented new problems. The practitioners dealing with electronic records in the 1970s were the first to address the issues of the relevance and applicability of archival concepts and principles to this new genre of records. Drawing upon both their archival training and their experiences with electronic records, these writers determined that

---

1 Ole Kolsrud, "The Evolution of Basic Appraisal Principles," *American Archivist* 55 (Winter 1992): 35-36; Donald R. McCoy, *The National Archives: America's Ministry of Documents, 1934-1968* (Chapel Hill: University of North Carolina Press, 1978), 179-82; Jane Smith, "Theodore R. Schellenberg: Americanizer and Popularizer," *American Archivist* 44 (Fall 1991): 316, 322-25. Schellenberg's major works are *Modern Archives: Principles and Techniques* (Chicago: University of Chicago Press, 1956); *The Management of Archives* (New York: Columbia University Press, 1965); and *The Appraisal of Modern Public Records*, National Archives Bulletin 8 (Washington, D.C.: National Archives, 1956). When I use Schellenberg in this article, I also include the other U.S. National Archives pioneers with whom he developed his concepts. See, for example, Philip C. Brooks, "The Selection of Records for Preservation," *American Archivist* 3 (October 1940): 221-34, and G. Philip Bauer, *The Appraisal of Current and Recent Records*, Staff Information Circular #13 (Washington, D.C.: National Archives, 1946), 1-25. The National Archives in this article refers to the National Archives of the United States. The National Archives was established in 1934. In 1949 it became the National Archives and Records Service, part of the General Services Administration. In 1985 it became an independent agency again, the National Archives and Records Administration.

traditional approaches were valid and useful with the new media, although some new procedures would be necessary.

The first practitioners of electronic records sought both to reach a broad consensus on this approach and to disseminate their shared views through a conference, "Archival Management of Machine-Readable Records," sponsored by the National Endowment for the Humanities in Ann Arbor, Michigan, in 1979. One summary presentation concluded that "it seems that traditional archival theory can be applied satisfactorily to organizing this material and making it useful. But it is equally clear that, because of the new machine-readable media . . . traditional practices will have to change to accommodate them." Thus, conference participants affirmed that Schellenberg's informational and evidential values remained relevant for appraisal and that traditional archival principles also should guide archivists' thinking about arrangement, description, storage, and access. Participants discussed new problems with electronic records, however, particularly those involving technological obsolescence and preservation. Conference participants also anticipated developments in office automation applications, such as word processing and electronic mail, that would later perplex or overwhelm archivists. It was these later developments that gave rise to arguments for overturning traditional archival theory and practice when dealing with electronic records.[2]

The Michigan conference was followed by a publication of the International Council on Archives, which signified that the broader archival community shared the North American electronic records custodians' confidence that archivists could apply traditional archival concepts to the new record forms. Written by Harold Naugler, the definitive 1984 Records and Archives Management Programme (RAMP) study on the appraisal of machine-readable records reinforced the electronic records practitioners use of traditional archival concepts with the new record forms. Writing from experience, Naugler called for content analysis of electronic records utilizing traditional appraisal considerations such as identifying evidential and information values. Naugler also wrote about significant new considerations in appraisal that the records and their media imposed, such as performing a technical analysis.[3]

---

2 Robert M. Warner and Francis X. Blouin, Jr., "Some Implications of Records in Machine-Readable Form for Traditional Archival Practice," in *Archivists and Machine-Readable Records: Proceedings of the Conference on Archival Management of Machine-Readable Records, February 7-10, 1979, Ann Arbor, Michigan,* ed. Carolyn L. Geda, Erik W. Austin, and Francis X. Blouin, Jr. (Chicago: Society of American Archivists, 1980), 245, 243-44. See also in the same publication Thomas E. Mills, "Archival Considerations in the Management of Machine-Readable Records in New York State Government," 104; Carolyn L. Geda, Erik W. Austin, and Francis X. Blouin, Jr., "Introduction," 9; William F. Rofes, "The Archival Snare: Mass and Manipulation," 112, 114-15; and Jerome M. Clubb, "Archival Implications of Technological and Social Change," 233-34.

3 Harold Naugler, *The Archival Appraisal of Machine-Readable Records: A RAMP Study with Guidelines* (Paris: United Nations Educational, Scientific and Cultural Organization, General Information Programme and UNISIST, 1984): 37-41, 57-82.

The new media practitioners also sought to educate archivists in managing electronic records. Beginning in the 1960s, various committees and task forces of the Society of American Archivists stressed the importance of educating archivists about computerized records. These groups used the annual meeting programs, publications, and particularly workshops to work toward this goal, so that more archivists would develop electronic records programs.[4] The emphasis on educating archivists showed a basic assumption: that archivists would and should manage electronic records in an archival setting, that is, valuable records would be transferred to an archives that would hold custody of them, preserve them, and make them available for use.

Terry Cook later labeled this first group of archivists who confronted electronic records issues "the first generation." He based his label on his assumptions about the records they managed (statistical databases), the techniques they employed (library cataloging), and their emphasis on informational rather than evidential value. His analysis is questionable, at least when examining the largest electronic records collection. Tom Brown's analysis of the holdings of the National Archives and Records Administration (NARA) showed that the "first generation" of archivists at NARA accessioned not only statistical databases but also other types of electronic records such as programmatic and text records. They appraised records for both evidential and informational values. Finally, they described electronic records according to NARA's archival description standards, not library standards. Brown concluded that Cook confused the technology that produced the records (mainframe computers) with the types of records the technology produced. He also demonstrated that the first generation at NARA did use archival models for functions such as description.[5]

A decade after the 1979 conference, there were still few functioning archival programs for electronic records.[6] During the 1980s, though, computer technology had become more complex. In particular, the use of electronic office applications, such as word processing and electronic mail, continued to grow, as did the resulting volume of electronic records and attendant preservation problems. Archivists struggled to understand the new technology and feared losing electronic records. While they knew they needed to address the new media, they remained reluctant to

---

4   Geda et al., "Introduction," 9; and Geda et al., "Introduction to Chapter 4," *Archivists and Machine-Readable Records,* 147; Thomas Elton Brown, "The Society of American Archivists Confronts the Computer," *American Archivist* 47 (Fall 1984): 366-82.

5   Terry Cook, "Easy to Byte, Harder to Chew: The Second Generation of Electronic Records Archives," *Archivaria* 33 (Winter 1991-92): 202-16; Thomas Elton Brown, "Myth or Reality: Is There a Generation Gap Among Electronic Records Archivists?" *Archivaria* 41 (Spring 1996): 234-38.

6   *Report of the Working Meeting: Research Issues in Electronic Records,* published for the National Historical Publications and Records Commission, Washington, D.C. (St. Paul, Minn.: Minnesota Historical Society, 1991), 20-21, discusses some of the reasons why so few programs existed.

do so. Archivists thus likely became vulnerable to arguments that electronic records were an altogether new phenomenon and that they should change or discard the traditional archival principles they used with paper records when they confronted electronic records. Since so many archivists lacked experience with electronic records, they probably also lacked a basis upon which to judge the validity and plausibility of arguments for new archival theories. In addition, Cook's article on the "first generation" might have given archivists the notion that the first practitioners and earlier writings couldn't help them.

Addressing the problems of volume and complexity of electronic records, some writers began formulating new ideas for dealing with such records. Influenced by the ideas of David Bearman, these writers called for a "new paradigm" to deal with electronic records.[7] They argued that archivists should change their focus, from the content of a record to its context; from the record itself to the function of the record; from an archival role in custodial preservation and access to a nonarchival role of intervening in the records creation process and managing the behavior of creators. In general, supporters of a new paradigm seldom referenced past archival literature or practice. They also focused more on appraisal than on other archival functions, largely because, in their new paradigm, archivists would not accept physical custody of electronic records and, therefore,

---

7 Ann Pederson, "Empowering Archival Effectiveness: *Archival Strategies* As Innovation," *American Archivist* 58 (Fall 1995) discusses Bearman's influence and his establishment of Archives & Museum Informatics (AMI) in 1986. During its first three years, "75-80 percent of the content of AMI publications [were] attributable to Bearman," Ann Pederson, "Do Real Archivists Need Archives & Museum Informatics?" *American Archivist* 53 (Fall 1990): 667-68. The percentage appears to be the same for later years. With volume 11, no. 1 (1997), Kluwer Academic Publishers became the publisher of the journal and announced that it would be peer reviewed. For the term "new paradigm," see Terry Cook, "Electronic Records, Paper Minds: The Revolution in Information Management and Archives in the Post-Custodial and Post-Modern World," *Archives and Manuscripts* 22 (November 1994): 305-15.

In this article I mainly discuss David Bearman's writings and some of the writings of Richard Cox, Margaret Hedstrom, Terry Cook, and Charles Dollar as being representative of the writers who call for a new paradigm for electronic records, although there are other such writers, particularly in Australia. Cook's writings present a problem. In the same 1997 SAA annual meeting session in which I gave the paper now revised and expanded as this article, a paper by Terry Cook presented some of the same criticisms of Bearman as mine, "Who Will Do It if We Don't: The Cultural Mission of Archives vis-a-vis Electronic Records." Cook's criticisms reflected the second part of an article he published just before the SAA meeting, "The Impact of David Bearman on Modern Archival Thinking: An Essay of Personal Reflection and Critique," *Archives and Museum Informatics* 11, no. 1 (1997): 15-37. This was an "invited" tribute to Bearman in a journal for which Bearman is editor-in-chief and which, at the time, was not peer reviewed. In this article, Cook crowned Bearman "the leading archival thinker of the late twentieth century," who alone stands with "giants" such as Sir Hilary Jenkinson and Schellenberg. Cook followed this fulsome praise with a discussion of some "incomplete or troubling" aspects of Bearman's vision. Cook then discussed seven "points" that criticized Bearman's ideas, leaving the reader puzzled about the preceding tribute. In the SAA paper, Cook said he was criticizing Bearman and acknowledged his own role in previously promoting Bearman's ideas. I cite some of Cook's promotional writings that support a new paradigm for electronic records; but since some of Cook's later criticisms of Bearman are similar to mine, I cite them as well.

would not need to preserve, describe, or provide access to them in an archival institution. Since archivists would not perform these traditional archival functions, the new paradigm writers did not identify educating archivists about managing electronic records as a major problem, in contrast to earlier writers. The lack of reference to traditional theory and practice also may have resulted from the writers' emphasis on what archivists regard as records management or record keeping, not archival work.[8]

The differences between traditional archival writers and those who support a new paradigm for electronic records emerge most clearly in certain aspects of the new paradigm: the definition of a record, appraisal, the records continuum, noncustody, and a new role for the archivist. Contrasts also appear in the two groups of writers' use of archival history and practice and their mode of expression, or style.

Definition of a Record

Supporters of a new paradigm for electronic records propose some ideas that have little precedent in the archival literature. For example, archivists should redefine a record as one with "evidentiality" or "recordness." Electronic records are only those with "evidence" of "business transactions." The writers argue that archivists "must focus on *evidence* not *information*." New paradigm supporters also denigrate the bulk of extant archival electronic records collections by proclaiming that "saving databases does not preserve evidence, only information." Most collections of electronic data "are not records because they cannot qualify as evidence."[9]

At least one writer goes to some lengths to make the new definition fit. Richard Cox quotes Schellenberg's definition of a record: "All books, papers, maps, photographs, or other documentary materials, regardless of physical form or characteristics, made or received by any public or private institution in pursuance of its legal obligations or in connection

---

8 The emphasis on recordkeeping is reflected in several research projects. The "Functional Requirements for Recordkeeping" project of the University of Pittsburgh School of Information Studies, led by David Bearman and Richard Cox, and projects at the University of Indiana and the City of Philadelphia to test the Pittsburgh model all fall more within what archivists regard as records management rather than archival work. Discussion of these projects is, therefore, outside the scope of this article. Since all three were funded by the National Historical Publications and Records Commission, links to information about them are included on the NHPRC's Web site, <www.nara.gov/nara/nhprc/ergrants.html>. Another project focusing upon recordkeeping but with a more archival framework, also excluded from this article, is at the University of British Columbia School of Library, Archives and Information Science, <www.slais.ubc.ca/users/duranti/>. Paul Marsden, "Counterpoint: When is the Future? Comparative Notes on the Electronic Record-Keeping Project of the University of Pittsburgh and the University of British Columbia," *Archivaria* 43 (Spring 1997): 158-73, compares the Pittsburgh and UBC projects and provides citations to numerous articles about these projects.

9 Richard Cox, "The Record: Is It Evolving?" *Records and Retrieval Report* 10 (March 1994): 12, (emphasis in original); David Bearman, *Electronic Evidence: Strategies for Managing Records in Contemporary Organizations* (Pittsburgh: Archives & Museum Informatics, 1994), 2, 285.

with the transaction of its proper business and preserved or appropriate for preservation by that institution or its legitimate successor as evidence of its functions, policies, decisions, procedures, operations, or other activities or because of the informational value of the data contained therein." Cox then concludes: "by the mid-twentieth century, there was firm sense of a record as a transaction and as evidence of transactions." This conclusion simply does not follow from Schellenberg's definition. When Schellenberg used the term "transaction of its proper business," he meant the whole activity of an organization and its conduct of business. His term is not the same as "business transaction," which is a much narrower construct.[10] Significantly, Cox ignores Schellenberg's phrase, "the informational value of the data contained therein," possibly because acknowledging such a value would refute his conclusion.

Both evidential and informational values are important for appraisal, and Schellenberg wrote that they were not mutually exclusive values. The problem with the new definition of a record — which appears to apply only to electronic records — is that the definition eliminates the concept of informational value. It also excludes records that do not document business transactions. Evidential and informational values form two ends of a pendulum's path. It might appear that the new definition of a record is merely a swing of the pendulum, that archivists are emphasizing one value over another. The new definition of a record is more than that, however, because it removes one-half of the pendulum's path.

The new definition of a record is too narrow. Using it, archivists would fill their archives with records that document only the "footprints of bureaucrats." Many, if not most, archives serve a higher purpose. Even national, state, and local government archives are also the "archives of governance," addressing the much broader role and responsibility of government within society. Even some government bureaucrats know that their organizational records provide documentary evidence of larger societal concerns. The value of archives is cultural and humanistic, not just bureaucratic. Archival programs that collect records or personal papers, which may contain electronic media, find the new definition bewildering. Personal papers may never show "evidence" of "business transactions," but such archival sources provide a wealth of information needed for society's memory. The new paradigm excludes personal papers and other similar documentary materials in the definition of archival records.[11]

---

10 Cox, "The Record," 10-11; Schellenberg, *Modern Archives*, 139.

11 Michael Fox coined the unpublished phrase "footprints of bureaucrats"; Ian E. Wilson, "Reflections on *Archival Strategies*," *American Archivist* 58 (Fall 1995): 422, 424, 426-27; Roy C. Turnbaugh, "Records and Evidence: From Theory to Reality," paper delivered at the annual meeting of the National Association of Government Archives and Records Administrators, Sacramento, California, 19 July 1997, 2-3, 6. After supporting a new definition of a record, Cook later wrote that this definition was too narrow. He then made the point about personal papers and private-sector archives in "The Impact of David Bearman," 29-30.

Defining a record exclusively as a business transaction eliminates documentary materials that may have permanent value, such as databases and personal papers. The definition could cause archivists to spend their time on the bulk of records of most agencies and large organizations: operating records, often known as "housekeeping" records. Such records provide definite evidence of business transactions, but archivists usually appraise them as nonpermanent. Schellenberg wrote that these types of records of individual transactions were seldom essential as evidence. The emphasis on *defining* a record thus obscures what archivists are trying to do: evaluate whether documentary materials have permanent value. So, in addition to being unnecessary, a new definition of a record seems to be an obstacle to archival work. Instead of asking whether documentary materials are records, archivists should ask if those materials are important. The concern should focus on the best evidence of the activities archivists are trying to document, not on the "evidence that best reflects an abstract conception of records."[12]

For more than 60 years, the National Archives, many state archives, and other archival organizations have used a definition of a record that is similar to Schellenberg's. The National Archives has been able to apply such a definition to records in all media — paper, maps, photographs, and electronic records — with no discernible problems. Even in the National Archives most celebrated lawsuit, *Armstrong v. the Executive Office of the President,* the courts did not find any deficiencies in the definition of a record in the Federal Records Act. Furthermore, redefining the legal definition of a record to better reflect electronic records "would make the definition itself subject to obsolescence."[13]

The new definition of a record raises troubling questions for archivists about why the traditional definition is inadequate. Supporters of a new definition of a record usually do not discuss or analyze what's wrong but, rather, declare what should be or is. It is also unclear why the new definition of a record applies only to electronic records and apparently not to records in other media, or what a collecting archives would do with such a definition.

Appraisal

Supporters of the new paradigm for electronic records call for bold, new ideas, but some are not so bold or new. Urging archivists to consider

---

12 Schellenberg, *Modern Archives,* 146; Kenneth Thibodeau, "Evidential Values and Archival Functions: Fundamental Challenges," paper delivered at the annual meeting of the Association of Canadian Archivists, Ottawa, 6 May 1997, 6. Thibodeau also shows that "databases provide substantial, unique and critical evidence of the conduct of affairs," 5-7.

13 Kenneth Thibodeau, "Managing Archival Records in the Electronic Age," in *Federal Information Policies in the 1990s: Views and Perspectives,* ed. Peter Hernon, Charles R. McClure, and Harold C. Relyea (Norwood, N.J.: Ablex Publishing Corporation, 1996), 284-85.

function in appraisal[14], as a historical review of archival writing shows, is not a new idea. More than 40 years ago, Schellenberg wrote that one of the three facts an appraiser should know was "the character of the functions performed by each office" and whether the functions were "facilitative" or "substantive." In his 1977 appraisal manual, Maynard Brichford discussed function, as did F. Gerald Ham in his 1993 appraisal manual, in the section on functional analysis.[15]

Some supporters of the new paradigm argue that the function of records is the only important appraisal criterion. They believe that archivists should not consider the contents of records and need not even look at records during appraisal. "We can decide in the abstract whether a function generates records that need to be retained," and archivists should "focus their appraisal upon the function or competence that produces records rather than the records themselves."[16] An appraisal archivist easily could find this approach troublesome or unworkable. For example, one important function of the U.S. Patent and Trademark Office (PTO) is granting patents. NARA appraised the important electronic patent records a few years ago. In 1996 the PTO submitted schedules for 54 additional electronic systems. The appraisal archivist could have considered only function, judged it to be an important one, not have looked at the records, and appraised all 54 databases as permanent. Instead, the archivist considered the content of all the databases and appraised only one as permanent.[17]

Supporters of new approaches to electronic records stress a need for new practices, but they fail to provide a convincing analysis of why traditional practices will not work. They also offer almost no examples of past or present practices. Those they do provide appear uninformed. For example, David Bearman and Margaret Hedstrom argue that "reviewing 100% of records created in order to select the less than 3% which should

---

14 David H. Thomas, "Business Functions: Toward a Methodology," 3, <http://www.lis.pitt.edu/~nhprc/Pub7.html> (accessed 26 July 1997).

15 Schellenberg, *Modern Archives*, 143; Maynard J. Brichford, *Archives and Manuscripts: Appraisal and Accessioning* (Chicago: Society of American Archivists, 1977), 4-5; F. Gerald Ham, *Selecting and Appraising Archives and Manuscripts* (Chicago: Society of American Archivists, 1993), 51-53.

16 Bearman, *Electronic Evidence*, 36; David Bearman, "Archival Strategies," *American Archivist* 58 (Fall 1995): 383; Charles M. Dollar, *Archival Theory and Information Technologies: The Impact of Information Technologies on Archival Principles and Methods* (Macerata, Italy: University of Macerata, 1992), 58, 76; Terry Cook, "Archives in the Post-Custodial World: Interaction of Archival Theory and Practice Since the Publication of the Dutch Manual in 1898," paper delivered at the XIII International Congress on Archives, Beijing, 1996), 13, 22-23. Cook later wrote that archivists do need to look at records in "The Impact of David Bearman," 33-34.

17 Michael L. Miller, "Is the Past Prologue? Appraisal and the New Technologies," in *Archival Management of Electronic Records*, Archives & Museum Informatics Technical Report No. 13, part II (Pittsburgh: Archives & Museum Informatics, 1991), 39-40, discusses the appraisal of PTO patent systems. I was the appraisal archivist for the 54 databases.

be saved . . . is inefficient."[18] In fact, few large archives in the United States review 100 percent of records. National Archives has not reviewed 100 percent of records for several decades, because it has mandatory general records schedules, or GRS. Congress gave the Archives legal authority to prepare GRS more than 50 years ago. NARA estimates that the GRS cover one-third of the total volume of federal records. In addition, many states and universities also have general records schedules.[19] The archivist in the PTO example above, by the way, did not write an appraisal for all 54 PTO databases. Most of them were already classified as temporary under the GRS.

New paradigm writers urge archivists to quit appraising and scheduling records when they are inactive, when they arrive at the archives, and even after they have been accessioned.[20] However, many, if not most, archivists in U.S. federal and state governments and universities and large organizations already appraise current, that is active, records. As practicing archivists understand, appraising current records is the whole point of records schedules. NARA has appraised active records in electronic form as well as paper for many years. In fact, the U.S. Code of Federal Regulations requires agencies to schedule new or changed records series within one year of their creation. Some states, such as Wisconsin, have similar regulations. In 1940 Philip C. Brooks wrote that appraisal is best performed as records are created. In 1956 Schellenberg called for appraisal of active records.[21] New paradigm writers thus tend to ignore both history and the practices of electronic records archives today.

The Records Continuum

Supporters of new approaches to electronic records go further than appraising active records. They urge archivists to intervene before the creation of electronic records and appraise records in the "concept stage," when creators are conceiving electronic records systems. Archivists "should appraise business functions, deciding before any records are created at all, what documentation it is desirable to create and retain for a

---

18 David Bearman and Margaret Hedstrom, "Reinventing Archives for Electronic Records: Alternative Service Delivery Options," in *Electronic Records Management Program Strategies,* Archives and Museum Informatics Technical Report No. 18, ed. Margaret Hedstrom (Pittsburgh: Archives & Museum Informatics, 1993), 86.

19 McCoy, *The National Archives,* 157; "Introduction to the General Records Schedules," *General Records Schedules,* Transmittal No. 7 (Washington, D.C.: National Archives and Records Administration, 1995), 1; Ham, *Selecting and Appraising Archives and Manuscripts, 29.*

20 Cox, "The Record," 12; Bearman and Hedstrom, "Reinventing Archives," 86; Bearman, *Electronic Evidence,* 29.

21 Code of Federal Regulations, Title 36, Part 1228, section 26 (a) (2); Ham, *Selecting and Appraising Archives and Manuscripts* 29; Brooks, "The Selection of Records for Preservation," 226; Schellenberg, *Modern Archives,* 26, 109.

given function." A closely related idea follows: there should be no distinction between archival and records management work. A "records continuum" should replace the concept of the life cycle of records.[22] The traditional life cycle delineates clear responsibilities to creators and records
managers for the primary value of records and to archivists for secondary
value, to use Schellenberg's definitions. In a records continuum, however,
archivists hold responsibility beginning before creation, through maintenance, preservation, and use. A records continuum would "mend the
Schellenbergian split between records managers and archivists."[23]

First of all, Schellenberg did not think archivists should become creators
of records. Nor do all those who write about electronic records today.
Contemporary writers who do not call for new archival theory and practice
for electronic records believe that archivists can give advice about creating
and managing reliable records. But if archivists usurp the role of creator by
defining what records should be created, archivists make records "less
genuine, less authentic," and thus sacrifice their highest virtue: neutrality.
Secondly, records managers seem to have disappeared in the new paradigm,
or archivists have replaced them. The supporters of the new paradigm
apparently think archivists should become a "new breed of revitalized
records manager," concentrating only on the records management portion
of Schellenberg's split and "merging the broader archival agenda with the
narrower records management or institutional agenda." Largely because of
Schellenberg, archivists recognize the importance of records management.
He worked as both an archivist and records manager and understood the
duties, roles, and principles of each profession. Archivists regard records
management as an important process of managing volume and identifying
and obtaining archival records. But for them, records management is not
the work they ought to do instead of archival work. If archivists follow the
advice of new paradigm writers, archivists' "primary mission, facilitating
more efficient functioning of our parent organizations" would become their
"only mission."[24] The protector of the archival side of Schellenberg's split
also seems to have disappeared.

Custody

Supporters of a new paradigm for electronic records promote the
notion of "post-custodialism," which defines a centralized archives as "an

---

22 Bearman, "Archival Strategies," 399. David Bearman, "Managing the Records Continuum,"
   Archives and Museum Informatics 10, no. 2 (1996): 133-36.

23 Cook, "Archives in the Post-Custodial World," n. 73.

24 Thibodeau, "Evidential Values and Archival Functions," 12; Luciana Duranti and Heather McNeil,
   "The Protection of the Integrity of Electronic Records: An Overview of the UBC-MAS Research
   Project," *Archivaria* 42 (Fall 1996): 60-62; Cook, "The Impact of David Bearman," 34-35. In this
   article, Cook apparently rethought the desirability of mending the split and wrote that archivists
   shouldn't become records managers. Turnbaugh, "Records and Evidence," 4.

archives of last resort." New paradigm supporters urge archivists to "cease being identified as custodians of records" because, among other things, this role "is not professional." An archives with custody is "an indefensible bastion and a liability." These writers maintain that creators of records or other institutions, whether they are archives or not, can take care of archival records.[25]

Schellenberg did not advocate noncustody, nor did traditional European or English archival writers. Schellenberg and the other National Archives pioneers knew all about noncustody, although their term surely would be "precustody." The U.S. government, by default, practiced noncustody for more than 150 years before the National Archives was established in 1934. The pioneers knew all about noncustody: records lost and damaged, others in vast disarray and a new National Archives to deal with the aftermath. They could not possibly wish that situation on later generations for records in any format.

Nor do several contemporary writers who argue for a rigorous custodial role for electronic records. These writers maintain that records creators face possible conflicts of interest. Shifting custodial responsibilities to creators "would leave the Oliver Norths of this world in charge of their records." Maintaining historical archival records in active systems could easily lead to their destruction, to gain disk space for example, or to changes that would alter their character. An archives also is committed to preserving records as created and as received. Furthermore, creators have little incentive to retain records — in any form — beyond their primary usefulness. Why would an organization allocate resources to a function that is not its primary mission? "Archives without custody would not be archives at all; they would simply disappear into the maw of a bureaucratic leviathan and with them the guarantees they offer the world of an uncorrupted and intelligible record of the past." The noncustody argument may have a deleterious effect as well, if archivists were to decide that "we'll be a post-custodial archives and require the records creators to maintain their own records. Then we won't have to worry about electronic records." While some archivists in Australia have embraced the noncustody argument, "it is striking that despite the fact that some of the most persuasive writings on the subject have urged traditional archives to take a non-custodial approach to the preservation of electronic records, no national archives in Europe, whether it has already begun an electronic

---

25 Dollar, *Archival Theory and Information Technology*, 54, 75; David Bearman, "An Indefensible Bastion: Archives as Repositories in the Electronic Age," in *Archival Management of Electronic Records*, Archives and Museum Informatics Technical Report No. 13, part I, (Pittsburgh: Archives & Museum Informatics, 1991), 14-24; Bearman and Hedstrom, "Reinventing Archives," 94; Cook, "Archives in the Post-Custodial World," 22-23.

records programme or is about to do so, has opted to take a non-custodial approach."[26]

The "New" Archivist

The new paradigm delineates a new role for archivists and, it seems, a new definition of an archivist as well. Traditionally defined, archivists appraise, arrange, describe, preserve, and provide reference and outreach for archival records. Supporters of new approaches to electronic records argue that archivists have failed in their traditional role. If archivists follow the new paradigm, a new definition of a record presumably means a smaller body of records with which to deal. Appraisal by function also reduces the workload. Within the ideal records continuum, creators will produce the records archivists want. Archivists wouldn't be burdened with physical custody or requests for records. The new paradigm sees archivists as regulators, auditors, and "internal consultants, defining record keeping regimes and tactics." Archivists can then "manage organizational behavior." Archivists will become, at best, only consultants and educators.[27]

If archivists follow the suggestions of David Bearman and Margaret Hedstrom, however, they could just as likely face a future with no role at all. Bearman and Hedstrom call for archivists to get others to adopt archival goals and thereby "co-opt their resources." They profess that archivists should get others, such as "representatives of the public," to select records, or use technology to automatically select records based on metadata. Interestingly, Bearman and Hedstrom don't suggest that

---

26 Thibodeau, "Managing Electronic Records," 282; Kenneth Thibodeau, "To Be or Not To Be: Archives for Electronic Records," in *Archival Management of Electronic Records*, Archives and Museum Informatics Technical Report No. 13, part I (Pittsburgh: Archives & Museum Informatics, 1991), 3, 11-12; Luciana Duranti, "Archives as a Place," *Archives and Manuscripts* 24 (November 1996): 250-53. Theodore J. Hull, "Reference Services for Electronic Records in Archives," in *Reference Services for Archives and Manuscripts*, ed. Laura B. Cohen (Binghamton, N.Y.: Haworth Press, 1997), 152-57, gives examples of agencies having little or no interest in maintaining records no longer needed for current business. Cook later made the same point about creators' unwillingness to retain archival records in "The Impact of David Bearman," 32-33. Terry Eastwood, "Should Creating Agencies Keep Electronic Records Indefinitely?" *Archives and Manuscripts* 24 (November 1996): 265. In this article, Eastwood dissects Bearman's arguments against custody and writes that "Bearman is wrong on *every* score," 259 (emphasis in original). Mark Conrad, "To Have and to Hold?: Archival Responsibility in the Electronic Age," *Irish Archives* 37 (Spring 1996): 37; Ken Hannigan, "A Summary on Electronic Records Management in the EU Member States: Relations Between Public Administrations and Archives Services," in *INSAR Supplement II: The Proceedings of the DLM-Forum on Electronic Records, Brussels, 18-20 December 1996* (Luxembourg: Office for Official Publications of the European Communities, 1997), 230.

27 Lewis J. and Lynn Lady Bellardo, comp., *A Glossary for Archivists, Manuscript Curators and Records Managers* (Chicago: Society of American Archivists, 1992), 3-4; Bearman and Hedstrom, "Reinventing Archives," 97-98; Pederson, "Empowering Archival Effectiveness," 442. Wilson, "Reflections on *Archival Strategies*," 427, points out that "the trend in government is strongly away from further control and regulation."

creators select records, a concept Sir Hilary Jenkinson once espoused that had, at least, precedent in the archival literature. If creators shouldn't select records, however, creators or perhaps users can describe them. Or technology can describe records, as in "self-documenting records." As for reference and access, "couldn't libraries provide access since they're in that business?" As for preservation, archivists should "have someone else keep records instead of archives." If all this doesn't work, they propose that archivists: 1) lend records to those who might use them, 2) give records to others, or 3) sell records "to those who want them most." Ann Pederson writes that if archivists *don't* follow Bearman's advice, they will become professionally obsolete.[28] It seems that if archivists *do* follow his advice, they will become obsolete. Obviously, Schellenberg did not suggest that the solution to archival problems was to eliminate archives and archivists.

Archival History and Practice

Reading Schellenberg and then reading the writings of supporters of the new paradigm for electronic records provides contrasts in the use, or lack thereof, of archival history and practice. Schellenberg found much previous archival writing limited in usefulness because of the problems he faced in dealing with the results of 150 years of non-custody and the continual creation of a mass of federal records. Nevertheless, he used parts of previous archival writings, applying them when he could. Ole Kolsrud writes that Schellenberg "elegantly represents a synthesis of American, English and German appraisal theory." Schellenberg thus developed his concepts in the context of both archival history and his own and others' experiences.[29] In contrast, supporters of the new paradigm for electronic records seldom ground their pronouncements in, or demonstrate an understanding of, Schellenberg or any historical archival theoretician. In the few instances when they do, the history seems distorted. For example, one writer incorporates Schellenberg's informational value when it supports documentation strategies but does not accept that value in writing about electronic records. Another writer broadly discusses 100 years of archival writings, but refers only to the writings of supporters of the new paradigm for electronic records, ignoring the first writers on electronic records. His conclusion from "studying the intellectual history

---

28 Bearman and Hedstrom, "Reinventing Archives," 88-95; Bearman, "Archival Strategies," 389, 394, 397, 400-406; Pederson, "Empowering Archival Effectiveness," 433.

29 Smith, "Schellenberg," 324; McCoy, *The National Archives*, 77-78; Kolsrud, "The Evolution of Basic Appraisal Principles," 36; Schellenberg, *Modern Archives*, 67-77, 133-39, 169-79, 195-203; T. R. Schellenberg, *The Management of Archives* (New York: Columbia University Press, 1965), 20-60.

of our profession," postcustodialism, seems to come only from the writings of new paradigm supporters, and not from writings of the preceding 90 years.[30]

Supporters of a new paradigm for electronic records usually don't cite historical sources; most of them cite themselves and each other. For example, in one Bearman article, 62 percent of the citations referred to his own writings. Another writer cited his own and other writings supporting a new paradigm 41 times in 36 footnotes. The practice of citing each other refers readers only to other new paradigm writers, who then proclaim a growing consensus for their ideas.[31]

In addition to using historical archival sources, Schellenberg and other National Archives pioneers were practitioners; they had experience. Their writings emerged from that experience and the real problems they faced. In addition, Schellenberg incorporated the archival experiences of other practitioners. In contrast, Bearman "is not an archivist, has never worked as an archivist, has never trained as an archivist — and moreover is proud of being such a professional 'outsider.'"[32] He is thus unable to incorporate an experience-based perspective. Surprisingly, advocates of the new paradigm who do have archival experience do not use it to support their new paradigm. These writers also do not use the experiences of archives that hold electronic records. Instead, they make generalizations based on little information, and this leads to some unfounded statements. For example, "the implications for archival institutions of assuming physical custody of electronic records have yet to be worked out." Preserving electronic records has "proved beyond the capabilities of every . . . archives in the world." Advocates of a new theory for electronic records argue that appraisal of electronic records has not assured their preservation or access. And one writer generalizes from the experience of *one* archives that, "projects that attempted to extract archival records from existing or inactive information systems confirmed that this approach is . . . usually futile."[33] While few archives have worked with electronic

---

30 Richard Cox, "The Documentation Strategy and Archival Principles: A Different Perspective," *Archivaria* 38 (Fall 1994): 11-36, and "The Record," 1-33. It seems to me that a documentation strategy depends on evaluating records for their informational value, because records of "business transactions" may document nothing larger than a bureaucracy or an organization. Perhaps this explains Cox's inconsistency. Cook, "Archives in the Post-Custodial World," 1-33.

31 David Bearman, "Documenting Documentation," *Archivaria* 34 (Summer 1992): 33-49; Cook, "Electronic Records, Paper Minds," 300-326; Margaret Hedstrom, "Teaching Archivists About Electronic Records and Automated Techniques: A Needs Assessment," *American Archivist* 56 (Summer 1993): 425 and n. 8.

32 Schellenberg, *Modern Archives*, 67-77, 133-39, 169-79, 195-203; Schellenberg, *Management of Archives*, 20-60; Cook, "The Impact of David Bearman," 15-16.

records, the National Archives has almost 30 years of experience in the administration of such records. Supporters of new approaches to electronic records have not tried to learn what NARA does or what it has learned about electronic records from its custodial experience. Instead, Bearman promulgated misinformation about NARA in order to conclude that its electronic records program was "dangerous, deluded and destructive."[34] Formulating theories lacking a basis in practice and not drawing upon their own experience, supporters of a new paradigm appear to read computer literature and decide that the latest technology is what archivists face, which isn't necessarily so. They then conclude that traditional archival theory and practice cannot accommodate the new technologies.

The approaches of supporters of a new paradigm thus raise questions about practitioners versus theorists. One opponent of archival education worried that the development of archival education would lead to a division between theorists and practitioners. He feared that theorists would come up with new models "whether they are needed or not" and impose those models upon practicing archivists "whether they are workable or not." Archivists apparently resist imposition, however, since one supporter of the new paradigm concedes that only a few archives have tested or used the new models.[35] Perhaps archivists do not find the proposed models workable. While not all archival education programs

---

33 Cook, quoted in Alf Erlandsson, *Electronic Records Management: A Literature Review* (Paris: International Council on Archives, December 1996), n. 259; Adrian Cunningham, "Journey to the End of the Night: Custody and the Dawning of a New Era on the Archival Threshold," *Archives and Manuscripts* 24 (November 1996): 317; Alan Kowlowitz, "Appraising in a Vacuum: Electronic Records Appraisal Issues — A View from the Trenches," in *Archival Management of Electronic Records*, Archives & Museum Informatics Technical Report No. 13, part II (Pittsburgh: Archives & Museum Informatics, 1991), 32, 35; Margaret Hedstrom, "Electronic Records Research: What Have Archivists Learned From the Mistakes of the Past?" *Archives and Museum Informatics* 10, no. 4 (1996): 319 (emphasis added).

34 Thomas E. Brown, "Myth or Reality," counters writings of Cook and Cox about the electronic records experiences of the National Archives. For a list of writings and presentations of National Archives staff about electronic records, see <www.nara.gov/nara/electronic/selpub.html>. David Bearman, "The Implications of *Armstrong v. Executive Office of the President* for the Archival Management of Electronic Records," *American Archivist* 56 (Fall 1993): 689. Bearman's article contains factual errors. For example, NARA has never claimed that changes in practice were unnecessary to cope with electronic records (689). In attributing this position to Acting Archivist Trudy Petersen, Bearman contradicts her published views, see n. 45. Also contrary to Bearman's undocumented assertions, NARA did have both experience and competence in processing electronic records (680) and has never based electronic records retention on "software utilities" (689). Because the *Armstrong* case was still under litigation at the time that Bearman's article was published, NARA could not respond. Neither the author nor the editor noted that Bearman was a consultant to the plaintiffs in the court case. Nor did they note that Bearman was a consultant to the Pittsburgh Project, whose functional requirements he endorsed in the article. Finally, they also failed to note that the principal investigator of the Pittsburgh Project, Richard Cox, was the editor of *American Archivist* at that time.

35 John Roberts, "Archival Theory: Myth or Banality?" *American Archivist* 53 (Winter 1990): 119; Hedstrom, "Electronic Records Research," 323.

are taught by and produce such theorists, the new archival theories do raise questions. What are students learning about electronic records in graduate programs? Are they reading only the writings of the supporters of the new paradigm, whose ideas are impressionistic, speculative, and, as yet, unproven? If so, how prepared are archival graduates to deal with electronic records in the real world? Schellenberg's admonition to the educator remains valid: "he should certainly learn before he ventures to teach."[36]

In working with electronic records, archivists need not and should not forget all the lessons they have learned with paper records. For example, one supporter of new approaches to electronic records worried, "is the record version my memorandum drafted for initial review, the second version sent to its intended audience, or the third version which has been modified by the recipient as he included the memorandum into a report?"[37] Why this is a problem with electronic records is unclear, since archivists have been appraising drafts of paper records for years. The writer appears to have forgotten provenance as well. As another example, NARA appraisal reports for electronic records first discuss the sufficiency of evidential and informational values, just as archivists do for paper records, and only discuss issues regarding the electronic format if they present a problem. Furthermore, NARA archivists describe electronic records using the same format that archivists use for records in other media, with only minor exceptions. The loss of records, however unfortunate, is not a phenomenon unique to electronic records. Being unable to accession electronic records due to technological problems is analogous to being unable to accession paper records due to irreparable damage.

Manner/Expression

Schellenberg realized that he did not have all the answers. Nevertheless, he tried to understand archivists' problems and to help and educate them. He wanted to "perk up the pride" of archivists and "bolster their faith in themselves and the significance of their profession."[38] In contrast to this esteem for archivists and archival work, supporters of the

---

36 Cook, "The Impact of David Bearman," 31, points out that Bearman is an idealist and conceptualizer who is impatient when "real-world" problems are said to block his approach. Schellenberg quoted in McCoy, *The National Archives*, 182. Inadvertently making my point about what students are learning, one of the external reviewers of this article wanted a discussion of Schellenberg's evidential and informational values because of a sense "that the present generation of archivists may not have read the 'classic' account on this in archival administration courses."

37 Cox, "The Record," 2.

38 McCoy, *The National Archives*, 77-78, 92-104, 168-89. The quotations are taken from page 181.

new paradigm seem to denigrate archival work and unduly alarm archivists about the problems. Some examples of this pessimism include statements that appraisal is "fatally flawed" and that if archivists resist new approaches, they "might soon be out of a job," facing "professional obsolescence." They claim that archivists suffer from "denial and self-delusion" and have a "victim mentality." They label archivists' efforts to manage electronic records "futile and professionally suicidal."[39] All this fatality imagery frightens and insults archivists. In contrast to Schellenberg, it does not educate them.

Supporters of new approaches to electronic records furthermore use confusing jargon and technobabble, both of which fail to enlighten archivists. Typical jargon includes "business acceptable communications," "enterprise or business systems analysis methodologies," and "semiotically constructed contexts of records creation." Archivists should become "documentary risk managers," "technology assessors," and "metadata auditors." Technobabble includes "metadata requirements" for "recordness," a "metadata encapsulated object," and "BLOB (binary large object)." Archivists undoubtedly need to be aware of business jargon. They must learn and be comfortable with technical terminology, particularly so that they can talk with technologists about electronic records. But archivists expect their colleagues to write in a language that archivists understand. They do not expect their colleagues to just appropriate jargon and technobabble without an attempt to educate. Since so many supporters of the new paradigm do just that, and offer alarmist imagery as well, the result is to exclude the majority of archivists from the dialogue about electronic records, rather than invite them to participate in it. Ann Pederson gives clues to the exclusionary nature of the group in an article about Bearman and his followers. She uses terms such as "close colleagues" and "circle of colleagues"; phrases such as "choosing collaborators carefully to include leading opinion shapers and disseminators"; and sentences such as "key ideas had circulated informally."[40] All of this implies a "we know best" aura. Nothing in the writings of the supporters of a new paradigm approaches Schellenberg's introductory statement to *Modern Archives:* "I do not believe that American methods of handling modern public records are necessarily any better than those of other countries; they are merely different."[41]

---

39 David Bearman, "Archival Methods," *Archives and Museum Informatics Technical Report* 9, no. 1 (Spring 1989): 10; Pederson, "Empowering Archival Effectiveness," 431-34, 439.

40 David Bearman, "Item Level Control and Electronic Recordkeeping," *Archives and Museum Informatics* 10, no. 3 (1996): 214-17; Bearman, *Electronic Evidence*, 283; Cook, "Electronic Records, Paper Minds," 318; Edith Cowen University, quoted in Erlandsson, *Electronic Records Management*, 26; David Bearman, "Virtual Archives," paper delivered at the ICA meeting, Beijing, 1996, 2, 4. <http://www.lis.pitt.edu/~nhprc/prog6.html> (accessed 2 August 1997). Pederson, "Empowering Archival Effectiveness," 433-34, 437.

41 Schellenberg, *Modern Archives*, x.

Conclusion

Supporters of new approaches to electronic records have made archivists think about what they do, and a reexamination of archival theory and practice is useful. But the price has been too high. Both the ideas of advocates of a new paradigm for electronic records and their manner of presentation have deterred archivists from learning about electronic records and from developing electronic records programs. The writing has little basis in archival theory and practice and contains alarmist language, unnecessary jargon, technobabble, and unclear new ideas. The writing thus seems to discourage new learning and to offer little useful advice. The understandable advice is noncustody, but it may convey a disturbing message: "somehow, magically, electronic records will be taken care of by the records creators. . . ." No wonder, then, that few archivists are developing electronic records programs.[42] While the supporters of a new paradigm did not cause this situation, they have done little to improve it.

Unfortunately, the supporters of new approaches to electronic records have served to divide the profession, because they exclude "that half [or more] of the archival tradition which focuses on the cultural, historical and heritage dimensions and uses of archives."[43] In particular, their narrow definition of a record and their arguments against archival custody of electronic records pertain, at best, only to organizational archives. These arguments do not hold any promise for noninstitutional archives and manuscript repositories. The new paradigm excludes them.

Electronic records undoubtedly present some new challenges. Archivists who have electronic records programs do not have answers for all of the problems. Solutions will come, as they have for other new types of records, from archivists' first examining what they know and the extent to which it is applicable, before dismantling archival theory and practice. Archivists should "start believing that traditional archival principles and theories . . . reconceptualized for an electronic world, may hold the key to prospering in the new environment we face."[44] Although this writer's reconceptualization was postcustodialism, tradition does offer help in dealing with new problems presented by electronic records.

Archivists should continue using established archival principles and practice in dealing with electronic records, as Trudy Peterson wrote a decade ago: "Managing machine-readable records does not . . . mean having to create the world of archival theory anew. The traditional

---

42 Conrad, "Archival Responsibility in the Electronic Age," 37; Margaret Hedstrom, *Electronic Records Research and Development: Final Report of the 1996 Conference held at the University of Michigan, Ann Arbor, June 28-29, 1996* (Ann Arbor: University of Michigan School of Information, 1997), 6; Hedstrom, "Electronic Records Research," 315.

43 Cook, "Impact of David Bearman," 36.

44 Cook, "Electronic Records, Paper Minds," 305.

archival principles — evidential and informational values, provenance, levels of arrangement and description — continue to undergird archival practice. That practice will grow and change, but the principles will endure."[45] Supporters of a new paradigm for electronic records need to demonstrate conclusively that this approach won't work and why, and their arguments need to draw on evidence based on archival history, traditional archival theory, and the experiences of practicing electronic records archivists.

More than 40 years ago, Schellenberg's concern was "how to meet current challenges on the basis of present practices and resources, not starting over again from scratch." In 1992 Ole Kolsrud reflected the same concern: "Whatever we do in the way of theorizing or reflecting upon the nature of our profession is an obligation of ours. . . . But to do so sensibly, we ought to be aware of how archivists elsewhere and before us have tried to come to grips with their task. There is a strange tendency, even among archivists, to start from scratch as happy amateurs every time the need to ponder what we are really doing is felt." [46]

---

45 Trudy Huskamp Peterson, "Machine-Readable Records as Archival Materials," XI International Congress of Archives (Paris: International Congress of Archives, 1988), 13. This article is similar, to an earlier one Peterson wrote, "Archival Principles and Records of the New Technology," *American Archivist* 47 (Fall 1984): 383-93. Supporters of the new paradigm do not cite or discuss Peterson or the other first writers about electronic records whom I noted earlier.

46 McCoy, *The National Archives*, 180; Kolsrud, "The Evolution of Basic Appraisal Principles," 37.

26

Digital Communications: Documentary Opportunities Not to Be Missed

ANNE GILLILAND-SWETLAND

Abstract: Drawing upon professional literature, electronic records, and digital library research initiatives at the University of Michigan, this paper examines the nature of and opportunities provided by digital· communications, primarily as evolving documentary media, but also as digital environments through which documentation may potentially be made more widely available and relevant. It cautions against utilizing a pure systems or risk management approach in identifying such materials for long-term retention and concludes with a discussion of the need to revisit the role of appraisal to establish and capitalize on the nature and use of digital communications.

In a recent article on the implications of the case of *Armstrong v. the Executive Office of the President*, David Bearman concluded that

> If archivists do not use this and other opportunities to articulate forcefully what we expect from records creators and systems designers and to extend our mission and authorities both legally and in practice, we will lose most of this record of the next decade and squander our role as protector of the public interest in documented and accountable government.[1]

While such proactive approaches are indubitably necessary to assist in the legal management of the digital communications record, they do not come close to covering the wider professional and cultural considerations of managing the "human record" in the evolving and expanding world of digital communication. Moreover, the constant exhortations in the archival literature for the profession to cast aside, or at least significantly augment its traditional roles and approaches by plunging into the stratosphere of high technology, have left many archivists feeling confused,

---

Reprinted with permission of *Archival Issues* 20, no. 1 (1995): 39-50.

1 David Bearman, "The Implications of *Armstrong v. the Executive Office of the President* for the Archival Management of Electronic Records," *American Archivist* 56 (Fall 1993): 689.

anachronistic, insecure, even stupid. Like a rabbit out of its burrow on a dark night, many an archivist, faced with venturing into the realm of electronic records, has found herself or himself frozen in the lights of oncoming traffic, unable to move either forward or backward, doomed to be roadkill on the information superhighway.

The time has come for archivists to reassert their interests and expertise with the documentary aspects and issues associated with preserving and accessing the human record. These are the aspects and issues that attracted many archivists to the profession and that will endure regardless, and as a direct result of, technological innovations and initiatives. Digital communications, both in the sense of transaction-interaction mechanisms and of documents, provide a strong focus in this respect. They are altering the nature of bureaucratic processes and transactions, personal interaction, information seeking and delivery strategies, and documentation itself, which is why they are already under study by communications researchers and organizational behaviorists, and by engineers, publishers, and information scientists involved in building "digital libraries." The archival profession should strive to bring its own, unique perspective to such research by identifying the uses and documentary natures of digital communications (especially what it is that they might reveal of changes in organizational, professional, and individual communication, and even changes in society and cultures); exploiting digital capabilities to track and harvest certain types of electronic interactions; and capitalizing upon these technologies for the ongoing dissemination, preservation, and use of archival materials.

The Nature of Digital Communications

The nature of digital communications in terms of content, context, structure, and use must be a central concern for any appraisal or selection process for these materials. This is so because archivists must be able to understand whether the digital communications they are appraising are potentially official records or offer new, enhanced, or additional documentation of a records mandate or collecting theme. Perhaps one of the most interesting aspects of electronic records, and one of the least treated by archival literature and practice, is their enormous potential to document contemporary culture and cultural and societal change due to the implementation of electronic information systems. Such change is manifested in many ways, including through developments in organizational structure and behavior, ethics, concepts of individual privacy and right to access records, ownership, and information use patterns, not to mention changes in the actual nature of the documentary record. To be truly effective in working with networked information and record-keeping systems and in interpreting their output, archivists must be aware of those systems' wide-ranging cultural, sociological, and legal implications. For example, Catherine Bailey has stated that "Electronic mail gives the illusion of privacy with none of the constraints of official correspondence."[2]

Of all the existing electronic information and recordkeeping systems, digital communications (also referred to as computer-mediated communications, or CMC) perhaps best demonstrate all the above manifestations. Digital communications have been in a rapid and exponential state of evolution since their inception, not just in terms of technology, but in terms of the extent and nature of their use at almost every level of society and in almost every country in the world. Identifying and addressing the changing documentary nature of such media is an area that gets to the heart of the archival role in society and is one that should receive much more attention in archival literature than it has to date.

CMC is really an umbrella term covering a multitude of different technologies, formats, genres, and environments, some of which are more clear cut and have more predictable uses, contents, and structures, and hence may be easier for archivists to identify and appraise, than others. CMC include the familiar electronic mail,[3] used for either one-on-one correspondence, or one-to-many mailings; the ubiquitous bulletin board, listserv, and news group formats for communication among many; and various conferencing environments available for self-selecting or self-contained groups to use in task-oriented and social discussion. CMC also include both refereed and unrefereed journals, especially in scholarly and research fields, and a burgeoning number of hypermedia "documents," such as those generated using Hypertext Mark-up Language (HTML) and disseminated over the World Wide Web. Already the addition of new capabilities to existing software make it difficult in some cases to identify where one format or genre ends and another begins. Many of these formats and genres will become obsolete with developing technology, while some will continue to evolve and become more complex before rigorous internationally accepted standards, predictable document structures, societal use norms, and agreed-upon policies are developed that may simplify CMC management by archivists and other concerned parties.

Of all these forms of CMC, the most widespread administrative and personal uses are probably made of textual electronic mail. With large-scale implementations already in place in the corporate environment in

---

2 Catherine Bailey, "Archival Theory and Electronic Records," *Archivaria* 29 (Winter 1989-90): 73.

3 Electronic mail has been variously defined. For example, Webster's *New World Dictionary of Computer Terms* (1992) defines it as "the process of sending, receiving, storing, and forwarding messages in digital form over telecommunications facilities"; and Rice and Bair as "the creation, editing, sending, receiving, storage, forwarding, and printing of text — all facilitated by the computer." See R. Rice and J. H. Bair, "New Organizational Media and Productivity," in *The New Media*, ed. R. E. Rice (Beverly Hills, Calif.: Sage), 191.

particular, advanced voice processing applications such as voice-to-text conversion and voice annotation are also being integrated, along with public key encryption (PKE), to make this once rather straightforward format increasingly complex. Electronic conferencing generates administrative materials in instances where it is used to provide an electronic forum for groups of administrators, committees, and research collaborators, but much of the impetus for electronic mail's development over 20 years ago was to provide for personal interaction. Indeed, extensive use is made of all forms of digital communications by individual users acting solely in a personal capacity, or appending personal communications to those that would otherwise be considered official. This personal involvement in digital communications provides an essential element to any discussion of their documentary nature.

Where CMC developments, users, and archivists are today is a far distance from the beginnings of the widespread use of CMC in the 1970s. Where they will be in 10 years will probably not resemble any situation archivists have previously encountered. It is this dynamism that, rather than being viewed by archivists as an obstacle to working with these media, should be seen as the key to the many potential benefits that may accrue both to the historical record and to archival practice. Archivists, records creators, and historical researchers alike need to be aware of the documentary potential of materials generated by CMC and the associated opportunities the technologies present to reach new user communities in new ways. Charles Dollar, writing in 1992, emphasized the power of technologies as instruments of change. He stated that a basic condition of modern life is

> . . . the power of technologies, particularly information technologies, to break down the social, cultural, and national differences in communication — one of the most fundamental of human activities. No cultural or national tradition will be immune from the pervasive power of information technologies over the next century. In the long run, therefore, social, cultural, and national traditions about archives are useful in providing us with a baseline against which to assess the nature of change occurring around us.[4]

Hugh Taylor is one of the only archivists to have written about changes in the resultant "record," that is, the potential of the output of such technologies to reflect their global societal and cultural impact. Taylor states that

---

4 Charles Dollar, *The Impact of Information Technologies* (Ancona, Italy: University of Macerata Press, 1991).

. . . there is a need to understand how various technologies impinge upon communication in such a way as to change the bureaucratic process and the meaning of the act or decision entered in the record, which may look the same but ceases to have the same authority, especially since the computer is already evincing certain characteristics analogous to preliterate authority.[5]

Unfortunately Taylor's observations appear to have largely escaped concrete application in the appraisal practices of archival electronic records programs and archival research into the management of CMC. Catherine Bailey has commented upon the documentary nature of electronic mail

Electronic mail is the nearest written equivalent to the correspondence of the pre-World War II era, when decision makers committed their thoughts, feelings and judgments to discursive prose in official letters. The letters conveyed information for an immediate purpose; they were not written with an eye to history, nor did they serve the purpose of most official letters today — after-the-fact confirmation of decisions already reached.[6]

Awareness of cultural and sociological changes brought about by networking are being investigated by disciplines other than archivists, however, especially in fields such as communications research and sociometrics.

In 1991, Roberta Corbin observed in an article about the proposed National Research and Education Network (NREN) that

The development of a new technology occurs in several phases. First is the replacement of traditional manual functions with automated ones. Next, people see the potential of using the technology, and new uses and ways of doing things are devised. Finally, society itself changes as a result of that technology. These societal changes are occurring with the development of networks on a local, regional, national, and international scale.[7]

In the aftermath of the ruling in *Armstrong v. the Executive Office of the President* that held, among other things, that some electronic mail may indeed have archival value and that the value may be greater, or at

---

5   Hugh Taylor, "My Very Act and Deed: Reflections on the Role of Textual Records in the Conduct of Affairs," *American Archivist* 51 (Fall 1988): 456-69.

6   Bailey, "Archival Theory and Electronic Records," 73.

7   Roberta A. Corbin, "The Development of the National Research and Education Network," *Information Technology and Libraries* 10, no. 3 (September 1991): 212-20.

least different, in its original digital form to its print-on-paper version, Corbin's observation would appear to be particularly pertinent. What Corbin describes is not exactly a continuum, but is rather the interaction of various stages. While her first stage, that of replacement of manual functions with automated ones, has already occurred in many administrative environments, administrative users, individuals, and society in general are all straddling various points in the second and third stages (that is, devising new uses and ways of doing things and eventually effecting societal change). Through the implementation of digital networking technology, digital documents are being created, annotated, and delivered, not only by and to government, corporate, and academic institutions, but also by and to individuals communicating in a personal capacity — the person on the street, even the child in the home. Integral to all of this for the archivist is the impact that changing technology has upon the nature of the resulting "record," its historical import, and the ways in which we access, validate, and correlate it.

The dynamism (perhaps even chaos) of, and researchers' associated lack of knowledge, or potentially, inability to know about, the extent and nature of the use of digital communications comprise some of the most difficult aspects to operationalize in research projects looking at CMC. This has proven to be a problem not only for archivists, but also for researchers such as those in organizational behavior and theory, communications research, and information science. As a result, it has proved difficult to develop studies that are high in internal and external validity that might help to characterize the nature and uses of CMC.

Much current research is being driven by the plans to develop the National Information Infrastructure (NII). This proposition calls for the investment of billions of dollars of government and corporate moneys in an unparalleled partnership to develop an "Information Superhighway." Coupled with this are new developments in "digital libraries," for which major monetary awards have recently been made by the National Science Foundation to several collaborative projects based at six major American universities: Carnegie-Mellon University, Stanford University, the University of California at Berkeley, the University of California at Santa Barbara, the University of Illinois, and the University of Michigan. The essence of the digital library concept is that

- heterogeneous and distributed files and databases are available, linked together, and frequently annotatable;
- library contents comprise multiple digital media (text, images, graphics, audio, video);
- library contents are universally accessible from work, school, and home through telecommunications networks;
- the library is designed for multiple and diverse user communities;

- the library is dynamic, in that the nature of both the digital library and its user communities should change as a direct result of their interaction with one another;
- the library is economically feasible, implying that it may well include commercial components; and,
- the development is frequently a collaborative venture.[8]

Major problems with the premises of the NII and the concept of the digital library, however, are that little is currently known or understood about the actual use and impact of digital communications networks. Perceptions that are most frequently cited, although little sound empirical evidence exists, are that such networking encourages intra- and interinstitutional as well as transnational collaboration; that it is a democratizing force that is breaking down hierarchical organizational and scholarly structures; that it can function almost as an instantaneous, synchronous medium and as a result may be more reflexive, spontaneous, candid, and informal. The findings of various research projects discussed below regarding who is creating materials and the "recordness" of those materials in terms of provenance and ownership, legal and fiscal values, validation and authentication, and documentary quality should demonstrate a number of concerns of interest to archivists.

Research into the impact of CMC upon organizational hierarchies, as well as the questions associated with the impact of such communications upon property rights and the scholarly review process, is currently being undertaken at the John F. Kennedy School of Management at Harvard University, in concert with the Consortium for Networked Information (CNI). Discussions so far circulated appear to affirm what has already been mentioned above, that is, democratization and flattening of existing hierarchies is occurring and considerably more publishing is being done digitally by those who actually create the publications and/or do the research. The result is a host of associated concerns with breakdowns in traditional validation mechanisms such as peer review and release of research results after approval by the top of the organization. Kahin and his associates feel that, particularly in young and emergent fields of research, digital publication and other digital communications may be used to gain rapid visibility and credit for a particular viewpoint or line of research.[9]

---

8 This definition is compiled from the request for proposals for digital libraries issued by the National Science Foundation, 1994; the proposal submitted by the University of Michigan School of Information and Library Studies et al.; and comments made by Nicholas Belkin at a presentation made at the University of Michigan School of Information and Library Studies in June 1994.

9 Brian Kahin, "Scholarly Communication in the Network Environment — Issues of Principle, Policy, and Practice," discussion paper, Science, Technology and Public Policy Program, John F. Kennedy School of Government, Harvard University; and the Coalition for Networked Information, 1992.

Research is also beginning to indicate different use patterns between male and female users, with women using digital communication capabilities to do more time-shifting to meet demanding schedules, as well as more peer networking.[10] Similar sorts of differences have been detected between senior and junior researchers and executives. Users frequently feel very proprietary toward materials created by the more individualized CMC genres such as electronic mail, even in the administrative environment, thus raising issues regarding ownership of such materials and the specifics of institutional information policy. The increasing level of collaboration between peers is making it much more difficult to define primary authorship of research projects and articles, and, more generally speaking, the provenance of documents. It is, of course, unknown at present what impact the implementation of realistic charges might have upon CMC use as a result of commercialization of the Internet and the developing National Information Infrastructure, since many of the heaviest users of the Internet (particularly those involved in education and academic research) currently experience it as an inexpensive if not free environment.

Bishop, Doty, and McClure, who have conducted several studies looking at the use of networks, claim little evidence documents how many researchers are regular users of the existing national network structure, what the vast majority of researchers use networks for, and how networks affect their work. Much of their study of network use has been conducted with the aid of federal funding in order to make policy recommendations for the proposed NII and combines traditional social science empirical methods with policy analysis. This research looked at three settings that have been major users of computer networking: private industry, academia, and federal laboratories. It found that little research on major policy issues related to the design and implementation of a national research network has been conducted and that increased end-user training and digital network policies are necessary to support and reinforce classical disciplinary and scientific norms such as peer review in order for researchers to feel comfortable using networks for formal functions.[11]

---

10 See, for example, Yvonna Lincoln, "Virtual Community and Invisible Colleges: Alterations in Faculty and Scholarly Networks and Professional Self-Image," paper presented at the Annual Meeting of the Associations for the Study of Higher Education, Minneapolis, Minn., October 29-November 1, 1992; and Kahin, "Scholarly Communications."

11 See Charles McClure, Ann P. Bishop, and Philip Doty, *The National Research and Education Network: Research and Policy Perspectives* (Norwood, N. J.: Ablex, 1991); Philip Doty, Ann P. Bishop, and Charles R. McClure, "Scientific Norms and the Use of Electronic Research Networks," *ASIS '91: Proceedings of the 54th ASIS Annual Meeting*, vol. 28 (Medford, N.J.: Learned Information Inc., 1991): 24-38; and Ann P. Bishop, Philip Doty, and Charles R. McClure, "Federal Information Resources Management (IRM): A Policy Review and Assessment" *ASIS '89: Proceedings of the 52nd ASIS Annual Meeting*, vol. 26 (Medford, N.J.: Learned Information Inc., 1989).

One concern voiced by many scholars and researchers is that academia, if not society, may be beginning to confuse digital information and databanks with knowledge. For example, Richard Wurman, writing about the "information revolution," cites a source who states that

> Information is not knowledge. You can mass-produce raw data and incredible quantities of facts and figures. You cannot mass-produce knowledge, which is created by individual minds, drawing on individual experience, separating the significant from the irrelevant, making value judgments.[12]

This concern was also implied in a 1987 article by Jay Bolter, writing about what he called the ". . . dichotomy between the spoken and the written language; between writing and memory; between technology and the human mind itself." Bolter goes on to discuss how it is a

> . . . short step from electronic reading to electronic writing — from determining the order of texts to altering their structure and content. Traditional writings such as encyclopedias had permanent hierarchies of knowledge due to their formats. Now we can rearrange and make links as we wish. Computerized text is becoming more eclectic: combining visual symbols and images in more complex ways (including iconographic writing). One way to characterize this whole complex of changes in structure and symbol is to say that the computer gives us a new space for reading and writing. Literate people not only speak differently from illiterates, but they think differently as well: they analyze, they categorize, they reason abstractly with much greater facility.[13]

This is an interesting point, given that there are many archivists who would see their role, as manifested in the activities of appraisal, description, and reference, in large part being that of turning information into knowledge, but who are finding that to be more challenging when working with digital materials:

> The quest for knowledge rather than mere information is the crux of the study of archives and of the daily work of the archivist. All the key words applied to archival records — provenance, respect des fonds, context, evolution, inter-relationships, order — imply a sense of understanding, of 'knowledge,' rather than the merely efficient retrieval of names, subjects, or whatever, all devoid of context, that is

---

12 Richard S. Wurman, *Information Anxiety* (New York: Doubleday, 1989).

13 Jay David Bolter, "Text and Technology: Reading and Writing in the Electronic Age," *Library Resources and Technical Services* 31 (January/March 1987): 12-23.

'information' (undeniably useful as this might be for many purposes). Quite simply, archivists must transcend mere information, and mere information management, if they wish to search for, and lead others to seek, 'knowledge' and meaning among the records in their care.[14]

In some respects, Jay Bolter's comment harks back to Hugh Taylor's concerns about subtle (and not so subtle) changes that may be taking place in the nature of the historical record. It would not be difficult, for example, for an archivist to perceive, when appraising existing electronic mail, whether electronic mail does indeed tend to be more candid and to reflect more collaborative relationships. Perhaps electronic mail might reflect government associating with the corporate sector and the individual citizen on a scale and of a nature quantitatively and qualitatively different than before CMC (for example, President Clinton's development of an "electronic White House"). It is certainly likely that the archivist will find that current CMC being appraised contain a much higher degree of mixture of personal and official communications within individual digital documents than is normally found in paper correspondence. It would be harder, however, for the archivist to identify whether the nature of the record and documentation of society in general is being fundamentally altered. Findings of the electronic conferencing project conducted at the University of Michigan in 1991-92 would suggest considerable new and different forms of documentation are being created on university campuses, especially those documenting the experiences of the ordinary person, as opposed to the central figure, or the office. Findings also point to the documentation of activities and social, political, and intellectual concerns that had not previously been possible to document through traditional record-keeping practices. The historical value of such interactions, however, are highly dependent upon how free individuals feel to speak their mind, whether or not membership of an online group has a critical mass and a strong organizer, and what costs are associated with system use.[15]

Obstacles to Archival Management

Many problems raised by digital communications for archival management are products of technological developments and legal interpretation and are germane to most digital systems. At this point, these prob-

---

14 Terry Cook, "From Information to Knowledge: An Intellectual Paradigm for Archives," *Archivaria* 19 (Winter 1984-1985): 28-49.

15 See Anne J. Gilliland-Swetland, Gregory T. Kinney, and William K. Wallach, *Uses of Electronic Communication to Document an Academic Community,* final report to the National Historical Publications and Records Commission on Grant No. 91-113 (Ann Arbor, Mich.: Bentley Historical Library, University of Michigan, December 1992).

lems are almost self-evident and have been discussed in some depth in the existing archival electronic records literature.[16] They include the facts that digital communications formats are constantly evolving and lacking in standards; no one is sure exactly how substantive or widespread are their administrative uses; it is unclear in many circumstances as to what extent such materials constitute public record, especially when communications frequently contain a mixture of official and private correspondence. User capabilities to create a document on a computer and send it electronically to one or more second parties (who in turn may modify it, add graphics, and so forth), make the establishment of provenance and version control problematic. The passage of digital communications materials through network gateways and individual electronic mailboxes in chronological rather than any more useful original order makes it difficult to identify the boundaries between systems, record series, and documents, yet archivists may have to work with such correspondence while it is still active, perhaps before the recipient has even read it and replied, or else risk losing it to a system purge or user deletion. Moreover, those who design communications systems and set communications and software standards still remain largely ignorant of archival needs.

Added to all of these is a set of obstacles acknowledged not only by archivists, but also by industry and scholarly and research communities, for example, too much to save (sheer volume); too hard to weed, filter, or appraise (depending upon one's perspective); media integration (e.g., images, voice processing); text encryption; lack of standard digital document structures; authentication and mutability; migration of "archived data"; and lack of standard end-user equipment.

Not so obvious and perhaps more difficult to resolve, are what might loosely be termed "philosophical" issues. Many of these are discussed from varying perspectives in the information and library sciences, business, and communications research literatures, although they receive significantly less attention in the archival literature. They include questions of assessing documentary value, establishing ownership of network materials, promoting user access, protecting personal privacy, even the ethics of managing digital materials.[17] Some of these questions have economic underpinnings, but many of them boil down, as Doty, Bishop, and McClure suggest, to a fundamental need for widespread user education

---

16 See, for example, Bailey, 180-196; Margaret Hedstrom, "The Electronic Records Challenge," *History News* 48, no. 4, (July/August 1993): 5-8; and Candace Loewen, "The Control of Electronic Records Having Archival Value," *Archivaria* 36 (Autumn 1993): 64-73.

17 For example, some users who do not trust or understand the archivist's motives may be prepared to destroy rather than hand over some material, especially in an environment such as academia, where a legal definition of what might be "a record" can be much less clear than in the government setting.

and the encouragement of appropriate societal and community norms regarding the use of computer networks and the secondary uses of materials created thereon. All of them should be of prime concern for archivists.

A Return to Appraisal

Much of the current archival literature follows in the same vein as the comment by David Bearman that is quoted at the beginning of this paper, that is, that digital materials should be managed within an electronic records management context, with heavy emphasis on the identification and retention of electronic records of evidentiary value. In fact, the terminology for this area is most telling: the profession talks in terms of "automated records and techniques" and "electronic records management," not in its usual bifurcated terms of administration of electronic "archives and manuscripts." The electronic records management approach may provide a cleaner and more administratively persuasive framework within which the fuzzy universe of digital materials can be examined, especially from the perspective of the National Archives. It is, at best, however, limiting from a true archival perspective, and at worst, actually precludes the identification, preservation, and use of those materials that the archivist often finds to be the richest in historical terms, those that are integral to the process of *überlieferung* or the handing down of culture to future generations. Perhaps the profession has become too confined within existing structures and constructs — rigid definitions of records, an implication of the exclusivity of evidential and informational values, and an over-reliance on the legal environment to set up operational parameters. Legislated law will never be sufficiently up-to-date to give archivists clear guidelines as to how to proceed in this area, and case law is never, by definition, proactive, and not necessarily made in the best interests of archivists.

In fact, the emerging digital communications environment raises surprisingly few new issues for archivists, and those it does raise are more often than not also issues for other professional communities. Rather, what digital communications do is force consideration of many documentary problems that archivists have long acknowledged and that they have attempted to address in recent years for more traditional materials through documentation strategies and other new approaches to archival appraisal (for example, how to document more than great white male-dominated institutions; or how to cope with evolving organizational hierarchies). It is now time for archivists to refocus their attention away from their awe of the actual communications technologies and systems and onto the documentary values of the materials they create. Appraisal is the key to this process.

The archival community has conducted very little substantive research into the conduct of appraisal for digital communications materials. This is in part due to the availability of large-scale, relatively inexpensive digital storage that allows more to be kept and in part to a lack of techniques for "weeding" vast files of communications materials. In many instances, the appraisal decision is reduced to a simple equation — keep all or nothing. Where appraisal does take place, however, it can strip away a large amount of "useless" materials to reveal a rich and novel documentary core while at the same time assisting individuals and organizations with the awesome task of managing digital information overload. What has been learned from several research projects conducted at the University of Michigan, both in appraising digital communications and using them as a major vehicle to develop collaborative digital libraries, is that they present tremendous opportunities for enhancing the quality and scope of existing documentation not only of administrative activities, but also of the human record, and then for delivering this record in the integrated, contextual manner that many researchers will come to expect as society becomes increasingly engaged in digital communication. For example, findings of the University of Michigan electronic conferencing appraisal project suggest that electronic conferences, as one form of digital communications, represent an untapped form of documentation regarding life on university campuses where they are widely used. While the utility of such documentation will depend upon the archival mission statement and collecting policy, it can be especially revealing of the experiences of the ordinary person, as opposed to the central figure or office, as well as documenting activities and social, political, and intellectual concerns (particularly those of minorities) that previously had been captured through traditional record-keeping practices.[18]

A twofold automated appraisal strategy that may well assist in this process is the use of communications systems design or expert "front ends" first to identify and tag on a collective level those digital communications materials that document core functions performed by the responsible agency, and second, to perform item-level appraisal that looks at the context, content, and structure of each individual digital communication. This promising approach, which has been tested as part of a doctoral research project for the appraisal of electronic mail at Michigan State University, will be further developed over the next year.[19]

---

18 For further information on this topic, see Anne J. Gilliland-Swetland, Gregory T. Kinney, and William K. Wallach, *Uses of Electronic Communication;* and Anne J. Gilliland-Swetland, "Documenting Student Life Through the Use of Computer Conferences," paper presented at the spring 1992 meeting of the Midwest Archives Conference, Chicago, Ill.

19 For more detailed documentation of this research, see Anne J. Gilliland-Swetland, *Development of an Expert Assistant for Archival Appraisal of Electronic Communications: An Exploratory Study,* Ph.D. diss. (Ann Arbor, Mich.: University of Michigan, 1995).

The fact that digital communications are created in digital formats also opens up possibilities of their being used as documentation, or perhaps more accurately, as data, by less traditional archival researcher communities such as discourse analysts, communications researchers, anthropologists, and sociologists who are seeking quantifiable digital data. The latter three, in particular, are evincing interest in triangulating quantitative with qualitative research techniques in studies that may take advantage of more traditional narrative records and even oral histories in concert with digital data accessioned by archivists. This implies factoring in the interests of these communities during the archival appraisal process (and possibly even the systems design process) so that the data needed by these communities can be automatically tracked, "harvested," and even delivered as part of the archival reference process. For example, the University of Michigan's digital library project (UMDL), which focuses on the area of earth sciences, is associated with an electronic scientific collaboration called the Upper Atmosphere Research Collaboratory (UARC). Project developers and organizational behaviorists have been studying the digital interactions of scientists involved with these projects in order to obtain more knowledge of the scientific and intellectual processes and group dynamics at work in these digital environments.

Conclusions

One of the most powerful effects of the decision rendered by Judge Charles Richey in the case of *Armstrong v. the Executive Office of the President* has been to make organizations across the country aware of the legal implications of electronic mail, thereby opening the political doors for archivists finally to begin to work with digital communications within their own organizations. This is only a part of the picture, however. While many of their contents may have little, if any, enduring value, digital communications materials are not ephemeral and should not be dismissed whole cloth if the "documents" they generate cannot neatly be fitted into a legal or formulaic definition of a "record." Digital communications represent a potentially rich source of documentation for many different facets of society, over and above its organizational activities. Archivists should seek to develop new appraisal strategies that enable them to identify that documentation and to develop new digital environments that enable them to disseminate it in a coherent, contextualized manner.

Moreover, archivists are in a position to take a leadership role in collaborative research projects with their colleagues and allies in related professional settings. It is fast becoming a truism to say that the archival profession needs more systematic research and evaluation. Truism or no, rigorous research and evaluation conducted in cooperation with nonarchival communities, such as the computing and telecommunications industries, organizational theorists, and communications researchers, will bring the archival profession closer to understanding and measuring the content and impact of the technology and its media within their implementation environment. In doing so, the archival profession should be raising its own profile and concerns, demonstrating its unique skills, and making itself and its collections an indispensable part of the National Information Infrastructure.

Part Nine:
Management

Archivists need to understand management concepts for two broad reasons. First, the relatively small size of many archival institutions means that most archivists at some stage of their career will assume managerial responsibilities. It is thus important to understand how organizations operate, how to formulate goals and objectives, and how to establish policies and priorities within the repository. Second, knowledge of management principles is an essential aspect of understanding how the organizations that archivists seek to document actually function. This will enable archivists to improve their ability to select, appraise, and manage archival records.

Despite the importance of management concerns to archivists, there is relatively little archival literature on the topic. The two articles in this section focus on efforts to understand archival users and funders. This is an extension of archival outreach (or "in-reach" within institutions), but it also requires archivists to consider their goals, priorities, and management styles.

In "Redefining Archival Identity: Meeting User Needs in the Information Society," Randall C. Jimerson argues that management concepts of marketing should be applied to archival decision making. This would further the client orientation advocated by Elsie Freeman Finch. John Grabowski advocates an extension of outreach to include building a larger advocacy base for archives in "Keepers, Users, and Funders: Building an Awareness of Archival Value." This type of advocacy should be built into the management operation of the archives, in order to ensure that users and resource allocators can be shown the value of archival programs.

27

Redefining Archival Identity: Meeting User Needs in the Information Society

RANDALL C. JIMERSON

Abstract: *To avoid becoming irrelevant in the modern information society, archivists must redefine their professional identity and role in society, learn new planning and marketing skills, and establish the importance of archives in meeting user needs. Responding to initiatives launched by the SAA Task Force on Archives and Society, the author argues that archivists should adopt a more user-friendly approach to marketing their services. Marketing differs from public relations and selling products by focusing on customers and their needs. Altering the profession's image requires that individual archivists redefine their own self-image, attitudes, and procedures.*

The Ghost of Archives Yet to Come visited me late one Friday afternoon. While refoldering Cooperative Extension Service records, I looked up and saw the black-shrouded apparition. It beckoned me to follow, and we soon stood in a gleaming air-conditioned room filled with banks of computers and display screens. A brightly colored sign on the door proclaimed DATA ARCHIVE. A digital calendar read 12 September 2001.

Efficient information processors busily answered inquiries about university policies and procedures, student academic and social records, alumni profiles, and faculty publications. Every terminal in the search room was occupied by students or faculty members, but most requests were handled through electronic mail and fax copiers. "Our goal is to provide immediate responses to all types of information needs relating to the university," the computer center manager explained. "Our success rate in satisfying client requests is 99 percent."

The Spirit led me from the room. In an instant, we were descending a dark stairway to the library basement. Following a narrow corridor, we came to a steel door with faded letters spelling UNIVERSITY ARCHIVES. Cautiously, I opened the door. The room was crowded with stacks of ancient Hollinger boxes. Piles of unprocessed papers covered several large tables.

Reprinted with permission from the *American Archivist* 52 (Summer 1989): 332-40.

"Ah. You must be a researcher," I heard a voice say. "I was hoping someone would come this week. What do you want? We have old yearbooks, catalogs, and noncurrent records of ; . ."

"Spirit, enough," I pleaded. "Let us turn back now." Mercifully, the Spirit led me quickly from the room.

"Before you leave, Spirit, tell me this," I beseeched him. "Are these the shadows of the things that *will* be, or are they only shadows of the things that *may* be?" The Ghost of Archives Yet to Come did not answer, but only pointed back to the future.

This vision still haunts me. Is this our future as archivists? Will we become quaint anachronisms in a world of instant data communication, high technology, and rapid change? Such questions are troubling. They strike at our professional pride, at our self-esteem. Pity the poor archivist of the future — shunted off to a basement corner, his disappearance unlamented, unnoticed. The motto for the high-tech future may well be: What is Past is — not Prologue, but — Irrelevant.

The twenty-first century is only a decade away. The challenge for archivists — as for our entire society — is to prepare for the increasingly rapid changes we will encounter in coming years. Already we have seen a major shift from an industrial society to an "information society," as John Naisbitt argued in his 1982 best-seller, *Megatrends*. Information is now the United States's major strategic resource. While industrial production declines, information-related jobs have become the major growth segment of the workplace. Computer literacy will soon be as essential as the "three Rs" were a generation ago. Thanks to satellite links, worldwide communication is instantaneous. As Naisbitt writes, the real importance of *Sputnik* was not that it launched the age of space exploration, but that it introduced the era of global satellite communication. We suffer from information overload. "We are drowning in information, but starved for knowledge," Naisbitt concludes. "Uncontrolled and unorganized information is no longer a resource in an information society. . . . The emphasis of the whole information society shifts, then, from supply to selection."[1] Archival appraisal skills should be highly valuable in meeting this challenge.

Professional Identity and Professional Planning

In the midst of these rapid changes in society, the archival profession is going through an identity crisis. The recent flurry of self-analysis efforts marks a healthy questioning of our professional identity. First, the state historical records assessment projects documented, graphically and in great detail, what we already knew about the "cycle of poverty" that hampers our efforts. Funded by the National Historical Publications and

---

1   John Naisbitt, *Megatrends: Ten New Directions Transforming Our Lives* (New York: Warner Books, 1982), 12, 24.

Records Commission, these assessment reports provided the first in-depth examination of national historical records programs since the New Deal. Both separately and cumulatively, they reveal the serious financial, personnel, and resource limitations under which archivists work to preserve our documentary heritage.[2]

Second, the Society of American Archivists' Task Force on Goals and Priorities (GAP) has provided a valuable planning tool to help us chart future directions and priorities. Its report, *Planning for the Archival Profession,* attempts to provide a framework for planning and decision making and "to promote consensus on major goals and objectives." Although many of the report's recommendations have been embraced by various SAA committees and section steering groups, archivists have been slow to institutionalize planning as an ongoing process.[3] This is particularly true for individual repositories. Few archival institutions have started systematic planning programs.

Even certification is primarily an effort in self-definition. It will provide employers, resource allocators, and others with one means of identifying experienced and knowledgeable archivists. Yet its more significant implication, it seems to me, lies in defining the boundaries of professional status. This has both positive and potentially negative connotations. It may enhance the status and self-image of archivists who become certified. But it could also drive a wedge between certified and noncertified archivists, just at the time that we need to broaden our professional networks and strengthen our ties with related professions.

The Task Force on Archives and Society is the only one of these self-analysis efforts that has looked outside the profession for answers. In particular, the Sidney Levy and Albert Robles report, *The Image of Archivists: Resource Allocators' Perceptions,* holds a mirror for us to see our public image. It isn't as pretty as we would like. Even our positive qualities actually become liabilities, as one summary indicates: "[W]e are well liked for our passivity; we are respected for our service, but service is by implication reward enough; we are admired for our curatorial ability, meaning we are quiet, pleasant, and powerless."[4]

To improve our status, however, we must understand how others see us. Then we can begin to change. Altering public stereotypes is not just a

2   Lisa B. Weber, ed., *Documenting America: Assessing the Condition of Historical Records in the States* (Atlanta: National Association of State Archives and Records Administrators, 1984).

3   *Planning for the Archival Profession: A Report of the SAA Task Force on Goals and Priorities* (Chicago: Society of American Archivists, 1986), 1. The continuation of the SAA planning process is shown in *An Action Agenda for the Archival Profession: Institutionalizing the Planning Process* (Chicago: Society of American Archivists, 1988).

4   Sidney J. Levy and Albert G. Robles, *The Image of Archivists: Resource Allocators' Perceptions* (Chicago: Society of American Archivists, 1984); SAA Task Force on Archives and Society, "Archivists' Resource Allocators: The Next Step," unpublished report (9 December 1985), 4.

public relations problem of "'educating the public." It requires us to change our own self-image, actions, and attitudes.

To succeed archivists must do two things. First, we must redefine our professional identity and our role in society. Then, we must develop a clear strategic vision for improving services and responsiveness to archival customers. For many of us, this will require a reconceptualization of traditional methods, theories, and assumptions. In order to change old habits we need professional development in communication techniques, management, strategic planning, negotiation, motivation training, marketing, public relations, the nature and use of power, and other skills.[5] It won't be easy. But it is necessary for survival. We can't afford *not* to change.

What Business Are Archivists In?

What business are we in? What business are we not in? What business should we be in? In order to define our professional identity, we must pay serious attention to these questions. Easy traditional answers won't be enough. Consider what happened to the railroads. As marketing expert Theodore Levitt has argued, the railroads lost their national prominence largely because they assumed they were in the railroad business. They should have realized they were in the transportation business. Likewise, Hollywood thought it was in the movie business. The advent of television — a strong competitor in the entertainment business — nearly destroyed Hollywood. In both cases, industry leaders were product oriented, instead of customer oriented.[6]

According to Levitt, an organization "must learn to think of itself not as producing goods or services but as buying custorners, as doing the things that will make people want to do business with it." He contends that an industry should develop backwards. Starting with a customer's needs, it should develop delivery systems to reach the consumer, then create things that will meet their needs, and finally find the necessary raw materials. "The purpose of a business is to get and keep a customer," Levitt argues. "Customers are constantly presented with lots of options to help them solve their problems. They don't buy things, they buy solutions to problems."[7] As the railroads discovered too late, people did not want to ride trains. They wanted to reach a particular destination. When they could do so more quickly by air, or more conveniently by car, they stopped riding trains.

---

5 Ibid., 6.

6 Theodore Levitt, "Marketing Myopia," *Harvard Business Review* 38 (July/August 1960): 45-46; Naisbitt, *Megatrends*, 85-88.

7 Levitt, "Marketing Myopia," 55-56; Theodore Levitt, *The Marketing Imagination* (New York: Free Press, 1983), xii, 1-19; Philip Kotler, *Marketing for Nonprofit Organizations,* 2nd ed. (Englewood Cliffs, N. J.: Prentice-Hall, 1982), 19-26.

Archivists can take a lesson here. We can't afford to continue making trains and preparing elaborate schedules, if people want quicker, more convenient transportation. Many have the illusion that a superior product will sell itself. It won't. It must meet a real customer need, not a hypothetical need derived from an existing product line. All too often archivists exhibit a product orientation, offering products and services that we think will be good for the public and are inherently desirable. When we take a more active stance, it often comes from a selling orientation, aimed at "persuading target audiences that they ought to accept the offering — that it is superior to any alternatives." Instead, we should adopt a marketing orientation: identify what information people need or want, then determine how to provide it, and finally discover where to find the raw materials.[8] It isn't enough to try to sell the goods we already have on our shelves.

What business are archivists in? All too often, we assume it is the business of preserving records of the past for future use. Similar perceptions affect our "sister" professions. As Philip Kotler and Sidney Levy reported in a 1969 article: "Most museum directors interpret their primary responsibility as 'the proper preservation of an artistic heritage for posterity.' As a result, for many people museums are cold marble mausoleums that house miles of relics that soon give way to yawns and tired feet." To counteract this, museums should pay closer attention to their users' concerns and needs. At the very least, public use and understanding of art should be part of their mission. As one marketing expert explains, art museums "compete with aquariums for family outings, and with movies and restaurants as places to socialize."[9] Archivists face similar challenges.

New Skills and Approaches

Archives compete with other information services and cultural organizations, both for limited budgetary resources and for customers. In order to ensure their survival, archives must gain recognition as useful — better yet, essential — programs. How can we do this? There are no easy answers. If we wish to avoid the fate suggested by the Ghost of Archives Yet to Come, there are at least six actions we can take, individually and as a profession. To improve our competitive position, we will need to develop new skills and change our approach to basic archival activities.

---

8 Alan R. Andreasen, "Nonprofits: Check Your Attention to Customers," *Harvard Business Review* 60 (May/June 1982): 106; Levitt, "Marketing Myopia," 54; Kotler, *Marketing for Nonprofit Organizations*, 21-23.

9 Philip Kotler and Sidney J. Levy, "Broadening the Concept of Marketing," *Journal of Marketing* 33 (January 1969): 11; Andreasen, "Nonprofits," 109; Kevin Flood presentation at New England Archivists' Marketing Workshop, Amherst College, 22-23 March 1985.

Redefining Professional Identity and Role.   We should begin
by redefining our professional identity and role in society. As Levy and
Robles state in *The Image of Archivists,* "To improve their situation,
archivists need to define more coherent identity objectives, and communicate greater freshness and distinctiveness in imagery by their training,
programs, self-assertion, publicity, advertising, and relevance to modern
life." The problem, which archivists share with librarians and others, is
not just how to project a more positive image, but how to reach agreement on exactly what image the profession wishes to send forth. Writing
about librarians, Cosette Kies states the problem faced by archivists: "It
should be no surprise, if we have no clear image of ourselves, that the
public does not understand our purpose either."[10]

In *Planning for the Archival Profession,* the SAA Task Force on Goals
and Priorities defines the profession's mission in the familiar triad of
archival functions: "To insure the identification, preservation, and use of
records of enduring value." This is how we usually define our business.
Yet it bears a distinct product orientation. It emphasizes the records, not
their informational content or the needs they satisfy. In discussing the
goal of "availability and use of records," however, the GAP report
acknowledges: "Archivists tend to think about their work in the order in
which it is performed. Inevitably, use comes last. Since use of archival
materials is the goal to which all other activities are directed, archivists
need to re-examine their priorities."[11] This begins to sound like a marketing orientation for archives.

Urging archivists to take a marketing approach, Kevin Flood, a
member of SAA's Task Force on Archives and Society, suggests a starting
point for defining what business we are in. We should stop thinking of
ourselves as custodians, Flood argues, and think of ourselves as "information processors with outreach and administrative responsibility."
These are action terms: information processors, not guardians; outreach,
not collecting records and waiting for the world to beat a path to our
doors. Flood advises us "to enter into the information mainstream, to
mold it to our needs, and to be part of the contemporary process instead
of just a passive custodian of the past." One reason the archival profession does not ocupy a more prominent social role, Flood contends, is
that it serves the ideology of the information custodian instead of the
needs of people.[12]

---

10   Levy and Robles, *Image of Archivists,* v; Cosette Kies, *Marketing and Public Relations for Libraries*
      (Metuchen, N. J.: Scarecrow Press, 1987), 45, 168.

11   *Planning for the Archival Profession,* vi, 23.

12   Kevin Flood, "Address Prepared for Task Force on Society [*sic*] Presentation," unpublished paper
      (September 1984), 7; Flood, Marketing Workshop.

Strategic Planning. As a second element in improving the competitive position of archives, strategic planning provides a process for defining our mission, goals, and objectives. In contrast to long-range planning, which is based on broad projections of internal growth and development, strategic planning "focuses on the external environment and the organization's ability to deal with it." Strategic planning clarifies the institution's purposes, provides a focus for program planning, and incorporate a systematic evaluation of alternatives. The process is based on the assumption that external conditions have a greater impact on the institution's ability to achieve its objectives than do the internal desires, goals, and intentions of managers and staff. Above all, it is action oriented. Grounded in a rigorous assessment of the organization's capabilities, strategic planning establishes goals and objectives, evaluates the potential impact of alternative choices, defines the necessary organizational changes to achieve desired results, and requires immediate actions.[13]

The GAP report has begun the process of planning the overall goals of the profession. Each repository should now undertake its own strategic planning process. This includes clearly stating the repository's mission, goals, and objectives. By linking these directly to the institution's mission and goals, the archives obtains credibility and recognition as contributing to essential programs. In addition, by evaluating strategic alternatives, the archives assumes an active posture in seeking external support, resources, and recognition. The planning process also provides a solid basis for setting internal objectives and priorities.

Educating Resource Allocators. One additional benefit of strategic planning is that it compels archivists to respond to external forces and power structures, particularly in regard to resource allocators. This is the third action we must take for survival — convincing resource allocators that archives are essential. Archives must learn to compete effectively with other units and agencies for support and resources. "To raise this sense of priority, archivists should bring more to the fore the essential character of the archives," Levy and Robles suggest. "Allocators know archives are necessary by law and for research. But the purposes, uses, and contributions of the archives have to be made more vivid — more explicit, more concrete, and repeated in varied ways."[14] Administrators require us to serve present needs. It is not enough to preserve the past (old musty documents) for the future (when we'll all be dead). If archivists cannot meet today's needs for information, we will fall by the wayside.

---

13   Alice McHugh, "Strategic Planning for Museums," *Museum News* 58 (July/August 1980): 23-27; Bruce W. Dearstyne, "Planning for Archival Programs: An Introduction," MARAC Technical Leaflet, Number 3, *Mid-Atlantic Regional Archivist* 12 (Summer 1983).

14   Levy and Robles, *Image of Archivists*, iv.

Our multiple roles serving researchers, administrators, and other information handlers provide us with strategic advantages. Information is power. Our importance as archivists comes not from hoarding information, but from our ability to process data and assist others in using it. By showing resource allocators how they can use archival information to advantage, archivists can enhance their claim on scarce resources.

In addition to the benefits derived from archival records, archivists have personal attributes that offer benefits to resource allocators. As stated in the SAA response to the Levy report, "Our training and interests stress the ability to analyze problems, develop hypothesis, draw conclusions, all of which makes us valuable as analysts in a variety of organizational settings."[15] We can apply our skills in information processing and analysis on a wider basis. This may include personal involvement on institutional committees and task forces. At the very least, archivists should be involved in planning and policy making for records management and data systems. Current record-keeping concerns should be integrated with efforts to ensure preservation of essential information.

Becoming User Friendly. Closely related to improving services and usefulness to resource allocators is a fourth, and perhaps most important, key to survival: becoming "user friendly." Archivists should adopt a marketing orientation to attract users and satisfy their needs for information. As Lawrence Dowler states, "If use is the measure and justification of archives, then reference should be first, not last, in operational priorities." All to often, we begin with the organization's needs and products, and then determine how to convince people to use archives. Instead, as Elsie Freeman [Finch] argues, we need to reconceptualize our basic services and procedures from the user's point of view. Advanced technologies and information systems may make archives a backwater, Freeman warns, "not because our material is irrelevant to current or retrospective questions but rather because of the difficulty users have in reaching the information hidden in the records we hold." Convenience is critical for most information seekers. As Flood notes, users will follow the path of least resistance in seeking information. They expect speed, accuracy, and integrity of information. To meet these demands, archivists must develop new findings aids based on the convenience of users, not of archivists.[16]

Greater rigor and imagination in studying users and potential users will disclose their needs. As Freeman suggests, "We must begin to learn systematically, not impressionistically as is our present tendency, who

---

15 "Archivists' Resource Allocators," 4.

16 Lawrence Dowler, "The Role of Use in Defining Archival Practice and Principles: A Research Agenda for the Availability and Use of Records," *American Archivist* 51 (Winter/Spring 1988): 84; Elsie Freeman [Finch], "In the Eye of the Beholder: Archives Administration From the User's Point of View," *American Archivist* 47 (Spring 1984): 112, 116; Flood, Marketing Workshop.

our users are; what kinds of projects they pursue, in what time frames, and under what sponsorship; and, most importantly, how they approach records." Valuable models for designing user studies have been offered by Paul Conway and William J. Maher. In addition to improving services to users, user studies may have a secondary benefit. "The more archivists know about the use of their holdings," Maher suggests, "the more ammunition they will have in the battle to convince people that archives really matter."[17]

In examining users of archives, the tendency has been to focus on archivists' needs. An instructive example of this is the effort by the Illinois State Archives to promote scholarly use of its holdings. The attempt failed, not because the records could not support scholarly use, but because the archives had not evaluated the needs of its users. It reminds one of Theodore Levitt's critique of Detroit's customer studies, which "only researched his preferences between the kinds of things which it had already decided to offer him."[18] A marketing orientation will ensure that archivists provide services based on the needs and desires of both users and potential users. A careful application of user studies can help us to identify these concerns.

We may need to begin by redefining our user constituencies. At the outset we need to recognize the various groups that make up our users. Archivists tend to develop finding aids and other services for scholarly researchers. Often, we have what Freeman characterizes as "adversary relationships" with genealogists and some other avocational users. The goal of archives, however, should be to encourage use of valuable records. All potential users of the archives should be assisted and appreciated. At the same time, archivists need to prioritize their decisions in order to focus on the groups that most need their materials and attention.[19]

Users can be a valuable constituency to assist archivists. For example, genealogists can be strong allies in seeking support for maintaining or expanding archival programs. Students and alumni of academic institutions, who often only want to see old yearbooks, campus papers, or course catalogs, can help justify the continuation of the archives. We should not underrate the value of nostalgia. It is a powerful motivation for many users of archival information. An important area for investigation would be the underlying human needs that archival research can satisfy. We know a lot about the basic properties of our products —

---

17 Freeman [Finch], "In the Eye of the Beholder," 112; William J. Maher, "The Use of User Studies," *Midwestern Archivist* 11 (1986): 15; Paul Conway, "Facts and Frameworks: An Approach to Studying the Users of Archives," *American Archivist* 49 (Fall 1986): 393-407.

18 Roy C. Turnbaugh, "Archival Mission and User Studies," *Midwestern Archivist* 11 (1986): 27-33; Levitt, "Marketing Myopia," 51.

19 Freeman [Finch], "In the Eye of the Beholder," 113; Flood, "Address for Task Force on Society," 12.

records, exhibitions, public programs — but very little about the psycho-logical and informational needs that motivate users. For example, some people have a need to know information from the archives. Others may have a "nice-to-know" attitude. Information may be either essential, valuable, or simply interesting for different users.[20]

Marketing Archives. The actual marketing of archives is a fifth step in guaranteeing survival. Marketing for archives includes four major steps: analyzing the community we wish to serve; identifying, segmenting, and selecting target groups; designing and promoting appropriate programs tailored to the needs of each target group; and managing the process through research, planning, and evaluation. According to marketing expert Philip Kotler, nonprofit organizations face different marketing considerations than businesses. Nonprofits have multiple audiences to serve. They have multiple objectives and must determine the relative importance of each. They provide services rather than physical goods. Finally, nonprofits are expected to operate in the public interest, since they often receive public funding, subsidies, or tax exemptions.[21] In order to market archival services, we must understand these factors and how to turn them to our advantage.

As an important aspect of marketing, archival outreach efforts should become a higher priority. Visibility is essential. As Sidney Levy concludes in his study of resource allocators, "Making archives a more common and accessible concept, and doing more to open them to use and visiting should diminish the various elements of dustiness and mustiness, sheer acquisitiveness, territoriality, and dead accumulation. Open houses, showcases, special events, celebrations, announcements of findings and distinctive uses of archives, etc., will convey a greater sense of vitality."[22] The best way to alter the public image of archives (and archivists) is to change our own attitudes and ways of doing things. Outreach is essen-tial, both to inform the public of archival resources and services and to demonstrate responsiveness to user needs.

Many archivists and resource allocators resist publicizing their archives. Some fear that overuse will damage fragile documents. Others think that "serious" researchers already know enough about archives. "I don't know if the public needs to be informed," one resource allocator stated. "Most people aren't interested and have no need for archives in their day-to-day lives."[23] This typifies the attitudes archivists must over-come if we are to gain resources and appreciation for the value of our

---

20 Levitt, "Marketing Myopia," 54; Kies, *Marketing and Public Relations*, 171.

21 Kies, *Marketing and Public Relations*, 74; Kotler, *Marketing for Nonprofit Organizations*, 9, 215-31.

22 Levy and Robles, *Image of Archivists*, v.

23 Ibid., 60-61.

profession. Through marketing and outreach, archivists need to identify how to satisfy people's daily needs for archival information and services.

Outward-looking Attitude. Finally, an essential key to survival is adopting a more positive, outward-looking attitude. Shouting "Archives are primary!" from the library steps won't help much. We need to show that they are. This will require anticipating and responding to user needs. Archivists will have to preserve the information people want, in formats they can use easily, with the quick access they demand.

Archivists are used to being humble. Compared to other virtues, however, modesty is highly overrated. In order to improve our status, we need to become unabashed promoters of archives. "Archivists need to translate their importance into more power," Levy advises. "That requires more self-assertion, more concerted action, being less sympathetic to or understanding of the resource allocators' budget problems."[24] Constituencies served well can be counted on for support and lobbying. Researchers, genealogists, administrative support staff, and other archives users should be called on to tell resource allocators how valuable archival services are to them.

Archivists can survive the transition to a high-tech information society if they redefine their professional identity and role in society, undertake strategic planning, respond to the needs of resource allocators and public users, adopt a marketing and outreach orientation, and take a more assertive, outward-looking stance. The archivist's aspiration, however, should not be merely to survive. As Theodore Levitt points out, "Anybody can survive in some way or other, even the skid-row bum. The trick is to survive gallantly, to feel the surging impulse of commercial mastery; not just to experience the sweet smell of success, but to have the visceral feel of entrepreneurial greatness."[25] This should be our goal. Archivists should strive to become integral parts of the information society.

My own encounter with the Ghost of Archives Yet to Come has changed my perception of the archivist's role in society. In my own vow to reform, to begin a new life as a user-oriented archivist, I can echo Ebenezer Scrooge: "I will live in the Past, the Present, and the Future. The Spirits of all three shall strive within me. I will not shut out the lessons that they teach." If Scrooge could change his ways, perhaps I can — perhaps all of us can. May our transformation be as successful as his. If it is we may earn the recognition Scrooge received (changing one word from Dickens's final tribute): "It was always said of him, that he knew how to keep Archives well, if any man alive possessed the knowledge."[26]

---

24   Ibid., iv.

25   Levitt, "Marketing Myopia," 56.

26   Charles Dickens, *A Christmas Carol* (London: Chapman and Hall, 1843), 165-66.

28

Keepers, Users, and Funders: Building an Awareness of Archival Value

JOHN J. GRABOWSKI

Abstract: *Archivists need to build an awareness of "archival value" among the general public if they are to command the support the profession deserves, and they need to work together with the community of public and academic historians in creating this awareness. The recent emphasis on outreach indicates that archivists are becoming aware of this need. But is outreach moving in the right direction? Merely educating the public about what archivists do is not enough. Archivists must create a larger body of users. By doing so, the profession will not only build a larger advocacy base for its fiscal support but will also help create a citizenry more aware of the sources and value of history and heritage.*

During the past decade, the archival profession has, for good reason, become obsessed with the issue of outreach. By *outreach* we mean the matter of educating the public, and those whom we choose to call "resource allocators," about the purpose and importance of what we, the custodians of Clio, do for a living. Paradoxically, we have at the same time become engaged in a process of professional definition that seems to be moving us away from a link with history, a link that may be far more critical for the well-being of the profession than are arguments about theory or vocational purity. It would seem that fragmenting the historical profession into obscure fields of specialization and creating a guild of archivists can serve only to counteract the benefits of outreach, for it divides us from our allies and, more critically, may tend to isolate us intellectually from the public, who, in the United States, are the ultimate source of all that we might consider support.

The professional fragmentation of those involved in the field of history is a matter that Theodore Karamanski of Loyola University and the Council of Public History addressed most adroitly in a 1989 Midwest Archives Conference meeting. At that meeting, Karamanski called into question the barriers that people who "do" history for a living have created

Reprinted with permission from the *American Archivist* 55 (Summer 1992): 464-72.

between their respective spheres of endeavor. He argued that the numbers of history practitioners are so small that any particular subdivision within the field can ill afford to set itself apart from its peers, whether that separation takes the form of certificates of specialization or an attitude of professional superiority. According to his argument, there are far too few "history" people in any of these professional disciplines to make any impact in advocating their work before legislative bodies and other resource allocators—entities that seemingly take little notice of heritage but that do seem to notice large numbers and noisy demands. By recognizing our common mission, working together, and marshalling our numbers in a single voice we might, Karamanski reasoned, have a better chance at advocating our individual and common causes.[1]

Such unity is a correct and necessary beginning if those who would preserve this nation's heritage are to have any impact on public and political attitudes that not only determine the resources allocated to Clio, but more important, set a societal standard for historical self-understanding. Yet, one wonders what the effect would be even if all of those professionals who "do" history for a living were to march in unison on the national Capitol or prepare a direct-mail lobbying campaign. Would such numbers be sufficient to impress public representatives accustomed to receiving millions of postcards and telephone calls from an organized citizenry upset about more popular issues ranging from abortion to zoological catastrophe? That seems doubtful. What the history profession needs, in addition to unified action, is the development of a large clientele that understands, respects, and, therefore, will advocate our cause. We, the keepers, need more users.

Archivists have tried to create a broader understanding of our mission. The number of outreach programs that have been discussed at so many of our professional archival gatherings during the past 10 years are evidence of that effort. Archivists, blessed or damned, if you will, with a professional moniker of great popular obscurity, have had a greater problem in creating an awareness of their importance among the public than have our colleagues in allied historical fields. We have tried mightily to remove the shroud (or is it a cloud of dust?) that surrounds us. Not that our efforts have been minor. Witness the activities of the Archival Roundtable of Metropolitan New York as it annually sponsors an "Archives Week" designed to inform the public about archival activities. This activity now will become national, and archivists in a number of cities and states are deciding what they will do for an archives week each

---

1   Theodore J. Karamanski, "Resolved: Graduate Study in Public History Shall Be Required for Archivists," unpublished paper delivered at the Midwest Archives Conference meeting in Chicago, May 1989. Karamanski's thoughts on this matter are further explicated in "Making History Whole: Public Service, Public History, and the Profession," *Public Historian* 12, no. 3 (Summer 1990): 91-101.

year.[2] Yet such activities seem not to have moved the public to a general awareness of what archivists do. (For most people, for instance, presidential libraries are not repositories but museums crammed with wax dummies, football helmets, and the gifts of foreign heads of state.) Despite the archivists' efforts at outreach, nationally syndicated cartoonist Jeff MacNelly can still equate archives with the messy desk of an idiosyncratic "Perfesser" and describe them as differing from a garbage dump only by lacking a flock of scavenging seagulls.[3] It might be appropriate to have the Society of American Archivists (SAA) fund a national survey to see how many Americans know what the term *archivist* means and, more important, to delve more deeply and learn how many have any inkling of where history comes from.

If the slide shows, archives week document examination opportunities, brochures, and preconvention publicity for professional meetings have done little to educate the public, what can we and our colleagues in allied fields do to educate the public and thus affect what we now call "resource allocators"? It is, one suspects, time for the keepers to strive not only to educate the public but also to create more users, on the assumption that someone who uses the product is more likely to value the industry that produces it. If we are to get a reasonable proportion of the gross national product in the era of the new free enterprise, we are going to have to get more customers.

The issue of bringing more users into the archives and manuscripts repositories of the land is not new or single-sided. Many of our colleagues in the field of business and institutional archives know how important broad service is to their survival in a larger corporate or bureaucratic environment: only useful parts of the corporate entity deserve to survive. It is those of us who preserve largely for research purposes — whether in governmental archives or manuscript repositories — who need to address the user issue in a broader sense. But we know the problems of increased usership. If we increase usership, we also endanger collections from overuse and overtax staff who must serve larger numbers of patrons. Is the price too high to pay for this gamble? Perhaps not. Creating a larger usership does not necessarily involve overstuffing our research rooms. All such methods, however, depend on people deriving "something" from archives other than awestruck reverence for famous signatures and fragile old documents. Several programs undertaken at the Western Reserve

---

2 Larry J. Hackman, "Archives Week in the United States?" *SAA Newsletter* (March 1991): 14, 20. In this article Hackman proposes that a national Archives Week be declared during the first week of October 1992, and he cites the successful programs undertaken as part of archives weeks throughout New York state.

3 In several of his *Shoe* comic strips, syndicated cartoonist Jeff MacNelly has made the connection between the unkempt desk of the "Perfesser" character and archives. The characterization of archives as   "a dump without seagulls" occurred in the 30 November 1990 strip.

Historical Society (WRHS) in Cleveland and other repositories in the state of Ohio have served to bring new faces into the research room and have provided funds and advocates in the state house in Columbus. Although much that follows relates to keepers and users, it should be clear that that relationship can and does have great impact on funders.

Primary among these user groups, and recently represented in a focused exchange in the *SAA Newsletter*, are genealogists.[4] There is no need to rehash the sometimes stormy relationship between archivists and genealogists or to debate the issue of good research versus bad research. Good research and bad research can characterize the work of any patron in our facilities, be that person a published scholar or a neophyte family historian. In many cases, archivists and genealogists need and can come to some accommodation, whether over the care that must be accorded to collections or the understanding of what constitutes legitimate research.

The bottom line here is that genealogists are the fastest growing group of researchers in many repositories. At the Western Reserve Historical Society, usage of the library has grown by more than 151 percent in the last 10 years, and most of this growth is genealogical in nature. The Ohio Genealogical Society claims over 20,000 members. At the Ohio Historical Society and at the member centers of the Ohio Network of American History Research centers, government records and other files draw considerable genealogical research.[5] Within the past two decades, genealogical societies have been started for people of African-American, Polish, Czech, and other "nontraditional," non-Anglo ancestries. Whether as a post-retirement activity in a national population with more golden agers than ever before, or as a class assignment in high schools or colleges running programs in family history or cultural awareness, the tracing of one's roots is a rapidly expanding activity, and it promises to produce more users of primary sources than we have ever seen before.

There can be many benefits of close work with family researchers. At WRHS, for example, the library has long had a genealogical advisory committee. Meeting monthly, this group has raised money to purchase books, microfilm, and microfilm storage cabinets. Good relationships last; the estate of one genealogist, left in total to WRHS in 1980, allowed the library to purchase the entire federal census for the United States on

---

4 Peter W. Bunce, "Towards a More Harmonious Relationship: A Challenge to Archivists and Genealogists," and Elizabeth Shown Mills, "Genealogists and Archivists: Communicating, Cooperating, and Coping!" *SAA Newsletter* (May 1990): 18-21, 24.

5 Approximately 75 percent of the people using the WRHS library on any given day are pursuing family history research. Conversations with representatives of the Ohio Network of American History Research Centers indicate that the bulk of research use with local governmental records held by those centers is done by genealogists. The size of the Ohio Genealogical Society (OGS) membership is based on 1992 figures. In 1992, OGS had over 100 chapters throughout the state. For chapter listings, see the *OGS Newsletter* for recent years.

microfilm. This served only to spur genealogical use and support of the library (patrons of the library are now helping WRHS underwrite the cost of purchasing the entire newly available 1920 U.S. Census).[6] This relationship has also proved a boon to the cliometricians in our general research population. The genealogical committee also provides a cadre of competent volunteers who work with the professional reference staff to keep the research room fully staffed. With an attendance that can exceed 100 people per day, WRHS greatly needs this help.[7] The committee, working with the library and manuscripts curator, is also a de facto field staff. In one instance, the committee will assist in a survey of local funeral home records that may result in a large-scale microfilming program directed toward such sources. Critics who see little use for these materials beyond the needs of family researchers should be aware that in Cleveland, Ohio, as in other cities, funeral record books often provide valuable historical detail on the customs and mortality statistics of ethnic and minority groups in the community.

There is, therefore, a relationship that can be of immediate fiscal benefit to a repository. Of greater import, however, is the potential of genealogists as lobbying agents. In a recent case that would have resulted in the partial sequestering of vital records, the Ohio Genealogical Society and its members pressured state officials by letter and telephone until the bill in question was rewritten so that certain vital information remained easily obtainable.[8] There is great potential here for the historical community, provided it builds bridges with the family researchers and makes its needs known. One has to be optimistic in believing that those who derive so much from the primary source can not only be educated about the precautions necessary for its use but also about the societal resources necessary for the continued preservation of such valuable materials.

Using archival material, and becoming aware of its vast potential, are the key elements in what has made genealogists advocates for archives.

---

6 John Hyde Gehrung, a member of the WRHS Genealogical Advisory Committee, left his entire estate to the society's library upon his death in 1980. The bulk of the proceeds were used to purchase the entire available U.S. Census microfilm, a move that vastly increased use of the library. Given this precedent, the library has proceeded to purchase additional census microfilm as it has become available, including the 1920 Census, which will cost over $114,000. This cost is being underwritten, in large part, by patrons and friends of the library.

7 Over 80 people volunteer to assist the WRHS reference staff. Two to six volunteers assist the two full-time staff members in the reference area on any given day. Their duties usually center around assisting genealogical researchers, making electrostatic copies, and handling written research requests on a fee basis (with the fee going to WRHS).

8 In 1987-88, the Health Department of Ohio introduced legislation (House Bill 790) relating to the maintenance and preservation of health records. A portion of the bill would have made it much more difficult for researchers to gain access to vital statistics. Lobbying by the state genealogical community was intense, and the "offending" portions of the bill were changed. Building coalitions with groups such as genealogists can provide archivists with the same clout when issues critical to the profession are being considered in the halls of government.

Fostering the use of archival material among other segments of the population is a wise program for the keepers of the past. Exhibits of our treasures, at archives week events or other occasions, are fine, but people must understand the personal utility of those treasures before they will ever become our advocates. In particular, we should build a new generation of heritage advocates by attempting to introduce students, from the elementary to the undergraduate level, to the sources of history. In several cases, the production of teaching packets of archival facsimiles, such as that produced by the New York State Archives, has served to move the collections to the classroom. It is equally possible to bring the classroom to the archives by making careful, prior arrangements with instructors and setting assignments that match neophyte researchers with carefully controlled collections.

Experience at WRHS has shown that collections can be successfully and safely presented to students from grade levels six and up. One particularly notable program in the library involves an annual visit of middle-level Montessori students for primary source research in local ethnic history. Library staff also work carefully with local university history departments in an effort to have professors interest their students in undertaking primary research for papers in a variety of courses. Outside of creating a new clientele, the library staff has always found it fulfilling to observe students as they find a sense of excitement and discovery, in reading a Civil War letter or reviewing the correspondence of a locally notable figure. Given the manipulation that history has undergone in some television miniseries and in the tabloid press, it seems imperative that methods courses not be limited to graduate-level history students, but instead be made a requirement of all liberal arts undergraduate students. An educated citizenry must know whence their past derives and be aware of the unscrupulous manipulation it might undergo.

One national program, National History Day, has tremendous potential for creating a new clientele and friends for a wide variety of repositories. Begun in Cleveland and now operating in almost every state of the Union, this program's intent is to introduce students to the "stuff" of history and, like local science fairs, to present awards for the best historical papers, projects, and presentations. This move to make history more popular is a program initiated by our colleagues in academe. Archivists and curators would be wise to participate as fully as possible in it, for History Day is too good an opportunity to miss. It offers the chance not only to build links with academic historians and secondary school teachers but also to bring young, new users to our collections. It has other satisfactions as well. One of the proudest moments for the staff of the WRHS library was when a project based on one of our collections received a national first-place award. The student who produced that project certainly knows what the keepers are about. It is not, perhaps, too much to suggest that SAA should establish a formal liaison with the governing board of History Day, in much the same manner that it keeps in contact with other professional organizations.[9]

User-keeper bridges can also be built with portions of the American population who may have felt left out of the historical mainstream; indeed, the young student who won the History Day prize based his project on the papers of a local African-American inventor. Once created, such relationships will have long-term benefits for the repository, the archival profession, and society. It is worth citing two particular WRHS programs, the Black History (now African-American) Archives and the Cleveland Jewish Archives.[10] The former program, begun as a collecting arm of the society's library in 1970, has greatly enriched the library's holdings relating to local African-American history. It has also created an increased awareness of the importance of history and of WRHS's commitment to history within the local African-American community. Located in a city with a population that is nearly 50 percent African-American, the society makes a concerted effort in this area as part of its general commitment to preserve all aspects of community history. Such interest and commitment do not go unnoticed by the local political establishment or funding agencies.

In 1991, the Cleveland Foundation, the city's pioneering community trust, awarded the society a three-year, $150,000 grant to revitalize its African-American collecting program. During this grant period the society's African-American Archives Auxiliary has been working to create an endowment fund that will permanently underwrite the position of associate curator for African-American history. [11] In embarking on the endowment drive, the auxiliary (composed largely of citizens interested in African-American history) is following the lead of the city's Jewish community, which has supported a Jewish history archives at the society for more than a decade.

When the society began extensive collecting in the city's ethnic communities in the early 1970s, the Jewish community was automatically

---

9 Information about History Day can be obtained by writing to the History Day Office, Department of History, Mather House, Case Western Reserve University, Cleveland, Ohio 44106. The national headquarters of History Day is in the process of moving to Washington, D.C., but the Cleveland connection will remain viable.

10 For information about the specialized collecting programs at the WRHS library, see John J. Grabowski, "Fragments or Components: Theme Collections in a Local Setting," *American Archivist* 48 (Summer 1985): 304-14, and Kermit J. Pike, "Western Reserve Historical Society," in *Encyclopedia of Library and Information Science* 33 (1982), 131-36.

11 It will take an estimated $400,000 to endow the African-American Archives. Members of the auxiliary, working with WRHS library and development staff, have prepared a program that will solicit support from various components of the African-American community — churches, businesses, the legal profession — and will inform them of the need to preserve their records in the archives. In this manner the archives becomes more than an abstract funding goal; it becomes a program that has specific benefit for a donor group.

targeted within this program. This move on the part of the society was well received by the organized Jewish community, as represented by the local Jewish Community Federation. This interest eventually led two prominent local Jewish families to fund a separate Jewish archives program in 1976 and then, with the assistance of other families and the federation, permanently to endow that program in 1981. Although focusing on the records of a specific segment of the community, this program nevertheless allows the society to work toward its goal of total community documentation.

The immediate benefits of working with groups outside of the historical mainstream can be seen elsewhere in the archival/historical community. Most notable here are the efforts of Rudolph Vecoli at the Immigration History Research Center at the University of Minnesota, and those of Mark Stolarek, former director of the Balch Institute for Ethnic Studies in Philadelphia. In both instances, Vecoli and Stolarek worked closely with ethnic groups not only to accumulate records but also to fund surveys, microfilming, and preservation projects.[12] What seems to be operative in all of these dealings with groups outside of the historical mainstream is a hunger for historical recognition, a realization on the part of those who have been on the outside of how important history is as a means of self-identification and cultural continuity, as well as a symbol of acceptance. It is a lesson all Americans should heed, and it is certainly one any practitioner of history should understand. To begin programs directed at nonmainstream history is not to suggest that those who practice history should "use" these groups. Rather, it is simply a statement that the legitimate recognition of the history of so-called minorities may carry benefits in addition to those that come with creating a more complete record of the past.

Although collecting and preserving the records of various constituencies in the American body politic does help build a larger awareness of the importance of archives and history, it is imperative that these and other records be brought out of their boxes if they are to have the maximum impressive effect. The work at WRHS with the African-American and Jewish communities and the work of Balch with various ethnic communities has been assisted by exhibitions that use archival materials and create a broader awareness of their importance to the study of history.[13]

---

12 For an overview of the program at the Immigration History Research Center (IHRC), see Rudolph J. Vecoli, "Diamonds in Your Own Backyard: Developing Documentation on European Immigrants to North America," *Ethnic Forum* 1 (September 1981): 2-16. The *IHRC News* published by the center also contains detailed information on IHRC programs that are supported by grants from various ethnic organizations. For the Balch Institute, see R. Joseph Anderson, "Building a Multi-Ethnic Collection: The Research Library of the Balch Institute for Ethnic Studies," *Ethnic Forum* 5 (Fall 1985): 7-19.

13 The Balch Institute has been particularly innovative in creating exhibits that focus on specific ethnic groups and that involve those groups in both the creation of the exhibit and the

One particular example at WRHS deserves attention. The accessioning of the more than 40,000 negatives of Cleveland African-American photographer Allen E. Cole was a major event in the history of the then Black History Archives project. At the time it occurred, it garnered little press coverage. However, only when a portion of the Cole negatives were selected, printed, framed, and exhibited did the Cole collection receive the recognition it deserved. That exhibit, which is now available for loan, receives frequent use throughout the year, and it brings to the library dozens of researchers who have now realized that it contains material relevant to their lives, families, and communities. The travels of such an exhibit are critical — it goes out to the community and enjoys an audience that might not think of stopping in an archives or a museum. Its travels also represent a means of creating users, those who read and view the exhibit but who do not necessarily come to the research room.

A recent exhibit created by the Jewish Archives, which celebrates the founding of the Cleveland Jewish community 150 years ago, has also been quite popular, both in and outside of the society's museum. Composed entirely of copies of documents and photographs, the "Founders" exhibit was designed for two purposes: to stand as a major museum display augmented by original materials and to travel on its own. In the museum, at a local mall, at a community theater, and at one of the city's major reform temples, it has attracted considerable attention and has served to lure both patrons and new collections to the Jewish archives. Its travels are important, for in a mall setting it will attract over 10,000 viewers a week, far more than the 1,300 who visit the society's museum gallery each week. Heritage becomes tangible only when seen. Hidden in a box, it becomes only another mystery to be associated with the arcane profession of archivist and the dull pursuit of history.

Creating this awareness of the holdings of archives and the richness of history is an important step in garnering more users and potential advocates. Traditional exhibits go a long way in stimulating awareness, but many archivists lack the facilities or the resources to mount an exhibit. However, most can still make their materials more visible and at the same time be at the popular edge of community interaction by using the broadcast media. The electronic media can be a tremendous resource for creating awareness and advocacy. Although the reference staff at WRHS often shudder at the prospect of dealing with another television film crew (who have a propensity to come in five minutes before their deadline), they know the relationship with television is essential if archivists are to create advocates among the public. The issue is how to control the media instead of letting it control you.

---

associated programming. The Balch newsletter, *New Dimensions*, details the exhibits mounted by the institute during the past several years.

A few examples can suffice here. Major events and anniversaries usually receive television coverage. Archives holding material relating to
these events should bring relevant collections to the attention of the
media. That means inviting them in before they descend on you.
Two minutes of evening news coverage relating to holdings on a Korean
War anniversary, the inauguration of a mayor, or the granting of woman
suffrage can let thousands of people into the mysteries of the document.
Certainly, working with the local media can be troubling in terms of
short deadlines and arguments for proper credit. However, a good relationship with a local television station may come in handy when a funding cut looms or some other threat confronts one's institution; producers
who know the value of a potential source may well be interested in
devoting air time that might protect that source.

In a broader sense, those allied with heritage preservation must learn
to work well with those in the media who are creating the new "consumer history," because the television documentary, the PBS special, and
their resulting videos for sale are the chief access routes to history for
many Americans. Making contact with documentary producers, being
aware of their needs, and giving them careful direction in the use of
one's collections can all pay off in new friends for history as people view
such excellent productions as the Ken Burns television history of the
American Civil War. This extraordinary program, which brings the history of the war into a popular, yet historically accurate perspective through
the use of still period photographs and quotations from a variety of manuscript and published sources, is a model of what good, popular history is
destined to be. More than any other recent production, the Burns history
epitomizes the rich potential of traditional historical source material
and provides testament to the importance of archival work in preserving
and presenting that material. One can only hope that those who have
viewed the series are fully aware of its origins and of the role of archivists
in making it possible. It might well be worth SAA's consideration to fund
a short documentary about the role archivists and historians play in
producing such works. This would be outreach at its most effective.[14]

Building an awareness of archival value, to the extent that substantial portions of the population understand and appreciate what we as
archivists do, is no easy task. It is advocacy that goes beyond the production

---

14 When the Burns series was shown on the local PBS affiliate (WVIZ) in Cleveland, interviews, in
    which Burns discussed his work on the project, were used as fillers after some of the series
    segments. Unfortunately, the importance of archives and manuscripts repositories in Burns's
    work was not clearly articulated during these interviews, although his dependence on archives
    has been clearly noted in some of the subsequent appearances he has made before groups of
    archivists and historians. Given Burns's high public visibility and forthcoming projects (including
    a documentary on baseball), the profession should seriously consider using Burns in an archives
    documentary.

of brochures and slide shows, though these may be necessary first steps in attracting people to our repositories. For some of us, it will involve a long step down from the ivory tower — the disavowal, if you will, of a priesthood of history. For others, it will involve coming home to the "why" of our profession from a sometimes obsessive sojourn with the "how." For almost all of us, it will involve extra work as we go out to talk with potential user groups and then carefully shepherd them through the intricacies of collection use. But such effort is necessary. If we say that we are preserving the nation's heritage, we and our colleagues throughout the history profession cannot narrowly define the owners of that heritage. We can only strive to make it broadly available in a manner commensurate with our duty to preserve and protect it. Only when a large number of users joins the small number of keepers and their historical allies in saying that archives, history, and heritage are important, will the funders respond in a manner that befits the work we do.

Contributors

David A. Bearman is president of Archives and Museum Informatics. He consults on issues relating to electronic records and archives, integrating multiformat cultural information and museum information systems and is founding editor of the quarterly journal *Archives and Museum Informatics*. Bearman is the author of over 125 books and articles on museum and archives information management issues. Prior to 1986 he served as deputy director of the Smithsonian Institution Office of Information Resource Management and as director of the National Information Systems Task Force of the Society of American Archivists from 1980 to 1982. From 1987 to 1992, he chaired the Initiative for Computer Interchange of Museum Information. In 1989 Bearman proposed Guidelines for Electronic Records Management Policy, which were adopted by the United Nations Administrative Coordinating Committee on Information Systems in 1990, and in 1995 he proposed a Reference Model for Business Acceptable Communications as part of a research program on functional requirements for electronic evidence. He is a fellow of the Society of American Archivists.

Frank Boles has been director of the Clarke Historical Library, Central Michigan University, since 1991. From 1982 to 1991 he worked at the University of Michigan's Bentley Historical Library. He has also served as an archivist at the Chicago Historical Society and as a program officer at the National Endowment for the Humanities. Both his bachelor's and master's degrees are from Wayne State University, where he also received his formal archival education. He received the Ph.D. in history at the University of Michigan and is a fellow of the Society of American Archivists.

Paul Conway has headed the Preservation Department at Yale University Library since 1992. Previously, he conducted research for three years at the National Archives and Records Administration, including a study of research use of archives and a review of how government agencies implement digital imaging technology. He began his professional career in 1977 as an archivist on the staff of the Gerald R. Ford Library. From 1988 to 1989 he was the preservation program officer of the Society of American Archivists. He has a master's degree in history and a Ph.D. in information and library studies, both from the University of Michigan. He is a fellow of the Society of American Archivists.

J. Frank Cook has been director of the archives at the University of Wisconsin-Madison, since 1971. He was assistant archivist there from 1965 to 1970. Cook has a B.S. degree in history from East Tennessee State University and M.S. and Ph.D. degrees in American history from the University of Wisconsin-Madison. Cook is a past president and fellow of the Society of American Archivists. He has served on SAA's Council, Executive Committee, and Editorial Board. He has taken on the responsibility of caring for SAA's archives. He is a founding member and former vice president of the Midwest Archives Conference.

Richard J. Cox is an associate professor at the University of Pittsburgh School of Information Sciences, responsible for teaching archives and records management. He has published over 130 articles on archives, records management, historical, and library and information science over the past quarter of a century. Cox has published five books on aspects of archival science since 1990, and he is currently completing another book on archives and records management policy. He is a frequent speaker at North American and international conferences. He is a fellow of the Society of American Archivists and edited the *American Archivist* from 1991 through 1995.

Timothy L. Ericson is currently assistant library director for Archives and Special Collections at the Golda Meir Library, University of Wisconsin-Milwaukee, a position he has held since 1989. He also teaches graduate level coursework in archival administration as an adjunct instructor for the university's Department of History and the School of Library and Information Science. Prior to 1989 he was the education officer for the Society of American Archivists, map curator and project archivist at the State Historical Society of Wisconsin, and university archivist/Area Research Center curator at the University of Wisconsin-River Falls. He also serves on Wisconsin's State Historical Records Advisory Board. He is a fellow of the Society of American Archivists.

Elsie Freeman Finch was director of Academic, Professional and Public Programs in the Education Division of the National Archives, where she directed programs designed to bring the records of the National Archives to the attention of a variety of users. She began her career in archives at Haverford College and later served as head of manuscripts collections at Washington University, St. Louis, and as assistant curator of manuscripts for the Smithsonian Institution's Archives of American Art. She holds an undergraduate degree in American history and literature and a master's degree in English literature. She is a fellow of the Society of American Archivists and has served on SAA Council and numerous committees. She is editor of the book *Advocating Archives* (SAA, 1994) and now lives in Ithaca, New York.

John A. Fleckner is chief archivist at the National Museum of American History, Smithsonian Institution. He directs the Archives Center, a manuscripts and special collections operation with special strengths in American consumer culture, the history of technology, and American music. Before joining the Smithsonian in 1983, Fleckner held a variety of archival positions at the State Historical Society of Wisconsin. He is a past president and fellow of the Society of American Archivists and has written on records surveys, Native American archives, and other topics.

Kenneth E. Foote is the Erich W. Zimmermann Regents Professor of Geography and director of the Environmental Information Systems Laboratory at the University of Texas at Austin. He teaches cultural and historical geography, American landscape history, and computer research techniques. His recent books include the co-edited *Re-reading Cultural Geography* (1994) and *Shadowed Ground: America's Landscapes of Violence and Tragedy* (1997). An early version of his article was presented at the 49th annual meeting of the Society of American Archivists in Austin, Texas, in October 1985. It was revised for publication in the *American Archivist* at the encouragement of then-editor David Klaassen. Many of the controversial sites mentioned in the article are discussed in greater detail in *Shadowed Ground*.

Anne Gilliland-Swetland is an assistant professor in the Graduate School of Education and Information Studies at UCLA where she teaches in the graduate specialization in Archives and Preservation Management. Prior to coming to UCLA in 1995, she was director of the SourceLINK Project in the University of Michigan Medical School Historical Center for the Health Sciences and taught courses in archival administration and electronic records management at the University of Michigan School of Information and Library Studies. She holds a Ph.D. from the University of Michigan, M.S. and C.A.S. degrees from the University of Illinois at Urbana-Champaign, and an M.A. from Trinity College Dublin. She is a fellow of the Society of American Archivists.

Luke J. Gilliland-Swetland is currently deputy director at the Japanese American National Museum in Los Angeles, California. Previously, he served as head of Research and Access Programs at Henry Ford Museum and Greenfield Village in Dearborn, Michigan. He holds an M.A. in American Studies and an M.L.S., both from the University of Michigan.

John J. Grabowski is director of research at the Western Reserve Historical Society and Krieger-Mueller assistant professor of public history at Case Western Reserve University. He has a Ph.D. in American history, with a supporting field in archives, from Case Western Reserve. He is the co-editor of *The Encyclopedia of Cleveland History* and *A Tradition of Reform* and is the author of a number of articles relating to urban and ethnic history and archives. In 1996-97 he served as senior Fulbright lecturer at Bilkent University in Ankara, Turkey.

Mark Greene is currently head of Research Center Programs at Henry Ford Museum and Greenfield Village. From 1989 to 2000 he worked at the Minnesota Historical Society where he was curator of manuscripts acquisition, with responsibility for acquiring and appraising business records, congressional collections, and records of philanthropy. At MHS he led two major reappraisal projects. He received his M.A. in history, with a cognate in archival administration, from the University of Michigan and served as archivist of Carleton College from 1985 to 1989. He has published many archival and historical articles, and in 1995 received the Margaret Cross Norton Award for the best article in *Archival Issues*, the journal of the Midwest Archives Conference. He is a past president of MAC and is currently editor of its journal. In addition, he is a member of the Council of the Society of American Archivists, where he also has served as chair of the SAA Manuscripts Repository Section, Congressional Papers Roundtable, and co-chair of the Committee on Education and Professional Development.

Margaret Hedstrom is associate professor at the School of Information, University of Michigan, where she teaches archives, electronic records management, and digital preservation. Before joining the faculty at Michigan in 1995, she was chief of State Records Advisory Services and director of the Center for Electronic Records at the New York State Archives and Records Administration. Hedstrom earned master's degrees in library science and history and a Ph.D. in history from the University of Wisconsin-Madison. She is a fellow of the Society of American Archivists and has served on several SAA bodies including Council, as co-chair of the Task Force on Organizational Effectiveness, and as chair of the Committee on Automated Records and Techniques. She was the first recipient of the annual Award for Excellence in New York State Government Information Services.

Linda J. Henry has worked with manuscripts, organizational, and public records in several institutions. Since 1991 she has been an archivist with the Center for Electronic Records of the National Archives and Records Administration. She is a fellow of the Society of American Archivists and has served as SAA treasurer and a member of Council.

Laura L. Bost Hensey is currently working as a records management analyst for North Carolina state government. After graduating from the University of Michigan School of Information and Library Studies, she was employed as a project archivist for the University Archives of Case Western Reserve University in Cleveland, Ohio.

Randall C. Jimerson is associate professor of history and director of the Graduate Program in Archives and Records Management at Western Washington University in Bellingham, Washington. He received the Ph.D. in American history at the University of Michigan. From 1979 to 1994 he was university archivist and director of the Historical Manuscripts and Archives Department of the University of Connecticut Libraries. Prior to that he worked as an archivist at the Bentley Historical Library and at Yale University. He has served on the Council of the Society of American Archivists and on its Executive Committee. A former president of the New England Archivists, he received its Distinguished Service Award in 1994.

Elisabeth Kaplan is the archivist at the Charles Babbage Institute for the History of Information Processing, University of Minnesota, Minneapolis. She has also worked at the Institute Archives at the Massachusetts Institute of Technology and the Audiovisual Department of the John F. Kennedy Library. She studied filmmaking at the Massachusetts College of Art and received a B.A. in history and an M.A. in history and archival methods at the University of Massachusetts, Boston. Her master's thesis was "Archivists, Historians and the Concept of Visual Literacy: Translating Audiovisual Information into Words."

Richard H. Lytle is director of the Oregon Master of Software Engineering Program, a statewide effort of four universities to provide education relevant to the needs of Oregon's high technology companies. During 1998 he was director of education and training services at CoreTech Consulting Group, King of Prussia, Pennsylvania. From 1987 to 1998, he was dean of the College of Information Science and Technology and Isaac L. Auerbach Professor of Information Systems at Drexel University, Philadelphia. Lytle was formerly director of the Office of Information Resource Management at the Smithsonian Institution, where he had responsibility for central computing, telecommunications, and information technology planning. Prior to his work at the Smithsonian Institution, he established information management programs at Washington University, Rice University, and the State of Illinois. He has degrees from Rice University, Washington University, and the University of Maryland, and is a fellow of the Society of American Archivists.

Avra Michelson received an M.A. in American studies from the State University of New York at Buffalo and an M.L.S. with a specialization in archives administration from the University of Michigan. She prepared her article while at the Bentley Historical Library at the University of Michigan. Since then she has worked in government, software engineering, and commercial enterprises as a systems administrator, trends forecaster, information technology consultant, and business planner. Currently she is a member of the Information Technology Center at The MITRE Corporation in McLean, Virginia.

Jeffrey Mifflin is currently archivist and curator of Special Collections at Massachusetts General Hospital in Boston. He holds an A.B. from Harvard University, an M.A. in history and archival methods from the University of Massachusetts-Boston, and an M.S. in library and information science from Simmons Library School. He has worked as an archivist at McLean Hospital, Harvard Business School, Pioneer Group, Inc., and the Massachusetts Institute of Technology.

James M. O'Toole is associate professor of history at Boston College. For 15 years he directed the M.A. program in history and archives at the University of Massachusetts-Boston. He has worked as an archivist at the New England Historic Genealogical Society, the Massachusetts State Archives, and the Archives of the Roman Catholic Archdiocese of Boston. He is the author of *Understanding Archives and Manuscripts* (SAA, 1990) and editor of *The Records of American Business* (SAA, 1997). He is a fellow of the Society of American Archivists and has served on SAA Council and numerous committees and boards.

Judith M. Panitch is research and special projects librarian at the University of North Carolina at Chapel Hill. Previously she was coordinator of the Modern Economic and Social History Preservation Microfilming Project at the Columbia University Libraries. She wrote the article included in this volume as part of her course work for an M.L.S. degree at the School of Information Science and Policy, University at Albany, State University of New York.

Christopher Ann Paton is archivist of the Popular Music Collection in the Pullen Library Special Collections Department at Georgia State University, where she oversees a collection that includes approximately 60,000 commercial and noncommercial disc and tape recordings.

Daniel V. Pitti is project director at the Institute for Advanced Technology in the Humanities (IATH) at the University of Virginia where he is responsible for project design in general and SGML and XML development in particular. Before coming to IATH in 1997, he was librarian for Advanced Technologies Projects at the University of California at Berkeley Library. For the past seven years Pitti has led a national and increasingly international effort to develop an encoding standard for library and archival finding aids known as Encoded Archival Description. He has an M.A. and a C.Phil. in history of religions from the

University of California at Los Angeles and an M.L.I.S. from the University of California at Berkeley.

Helen Willa Samuels was trained as a librarian at Simmons College after receiving her bachelor's degree from Queens College in New York City. She began work at the Massachusetts Institute of Technology in 1977 as institute archivist and served in that capacity until 1997, when she moved to the Provost's Office where she has worked on information policy and educational technology issues. Her research and publications examine the documentation of science, technology, and institutions of higher education. She is a fellow of the Society of American Archivists. Her book, *Varsity Letters: Documenting Modern Colleges and Universities* (SAA, 1992), received SAA's Leland Prize.

Elizabeth Yakel is an assistant professor at the University of Michigan School of Information where she teaches in the areas of archives and records and preservation. Previously, she taught at the University of Pittsburgh. She has also served as a research assistant at the Collaboratory for Research on Electronic Work at the University of Michigan. Her archival experience includes working on the Vatican Archives Project and serving as archivist and records manager for the Maryknoll Missioners and the Archdiocese of Detroit. She earned a master's in library science and a Ph.D. from the University of Michigan. Her doctoral dissertation won an award from the Association of Library and Information Science Education. Yakel is a fellow of the Society of American Archivists and has served on SAA Council and as chair of the Committee on Education and Professional Development.

Julia Marks Young is head of the Special Collections Department and director of the Southern Labor Archives at Georgia State University's Pullen Library. She has taught archival administration courses since 1983, and previously held archival positions at the Superconducting Super Collider Laboratory, the University of Southern Mississippi, and the University of Michigan. She served as a member of the SAA Task Force on Institutional Evaluation and as editor of the *American Archivist*. She holds an M.L.S. with a specialization in archives administration from the University of Michigan and an M.A. from Auburn University.

Index